# Avro Aircraft

## since 1908

Vulcan prototypes VX770 and VX777 formating with Avro 707As WZ736 and WD280, Avro 707B VX790 and Avro 707C WZ744 before appearing at the 1953 Farnborough Air Show. (*Avro*)

# Avro
# Aircraft
## since 1908

## A J Jackson

Revised and Updated
by
R T Jackson

PUTNAM

BY THE SAME AUTHOR

*Blackburn Aircraft since 1909*
*British Civil Aircraft 1919–1972 (three volumes)*
*De Havilland Aircraft since 1909*

© A J Jackson 1965
New material © R T Jackson 1990

*First published 1965*

This edition published in Great Britain in 1990 by
Putnam Aeronautical Books, an imprint of
Conway Maritime Press Limited
24 Bride Lane, Fleet Street
London EC4Y 8DR

*British Library Cataloguing in Publication Data*
Jackson, A. J.
Avro aircraft since 1908. -2nd ed.
1. Avro aeroplanes, history
I. Title
623.746

ISBN 0-85177-834-8

Typeset by Lasertext Ltd, Stretford, Manchester
Printed and bound by The Alden Press, Oxford

# CONTENTS

# FOREWORD

*The first edition Foreword that follows has been amended to take into account changes made in the content and format of the book as it is now presented in this, its second edition.*

The career of Alliott Verdon Roe, founder and first designer of the great British aircraft manufacturing firm of A. V. Roe and Co Ltd, who flew model gliders from the ss *Inchanga* in 1901–02, won prizes for rubber driven models in 1907, made the first sustained flight in an all-British aeroplane in 1909 and was knighted for services to aviation in 1929, is covered briefly in the Introduction along with the fortunes of the company that bore his name. However, the main purpose of the book is to record as completely as possible all aeroplanes which have borne the Avro trademark, together with something of their technical details and operational histories.

From 'stick and string' days at Brooklands, Shoreham and Manchester, the story covers the First World War era and the production of that now-legendary masterpiece, the Avro 504 in all its variants. Their descriptions spread through the book in type number sequence. Hamble, birthplace of classic Avro seaplanes, where Bert Hinkler tested military and civil proto-types designed by Roy Chadwick between the wars, was the scene of early autogiro experiments which qualify for chapter status because complete Avro airframes were used.

In 1928 'A.V.' left the firm and the story moves again to Manchester where in 1936 the company became a member of the Hawker Siddeley Group. It tells of world sales of Avian and Tutor derivatives and production of those giants of the Second World War, the Anson and Lancaster. From the York and a series of interim passenger transports it proceeds to the mighty Vulcan delta bomber and comes finally to the turbine-powered Avro 748, last aircraft to originate with the Avro prefix. Later designs had H.S. designations resulting from a change of company style to the Avro-Whitworth Division of Hawker Siddeley Aviation effective from July 1, 1963.

Painstaking research has brought to light unpublished material which disproves a number of long-accepted theories, but definite records do not go back beyond 1912, a period when A. V. Roe was preoccupied with the basic problem of getting off the ground and found little time for making notes. The frequency with which his primitive machines were reconstructed, coupled with the vague and indefinite information given by a (then) inexpert Press and the fallibility of human memory, has led to the identity of several of these early aeroplanes being misrepresented or going entirely unrecorded. Descriptions are often contradictory and many statements for which there is no justification have attained a false air of authenticity through constant repetition, the Roe III triplane in particular having come down the years in a welter of conflicting statements. Thus it may never be possible to write a full history of 1908–11 Avro aeroplanes and relevant chapters of this book are therefore presented in as much confirmed detail as possible, without any claim to completeness, in the earnest hope that they form the most satisfactory record published so far.

Completed aircraft account for only some 30 per cent of Avro designs. A list of all unbuilt projects is given therefore in an appendix, together with details of four types built for other firms, and four built by A. V. Roe Canada Ltd. Having no Avro origins, Hawker Audax, Bristol Blenheim and English Electric Canberra aircraft built by the firm are not discussed, though their identities are listed in Appendix A.

New material made available from Avro records has made possible complete listings of production aircraft. Initial markings alone are quoted except where susequent identities are demanded by the story and in the unique Avro 504K joyriding saga. Similar treatment for the civil Anson is beyond the scope of the present volume.

The author acknowledges with gratitude enthusiastic help given by several specialists whose contributions have enriched this work, notably D. E. Monk; H. Holmes; C. H. Barnes; J. M. Bruce MA; J. A. Bagley BSc; H. F. Cowley; W. Duigan of Geelong, Australia (1911 biplane photographs); F. G. Miles; K. M. Molson, Curator of the Canadian National Aviation Museum (early Canadian data and photographs); P. W. Moss; Bruce Robertson; D. E. Roberts BSc; H. E. Scrope; E. Taylor; L. E. Bradford who prepared the three view drawings; and the author's wife who typed the manuscript so expertly.

Valuable assistance was also received from the Avro-Whitworth Division of Hawker Siddeley Aviation; Rolls-Royce Ltd; H. F. King MBE, Editor of *Flight International* and Miss A. Tilbury (*Flight* photographic department); D. Dorrell, Editor of *Air Pictorial*; J. W. R. Taylor, Editor of *Jane's All the World's Aircraft*; J. H. Blake, Editor of the *Royal Aero Club Gazette*; the Editor of *Lloyd's List and Shipping Gazette*; F. H. Smith, Librarian of the Royal Aeronautical Society; the Airworthiness Department of the Ministry of Aviation; the photographic section of the Imperial War Museum; and J. A. Pryor and D. P. Woodhall of the Air Historical Societies of Australia and New Zealand respectively.

The following gentlemen have also contributed materially to the completeness of this book: R. C. B. Ashworth; C. A. Nepean Bishop ARAeS; T. W. Boughton, J. Hopton and C. A. Lynch (Australia); P. T. Capon; J. R. Ellis (Canada); C. A. van der Eyk (Netherlands); J. S. Havers; W. K. Kilsby; H. Kofoed (Denmark); G. S. Leslie; C. Longworth-Dames; O. G. Nordbø (Norway); and E. Rerren (Belgium).

A. J. J.

Leigh-on-Sea, January 1965

# FOREWORD TO SECOND EDITION

Regrettably my father, A. J. Jackson, did not live to complete a second edition of *Avro Aircraft since 1908*. However his notes, including additional text relating to overseas Avro 504Ks and the Avro 671/Cierva C.30A, and above all his extensive personal archive have made the task of updating the book a relatively straightforward one. The archive is now in the ownership of my elder brother, Squadron Leader D. H. Jackson, and particular thanks are due to him for his support and encouragement.

Valued assistance has also been received from J. A. Bagley BSc, former Curator of the Science Museum's Aeronautical Collection, who was largely responsible for updating the chapter on the Roe I Triplane; J. M. Bruce MA, who not only supplied information on pre-1918 aircraft but together with his colleague G. S. Leslie provided a number of historically important photographs; Peter Connon, whose extensive research for his books on the history of aviation in the Cumbria, Dumfries, and Galloway region provided new information and photographs of the Lakes Water Bird and Lakes Sea Bird; Philip Jarrett, who provided much information on A. V. Roe's early years; and K. A. Molson, whose knowledge of Canadian aviation has added much to this book.

In addition grateful thanks are due to P.G. Murton BA, ALA, Keeper of Aviation Records at the RAF Museum, Hendon, the staff of the National Motor Museum at Beaulieu and the following gentlemen (and one lady) who have all made an important contribution; R. C. B. Ashworth; Ernest Brook, Editor of *The Rolls-Royce Magazine*; G. M. K. Fraser; M. J. Hardy; E. A. Harlin (for a letter written in 1973); H. R. Harrison; Harry Holmes, Public Relations Manager, British Aerospace Civil Aircraft Division, Woodford; Allan L. Montgomery, Curator of the US Army Transportation Museum, Fort Eustis, Virginia; Francesca Riccini, Assistant Curator, Science Museum Road Transport Collection; Richard Riding, Editor of *Aeroplane Monthly*; Bruce Robertson; Johan G. H. Visser; J. Wells; Howard S. Wolko of the National Air and Space Museum, Washington DC; and Humphrey Wynn.

R. T. J.

Leigh-on-Sea, July 1990

# Introduction

**The Early Years**

Edwin Alliott Verdon Roe was born at Patricroft near Manchester on April 26, 1877, the fourth child of Dr Edwin Hodson Roe and his wife, the former Sofia Verdon.

At the age of eight the young Alliott, as he preferred to be called, was sent away to school at Haliford House near Brooklands with his younger brother Humphrey, later transferring to Shorne College in Buckinghamshire. At the age of eleven, still in company with his brother, he started at Bewshers, the preparatory school for St Paul's, where later it was said he preferred sport to academic study. Despite this he displayed a talent for inventiveness and was only thirteen when he took out his first patent, that for a carpet brush with a reversible bristle head.

By the time he was fourteen, Alliott was keen to leave school and see the world. The opportunity to do just that came when a friend of his father, a civil engineer in British Columbia, agreed to teach him surveying. Alliott sailed from Liverpool aboard the *Labrador* early in March 1892.

A.V. Roe with his 1907 prize winning model.

The Avro Type E prototype and the Burga Monoplane under construction at the Brownsfield Mills works in early 1912.

Unfortunately his arrival in Canada coincided with a slump caused by a drop in the price of silver resulting in little work for surveyors and Alliott was soon obliged to turn to tree planting, and later fishing to earn his living. The depression continued into the new year and Alliott decided to return to England but not before his interest turned to engineering.

In the summer of 1893 Alliott started as an apprentice at the Lancashire and Yorkshire Railway Works at Horwich, Lancashire. Here his talent for invention again came to the fore with novel modifications to lathes allowing him to appreciably increase output and thus his earnings to time and a half. After completing his five-year apprenticeship, Roe's certificates of proficiency from the Mechanic's Institute enabled him to gain employment on torpedo work at Portsmouth Dockyard. However he soon decided to join the Royal Navy and went to King's College, London, to study Marine Engineering. He was not however successful in all the subsequent examinations held at the Royal Naval College, Greenwich, and he was not accepted for a naval career. Despite this his passes in the technical subjects and mathematics were deemed sufficient qualifications for entry into the merchant marine and he was appointed Fifth Engineer of the SS *Jebba*, a steamer of the British and South African Royal Mail Company on the West African run. After three voyages, and promotion to Fourth Engineer, Roe transferred to another of the company's ships the SS *Cameron* but his seagoing career was interrupted by a severe attack of malaria. After a slow recovery he made seven voyages to Batoum on the Black Sea aboard the SS *Caucasian* before joining the SS *Inchonga* on her voyages to Durban and

Capetown as Third Engineer. It was on these voyages in 1902, which were to be the last of his Merchant Navy career, that Roe's mind first turned to the problem of flight, his interest aroused by the sight of the soaring albatross.

Roe's first model, that of an albatross, did not fly but after much experimentation he eventually succeeded in making models of varied designs (monoplanes, biplanes, triplanes and multiplanes, some of which were canards) which glided reasonably well. On leaving the sea, Roe became a draughtsman in the motor-car industry with Brotherhood Crockers, the firm which later became the Sheffield Simplex Motor Car Company, and was responsible for designing a clever gear change mechanism which saved the firm from having to pay substantial patent fees for the use of the Mercedes system. Throughout this period, Roe's thoughts remained firmly on the problems of flight and model making continued.

On January 24, 1906, the *Times Engineering Supplement* published a letter from Roe which aimed to combat the prevailing scepticism on aviation matters. In this he reported success with 3 ft long dart models fitted with combined vertical and lateral rudders and announced his intention to try for both the £2,000 Deutsch-Archdeacon Prize of the French Aero Club and the substantial prize offered by Sir David Salomons, Bart, for the first successful mechanical-driven Wright-type aeroplane built in Britain. Roe added 'If immediate steps are taken, I see no reason why a motor-driven aeroplane should not be gliding over England by the middle of the summer'. However his optimism was not shared by *The Times* whose memorable footnote suggested that all attempts at artificial aviation were not only dangerous to human life but doomed to failure from an engineering standpoint.

A.V. Roe (*left*) and H.V. Roe (*RAF Museum*)

In December 1903 Roe heard of the successful powered flights by the Wright brothers in the United States but it was not until news came of their success with the Flyer in 1905 that he first wrote to Wilbur Wright. This was February 1906 and the following month a very friendly reply was received which provided A. V. Roe with much encouragement in his aim to pioneer powered flight in Britain. In his letter, Roe had mentioned that he had procured space at the Motor and Aeronautical Show to be held at the Agricultural Hall, Westminster, from March 24 to 31, 1906. Here he displayed several Wright-type paper gliders and a larger Wright-Roe 'combination' type with wing-warping and rudder controls.

By now Roe had decided to devote himself entirely to aviation and in early April 1906 applied for the post of Secretary to the Aero Club (later the Royal Aero Club). For this he was interviewed by two members of the committee, the Hon C.S. Rolls and Mr Stanley Spooner, and much to his surprise was appointed. However after only a few weeks with the club he left to work as draughtsman for a Scotsman, Mr G.L.O. Davidson, in Denver, Colorado. Roe's new employer had ambitious plans to build a steam-powered passenger carrying 'helicopter' (actually more like a VTOL airliner) but before it was completed Roe returned to England to finish work on the associated British patent drawings but a dispute resulting from non-payment of salary led to the need for new employment. The 'helicopter' meanwhile had been damaged after rising slightly into the air when the two 20 hp Stanley steam engines were started and the project was terminated.

On November 18, 1906, Roe wrote to B.F.S. Baden-Powell, President of the Aeronautical Society of Great Britain saying 'I am very anxious to join some one in making and experimenting with a motor driven aeroplane, and now you are going in for this perhaps we could come to some arrangement, or do you think I could join the staff at Aldershot?' Baden-Powell, though no longer at Aldershot, offered to help if he could. The following day, November 19, 1906, Roe submitted his application for a patent concerning the stability and control of an aeroplane. The auxiliary surface was in front of the wings, elevating or depressing it raised or lowered the nose and turns were achieved by warping the extremities. A significant step forward was the use of a single control wheel. Warping resulted from the turning of the wheel and control of the fore-plane was exercised by raising or lowering it.

At this time a number of newspapers and magazines began offering cash prizes for aviation achievements providing the incentive to experiment. However Roe and other aspiring aviators were held back by the problem of finance, the cost of building a full-size aeroplane being significant. Roe's models were now quite sophisticated and had reached heights of 100 ft. Pictures of several of them were published early in 1907 and one of them, a biplane with a forward steering plane, was very similar in layout to that depicted in his patent drawings.

Roe first revealed that he was constructing a full-size aeroplane in a letter to *The Car* that was published on January 30, 1907. Nevertheless model

The Avro works at Clifton Street, Ancoats, Manchester. (*RAF Museum*)

building continued and prizes obtained used to help finance the full-size machine. Five Roe models were entered in a display of model aeroplanes that formed part of the International Motor Car Exhibition held at the Royal Agricultural Hall from April 6 to 13, 1907. In conjunction with this *The Daily Mail* offered cash prizes totalling £250 for models weighing between 2 and 50 lb which were capable of flying above 50 ft under their own power from a launch point no more than 5 ft above ground level. The judges were to consider the length of the flight, practicability, stability, steering power, speed, excellence of design and construction, the method of launch and 'available lifting power'.

The prize trials took place at Alexandra Palace on April 15 and began with indoor tests. Only Roe and a Mr W.F. Howard produced models capable of achieving credible flight with Roe's 9ft 6 in span rear steering plane model outperforming all others. It made two flights of 60 ft and 78 ft and after more rubber had been added 'to increase the motive power' achieved 'a beautifully even flight' of 85 ft. Despite this success, much to Roe's chagrin, it was decided that none of the models deserved the £150 first prize and he was awarded instead the £75 second prize.

The full-size Roe biplane, under construction in the coach-house at Putney owned by his brother, Dr Spencer Verdon Roe, was now well advanced and a picture of Roe seated in the partly completed frame was published in the June 1907 issue of *Ballooning and Aeronautics*. The Biplane was reportedly complete in August but due to the continuance of the motor racing season it was not until mid-December 1907 that trials began on the Brooklands track.

## A.V. Roe and Company

A.V. Roe's first business partner was the J.A.P. engine designer, J.A. Prestwich. Together they formed the JAP Avroplane Company on September 15, 1908, with capital of £100 but the partnership was amicably dissolved in November 1909 following a disagreement over the size of triplane to be manufactured. The larger of the two triplanes that were then under construction was disposed of at auction.

To finance his experiments, Roe borrowed money from both his father and his brother, H.V. Roe who was by now a successful businessman and owner of H.W. Everard and Company, the manufacturers of 'Bulls-Eye' braces. 'H.V.', who had been very close to his brother since childhood, agreed to enter into partnership with 'A.V.' on April 27, 1909, and the deal was sealed by the payment of £1. This agreement laid the foundations of A.V. Roe and Company which was formed on January 1, 1910. Attempts to gain outside financial backing failed and the new enterprise was solely financed by H.V. Roe. In the new company 'A.V.' had responsibility for inventing and 'H.V.' for finance, organisation and management. It was planned that fifty per cent of any profits would go to each brother but in the event of the firm being a financial failure 'H.V.' would shoulder all responsibility leaving 'A.V.' free from debt. So that 'H.V.' could oversee the new company, its workshops were established in the factory of Everard and Co. at Brownsfield Mills, Ancoats, Manchester, rather than near London as 'A.V.' had hoped. The first product was the Roe II triplane *Mercury*. Flight testing however took place at Brooklands whose new enlightened management had established a flying ground in the centre of the track. 'A.V.' was quick to rent one of the newly erected sheds at £100 per annum and returned there after a nineteen-month absence on March 1,

R.J. Parrott (*left*) and Roy Chadwick.

F.P. Raynham (*left*) and James Grimble Groves. (*RAF Museum*)

1910. The Avro Flying School was established there later the same year but the level of activity at Brooklands led to the school being transferred to Shoreham the following year. Here seaplane flying was also possible from the nearby River Adur.

A number of youngsters had now joined the firm, including R.J. Parrott who was taken on as A.V.'s assistant and draughtsman in 1909 after responding to an advertisement placed in the *Engineer*. A talented engineer, he was to later become Works Manager and a major figure in the company as would Roy Chadwick who joined the firm in 1911. Roy Chadwick who by the end of the First World War was established as the firm's chief designer was involved in the design of all Avro aircraft until he was tragically killed in the crash of the Tudor 2 prototype on August 23, 1947. Another of the great men of aviation, the skilful test pilot, F.P. Raynham also joined the firm in 1911.

The question of finance for the new company remained to the fore and from February 1911 attempts were made to find a third partner willing to invest considerable capital in the fledgling A.V. Roe and Company. One enthusiastic supporter, C.R.L. 'Kenworthy, being under 21, was prevented from joining the partnership by his mother and her solicitor and a proposal to establish the firm of Avro Schools Ltd with backing from F.S. Barnwell in December 1911 was similarly stillborn. The quest for a backer continued but advertisements placed in the *Manchester Guardian* in April 1912 drew not a single reply and approaches made to a number of firms, including Crossley Motors, Vickers, Sir W.G. Armstrong Whitworth and Company and the Sheffield Simplex Motor Car Company, were equally abortive. The general concensus at the time was that aviation was too much of a risk venture. Finance thus remained the responsibility of H.V.

Roe and before the business finally became a success he had invested some £10,000 in it.

Towards the end of 1912 the company was looking more secure and James Grimble Groves, a member of a prominent brewing family, offered financial help resulting in the firm becoming a limited company with £30,000 capital on January 11, 1913. Members of the board were Groves, Chairman, the two Roe brothers, joint Managing Directors, and a Capt Lutwyche. In April 1913, the workshops at Brownsfield Mills were vacated and A.V. Roe and Co Ltd moved to new premises at Clifton Street, Miles Platting, Manchester. A blow was dealt the company when Groves died on June 23, 1914, but his family retained their interest in Avro until December 1916 when their shareholding was bought by H.V. Roe.

The coming of the First World War led to a massive expansion in aircraft production and large orders were placed for the legendary Avro 504. The new premises at Clifton Street were too small for the required large-scale production and it was necessary for the company to rent larger premises from the nearby company of Mather and Platt at Newton Heath. From October 1914 the Clifton Street works were relegated to the role of Woodworking Department. A piece of land adjacent to the Mather and Platt's extension was acquired later with the intention of building a large new factory but this was not fully complete until 1919.

In 1916, with the testing of naval aircraft in mind, A.V. Roe decided to establish a new Avro factory at a waterside location. Sites in Lancashire and near Brighton were considered but the final choice was Hamble on Southampton Water. Here it was intended to build not only a new works but a garden city for the company's employees but after only the hangars and 24 houses had been built the shortage of wartime materials halted the scheme. Apart from the production of some Avro 504s at the end of the war, Hamble was used solely as an experimental shop, R.J. Parrott being its General Manager.

Also during 1916 the prospect of the new works at Hamble and the expectation of large orders for both the Avro 529 bomber and Avro 530 fighter spawned a proposal to split A.V. Roe and Co Ltd into two with effect from December 31, 1916. A new company 'A.V. Roe (Southampton) Ltd' was to be established at Hamble with responsibility for obtaining orders for the Type 530, the original company retaining responsibility for obtaining orders for the Type 529. Production of both types was to be shared equally between both companies. However with the curtailment of the building at Hamble and the failure to secure production orders for either the Avro 529 or 530 the scheme was shelved.

In 1917 Humphrey Roe decided to join the Royal Flying Corps and left the company on July 31 receiving some £20,875 for his shareholding. By this time one of 'A.V.'s' inventions, the Avro strainer, a device to adjust the tension of interplane bracing wires, alone was earning the company some £40,000 annual profit.

Throughout the war business had been good and profits high but the

R.H. Dobson

armistice in November 1918 resulted in the wholesale cancellation of contracts and a major slump in the company's fortunes. Many Avro workers were laid off and those remaining found themselves producing such non-aeronautical items as baby carriages and billiard tables. Steps were also taken to diversify into large-scale motor car production and a small 10 hp car was designed. However after only a small number had been produced production ceased in May 1920 as a result of Crossley Motors acquiring a controlling interest in A.V. Roe and Co. Crossley car bodies were then set to be added to the list of products being manufactured in the Avro works but the production was thwarted by a recession in the motor industry.

In a further attempt to increase the company's income in the difficult postwar years, the Avro Transport Company was established to exploit the keen public interest in flying. Joy riding centres were established in the summer of 1919 at the company's base at Alexandra Park aerodrome, Manchester, and at many coastal resorts. The company also inaugurated the first scheduled domestic air service in Britain on May 24 when four three-seat Avro 504Ks flew from Alexandra Park to Blackpool via Southport. One of the passengers was Avro director John Lord who in earlier times was General Manager of Everard and Co and became sole proprietor of that firm when H.V. Roe joined the RFC. He joined the Avro Board in 1917.

By 1920 the depression was beginning to bite and there were no longer large and eager crowds anxious to fly. Joy riding plans were therefore

Tutor production at Newton Heath in 1935. (*British Aerospace*)

Woodford in 1940 with Ansons and Blenheims outside the flight sheds. (*British Aerospace*)

cancelled in April 1920 and the Avro Transport Company fleet was sold. A few months later, in August 1920, Newton Heath became the head office of A.V. Roe and Co and in the same year 'A.V.' received the first of his honours, the OBE.

The Air Ministry's lease on Alexandra Park aerodrome expired in 1924 and Avro was obliged to seek an alternative site for the testing of their aircraft. Land at New Hall Farm was acquired and a hangar erected on what was to become the Woodford aerodrome we know today. The early twenties were lean years for Avro and the firm was largely kept in business by building small production batches of Avro 504s for the Royal Air Force and refurbishing many examples of the same type both for the RAF and for a number of overseas air forces.

In 1928 A.V. Roe sold his interest in the company to Sir John Siddeley, the head of Sir W. G. Armstrong Whitworth Aircraft Ltd. On leaving the firm 'A.V.', who was subsequently knighted in the 1929 New Years Honours and took the surname Verdon-Roe in honour of his mother in 1933, acquired together with John Lord a controlling interest in the famous Cowes boat building firm of S.E. Saunders Ltd. The company's name was changed to Saunders-Roe Ltd and the firm turned its attention to the production of flying-boats. Sir Alliott was still President of Saunders-Roe at the time of his death on January 4, 1958.

Following the takeover by the Siddeley Group, the Avro design and development staff were moved from Hamble to Manchester but the Hamble premises remained in Avro ownership until they were taken over by Air Service Training Ltd in April 1931. In the first years of the new decade prosperity returned to Avros with healthy orders being received for Avians, Tutors, 626s and Cadets. The next major landmark in the history of Avro was when in July 1935 the company became a subsidiary of the newly created Hawker Siddeley Aircraft Co Ltd. By the following year Roy Chadwick was on the Board of A.V. Roe and Co as was R.H. Dobson (later Sir Roy Dobson, CBE), who had joined the company in 1914 and went on to become Managing Director in 1941, Managing Director of the whole Hawker-Siddeley Group in 1958, and their Chairman in 1963.

The expansion of the RAF from the mid-thirties led not only to Avros receiving orders for 287 Hawker Audaxes in addition to their own aircraft but also the establishment of new government sponsored aircraft factories. One of these was Chadderton near Manchester which was handed over to A.V. Roe and Co in 1938. By the outbreak of the Second World War both Chadderton and Newton Heath were in full production producing Ansons, Manchesters and Bristol Blenheims. Assembly of all these types took place in large new hangers erected at the firm's Woodford aerodrome which was also soon to be the site of additional production facilities. Use was also made of hangar space at Ringway Airport Manchester. Lancaster production began in 1941 and to meet the volume of orders received for both this and the Anson a new shadow factory was established at Yeadon aerodrome near Leeds. Production of the Anson at Yeadon reached 130 aircraft a month during 1943 and 1944. As in the First World War Avro aircraft were also built in large numbers by sub-contractors.

Peace in 1945 led to the cancellation of orders and the company once again contracted. Civil aircraft again rolled off the production lines but the company remained in the military market producing Lincolns, then Shackletons and later the revolutionary delta wing Vulcan. Throughout the period the company continued to slim down until by the early 1960s only the Woodford and Chadderton factories remained. On July 1, 1963, the great name of Avro disappeared when the company was restyled the Avro-Whitworth Division of Hawker Siddeley Aviation Ltd. From that date the Avro 748, which was then in production, became the H.S.748. The type, which remained in production longer than any other Avro design, even the legendary 504, underwent a further and final name change when British Aerospace was established on April 29, 1977.

A. V. Roe with his biplane in the famous 'Avroplane' shed at Brooklands in December 1907.

# Roe I Biplane

A. V. Roe's first man-carrying aircraft was a canard biplane of wire braced, wooden construction, similar to the Wright-type model with which he won £75 at Alexandra Palace in April 1907. The aircraft was built round a large white wood, three bay, triangular structure mounted on four home-made pneumatic tyred wheels, the front pair being steerable. The pilot sat in the forward part of the machine and a 6 hp J.A.P. air-cooled motorcycle engine was situated amidships, driving a 6 ft 2 in diameter two bladed paddle-like pusher airscrew of 3 ft pitch through five feet of extension shafting which formed the apex of the central structure. Wing construction was primitive, the kauri main spars being external and therefore thin to reduce drag. For rigidity it was necessary to employ a large number of bracing wires and kingposts with the result that the cotton covering could only be applied to the underside of each wing, the erroneous belief being that lift was only generated by pressure on the undersurfaces. The covering was then tightened with a coat of size and the whole wing structure braced from three much taller kingposts. There were no ailerons and no rudder but a car-type steering column warped and pivoted the large front elevator and so gave both lateral and fore-and-aft control. A. V. Roe was the true inventor of the single-lever type of control and had patented such a system as early as 1906, ante-dating the claims of Continental inventors by several years.

The Roe I biplane at Brooklands in 1908 showing the 6 hp twin-cylinder J.A.P. engine amidships. (*Courtesy the Royal Aeronautical Society.*)

The Roe I biplane was built in the stables behind the surgery of A. V. Roe's brother Dr. S. Verdon Roe at 47 West Hill, Putney, London, and on completion in September 1907 was taken to Brooklands, where Roe hoped to make an attempt to win at least two of the prizes on offer for successful powered flight. The Brooklands Automobile Racing Club had offered £2,500 for the first flight round their three-mile circuit before the end of that year, stipulating that it should be completed at not less than 10 mph and at a height of between 30 and 50 ft, and *The Graphic* and *Daily Graphic* were offering £1,000 'to the inventor who first produces a machine which, being heavier than air, shall fly, with one or more human passengers, between two given points not less than one mile apart.'

Although a great deal of taxying was done along the concrete track, the 6 hp engine was not powerful enough and the biplane flew only when towed by friendly racing motorists. Such flights were successful on straight tows, but turns resulted in sideslips and damage until Roe designed a quick-release which enabled him to cast off at will and make controlled landings. In this way he learned the feel of the controls but the end of the year came without the prize being awarded.

A. V. Roe working on the Roe I biplane after it had been fitted with a 24 hp eight cylinder Antoinette.

2

'A.V.' then negotiated the loan of a 24 hp Antoinette eight cylinder, water-cooled engine designed and built in France by Levasseur. It had copper water jackets and direct petrol injection and on its arrival in May 1908, gave Roe the extra power he so badly needed. To carry the increased weight, extra wing area was provided by inserting short stub wings at mid gap in the inner wing bays. Unfortunately the extra power was more than his airscrews could absorb and many blade failures occurred, but the trouble was eventually cured and in the early morning of June 8, 1908, he succeeded in taking the biplane off under its own power and in making several hops at a height of 2 to 3 ft. above the track. A. V. Roe did not publicise his achievement and two years passed before he let it be known that he had left the ground in 1908. In 1928–29 the Gorrell Committee of the Royal Aero Club disallowed his claim to have been the first to fly in Britain on the grounds that he had not been airborne for a sufficient distance, ruling that the first Briton to do so had been J. T. C. Moore-Brabazon in a Voisin biplane at Eastchurch nearly a year later.

During his long stay at Brooklands, Roe received no encouragement from his landlords. Indeed, the Clerk of the Course, E. Rodakowsky was at times openly hostile to aeroplanes, and at the start of the 1908 motor racing season insisted that Roe's shed be painted dark green and be moved from its original site alongside the finishing straight, close to the judge's box, to the other side of the paddock. The shed was also pressed into service as a refreshment room on race days and it was on the first such occasion that Rodakowsky ordered Roe's biplane to be lifted over 5 ft railings into an adjoining field. During this exercise, track attendants stumbled under the load in the gusty conditions and dropped the machine into a dried-up dyke breaking some ribs. Some further damage was caused by mishandling but the machine was repaired and six trials were possible before Roe was evicted from Brooklands on July 17, having been given two weeks' notice on July 4. The Antoinette engine was then returned to France as Roe could not afford to buy it and the biplane dismantled. A wheel and a few other selected parts were kept by Roe to remind him of some of the ingenious constructional methods he had used. In later years these items were preserved in a glass case at his home as part of the Roe private aeronautical collection.

## SPECIFICATION AND DATA

*Construction:*   By A. V. Roe at 47 West Hill, Putney, London, S.W.15

*Powerplants:*   One 6 hp J.A.P.
One 24 hp Antoinette

*Dimensions:*   Span 36 ft (upper wing)   Length 23 ft
30 ft (lower wing)

*Weights:*   Tare weight 350 lb   All-up weight 650 lb
Weight of Antoinette engine (without radiator) 98 lb

A. V. Roe at Blackpool with the first Roe I triplane in October 1909. (*Flight photo 0140*)

# Roe I Triplane

After his eviction from Brooklands, A. V. Roe turned his attention to a triplane design. In January 1909 he filed a patent for a novel control system applied to a tandem triplane arrangement. The main wings provided control in the pitching plane by varying incidence, operated by fore and aft movements of the pilot's control lever. Side to side movement of the same lever warped the centre wing, and the upper and lower wings were warped in unison by the rear wing struts acting as push rods. The rear triplane unit acted simply as a fixed lifting surface; a rudder behind this was operated in consort with the wing warping.

Early in 1909, Roe began work on two triplanes for which engine manufacturer J. A. Prestwich agreed to supply two of his J.A.P. engines. The larger machine, intended to have a 35 hp engine, was apparently built with financial support from motor dealer George Friswell, but before it was completed the partnership was dissolved. The incomplete airframe was subsequently auctioned at Friswell's Sales Rooms in Albany Street, London, where it realised £5 10s (£4 19s after commission).

For his own use, Roe designed a machine to use a four-cylinder inline engine of 10 hp. Unfortunately this engine failed on test in the J.A.P. factory, so Prestwich agreed to build a two-cylinder engine of similar power. Until this was ready, Roe had to install the 6 hp engine from his Brooklands biplane.

The new triplane closely resembled the patent drawings. The two sets of wings were joined by a fuselage of triangular section, with three deal longerons joined by cross struts and wire braced. The main undercarriage consisted of two cycle wheels in reversed forks, with a smaller cycle wheel

4

under the rear fuselage ahead of the tail unit. The wings were each made in three panels, with internal wooden structure of spars and ribs. For lightness and cheapness, the surfaces were covered with wrapping paper with open weave fabric backing. A coat of yellowish varnish earned the machine the ironic name of *Yellow Peril* later in its career.

The components of both triplanes were made at Putney early in 1909 while Roe sought a flying ground. After a protracted search, he found the open space of Walthamstow Marshes alongside the River Lea in Essex, where he was able to rent an arch under the Great Eastern Railway's bridge across the river. Erection of the two triplanes under the archway probably began in March, and after the larger unfinished machine had been removed, taxying trials with the 6 hp engine began in April. By this time, Roe's younger brother Humphrey had agreed to provide financial support. He owned a factory in Manchester whose best-known product was gentlemen's trouser braces sold under the trade-mark 'Bulls Eye'; in recognition of this sponsorship, A. V. Roe added the name 'Bulls Eye' to the side of the triplane, which already carried his own trade name 'Avroplane'.

The new J.A.P. engine arrived about the end of May. It was a V-Twin with the same 50 degree angle as the 6 hp engine but had mechanically operated overhead valves and, from mid-June, a Simms magneto replacing the battery and coil ignition. Although it only provided 9 hp instead of the promised 10 hp, this was sufficient to enable Roe to get airborne for brief hops from June 5, making (in his own words) 'dozens of short flights up to 50 ft in length at a height of 2–3 ft, which were hardly more than jumps.'

The propeller was mounted on a drive-shaft above the engine, with belt-drive from a pulley on the engine to a larger pulley on the propeller shaft. Varying pulley size allowed different gear ratios, and the pitch of the

The first Roe I triplane outside the famous railway arches at the Lea Valley in Essex. (*The Science Museum photo 395/66*)

5

propeller blades could be adjusted on the ground between flights. After a series of trials in which Roe investigated the effect of these variations, and also refined his piloting technique, on Friday July 23 he made three flights of about 900 ft at an average height of 10 ft, thus becoming the first to fly an all British aeroplane with a British engine over British soil.

Further flights were made during the next two months, interspersed with mishaps leading to repairs and modifications. Skids were fitted under the wing tips, and later removed; the pilot's seat was moved forward, and then the engine was moved forward, so that the drive wheel on the propeller shaft was ahead of the centre wing spar. Finally, the belt-drive was replaced by a motor cycle chain between pinions on the engine and propeller shafts.

In this form, and with the vertical fin surfaces in the tail unit removed, the first triplane appeared at the Blackpool meeting of October 18–24. It made a few short hops of up to 150 ft on October 19 but according to contemporary reports it was suffering from engine trouble; Roe himself later suggested that the main trouble was heavy rain soaking the paper covering.

Roe took two machines to Blackpool; the second aircraft was similar to the original, but was designed to have a new four-cylinder engine which was intended to produce 20 hp but which seems to have only produced about 14 hp. This new engine arrived in Blackpool at mid-week and Roe had the second aircraft ready to fly by October 21, but storms prevented any further flying.

Blackpool Week 1909 ended the active career of the first Roe I triplane. It made a brief reappearance at an aero exhibition held at Belle Vue Gardens, Manchester, January 1–3, 1914, spent 11 years in storage at the Manchester factory, and was presented in 1925 to the Science Museum at South Kensington, London where it remains on permanent exhibition.

The airframe of the second Roe I triplane closely resembled that of the

The second Roe I triplane, identified by cylindrical fuel tank, tail skid and tapered fuselage, in flight at Wembley, December 1909. (*Courtesy P. T. Capon*)

'Two-and-a-Bit Plane'—the second triplane with extended biplane wings, tail wheel and *Mercury* undercarriage at Brooklands 1910. (*Flight*)

first but fortunately there were several prominent recognition features which made it easily distinguishable from its forebear. Whereas the earlier aircraft had a fuselage of constant depth and large tail wheel, the second fuselage was tapered towards the rear and equipped with a long tail skid. There were also additional struts in the undercarriage. The first machine had a small fuel tank mounted on a fuselage longeron but the second had a narrow, cigar-shaped tank on struts ahead of the pilot to give a greater head of fuel. It must also be remembered that only the first triplane bore the fuselage inscription 'Bulls Eye Avroplane' under which appeared a clearly painted figure 3, indicating that the inventor regarded it as his third individual aeroplane. He had meanwhile been evicted from Lea Marshes and on his return from Blackpool, transferred to Old Deer Park, Richmond, Surrey. The new site proved unsuitable and late in November 1909 he moved to Wembley Park, Middlesex, where on December 6 the second Roe I triplane made its first exploratory flights with encouragingly few mishaps. The bigger engine improved the performance to the point where local authorities sportingly felled a number of trees to enable him to fly a circular course and land back at his starting point. Attempts to improve the control system were not always successful as on Christmas Eve 1909 when Roe found it impossible to lift the port wings quickly enough and sideslipped into the ground, once more demolishing the port mainplanes.

In January 1910, with financial help from his brother H. V. Roe, the private firm of A. V. Roe and Company was formed with workshop space in the factory of Everard and Company at Brownsfield Mills, Manchester. Wembley Park flying ground was retained until Maj Lindsay Lloyd converted the centre of Brooklands track into an aerodrome. 'A.V.' then returned to the scene of his 1908 experiments and made three half-mile introductory flights there on March 11, 1910. He then left for London to look after his new Roe II triplane, the first example of which, named *Mercury*, was that day introduced to the public at the Olympia Aero Show.

7

The Avro 'Friswell' triplane (*right*) under construction alongside the first Roe I triplane in the railway arches at the Lea Valley. (*The Science Museum photo 624/78*)

No doubt influenced by the success of contemporary biplanes, he later tried out this configuration using the second Roe I triplane as a guinea pig. All three outer wing panels were removed and the top two replaced by others similar to, but longer than, those of the Roe II *Mercury*. At the same time a *Mercury*-type bottom centre section and improved undercarriage were fitted. The tail wheel from the original Roe I triplane was borrowed and fitted into a strengthened mounting, a piece of cannibalism which explains its absence from the Science Museum exhibit to this day. When flown in this guise at Brooklands on Easter Monday 1910, the aircraft was nicknamed the 'Two-and-a-Bit Plane' but the advent of newer designs speedily ended its career and the old aircraft was dismantled at Brooklands at the end of the following month.

## SPECIFICATION AND DATA

| | |
|---|---|
| *Construction:* | By A. V. Roe at 47 West Hill, Putney, London, S.W.15; erected at Lea Marshes, Essex (1st machine) and Blackpool, Lancs (2nd machine) |
| *Powerplants:* | One 10 hp J.A.P.   One 20 hp J.A.P. |
| *Dimensions:* | Span 20 ft 0 in   Length 23 ft 0 in<br>Wing Area 285 sq ft<br>Tailplane span 10 ft 0 in   Tailplane area 35 sq ft |
| *Weights:* | Tare weight 300 lb   All-up weight 450 lb |
| *Performance:* | Speed 25 mph   Range 500 yards |
| *Production:* | No.1 Fitted with two-cylinder 10 hp J.A.P., small fuel tank and tail wheel; preserved without engine or tail wheel at the Science Museum, South Kensington, London<br>No.2 Fitted with four-cylinder 20 hp J.A.P., raised cylindrical fuel tank and tail skid; wings and undercarriage modified 4.10; dismantled at Brooklands 5.10 |

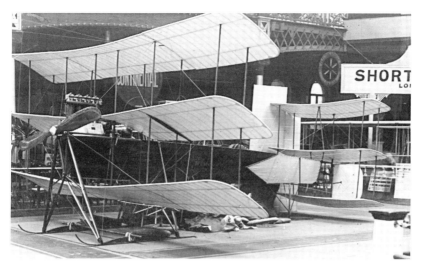

The first Roe II triplane *Mercury* at the Olympia Aero Show, London, in March 1910 in its initial form with warping wings. (*Flight*)

# Roe II Triplane

First product of the newly formed A. V. Roe and Company was a single seat triplane known as the Roe II. This was approximately equal in size to the original machine but was fitted with a 35 hp Green four-cylinder, water-cooled engine driving a birch two-bladed, adjustable-pitch airscrew. Cooling was by means of two spiral tube radiators built into, and fitting flush with, the sides of the front fuselage. The new triplane was structurally superior to its predecessors, with silver spruce struts and spars, and an ash fuselage covered with Pegamoid fabric. The undercarriage was a rigid triangulated structure to which the two-wheeled axle was secured by rubber shock absorber cord. Climbing and diving control was improved by pivoting the entire triplane tail and linking it to the mainplane variable incidence gear, the range of movement being from four to eleven degrees of incidence.

Named *Mercury* with due ceremony by the Lord Mayor's daughter, the first Roe II triplane occupied the place of honour at the Manchester Aero Club's model aircraft exhibition at White City, Manchester, on March 4, 1910, and although it had not yet flown, was priced at £550 (with tuition). A week later it was again exhibited at the London Olympia Aero Show of March 11–19, where the Prince and Princess of Wales were shown round the machine by A. V. Roe and an order was received from W. G. Windham, later Sir Walter Windham MP, a manufacturer of motor car bodies at Clapham Junction. References to the sale of yet another Roe II triplane to the Rangie Cycle Company appeared in several publications at the time but there is no evidence that such an aircraft was ever built.

9

The exhibition machine *Mercury* was retained by A. V. Roe for school and experimental use but when flight trials began at Brooklands, it rolled on take-off and twice landed upside down. The second crash (by pupil Job), April 17, 1910, resulted in the destruction of the undercarriage and most of the mainplanes. During reconstruction Roe took the opportunity of correcting the C. G. position by moving forward the pilot's seat, and abandoned wing warping. The control column was remounted on a universal joint, large unbalanced ailerons were hinged to the trailing edge of the top wing, and a tall rectangular rudder more than twice the area of the original was fitted. Ten days were sufficient to complete this work and *Mercury* was out again for taxying trials on April 27.

W. G. Windham's aircraft was delivered to Brooklands early in May and assembled during Whitsun. First hops were made on May 26 by A. V. Roe who then handed it over to the owner for some preliminary taxying. The amount of flying done on this machine is uncertain but it is known that Windham landed in soft ground at Brooklands on July 12 and turned the triplane over on its back.

Accidents to *Mercury* were now much less frequent and on Thursday June 2, Roe made several circuits of Brooklands at a height of 20 ft and executed a number of fairly steep turns. At the end of July it was dismantled and taken to Weybridge station along with its successor, Roe III, for

*Mercury* with ailerons fitted, after one of its several mishaps at Brooklands later in 1910. (*Courtesy the Royal Aeronautical Society*).

The Roe II triplane at the Manchester Aero Club exhibition in March 1910.

despatch by rail to the Blackpool Flying Meeting of August 1, 1910. Hopes of winning the prize money so necessary for future experiments were dashed when sparks from the engine of the LNWR goods train set fire to their truck while puffing up an incline near Wigan on July 27. Both aircraft were reduced to ashes.

## SPECIFICATION AND DATA

*Manufacturers:*    A. V. Roe and Company, Brownsfield Mills, Great Ancoats Street, Manchester; and Brooklands Aerodrome, Byfleet, Surrey.

*Powerplants:*    One 35 hp Green

*Dimensions:*    Span 26 ft 0 in    Length 23 ft 0 in    Height 9 ft 0 in
Wing area 280 sq ft

*Weights:*    Weight of engine without flywheel 150 lb
All-up weight 550 lb

*Performance:*    Maximum speed 40 mph

*Production:*    No.1 *Mercury*, Avro experimental, burned out near Wigan 27.7.10
No.2 For W. G. Windham, Brooklands.

11

The Roe III triplane (35 hp J.A.P.) with ailerons fitted to the top wing. (*Courtesy the Royal Aeronautical Society.*)

# Roe III Triplane

The 'prototype' Roe III was a two-seater, structurally similar to Roe II, but with the important difference that the mainplanes were fixed to the fuselage, climbing and diving being effected for the first time by means of a tail elevator. The aspect ratio was 8 and the bottom wing was cut back to a span of only 20 feet. The lifting tail remained, but as a result of experiments with the triplane *Mercury*, lateral control was by means of ailerons (5 ft span by 2 ft chord), this time hinged to the rear spar of the top wing so that they were slightly inset. By this time the functions of the rudder were better understood and this organ was increased in size to a rectangle equal in height to the maximum tailplane gap as on the modified Roe II. A more robust undercarriage was of the twin-skid, four wheel Farman type and the engine a 35 hp J.A.P. eight-cylinder vee air-cooled unit.

First taxying trials were made at Brooklands by A. V. Roe on the evening of June 21, 1910, and the first straights were flown in a tricky wind on June 24. Flight times gradually increased until on July 4 he made a best flight of 11 minutes (with 'just a touch' after $3\frac{1}{2}$ minutes) and later in the day carried his mother and several other passengers. Roe seldom exceeded 20 minutes in the air in the 'prototype' Roe III because the J.A.P. engine had a tendency to overheat and cover pilot and passenger with sooty oil ejected from the scavenging holes at the base of the cylinder walls. Carburettor fires were frequent but Roe persevered until on July 9 he remained aloft for 25 minutes and made comparatively steep turns. He also practised figure eights in readiness for Royal Aero Club tests which he passed on this aircraft on July 20. Aviator's Certificate No.18 was issued to the great pioneer on July 26, but within a year he had given up piloting in favour of designing and did not take the Air Ministry's 'A' Licence tests when they came into being in 1919. He kept no log books and did not know how many hours he had flown as a pilot. The J.A.P. engined Roe III was advertised secondhand by the makers for £250 in May 1911 but its ultimate fate is uncertain.

The three subsequent triplanes of this type (all powered by 35 hp Green four cylinder, water-cooled engines) had the span of the top mainplane increased to 31 ft and were fitted with ailerons hinged to the rear spar of the centre wing. First of these, identified by rounded corners to the trailing edge of the rudder and by fuselage covering applied only in the region of the cockpits, was a special slow flying aircraft with a more heavily cambered wing section for instructional use at the Avro School. Piloted by the designer, this triplane first flew at Brooklands on July 9, 1910, and its performance was at once encouraging. Both Roe and Pixton carried passengers on July 13 and one another on the following day. At the end of the month the machine was sent by train from Weybridge to the Blackpool meeting only to be destroyed by fire en route, as was the Roe II *Mercury*.

Determined to compete, Roe and Pixton hastily brought spare components from the Manchester works to Blackpool and arranged for a new engine to be delivered direct from the Green factory. Work started on Thursday July 28 and the finished aircraft flew on Monday August 1, much of the erection

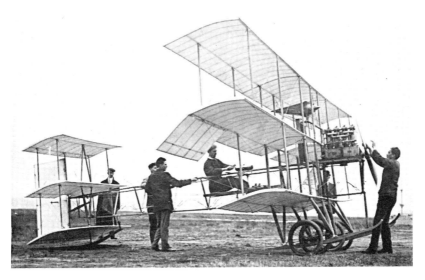

A. V. Roe seated in the 35 hp Green engined Roe III triplane at Squantum Point, Boston, USA in September 1911. (*Courtesy H. F. Cowley*)

13

A. V. Roe flying the third Roe III triplane at the 1910 Blackpool Meeting.

having been done by Roe himself during the previous night. There was not even time to cover the fuselage. Three attempts were made to take off, during which a tyre burst and some rubber shock absorbers snapped. Two struts were broken on landing but not before Roe had made four circuits of the course, at least two with passengers (who could face forward or backward according to taste). For this he received a special merit award of £50. August 2 dawned wet and windy but after repairs Roe succeeded in making two more short hops at 7.30 p.m. and on the following afternoon left the ground in a much more lively manner. In turning, the wind carried him dangerously close to one of the pylons, to avoid which he had no alternative but to make a crash landing, breaking several more struts, the airscrew and one mainplane.

Visitors to the Blackpool meeting included J. V. Martin, Organiser of the Harvard University Aeronautical Society, who ordered a Roe III triplane which was built, crated and despatched (without engine) to the USA by August 13! A. V. Roe and Claude Grahame-White were also invited to fly at the Boston Aviation Meeting scheduled to open on September 2. They left in the White Star liner *Cymric* on August 23, Roe taking with him the makeshift Blackpool triplane in a 40 ft packing case. Arriving at Boston on September 1, they collected the Harvard Society's triplane (which had been stored at East Boston Docks since its arrival in the Cunarder *Ivernia* a week previously), and took all the aircraft by lighter to the airfield at Squantum Point. Here Roe and mechanics Pixton and Halstead complete the erection of the Blackpool triplane on September 3, but flights begun on September 6 were disappointing, the longest being 75 ft at a height of 10 ft. At 5 p.m. the engine failed and the triplane landed heavily in front of the grandstand, damaging the starboard mainplanes and

14

undercarriage. Local woodworker C. H. Metz made a new airscrew and at 6.30 p.m. on September 8 Roe succeeded in leaving the ground properly for the first time, reaching a height of 30 feet. When he shut off the engine to land, however, a sudden gust caused the aircraft to swerve to starboard and dig the right undercarriage skid into the ground, causing it to swing round with major breakages. Roe was unhurt and more determined than ever to show the Americans that his triplanes were more than just interesting freaks. On September 9 he secured permission from Harvard to erect the Society's triplane and fit it with the 35 hp Green engine taken from the wreck. Erection was completed and engine runs made on September 12 and it is said that the aircraft was slightly heavier than its predecessor and had two instead of four wheels. Two days later, amid the applause of 10,000 spectators, successful flights were made up to a height of 50 feet but the engine still refused to give full power. After tinkering with it for most of September 15, Roe made a good take-off at 4.20 p.m. and flew the length of the field. In attempting to round the pylon, he sideslipped into the ground from 50 feet, totally wrecking the port side of the aircraft and suffering a severe scalp wound. A cordon of police saved the wreck from souvenir hunters and after A. V. Roe returned to England, Pixton built a new triplane for Harvard out of the remains of the other two. He then sold the surplus spares to the local aircraft firm of Burgess and Co and Curtiss of Marblehead to raise money for his passage home, leaving Harvard with their machine untested in the air.

## SPECIFICATION AND DATA

*Manufacturers:* A. V. Roe and Company, Brownsfield Mills, Great Ancoats Street, Manchester; and Brooklands Aerodrome, Byfleet, Surrey

*Powerplants:* One 35 hp J.A.P.
One 35 hp Green

*Dimensions:* Span (upper) 31 ft 0 in, (lower) 20 ft 0 in
Length 23 ft 0 in    Wing area 287 sq ft
Tailplane area 75 sq ft

*Weight:* All-up weight 750 lb

*Production:* No.1 Prototype with 35 hp J.A.P., first flown 24.6.10, up for sale 5.11
No.2 Avro School machine, first flown 9.7.10, burned out 27.7.10
No.3 Blackpool makeshift machine, first flown 1.8.10, crashed at Boston, USA 8.9.10
No.4 Harvard Aeronautical Society machine, first flown (and crashed) at Boston, 15.9.10

*Note:* A work of reference of the period states that a triplane of this type was built for the great pioneer pilot Cecil Grace. This aircraft is conspicuous by its absence from contemporary records and diligent research by the author only makes it evident that no such aircraft existed.

15

The Roe IV triplane. (*Flight*)

# Roe IV Triplane

The last of A. V. Roe's primitive triplanes, completed in September 1910, was a single seater structurally similar to its predecessors and powered by a 35 hp Green water-cooled engine, the radiator for which was mounted in the centre section gap. The shortened bottom wing was retained but the wing chord was somewhat reduced. Despite the improved lateral control given by ailerons, the Roe IV triplane reverted to wing warping, effected by rotating a control wheel mounted on a column which moved fore and aft for diving and climbing. The tailplane was triangular in shape and for the first time of the non-lifting monoplane type equipped with movable elevators. The familiar four-wheeled undercarriage of the previous triplanes was also a feature of Roe IV.

By the middle of 1910 'A.V.' was fast becoming interested in building a biplane, with the result that only one Roe IV was constructed. It was used almost exclusively for instructional work at the Avro Flying School at Brooklands where pupils found it rather sensitive on the controls and more difficult to master than the earlier machines. Needless to say it was broken many times as on October 10, 1910, when, in the words of an onlooker, 'a pupil rose unsteadily and after 225 yards slowly sideslipped into the sewage farm, completely smashing the starboard mainplane.' Such incidents were so frequent that they excited little comment and the aircraft structure was so simple that even major damage could often be put right the same day.

Several famous pilots were trained on the Roe IV triplane, including Hubert Oxley and C. Howard Pixton, the former starting his training with a flourish by attempting to take off down wind without previous experience and nosing over in the sewage farm on October 17, 1910. Pixton, practising figure eights at 200 ft on November 8 for his Royal Aero Club certificate, sideslipped Roe IV into the ground, where it caught fire and suffered extensive damage. Nevertheless the machine was out again on November 17, back in the sewage farm by December 4 and carried Pixton successfully through the tests for his aviator's certificate on January 24, 1911. It continued to suffer at the hands of trainees such as F. Conway Jenkins, Gordon Bell, R. C. Kemp and Lt W. D. Beatty, until the last mentioned slipped in and badly wrecked it on February 14, 1911. This time the damage took a fortnight to repair and the opportunity was taken to insert a 4 ft extension piece into the fuselage.

Pixton made the first test flight in the revised Roe IV on March 1 and managed to coax it up to 750 ft. This performance contrasted sharply with the usual 150 ft ceiling associated with this machine. A week later, on March 8, engine trouble compelled R. C. Kemp to abandon the tests for his certificate and soon afterwards (certainly no later than August 1911) the Roe IV was dismantled and replaced at the Avro School by the Type D biplane of superior performance.

The Roe IV triplane at Brooklands.

## SPECIFICATION AND DATA

*Manufacturers:*   A. V. Roe and Company, Brownsfield Mills, Great Ancoats Street, Manchester; and Brooklands Aerodrome, Byfleet, Surrey.

*Powerplant:*   One 35 hp Green

*Dimensions:*   Span (upper) 32 ft 0 in, (bottom) 20 ft 0 in
Length 30 ft 0 in (increased to 34 ft 0 in February 1911)
Height 9 ft 0 in    Wing area 294 sq ft

*Weights:*   Airframe less engine 350 lb    All-up weight 650 lb

*Production:*   One aircraft only, completed 9.10, withdrawn from use at Brooklands about 8.11

17

The original Avro Type D biplane with transverse radiator. (*Flight*)

# Avro Type D

In 1911 A. V. Roe abandoned the triplane configuration and designed a biplane which bore a close resemblance to the Roe IV. It was a two-seater with triangular girder fuselage, twin undercarriage and the same type of cumbersome, triangular monoplane tail. This was replaced almost at once by one of rectangular shape. As on Roe IV, lateral control was by means of wing warping but the passenger seat was placed at the C.G. so that the machine could be flown solo without ballast. Power was supplied by a 35 hp Green, the radiator for which, placed vertically behind the engine at right angles to the direction of flight, distinguished this machine from later aircraft of the same type. It is probable that the engine was that knocked down to A. V. Roe for £67 10s. when the assets of the Scottish Aviation Syndicate were auctioned at Brooklands on December 17, 1910.

In later years aircraft of this type became known as the Avro Type D even though no reference seems to have been made to Types A, B, or C. These, of course, would have been designations posthumously applied to the early triplanes.

The first Avro Type D was erected at Brooklands in March 1911 and first flown on April 1 by C. Howard Pixton (who later took Mrs Roe up in it). He declared it stable, viceless and easy to fly, characteristics confirmed by Gordon Bell and effectively demonstrated on April 11 by Lt Wilfred Parke RN who, without having been in an aeroplane before, flew the length of the aerodrome. Numbered 1, it was flown in the Brooklands–Shoreham race by Pixton on May 6, 1911—the first event in which the Avro entry was not flown by the designer. Pixton lost time at the start because he was flying round in an attempt to win the £500 Manville endurance prize with passenger. He had completed 26 minutes 30 seconds before noticing competitors taking off at the start of the race. He had no map, no cross country experience, and the Type D had never before been flown outside Brooklands Aerodrome. Nevertheless he made a hasty landing to refuel and set off after the others. He lost his way and took three hours for the trip, landing en route at Plumpton Racecourse, seven miles short of his destination. On the way back he spent two days at a flying demonstration at Oakwood, Haywards Heath, returning to Brooklands on Monday May 9 after a very turbulent trip via Dorking. On May 12 he flew the Type D to Hendon in 48 minutes to give a flying display before the Parliamentary Aerial Defence Committee, during which he carried the famous Cdr Sampson RN as passenger and sent A. V. Roe solo in the machine for the first time. Pixton flew home to Brooklands next day and on May 19 made a nonstop flight of 1 hour 30 minutes towards the Manville prize. On June 11 the Type D climbed to a considerable height with the 12 stone Pixton and a 14 stone passenger.

After a flight at Brooklands in June 1911, Cdr Schwann (later AVM Sir Oliver Schwann KCB, CBE) of the Naval Airship Tender *Hermione*, bought the Type D for £700. It was despatched by rail to Barrow-in-Furness where the original triangular tailplane was replaced, the wheels removed and the skids lashed directly to a series of float undercarriages designed by Schwann and his associates and built by naval personnel. The drag of the floats was partially offset by repositioning the radiator horizontally on top of the centre section and by covering the rear fuselage with fabric.

During first taxying trials on August 2 in the 9 ft deep Cavendish Dock on Schwann's narrow flat bottomed Mk.I floats, the aircraft assumed such a tail-down attitude on the water that the small tail float caused excessive wash. This and the fin were therefore removed and the rudder moved upward along the hinge line to clear the water. Later the rudder was raised still further till the lower edge was in line with the bottom of the fuselage.

The special Type D with E.N.V. engine at Brooklands on the eve of the Circuit of Britain Race, July 1911.
*(Courtesy C. H. Barnes)*

Cdr Schwann with the Type D seaplane at Barrow-in Furness, August 1911. (*Avro*)

Maximum speed was only 18 knots and the machine eventually capsized. Report R & M 69 deals at length with Schwann's further experiments with seven different types of single and twin float undercarriages. Limited success came on November 18, 1911, after the Green Engine Co Ltd had coaxed an extra 10 hp out of the engine by fitting additional open exhaust ports, and float design had reached the Mk.VII stepped type. On that day the Type D lifted on to the step for the first time and left the water rather unexpectedly, reaching a height of 15–20 ft. Schwann was not at that time a qualified pilot and the aircraft fell back into the water and capsized. After salvage and reconstruction, trials were resumed by S. V. Sippe who made the first of a series of short flights at Barrow on April 9, 1912, during which he reported favourably on the feeling of acceleration from the unstick speed of 25 mph to the flying speed of 40 mph. It became the first seaplane ever to take off from British sea water. On April 12 Sippe made two or three circuits of the dock and reached a height of 160 feet. The seaplane was then handed over to the owner who had just qualified as a pilot at the Bristol School on Salisbury Plain. The feasibility of marine aircraft had been proved but the rate of climb of the Type D seaplane was poor due to an increase in all-up weight to 1,000 lb (an accurate figure obtained by weighing the machine in the airship shed at Barrow). Endurance was but 20 minutes— the time taken for the cooling water to boil away, so a 50 hp Gnome rotary was fitted in an attempt to improve the performance, but there are no recorded flights with this engine.

The sale of the Type D biplane reduced the Avro School to only one aircraft—the Roe IV triplane. Pending delivery of new machines from Manchester, A. V. Roe acquired a secondhand Gnome-engined Farman pusher purchased in Newcastle. The crates housing this relic were too big for railway trucks and travelled south by sea at a cost of £25. This charge

20

contrasted sharply with that for Avro aircraft, which broke down into sections to fit into a single crate, the Manchester–Brooklands rail charge for which was a mere £1 16s. 6d.

The next Avro aircraft was a modified Type D built to compete in the £10,000 *Daily Mail* Circuit of Britain Race. It was a sesquiplane with upper and lower spans of 33 and 23 feet, powered by a 60 hp E.N.V. eight-cylinder, water-cooled engine. Like all subsequent machines of the type, its fuselage was increased in length from 26 ft to 28 ft, but it was the only one, apart from the prototype, to be fitted with the large triangular tailplane. Construction took place at Manchester during June 1911 under the watchful eye of the pilot, R. C. Kemp, and first taxying trials were made at Brooklands by A. V. Roe on July 18. First flights made by Kemp later in the day showed the machine to be fast, but the engine overheated and the rate of climb was poor with full load of petrol and oil. Without A. V. Roe's approval, extensions were hurriedly fitted to the lower wing, making it equal in span to the upper and increasing the wing area by 50 sq ft. After an initial test circuit at 100 ft on July 22, morning of the race, Kemp climbed to 800 ft but during a fairly steep descent at half throttle the extension to the port lower mainplane failed at 150 ft. Although he jerked on full right rudder and full left warp, the machine spun into the ground wingtip first and broke up. Miraculously Kemp stepped unhurt from the wreckage.

The third Type D, the assembly of which was completed at Brooklands

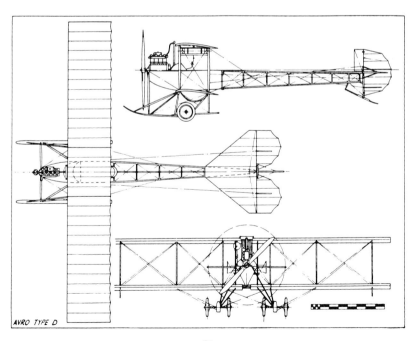

AVRO TYPE D

on September 9, 1911, was almost identical with the first but distinguishable from it because drag had been reduced by fitting the radiator in a sloping position behind the engine. Minor differences included straighter front skids, a covered fuselage and no fin. First straight hops were made by F. P. Raynham on September 11 and after adjustments a flight to 600 ft was made on September 17. Although intended as a school machine, it was entered for the Michelin Speed Prize but during his flight to Hendon to compete on September 21, Raynham ran into thick fog. In attempting to 'press on' with primitive instruments, he made what may have been the first recorded spin and recovery, afterwards landing at New Barnet to ask his way. Unsatisfactory experiments with a new airscrew, and sagging wing fabric compelled him to give up the attempt. He therefore returned to base, arriving over Brooklands at 1,000 ft on the evening of September 24 and by the end of the month the Type D was in full time use by the Avro School.

Delivered at Brooklands on September 30, 1911, the fourth Type D was a single-seater but otherwise identical with the equal-span school version, except for the radiator which was fitted vertically behind the engine in line with the direction of flight. The engine was a specially tuned Green giving 45 hp and identified by holes at the base of the cylinder walls which improved scavenging. After some trouble with slack fabric, satisfactory first flights on October 12 again raised Raynham's Michelin hopes and although he reached 1,000 ft with 5 hours' fuel (13 gallons) during a practice flight two days later, bad weather on October 15, last day of the competition, ruined his chances. With an eye on the Michelin long distance prize, he coaxed the machine off on October 18 with 8 hours' fuel (24 gallons) but the attempt came to an abrupt end when the machine forced landed in the sewage farm with an iced-up carburettor on October 27, only three days before the closing date.

The fifth Type D was an improved sesquiplane version generally similar

F. P. Raynham seated in the fourth Type D at Brooklands in October 1911. (*Courtesy C. H. Barnes*)

The fifth Type D was the improved sesquiplane version. (*Courtesy C. H. Barnes.*)

to, and having the same dimensions as, the ill-fated Circuit of Britain machine. The engine was a 35 hp Green.

The sixth machine was a single-seater powered by a new 35 hp five-cylinder Viale air-cooled radial which had been delivered to A. V. Roe on September 30, 1911. The installation was done by Maurice Ducrocq (British concessionaire for Viale engines) and his apprentice Jack Alcock. Work was completed on October 6 but it was not until November 20 that first flights were made by F. P. Raynham. The Viale-powered Type D proved very manoeuvrable and flew strongly in the hands of a number of school pilots. On December 6 Raynham used it for joyriding by removing the fuselage petrol tank to make room for a passenger to kneel facing him. On December 27 Wilfred Parke climbed the machine to 2,500 ft over Addlestone as a prelude to his 'Superior Brevet' tests and S. V. Sippe gained his Aviator's

The sixth Type D after its forced landing at Abingdon on January 13, 1912. (*RAF Museum*)

23

Certificate on it on January 8, 1912. During an attempt to fly to Oxford as part of his tests on January 13, Parke followed the Thames until poor visibility forced him down at Abingdon where he broke two bracing wires and damaged the undercarriage and mainplanes. On the following morning the machine was dismantled in 65 minutes and temporarily stored in a local garage. The 'broken parts' of the machine were subsequently sent to the Avro works at Manchester, arriving there on February 16, 1912. The necessary repairs were reportedly almost complete by the end of the same month but there is no record of the aircraft ever having flown again and its Viale engine was installed in the Avro Type F cabin monoplane in the following April.

It is believed that only seven Type D biplanes were produced at the Manchester works. Advertisements making a special offer of 12 Type Ds at a reduced rate of £400 each during October and November 1911 can only be regarded as a publicity stunt. There is no evidence that any orders were placed.

In October 1912 the Avro School moved from Brooklands to the new aerodrome at Shoreham-by-Sea, Sussex, and became the Avro Flying School (Brighton) Ltd with A. E. Geere as CFI. Last noteworthy flights before the transfer were made in mid-August by Wilfred Parke in the old sloping radiator Type D to Staines, Ripley, Hounslow Heath and Walton. The machine was used for instruction at Shoreham during 1913 and became well known along the South Coast as did the school's 45 hp Green engined

The 50 hp Isaacson engine installed in the seventh Type D. (*Courtesy Philip Jarrett*)

Type D, Type D with 50 hp Isaacson seven-cylinder radial, and the Avro Type E prototype described later.

The Isaacson-engined machine was the seventh and apparently final Type D manufactured. Recorded in the Avro works' log as being under construction on October 31, 1912, the airframe was complete by November 29, 1911, though the engine was not delivered to the factory until December 4, 1912. Its first flight date is not recorded.

## SPECIFICATION AND DATA

*Manufacturers:*   A. V. Roe and Company, Brownsfield Mills, Great Ancoats Street, Manchester; and Brooklands Aerodrome, Byfleet, Surrey; and Shoreham Aerodrome, Sussex.

*Powerplants:*   One 35 hp Green
One 45 hp Green
One 35 hp Viale
One 50 hp Isaacson
One 60 hp E.N.V. Type F

*Dimensions, Weights and Performances:*

|  | Standard | Seaplane | Sesquiplane |
|---|---|---|---|
| Span, upper | 31 ft 0 in | 31 ft 0 in | 33 ft 0 in |
| Span, lower | 31 ft 0 in | 31 ft 0 in | 23 ft 0 in |
| Length | 28 ft 0 in* | 26 ft 0 in | 28 ft 0 in |
| Height | 9 ft 2 in | — | 9 ft 2 in |
| Wing area | 310 sq ft | 310 sq ft | 279 sq ft |
| All-up weight | 500 lb | 1,000 lb | 550 lb |
| Speed | 45–50 mph | 40 mph | — |
| Range | 100 miles** | — | — |

*Prototype 26 ft 0 in    **With Viale engine.

*Production:*

No.1 Prototype, 35 hp Green, transverse radiator, first flown 1.4.11, converted to seaplane, last mentioned 4.12;

No.2 Circuit of Britain machine, E.N.V. engine, first flown 18.7.11, crashed at Brooklands 22.7.11;

No.3 School machine, 35 hp Green, slanting radiator, first flown 11.9.11, withdrawn from use at Shoreham 5.14;

No.4 Single-seater, 45 hp Green, fore-and-aft radiator, first flown 12.10.11, withdrawn from use at Shoreham 5.14;

No.5 Improved sesquiplane, believed that advertised for sale at Shed 4, Brooklands, 5.12 and that reported scrapped near the petrol store 12.12;

No.6 School machine, Viale engine, first flow 20.11.11, crashed at Abingdon 13.1.12;

No.7 School machine, Isaacson engine, withdrawn from use at Shoreham 5.14.

Capt. E. W. Wakefield's Avro-Curtiss seaplane flying over Windermere, January 1912. (*Manchester Guardian.*)

# Avro Curtiss-type

In the summer of 1910 A. V. Roe and Company declared its willingness to build aeroplanes to other people's designs and the first such aircraft was a Farman-type biplane for the Bolton business man and manufacturer of Avro aero engines, Maurice F. Edwards. Bolts, fittings and bracing wires were also supplied to Miss Lilian Bland who built and flew the Mayfly biplane of her own design at Carnamony, Belfast. Each of these aircraft was fitted with one of the few examples of the 20hp two-cylinder, horizontally-opposed, air-cooled Avro engines. The Farman-type evidently did not met with much success as 18 months later, at the end of 1912, the engine and airframe were advertised for sale in new condition for £45 and £60 respectively.

A Curtiss-type, of the familiar outrigger-tail and front-elevator variety with 50 hp Gnome rotary, was built in 1911 to the order of Capt E. W. Wakefield of Kendal. Neither this nor the Farman-type mentioned above was given an Avro designation. Mainplanes were of unequal span and lateral control was by four ailerons on the upper mainplane, the inner and larger pair having semi-circular trailing edges. It was built at Manchester and delivered at Brooklands for test flying on May 25, 1911, though it did not fly until June 19.

After a short period with the Avro School during which it was flown by F. P. Raynham, R. C. Kemp, F. Conway-Jenkins and Louis Noel, the Avro-Curtiss was dismantled on July 7, 1911, and transferred to Lake Windermere where Capt Wakefield replaced the wheels by a single 12 ft, three step, canvas covered mahogany float built by Messrs Borwick and Sons of Bowness-on-Windermere and small cylindrical floats were fitted below the wingtips. During the course of the re-erection and modification much dissatisfaction was expressed with the standard of the machine's construction and over the discovery of a crack below one cylinder of the Gnome engine. Legal proceedings were begun against A. V. Roe and Company with Capt Wakefield claiming £212 for the engine and £50 on account of the Curtiss-type not being built to contract but there was no recorded outcome to the case. The aircraft made its first flight in marine form on November 25, 1911, piloted by H. Stanley Adams, a former pupil of the Avro School. The success of the first test flights prompted Wakefield to invite the press to view an exhibition flight two days later. The event was reported at some length in *The Westmoreland Gazette* and the reference to the machine's bird-like properties are thought to have prompted the adoption of the name 'Lakes Water Bird' by which the machine was subsequently known. Water Bird was the first consistently successful seaplane in the United Kingdom and during the next few months its fame spread quickly and a considerable waterborne joyriding business was done. Sixty flights were made in the first 38 days, the best being of 20 minutes duration up to a height of 800 ft. On December 7, 1911, Stanley Adams flew the whole length of the lake at a speed of approximately 40 mph at a height of between 60 and 100 ft. These operations continued throughout the winter, but the night of March 29–30, 1912, brought gales which demolished the lakeside hangar at Cockshott and damaged Water Bird beyond repair. Its float, tailplane and rudder (the last still proudly displaying the legend 'A.V. Roe and Company, Manchester') are still in the possession of the Wakefield family at Windermere.

The Avro Farman type under construction.

27

H. Stanley Adams with the Avro Curtiss-type on November 25, 1911. (*Lord Wakefield of Kendal via Peter Connon*)

Water Bird's successor, identical, but entirely designed and built at Windermere by Capt Wakefield's Lakes Flying Company later in 1912, was known as Water Hen. Its only Avro component was the airscrew and at first it could be distinguished from its Avro-built forerunner by the wingtip floats and straight trailing edges to the ailerons. These were mounted parallel to the chord line of the mainplanes instead of at a considerable angle to it. They were later remounted in the angled position but by that time more drastic modifications had been made and all similarity to Water Bird ceased.

## SPECIFICATION AND DATA

*Manufacturers:*    A. V. Roe and Company, Brownsfield Mills, Great Ancoats Street, Manchester; and Brooklands Aerodrome, Byfleet, Surrey.

*Powerplant:*    One 50 hp Gnome

*Dimensions:*    Span (upper) 41 ft 0 in, (lower) 32 ft 0 in
Length 36 ft 5 in    Wing area 365 sq ft

*Weights:*    Tare weight 780 lb    All-up weight 1,130 lb

*Performance:*    Maximum speed 45 mph    Ceiling 800 ft

*Production:*    One aircraft only, first flown as landplane 6.11; first flown as seaplane 25.11.11, damaged beyond repair at Cockshott, Windermere, 30.3.12

The Duigan biplane in its original form with 40 hp horizontally opposed Alvaston engine.
(*Courtesy W. Duigan.*)

# The Duigan Biplane

John R. Duigan was an Australian who designed and built a Farman-type biplane at Mia Mia, Victoria, in 1910 and flew it before a very large crowd at Bendigo Racecourse, Melbourne, on May 3, 1911. A series of accidents convinced Duigan that he needed proper flying instruction and some weeks later he sailed for England, arriving in August 1911. Two months elapsed before he joined the Avro School at Brooklands, having by then already placed an order for a private Avro aeroplane. In November he went to Manchester to see it built.

The machine was a two-seat, dual control biplane, similar to Type D but fitted with a square rudder, steel framed tailplane and square instead of triangular section fuselage. The seats were arranged so that the occupants' heads were raised just above the padded rim of an elliptical opening and celluloid windows were provided in the floor to give downward view. Following current Continental practice, Roe tried a newer wing section having 'Phillips entry' whereby the chord line of the wing was horizontal in level flight. Wing warping was employed for lateral control and wing spars were of English ash with poplar ribs, rounded wingtips being formed from rattan cane. As usual, the whole machine was built in sections, easily dismantled for transport, the fuselage consisting of two halves bolted together behind the rear cockpit. The engine was a 40 hp horizontally opposed Alvaston driving an Avro airscrew of kauri pine and cooled by large spiral tube radiators on each side of the front cockpit.

The undercarriage was a complete departure from normal Avro practice, incorporating a Nieuport-type leaf-spring axle and centre skid with bracing wires to flatten long grass and prevent nosing over. This type of undercarriage proved so successful that in modified form it was used on Avro aeroplanes for a generation.

J. R. Duigan flying the biplane with 35 hp E.N.V. engine at Brooklands April 1912. (*Courtesy W. Duigan*)

First straight hops were made by Duigan at Huntingdon Racecourse flying ground early in December 1911 but in spite of experiments with different airscrews the machine was very loath to leave terra firma. Considering it advisable to return to the Avro fold, Duigan took the machine to Brooklands where a 35 hp E.N.V. engine was fitted and he met with more success. On March 10 several long straight flights were made but the aircraft was sadly underpowered and only flyable in good weather. Duigan then made and fitted an airscrew of his own design and working as his own mechanic, tuned the E.N.V. engine to such good effect that on April 13 he succeeded in flying several times round Brooklands track. On April 19 he flew figure eights at 300 ft and on April 20 successfully completed tests for his Aviator's Certificate (No.211), the aircraft having completed four hours in the air up to that date entirely without damage. Passenger flights, not so successful on low power, were confined to straights within Brooklands track. Duigan's best solo flight in his machine, consisting of an hour's circuits over Addlestone at an altitude of 400–600 ft, was made on April 30. His final recorded flight was on May 15.

The Lakes Sea Bird at Hill of Oaks, Lake Windermere in 1915. (*F. Herbert courtesy Peter Connon*)

30

Having achieved his objectives, Duigan returned home. There he built a very similar machine to the Avro which crashed on its first flight on February 17, 1913. His British aeroplane was put up for sale with engine for £380 but was almost immediately reduced to £180, no doubt because the engine had been sold separately. The airframe was purchased by the Lakes Flying Company and it was delivered to Windermere on June 4, 1912. Here it was rebuilt as the centre float seaplane Sea Bird which H. Stanley Adams flew off the lake for the first time on August 28, 1912. The company entirely redesigned the front end of the fuselage to accept a 50 hp Gnome rotary, the upper half of which was cowled and gave a cocked-up appearance to the nose. New three-bay, warping mainplanes of Eiffel 12 section and 8·5 aspect ratio were also fitted. The machine proved much faster than the old Avro-built Water Bird and after it has been fitted with an improved twin float undercarriage, carried large numbers of holiday makers during 1912–13.

At the end of 1912 the machine was tested with an amphibious undercarriage but trials came to an end on December 18, 1912, when Sea Bird piloted by Lt J.F.A. Trotter was caught by a gust of wind and the lower port wing struck the water. In January 1915 the Lakes Flying Company was taken over by the Northern Aircraft Company Ltd and thereafter the machine was generally referred to as the Avro Biplane Tractor. It was equipped with dual control soon after and at the beginning of June was fitted with new floats. Unfortunately, pupil R. Buck took off in the Avro for his *Vol-plane* test on June 5 unaware that the latter had altered the centre of gravity. On switching off the engine to begin his glide approach, Buck failed to lower the nose sufficiently and the machine stalled at 300 ft, crashing into the lake tail first. Miraculously Buck was unhurt but the Sea Bird was destroyed.

## SPECIFICATION AND DATA

*Manufacturers:*    A. V. Roe and Company, Brownsfield Mills, Great Ancoats Street, Manchester; and Brooklands Aerodrome, Byfleet, Surrey.
Rebuilt by The Lakes Flying Company, Cockshott, Lake Windermere, Westmorland

*Powerplants:*    (Duigan) One 40 hp Alvaston
                      One 35 hp E.N.V. Type D
(Sea Bird) One 50 hp Gnome

*Dimensions:*    (Duigan) Span 34 ft 0 in   Chord 4 ft 6 in
(Sea Bird) Span 39 ft 4 in   Length 29 ft 4 in
                    Height 10 ft 6 in   Wing area 350 sq ft

*Performance:*    (Duigan) Speed 40 mph
(Sea Bird) Maximum speed 62 mph

*Production:*    One aircraft only, first flown 2.12; converted into the Lakes Sea Bird 10.12, crashed at Windermere 5.6.15

The Avro Type E prototype with 60 hp E.N.V. engine. (*Flight photo 029*)

# Avro 500 (Type E) and Avro 502 (Type Es)

The first War Office military aircraft specification, issued in 1911, called for a two seater to carry a 350 lb load in addition to essential equipment and have an endurance of $4\frac{1}{2}$ hours, initial rate of climb of 200 ft/min, maximum speed 55 mph, ability to maintain 4,500 ft for one hour, and be capable of delivery to Salisbury Plain in a crate. Competing firms had only nine months in which to design, build and test.

A. V. Roe and Company met this specification by building a new two seat biplane, very similar in design and construction to the previous year's Duigan machine. The built-up box-girder fuselage was again of square section, fabric covered in the rear and metal clad forward. It was more streamlined than the Duigan with pilot and passenger seated at the widest part with their heads protruding through padded openings in the top. Small celluloid panels were again provided in the floor to give downward vision. The mainplanes used ash spars and an improved, double-surfaced section covered with Pegamoid fabric. They were detachable in three sections for ground transport. The undercarriage was of the Duigan type with centre skid and leaf-spring axle, the tail being carried on a rubber-sprung skid.

A 60 hp E.N.V. watercooled engine was mounted on the top longerons and drove a 10 ft Avro airscrew. The main fuel tank was in front of the passenger and twin gravity tanks were fixed to the centre section struts. Known originally as the 'Military Biplane', but in later years as the Type E prototype, the machine was first flown at Brooklands by Wilfred Parke on March 3, 1912. It was obvious from the outset that this was no ordinary aircraft but one with that rare quality, a reserve of power. This encouraged its entry for the Mortimer Singer prize. Test flying took but a few days, during which it was promptly dubbed *Elinor Glyn* (after a well-known novelist of the period) and on March 23 Parke climbed to 1,000 ft in under six minutes and 2,000 ft in 13 minutes with a heavy passenger (R. L. Charteris).

Cooling was by spiral tube radiators on each side of the front fuselage, augmented by two smaller units on the centre section struts on each side of the passenger's head. On April 20 Parke suffered partial engine failure when taking off for Hendon to compete for the prize. The hurried landing ripped off undercarriage and mainplanes and when the aircraft rolled on its side the auxiliary radiators folded over the front cockpit and engineer W. H. Sayers had to be extricated through a hole cut in the side. In the interest of future passengers the machine was rebuilt with only the lower radiators fitted. Parke successfully piloted the machine through Farnborough trials in June 1912 after which it returned to Brooklands to become a flying test-bed for the new 60 hp A.B.C. engine. First straight hops with this power unit were made by F. P. Raynham on August 31 but it was not until October 18, when several engine and airframe adjustments had been made, that it flew strongly in the hands of the A.B.C. representative R. L. Charteris. In 1913 the E.N.V. engine was reinstalled and the aircraft sent to Shoreham and there flown by experienced pilots of the Avro School, such as H. R. Simms and H. S. Powell. On June 29, 1913, pupils were allowed to fly it for the first time but in the afternoon it stalled on a turn, crashed and was destroyed by fire. Pilot R. N. Wight received fatal injuries, the first ever in an Avro aircraft.

Although he had created a remarkable aeroplane, A. V. Roe was not altogether satisfied. He therefore built an almost identical machine and fitted the 50 hp Gnome seven-cylinder rotary taken from the superannuated Avro School Farman when it was dismantled in November 1911. The Gnome, only a fraction of the weight of other engines of similar power, gave the machine a much enhanced performance and during first flights at Brooklands by Parke on May 8, 1912, the machine reached 2,000 ft in five minutes. The next day he flew 17 miles to Laffan's Plain in 20 minutes and completed all official trials the same afternoon. Officialdom was impressed and after some haggling over price, the War Office bought it and ordered two others with dual control. One of these is said to have been tested to destruction under ground load, but it is now clear that the Avro 500 in question was merely proof loaded as part of the acceptance trials.

The Avro 500 prototype with 50 hp Gnome rotary engine and the original sprung rudder. (*Flight photo 044*)

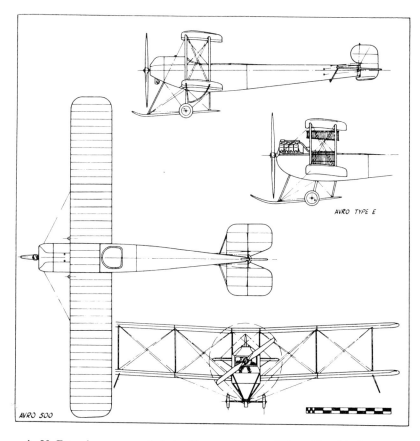

AVRO TYPE E

AVRO 500

A. V. Roe always regarded the Gnome powered Type E as his first really successful aeroplane. Dismissing all previous machines as mere experiments he gave it the imposing type number 500, first of the Avro series which continued in use throughout the firm's existence.

Wilfred Parke first flew the second Avro 500 at Brooklands on June 5, 1912, and delivered it to Farnborough in 23 minutes later in the day. Although so many Avro aircraft had first seen the light of day in Manchester, the inhabitants of that city had not at that time seen one in the air. To remedy this the third Army machine was 'borrowed' on June 28, taken from the factory to Eccles Cricket Ground and next day flown over Chorlton by Parke. Flights were made from Old Trafford over the Docks on the following day and from Fallowfield on July 5. After minor repairs the machine was then flown to Brooklands for normal flight test by Parke (with Gordon Bell as passenger) on July 19 before delivery by Raynham on July 22. The three Avro 500s joined the strength of the Central Flying School, Upavon, with serial numbers *404*, *405* and *406*. They were flown by pilots who later became famous, such as Maj Brooke-Popham (later Air Chief

34

Marshal Sir Robert Brooke-Popham, Governor of Kenya) and Lt-Col Cook RA who made a notable flight to Portsmouth in *404* on August 8, returning via Lee-on-Solent (50 miles) in 40 minutes on August 17. The Avro 500 rapidly established itself as the best available trainer, resulting in a further order for four two-seaters in November 1912 and another for five single-seaters to equip No. 3 Squadron, Netheravon, in January 1913. The latter were given the Avro type number 502 though in military service they were simply known as the Avro Type Es in order to distinguish them from the two-seat Type E (Avro 500).

Years of endeavour were being rewarded. To A. V. Roe fell the honour of escorting HM King George V round the second machine of the two-seater batch at the Olympia Aero Show of February 14–22, 1913. With total orders at the dozen mark the firm had become sufficiently stable financially to re-form as a limited company on January 11, 1913, and to move into larger premises at Clifton Street, Miles Platting, Manchester, in the following April. War Office orders were completed in June 1913 (the penultimate single-seater was tested at Shoreham by F. P. Raynham on June 12). The Air Department of the Admiralty also received two Avro 500s, both of which were stationed at Eastchurch. The first, *41*, was delivered in March 1913 and the second, *150*, in February of the following year.

J. Laurence Hall in the 'civil' Avro 500 at Hendon in January 1914. Typical of late production 500s it had the 'comma' rudder and inversely tapered ailerons. (*Flight*)

The RNAS Avro 500 *939* pictured at Hendon in late 1914 with twin skid undercarriage and oversize wheels. (*Courtesy the Royal Aeronautical Society*)

RFC Avro Type E (Avro 500) *448* in service at the Central Flying School, Upavon. (*J. M. Bruce/G. S. Leslie Collection*)

During the short Service life of the Avro 500, several important modifications were made. The prototype had no tail skid and depended on a steel shoe screwed to the bottom of the rudder. It was a weak arrangement and the rudder was redesigned to absorb landing shocks by sliding vertically up the kingpost against the action of a coiled spring. By mid-1913 this still somewhat hazardous system had been abandoned in favour of an ordinary bungee-sprung tail skid and the now-famous comma-shaped Avro rudder. Lateral control on all War Office Avro 500s and Avro 502s was by wing warping but modified outer wing panels incorporating inversely tapered ailerons on top and bottom wings were fitted later. At least *406* was further modified with constant chord ailerons, while in several instances the looped wing tip skids were replaced by braced bamboo rods with, or without, a small wheel at the tip.

A few machines remained in commission throughout the early years of the First World War and one was locally re-engined at Chingford with a 100 hp Gnome fourteen-cylinder rotary.

There were at least three other Avro 500s in addition to War Office and Admiralty machines. The first, of the sprung rudder type, was built for the Portuguese Government and paid for by public subscription. Despatched to Lisbon in September 1912 in charge of H. V. Roe, Copland Perry (pilot) and W. H. Sayers (engineer), it was unloaded on October 7 and conveyed by bullock cart to the flying ground at Belem. It was erected and flown on successive days, after which trial flights were made up the Tagus to Lisbon with the name *Republica* in large red letters on the fuselage and in green under the mainplanes. The machine was handed over to the Minister of

War before 20,000 people on October 16 but the next day Perry just failed to reach the aerodrome when an exhaust valve on the Gnome jammed open. He put the Avro down gently in shallow water from which it was salvaged without damage, cleaned down, greased and stored for the winter.

The best known of all Avro 500s was probably that flown by F. P. Raynham to the Burton-on-Trent Meeting of August 2–5, 1913, during which he carried numerous passengers and won the quick starting and cross country races. As if to underline the fact that this was no 'stick and string' freak, Raynham flew the machine south to Brooklands after the meeting and on August 9 raced it from scratch into second place in the six laps speed race at the Hendon August Meeting. Raynham then became so fully engaged in demonstrating the new Avro 504 prototype that the faithful 500 languished at Brooklands until he was free to give dual instruction to H. V. Roe and C. F. Lan-Davis. The latter bought the machine in December 1913 and gained his Aviator's Certificate on it on March 24, 1914. He first kept the machine at Brooklands but it was later based at Hendon where Lan-Davis fitted an elaborate array of instruments. He also attempted to mass balance the elevator by fitting broomsticks which projected forward at each end.

The other 'civil' Avro 500, delivered Brooklands-Hendon by F. P. Raynham on January 22, 1914, was used for display and instruction by J. Laurence Hall whose name appeared large on the fuselage. Two months later Hall succeeded in looping the machine to show that standard British aircraft were quite as manoeuvrable as the special lightweight French machines of the period. He flew hundreds of trouble-free hours in it and made numerous cross country flights including a 45 minute trip from Shoreham to Hendon with a lady passenger on July 14. An order for four Avro 500s by the Royal Aero Club was frustrated by the outbreak of the

Single-seat Type Es (Avro 502) *291* was the last of five delivered to No. 3 Squadron at Netheravon in 1913.

First World War but the Hall machine continued in instructional use at Hendon until commandeered by the War Office in September 1914 and allocated the RFC serial *491*.

## SPECIFICATION AND DATA

*Manufacturers:*  A. V. Roe and Company (reconstituted as A. V. Roe and Co Ltd, 11.1.13), Brownsfield Mills, Great Ancoats Street, Manchester (moved to Clifton Street, Miles Platting, Manchester 4.13); and at Shoreham Aerodrome, Sussex

*Powerplants:*  (Type E prototype)  One 60 hp E.N.V. Type F
One 60 hp A.B.C.
(Avro 500)  One 50 hp Gnome
One 100 hp Gnome

*Dimensions:*  Span 36 ft 0 in  Height 9 ft 9 in
Length (Type E prototype) 30 ft 6 in
(Avro 500)      29 ft 0 in
Wing area 330 sq ft

*Weights:*  (Type E prototype)
Tare weight 1,100 lb  All-up weight 1,650 lb
(Avro 500) Tare weight 900 lb  All-up weight 1,300 lb

*Performance:*  (Type E prototype)
Maximum speed 50 mph
Initial climb 170 ft/min  Endurance 6 hours
(Avro 500) Maximum speed 61 mph
Initial climb 440 ft/min

*Production:*
**Type E**
Prototype only, first flown at Brooklands 3.3.12, destroyed by fire at Shoreham 29.6.13

**Avro 500**
(i)  To War Office contract March 1912

*404* – first flown at Brooklands 8.5.12, delivered to Farnborough 9.5.12, thence to CFS Upavon
*405* – first flown at Brooklands 5.6.12, delivered to Farnborough 5.6.12, thence to CFS Upavon
*406* – first flown at Manchester 28.6.12, delivered to Farnborough 22.7.12, thence to CFS Upavon

(ii) To War Office contract December 1912

*430*
*432*  delivered to CFS Upavon 20.1.13, 24.2.13,
*433*  20.3.13 and and 17.4.13 respectively
*448*

(iii)  To Admiralty contract 1913

*41* – delivered to Eastchurch 3.3.13, to Hendon 9.14
*150* – delivered to Eastchurch 23.2.14

(iv)  Other machines

1.  For the Portuguese Government – handed over in Lisbon 10.10.12, named *Republica*
2.  Demonstrator, first flown 7.13, sold to C.F. Lan-Davis 12.13, awaiting more powerful engine at Hendon 8.14, believed to have been the Avro 500 that was in RNAS service at Hendon from October 1914 and carried the military serial *939*.
3.  To J. Laurence Hall, Hendon 22.1.14, commandeered 9.14 and allotted RFC serial number *491*.

**Avro 502**

(i)  To War Office contract January 1913

*285*
*288*  delivered to No.3. Squadron, Netheravon, 3.4.13, 30.4.13
*289* } 14.5.13, 28.5.13, 21.6.13 respectively, all to No.5 Squadron
*290*  by January 1914 and to the CFS by September 1914
*291*

*Republica* being recovered from the shallows of the River Tagus after Copland Perry's forced landing on 17 October 1912. (*RAF Museum*)

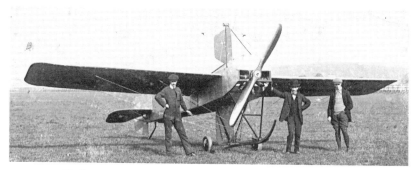

The Burga monoplane at Shoreham in November 1912. (*Courtesy C. H. Barnes.*)

# The Burga Monoplane

In 1912 A. V. Roe and Company built a shoulder-wing monoplane to the designs of Lt Burga of the Peruvian Navy, who wished to try out some highly original ideas on aircraft control. The machine was constructed at Brownsfield Mills at the same time as the Avro Type E prototype and used the same tail and undercarriage, but the fuselage was much slimmer and the engine a 50 hp Gnome rotary.

Rectangular monoplane wings were wire braced to strong points on the undercarriage and to a pylon built over the fuselage. There was no wing warping, lateral control being obtained by two 'rudders', one above and one below the fuselage, working in opposite directions. The design made provisions for wings of varying camber which fitted at varying angles of incidence to give the machine any desired performance.

Construction of the Burga at Brownsfield Mills was evidently undertaken on an intermittent basis as other work allowed. It was first mentioned in the Works Log in February 1912 but by the end of March had been

The Burga Monoplane at Shoreham in November 1912 with H. R. Simms in the rear cockpit and Lt Burga in the front. (*P. F. Wright via Philip Jarrett*)

40

dismantled and removed to a cellar, ending up the following month suspended from the boiler house roof. There it remained until June 3 when it was re-erected and the left wing doped in time for the machine to be inspected by visiting VIPs the following day. Work started on the engine in July and the top wing bracing was finished in August. A further two months elapsed before the whole machine was completed and it was finally dispatched from the factory on October 15, 1912.

Lt Burga took a shed at Shoreham where the machine was test flown on November 20, 1912, by H. R. Simms. The mainplanes fitted were those best suited for maximum speed and the pilot reported that it was certainly fast and had a good rate of climb. Further taxying trials were made by H.S. Powell in the following month shortly before the machine was seriously damaged in an accident. This resulted in the Burga monoplane being returned to the Avro Works at Manchester in January 1913 for repair and it was not heard of again.

The Burga Monoplane after its accident at Shoreham in December 1912. (*P. F. Wright via Philip Jarrett*)

## SPECIFICATION AND DATA

*Manufacturers:*  A. V. Roe and Company, Brownsfield Mills, Great Ancoats Street, Manchester; and Shoreham Aerodrome, Sussex

*Powerplant:*  One 50 hp Gnome

*Dimensions:*  Length 29 ft 0 in

*Production:*  One aircraft only, first flown at Shoreham 20.11.12

41

The Avro Type F cabin monoplane showing the famous 35 hp Viale radial engine which is now preserved for all time. (*Flight photo 09*)

# Avro Type F

In the spring of 1912 A. V. Roe's fertile mind conceived the idea of an enclosed aeroplane affording the occupants complete protection from the elements. He straightway designed two such machines, the first of which was a single seat, mid-wing monoplane known as the Type F.

Structurally similar to the Avro 500, it used the same undercarriage, tail unit and small rudder (this time linked to a steerable tail skid), but there the similarity ended. The box-girder fuselage was of streamlined shape built up from four wooden longerons and cross struts, reinforced by triangular plywood stiffeners in each bay and braced internally with piano wire. By unlacing the fabric half way along the rear fuselage to expose steel jointing plates, the fuselage could be taken apart quite easily to facilitate packing. Its maximum width was only 2 ft but there was sufficient depth for the pilot to sit wholly inside with a somewhat restricted view through a number of celluloid windows. Entry was through a sheet aluminium trap-door in the roof and large circular holes were provided in each side through which the head could be thrust when flying in poor visibility. Fuel and oil tanks were situated inside the fuselage, remote from the engine to reduce risk of fire.

The mainplane, constructed in two halves round a built-up front spar, was mounted on the centre line of the fuselage and braced by wires to a stout kingpost under the fuselage and to a pylon of steel tubes on top. Lateral control was by wing warping.

The Type F monoplane was erected at Brooklands in April 1912 and Wilfred Parke made the first take-off on May 1, climbing the machine steeply on half throttle. It was the first flight in the world by an aeroplane with a totally enclosed cockpit. Critics predicted that oil thrown back by the 35 hp Viale five cylinder radial engine would completely obscure the pilot's vision but this proved not to be the case. It was a carefully maintained engine well known to Parke, being that taken from the Type D school machine which he had flown from Brooklands to Abingdon in the previous January. First circuits were made on May 3 and test flying continued until May 17 when, during a flight over Chertsey, 1,000 ft was reached for the first time. On May 25 it was decided to show the machine at Hendon but the engine failed soon after take-off and in the ensuing forced landing at Weybridge, Parke hit a fence and turned over. There was little damage and the Type F was dismantled by four men in 25 minutes for return to the workshops.

For some months the machine languished at Brooklands until taken out by R. H. Barnwell on September 13. After one or two straight hops, the front part of the skid was broken in landing and the aircraft turned over, suffering serious damage in the process. Barnwell was unhurt but it is evident that the Type F did not fly again.

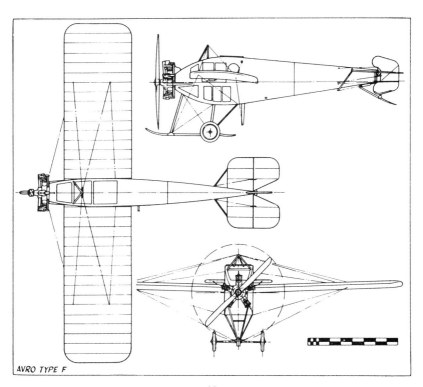

AVRO TYPE F

The Avro Type F at Brooklands. (*Flight*)

## SPECIFICATION AND DATA

*Manufacturers:*    A. V. Roe and Company, Brownsfield Mills, Great Ancoats Street, Manchester; and Brooklands Aerodrome, Byfleet, Surrey

*Powerplant:*    One 35 hp Viale

*Dimensions:*    Span 28 ft 0 in    Length 23 ft 0 in
Wing area 158 sq ft

*Weights:*    Tare weight 550 lb    All-up weight 800 lb

*Performance:*    Maximum speed 65 mph    Initial climb 300 ft/min

*Production:*    One aircraft only, first flown at Brooklands 1.5.12, damaged beyond repair at Brooklands 13.9.12. Engine preserved at the Science Museum, London.

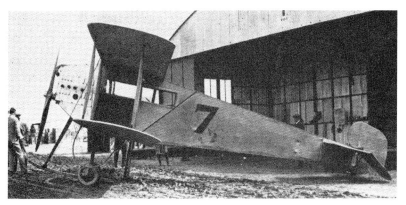

The Avro Type G cabin biplane, 60 hp Green engine, at Larkhill in August 1912. (*Avro*)

# Avro Type G

A. V. Roe's second cabin aeroplane was a two seat biplane designed specifically for the Military Aeroplane Competition of August 1912, and today historically important as the world's first cabin biplane. Very similar structurally to the Type F, the fuselage filled the whole mainplane gap and was again very narrow with a maximum beam of 2 ft 3 in tapering to only 15 in at the front end. This was made possible by the use of a slim inline engine mounted on steel bearers and enclosed in louvred cowlings with the main exhaust taken over the roof. As on the Type E prototype, cooling was by means of spiral tube radiators on each side of the cabin, entry to which was through triangular doors hinged to slanting struts in the sides of the fuselage. Mainplanes, undercarriage and tail unit were identical with those of the Avro 500. Once again there was no vertical fin and the steel shod rudder also acted as tail skid. Lateral control was by wing warping with a maximum warp at the tip of 18 in.

Two Type G biplanes were laid down. One with a 60 hp Green engine to be flown by Wilfred Parke with competition number 6 and a second, numbered 7, for R. L. Charteris of the All-British Engine Co Ltd with a 60 hp A.B.C. eight-cylinder engine. Unfortunately this A.B.C. engine was not ready in time and as a matter of expediency No.7 was completed with the Green engine in place of No.6.

There was no time for test flying and the aeroplane was delivered in a crate direct to the competition ground at Larkhill on Salisbury Plain and there flown for the first time by Wilfred Parke. On August 7, 1912, he took off at the start of the 3 hours endurance test but after half an hour turbulent conditions compelled him to give up. Hurriedly landing down wind, he overturned and so damaged the machine that it had to be sent back to Manchester for repair. Exactly a week later on August 14, the machine returned, no doubt incorporating many components of the unfortunate

45

No.6. During the resumed trials Parke demonstrated the machine's all-weather qualities by flying in a rainstorm for 37 minutes and for half an hour in a wind of 40 mph.

At 6.04 a.m. on Sunday August 25, 1912, Parke again started on the endurance test carrying Lt Le Breton as passenger. Just after 9 a.m. he commenced a series of steep dives to relieve the monotony and in so doing spun off a turn, but Parke's cool head and analytical mind were equal to the situation and he soon discovered that if the stick were central, recovery was possible by applying full opposite rudder. He was the second pilot to survive a spin but the first to do so before competent observers. In the ensuing discussions he gave a lucid account of what had taken place and today 'Parke's Dive' is recognised as an important milestone in the development of flying techniques. Later in that eventful day H. V. Roe flew as passenger to Upavon and became the first person to type a letter in an aircraft in flight.

The Type G cabin biplane was an easy winner in the assembly test in a time of 14½ minutes compared with the 9 hours 29 minutes of the Farman biplane and although the accident left insufficient time for the compilation of all the required data, the Avro company was awarded £100 for attempting all the tests. The Type G failed to secure a major award because the initial rate of climb was poor (9 min 30 sec to reach 1,000 ft).

F. P. Raynham flew the machine home to Shoreham on October 11 but it had been in the open for so long that both engine and rigging needed attention. He therefore took the machine to Brooklands for adjustments on October 21 in 45 minutes and next day made an attempt to win the British Empire Michelin endurance prize. A broken water connection ended the flight after 3½ hours but on October 24 he established a duration record for all-British aeroplanes with a time of 7 hours 31 minutes. Competing against

The Type G being assembled at Larkhill in August 1912. (*J. M. Bruce/G. S. Leslie Collection*)

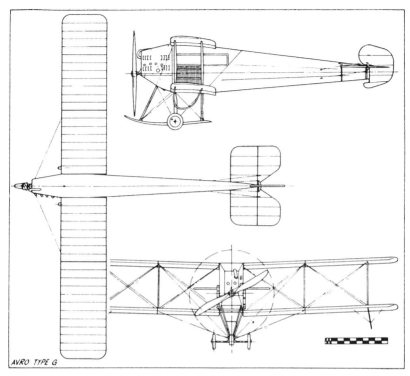

AVRO TYPE G

Harry Hawker in the Sopwith Wright biplane, Raynham flew round Brooklands all day with the Green engine throttled right back to conserve fuel until forced to land through shortage of oil. His record stood for only an hour as Hawker went on to establish a new record of 8 hours 23 minutes and win the £500 prize. The Type G biplane was afterwards flown back to Shoreham where it was last heard of in February 1913 hangared with the Type D biplanes of the Avro School.

## SPECIFICATION AND DATA

*Manufacturers:*  A. V. Roe and Company, Brownsfield Mills, Great Ancoats Street, Manchester; and Brooklands Aerodrome, Byfleet, Surrey

*Powerplant:*  One 60 hp Green

*Dimensions:*  Span 35 ft 3 in   Length 28 ft 6 in
Height 9 ft 9 in   Wing area 335 sq ft

*Weights:*  Tare weight 1,191 lb   All-up weight 1,792 lb

*Performance:*  Maximum speed 61.8 mph   Initial climb 105 ft/min
Range 345 miles

*Production:*  One aircraft only, second machine not completed.

47

The original Avro 503 seaplane moored at Shoreham in June 1913. (*Courtesy the Royal Aeronautical Society*)

# Avro 501 and Avro 503 (Type H)

The choice of Shoreham as the Avro company's new flying ground when it moved from Brooklands in the autumn of 1912 was largely the result of Cdr Schwann's successful waterborne experiments and Avro's awakening interest in seaplanes. It was an ideal site with Shoreham Harbour close at hand and it was from the adjacent River Adur that the Avro Type H seaplane made its first take-off. Construction of this machine followed tests on Windermere by H. Stanley Adams in January 1913 with the Avro 501 which, apart from a considerable strut-braced top wing overhang, was similar to an enlarged float-equipped Avro 500. Built at Brownsfield Mills in November 1912 and powered by a 100 hp Gnome, the Avro 501 first flew as an amphibian with a sprung central float designed by O. T. Gnosspelius, 15 ft long and 7 ft wide from which projected three small wheels, two in the rear and one forward. With so narrow a float an aircraft with a wing span of 47 ft 6 ins could be expected to heel over when steerage way was lost, and for this reason small wing tip floats were fitted and inclined to sit squarely in the water. This arrangement proved unsatisfactory and Gnosspelius replaced it with a twin float unit without wheels which made the aircraft sufficiently seaworthy to interest the Admiralty, to whom it was eventually delivered in the Isle of Grain. In the light of experience at Barrow, the airscrew leading edges were sheathed with brass to prevent damage from flying spray and the tail float was bolted directly to the old-style sprung rudder for steering on the water.

Also powered by a 100 hp Gnome, the Type H (later known as the Avro 503), was a slightly larger version of the Avro 501 but with less mainplane overhang and no inclined struts. Following standard Avro practice, the new seaplane was built with an eye to quick dismantling and was constructed round a 9 ft centre section to which were bolted fuselage, undercarriage and outer wing panels. The upper mainplane, 3 ft greater in span than the lower, was fitted with large inversely tapered ailerons but none was fitted

48

to the lower wing. Two-step, internally sprung floats, 14 ft long and 2 ft 6 in wide, set at a track of 6 ft 6 in, were covered with rubberised material and attached to the aircraft by 14 tubular steel struts bound with varnished fabric.

Such was his confidence in the Type H that F. P. Raynham made the first take-off from the Adur in sea mist on May 28, 1913, carrying passenger Jack (later Sir John) Alcock, two hours' fuel and an anchor. The aircraft became airborne after a run of only 60 yards and cleared the adjacent railway bridge by 100 ft. Next day, again carrying the future conqueror of the Atlantic, Raynham made a first landing on the open sea outside Volk's seaplane hangar opposite Paston Place, Brighton. A float was damaged on take-off so a landing was made in Shoreham Harbour where the aircraft was hastily beached. After some local strengthening of the nose of each float the machine was out again on June 12 and two days later Raynham made an hour's demonstration flight over Brighton carrying Lt J. W. Seddon RN, Inspector of Naval Aircraft. Despite the weight and drag of the floats, the Type H climbed to 1,300 ft in 5 minutes.

The Avro 503 was then flown by Capt Schultz, a German naval officer who had made several visits to the works while it was under construction, and before the month was out the machine was purchased by the German Government, dismantled and packed for shipment. Flown by Lt W. Langfeld it became on September 3, 1913, the first aircraft to cross the 40 miles of North Sea from Wilhelmshaven to the Island of Heligoland, a successful return trip to Cuxhaven being made on September 15. An Avro 503 seaplane was also ordered by the Peruvian Government but the outbreak of the First World War prevented delivery and it is believed to have been turned over to the British Admiralty.

Three other 100 hp Gnome-powered Avro 503s were built—all to Admiralty order for use by the Royal Naval Air Service. The float undercarriage of the old Avro 501 having proved far too heavy, the Admiralty agreed to accept it as a landplane. A. V. Roe thereupon devised a two-wheel, twin-skid undercarriage but the track was still too narrow to support the aircraft vertically at rest and stout wing tip skids were necessary.

The Avro 501 in landplane form with naval serial *16* at Eastchurch 1913. (*Courtesy C. H. Barnes*)

In land-plane form, with large inversely tapered ailerons replacing the constant chord units, the Avro 501 was so quaint a structure that it soon earned the name 'Rickety Ann'. After delivery to Eastchurch it had to be lightened and several airscrews tried before F. P. Raynham could complete the acceptance tests. Bearing naval serial *16* it was flown to Shoreham on June 2, 1913, by Raynham with Lt Seddon as passenger.

The first RNAS Avro 503 seaplane, *51*, was delivered in crates to the Isle of Grain on September 8, 1913. It easily passed its RNAS trials there on September 25, 1913, when, piloted by F. P. Raynham, it reached a speed of 64 mph and climbed to 3,000 ft in 19 minutes with full tanks (36 gallons of petrol and 10 gallons of oil giving 4 hours' endurance) while carrying a passenger and wireless equipment. The second machine, *52*, was delivered to the Isle of Grain on October 7, 1913, and the third, *53*, on October 15, 1913. This last machine incorporated some undefined improvements. All three machines were later converted to landplanes and were in use at Eastchurch in September 1914. No. *52* remained active until January 1916.

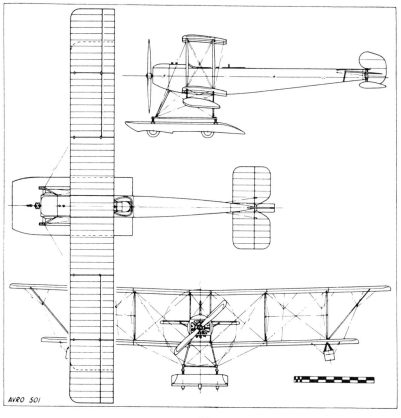

AVRO 501

The second RNAS Avro 503 in landplane form at Chingford in 1915. (*J. M. Bruce/G. S. Leslie Collection*)

## SPECIFICATION AND DATA

*Manufacturers:* A. V. Roe and Company (reconstituted as A. V. Roe and Co Ltd 11.1.13), Brownsfield Mills, Great Ancoats Street, Manchester (moved to Clifton Street, Miles Platting, Manchester 4.13); and Shoreham Aerodrome, Sussex

*Powerplant:* One 100 hp Gnome

*Dimensions, Weights and Performances:*

|  | Avro 501 seaplane | Avro 503 seaplane |
|---|---|---|
| Span, (upper) | 47 ft 6 in | 50 ft 0 in |
| Span, (lower) | 39 ft 6 in | 47 ft 0 in |
| Length | 33 ft 0 in | 33 ft 6 in |
| Height | 12 ft 6 in | 12 ft 9 in |
| Wing area | 478 sq ft | 567 sq ft |
| Tare weight | 1,740 lb | — |
| All-up weight | 2,700 lb | 2,200 lb |
| Maximum speed | 55 mph* | 50 mph |
| Initial climb | — | 225 ft/min |

*Landplane 65 mph

*Production:*

Avro 501 seaplane, first flown on Windermere 1.13, converted to landplane serial *16*, still airworthy in 1914

Avro 503 prototype first flown at Shoreham 28.5.13, to the German Navy 6.13 with serial *D12*

Three Avro 503 seaplanes with serials *51*, *52* and *53* built for the RNAS and delivered to the Isle of Grain. All later converted to landplanes before September 1914. *51* crashed at Chingford 11.8.15, *52* withdrawn from use 1.16, *53* withdrawn from use at Eastchurch 11.15

51

The prototype Avro 504 at Hendon, September 1913, in its original form with square cut engine cowling and warping 'ailerons'.

# Avro 504 to Avro 504H

Design work on a successor to the Avro 500, begun at Brownsfield Mills in November 1912, was completed at the new Clifton Street works early the following year, Messrs Chadwick and Taylor being responsible for the fuselage and undercarriage and H. E. Broadsmith the wings. Designated Avro 504, it was very lightly constructed with a rectangular section, wire braced, box-girder fuselage built from four ash longerons channelled for lightness and strengthened by flanges. Cross struts were of spruce. For maximum view the pilot sat in the rear, the passenger occupying the front cockpit, from the corners of which four ash struts supported the centre section. Equal span, two bay wings were rigged with 2 ft stagger and braced by streamline section, hollow spruce interplane struts pin-jointed to the spars. Each wing panel consisted of five main ribs with spanwise stringers supporting a number of contour-forming strips of wood anchored to leading and trailing edges. Lateral control was by inversely tapered ailerons rigidly fixed at the inner end, the widened outer ends of which were warped by means of cables.

Although similar to that of the Avro 500, the undercarriage was a much improved and simplified unit. An ash skid was anchored to the fuselage by steel V struts as before, but the axle was no longer bolted to it and was no longer a laminated spring. Instead, a simple steel tube axle was used in conjunction with two main undercarriage legs having built-in rubber shock absorbers (8 ft 8 in of bungee cord wound round the two halves of the leg) in streamlined cases. The tail skid was attached to the bottom of a comma-type rudder.

In design, construction and performance the Avro 504 was considerably in advance of other 1913 types and benefited from the use of an improved wing section. Power was supplied by one of the new 80 hp Gnome rotaries (the actual power output of which is said to have been nearer 62 hp) installed in a square section cowling bulged on top and sides.

To give it the widest possible publicity the Avro 504 was entered for the 1913 Aerial Derby and consequently was built in considerable secrecy. Its arrival at Hendon on September 20, 1913, morning of the race, was therefore something of a sensation as it was obviously very fast and the impression of speed was heightened by its staggered mainplanes. When F. P. Raynham crossed the finishing line in fourth place at an average speed of 66·5 mph, few realised that the Avro 504 was virtually untried, having been delivered at Brooklands only three days before (September 17), and flown for the first time on the following day.

After the Aerial Derby the Blackburn Aeroplane and Motor Co Ltd issued a challenge to its Lancashire rivals and on September 29 Raynham flew the Avro 504 from Brooklands to Leeds for a race against a new Blackburn monoplane flown by Harold Blackburn. The 100 mile race was held on October 2 over a course starting and finishing at Leeds and passing over York, Doncaster, Sheffield and Barnsley. With H. V. Roe as passenger, Raynham flew neck and neck with Blackburn until bad visibility forced him to land near Barnsley.

Although basically a sound aeroplane the 504 needed modification and went back to the Manchester works where the engine mounting was changed for an improved version carrying more streamlined cowlings. Aileron control was also lightened by replacing the warping arrangement with constant chord hinged ailerons with wires to complete the circuit in place of the original rods. The wing structure was strengthened by replacing the hollow

The 504 prototype at Paignton, Devon, in April 1914 rebuilt as a seaplane with rounded cowlings and constant-chord ailerons.

Production Avro 504 *785* was one of 44 machines that comprised the first war order. (*J. M. Bruce/G. S. Leslie Collection*)

pin-jointed interplane struts by solid ones fitted in metal sockets. Redelivered at Brooklands at the end of October, the 504 was flown a great deal by Raynham during the following month. He made a forced landing at Horley with a broken carburettor control during the Hendon–Brighton–Hendon race on November 8; flew from Brooklands to Farnborough and back on November 15; gained second place in the Shell Trophy Race at Hendon the same afternoon and broke the lap record at 73 mph; spent a week on day and night flying at Shoreham and flew to Farnborough for official tests on November 24. With a passenger and fuel for three hours the Avro 504 clocked 80·9 mph over the measured mile and climbed to 1,000 ft in 1 min 45 sec.

An outstanding performance put up by Raynham on February 4 was a climb to 15,000 ft over Brooklands. This exceeded the existing British altitude record by almost 2,000 ft but was not an officially observed record. During the descent Raynham shut off his engine, put the machine into a

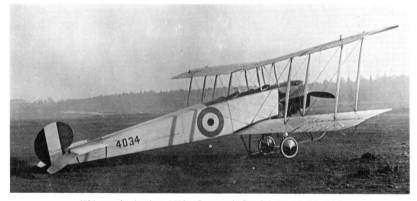

*4034*, a production Avro 504A. (*Courtesy the Royal Aeronautical Society*)

glide, and 25 minutes later was at 5,000 ft over Hendon some 20 miles away. He then spiralled down to a landing, still without using his engine. Carrying R. J. MacGeagh Hurst in the front seat Raynham made an officially observed climb to a record height of 14,420 ft over Brooklands on February 10.

Later in the season the machine was purchased by the *Daily Mail* and toured the country giving passenger flights piloted by F. P. Raynham and G. Lusted. A. V. Roe and Co built an interchangeable twin float undercarriage so that the machine could be flown off the sea at coast resorts. At the same time the original 80 hp Gnome was replaced by an 80 hp Gnome Monosoupape which was supposed to give more power but which in fact gave only trouble. First flights as a seaplane took place at Paignton in April 1914, after which it visisted Falmouth, Southport and Ireland, but when war was declared on August 4 the machine was at Shoreham where it was immediately commandeered. Two days later the career of this historic

Production Avro 504B serial *1032*, with cut-away cockpit sides and tail skid pylon. (*Courtesy the Royal Aeronautical Society*)

aeroplane ended when the engine failed as Raynham took off to deliver it to the RNAS. With no height in hand there was no alternative to putting the machine down on land where it was damaged beyond repair.

Series production of the Avro 504 began in the summer of 1913 when the War Office placed a contract for twelve machines. This brought about some restressing of the wings to comply with their strength requirements which included doubling the depth and width of the rear spar. Others were built for non-military and experimental purposes, one of which was exhibited at Belle Vue, Manchester, on January 1–3, 1914, and another, delivered at Brooklands on February 16, was fitted with the first Armstrong Whitworth-built 100 hp A.B.C. engine. After endless engine runs Raynham made what was possibly its only flight with this engine early in April. Drawings were also prepared for the installation of a 65 hp Austro-Daimler engine but as far as is known this scheme was shelved. A third Avro 504 was exhibited with rubber-sprung float undercarriage at the Olympia Aero Show in March 1914 and another was delivered to Harold Blackburn at Southport in July. In common with thousands of Avro 504 variants built in later years, these aircraft were noticeably different from the prototype because the top longerons sloped downwards aft of the cockpits to make the fuselage symmetrical in side elevation.

Two Avro 504s, almost the last of the twelve War Office machines, were delivered at Brooklands on June 5, 1914, and it was in one of these on June 12 that F. P. Raynham succeeded in looping a 504 for the first time. They were delivered next day to Farnborough where *376* (the first machine of the batch) was tested to destruction during July. A few Avro 504s were among the aircraft of No.5 Squadron RFC when it left for France on August 13, one of which became the first British aeroplane brought down

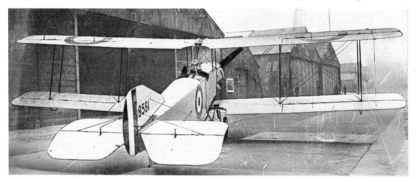

An RNAS anti-Zeppelin Avro 504C.

by the Germans when Lts V. Waterfall and C. G. G. Bayly were hit by infantry fire in Belgium on August 22. In mid-October, *383*, another Avro of the squadron was fitted with a Lewis gun by 2nd-Lt L. A. Strange whose gunner, Capt L. da C. Penn-Gaskell, strafed a troop train at Perenchies and forced down an Albatros two-seater near Neuve-Église a month later. Only a few Avro 504s saw front-line service and the greatest number in RFC squadrons in France at any one time was thirteen.

The Admiralty placed an order in the spring of 1914 for one Avro 504 and for six others a few months later. The first of these was delivered to the RNAS Eastchurch Squadron on November 27, 1914. Armed with four 16 lb bombs and piloted by Flt Sub-Lt R. H. Collet, an attempt to bomb the Bruges submarine depot on December 14 was foiled by bad visibility and an attack was made on the Ostend–Bruges railway instead. Very few offensive sorties were made by the Avro 504, the most ambitious being the brilliant and historic raid on the Zeppelin sheds at Friedrichshafen. A special flight of four machines formed at Manchester in October 1914 by Sqn Cdr P. Shepherd, was equipped to carry four 20 lb bombs per aircraft and shipped from Southampton to Le Havre. They arrived at Belfort by train on the night of November 13, 1914, and were hidden in a barn for fear of arousing the suspicions of local spies. It was not possible to flight test them and the first machine, *874*, took off untried at 9.30 a.m. on November 21 piloted by Sqn Cdr E. Featherstone Briggs. Flt Cdr J. T. Babington then left in *875* followed by Flt Lt S. V. Sippe with five minutes separation in *873*. Flt Sub-Lt R. P. Cannon's machine *179* (the first Avro 504 built for the RNAS) broke its tail skid and could not go. The raiders followed the Rhine at 5,000 ft, crossed Lake Constance at 10 ft and put several bombs into the airship sheds from 1,200 ft. They narrowly missed destroying naval Zeppelin *L.7* but hit the gas plant which exploded with considerable violence. Briggs was shot down but the others made the 125 mile return trip in safety after four hours in the air. Flown by Flt Lt H. L. Rosher, Sippe's Avro *873* was one of five belonging to No.1 Sqn RNAS which twice bombed Ostend and on March 24, 1915, destroyed two U-boats in an attack on the submarine depot near Antwerp. Together with *179* and *875*, it survived to return to England for overhaul and transfer to school work. A pioneer Zeppelin interception was also made by an Avro 504 from RNAS Westgate piloted by Flt Sub-Lt Mulock who made contact with *LZ.38* in the early hours of May 17, 1915. The airship climbed too rapidly for him to use his armament of two hand grenades and two incendiary bombs but later the same night the Avro 504 *1009*, piloted by Flt Cdr A. W. Bigsworth, pursued *LZ.39* towards Ostend with more success. He managed to gain sufficient height to drop four 20 lb bombs on the airship's stern and caused slight damage by fire which led to a heavy landing at Evère, Brussels.

When the Avro 504 was relegated to training, a duty it was destined to fulfil with distinction for over 15 years, A. V. Roe and Co designed and supplied a self contained dual control unit comprising seats, control columns and rudder bars. Later in 1915 converted machines were joined by a number specifically built as trainers, total Avro 504 production amounting to at

*796*, one of only six single-seat Avro 504Ds.

least 88 aircraft. As the war progressed, modification gave rise to a series of variants. The Avro 504A, built for the RFC, was a strengthened version with wide-chord interplane struts and ailerons of reduced span. The lower wing roots were sometimes stripped of fabric to improve the downward view and *2905*, delivered on January 17, 1916, was used at Farnborough for fabric tests. At least *B3103* was fitted with an improved undercarriage having rear shock legs and front radius rods for use by the CFS Communications Flight at Lopscombe Corner, Salisbury, in 1918.

The Admiralty insisted on wing spars of greater cross section and was supplied with a drastically modified version known as the Avro 504B. It reverted to long-span ailerons and was identified by a large, unbalanced rudder hinged to a considerable dorsal fin. The top longerons were recessed to provide curved cut-outs in the sides of the rear cockpit. A stout ash tail skid, sprung with rubber cord and hinged to a pylon under the rear fuselage, became standard fitment on this and all subsequent 504 variants. A few RNAS Avro 504Bs were used operationally at Dunkirk, including *9890* and *N5267* which had forward-firing guns and interrupter gear.

The majority of Avro 504Bs were naval trainers and late production models had the 80 hp Le Rhône, provision for Scarff ring and no cut-outs to the rear cockpit. At least one was used in early deck landing arrester gear experiments. In the coastal reconnaissance role the endurance was increased to $4\frac{1}{2}$ hours but this soon proved insufficient and 80 examples of a single-seat version having 8 hours endurance were built. Powered by an 80 hp Gnome and known as the Avro 504C, it had a large cylindrical fuel tank in place of the front cockpit and a gap in the top centre section through which a Lewis gun could fire incendiary ammunition upward at an angle of 45 degrees. The RFC equivalent, conceived in 1915 under the designation Avro 504D, retained the balanced comma-type rudder and short-span ailerons, but had the recessed longerons and wing root modifications of the Avro 504C. Only six 504Ds were built and delivery began in August 1915.

The unique Hawk-engined Avro 504F *8603*. (*via Philip Jarrett*)

*9277, one of the ten Avro 504E biplanes. (Imperial War Museum photo Q.67065.)*

Modification on this scale led to a severe weight penalty and additional power had become a dire necessity. The next RNAS variant, the Avro 504E, was therefore fitted with the 100 hp Gnome Monosoupape. At the same time the rear cockpit was moved farther aft and the change of C.G. position caused by installing the main fuel tank between the cockpits was counteracted by reducing the stagger from 24 to 9 in. Centre section struts were then repositioned to converge towards the top in side elevation. The 504E also reverted to the straight top longerons of the prototype but was fitted with the fin, rudder and ailerons of the 504B. Ten were built, some of which were used at Chingford and Fairlop and one at Cranwell.

Designation Avro 504F was given to a single Avro 504C, *8603*, fitted at the suggestion of the Admiralty with a 75 hp Rolls-Royce Hawk six-cylinder in-line engine. It was evidently an unsuccessful union as a contract for 30 Avro 504F aircraft was cancelled and replaced by one for the 80 hp Gnome version.

Designation Avro 504G was used by the RNAS for the 80 hp Gnome-powered Avro 504B conversions having racks for practice bombs, synchronised front Vickers guns and a Scarff ring for a Lewis gun on the rear cockpit.

Last of the early exploratory variants was the 504H, a strengthened 504C fitted under the supervision of Sqn Cdr E. H. Dunning in 1917 with catapult pick-up points and a special padded seat. Piloted by Flt Cdr R. E. Penny this machine later became one of the first aircraft successfully launched by catapult.

At this stage of the war orders for the several variants were far in excess of production capacity at Manchester and a number of sub-contractors were brought in as listed in the data section.

# SPECIFICATION AND DATA

*Manufacturers:*  A. V. Roe and Co Ltd, Clifton Street, Miles Platting, Manchester
The Bleriot & Spad Aircraft Works, Addlestone, Surrey
The Brush Electrical Engineering Co Ltd, Loughborough
The Eastbourne Aviation Co Ltd, Eastbourne
The Humber Motor Co Ltd, Coventry
Parnall and Sons, Mivart Street, Eastville, Bristol
The Regent Carriage Co Ltd, Fulham, London
S. E. Saunders Ltd, East Cowes, Isle of Wight
The Sunbeam Motor Car Co Ltd, Wolverhampton

*Powerplants:*  (Prototype) — 80 hp Gnome
80 hp Gnome Monosoupape
(Avro 504 and 504A) — 80 hp Gnome
80 hp Le Rhône
80 hp Clerget
100 hp A.B.C.
(Avro 504B) — 80 hp Gnome
80 hp Le Rhône
(Avro 504C and 504D) — 80 hp Gnome
(Avro 504E) — 100 hp Gnome Monosoupape
(Avro 504F) — 75 hp Rolls-Royce Hawk
(Avro 504G and 504H) — 80 hp Gnome

*Dimensions:*  Span 36 ft 0 in   Length 29 ft 5 in
Height 10 ft 5 in   Wing area 330 sq ft

*Weights and Performances:*

| | Prototype | Avro 504 landplane | Avro 504 seaplane | Avro 504A Le Rhône |
|---|---|---|---|---|
| Tare weight | — | 924 lb | 1,070 lb | 1,050 lb |
| All-up weight | 1,550 lb | 1,574 lb | 1,719 lb | 1,700 lb |
| Maximum speed | 81 mph | 82 mph | 75 mph | 86 mph |
| Climb to 3,500 ft | 7 min* | — | — | 7 min** |
| Endurance | 3 hours | — | — | 4½ hours*** |

*With 80 hp Gnome Monosoupape.   **With 80 hp Gnome 9 min 30 sec
***With Avro 504C and 504D 8 hours.

*Avro 504 Production:*

| Quantity | For | Remarks |
|---|---|---|
| 1 | Avro | Prototype, first flown 18.9.13, crashed at Shoreham 6.8.14 |
| At least 4 | Avro | Exhibition, private and experimental aircraft |
| 12 | War Office | Constructor's numbers A.V.R.1 to A.V.R.12, serials *376, 390, 397, 398, 637, 638, 652, 665, 683, 692, 715* and *716* |
| 1 | Admiralty | Serial *179* |
| 44 | War Office | First war order for the Army, serials *750* to *793* |
| 6 | Admiralty | Covering order for machines taken out of Army contract for Friedrichshafen raid, serials *873* to *878* |

60

## Avro 504A Production:

| Serial range | Manufacturer | Serial range | Manufacturer |
|---|---|---|---|
| 2890 to 2939 | A. V. Roe | A8501 to A8600 | A. V. Roe |
| 4020 to 4069 | A. V. Roe | *A976 to A9812 | Saunders |
| 4737 to 4786 | A. V. Roe | *B901 to B1000 | A. V. Roe |
| 7446 to 7455 | A. V. Roe | B3251 to B3300 | Humber |
| 7716 to 7739 | A. V. Roe | *B4301 to B4350 | A. V. Roe |
| 7943 to 7992 | A. V. Roe | B4351 to B4400 | Contract cancelled |
| A412 to A461 | Saunders | **B8581 to B8780 | Parnall |
| A462 to A511 | Bleriot & Spad | B8781 to B8830 | Contract cancelled |
| A512 to A561 | A. V. Roe | **C551 to C750 | Humber |
| A1970 to A2019 | Bleriot & Spad | **D1601 to D1650 | Eastbourne |
| A2633 to A2682 | A. V. Roe | **D6201 to D6250 | Humber |
| A3355 to A3404 | Saunders | **D8251 to D8300 | A. V. Roe |
| A5900 to A5949 | A. V. Roe | | |

*Some completed as Avro 504J
**Some completed as Avro 504J or Avro 504K

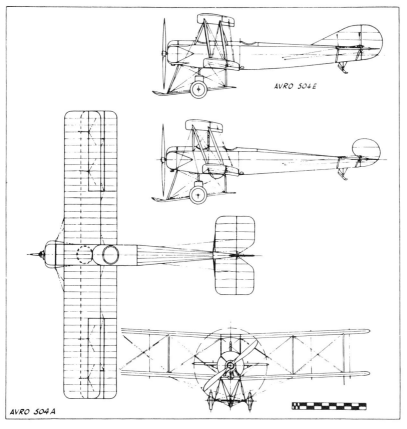

AVRO 504E

AVRO 504A

## Avro 504B Production:

| Serial range | Manufacturer | Serial range | Manufacturer |
|---|---|---|---|
| 1001 to 1050 | A. V. Roe | N5800 to N5829 | Parnall |
| 9821 to 9830 | A. V. Roe | N6010 to N6029 | Parnall |
| 9861 to 9890 | Parnall | N6130 to N6159 | Sunbeam |
| N5250 to N5279 | Sunbeam | N6650 to N6679 | Parnall |
| N5310 to N5329 | Regent | | |

Notes: (i)   Initial deliveries in batch 1001 to 1050 were type 504
      (ii)  1005 to 1008 and 1020 to 1025 transferred to RFC as 2857–2860, 4221–4225 and 4255.
      (iii) N6010 to N6029 to RFC as A9975–A9977, B382–B385, B389–B392, B395–B396, B1390 and
            B1391.
      (iv)  N6650 to N6656 to RFC as B1392–B1394 and B1397–B1400.
      (v)   N5800 to N5829 believed completed as Avro 504G

## Other variants:

| Serial range | Type | Manufacturer | Serial range | Type | Manufacturer |
|---|---|---|---|---|---|
| 794 to 799 | 504D | A. V. Roe | *8574–8603 | 504C | A. V. Roe |
| 1467 to 1496 | 504C | Brush | 9276 to 9285 | 504E | A. V. Roe |
| 3301 to 3320 | 504C | Brush | | | |

*8603 fitted with 75 hp Rolls-Royce Hawk as the single-seat Avro 504F.

## Service Use:

A complete record of machines held on charge by individual squadrons no longer exists, but specimen serial numbers are given where possible.

(a) In France: No.1 Sqn. RFC, 752–755, 758, 769, 773, 784, 2857–2860, 4223; No.5 Sqn. RFC, 383, 568, 637, 715, 750, 755, 782, 783, 4225; No.23 Sqn RFC, 4741; Nos.1 and 3 Sqns RNAS; the Belfort Zeppelin Flight (1914), 179, 873–875.

(b) Overseas: Aboukir, A266, A545, A547, D5479; No.2 Wing, Imbros, 1040–1043.

(c) Home Defence: Nos.33, 51, 75, 76, 77 and 90 Sqns. RFC

(d) RNAS Stations at Cranwell, 1028, 1492–1494, 2930, 3302, 3318, 9278, 9821, 9822, 9862–9864, 9870, N5271, N6654, N6666; Chingford, 876, 1031–1034, 9277; Dover, 1034; Frieston, N6158; Manston, 9880; Port Victoria, 1046; Redcar, 2929, 2933, 2934, 8594, 8600, 9865–9867, 9869, N5264, N5266; Westgate; Great Yarmouth.

(e) Training: No.31 Sqn., A426, C4436; No.35 Sqn., A8505; Flying Instructors' Schools at Gosport, A9799, A9810–A9812, B987, B3101–B3104, B3131, '55, '58, '59, '65, '67, '69, '72, '74, '96, B4222, '23, '42, '43, '45, '46, '49, '50, '63, '65, '66, C606, '08, '09, C4344, C4431–C4433, C4447–C4452, D41, D42; Shoreham; Lilbourne; Redcar; Ayr; Curragh (Ireland).

(f) Working-up squadrons: Nos.24, 40, 45, 65, 186, 188 and 190 Sqns RFC.

Avro 504J *C4451* on which HRH Prince Albert learned to fly, showing the characteristic lobed cowling.
(*Imperial War Museum photo Q.67100.*)

# Avro 504J and Avro 504K

In the autumn of 1916 a more powerful version of the Avro 504A with the 100 hp Gnome Monosoupape was produced for the RFC. This variant, designated 504J and known in the RFC as the 'Mono Avro', was externally identical with the earlier type and large numbers ordered as 504As were completed as 504Js.

Among the first recipients of the Avro 504J was the School of Special Flying founded at Gosport in July 1917 by Maj R. R. Smith-Barry. Here (and later at similar schools at Shoreham, Lilbourne, Redcar, Ayr and Curragh) instructors were introduced to Smith-Barry's revolutionary flying training technique, a system based on demonstration and explanation by an instructor who was in verbal communication with the pupil. The 'Gosport' speaking tubes specially designed for this purpose were still to be found in club aircraft half a century later. The Avro 504J was fully aerobatic and made an ideal training aircraft because its light and powerful controls quickly showed up faults in a pupil's flying. It is now historically important as the aeroplane which made possible a system of training which, in modified form, became part of the RAF's Flying Training School syllabus for more than 40 years. As the standard RFC trainer, the Avro 504J was ordered in such quantity that contracts were placed with additional sub-contractors. Components for Avro-built machines were constructed in Manchester for erection at the company's new aerodrome at Hamble.

In his memoirs C. A. Nepean Bishop recalls that the Gosport School Avro 504J *C4448* was the personal machine of Capt Williams whose favourite trick was to land between the hangars, touch down on the tarmac, swing completely round and finish the landing run inside 'C' Flight hangar. Among other Gosport instructors were Maj E. L. Foot who was to become well known as airline, test and sporting pilot in the years immediately after the War, and Capt Duncan Davis, manager of Avro's South Coast joyriding aircraft in 1919–20 and CFI of the Brooklands School of Flying in the

1930s. A distinguished pupil was HRH Prince Albert (later King George VI) who learned to fly on *C4451*. In 1918 a team of instructors took four Mono Avros across the Channel to demonstrate the Gosport system to the French.

By the end of 1917 the 100 hp Gnome Monosoupape was outmoded as a front line powerplant and British production of this engine was allowed to tail off. To prevent interruption of Avro 504J production through engine shortage, all surplus rotaries, including 80 hp and 110 hp Le Rhônes as well as 130 hp Clergets, were collected from English and French aerodromes. There was no difficulty in fitting the 80 hp Le Rhône and a number of 504Js were thus powered, but it was necessary to modify the front fuselage before larger engines could be installed. Following the trial installation of a 130 hp Clerget in *B3157* for Smith-Barry at Gosport at the end of 1917, the Technical Dept of the Air Board asked A. V. Roe and Co to produce adaptors and a new type of universal engine mounting. In the older machines this was of the two bearer type, the front bearer being in the form of a ball race supported on four tubular arms forming extensions to the fuselage longerons. This 'spider' was now replaced by an overhung mounting designed by H. E. Broadsmith which consisted of two bearer plates which would accept any suitable engine and allow the use of a smooth open fronted cowling. Irrespective of the type of engine fitted, aircraft built with this mounting were known as the Avro 504K, even though many had been ordered as 504Js or even 504As as shown in the table on page 61. The original 'Clerget Avro' *B3157* joined 'F' Flight, School of Special Flying, and crashed at Gosport on March 2, 1918.

With standardisation accomplished the way was clear for greatly increased production and the Avro company was authorised to plan the construction of 100 machines a week, plus spares. They were also required to produce

Avro 504J *B3103* of the CFS Communication Flight at Lopscombe Corner, Salisbury, in 1918 with modified undercarriage. (*Courtesy C. H. Barnes.*)

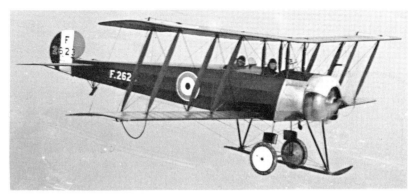

Avro 504K *F2623* during a postwar instructional flight over Salisbury Plain.

20 sets of knock down parts per week for assembly at the Eastern Aircraft Factory at Aboukir, Egypt and by the Armistice production had reached eighty Avro 504Ks a week, including twenty sets of components for Aboukir.

As a result of demonstration flights over Washington by Avro 504J *C4312* imported by the British Mission under Col Lee in the winter of 1917–18, fifty-two Le Rhône engined 504Ks were purchased by the Americans in July 1918. These were used by the AEF for advanced training at No.3 Instruction Centre, Issoudun, France, and after the War survivors were shipped to the USA, where one or two still exist.

Major modification of the Avro 504J was confined to the fitting of short-span, single-bay wings and curved fin to *B4264* at Gosport in January 1918. Standard 36 ft mainplanes were eventually replaced, rigged experimentally with the gap reduced from 5 ft 6 in to 5 ft 1¼ in. In March 1918 the same set of short-span wings was fitted temporarily to *B3155*, a two-seater with shortened fuselage and armed with a Lewis gun. In the following May it flew as a single-seater with the fuel tank in the front cockpit, and this led logically to the first of a number of 110 hp Le Rhône engined single-seat

The single-bay Avro 504J *B4264* at Hamble. (*J. C. C. Taylor*)

65

504Ks for high altitude work with Home Defence Squadrons in the north of England. These had the gravity tank repositioned to port to make way for a Lewis gun on the top centre section, and with front cockpit faired in could reach 18,000 ft. Some were fitted later with a low drag V-type undercarriage similar to that of the Avro 521. Two so modified were flown at Gosport—*C605* with 130 hp Clerget on June 15, 1918 and *C604* with Le Rhône on February 3, 1919.

Total wartime production of Avro 504s of all marks exceeded that of any other type of British aeroplane but the oft quoted figure of 8,340 aircraft (3,696 by A. V. Roe and 4,644 by sub-contractors) is obviously in excess of the actual total. Nine were delivered to the Expeditionary Force in France in 1914; 4,771 to training units; 274 to Home Defence Units; 392 to the Middle East Brigade and 52 to the Americans. When the RFC and RNAS

A high altitude Home Defence Avro 504K single-seater with Lewis gun on the top centre section.
(*Imperial War Museum photo Q.67264.*)

came under unified command on April 1, 1918, Avro 504Js and Ks were in use with almost every Service unit in Britain so that on October 31, 1918, there were 2,999 on RAF charge (including 2,267 at flying schools and 226 on Home Defence). One hundred and eleven were in Egypt and Palestine, where some were pressed into emergency air mail service during the Egyptian rising of March–April 1919.

In 1919 the Sunbeam Motor Co, sub-contractor for the Avro 504B, J and K, fitted one of its 100 hp water-cooled Dyak airship engines into a 504K airframe. With brass nose radiator and attendant plumbing it was a heavy powerplant which substantially reduced payload. Conversions were consequently few but two were supplied to Norway in 1920 and several were built for civil use with the Dyak engine in Australia in 1922.

The Royal Aircraft Establishment found the 504K a most useful test vehicle in the years immediately after the war, and each of Farnborough's

Avro 504K with 100 hp Sunbeam Dyak.

resident machines was used for a wide variety of experimental flying. One important phase was flight testing a number of wings designed by Boulton and Paul, Humber, Vickers and the Steel Wing Company with metal spars and/or ribs. The metal wing programme was initiated partly through timber shortage but chiefly because seemingly identical wooden spars varied considerably in strength and weight. Minor experimental devices flown on

The Avro 540, a postwar gunnery trainer version of the Avro 504K.

the 504Ks ranged from a Leitner-Watts metal airscrew to a windmill-driven clear vision rotating windscreen.

A postwar gunnery trainer version of the Avro 504K (130 hp Clerget) was designated Avro 540 but differed from standard only in the region of the rear cockpit which was strengthened and built up to take a Scarff mounting for a rear gunner. There was no new production, the few that existed being converted 504Ks.

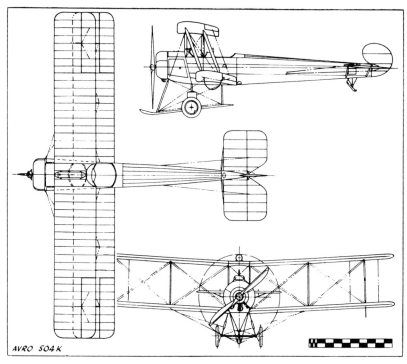

AVRO 504K

Of greater importance was the 504K's contribution to low speed flying research in the course of which *H2402* was fitted with a V-type undercarriage, water ballast tanks near the C.G. and in the tail, as well as an immense fin and unbalanced rudder. Eleven gallons of water could be pumped into the rear tank in the air to enable the aircraft to fly at very large angles of incidence (up to 35 degrees) with the object of exploring controllability in stalled flight and so reduce the risk of hitting the ground in a nose-down attitude as described in R. & M. 991. In the event, *H2402* experienced almost uncontrollable longitudinal oscillations and a second machine, *F8940*, with similar undercarriage, fin and rudder, was flown with variable-incidence tailplane and lead weights up to 80 lb over the tail skid. Large range differential ailerons allowing upward angles in excess of 90 degrees and interconnected with leading-edge slots, were actuated by a wheel mounted on the control column. Research also embraced balanced

*F8940*, one of the Avro 504Ks modified at the RAE, Farnborough, in 1922 for low speed lateral control tests.
(*P. T. Capon.*)

ailerons mounted at mid-gap and concluded with flight tests by *E3269* equipped with Handley Page slots inter-connected with Frise-type balanced ailerons. This aircraft was demonstrated sensationally by F/Lt P. W. S. Bulman at Farnborough on April 15, 1925. A list of the main experimental machines appears in the data section.

The 504Js were declared obsolete in September 1921 but the 504K remained in service as the standard RAF trainer with the CFS and Nos.1, 2, 3, 4 and 5 Flying Training Schools until the late 1920s. It also served with No. 24 (Communications) Squadron; with Nos.600, 601, 602 and 603 Auxiliary Air Force Squadrons; and with Fleet Air Arm training units at

The 'fireproof' Avro 504K *D9068* with 170 hp A.B.C. Wasp I engine.

Netheravon and Leuchars. It took part in Hendon RAF Displays, beginning in 1920 when F/O Quinland cavorted 'L'Avro Comique' *B3292* with extra large four-speed and reverse gear-box, be-cobwebbed undercarriage, vacuum cleaner, anchor, kettle, flue pipe, jazz painted interplane struts and four dummy heads! The Display of July 3, 1921 included a standard Avro race won for Kenley by F/O P. Murgatroyd who won again in the following year while representing Cranwell. Crazy flying by F/Lt Jack Noakes in 1921 and F/Lt W. H. Longton in 1922 brought congratulations from King George V. The Avro 504K made its final appearance in a star role in 1923 as the 'Orva Mayfly', which paraded in front of the crowd with 'A.B.C. Lion' engine, wireless clothes line, kettle, chimney, six-inch gun and carrot accelerator!

The last Avro 504Ks, built by A. V. Roe to Contract 707157/26, appeared in two batches. The first 40, delivery of which was completed on November 11, 1926, were followed by 10 delivered by January 17, 1927.

In 1990 three Avro 504Ks survived in the United Kingdom in military markings, *D7560*, fitted with the wings of *E3104*, property of the Science Museum, London, was on permanent exhibition. The Royal Aeronautical Society's *G-ABAA* painted as *H2311* was undergoing restoration for display at the Greater Manchester Museum of Science and Industry and the Shuttleworth Collection's *H5199*, which had previously carried the fictitious marks *E3404*, was airworthy at Old Warden.

*G-ABAA* which was flown from Scotland by F/Lt Birch to join the Nash Collection at Brooklands in 1938 was overhauled by A. V. Roe and Co for the Royal Aeronautical Society in 1950 and flown at the Farnborough RAF display by Gp Capt L. S. Snaith in July of that year. After a period in store at Hendon and London Airport, it was transferred to Upavon in 1962 and was later held in store at Henlow before being transferred to Manchester. The Shuttleworth machine, c/n R3/LE/61400, which had been stored for many years at Old Warden was rebuilt by apprentices at the Chadderton works of A. V. Roe and flew again in 1955. It later took part in the film *Reach for the Sky*.

## SPECIFICATION AND DATA

*Manufacturers:*  A. V. Roe and Co Ltd, Park Works, Newton Heath, Manchester; and Hamble Aerodrome, near Southampton, Hants.
Australian Aircraft and Engineering Co Ltd, Sydney, NSW, Australia
The Brush Electrical Engineering Co Ltd, Loughborough
Canadian Aeroplanes Ltd, Toronto, Canada
The Eastbourne Aviation Co Ltd, Eastbourne
The Grahame-White Aviation Co Ltd, Hendon Aerodrome, London, N.W.9
Harland and Wolff Ltd, Belfast
The Henderson Scottish Aviation Factory, Aberdeen
Hewlett and Blondeau Ltd, Oak Road, Leagrave, Luton, Beds.

The Humber Motor Co Ltd, Coventry
Morgan and Co, Leighton Buzzard, Beds.
Nakajima Hikoki Seisaku Sho, Ohta-Machi, Tokyo, Japan
Parnall and Sons, Mivart Street, Eastville, Bristol
Frederick Sage and Co Ltd, Peterborough and London
S. E. Saunders Ltd, East Cowes, Isle of Wight
Savages Ltd, King's Lynn, Norfolk
Société Anonyme Belge de Constructions Aéronautiques, Haren, Brussels, Belgium
The Sunbeam Motor Car Co Ltd, Wolverhampton
Yokosuka Naval Arsenal, Japan

Powerplants:    (Avro 504J)  One 80 hp Le Rhône
                            One 100 hp Gnome Monosoupape
                (Avro 504K)  One 90 hp RAF.1A
                            One 100 hp Gnome Monosoupape
                            One 90 hp Thulin
                            One 100 hp Curtiss K.6
                            One 100 hp Sunbeam Dyak
                            One 110 hp Le Rhône
                            One 130 hp Clerget
                            One 150 hp Bentley B.R.1
                            One 170 hp A.B.C. Wasp I
                            One 220 hp Hispano-Suiza

Dimensions:     Span 36 ft 0 in   Length (rotary engines) 29 ft 5 in
                (Dyak) 28 ft 11 in   Height 10 ft 5 in
                Wing area 330 sq ft

Weights and Performances ( Avro 504K ):

|  | 100 hp Gnome Monosoupape | 110 hp Le Rhône | 100 hp Dyak |
|---|---|---|---|
| Tare weight | 1,100 lb | 1,231 lb | 1,320 lb |
| All-up weight | 1,800 lb | 1,829 lb | 1,857 lb** |
| Maximum speed | 82 mph* | 95 mph | 70 mph |
| Cruising speed | — | 75 mph | — |
| Climb to 8,000 ft | — | 6·5 min | — |
| Service ceiling | 13,000 ft | 16,000 ft | — |
| Endurance | 3 hours | 3 hours | 2¾ hours |
| Range | — | 250 miles | |

*At 6,500 ft    **2,400 lb with 220 hp Hispano-Suiza (see page 87).

Avro 504J Production:

| Serial range | Manufacturer | Serial range | Manufacturer |
|---|---|---|---|
| B3101 to B3250 | A. V. Roe | D4361 to D4560 | Sunbeam |
| B4201 to B4300 | A. V. Roe | *D5451 to D5550 | A. V. Roe |
| C4301 to C4500 | A. V. Roe | *D6251 to D6400 | Brush |
| *C5751 to C6050 | Harland & Wolff | *D7501 to D7800 | A. V. Roe |
| D1 to D200 | A. V. Roe | E1601 to E1900 | A. V. Roe |

*Some completed as Avro 504K and Avro 504N.

*Avro 504K Production:*
## (a) Wartime deliveries

| Serial range | Manufacturer | Serial range | Manufacturer |
|---|---|---|---|
| *D1976* to *D2125* | Sage | *E3254* to *E3403* | *Parnall |
| *D5851* to *D5950* | Henderson Scottish | *E3404* to *E3903* | A. V. Roe |
| *D7051* to *D7200* | Hewlett & Blondeau | *E4104* to *E4303* | Humber |
| *D8251* to *D8300* | Humber | *E4324* to *E4373* | Eastbourne |
| *D8781* to *D9080* | Grahame-White | *E6737* to *E6786* | Morgan |
| *D9281* to *D9380* | Parnall | *E9207* to *E9506* | Grahame-White |
| *E301* to *E600* | Harland & Wolff | *F2233* to *F2332* | Brush |
| *E2901* to *E3050* | Morgan | *F2533* to *F2632* | Sunbeam |
| *E3051* to *E3150* | Savage | *F8696* to *F8945* | Sage |

*c/n commenced P.L.6000.

## (b) Later deliveries

| Serial range | Manufacturer | Serial range | Manufacturer |
|---|---|---|---|
| *\*F9697* to *F9922* | Hewlett & Blondeau | *H6543* to *H6842* | Humber |
| *H202* to *H350* | Henderson Scottish | *H7413* to *H7562* | Hewlett & Blondeau |
| *H1896* to *H2145* | Sunbeam | *H9513* to *H9812* | Grahame-White |
| *H2146* to *H2645* | A. V. Roe | *H9813* to *H9912* | Sage |
| *\*H2946* to *H3195* | Brush | *†J731* to *J1230* | A. V. Roe |
| *H5140* to *H5239* | A. V. Roe | *\*\*J6896* | R.A.F. Halton |
| *H5240* to *H5289* | Eastbourne | *J8331* to *J8380* | A. V. Roe |

*Some completed as Avro 504N.
**Built from parts of *H2976* and *H6593*.
†Contracts awarded November 1, 1918, for the construction of *J2142* to *J2241* (Henderson Scottish); *J3992* to *J4091* (Hewlett and Blondeau); *J5092* to *J5191* (Sage); and *J5492* to *J5591* (Savage) were cancelled.

*Service Use:* (With specimen serials as on page 62).

(a) By the RAF at East Retford, Throwley, and Newmarket; Central Flying School, Upavon, *E3567, H2930;* Nos.1, 2, 3 and 5 Flying Training Schools; No.4 Flying Training School, Abu Sueir, *E3493, E3545, H3026, J8376;* RAF College, Cranwell, *F8798, H7417;* No.10 Training Sqn, Gosport, *D4388, D4441, D7051;* No.186 Development Sqn; No.24 (Communications) Sqn; Nos.600, 601, 602 and 603 Sqns, Auxiliary Air Force.

(b) By the American Expeditionary Force, Third Instruction Centre, Issoudun, France, *D9038* (renumbered *1668*).

(c) By Fleet Air Arm training units at Leuchars and Netheravon.

*Experimental Avro 504Ks used at the RAE, Farnborough:*

*D8837*   Used for static strength tests prior to 3.19
*D9068*   The 'fireproof' Avro, fitted with 170 hp A.B.C. Wasp and flown 19.2.20 to 3.6.20 when crankshaft failed. Flown again 28.9.22. (*see* page 113).

*E3269*  CTE petrol control valve tests 9.18; metal (including Vickers) wing tests 4.7.19 to 1.6.20; turn indicator tests 5.20; plug, fuel, temperature and Tampier Needle/Bloctube carburettor tests by C Flight up to 6.22; further steel wing tests 8.22; lateral control at low speeds until 2.5.25

*E3621*  Steel spar tests commenced 20.5.19, destroyed 14.7.19 in fatal air collision over Farnborough with S.E.5A *D7014*

*F2234*  Stall indicator, Holt flare, navigation light and Adamchick undercarriage tests 11.6.23 to 24.4.25

*F8857*  Parachute tests 2.7.19 to 3.11.19; turn indicator tests 13.1.20; accident taking off from Laffan's Plain 16.1.20

*F8940*  Steel wing and accelerometer tests 28.7.21 to 11.21; low speed lateral control tests up to 8.22; F/O Bouchier flew it in landing contest, Hendon 29.6.22; automatic control recorder tests from 11.8.22; airscrew tests 4.23

*H2202*  From Martlesham 28.7.22 for Tampier needle/Bloctube carburettor tests by Engine Research Flt, left for Kenley 18.12.22

*H2214*  Leitner-Watts steel airscrew tests, commencing with ground runs 20. 9.21; lateral control tests 8.22; automatic control recorder tests 15.9.22 to 20.6.23; lateral control movement recorder tests from 26.6.24

*H2365*  To Wireless and Photographic Flt 17.6.24 for short wave telephony and night flying equipment trials to at least 7.2.25

*H2402*  Steel wing tests 22.1.19 to 1.3.20; revolving clear view windscreen tests 10.11.20 to 1.12.20; instrument, control column force recording, accelerometer, low speed lateral control, fuel pump, Mk.IV sextant and clinometer tests by A Flight up to 8.22; undercarriage collapsed 18.3.25

*J7555* and *J7556*  Two Avro 504Ks *A 101* and *A 102*, equipped with Sperry Mark A gyroscopes and radio control gear, were acquired 8.24 from the Sperry Gyroscope Co, New York. To the RAE Instrument Flt 1.11.24 for research into automatically controlled flight. The aircraft were re-serialed *J7555* and *J7556* though only the latter was used; flown on six occasions 3.25 to 12.26.

The Golden Age of barnstorming—Martin Hearn riding the top wing of Aviation Tours' Avro 504K
*G-EBYW circa* 1933.

# Avro 504K (civil)

The vast armada of Avro 504Ks rendered surplus by the 1918 Armistice included not only wartime training veterans but also large batches of new machines at storage units or still in the factories. An offer by A. V. Roe and Co to repurchase them *en bloc* was refused on the grounds that the Disposal Board found it impossible to compute the precise number of saleable aircraft. Sales therefore began by public auction at No.1 Aircraft Salvage Depot, Hendon, but in 1920 Handley Page Ltd bought all Disposal Board stocks and the 504Ks were thereafter marketed by its subsidiary, the Aircraft Disposal Co Ltd of Croydon. Trade was brisk despite the late G. P. Olley's forced landing on March 31, 1920, in Southwark Park pond in the company's demonstrator *G-EAHW* (130 hp Clerget). Foreign and Commonwealth governments made considerable inroads into stocks but even greater numbers were sold for civilian use. Low first cost and a seemingly endless spares backing, made the Avro 504K the only military aircraft of the period to find lasting favour as a civil type. Between 1919 and 1930 over 300 were allotted civil registrations in Britain alone and before the advent of the D.H. Moth in 1926 the Avro 504K was the most common British aeroplane. The majority had the dual controls removed and the decking cut away to make room for a third seat but a few were used for flying instruction and the total included a number ferried abroad in temporary civil marks.

Civil flying was sanctioned in Britain at Easter 1919, a memorable Bank Holiday when A. V. Roe's immortal trainer embarked on an even greater career as a pleasure trip machine. Its usefulness extended over two decades and its name will be linked for ever with the halcyon days of itinerant joyriding, the story of which falls into four clearly defined periods.

Excited by the deeds of great wartime pilots, the public developed a thirst for flying which earned every airworthy 504K a handsome living for the rest of 1919. Despite an ambitious essay into organised pleasure flying by the Avro company, lesser concerns also made a great deal of money, particularly in Scotland. Quick to fill the gap when Avro withdrew from the business in 1920, many former RAF pilots bought 504Ks in the hope of reaping similar rewards but over 50 such mushroom enterprises were ended within the year by the trade slump. The third period, which lasted until the end of the decade, saw Avro pleasure flight business reduced to a number of old established firms run by a handful of seasoned pilots whose lives were dedicated to the game. Their eventual absorption into the great air displays of the 1930s brought the career of the 504K to an end as it had begun, in organised joy flying on the grand scale.

*Genesis*    A. V. Roe and Co started operations at Hamble at Easter 1919 with three Avro 504Ks (100 hp Gnome Monosoupape) in military marks. Piloted by G. L. P. Henderson, H. A. Hamersley, F. Warren Merriam and others, they carried 359 passengers at £1 a head on the first day! Some 3½ weeks later the Avro Transport Company was set up to run a daily return service between Alexandra Park, Manchester and Blackpool Sands via Southport. The inaugural flight, made on May 24 by four 3-seat 504Ks (110 hp Le Rhône), carried Avro director John Lord and a selection of civic dignitaries. During the 18½ week life of the service, bad weather only prevented 28 of the 222 scheduled flights and when the route closed for the winter (and for ever) on September 30, 8,730 miles had been flown without a forced landing.

Inspired by results at Hamble, the Avro Transport Company launched a nation-wide joyriding programme and put G. L. P. Henderson in charge.

Avro Transport Company joyriding 504K *E4359/G-EABJ*, Fleet No. 3, on the beach at Blackpool in 1919. (*Courtesy J. C. C. Taylor*)

75

As prelude to this assignment he flew a brand new 504K (110 hp Le Rhône) *H2586/G-EAEV* into 6th place in the Aerial Derby at Hendon on June 21, 1919, at an average speed of 75·22 mph. The leading pilots of the day whom he had appointed to take charge of 'Southern Area' operations were already hard at it at Hounslow Heath (Maj A. G. Taylor); Manston (Capt Duncan Davis); Southsea/Eastney (F/Lt E. A. Sullock); Weston-super-Mare sands (Capt D. G. Westgarth-Heslam); Brighton/Patcham/Blatchington Farm (Capt D. I. M. Kennard); Swansea/Brynmill (F. G. M. Sparks); and Porthcawl (Capt E. D. C. Herne). The 'Northern Stations' were Blackpool South Shore (Capt W. G. R. Hinchliffe); Southport/Birkdale Sands (Capt Collison); Fleetwood/Scale Hall and Morecambe Sands (Lt Macrae); Rhyl (Capt E. Maitland Heriot); Liverpool/Waterloo Sands (machines diverted from the Manchester–Blackpool service on Wednesdays and Saturdays); Manchester/Alexandra Park (Lt-Col G. L. P. Henderson); and Isle of Man/Douglas Promenade/Ramsay (Lt G. B. Moxon). Avro 504L seaplanes and Avro 536 five seaters were also used as detailed in their own chapters.

During Wakes Weeks, industrial workers, coal miners and the like spent lavishly on longer flights, looping and inverted flying and by August 1 over 10,000 passengers had been carried at Blackpool alone. Similar figures were returned at Southport where flying often continued by moonlight and one woman passenger had 15 stunt flights within a week. In mid-August a gale of unprecedented fury struck the coast, wrought havoc among Avros pegged down with sandbags on the beaches and reduced the number in service on August 31 to 17.

At Hounslow Heath where 6,400 passengers were carried during the season, Avro 504K *E3289/G-EAAM* and Avro 536 *K-105/G-EAAP* were chartered by the *Evening Standard* in July for daily newspaper flights to Brighton and Southsea. Another made an incredible eight hour flight from Perth to Hounslow on August 12 with 60 brace of grouse.

Let by *G-EAIH*, '*II* and '*IJ* which left the Manchester works on July 28, 1919, nine Avros (including *G-EAJQ*, '*JU*, a 536 and two 504Ls) attended the First Air Traffic Exhibition at Amsterdam in August 1919. A sustained demand for joy flights kept them in the Netherlands and the last two did not arrive back at Lympne until January 3, 1920. Meanwhile a rail strike in Britain had brought almost the entire fleet to Hounslow to convey passengers, newspapers, films and light freight to the provinces. The return flights were offered as a daily service to London and once again demand was far in excess of available seats. When petrol restrictions brought the season to an end the Avro Transport Company had carried over 30,000 people and flown the equivalent of $12\frac{1}{2}$ circuits of the earth. The craze for flying bordered on hysteria. Garden parties without a 504K were considered unfashionable and the Swansea machine was frequently 'detached' to the Abernant Hotel, Llanwrtyd Wells, for this purpose, and when the Town Crier flew over Swansea ringing his bell in flight, the local police could hardly control the resultant crowd of would-be aviators.

Hounslow was not the only 504K pitch in the London area. Prewar

76

The Navarro Aviation Co's Avro 504K *D9304*/*G-EAEA* joyriding at Whitstable, Kent, in 1919. Like so many contemporary civil aeroplanes, it flew in drab military green with RAF serial.

premises were reopened at Hendon by the Grahame-White Aviation Co Ltd as the London Flying Club, a centre of fashionable society equipped with 12 Avro 504Ks acquired from the nearby Salvage Depot. Painted in carroty pink, they carried enlarged versions of their RAF serials until full civil markings on white rectangles were applied some months later. Instruction was available and an attempt was made to revive Saturday afternoon pylon racing but the Avros were engaged mainly on joy flights, 5,100 tickets being sold in the public enclosures that season. They also carried the *Daily Mirror* to the Midlands during the railway strike but the concern degenerated into a country club and flying ceased at the end of 1920. Across the road at Stag Lane, the London and Provincial Aviation Co Ltd used a single machine, *G-EABT*, which was later flown at Yarmouth by T. Neville Stack and George Lusted. An eight-strong fleet (110 hp Le Rhône engines), flown at Northolt by the Central Aircraft Co Ltd included *G-EAGI* fitted with the V-strut undercarriage of the Home Defence fighter variant. When the firm closed in 1921, chief pilot Herbert Sykes left to continue Avro joyriding on his own account at Kingsbury, Middlesex, with tours in the Midlands each summer, each of his machines being appropriately named *Psyche* in turn.

Vickers Ltd opened south of the Thames with *G-EACV*, '*DS*, '*EY* and '*EZ* at Joyce Green, Kent. Two of these did a roaring trade at Kings Heath, Birmingham, in August and on October 10 another, piloted by Capt Simpson, made commercial aviation history by carrying 333 lb of tinned fish from Newcastle to Turnhouse. Croydon figured as an Avro 'pitch' from August 1919 when Aircraft Transport and Travel Ltd started joyriding with *G-EAIO*–'*IS* and Sir Philip Sassoon, who was just about the first owner of a private 504K, commuted to and from Lympne in *G-EANN*.

Coastal resorts outside the Avro company's network were served in 1919–20 by the Eastbourne Aviation Co Ltd with 504L seaplanes and two 504Ks; by the Bournemouth Aviation Co Ltd with five; and by the Navarro Aviation Co Ltd with three. The Bournemouth outfit ran a service to Weymouth and worked inland towns as far as Bath, while Navarro's machines *G-EADY*, '*EA*, '*EB* and '*JP* enjoyed lucrative seasons at Southend and

Whitstable. Among the first concerns to offer flying instruction was the Cambridge School of Flying Ltd of Hardwick to which record crowds were drawn by F. J. Ortweiler's aerobatics in *E3501/G-EAEC* in August 1919. Their other machine *E4118/G-EAHL* did good business at Hunstanton and during August and September 1919 two new Humber-built 504Ks *G-EAGV* and *'GW* ran a Harrogate–Hull–Scarborough service for the North Sea Aerial Navigation Company of Leeds.

Aerial Photos Ltd of Edinburgh, owners of three (later six) 504Ks made a vigorous pleasure flight tour of St Andrews, Rothesay, Dundee, Perth, Berwick and Montrose. They carried 1,509 passengers, one of whom flown at North Inch, Perth, was the young Earl of Kinnoull, who four years later became the owner of private 504K *G-EAMZ*. The Ayr–Glasgow area was served by *G-EADH*, *'HY*, *'HZ* and *'IA* of the West of Scotland Aviation Co Ltd, Renfrew.

Smaller concerns of the period were run by Telford Rogers at Birmingham with *G-EAFQ*; *G-EAHO* (H. V. David) crashed at Aberystwyth after only three weeks; C. A. Crichton (Northern Aircraft Transport and Travel Co Ltd) flew *'GZ* at Sunderland; and W. G. Pudney toured rural Essex with *'JZ*, *'MI* and *'RP*. Probably the first British 'executive' aeroplane was Avro 504K *G-EANT* commissioned at Brooklands in October 1919 to assist Godfrey-Nash motor racing interests. J. D. V. Holmes, an ex-RAF pilot whose brother F. J. V. was a skilled aircraft engineer, pooled all available cash in May 1919 with the newly demobilised Alan J. Cobham, and bought *G-EACL*, first 504K sold by the Aircraft Disposal Co Ltd. After its conversion to three-seater by Avro at Hamble, Cobham commenced joyriding at Newbury, Wantage, Oxford and Aylesbury, but two months later *'CL* overturned in a hayfield near Northampton, after which the replacement *G-EAIB*, worked Leicester, Nottingham and elsewhere.

*The Lean Years*  Foreseeing the end of the boom, Avro left the joy flight business but the Holmes brothers continued through the winter at Bradford, Middlesbrough and Newcastle, Cobham alone carrying 6,000 passengers. Wing-walking was introduced by F. J. V. Holmes and R. Graham-Woolland at Leicester on August Monday 1919 and served to draw the crowds. *G-EASF*, destined to become the most famous of all joyriding 504Ks, was first flown at Warrington and Bolton in 1920 under Cobham and Holmes Aviation Co ownership but much of the income came from free flights paid for by local newspapers. When Cobham left to join de Havillands his place was taken by J. C. C. Taylor, an experienced pilot and engineer. Former Avro Transport machines *G-EAHZ* and *'KX* were acquired to work the lucrative South Wales beaches but *'IB* was sold. After overhaul at Manchester it was flown to Priory Heath, Ipswich, in $2\frac{1}{2}$ hours by Capt Anderson of the Anderson and Pool Aviation Co on July 2, 1920. To attract custom, fares came down to 15s 6d, a move found expedient by concerns such as J. M. Drysdale's Oxfordshire Aviation Co which based

*G-EAGI*, one of the Central Aircraft Co's Northolt-based instructional 504Ks, retained the V-type undercarriage of the Home Defence fighter version.

*G-EADU* and '*GT* at Caversham, Reading; J. Blake's taxi service between Liverpool and the Isle of Man, flown by *G-EAFD* during the T.T. Races in June 1920; Ingham and Little (the Border Aviation Co) at Carlisle and Scarborough with *G-EANQ* in 1920, and at Cockermouth and Heysham with *G-EAIA* in 1921; Summerfield and Company on the East Coast with *G-EADR* and '*EB*; and A. A. Mitchell (the Scottish Aerial Transportation Company) of Craiglockhart who carried passengers over Edinburgh in *G-EAQU*, '*QV* and four others hired from Aerial Photos Ltd. By this time Croydon joyriding was in the hands of W. G. Chapman (Leatherhead Aviation Services) with the ex-Cambridge *G-EAHL*. He also sold flights at Reading, Leatherhead, Guildford and Chessington but withdrew from the business when his new 504K *G-EBAV* crashed at Slough on August 20, 1922. F. G. M. Sparks and E. A. Sullock formed the Welsh Aviation Co Ltd in November 1920 to revive the Swansea trade with *G-EAWK*, '*WL* and '*WM* but optimism went unrewarded and after one season they were bought out by local turf accountant Evan Williams. Only 71 hours were flown in 1922 and the new owner was drowned with pilot F. Bush when '*WK* fell into the sea in the following October.

Alexandra Park, birthplace of the 504K, housed the Midland Aviation Company equipped with *G-EADP*, '*GB* and '*LE*. It was a typical 'one season' outfit, taken over in 1922 by the Manchester Aviation Co Ltd which, with a smaller concern called Manchester Airways operated all over Lancashire. Three Avros *G-EADP*, '*ZW* and '*ZX* alone survived this ordeal to found the Northern Aviation Co Ltd in 1924. In the south C. L. Pashley (CFI of the Southern Aero Club until 1965) took 504K *G-EATU* to Shoreham for instruction and joyriding, while a more ambitious project, inaugurated by the Royal Aero Club in July 1921, sought to provide aeroplanes for the use of members. The Aircraft Disposal Co delivered *G-EAXY*, '*YB* and '*YC*, newly overhauled, which were raced enthusiastically at Croydon in September 1921 but lost in accidents soon afterwards.

79

Frank Neale (the Essex Aviation Company) who acquired *G-EBCK* from F. J. V. Holmes in 1923, did well at Epping and also on Margate beach. In the same year J. M. Drysdale's old machine *G-EADU* was sold to Renfrewshire Flying Services to join '*JZ* at the game in southwest Scotland. They were not alone at Renfrew as William Beardmore and Co Ltd was awarded a Reserve Training contract and purchased *G-EAHY* from the West of Scotland Aviation Co Ltd, *G-EBFV* from F. J. V. Holmes and *G-EBGY*, '*GZ* and '*IS* newly civilianised by A. V. Roe and Co. These and *G-EBXA* (a crash replacement) flew hundreds of hours per annum until the three survivors were replaced by Bristol Type 89As in 1927 and sold to the North British Aviation Co Ltd at Hooton for joyriding in 1929. *G-EBLA*, originally the Reserve Training 504K at Brough, was also sold for joyriding but fell into the sea at Weymouth on June 6, 1928.

The 1923 Air Ministry Light Aeroplane Trials awakened interest in private flying and several 504Ks were thus used, including *G-EAMZ* (130 hp Clerget). This came out of storage as a mount for pioneer Avro test pilot F. P. Raynham in the Grosvenor Trophy Race on June 23. With rear seat faired over he flew round the Lympne–Castle Bromwich–Filton circuit at an average speed of 96·1 mph and came second. In June 1925 '*MZ* was sold to the Earl of Kinnoull (whose enthusiasm for the 504K dated from a pleasure flight at Perth in 1919) for whom Beardmore test pilot Maurice Piercy made the delivery flight to Le Bourget where it crashed only a few days later. Flying from Hendon and Brooklands, *G-EASB* was widely publicised in 1925 as the mount for the first 'aerial commercial travellers', (Tellus Super Vacuum Cleaner representatives), flown about the country by J. C. P. Phillips and C. P. B. Ogilvie. G. V. Peck (the Southern Counties Aviation Company) painted up *G-EASG* as the concern's 'A Flight' and a new machine *G-EBKS*, built from spares, as 'B Flight'. Working from Brooklands they were a familiar sight in the south and a third machine *G-EAAY* was added in 1926. This 'evergreen' was soon acquired by F. G. Miles of Shoreham along with *G-EBJE* which had been at Brooklands for some months as the private aeroplane of racing driver John Cobb. Although he is well known as the founder of Miles Aircraft Ltd, few realise that F. G. Miles flew over 2,000 hours in Avro 504Ks. In 1927 the Gnat Aero Co Ltd (forerunner of the Southern Aero Club) was formed at Shoreham with *G-EAJU*, '*TU* and *G-EBYB* and successfully worked the South Coast, a task in which *G-EBJE*, '*VL* and *G-AACW* of Southern Aircraft Ltd also joined in 1928. 'Opposition' in the area was provided by the irrepressible Dudley Watt operating from Ford, Sussex, with *G-AADY*, '*FJ* and *G-ABBF*. Other prominent members of the fraternity at that time were Messrs Thomas, Griffiths and Rimmer (South Wales Airways) of Porthcawl and Swansea who kept *G-EBNH*, '*SG*, *G-AASS*, *G-ABLV* and '*LW* in turn in their hillside hangar at Wenvoe; Messrs L. Lewis and L. A. Jackson (later of the Shuttleworth Trust) who ran L. J. Skytrips Ltd in the Home Counties; and Western Aviation Ltd which worked the West Midlands with the blue and cream striped *G-EBQR* and '*XV*.

*Renaissance*     Interest in the 504K as a private aeroplane revived in 1926. It was not easy to fly, but once mastered, was a real 'pilot's aeroplane', but unfortunately stayed economically in the air solely by joyriding's high utilisation. Thus C. L. Kent's *G-EBKR*; J. C. Don's ex-Gnat *G-EAJU*; *G-EBSJ* flown at Maylands by Battlesbridge flour miller A. H. Matthews; and L. E. R. Bellairs' *G-EBVL*; soon returned to barnstorming, the last at Christchurch with F. C. Fisher. Of unique interest was *G-EBWO* rebuilt with a 100 hp Anzani radial at Woodley in 1928 by Philips and Powis Ltd for Dr M. C. Wall (see also pages 114 and 116). After a few months it joined standard 504K *G-AAGG* at the Phillips and Powis flying school.

As the decade drew to its close another crop of small operators appeared which included R. J. Bunning at Pontypool with *G-EBSM*; Midland Aero Flights Ltd with *G-EBYE*; Inland Flying Services Ltd of Maylands who worked Essex fields with *G-AAFE* and *'FT*; and Aeroplane Services which spent the 1929 season at Southend using *G-AAEZ* in competition with Surrey Flying Services' *G-EBYW* at Shoebury. The latter was sold in 1930 to Aviation Tours Ltd which plied its trade in the west country with some success, took over Western Aviation Ltd in 1933 and expanded its fleet to five – *G-EBQR*, *'XV*, *'YW*, *G-AAYM* and *G-ABAA*. Airframes were by that time in very short supply and the last of these grand old biplanes were built from spares by Kent Aircraft Services Ltd who produced seven with private constructor's numbers K.A.S.1 to 7 at Kingsdown, Kent, in 1930–31; by G. and H. Aviations Ltd at Stag Lane in 1930 (*G-ABAA* and *'AB*); by the Essex Flying Club who built *G-ABWK* and *'YB* in a garage at Orsett, Essex, in 1932; and by C. B. Field who constructed *G-ABSL* – *'SN*, *G-ACAU* and *'AV* at Kingswood Knoll, Surrey, in 1932–33. The Kent Avros flew at seaside resorts, one at Ramsgate piloted by E. Bicknell of Thanet Aviation Ltd and another at Gravesend by P. H. Meadway. The Essex Avros, intended for a club at Abridge, went instead to Springfield, Chelmsford, in a second vain attempt to form a club. C. B. Field's machines were all sold to small concerns and on September 24, 1932, *G-ABSN* (130 hp Clerget) forsook its pitch at Herne Bay when London and Provincial's pilot Pegg averaged 59 mph in the Hillman Trophy Race from Maylands to Clacton and back and came 7th.

*Grand Finale*     The useful life of the old 504K ended in the mid-30s in service with the big names of joyriding. The first of these came into existence on August 25, 1921, when the Holmes brothers re-formed as the Berkshire Aviation Co Ltd (later restyled Berkshire Aviation Tours Ltd), operating initially at Porthcawl. Here A. L. Robinson joined O. P. Jones (later famous as the bearded Imperial Airways and BOAC Captain) on the payroll. The latter had been with the Holmes since February 1920, first flying commercially for them at Carlisle the same month. He, alone had carried 10,000 passengers by the end of 1921 (8,000 in *G-EASF*) but left to form his own company with A. N. Kingwill in 1922, using

For over a decade three of the greatest names in joyriding were those of Surrey Flying Services Ltd, the Cornwall Aviation Co Ltd and the Brooklands School of Flying Ltd, represented here by *G-EBDP* (1922–1930); *G-EBIZ* (1924–1935); and *G-AAEM* (1929–1931).

Avros *G-EADH* and *G-EBCB*. Robinson (who succeeded in carrying 155 passengers in one day in *G-EAKX* at Wells on May 14, 1922) also went to Imperial Airways in 1924, being replaced by J. D. Parkinson who alone carried 34,000 passengers, 10,000 of them for Berkshire in 1925. Overhauls continued at East Hanney where six more 504Ks were stripped and rebuilt as *G-EBCK*, '*FV*, '*IN*, '*KB*, '*KR* and '*KX* before 1926, the year the firm moved to Witney Aerodrome, Oxford. Scarcely any part of England and Wales escaped their attention and the firm's passenger figures to the end of 1925 exceeded 32,000. Berkshire amalgamated with Northern Air Lines in May 1929 to form Northern Air Transport Ltd with 16 aircraft, the largest 504K fleet since 1919. James Orrell, later chief test pilot of A. V. Roe and Co was the pilot of Northern's oldest Avro, the famous *G-EASF*, at Rochdale in 1931.

Surrey Flying Services Ltd, formed at Croydon in 1922 by A. F. Muir and W. F. Grant with two Clerget Avros, *G-EAWI* and '*WJ* (in which Capt Muir made charter flights to Cardiff, Dublin, Brussels and the battlefields) were precursors of a large fleet of blue and silver 504Ks which became an integral part of the Croydon scene for more than a decade. Short trips were reduced to 5s, countless thousands of which were sold by the indefatigable Joe Chamberlain at the Purley Way gate. In addition to 13 for its own use the firm also reconditioned 504Ks for other companies and as late as 1934 their last serviceable machine, *G-AAAF*, was still ambling off Croydon's turf in an aroma of castor oil to return to the accompaniment of never-to-be-forgotten blips of the rotary engine and with the wheels still spinning.

The only other firm to operate on any scale was the now almost legendary Cornwall Aviation Co Ltd formed in September 1924 by Capt Percival Phillips DFC and F. L. Hill, garage proprietors of St Austell. Their first machine *G-EBIZ*, resplendent in pillar box red and built by Berkshires at Witney, worked Margate beach. As business increased, other red Avros flew from fields all over the Home Counties and by 1930 the fleet consisted of *G-EBIZ*, '*NR*, '*SE*, *G-AAAF* and '*YI*. Each winter they were overhauled in the garage at St Austell and in the spring flew out of a nearby field at Ventonwyn. Maintenance 'on location' was very difficult because the man-in-the-street who saw a partly dismantled aeroplane took it for granted that an accident had occurred. To prevent unwarranted loss of trade the Avros were taxied under a tree at nightfall and a spare engine installed secretly by means of block and tackle in the light of car headlamps. It spoke well for the superannuated 1913 design that 20 years later it could still make up to 40 take-offs a day, every day, and take the punishment involved in miles of taxying over rough ground. In the summer pilots and engineers lived a nomadic existence and flew the Avros from field to field laden with tool chests and spares, and with bedding, tents and passenger ladders lashed to the undercarriage and between the interplane struts.

In 1932 they teamed up with Sir Alan Cobham's National Aviation Day Display but at the end of the 1933 season the Cornwall fleet disbanded to

The indestructible *G-EASF* which carried over 8,000 passengers in 1921 and was still in use for joyriding in 1935.

make way for Capt Phillips' new company. At the time of his death in 1938 Capt Phillips had carried over 91,000 passengers, nearly all of them in *G-EBIZ*.

'Cobham's Circus' succeeded in its aim of fostering airmindedness largely through the imaginative use of the red Cornwall 504Ks which enabled passengers to take part in the events. In 1933 the silver and black fleet of the North British Aviation Co Ltd was enlisted to enable two separate tours to take place simultaneously. Founded at Hooton in 1929 by E. E. Fresson and L. J. Rimmer with *G-EBGZ*, '*IS* and '*XA*, it normally worked Cheshire and Lancashire but in 1931 made a Lakeland tour with a base at Keswick. In 1933 L. J. Rimmer and W. 'Jock' Mackay bought up the remaining stock of the late Northern Air Transport Ltd and the augmented fleet of fourteen Avro 504Ks was used by Cobham again during the 1934 season. A series of accidents in which Mackay was killed in an Avro 504N left them with only the seemingly indestructible *G-EASF* with which to finish the 1935 season. At the end of that year the Air Ministry refused to renew Certificates of Airworthiness for rotary engined aircraft and the heyday of the Avro 504K in Britain was over.

Full details of all British Civil Avro 504Ks will be found in Appendix F.

The Dyak engined 504K c/n D.1 (later *G-AUBG*), built at Mascot by AAEC Ltd, from imported parts in 1920.

# Avro 504K (overseas)

In 1919–20 the British Government made each Dominion an Imperial Gift of surplus Avro 504Ks and other aircraft, and during the next 12 years large numbers of additional 504Ks were stripped, overhauled and test flown at Croydon by the Aircraft Disposal Co for military and civil use overseas. Vickers Ltd and A. V. Roe and Co were also heavily engaged, the latter completing one hundred 504Ks in 1921 alone. Manufacturing rights were also sold in Japan and elsewhere.

*Australia*    Equipment of the Australian Flying Corps in 1920 included 48 Imperial Gift Avro 504Ks. They carried *A3* serials and later served with the RAAF until replaced by D.H. Moths in June 1928. At least ten others were acquired by short lived joyriding outfits such as Kingsford Smith's Diggers' Co-op Aviation Co Ltd but few made money although Normal Brearley flew 80 passengers Perth–Kalgoorlie in two machines (100 hp Gnome Monosoupape) in October 1919 and C. A. Butler carried 62 at Adelaide. The Australian civil register was not established until June 1921 and all flew in old Service colours.

Avro manufacturing and sales rights were vested in H. E. Broadsmith, former manager of the Manchester works, who left for Sydney with four 504Ks which had been allotted (but never carried) British marks *G-EAIV* – *'IY* in the name of the Australian Aircraft and Engineering Co Ltd which Broadsmith had formed in association with Capt Nigel Love and Lt Warneford. He also took components for 15–20 additional 504Ks. On arrival three were converted to three-seaters and fitted with 130 hp Clerget engines at Mascot, where the first joyride took place on January 9, 1920. They carried no markings other than 'AVRO' and AAEC titling. Capt Love used the first machine for the first inter-city flight to Melbourne and a tour of the outback for a paint firm (September 7–October 18, 1920). He also won the handicap section of the first Australian Aerial Derby on November 27, 1920.

The company's second 504K (first flown as a 504L at Manly Bay, Sydney) was exhibited at the Brisbane Show and afterwards carried several thousand joyriders at Eagle Farm Racecourse, piloted by F. L. Roberts who on June 26, 1920, flew the first air mail 87 miles from Lismore to Tenterden. Capt Wilson in the third Avro dropped foodstuffs to valuable sheep in flooded country, but of the three Clerget machines, only *G-EAIV*/*G-AUCB* survived to receive civil marks in 1921. Lt Adair delivered the fourth (110 hp Le Rhône) to the Queensland Northern Graziers Association at Brisbane on August 13, 1920, after a record flight of 240 miles between Newcastle and Grafton. This machine became *G-AUBE* in 1921.

Broadsmith began the erection of 504Ks from imported parts in 1921 and fitted some of them with Sunbeam Dyak engines. The first, *G-AUBG* for the infant QANTAS, carried 283 passengers and flew 7,400 miles in a few months, while the second, built for P. Hogarth, was delivered 1,845 miles to Clio Station, North Queensland by J. Treacy in 20 flying hours. It was eventually registered to A. J. Driver, Brisbane, as *G-AUEO* in 1924. The third and fourth, believed *G-AUCD* and '*CE* (Clerget engines), were followed by seven more Dyak 504Ks including *G-AUBS* for Percy Heyde of Nimmitabel, NSW, and two unregistered examples for inter-railhead connections of Auto Aero Services Ltd.

In 1922 AAEC received a contract for six 504Ks (Clerget) for the RAAF. These were built at Mascot from selected Australian timber which proved equally strong for a weight penalty of only 80 lb. Serials were *A3-48* to *A3-53* and the first, named *Mary* by the wife of the Prime Minister, was handed over at Mascot on June 16, 1922, for acceptance tests by the well known Bristol designer Sq Ldr F. S. Barnwell.

The special Avro 504K with modified undercarriage and tail assembly, believed *G-AUDM*, showing the revised side cowlings of later Dyak powered machines. (*Courtesy W. Boddy*)

The 504K played a notable part in later Aerial Derby Races as in 1922 at Sydney when Dyak Avros *G-AUBJ*, *'CZ* and a third (believed *G-AUDM*) with improved V-strut undercarriage, unbalanced rudder and triangular fin, were on the line. Capt E. W. Percival, who had earlier fitted *G-AUDA* with a 90 hp RAF IA, came fourth in the 1924 Derby in *G-AUEP* which had been modified to take the big 220 hp Hispano-Suiza engine, competing against H. C. Miller who had replaced the Dyak in *G-AUDR* by a 100 hp Curtiss K-6 taken from a Curtiss Seagull, a combination which won the major prizes.

*Aircraft details:*

### (*a*) Imperial Gift machines
*A3-1* to *A3-48* including *A3-1* to *A3-9* (ex *H2171–H2179*); *A3-16* to *A3-19* (ex *H3033*, *'36*, *'37*, *'38*); *A3-21* to *A3-23* (ex *H3040*, *'41*, *'43*); *A3-27* to *A3-33* (ex *E3742–'46*, *'49*, *'50*); *A3-36* to *A3-41* (ex *H9835* and *'40*). *A3-47* (ex *H3042*). Based at Point Cook, 12 with No.1 FTS and 36 in reserve at No.1 Aircraft Depot.

### (*b*) Built by the Australian Aircraft and Engineering Co Ltd.
Imported aircraft: *G-EAIV–'IY*, c/n AAEC.1–AAEC.4, *'IV* became *G-AUCB* 6.21, s.o.r. 6.23; *'IW* and *'IX* flown without marks, one crashed at Goulburn, NSW; *'IY* became *G-AUBE* 6.21, s.o.r. 6.23. All were 130 hp Clerget powered except *G-AUBE* which had a 110 hp Le Rhône.
Erected from imported components: (Clerget) *G-AUCD* and *'CE*, c/n AAEC.5 and AAEC.6, s.o.r. 6.23 (Dyak) *G-AUBG*, c/n D.1, QANTAS, converted to Avro 548A, s.o.r. 4.32; *G-AUEO*, c/n D.2, P. Hogarth, s.o.r. 3.30; *G-AUBJ*, c/n D.5, Chapman Aerial Services, Sydney, s.o.r. 2.28; *G-AUBS*, c/n D.6, P. Hyde, Nimmitabel, NSW, s.o.r. 6.22; *G-AUCZ*, c/n D.7, A. G. McKeahnie, Queanbeyan, NSW, crashed at Smeaton, Victoria, 9.6.30; *G-AUDM*, c/n given as 1000DC but believed D.8 with modified tail, A. D. Reid, Taree, NSW, s.o.r. 11.25; *G-AUDR*, c/n D.9, M. Cox, Mascot, temporarily with Curtiss K-6 in 1924, s.o.r. 6.26.
Built from Australian materials: *A3-49* to *A3-54*.

### (*c*) Other Civil Avro 504Ks
*G-AUBA/H2030*, G. M. Elwyn, Inglewood, Q, s.o.r. 4.28; *G-AUBL/D6396*, s.o.r. 1.25, and *G-AUBM/H2846*, the Orva Commercial Aviation Co, crashed before registration; *G-AUBP*, J. Austin, Mudgee, NSW, dismantled 6.23; *G-AUBQ*, Diggers' Co-op Aviation Co, crashed at Cowra, NSW, 18.7.21; *G-AUBR/H1909*, Diggers', crashed at Wagga, NSW, 19.9.21; *G-AUCG*, Butler-Kauper Aviation Co, crashed at Minalaton, SA, 10.1.22; *G-AUCI/H1973*, re-registered to F. J. Barnes 1924 as *G-AUEN* burned out at Perth, WA, 27.10.26; *G-AUCJ/E3432*, Geelong Air Service, s.o.r. 6.29; *G-AUCL*, West Australian Airways Ltd, s.o.r. 6.31; *G-AUCN*, Mildura Aircraft Ltd, crashed at Mildura, V, 10.2.22; *G-AUCY/H7499*, Macpherson and Farmer, Melbourne, crashed 4.11.25; *G-AUDA/D5512*, Aero Flight Aviation Co, Brisbane, burned out 20.11.24;

*G-AUDQ/E3501* ex *G-EAEC*, A. W. Vigers, wrecked by gale, Melbourne 5.23; *G-AUEC/H1960*, L. H. Holden, Sydney; *G-AUEP*, E. W. Percival, to Airgold Ltd, burned out at Lae, NG, 6.6.28; *G-AUEW*, D. G. Brim and Sons, Milton, NSW, rebuilt 1928 with 90 hp Renault later re-engined with 120 hp Airdisco, s.o.r. 10.29; *G-AUFP/E3363*, Larkin Aircraft Supply Co, crashed at Wallacedale, V, 3.1.27; *G-AUGP*, Larkin Aircraft Supply Co *Pilot Bird*, crashed at Melbourne, V, 21.3.30.

Note: All Clerget-engined apart from *G-AUCJ*, '*CL* (100 hp Monosoupape); *G-AUDA* (90 hp RAF 1A); *G-AUEP* (220 hp Hispano-Suiza).

*Belgium*      Demonstrations at Brussels in August 1920 by Avro 504Ks *G-EAHX* and '*VD* led to the placing of Contract 45/21 with Vickers Ltd in 1921 for 12 machines to re-equip the 8th (Flying School) Group of l'Aéronautique Militaire. The order was made up of six converted by A. V. Roe and Co at Hamble and flown out with Belgian civil marks, and six redundant Avro Transport Company machines originally converted for joyriding in 1919. A further 38 obtained from the Aircraft Disposal Co in 1922 included 18 flown from Croydon to Brussels in British civil marks November 1921–July 1922. One other, *O-BADB*, was flown out by A. H. Forson for the pioneer airline SNETA on March 24, 1921.

Further needs were met by the construction of 27 Avro 504Ks (80 hp Gnome or 130 hp Clerget) under licence at Evère by SABCA. *A-51*, first of these, was specially equipped and flew inverted for 2 min 27 sec piloted by G. F. van Damme of the Belgian Army Flying School, Wevelghem. Thirteen outdated SABCA 504Ks were sold for civil purposes 1934–38.

*Aircraft details:*

### (a) Purchased in the United Kingdom

Belgian Air Force serials *A-1* to *A-50*; *A-1* to *A-6* ex *H1907*, *H1971*, *H1975*, *H1976*, *H1979*, *H1980*; *A-7* to *A-12* prepared by A. V. Roe and Co, Hamble, c/n 5011–5016, Cs of A★ 22.4.21. Flown out as *O-BADG* to

*OO-BOB*, a SABCA-built Avro 504K with a 90 hp Renard engine and modified undercarriage.
(*J. M. Bruce/G. S. Leslie Collection*)

'*DI* and *O-BADK* to '*DM*. Others included former Avro Transport Company machines *G-EABP*, '*DM*, '*DN*, '*IH*, *J749/G-EAND* and *J753/G-EANG* delivered 6.21, and the following overhauled by the Aircraft Disposal Co and flown out by Capts Hayns, M. Pearcy, E. L. Foot, A. F. Muir, R. H. Stocken and F. T. Courtney: *G-EAZG/H6605*, '*ZK/H6611*, '*ZQ/H2516*, '*ZR/H2553*, '*ZS/H2558*, '*ZU/H2509*, '*ZV/H2565*, *G-EBAF/H7467*, '*BP/H6653*, '*CC/H6656*, '*CD/H7487*, '*CF/H2065*, '*CO/H7482*, '*CR/H7474*, '*CS/H2062*, '*CT/H2071*, '*DC/H2060*, *DJ/H2052*. *G-EAZF/H7426* and *ZL/H6601* crashed on test at Croydon and were replaced.

*Used throughout to indicate 'Certificate of Airworthiness'.

(*b*) **Built by SABCA**

Belgian Air Force serials *A-51* to *A-78*, the last of which was delivered on 20.4.27, thirteen were later civilianised 1934–38 as *OO-ANS*, '*NW*, '*NY*, '*PA*, '*PB*, '*PD*, '*PE*, '*PK*, '*PL*, '*PN*, '*PX*, '*PY* and *OO-BOB*. Some were fitted with 90 hp Renard engines.

*C1502*, second of the two Avro 504Ks built at Toronto by Canadian Aeroplanes Ltd and incorporating a third undercarriage strut. (*Canadian National Aviation Museum*)

*Canada*     In 1918 a contract placed with Canadian Aeroplanes Ltd, Toronto, for 500 Avro 504Ks (130 hp Clerget) was ended by the Armistice when only two had been completed. Their V-type undercarriages had a third bracing strut and differed considerably from the British original.

After the war Canada received 63 Imperial Gift 504Ks which, from August 16, 1920, were used in lettered markings at Camp Borden, Ontario, for pilots' refresher courses. Some were employed by the Air Board for forestry patrol or aerial photography, *G-CYAC* making the first Canadian Air Force survey of Ottawa. Survivors of the 49 Avro 504Ks at Camp Borden at the beginning of 1922 were reconditioned by the Laurentide Air

Service, Quebec, in 1924 and others were reworked by Canadian Vickers Ltd and the Ottawa Car Co, some as Avro 504Ns.

Seven 504Ks (110 hp Le Rhône) were imported privately by the Canadian Aircraft Co Ltd of St Charles, Winnipeg, for conversion to three-seaters for joyriding. One of these, *G-CAAE*, came from the London Flying Club, Hendon; and *G-CAAR* made a 400 mile electioneering trip through Manitoba during 1920. On October 15–16, 1920, H. Dougall and F. H. Ellis flew *G-CABV* 487 miles from Winnipeg to The Pas, Manitoba, the longest commercial trip in Canada up to that time. Named *Thunderbird* by the Cree Indians, *'BV* was the first aircraft to fly north of latitude 53 degrees.

*Aircraft details:*

(*a*) **Built by Canadian Aeroplanes Ltd, Toronto**
*C.1501* and *C.1502* completed 10.18 and 11.18 respectively.

(*b*) **Imperial Gift aircraft registered to the Canadian Air Force (later the RCAF)**
*E361–E363/G-CYEE\**, *'AC*, *'AI*; *H1917/G-CYAL*; *H2041–H2049/ G-CYAX\**, untraced (1), *G-CYAP*, *'AS\**, *'DA\**, *'CY*, *'FI*, *'AQ*, *'CX*; *H7461–H7462/G-CYAR*, *'FE*; *H9552–H9558/*untraced (1), *G-CYFJ*, untraced (1), *G-CYFG*, *'FO*, untraced (1), *G-CYFF*; *H9621–H9633/G-CYCS*, *'AA*, untraced (1), *G-CYBH*, *'BL*, *'AV*, *'AT*, *'AW*, *'AU*, *'CZ*, *'FM*, *'FN*, untraced (1); *H9665–H9666/G–CYCU*, *'EI*; *H9668–H9672/G-CYCT*, *'CD*, *'BM*, *'CR*, *'BG*; *H9690/G-CYCA*; *H9714–H9715/G-CYCH*, *'BK*; *H9717/G-CYCK*; *H9722/G-CYFH*; *H9727/G-CYEH*; *H9729/G-CYEG\**, *H9732/G-CYCJ*; *H9735–H9745/G-CYFL*, *'CI*, *'CB*, *'AM*, *'CL*, *'BS*, *'CM*, *'BZ*, *'FK*, *'BD*, *'BR*; *H9749* and *H9755/*untraced (2).

*Note:* (i) Avro 504L seaplanes are marked with an asterisk. (ii) Two of the untraced aircraft were registered *G-CYHA* and *'HD*. (iii) *G-CYAM*, *'AU*, *'AV*, *'CM* and *'CZ* were allotted constructor's numbers C.V.16, 15, 19, 17 and 18 after reconstruction by Canadian Vickers Ltd. (iv) *G-CYAQ* and *'CX* later rebuilt as Avro 504N. (v) *G-CYAQ* and *'CM* later allotted RCAF serials *2* and *13*. (vi) *G-CYBH* crashed 22.10.25.

(*c*) **Avro 504Ks imported 1920 for commercial use**
*G-CAAE/D6202*, ex *G-EABO*, Canadian Aerial Services, Montreal, crashed at St Louis, PQ, 22.5.22; *G-CAAQ/H2292*, Canadian Aircraft Co Ltd, Winnipeg, to W. P. A. Straith, Winnipeg, after accident 19.8.23 written off 31.3.29; *G-CAAR/D9076*, Canadian Aircraft Co Ltd, Winnipeg, crashed at Fort Frances, Ontario, 26.8.20; *G-CABD/D8842*, Bishop-Barker Aeroplanes Ltd, Toronto, flown as *D8842*, s.o.r.\* 7.24; *G-CABP*, Edmonton Aircraft Ltd, s.o.r. 1.21; *G-CABS/D8997*, A. E. Bingham, Winnipeg, flown as *D8977*, crashed on test 16.7.20, rebuilt as Avro 548 *G-CACI*; *G-CABV/F9738*, Canadian Aircraft Co Ltd, Winnipeg, s.o.r. 7.24.

*\*Used throughout to indicate 'struck off register'.*

*China*    Twenty Avro 504Ks ordered by the Chinese Government from
Vickers Ltd on August 12, 1919, were mainly unused Harland and
Wolff-built machines, 18 of which were exported with British Certificates of
Airworthiness dated March 10, 1920, and two others as instructional
airframes or spares. First deliveries, which reached China in July 1920,
were used at the Nanyuan Training School, Peking, but a number were
seized by local warlords and only a few remained in Government hands at
Tsing Ho in 1923.

*Aircraft details:*
  E366, 368, 370, 373, 376, 377, 379, 380, 393, 397, 400, 409, 421; E9484,
9486, 9489; E9504; H9579; and two others.

*Denmark*    Six Avro 504Ks bought from the Aircraft Disposal Co by the
Danish Navy, arrived at Copenhagen by sea on December 29,
1920, and were erected at the Naval Flying School, Avedøre. They moved
to Kastrup in 1923 and to Ringsted in 1926. Three were lost in crashes but
two of them, serials *104* and *106*, survived for conversion into 504Ns in
1928 at the expense of *105* which was broken down for spares.

Det Danske Luftfartselskab (DDL) obtained three 3-seat 504Ks from
the same source for joyriding in 1919. Two of them, *H2549* and *H2556*
(110 hp Le Rhône), already certificated in Britain as *G-EAJE* and *'JF* to
DDL pilot Capt J. D. Atkinson, reached Copenhagen by sea on August 8,
1919, but the third (unregistered) was shipped from Leith to Iceland in
charge of Capt C. Faber who began pleasure flying at Reykjavik on
September 3. Operated by Flugfélag Islands (not the later company of that
name), the machine made a landing at the remote Westmann Islands and
carried 140 passengers in three weeks. Faber then returned to Denmark
and F. Frederickson used the Avro for fishery patrol in 1920.

Only the first of Atkinson's machines, which had been re-engined with a
150 hp Bentley B.R.1, received a Danish civil registration but when joyriding
petered out in 1921 both were acquired by the Danish Army which also

Det Danske Luftfartselskab's first Avro 504K *G-EAJE* in Danish marks as *T-DOLM* in 1921. (*Royal Danish Air Force*)

91

Danish Navy Avro 504K *H2023/104* at Kastrup in 1923. (*Courtesy H. Kofoed*)

took over the repatriated Icelandic machine in June 1922. They were re-serialled *Avro 1*, *Avro 2*, and *Avro 3* but the first two crashed at Klovermarken early in 1922 and were replaced by two new Avro 504Ks bought from A. V. Roe and Co without engines. Bentley B.R.1s were installed on arrival and all three remained in service until replaced by D.H. Moths in 1929.

*Aircraft details:*

### (*a*) **Danish Navy**

*H2217*/Danish Navy *101*, flew 94 hr 39 min, crashed at Kastrup 28.8.23; *H2472/102*, crashed at Kastrup 5.5.25; *H2021/103*, flew 150 hr 3 min, crashed at Kastrup 13.8.23; *H2023/104*, flew 187 hr, converted to 504N serial *112* in 1928; *H2430/105*, flew 197 hr 30 min, to spares 19.1.28; *H2027/106*, flew 110 hr 25 min, converted to 504N serial *111* in 1928.

*Note:* (i) British Cs of A issued to all six 16.11.20. (ii) *H2430* replaced *H2256* destroyed during engine run at Croydon 24.11.20.

### (*b*) **Det Danske Luftfartselskab**

*G-EAJE/H2549*, C of A 1.8.19, re-registered 1921 as *T-DOLM*, to the Danish Army 12.11.21 as *Avro 2*, crashed at Kløvermarken 11.4.22; *G-EAJF/H2556*, C of A 1.8.19, to the Danish Army 12.11.21 as *Avro 1*, crashed at Kløvermarken 24.6.22; *H2545*, 110 hp Le Rhône, Flugfélag Islands, to the Danish Army with Bentley B.R.1 as *Avro 3* 6.22, s.o.c.* 1.31.

*Used throughout to indicate 'struck off charge'.

### (*c*) **Danish Army**

Serials *Avro 1* and *Avro 2* used again for replacements obtained from A. V. Roe and Co without engines and fitted in Denmark with Bentley B.R.1s. Test flown at Kløvermarken 8.23 and 7.23 respectively, s.o.c. 1.31.

The Finnish Air Force ski-equipped Avro 504K *AV-57* was supplied by the Aircraft Disposal Co in 1926 as *G-EBNU* (visible under lower mainplane).

*Estonia*    Aeronaut AS inaugurated an airmail service between Reval and Helsinki, with Avro 504Ks (130 hp Clerget) on February 7, 1920. Landings were made in the ice-bound harbours by British pilots Emery and Swatridge. At least nine 504Ks (130 hp Clerget) were acquired by the Estonian Air Force in 1921, serials *15–23*, including *15/E9467*, *18/E3145*, *21/E9493* and *23/E9494*.

*Finland*    One Avro 504K *G-EBNU/E448* was supplied by the Aircraft Disposal Co to the Finnish Air Force in 1926. It was issued with a British C of A on April 23 of that year, was delivered on September 22, and flew in Finland with a ski undercarriage. Given serial *AV-57* it was withdrawn from use after an accident on November 11, 1930, but was then placed in storage, for many years at the Finnish Air Force Museum at Vesivehmaa. In 1968 it was transferred to Rissala for restoration and in 1979 was put on permanent display at the newly opened Aviation Museum of Central Finland, Tikkakoski.

*India*    The Imperial Gift of 100 aircraft for India included 18 presented to the Indian States. Many were Avro 504Ks, surplus examples of which were returned to the Public Works Dept, Aviation Branch, and then given to individuals attempting to open up commercial aviation in India. Their subsequent activities are obscure and none appeared in the register of Indian civil aircraft.

*Ireland*    In 1921 the Irish Air Corps purchased five Avro 504Ks from the Aircraft Disposal Co, and one from the Central Aircraft Co, Northolt, for reconnaissance, leaflet dropping and train escorting. They afterwards formed the equipment of 'A' Flight of the flying school at Baldonnel.

*109*, a ski-equipped Avro 504K of the Imperial Japanese Navy. (*Courtesy Philip Jarrett*)

Joyriding by civil 504Ks occurred only in 1932 when two aircraft bought from Northern Air Transport Ltd, Manchester, were operated on a roving basis by Irish Air Lines of Waterford.

*Aircraft details:*

(*a*) **Irish Air Corps**
*Nos.I, II, III, IV* and *V* (ex *H2500, H2073, H2075, E359* and *H2505*); *D7588/G-EADQ.*

(*b*) **Irish Air Lines, Waterford**
*EI-AAM* ex *H9833/G-AAYH*; *EI-AAN* ex *J8371/G-ABHP*; both withdrawn from use 1932.

*Japan*     A British mission to the Imperial Japanese Navy in April 1921 led by the Master of Sempill, took with it twenty Avro 504Ks. On arrival, one serialled *108* was displayed at the Yoyogi parade ground, Tokyo, to publicise the opening of a waterside training base at Kasumigaura also suitable for Avro 504L seaplanes. In the same year A. V. Roe and Co sold 504K manufacturing rights to Japan for £30,000 as well as 48 complete aircraft to the Japanese Army, including eight redundant 1919 joyriding conversions. Japanese 504Ks were built by the Nakajima Hikoki Seisaku Sho (Nakajima Aircraft Manufacturing Co) at Ohta-Machi, Tokyo, and fitted initially with 150 hp Bentley B.R.1 engines. As these wore out they were replaced by 110 hp Le Rhônes built under licence by the Tokyo Gasu Denki (Tokyo Gas and Electric Industry Co). Over 75 flew in civil markings alone, at least three were still active in 1928, and in 1934 a solitary example was still used by Nihon Koku Kabushiki Kaisha (Japan Air Transport Co), Tokyo.

*Aircraft details:*

(*a*)     **From A. V. Roe and Co Ltd**
*J754/G-EANP*; *J757–J763/G-EANX* to *'OD*; at least *J-BAXG* and *J-TEEJ*, Avro (Hamble) c/n 5030 and 5044.

Mexican Air Force Avro Anahuacs had Avro 504N style undercarriages. (*J. M. Bruce/G. S. Leslie Collection*)

(*b*) **Nakajima-built 504Ks**

*J-BAAK, 'AP, 'BD, 'BM, 'BP, 'CA, 'CB, 'CD, 'DG, 'ED, 'EH, 'FD,
'FL, 'GA, 'GL, 'HD, 'HI, 'IH, 'JH, 'KD, 'LA, 'MD, 'OD, 'OL, 'PD, 'QG,
'QH, 'RB, 'RD, 'SF, 'TB, 'TY, 'VB, 'VF, 'WD, 'XB, 'XL, 'YD, 'ZD;
J-BBUD, 'YB; J-BCAD, 'EE, 'EF, 'EG, 'FO; J-BDAB, 'YB;
J-BEAB, 'FD, 'MB, 'YB; J-BFIB; J-TACG, 'GK; 'VY; J-TEEH, 'FI,
'IN, 'TZ; J-TIHN, 'IO, 'JP, 'MS, 'NT, 'QW, 'VB, 'YE, 'ZE; J-TOOT,
'PU; J-TUEL, 'SZ, 'UB.*

*Malaya*      One Avro 504K was shipped to Penang in 1920 for a Chinese,
              Tsoe K. Wong, who had built and flown biplanes of his own
design at Shoreham 1913–14. The 504K stalled on a climbing turn on its
first take-off and the pilot L. J. Pugh, late of the Avro Transport Company,
Southport, was killed.

Three of the sixteen Avro 504Ks built in the Netherlands East Indies Army workshops. (*Courtesy Johan G.
H. Visser*)

95

*Mexico*  At least one Avro 504K, *E9441*, was imported from the UK
and a modernised version resembling the Avro 504K Mk.II was
built under licence at Balbuena for the Mexican Air Force. These new
aircraft were dubbed Avro Anahuacs and served with the Air Force flying
school at Balbuena 1922–30 after which some were sold for civil use. During
their careers they were fitted with a variety of engines, including the 80 hp
Gnome, 90 hp Curtiss OX-5 and 150 hp Hispano-Suiza.

*Netherlands Indies*  Thirty-six Avro 504Ks (130 hp Clerget) delivered to
the Netherlands Indies Army Air Arm 1919–22,
were supplemented by sixteen updated machines (110 hp Le Rhône) built
in the Air Arm's own workshops at Andir from 1924. Those bought in the
UK were delivered by Vickers Ltd in three batches of 12, to contract 269/19
on May 31, 1919; to 453/19 on December 18, 1919; and to 640/22 on
November 8, 1922. They were stationed at Kali Dvatch and bore the serials
*A-21* to *A-56*, one was formerly *H9769*. The locally built machines had
serials in the range *AL-57* to *AL-73* and all surviving 504K aircraft were
re-engined with the 130 hp Armstrong Siddeley Mongoose in 1933. The
type remained in service until 1936.

*New Zealand*  As she had no Air Force, only two of the twenty-one
Imperial Gift Avro 504Ks accepted by New Zealand in
1920 were retained by the Government for official use. They were based at
Sockburn, Christchurch, and the rest distributed on loan to the Canterbury
Aviation Company, Sockburn; the New Zealand Flying School, Auckland;
and the New Zealand Aero Transport Company, Timaru. A few of these
eventually received civil marks.

Four 504Ks (*D6243, E4153, E4237, E4242*) had been bought earlier from
the Disposal Board in England by Capt Euan Dickson of the Canterbury
Aviation Company. These arrived by sea on January 14, 1920, and *E4237*
was flown Sockburn–Fairlie–Mt Cook with two passengers on May 21, by

*201*, first of the 1929 NZPAF Avro 504Ks, after being converted to *ZK-ACN* in 1934 and repaired with the
wings of *206/ZK-ACS*. (*Courtesy C. Longworth-Dames*)

96

Capt Dickson who also made the first flight across Cook Strait while en route Sockburn–Trentham, Wellington, in *D6243* on August 26. The company's fleet rose to eleven 504Ks when seven others were loaned by the Government. On December 23, 1921 *E9432 High Jinks* was flown by Capt L. Brake via Napier to Gisborne where pleasure flights were made from Waikanae Beach.

The New Zealand Flying School received one 504L, *H2990*, and five 504Ks, four of which were converted into three-seaters and two into 504Ls.

Capt R. Russell flew one from Auckland to Wanganui and continued in *F9745* to New Plymouth on October 5, 1920. There it spun in from 200 ft on November 9, the local mayor, pilot and another passenger being killed. The New Zealand Aero Transport Company also received six machines, all of which were 504Ks and included *E9429* which made a pioneer flight from Wellington to Nelson on November 11, 1921, piloted by Capt Fowler. Another of the firm's pilots, Capt M. W. Buckley, acquired *H5241* and named it *Blazing Arrow*. Trading as the Arrow Aviation Company he undertook joy flying at the 1923 Hokitika Exhibition, and made the first photographic flights over the Franz Josef Glacier. Leaving Greymouth on June 4, 1924, he also made the first flight from Westland to Canterbury, crossing between Mt Rolleston and Mt Frankton at 7,500 ft and covering the 128 miles to Wigram in $1\frac{3}{4}$ hours.

In 1923 the New Zealand Government formed an air arm by purchasing the assets of the Canterbury Aviation Company together with Sockburn Aerodrome which it renamed Wigram. Initial equipment included *E3137* and *H1965*, retained by the Government in 1920, and the Canterbury machines, all of which reverted to unprefixed military serials. Many served later with the NZ Permanent Air Force for which six replacement aircraft were erected locally in 1925 using new airframes obtained from A. V. Roe & Co and engines previously supplied as part of the Imperial Gift.

*Aircraft details:*

(*a*) **Purchased in the UK by the Canterbury Aviation Company 7.19**
*D6243*, *E4153*, *E4237* and *E4242* (later *G-NZAK*)

(*b*) **Imperial Gift aircraft**
*E3137*, '42, *E9424*, '27, '29, '32, *F9745*, *H1952*, '58, '64, '65, '66, '68, '70, *H2986–H2990*, *H5240*, '41.

(*c*) **Imperial Gift aircraft loaned to civil operators**
New Zealand Flying School: *F9745* (crashed at New Plymouth 9.11.20), *H2986* (see also 504L chapter), *H2988*, *H2989/G-NZAA*, *H5240/G-NZAB* (to the Aerial Transport Co, Hastings), *H2990/G-NZAC* (see also 504L chapter). Canterbury Aviation Company: *H1952*, '58, '68, '70, *E9432/ G-NZAF High Jinks*, *H1964/G-NZAG* (crashed near Wigram 17.2.24), *H2987/G-NZAJ*, New Zealand Aero Transport Company: *E9429* (crashed at Hawera 5.1.22), *H1966/G-NZAL*, *E3142/G-NZAN*, *H5241/*

*N-37*, the Avro 504K fitted with 140 hp Hispano-Suiza HS 8Aa and cabin top for Lt Christian Hellesen in 1929. (*Courtesy O. G. Nordbø*)

*G-NZAO* (to M. W. Buckley 1923 as *Blazing Arrow*), *E9424/G-NZAP*, *E9427/G-NZAR* (cabin conversion, crashed 6.1.22).

### (*d*) Avro 504Ks erected at Wigram for the NZPAF 1929

NZPAF serial *201*, c/n A.201, first flown 1.9.25; to L. Brake and J. Paul 1934 as *ZK-ACN*; *202*, c/n A.202, to F. C. Norton 1934 as *ZK-ACU*, burned out 1936; *203*, c/n A.203, to Claridge, Wilcombe and Atkinson 1934 as *ZK-ACT*, to R. D. Downey, scrapped 1937; *204* and *205*, c/n A.204 and A.205, were written off at Wigram; *206*, c/n A.206, to J. Paul 1934 as *ZK-ACS*, to P. H. Wilton, scrapped 1938.

*Norway*    Two ex-RFC 504As (80 hp Le Rhône) erected at Kjeller by the Norwegian Army Air Force on February 14, 1918, were allotted serials *F-1* and *F-7* (later changed to *101* and *103*). The former crashed at Kjeller on September 30 and was rebuilt with a 90 hp Thulin (Swedish-built Le Rhône). The Army then acquired three Avro 504Ks in England. Two with 100 hp Sunbeam Dyak engines which arrived at Kjeller on November 2, 1920, were commissioned in July 1921 as *103* (reallocation) and *105*. The third 504K (110 hp Le Rhône) was presented by explorer Roald Amundsen but crashed on its first test flight on June 30, 1922, both occupants being killed.

The first civil flying school was started at Gardermoen in the summer of 1919 by Norsk Aeroplanfabrikk AS with one unregistered Avro 504J (100 hp Gnome Monosoupape), and at least one other 504A was also imported. Intended for naval training, the identity of the latter has not survived but after storage at Tønsberg, 1919–26, it was fitted with a 140 hp Hispano-Suiza HS 8Aa water-cooled engine for the firm's proprietor Lt Christian Hellesen. Registered *N-5*, its end came swiftly and Hellesen then acquired two 504Ks one being *101*, the original Norwegian Army 504A. Both were rebuilt with Hispano engines and were registered *N-29* and *N-37* respectively, the latter having enclosed cockpits and ski undercarriage.

*Aircraft details:*

### (a) Norwegian Army Air Force

Avro 504A, *101* ex *F-1* ex *B4305*, rebuilt with 90 hp Thulin, sold to Lt C. Hellesen; Avro 504A, *103* ex *F-7* ex *B4306*, crashed at Kjeller 1.4.19; Avro 504K, *103* (second use of serial), Dyak engine; Avro 504K, *105*, Dyak engine, crashed at Kjeller 29.10.23; Avro 504K, *107*, Le Rhône engine, crashed at Kjeller 30.6.22.

### (b) Civil aircraft (Hellesen Hispano conversions)

*N-5*, ex *101*, Norwegian C of A issued 9.4.27, crashed at Geilo 13.4.27; *N-29*, believed Canadian-built, converted 1929, marks re-issued to Klemm L.20 in 1933; *N-37*, converted 1929, sold 19.2.29 to J. Strandrud, s.o.r. 7.31.

*Portugal*     Thirty Avro 504Ks (110 hp Le Rhône) ordered by the Portuguese Government from Vickers Ltd under Contract C.1113/23 dated November 10, 1923, were entirely reconditioned at the Manchester works of A. V. Roe and Co and allotted constructor's numbers accordingly. Bearing serials *1–30*, they were all delivered in Portugal by May 20, 1924, and many were still in use at the Cintra flying school in 1927 and four were flying with the Grupo de Esquadrilhas de Aviação 'Republica' as late as 1934.

The Avro 504K at Manchester before delivery to the Portuguese Government in May 1925.

*Aircraft details:*

Serials *1–10*, British Cs of A issued 15.5.24, c/n R3/LE/12065, '84, '82, 12167, 12099, 12150, 12235, '01, 12320, 12218; serials *11–30*, British Cs of A issued 17.5.24, c/n R3/LE/12116, '33, 12286, '69, 12303, 12252, 12337, '54, '71, '88, 12405, '22, '39, 12541, 12473, '90, 12507, '24, 12456, 12558.

*South Africa*     Imperial Gift 504Ks formed the equipment of SAAF training, photographic and artillery spotting units until replaced by Avro 504Ns in 1927. For pleasure and charter flying three Le Rhône engined three-seaters were shipped to Johannesburg in July 1919. These had been allotted British marks *G-EAFU*, *'FV* and *'FW* in the name of the South African Aerial Transport Company, sole Avro agents for the territory. Named *The Rand Queen*, *Natalia* and *Orangia* at Baragwanath Aerodrome on October 25 and piloted by Maj A. M. Miller, Capt Ross and Capt Rutherford, they penetrated to all parts of the Union. Rutherford gave pleasure flights in the Northern Transvaal to former Boer War leaders Gen T. E. Botha and Capt de Jager, while Miller made a long distance flight to Kimberley and on November 15 flew to Durban for the *Johannesburg Star*, dropping 1,200 copies of the newspaper en route. One of two additional machines acquired in December 1919 was flown by Rutherford to Bulawayo where it was named *Rhodesia* in June 1920 and twice filmed the Victoria Falls. One Avro hired by the Union Air Force made unsuccessful rain making experiments on October 5, 1920, by dropping sand on clouds at a height of 5,000 ft.

Although *Natalia* had rescued the crew of Handley Page O/7 *G-EANV* when it crashed at Beaufort West on February 23, 1920, and over 5,000 passengers had been carried in 15 months, the company was wound up and surviving Avros *Natalia*, *Griqua* and *Rhodesia* auctioned. Two continued operations with former SAAT pilots of the Ross-Thompson Aviation Company and on March 24, 1921, Maj Honnett established a South African commercial height record by flying one of them over the Drakensberg Range with two passengers and luggage. The third crashed on take-off from Baragwanath on December 15, 1920, killing purchaser S. Brick, his wife and pilot F. V. Preller. Ross-Thompson 504Ks barnstormed for 18 months before sale in Southern Rhodesia where one crashed at Rusapi through elevator control failure in 1921.

*Aircraft details:*

(*a*) **Imperial Gift aircraft**
Surplus RAF Avro 504Ks re-serialled from *401* to at least *414*.

(*b*) **South African Aerial Transport Company**
*G-EAFU/H2583*, *G-EAFV/H2584*, *G-EAFW/H2591*, British Cs of A issued 10.7.19. They were named *The Rand Queen*, *Natalia* and *Orangia* but the order is uncertain. Two others, *Rhodesia* and *Griqua*, were bought 12.19. One crashed at Baragwanath 15.10.21, one at Rusapi, Southern Rhodesia, 1921.

*South America*    Argentina accepted the gift of one Avro 504K from the
                   Aircraft Disposal Co in 1921 and purchased eight more
on condition that the firm supplied an instructor for the flying school at El
Palomar. A tenth 504K (110 hp Le Rhône) was used by the Tucuman Civil
Aviation School under Capt S. H. Holland, but this was written off at Lules
in April 1920.

Four Avro 504Ks (100 hp Gnome Monosoupape, 110 hp Le Rhône or
130 hp Clerget engines) bought in England for the Brazilian Naval Air
Service were joined by eight others in 1921. Ten reconditioned machines
(110 hp Le Rhône) supplied to the Chilean Government by A. V. Roe and
Co in 1921 were used by the Military Aviation Service flying school at Lo
Espejo and included at least two unused Avro Transport Company civil
conversions and one aircraft, serial 82, named *Curico*. In 1924 the Guatem-
alan Air Force also purchased a number of Avro 504Ks.

The Peruvian Ministry of War placed a third and final order with
Vickers Ltd on March 13, 1922, for four Avro 504K trainers to Contract
C.137/22/160, delivery of which was completed on August 3, 1922. They
were erected on Lima Racecourse and flown to the training base at Las
Palmas. These and machines from two earlier batches of four in 1920–21
to Contracts 275/20 and 34/21 were still used for training by the Peruvian
Navy in 1925. Four Avro 504Ks were in use by the Uruguayan Air Force
at San Fernando Aerodrome, Montevideo, in 1920.

*Aircraft details:*

   *Argentina: E9428, '30, H1913, H2024, '26, H6603, H7422, '92, '97*,
British Cs of A issued 25.4.21: Brazil: *A2/H2024, A3/H2026, A4/H7479,
A6/H9608, A7/H2568, A8/H9660, A9/H7473, A11/E9463, A12/H9618,
A14/H2504, A15/E446, A17/H9591*. Chile: *G-EAMO/J746, G-EANE/
J751*, and eight others. Guatemala: no information: Peru: *E372, E391,
E395, E399*, British Cs of A issued 1.3.20 and eight others: Uruguay:
no information.

*Spain*    One Avro 504K overhauled at Hamble by A. V. Roe and Co was
           flown to Spain in August 1919 by Capt Truelove, had red
mainplanes and yellow fuselage, and was maintained by the Air Force for
the personal use of King Alphonso. Additional machines were delivered to
military flying schools in 1923 and one civilianised as *M-AIAI* in June
1924. Four sold to the Spanish Royal Naval Air Service by the Aircraft
Disposal Co in 1925, were based at Barcelona.

*Aircraft details:*

   *E434, 445, 450, H2057* to the Spanish Royal Naval Air Service with
British Cs of A issued 30.6.25.

*Sweden*   The first two Swedish Avro 504Ks (110 hp Le Rhône), *E3115*
           and *H1955*, were imported by the P.O. Flygkompani which
operated from Barkaby and bore the initials of founder Lt Per Oscar

Herrström who employed several British pilots including G. L. P. Henderson and A. B. H. Youell. Although surveyed by the Swedish authorities on July 11, 1919, and allotted civil marks *S-AAC* and *'AD*, they flew with RAF serials and the letter *S* on the fuselage, and visited many provincial cities, taking off from deep snow in 25 degrees of frost. Engines were warmed for starting by a lighted blowlamp placed in the engine bay. On June 2, 1920, a few experimental Stockholm–Helsinki flights were made. An anonymous 504K (130 hp Clerget), flown out by Capt Saunders in October 1919, was not approved at survey on December 18 and not used. One machine flown temporarily as a seaplane and three others used in North Sweden in 1921 are discussed in the Avro 504L chapter.

Two 504Ks (130 hp Clerget) ordered from A. V. Roe and Co by the Swedish Navy on October 27, 1923, were shipped from Hull on January 18, 1924. Numbered 6 and 7 (6 on skis) they were joined later by three others (believed *8, 9* and *10*) ordered on September 22, 1924. After the formation of Flygvapnet in 1926 they were renumbered *064* and *072–075* under the designation Sk 3. When *074* was struck off charge on June 30, 1928, it was auctioned at the Ljungbyhed Flying School and almost certainly became civil as *S-AABT* two weeks later.

*Aircraft details:*

(*a*) **Civil**

*S-AAC/E3115* and *S-AAD/H1955*, Swedish Cs of A issued 11.7.19, P.O. Flygkompani; *S-AABT*, c/n R/R3/CL/10688, believed ex *074*, Swedish C of A 21.8.28 to S. J. Mansson, Gothenburg, last owner T. C. J. Wahrgren, Gällivare, crashed 14.5.31 as *SE-ABT*; *SE-ACC*, c/n given as 2289/5652, Swedish C of A 30.10.29, ex-Flygvapnet, T. C. J. Wahrgren, Gällivare, last owner F. A. Oberg, Hudiksvall 5.31.

(*b*) **Military**

Swedish Navy *6–10* became Flygvapnet *064* and *072–075* in 1926, s.o.c. 9.9.27, 25.11.27 (crashed near Ljungbyhed 17.11.27), 30.6.28, 30.6.28, 13.3.28 and 12.4.28 respectively.

*Switzerland*    Avro 504Ks *G-EAKR* and *'KV* (130 hp Clerget), overhauled by A. V. Roe and Co at Alexandra Park in August 1919 for the Swiss Aero Club, were ferried via Hounslow on September 17, 1919, by Capts E. Bradley and H. M. Goode. *G-EAKV* arrived at Lausanne three days later via Paris, Dijon and the Jura Mountains, but *'KR* was damaged beyond repair in a forced landing at Les Laumes-Alèsia in the Côte-d'Or on September 20. *G-EAKV* crashed while avoiding high tension cables while joyriding at Nyon on November 2 but was rebuilt for the Lausanne Aéro École d'Aviation. The school erected a second Avro (110 hp Le Rhône) from spares. It first flew on February 21, 1920, piloted by Bradley.

The Avro 504K used as a test-bed for the Fairchild Caminez engine. (*J. M. Bruce/G. S. Leslie Collection*)

*Aircraft details:*

*G-EAKR/E4246*, C of A issued 19.9.19, forced landed in the Côte-d'Or 20.9.19; *G-EAKV/J803*, C of A issued 17.9.19, to the Lausanne Flying School as *CH-10*, written off 1921; *CH-39* built from spares at Lausanne 1920, crashed at Blecherette 3.6.22.

*United States*   Flights over Washington by Col C. F. Lee in Avro 504J *C4312* during 1917 were followed by inspection by the Dayton-Wright Airplane Company at Dayton, Ohio, and evaluation at McCook Field under project number P-25. The result was an order for 52 Avro 504Ks (100 hp Gnome Monosoupape or 80 hp Le Rhône) for the American Expeditionary Force 3rd Instruction Center at Issoudun, France, in July 1918. After the war they were shipped to the USA and taken over with all available spares by the Interallied Corporation, one forming the only British exhibit at the Chicago Aero Show in January 1920. A Miss Nellie Brown Duff bought one but the majority were sold to barnstormers, not the least of whom was Charles Kingsford Smith (later Air Commodore Sir Charles Kingsford Smith) who in 1920 toured California with a 504K of the Moffett-Starkey Aero Circus as pilot and stunt man. In June 1920 Lts Runser, Turner and Freeland flew round the USA in a Clerget Avro with the intention of giving flights in every State, and early in the following year the Lawrence Sperry Aircraft Co Inc acquired all remaining stocks from Interallied. As late as 1928 there were still fifteen on the US civil register, at least two of which were preserved, *NC5918*, originally *A1958*, restored to flying condition as *N8736R* by Cole Palen of Old Rhinebeck, NY, but sold to the Canadian National Aeronautical Collection as *G-CYFG* in 1966 and *NC710* kept in the Thompson Products Museum, Cleveland, Ohio. The latter had a 504L fin and last flew at Arcola Airport, New Jersey, in 1936. A third 504K, ex *D8971*, stored for many years in Connecticut was sold to the RCAF in 1966 and later flew as *G-CYCK*. A fourth machine, ex *B3182*, stored in Mexico until 1968, made its first post-restoration flight at Boise, Idaho, in August 1972.

*Aircraft details:*

### (*a*) **Evaluated at McCook Field**

Avro 504J *C4312*, project number P-25, British demonstrator 1917–18; US serial *94022*, project P-118, 100 hp Gnome Monosoupape, crashed, pilot, Capt Inglis; project P-119, no information; *94023*, P-141, surveyed 25.10.20; *94062*, P-142, salvaged aircraft. One was used as a test-bed for the Fairchild Caminez engine.

Seven shipped to the USA after 1918 were *62953–59*.

### (*b*) **Civil conversions**

At least *N-ABCA*, *'CC* and *'CE* (1922 Registry).

*NC156, 206, 218, 260, 710, 1286, 1864, 2490, 2718, 3170, 5244, 5664, 5918, 7468, NC868M* (1928 Registry).

*USSR*   Copies of the Avro 504K known as the U-1 Avrushka were built in Russia, using as a pattern an example shot down by the Red Army during the civil war. Altogether, over 700 were assembled at the Dux factory near Moscow during the early and mid-twenties.

*Note:* The following Avro 504Ks were sold abroad but remained untraced. *D1613* and *F2574* by Handley Page Ltd, Cs of A 7.5.20; *H1978* and *F8828* by Handley Page Ltd, Cs of A 16.11.20; *G-EBEL/E3291* and *E4201* by the London Aviation Company, Cs of A 15.8.22; *G-EBGV/E9358*, C of A 26.6.24, *E442* and *H2551*, Cs of A 22.9.25, *H6654*, C of A 2.10.26, all by the Aircraft Disposal Co.

The Avro 504K Mk.II prototype. (100 hp Gnome Monosoupape.)

# Avro 504K Mk.II

In 1924 the Hamble works produced a hybrid trainer known as the Avro 504K Mk.II and consisting of a flat sided 504K fuselage married to 504N-type undercarriage and mainplanes. The reasons underlying the creation of this strange variant were twofold, firstly to enable air forces of the smaller nations to modernise their 504K trainers using Avro-built conversion kits, or alternatively to provide low price 504N equivalents powered by cheap surplus 100 hp Gnome Monosoupape rotaries. While there is no record of conversions taking place overseas, a very similar machine, named the Avro Anahuac, was built under licence in the Mexican Air Force workshops at Balbuena, serials round and about 53.

The Avro 504K Mk.II was shelved but in 1935 four ex-RAF Avro 504N airframes, long stored at Croydon, were brought out and converted into joyriding three-seaters with 130 hp Clerget engines. They were therefore equivalent to the Avro 504K Mk.II of 11 years previously, differing from the prototype only in the type of engine, rounded sides, untapered ailerons, absence of wingtip skids and fuel tankage. The 1935 machines had one 18 gallon tank under the port upper wing root in the manner of the Mongoose-powered civil Avro 504N instead of the slim centre section tank of the prototype.

They were registered *G-ADGB*, *'GC*, *'GM* and *'GN* but work on *G-ADGC* was not completed. The other three endured one season's joyriding at Camber Sands, Sussex, with Zenith Airways, although *'GM* and *'GN* were nominally owned by Aircraft and Autos Ltd and Aviation Commerce Ltd of Croydon respectively. None flew after 1935 except *'GM* which was acquired by Brooklands Aviation Ltd, for joyriding at Shoreham. In the winter it was employed on school work at Brooklands and was destroyed there in a hangar fire on October 24, 1936.

## SPECIFICATION AND DATA

*Manufacturers:* A. V. Roe and Co Ltd, Newton Heath, Manchester, and Hamble Aerodrome, near Southampton, Hants.

*Powerplants:* One 100 hp Gnome Monosoupape
One 130 hp Clerget

*Dimensions:* Span 36 ft 0 in   Length 28 ft 6 in
Height 10 ft 11 in   Wing area 320 sq ft

*Weights:* All-up weight 2,155 lb

*Production:*

| RAF Serial and Registration | | C of A Issued | Details |
|---|---|---|---|
| — | — | — | Prototype, built Hamble 1924 |
| J8758 | G-ADGB | 19. 6.35 | Zenith Airways, Camber; s.o.r. 6.36 |
| J9689 | G-ADGC | nil | Zenith Airways, Camber; s.o.r. 1.36 |
| K1962 | G-ADGM | 11. 7.35 | Aircraft and Autos Ltd; 6.36 Brooklands Aviation Ltd; destroyed by fire at Brooklands 24.10.36 |
| H2962 | G-ADGN | 10. 8.35 | Aviation Commerce Ltd; s.o.r. 3.38 |

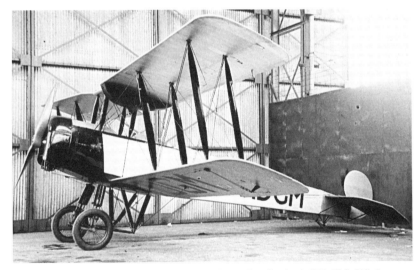

G-ADGM, one of the 130 hp Clerget conversions made at Croydon in 1935. (*E. J. Riding*)

The prototype Avro 504L two-seater *G4329* on the beach at Hamble early in 1919, showing the original four-strut undercarriage.

# Avro 504L

First peace-time 504K variant was the Avro 504L training seaplane. The prototype conversion, *C4329*, used two wooden, pontoon-type, single-step main floats, each attached to the fuselage by two steel struts, as well as tail and wingtip floats bolted directly to the main structure. A large curved fin was fitted to compensate for the extra keel surface forward and the fairing of the fuselage sides was improved to conform more closely to the shape of the cowling. To give a reasonable take-off performance the higher powered 130 hp Clerget was fitted and trials conducted at Hamble in February 1919 led first to the fitting of a four-bladed airscrew and the removal of the small wingtip floats. Later the main undercarriage was strengthened by means of an additional strut to the rear of each float.

The Avro 504L did not meet any RAF requirement and was not adopted; nevertheless the Avro company built a considerable number of float undercarriages. The Hamble works also produced seven short-range float-equipped three-seaters for the Avro Transport company. Still more power was needed and a proposal to fit the new 170 hp A.B.C. Wasp I radial was turned down after trials with this engine in *K-147*, a 'guinea pig' 504K from the same production batch. The 150 hp Bentley B.R.1 rotary therefore became the standard engine and drove a two-bladed airscrew.

*G-EANB*, last of the seven, was certificated too late in the season to be gainfully employed but the other six were all used for joyriding. Piloted by Capt F. Warren Merriam one worked the Isle of Wight resorts and Hayling Island, and the others went to Paignton, Devon. Flights over Torbay and to Teignmouth proved very popular and 250 passengers were carried during August–September 1919. On August 25, two 504Ls (in all probability *K-145* and *G-EAJX*), flew along the South Coast en route to an autumn joyriding season at the First Air Traffic Exhibition, Amsterdam. One refuelled in Dover Harbour but the other was forced to alight off Ramsgate with petrol shortage and had to be towed in. Their replacements *G-EALH* and *'LI* were withdrawn to Hamble but *K-146* (Capt Evans) was wrecked off Alderney in fog on October 5 while carrying newspapers to Guernsey.

Operations begun on Windermere under C. Howard Pixton on August 4, 1919, were quite remarkable. His aircraft were not true 504Ls but float-equipped 504Ks (130 hp Clerget) and without the third undercarriage strut. In common with the majority of Avro Transport Company machines at that time, they flew with enlarged Service markings, in this case *H2581* and *'82* (later *G-EADJ* and *'DK*). They used the slipway and hanger at Bowness formerly occupied by the Lakes Flying Company and continued the lucrative pleasure flights pioneered eight years earlier by the Avro-built *Water Bird*. The suspension of night mail boat services to the Isle of Man also gave Pixton the opportunity of making twelve 90 minute early morning crossings to Douglas with 3 cwt parcels of the *Daily News*.

The Eastbourne Aviation Co Ltd embarked on a South Coast joyriding season of its own and produced six float-equipped 504Ks. These were also without the third undercarriage strut, and the three occupants sat one behind the other in separate cockpits. The enterprise ended late in 1920 with a seaplane race as grand finale at Hove, Sussex, on August 19 during which *G-EAJH* sank with a collapsed undercarriage. Maj J. P. B. Ferrand carried 350 passengers in the former Windermere machine *G-EADK* at Folkestone in 1920 but Avro waterborne activities then ceased round the British Isles. In 1921 the Aircraft Disposal Co Ltd sold the new production 504L *G-EANB* and two others (almost certainly *H1911* and *'12*) in Sweden to Kungl Vattenfallsstyrelsen (Royal Waterfalls Committee) as *S-IAA*, *'AB* and *'AG*. They were used in connection with power station construction in North Sweden. Later two were flown inside the Arctic Circle for seven months by Gosta Hulstrom and Ing Homen who made 106 return journeys between Projus and Suorva, flew 23,820 km in 202 hours 53 minutes flying

*K-144/G-EAFB*, first of the Eastborne Aviation Co Ltd's joyriding 504Ls (three individual cockpits), taxying out at Hove, Sussex, in August 1920. (*Courtesy the Royal Aero Club*)

Canadian Air Board forestry patrol Avro 504L *G-CYAX*, showing the revised undercarriage strutting used on the majority of conversions. (*RCAF*)

time and carried 362 passengers plus 6,681 kg of mail. One Eastbourne 504L, *G-EASD* purchased for £400 by Ing G. Spaak, also went to Sweden in 1921.

Activities elsewhere were confined to idyllic flights from Bermudan beaches in 1920 by two 504Ls of the Bermuda and Western Atlantic Aviation Co Ltd; from Manly Bay, Sydney Harbour, by one of the Australian Aircraft and Engineering Company's imported machines (without dorsal fin) and later by two Imperial Gift 504Ls of the RAAF; at Mission Bay, Auckland, by three Imperial Gift aircraft of the New Zealand Flying School; in Canada where a few Imperial Gift float undercarriages were brought into use to enable 504Ks to operate from lakes on forestry patrol; and at Valparaiso where three 504L trainers (130 hp Clerget) were used by the Chilean Naval Air Service.

A British Mission led by Col the Master of Sempill, sent out to advise the Imperial Japanese Navy in 1921, took with it a selection of British machines including ten Hamble-built Avro 504Ls. Maj Orde-Lees and Mr H. Crisp trained the first Japanese naval pilots on these at Kasumigaura, near Tokyo, from which on September 3, 1921, they made a mass formation flight to escort the Crown Prince's warship and all alighted in Yokosuka Harbour. When Japan purchased the manufacturing rights from A. V. Roe, Bentley-powered 504Ls were built for the Navy by Nakajima. They were without the strengthened undercarriages and their performance deteriorated considerably when the B.R.1s wore out, the only available replacement engine being the licence-built 110 hp Le Rhône (see page 94). One Avro 504L remained in service with the Japan Air Transport Research Institute of Osaka until 1927.

# SPECIFICATION AND DATA

*Manufacturers:*  A. V. Roe and Co Ltd, Hamble Aerodrome, near South-ampton, Hants.
The Eastbourne Aviation Co Ltd
Nakajima Hikoki Seisaku Sho (Nakajima Aircraft Manufac-turing Co), Ohta-Machi, Tokyo, Japan

*Powerplants:*  One 110 hp Le Rhône
One 130 hp Clerget
One 150 hp Bentley B.R.1

*Dimensions:*  Span 36 ft 0 in  Length 32 ft 1 in
Height 11 ft 4 in  Wing area 330 sq ft

*Weights:*  Tare weight 1,408 lb  All-up weight 2,006 lb

*★Performance:*  Maximum speed 87 mph  Cruising speed 75 mph
Initial climb 650 ft/min  Endurance 2 hours
★With 130 hp Clerget engine.

*Production:*

   (*a*) **By A. V. Roe and Co Ltd**
   *C4329*, Clerget-engined prototype; c/n A.T.C.4, C of A 16.5.19, *K-106*/
*G-EAAO*, sold abroad 31.7.19; A.T.C.12 and 13, Cs of A 12 and 7.8.19, *K-145*/
*G-EAFF* sold in Belgium 7.21 and *K-146*/*G-EAFG* wrecked off Alderney
5.10.19. A.T.C.15-18, *G-EALH*, C of A 26.8.19; *'JX*, C of A 20.8.19; and *'LI*,
C of A 3.9.19; all s.o.r. 10.20. A.T.C.18, *G-EANB*, C of A 6.11.19, to Sweden
7.21 as *S-IAA Masen*, re-registered *S-ABAA* in 1923, s.o.r. 16.10.26
   (*b*) **504K conversions by A. V. Roe and Co Ltd**
   *G-EADJ*/*H2581*, C of A 26.6.19; *G-EADK*/*H2582*, C of A 2.8.19;
*G-EAGU*/*H2585*, C of A 16.8.19; *G-EAKA*/*H2590*, C of A 27.8.19; sold abroad
8.21; *G-EALB*/*H2589*, C of A 17.9.19
   (*c*) **By the Eastbourne Aviation Co Ltd**
   c/n E.1-E.6: *K-144*/*G-EAFB*, C of A 22.7.19; *G-EAJH*, C of A 22.8.19, sank
off Hove, Sussex, 19.8.20; *G-EALO*, C of A 19.9.19, crashed 2.21; *G-EANS*,
C of A 20.10.19, crashed 9.20; *G-EASD*, C of A 1.6.20, to Sweden 3.21 as
*S-AAP*, re-registered *S-AHAA* in 1923 and *SE-HAA* in 1928; *G-EASE*, C
of A 10.9.20
   (*d*) **Imperial Gift conversions**
   *G-CYAS*/*H2044*, *G-CYAX*/*H2041*, *G-CYDA*/*H2045*, *G-CYEE*/*E361* and
*G-CYEG*/*H9729* for Canadian Air Board forestry and fire patrols; *A3-46*/*H3034*
and *A3-47*/*H3042* by the Royal Australian Air Force; *H2986*, *H2988* and
*G-NZAC*/*H2990* by the New Zealand Flying School, Auckland
   (*e*) **Other conversions**
   *S-IAB* and *S-IAG*, believed ex *H1911* and *H1912*, Cs of A issued 21.1.21.
*S-IAB* re-registered *S-AAAA* in 1923, s.o.r. 16.10.26; *S-IAG* destroyed by
gale 12.22
   (*f*) **By Nakajima**
   Imperial Japanese Navy serials commencing *J. N. 752* in 1921, reaching at
least *R.603*, *R.604* and *R. 605* in 1926

The Avro 504M three-seat cabin machine *K-134/G-EACX* at Hendon in July 1919.

# Avro 504M

In the spring of 1919 Hamble was very busy converting Avro 504Ks for the Avro Transport Company and produced the seven 504Ls, a number of Avro 536 five-seaters and single examples of two dissimilar cabin variants. First of these, built in April of that year, was the Avro 504M, a standard 504K modified above the top longerons to form what was a claustrophobic enclosure accommodating two passengers in staggered seats behind the pilot.

A curved plywood roof with two glazed portholes in each side was hinged along the port longeron. After it was opened the pilot entered by raising a further section of roofing, and once in, viewed the landscape through five vertical Triplex panels mounted round the edge of the cockpit. A light fabric-covered structure faired the cabin smoothly into the tail and additional side area was compensated by the addition of a 504L-type dorsal fin. Despite the considerable weight penalty, improved streamlining made it faster than the standard 504K.

The Avro 504M was unusual among British civil Avros in having a 100 hp Gnome Monosoupape nine-cylinder rotary. Application for the temporary registration *K-134* was made on May 13, 1919, and, though not officially certificated until June 25, it flew from Hounslow to Margate and back on May 28 and was noted arriving at Southsea Common from Hamble on June 23. The Avro 'Limousine' as it was dubbed, made headlines when, on June 26, Lt R. S. Park flew it to Chorley Wood Common, Bucks. to pick up a newly married pair, Mr R. Hamilton and his wife Nora, outside the church. After a refuelling stop at Bournemouth, the 504M landed the honeymoon couple at Fowey, Cornwall, in an elapsed time of four hours. The machine then returned to Hounslow Heath and spent the rest of the summer doing a roaring trade among ladies wishing to fly over London without donning special flying kit. Avro's manager G. L. P. Henderson made many charter flights in it including return trips to Aintree on July 8

111

The Avro 504M at Hounslow Heath in August 1919 with permanent registration *G-EACX*, allotted on July 31.

and Brighton on July 13. Its one recorded overseas flight took place in the early hours of September 6 when Capt R. T. Fagan flew nonstop from Hounslow to Le Bourget in 2 hours 45 minutes with Norwegian passengers Robshon and Waase.

Many hours were flown during the railway strike, by which time the permanent marking *G-EACX* had been applied but the C of A was not renewed in 1920, no doubt due to the very cramped accommodation of such a primitive conversion. When the Japanese acquired 504K manufacturing rights in 1921, they quickly produced a 504M equivalent known as the Aiba Tsubami IV with 130 hp Gasuden Jimpu engine, one example of which, *J-BABC*, was still in use in 1928.

## SPECIFICATION AND DATA

*Manufacturers:*  A. V. Roe and Co Ltd, Hamble Aerodrome, near Southampton, Hants.

*Powerplant:*  One 100 hp Gnome Monosoupape B.2

*Dimensions:*  Span 36 ft 0 in    Length 29 ft 5 in
Height 10 ft 5 in    Wing area 330 sq ft

*Weights:*  Tare weight 1,220 lb    All-up weight 1,975 lb

*Performance:*  Maximum speed 98 mph    Cruising speed 85 mph
Climb to 8,000 ft 5·5 min    Endurance 3 hours

*Production:*  One aircraft only, *K-134/G-EACX*, c/n A.T.C.10; sole owner A. V. Roe and Co Ltd; C of A issued 25.6.19, not renewed in 1920

112

Danish Navy Avro 504N *112*, converted from Avro 504K *104* in 1928. See page 92. (*Royal Danish Air Force*)

# Avro 504N

Rapid wartime development of inline vee and radial type engines made possible two parallel 504K postwar modernisation programmes. The first, resulting in the Avro 548 and 552, is described elsewhere, but the front fuselage of the 504K was more suited to the radial and it was an engine of this type which eventually powered the last major variant, the Avro 504N.

Early in 1919 Avro's 504K 'hack' *K-147* flew at Hamble with a 170 hp A.B.C. Wasp I and in the following year *D9068* flew at the RAE, Farnborough, with this engine as the so-called 'fireproof' Avro. The Wasp was chosen in this case as an example of an up-to-date engine to see if the fireproofing scheme, comprising aluminium/asbestos bulkhead, steel-tube engine mounting, external fuel lines and tanks under the lower wing, would be effective for radial engined types of the future. Trials described in R & M 691 began on February 19, 1920, and continued until June 3 when the engine crankshaft failed, delaying further flights until September 28, 1922.

The Cosmos Engineering Co Ltd also equipped 504K *G-EADL* at Filton as test-bed for their new 100 hp Lucifer three-cylinder radial (later known as the Bristol Lucifer). Test flying was undertaken by Capt Norman Macmillan but ended abruptly when '*DL* broke its back in a difficult forced landing at Kingswood through engine failure in January 1920. The replacement aircraft *G-EAJB*, on loan from Avro, incorporated the airframe modifications necessary to keep pace with more efficient and powerful engines. The skid-type undercarriage remained, but the famous elastic shock absorbers gave place to a new semi-oleo type in which half the travel was taken by an oil dashpot before picking up rubber-in-compression.

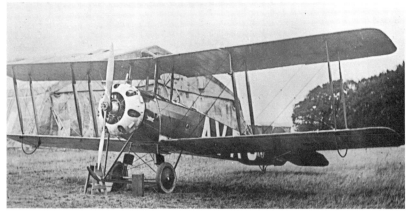

*K-147*, c/n A.T.C.14, fitted experimentally with a 170 hp A.B.C. Wasp I radial engine.

The Lucifer-engined Avro 504K *G-EADA* after installation of prototype N-type undercarriage in 1923.

Tapered ailerons were also fitted to lighten lateral control and harmonise them with the near-perfect rudder and elevators.

Early in 1922 the Hamble works fitted *G-EADA* (one of the old Avro Transport Company 504Ks) with a Bristol Lucifer, and modified two Service machines *E9265* and '66 to take the higher powered 150 hp Armstrong Siddeley Lynx seven-cylinder radial, but all three retained the skid undercarriage. Hinkler flew both Lynx Avros to Croydon for demonstration in May 1922 and *'DA* flew in the first King's Cup Race there on September 8, 1922. Piloted by Maj C. R. Carr it forced landed at Halifax. Although often referred to as the 504N prototypes, they were, more accurately, a first intermediate type. Nor were they the only examples. Years later in 1928 Phillips and Powis Ltd, Woodley, fitted 504K *G-EBWO* with a 100 hp Anzani radial and tapered ailerons for private owner Dr M.

C. Wall and in 1932 Armstrong Siddeley Mongoose engines were installed in 504Ks by Air Travel Ltd, Penhurst. The last example was *G-ABVC* flown by H. C. Chater with a Lucifer at Lympne in 1935.

A slightly more advanced interim type was a dual control trainer version with oleo sprung skid-type undercarriage and Lynx engine. Four of these, *G-EBHC*, *'HD*, *'HE* and *'HT* were supplied to Armstrong Whitworth Ltd in 1923 for use at the A. W. Reserve Flying School at Whitley. In 1931 the survivors, *G-EBHD* and *'HE*, were sold for joyriding to R. O. Roch (Modern Airways Ltd) and L. J. Rimmer (North British Aviation Co Ltd) respectively, the latter being reconverted to Avro 504K (130 hp Clerget).

Avro 504K *G-EADL* used by the Cosmos Engineering Co Ltd to airtest their 100 hp Lucifer radial at Filton 1920.

The second Lucifer test-bed *G-EAJB*, with semi-oleo skid-type undercarriage. (*Bristol*)

115

*E9265*, first of the two 150 hp Armstrong Siddeley Lynx engined interim prototypes.

Avro 504K *G-EBWO Bluey* of the Phillips and Powis Flying School with 100 hp Anzani radial.

Work was also in hand at Hamble on the now-famous N-type undercarriage. This consisted of two main legs coupled to the axle, which in turn was hinged by two horizontal tubes to the bases of two tubular steel Vs behind, and in line with, the main legs. Shock absorbers were of the semi-oleo type and the prototype undercarriage was fitted to *G-EADA* for participation in the 1923 Grosvenor Trophy Race at Lympne. Piloted by H. A. Hamersley, it came fourth at an average speed of 71.2 mph and afterwards went to Farnborough for undercarriage trials.

As a result of further Lucifer engine tests at Filton and Croydon with Avro 504K *G-EBFB*, the Aircraft Disposal Co produced four 504Ns with this engine (*E444, H2512, H2562* and *F8841*) for export to Argentina. These had standard 504K mainplanes and represented the penultimate stage in 504N development. The final product emerged at Hamble in the

116

following year when the Air Ministry ordered two trainer prototypes with alternative power plants. Both were conversions of new airframes caught in the Manchester factory when contracts were cancelled in 1918, the first *J733* having a Lucifer and the other *J750* the new 180 hp Lynx. These machines had all the final airframe modifications, viz. cutaway centre sections and wing roots to improve forward and upward visibility from both cockpits, 18 gallon fuel tanks under each upper mainplane, adjustable tailplanes and additional stringers to round out the fuselage sides. Martlesham trials resulted in the adoption of the Lynx powered versions as the RAF's new standard trainer and large scale production began in Manchester. Refinements embodied in a special lightweight aircraft *F2575*, consisting of streamlined engine cowlings with spinner, slimmer fuselage without top decking, and elevator controls re-routed externally (as on the Avro Baby and 548 prototype) were not adopted. This machine later formed the firm's exhibit at the Third Czechoslovakia International Aeronautical Exhibition at Prague May 31–June 9, 1924.

Production Avro 504Ns began with *J8496* in 1927 and 511 were built, ending with *K2423* in March 1932. Early versions had wooden fuselages and tapered ailerons but later models, to Specification 6/30, had fuselages of welded steel-tube and rectangular Frise-type ailerons. Government economies kept procurement below minimum requirements but deficiencies were met by converting about 100 exceedingly ancient 504Ks to N standard. One of these, *D6382*, served with No.2 FTS Digby, and credit must be given to this unit for popularising the crazy flying act first seen at the 1927 Hendon RAF Display. One of the pilots on that occasion was F/O Frank Whittle who later perfected jet propulsion. Similar exhibitions of hilarity in 504Ns were among the chief Display attractions up to 1933. In a more

*J733*, first true Avro 504N prototype, with Lucifer engine and N-type undercarriage.

117

Trials aircraft *F2575* with Lynx engine, streamlined front fuselage, and external elevator control circuit.

serious vein, the machine was historically important as the first RAF instrument flying trainer. For this purpose six aircraft of 'E' Flight, CFS, Wittering, were rigged with one degree less dihedral to reduce their inherent stability and fitted with blind flying hoods and Reid and Sigrist turn and bank indicators.

No history of the 504N would be complete without mention of the famous Hamble-built 'hack' *G-EBKQ*, Hinkler's mount in the 1925 King's Cup Race. In March 1926 *'KQ* was fitted with thick biconvex RAF 30 section mainplanes housing the fuel tanks, Frise ailerons on the bottom plane only, simplified wing and undercarriage strutting under the designation Avro 582. It appeared thus in March 1927 at the Norfolk and Norwich Aero Club meeting; at Bournemouth when H. A. Hamersley raced it during the Easter Meeting; and on July 3 when Alan Goodfellow flew the Bishop of Willochra, South Australia, on an urgent Sunday journey from Woodford to Croydon. At a later date *'KQ* was fitted with long exhausts linked under the tailplane as on skywriting S.E.5As, and later still reverted to standard 504N configuration. It then went to Filton as a more suitable test-bed for the new 210 hp Bristol Titan than the venerable *G-EAJB*. On its return to Hamble in 1930 the machine was equipped with twin metal floats and Mongoose engine as a penguin trainer for Air Service Training. Despite the low power it could be coaxed off the water under favourable conditions by experienced instructors and was often in the air over Southampton Water.

The Avro 504N had a considerble association with marine aviation, a 'one-off' conversion *J7301* having flown at Gosport and at RAE, Farnborough, with the primitive claw-type arrester gear under the axle in July

1924. Unarrested deck landing trials were made later on an aircraft carrier at sea by *K1813*.

A. V. Roe and Co also delivered 504Ns to Belgium, Brazil, Chile, Denmark, Greece, Japan, Peru, South Africa and Sweden. Siam also adopted the 504N after comparative trials with a Consolidated PT-1. A number were equipped with float undercarriages and dorsal fins under the designation Avro 504O, those for Chile being unique in retaining the seaplane fin during test flights on wheels. Floats were V-bottomed to make shock absorbers unnecessary and were of two types, either boat-built and double skinned with mahogany, or of duralumin. The Danish Navy had six Avro 504Ns, one of which, *107*, was delivered from Avro on September 28, 1925, while two others were local 504K conversions (one became civil in 1936) and the remaining three were built under licence by Orlogsvaerftet (Danish Naval Shipyard). One of the latter, *110*, is preserved in the Arsenal Museum at Copenhagen. Licence-built 504Ns were produced by SABCA in Belgium and by the Royal Thai Aeronautical Service Workshops. During 1926–28 Canadian Vickers Ltd converted at least 22 RCAF Avro 504Ks to N standard, and fitted some with ski undercarriages. One Canadian example was the single float seaplane *G-CYGK* powered by a 200 hp Wright Whirlwind J-4 and another *G-CYHE* flew with a Hamilton Standard ground-adjustable variable-pitch airscrew.

In 1920 the Japanese Yokosuka Naval Arsenal produced a navalised adaptation of the Avro 504K known as the Yokosuka K1Y1. This was developed as the K2Y1 with V undercarriage and 130 hp Armstrong Siddeley Mongoose in 1928; and as the K2Y2 Type 3 with 130 hp Gasuden Jimpu radial in 1929. Production, initially by the Watanabe Iron Works, was continued by the Kyushu Aircraft Company and others until 1940.

When the Avro 504N was declared obsolete by the RAF in 1933, some were reduced to instructional airframes and others were sold to civilian operators. With the exception of *G-ACZC*, flown privately from a field at Marlborough by the Earl of Cardigan, they were employed mainly for joyriding or towing advertisement banners. The first three civil conversions, made by F. J. V. Holmes' new firm Air Travel Ltd at Penshurst, Kent, were merely 504Ks with 150 hp Armstrong Siddeley Mongoose IIIA radials. Air Travel Ltd later moved to Gatwick and there overhauled a number of ex-RAF 504Ns which toured with Sir Alan Cobham's National Aviation Day Displays and British Hospitals Air Pageants Ltd, 1934–35, and finally with C. W. A. Scott's Air Display in 1936. A later conversion turned the wheel full circle when C. B. Field revived the original 504N alternative by fitting a 115 hp Bristol Lucifer IV into *G-AEAA* to private order at Kingswood Knoll, Surrey.

With one tank removed and operating on reduced fuel load, the low-powered Mongoose 504N was an extremely economical aeroplane for short pleasure flights. Several of the Lynx-engined variety, equipped either with under-wing rollers or a quick release gear under the tail for banner towing, infested British skies for several years, exhorting the masses to buy well-

The famous *G-EBKQ* in Avro 582 configuration with RAF 30 section mainplanes at Bournemouth in April 1927.

*G-EBKQ* at Filton in 1928 as test-bed for the 210 hp Britsol Titan radial. (*Bristol*)

*G-EBKQ/K-8* taking off opposite the Hamble slipway after reconstruction in 1930 as Air Service Training's Mongoose-engined Avro 504O with metal floats. (*Flight photo 12327*)

120

known brands of almost everything. They were operated by Aerial Sites Ltd, Hanworth (2 aircraft); Plane Advertising Ltd, Heston (4); Publicity Planes Ltd, Hanworth (2); and Air Publicity Ltd (8). Three which later found their way into club use were *G-ACOM* (Herts and Essex Aero Club, Broxbourne); *G-ADBD* (Aero 8 Club, Ashingdon, Essex); and *G-AECS* (Bournemouth Flying School, Christchurch).

The brothers L. G. and L. J. Anderson of Hanworth were responsible for a number of conversions including *G-ADBO-'BS* for joyriding in 1935 and two others, *G-AECR* and *'CS*, (Mongoose-powered), toured with Irish Air Displays Ltd in 1937. An attempt to tow banners in Ireland with Plane Advertising Ltd's *G-AEIJ* ended in the Irish Sea on January 21, 1937. On July 24 of that year Capt Percival Phillips (managing director of Air Publicity Ltd and founder of the Cornwall Aviation Co Ltd in 504K days), astonished the whole flying fraternity by winning the Devon Air Race at Exeter. With his wife as passenger and flying banner towing 504N *G-ADEV*, he completed the course at the incredible average speed of 103 mph. He did even better in the Thanet Air Race at Ramsgate on August 21 and averaged 103·75 mph, but the handicappers had his measure and *'EV* came only fourth.

In 1940 seven civil Avro 504Ns were recalled to duty by the RAF. Three formed the Special Duty Flight at Christchurch, whence they towed gliders 40 miles out to sea for experiments in radar detection of wooden aircraft. Three others were used at the RAE, Farnborough, and at the Development Unit of the Central Landing Establishment at Ringway to develop glider-towing techniques for the future Airborne Forces.

A Chilean Naval Air Service Avro 504O, with dorsal fin, mounted on a land undercarriage for test flying at Hamble 1929.

121

## SPECIFICATION AND DATA

*Manufacturers:*  A. V. Roe and Co Ltd, Newton Heath, Manchester, and Hamble Aerodrome, near Southampton, Hants.

Canadian Vickers Ltd, Vickers Works, Maisonneuve, Montreal, Canada

Sociètè Anonyme Belge de Constructions Aèronautiques, 1362 Chaussée de Haecht, Haren, Brussels, Belgium

Orlogsvaerftet (Danish Naval Shipyard), Copenhagen, Denmark

Royal Thai Aeronautical Service Workshops, Don Muang, Bangkok, Siam

*Powerplants:*  One 100 hp Bristol Lucifer
One 115 hp Bristol Lucifer IV
One 150 hp Armstrong Siddeley Mongoose IIIA
One 180 hp Armstrong Siddeley Lynx I (or III)
One 215 hp Armstrong Siddeley Lynx IVC
One 200 hp Wright Whirlwind J-4

*Dimensions, Weights and Performances:*

|  | Avro 504N | | | Avro 504O | |
|---|---|---|---|---|---|
| Engine | Lynx I | Lynx IVC | Mongoose IIIA | Lynx IVC | Lynx IVC |
| Floats | — | — | — | wooden | metal |
| Span | 36 ft 0 in | 36 ft 0 in | 36 ft 0 in | 36 ft 0 in | 36 ft 0 in |
| Length | 28 ft 5½ in | 28 ft 11 in | 28 ft 11 in | 31 ft 7 in | 30 ft 0 in |
| Height | 10 ft 10 in | 10 ft 10 in | 10 ft 10 in* | 11 ft 10 in | 11 ft 10 in |
| Wing area | 320 sq ft | 320 sq ft | 320 sq ft | 320 sq ft | 320 sq ft |
| Tare weight | 1,555 lb** | 1,584 lb | 1,392 lb* | 1,973 lb | 1,827 lb |
| All-up weight | 2,166 lb** | 2,260 lb | 2,240 lb | 2,663 lb | 2,483 lb |
| Maximum speed | 100 mph** | 100 mph | 90 mph | 96 mph | 97 mph |
| Cruising speed | 85 mph** | 85 mph | 80 mph | 80 mph | 80 mph |
| Initial climb | 800 ft/min** | 770 ft/min | 625 ft/min | 610 ft/min | 650 ft/min |
| Ceiling | 19,400 ft*** | 17,000 ft | 14,700 ft | 13,500 ft | 14,500 ft |
| Range | 255 miles | 255 miles | 320 miles | 240 miles | 240 miles |

*With Lucifer IV engine, 10 ft 5 in and 1,518 lb respectively.
**F2575 1,456 lb, 2,066 lb, 95 mph, 75 mph, 750 ft/min, 16,000 ft respectively.

*Production:*
## (a) Development aircraft

| Constructor's No. (or RAF serial) and Registration | | C of A Issued | Details |
|---|---|---|---|
| A.T.C.14 | K-147 | nil | Wasp I; converted 1920 to Avro 548 |
| D9068 | — | nil | Wasp I; 'fireproof' Avro at RAE 1920–22 |
| E4348 | G-EADL | nil | Lucifer; crashed at Kingswood, Bristol, 1.20 |
| H2598 | G-EAJB | 20.8.19 | Lucifer; converted 1927 to Avro 548 |
| E4221 | G-EADA | nil | Lucifer; s.o.r. 1924 |
| H2518 | G-EBFB | nil | Lucifer; s.o.r. 1.25 |
| 5104 | G-EBKQ | 2.7.25 | Lynx IVC; first flown at Hamble 2.7.25; 3.27 to Avro 582; Titan test bed 1928; to Air Service Training Ltd, Hamble, as Avro 504O (Mongoose), C of A reissued 14.6.30; sometime with Class B marking K-8; s.o.r. 11.35 |
| R3/CN/126 | G-EBVY | 1.2.28 | Lynx IVC; 11.32 L.G. Anderson, Hanworth; crashed at Tooting, London, 30.1.35 |

122

## (b) Prototype aircraft

*E9265, E9266, F2575, J733, J750.* Also *J7301* to Contract No. 492529/24

## (c) Interim aircraft for Armstrong Whitworth

| Constructor's No. and Registration | C of A issued | Details |
|---|---|---|
| R3/LY/10331  *G-EBHC* | nil | Registration 20.7.23, destroyed by fire at Whitley 3.8.23 |
| R3/LY/10348  *G-EBHD* | 1. 8.24 | 1.31 to R. O. Roch, Hanworth; 3.32 Modern Airways Ltd, s.o.r. 9.36 |
| R3/LY/10365  *G-EBHE* | 12.12.23 | Converted 1932 to Avro 504K (see page 115) |
| R3/LY/10382  *G-EBHT* | 14. 2.24 | Replacement for '*HC*; 3.32 Modern Airways Ltd; crashed at Porthcawl, Glamorgan, 25.6.32 |

## (d) RAF production batches

| Requisitioned | Quantity | Serials | Requisitioned | Quantity | Serials |
|---|---|---|---|---|---|
| March 1927 | 100 | *J8496–J8595* | September 1929 | 25 | *K1038–K1062* |
| March 1927 | 100 | *J8676–J8775* | 1930 | 12 | *K1242–K1253* |
| December 1927 | 50 | *J8975–J9024* | 1931 | 26 | *K1798–K1823* |
| March 1928 | 20 | *J9415–J9434* | 1932 | 35 | *K1956–K1990* |
| June 1928 | 40 | *J9253–J9292* | 1933 | 78 | *K2346–K2423* |
| September 1929 | 25 | *J9683–J9707* | | | |

## (e) RAF conversions from Avro 504K

Around one hundred aircraft including *D4430, D4432, D4452, D6382, D6383, D6388, D9021, D9092, D9290, E430, E3327, E3460, E9408, F2269, F2286, F2588, F8713, F8812, F8813, F9705, H2618, H2962, H2995, H2972, H3105, H5196, H5199, H7534, H9821, H9866, H9870, J731, J735, J738, J869, J875.*

## (f) Export orders

*Belgian Air Force:* Avro 504Ns c/n 373–382, Cs of A issued 14.12.29; c/n 480–484, Cs of A issued 19.1.31; c/n 492–493, Cs of A issued 14.3.31, allotted serials *X1–X17*

*Brazilian Naval Air Service:* Avro 504N/504Os c/n 439–442 delivered 5.30

*Chilean Naval Air Service:* Avro 504Os c/n 355–360, serial numbers *82–87*, completed 17.8.29, based at El Bosque

*Danish Navy:* Six Avro 504Ns, including five produced in Denmark, locally designated L.B.1 (Land Biplane 1)

| Constructor's No.* and Serial | On Charge | Details |
|---|---|---|
| —  *107* | 28. 9.25 | Crash off Copenhagen 9.8.26 |
| 43  *108* | 11. 3.26 | Crashed at Ringsted 16.5.29 |
| 49  *109* | 2. 5.27 | Crashed at Ringsted 30.5.29 |
| 50  *110* | 2. 5.27 | To the Arsenal Museum, Copenhagen, 1935 |
| —  *111* | 1927 | ex 504K *106*, crashed at Avnø 20.6.28 |
| —  *112* | 1929 | ex 504K, *104*, s.o.c. 13.7.36, sold as *OY-DEL*, seized by Germans 1940 |

*Orlogsvaerftet constructor's numbers.

The single-float seaplane version *G-CYGK*, c/n C.V.29, with 200 hp Wright Whirlwind J-4, built by Canadian Vickers Ltd 1926, (*RCAF*)

*Royal Hellenic Naval Air Service:* Six Avro 504N/504Os were supplied in 1925 to Works Order 7787 for training schools at Tatoi and Phaleron Bay, a few of which were still in service with the Royal Hellenic Air Force in 1940. Original serials around and about *E-14* and *E-15*

*Japan:* One Avro 504O supplied 1.27 to Works Order 8430

*South African Air Force:* Avro 504Ns were supplied as 504K replacements in 1927

*Royal Thai Air Force:* Twenty Avro 504Ns, c/n 390–409 supplied 3.30

*Royal Swedish Air Force:* One Avro 504N, serial *64*, Flygvapnet designation Sk 3A, delivered at Malmslätt for evaluation 28.4.26, crashed on take-off 11.4.27

### (*g*) Conversion and construction by Canadian Vickers Ltd

*G-CYAQ*, later RCAF *2*, *G-CYAR/1*, *G-CYAV/50*, *G-CYAX/14*, *G-CYBL/53*, *G-CYBM/52*, *G-CYCD/51*, *G-CYCA/13*, *G-CYCX/3*, *G-CYEH/54*, *G-CYEI/4*, *G-CYFG/5*, *G-CYFH/6*, RCAF *7, 9, 15, 44–48* and *49*, ex *H9623*; Construction: *G-CYGK* (c/n. C.V.29), later RCAF *12*, built 1926; RCAF *32–43* (c/ns C.V. 59–70) built 1928

### (*h*) Built under licence by SABCA

31 built for Belgian Air Force with serials *X18-X48*. 15 ordered in 1934, 10 in 1937 and 6 in 1939

*RAF Service Use:* (with specimen serials)

Central Flying School, Upavon, *H5185*, *H9870*, *J8548*, *K1042*, *'50*, *K1244*, *'46*, *K1963*, *'84*, *K2346*, *'74*, *'75*, *'77*, *'78*, *'81*; No.1 FTS, Netheravon, *J8745*, *'72*, *J9012*, *K1051*, *K1818*, *K2419*, *'23*; No.2 FTS, Digby, *D6382*, *F8812*, *H9821*, *'66*, *J9018*, *J9265*, *J9688*, *'90*, *K1815*; No.3 FTS, Grantham, *E3327*, *J8709*, *'53*, *'54*, *'74*, *J9687*, *K1056*, *'59*, *K1822*; No.4 FTS, Abu Sueir, *F2286*, *F9705*, *H3105*, *J8695*, *J8715*, *J8975*, *'77*, *'90*, *'91*, *K2359*, *'84*, *'85*, *'89*, *'91*, *'99*,

*K2405*; No.5 FTS, Sealand, *H2618, H3460, J8518, '24, '33, '35, J8677, J9007, J9428, '31, K1046, '47, '53, K1975, '90, K2347, '49, '51, '54*; No.23. ERFTS, Rochester, *K2400, '01, '08, '11, '17, '19, '20, '23*; Oxford University Air Sqn, *K1243, '47, K1802, '12, '18, '19, K1962, K2367, '71*; Cambridge University Air Sqn, *K1241, K1813, '15, '43, K1961, '66, K2367*; RAF College, Cranwell, *H9826, J8709, J9693, K1808, K1966, '87*; No.7 Sqn, *K1963, '68, '69*; No.24 Sqn; Station Flight, Duxford, *J8758*; No.500 Sqn AAF, *K1811, K2407, '12*; No.501 Sqn, *J8689*; No.502 Sqn, *J8738*; No.503 Sqn, *J8592, J9271, K1965, K2368*; No.504 Sqn, *H2995, J9265, J9703*; No.601 Sqn, *J8504, '05, K1971*; No.602 Sqn, *K1982*; No.602 Sqn, *K1822, K2417*; No.604 Sqn, *K1043*; No.605 Sqn, *J738, J8689*; No.607 Sqn, *K2364*; No.1 AAS, *K2365*

Avro 504N *G-ACCX* of Air Travel Ltd, a special conversion with 150 hp Armstrong Siddeley Mongoose IIIA engine and 504K type undercarriage. (*Hunting Aerosurveys*)

*British civil conversions (radial engined Avro 504Ks):*
*G-ABVC/F8834*, Lucifer, C of A 9.6.33, H. C. Chater, Lympne, s.o.r. 11.45; *G-ABVH/J8372* (C of A 8.4.32, s.o.r. 12.46), *G-ABVY/H2524* (C of A 21.5.32, s.o.r. 10.36) and *G-ACCX* (C of A 8.4.33, crashed at Stewkley, Bucks, 19.6.34) all Mongoose IIIA, F. J. V. Holmes, Penshurst, Kent

*British civil conversions 1934–36 (Avro 504N):*
*G-ACLV/J8573* Air Travel Ltd; *G-ACNV/K1808* Air Pageants Ltd; *G-ACOD/F8713* Air Travel Ltd (air collision with Westland Wessex *G-ADFZ* over Blackpool 7.9.35); *G-ACOK/F2588*★ National Aviation Day (crashed at Rhyl 14.8.38); *G-ACOM/E430*★ Air Travel Ltd; *G-ACPV/K1250* Aerial Sites Ltd, to Publicity Planes Ltd 3.38 (impressed 1.41 as *BV209*); *G-ACRE/E9408* Air Publicity Ltd (crashed at Gamlingay, Cambs. 13.2.38); *G-ACRS/K1802* National Aviation Day (crashed at Cove, Hants. 1.7.34); *G-ACZC* Earl of Cardigan (impressed 6.40 as *AX854/2453M*); *G-ADBD/K1245*★ National Aviation Day; *G-ADBM/K1055* Air Publicity Ltd (impressed 6.40 as *AX871*, crashed at Hawkinge 1.8.40); *G-ADBO/K2354* Air Publicity Ltd; *G-ADBP/K2353* Air Publicity Ltd (impressed 6.40 as *AX874*); *G-ADBR/K1819* Air Publicity Ltd; *G-ADBS/K1251*★ L. G. Anderson (crashed at Bodmin, Cornwall, 16.8.35); *G-ADDA/K1810* Air Publicity Ltd; *G-ADEI/E3460* H. B. G. Micklemore (crashed at Hanworth 16.5.39); *G-ADET/J8533* Air Publicity

Ltd (impressed 6.40 as *AX875*); *G-ADEV/H5199* Air Publicity Ltd (impressed 9.40 as *BK892/3118M*); *G-ADFW/K1061*★ Lincolnshire Flying Services Ltd, Louth; *G-AEAA*, c/n 14★★, F. C. J. Allen, Ford; *G-AECR/K2396*★ L. J. Anderson (sold abroad 3.38); *G-AECS/J8548* L. J. Anderson; *G-AEDD/K1823* Plane Advertising Ltd (crashed at Walsall, Staffs, 13.3.39); *G-AEGW/J9702*★ L. J. Rimmer (destroyed in hangar fire at Hooton 8.7.40); *G-AEIJ/J8507* Plane Advertising Ltd (lost in the Irish Sea 21.1.37); *G-AEMP/J9017* Plane Advertising Ltd (impressed 1.41 as *BV208*); *G-AFRM/K1964* Martin Hearn Ltd (destroyed in hangar fire at Hooton 8.7.40)

★150 hp Mongoose IIIA.   ★★115 hp Bristol Lucifer IV (C. B. Field conversion).

*Note:* Only the principal operator of each aircraft is given.

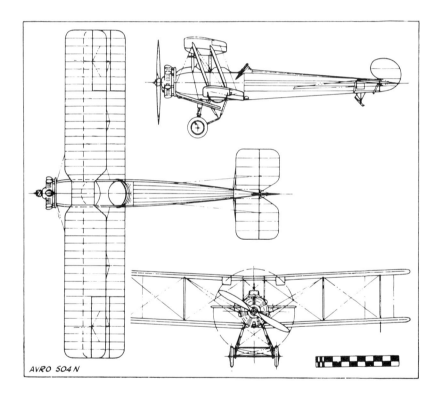

AVRO 504N

126

The Avro 504Q *G-EBJD* being launched at Hamble in 1924. (*Courtesy J. C. C. Taylor*)

# Avro 504Q

Designation Avro 504P was allotted to a proposed variant of the 504N having two seats side by side. Although this was never built, preparatory work for widening the fuselage undoubtedly assisted in the construction of the Avro 504Q, a special three-seat seaplane assembled at Hamble in 1924 for the Oxford University Arctic Expedition. Registered *G-EBJD* and powered by a 160 hp Armstrong Siddeley Lynx, the 504Q somewhat resembled the Avro 546 with open pilot's cockpit ahead of a glazed cabin, and a large dorsal fin at the rear.

Entry to the cabin was by a door in the starboard side and there was a sliding hatch in the roof through which the navigator could work in the open or pick up moorings. A Norwegian sledge was carried under the rear decking and a close-fitting engine cowl was stowed aboard in readiness for flying in sub-zero temperatures. In addition to the usual external 504N-type fuel tanks a large streamlined tank was fitted in the centre section and long wooden, single-step floats, strengthened to act as skis for landing on snow, made a tail float unnecessary.

The Avro 504Q was test flown from Southampton Water by H. J. Hinkler before despatch to Newcastle for shipment to Spitzbergen in the ss *Polar–bjørn*. With it went G. (later Sir George) Binney leading the expedition, A. G. B. Ellis first pilot, J. C. C. Taylor pilot and engineer, and Capt (later Sir Frederick) Tymms as observer, who, assisted by other members of the Expedition, erected the machine in four days and nights at an abandoned whaling base at Green Harbour, well within the Arctic Circle. Piloted by Ellis and carrying Binney as passenger, the 504Q left Green Harbour for Liefde Bay on July 15 but was forced down on the sea by engine failure. It was salvaged after a battle with heavy seas lasting 18 hours and taken to Liefde Bay for complete engine overhaul, but during later operations the long suffering undercarriage collapsed when the aircraft failed to clear the land on take-off from Treurenberg Bay. Even then repairs were somehow completed in ten days despite the primitive working conditions. In the course of a survey flight over North East Land (an island lying north east of Spitzbergen) in appalling flying conditions on August 8, 1924, *G-EBJD* reached latitude 80 degrees 15 minutes, the farthest north ever reached by an aeroplane up to that time. At the conclusion of the Expedition's work the Lynx engine was removed for return to the United Kingdom but the airframe was left at Liefde Bay to test the effect of prolonged Arctic weathering on fabric covered wooden structures. When rediscovered by a later expedition in 1932 it was still in reasonable condition but had been partly eaten by polar bears.

## SPECIFICATION AND DATA

*Manufacturers:*  A. V. Roe and Co Ltd, Newton Heath, Manchester; and Hamble Aerodrome, near Southampton, Hants.

*Powerplant:*  One 160 hp Armstrong Siddeley Lynx serial number A.S.17

*Dimensions:*  Similar to Avro 504N

*Weights:*  All-up weight 3,232 lb

*Performance:*  Maximum speed 85 mph   Cruising speed 63 mph

*Production:*  One aircraft only, *G-EBJD*, c/n 5103, registered 12.6.24 to the Oxford University Arctic Expedition, no C of A, abandoned at Liefde Bay, Spitzbergen, 9.24, s.o.r. 6.25

First Pilot A. G. B. Ellis with the Avro 504Q at Spitzbergen.

*G-EBNE*, prototype Avro 504R Gosport. (100 hp Gnome Monosoupape.)

# Avro 504R Gosport

First flown in June 1926, the Avro 504R Gosport was the ultimate variation on the 504 theme and an attempt to produce a low-powered version with a performance equal to that of the RAF standard 130 hp Clerget 504K trainer. The 100 hp Gnome Monosoupape was chosen and a new light-weight engine mounting devised specially for it. Then by reworking and improving every part of the airframe to reduce the gross weight from 1,830 lb to 1,690 lb, virtually a new aeroplane was created with all the characteristics of the Avro 504J. Tapered ailerons were fitted and all the old delightful handling characteristics were recaptured so that for a time the machine was referred to as the Avro 504J Mk.II. Cooling efficiency was improved by increasing the size of the front opening of the engine cowling, wing roots were cut back to improve the view as in the Avro 504N and a steerable tail skid fitted.

Two prototypes, *G-EBNE* and *'NF*, were built at Hamble the first of which became the firm's experimental 'hack' while the second was presented to the Lancashire Aero Club by Sir William Letts, Managing Director of A. V. Roe and Co at Woodford on April 16, 1926. Demonstrated by Avro test pilot H. J. Hinkler at the club's meeting two days later, it was used for instruction until Hinkler borrowed it on July 14 for a flight to Croydon for demonstration before the representatives of foreign governments. He also showed off the third Gosport *G-EBOX* (Manchester built) at a Yorkshire Aero Club meeting at Sherburn-in-Elmet during August with his usual artistry, resulting in the immediate sale of *'OX* abroad and in a number of overseas contracts.

Erratic engine behaviour kept *'NF* in its hangar at Woodford and so few flights were made that in the following November the Avro company replaced it with *G-EBQL*, second of their new Avian I light aeroplanes.

Gosport *G-EBPH* as the Avro 585 with Avro Alpha engine and N-type undercarriage, leaving Woodford for the Helvellyn flight on December 22, 1926.

Thereafter '*NF* flew only at long intervals eventually spinning in with two club members near Stockport in the autumn of 1928.

It was evident that without a modern power plant the Gosport would never achieve the standards of serviceability needed for military training schools. Plans to install a 100 hp Bristol Lucifer radial under the designation Avro 504S were eventually dropped in favour of a 100 hp Avro Alpha five-cylinder-radial specially designed for it. This engine was later built in small numbers by Crossley Ltd who had a financial interest in A. V. Roe and Co but production ceased when Armstrong Siddeley took over. The first engine of this type was installed in the fourth Gosport, *G-EBPH*, built at Manchester in September 1926 which differed from earlier machines only in the shape of the nose and in the use of narrow-chord hollow steel interplane struts.

Wishing to impress on the public that the aeroplane had become a useful and unique means of transport, the Director of Civil Aviation, Sir Sefton Brancker, persuaded Hinkler and the Lancashire Aero Club chairman J. F. Leeming to make a landing on the summit of Helvellyn (3,118 ft). Before this exploit, successfully accomplished on December 22, 1926, a 504N-type undercarriage was fitted with which *G-EBPH* became the Avro 585. A solitary climber (Prof Dodds of Birmingham University) signed a certificate showing that he had seen '*PH* land on the mountain. Taking off over Striding Edge, the machine then returned to Woodford and in 1928 was 'posted' to Hamble where its engine was eventually donated to an early autogiro.

The first prototype Gosport *G-EBNE*, flown in the 1926 Bournemouth Easter Races by Hinkler and by Schneider Trophy pilot H. R. D. Waghorn

130

in 1927, was also used in the search for an alternative power plant, undergoing experimental fitment at Hamble with a 140 hp Armstrong Siddeley Genet Major in July 1928. It later flew with Class B marking *K-6* and when Air Service Training Ltd moved into Hamble in May 1931, *'NE* became an instructional airframe and was still there in 1935.

Final choice of engine fell midway between the Alpha and the Lynx so that the fifth Gosport, *G-EBUY*, built at Manchester late in 1927, was powered by a 150 hp Armstrong Siddeley Mongoose. It retained the slim interplane struts but reverted to the skid undercarriage and carried fuel in two $12\frac{1}{2}$ gallon 504N-type tanks under the upper mainplane. *G-EBUY* appeared at several meetings during 1928 but left the civil register in January 1929 and there is little reason to doubt that it was the Gosport evaluated by the RAF at Martlesham in the same months as *J9175*. No Air Ministry contract was placed and the final civil machine *G-AACT* was eventually destroyed in an accident.

*G-EBNE* at Hamble in July 1928 with experimental 140 hp Armstrong Siddeley Genet Major IA installation. (*P. T. Capon*)

The final, Armstrong Siddeley Mongoose powered version of the Gosport. (*Crown Copyright Reserved*)

The first of ten Gosports built for the Argentine Military Air Service, before delivery in June 1927.

Production Mongoose Gosports, simlar to *G-EBUY* but with the engine mounted uncowled as in the 504N, were supplied to the Estonian Air Force at Tallinn in November 1928 (still in use in 1940) and to the Peruvian Army Aviation Service. Ten were delivered to the Argentine Military Air Service in June 1927 and the Military Aviation Factory (Fábrica Militar de Aviones) opened at Cordoba, Argentina, on October 10, 1927, built one hundred Avro 504R Gosport trainers under licence, the first of which made its first flight at the El Palomar School on October 2, 1928.

## SPECIFICATION AND DATA

*Manufacturers:*  A. V. Roe and Co Ltd, Newton Heath, Manchester; and Hamble Aerodrome, near Southampton, Hants.
Fábrica Militar de Aviones, Cordoba, Argentina

*Powerplants:*  One 100 hp Avro Alpha
One 100 hp Gnome Monosoupape

Line up of Estonian Air Force Avro 504R Gosports.

132

One 140 hp Armstrong Siddeley Genet Major IA.
One 150 hp Armstrong Siddeley Mongoose

*Dimensions:*     Span 36 ft 0 in    Length 28 ft 11 in
Height 10 ft 8 in    Wing area 320 sq ft

*Weights:*     (Gnome Mono)
       Tare weight 1,107 lb    All-up weight 1,676 lb
(Mongoose)
       Tare weight 1,297 lb    All-up weight 1,907 lb

*Performance:*     (Gnome Mono)
       Maximum speed 87 mph    Cruising speed 70 mph
       Initial climb 670 ft/min    Range 140 miles
(Mongoose)
       Maximum speed 95 mph    Cruising speed 75 mph
       Initial climb 700 ft/min    Ceiling 12,000 ft
       Range 340 miles

*Production:*

### (a) Prototypes

| Constructor's No. and Registration | | C of A Issued | Details |
|---|---|---|---|
| 5110 | *G-EBNE* | 15.6.26 | Gnome Mono; flown with Genet Major 1928, later as *K-6*, instructional airframe Hamble 1931 |
| 5111 | *G-EBNF* | 6.7.26 | Gnome Mono; Light Planes (Lancs) Ltd,★ Woodford, crashed at Bramhall, Cheshire 21.10.28 |
| R3/G/80086 | *G-EBOX* | nil | Gnome Mono: sold abroad 8.26 |
| R3/R/70000 | *G-EBPH* | 9.12.26 | Alpha: converted to Avro 585, crashed 1.30 |
| R3/CN/100 | *G-EBUY* | 26.11.27 | Mongoose: to the RAF 1.29 as *J9175* under Contract 787175/27 |
| R3/CN/238 | *G-AACT* | nil | Mongoose: crashed 1.30 |

★Trading as the Lancashire Aero Club.

### (b) Subsequent

Argentina: Ten delivered 6.27, and 100 built under licence
Estonia:     At least six, including *107, 109, 111* and *115* delivered 11.28
Peru:       An unspecified number

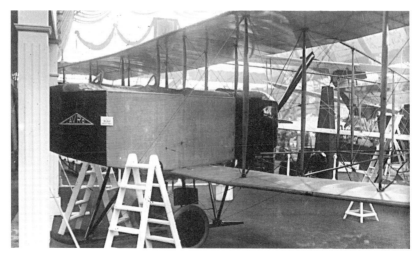

The Avro 508 reconnaissance pusher at the Olympia Aero Show, London, in March 1914. (*Flight*)

# Avro 508

The Avro 508 was a two-seat reconnaissance biplane built at the Manchester works in December 1913 and delivered at Brooklands for erection and test a month later. Following contemporary practice it was a twin boom, three-bay pusher biplane of fabric-covered wooden construction having equal span mainplanes structurally similar to those of the Avro 504 prototype. A wide centre section carried the first pair of interplane struts at its extremities, the dihedral commencing at this point as on the Avro 503. Ailerons were used for lateral control and the machine was noteworthy as the first Avro type to have aileron cables located inside the wing leading-edge and running over buried pulleys.

A capacious square-section nacelle, built up from four ash longerons and spruce cross-struts, accommodated two crew in tandem. The observer/gunner sat in the nose for maximum field of vision with the pilot behind. Fuel and oil tanks were located behind the pilot's seat and just ahead of an 80 hp Gnome rotary engine mounted on steel-tube bearers. The use of standard Avro cowlings and centre skid undercarriage heightened its likeness to a back-to-front Avro 504. Tail booms were of steel tubing braced by streamline-section spruce struts, the rear extremities of which were built into the tailplane structure. For ease of dismantling, the booms were jointed just ahead of the tailplane leading-edge. The rudder was an elongated version of the famous comma type, somewhat like an artist's palette.

The Avro 508 was not adopted for the Royal Flying Corps and the single machine built made but two public appearances. The airframe was shown without covering at an exhibition at Belle Vue Gardens, Manchester, on

134

January 1–3, 1914, and the complete aircraft was shown on the Avro stand at the Olympia Aero Show, London, on March 16–25, 1914.

In late April 1915 the Avro 508 was operational at Brooklands, but following the company's failure to secure orders for the type, it was apparently disposed of to the Hall Flying School at Hendon in whose sheds it was noted in a dismantled state and engineless in April 1916. At that time, the school expressed the intention of fitting dual controls and using the machine for carrying passengers as well as for instruction. Of note is that they expected the Avro 508 to be of particular use during windy conditions when it was adjudged capable of climbing to a height where 'the wind was steadier than nearer the ground'. However, it is not known if the machine was ever erected at Hendon and pressed into service.

## SPECIFICATION AND DATA

*Manufacturers:*  A. V. Roe and Co Ltd, Clifton Street, Miles Platting, Manchester; and Brooklands Aerodrome, Byfleet, Surrey

*Powerplant:*  One 80 hp Gnome

*Dimensions:*  Span 44 ft 0 in   Length 26 ft 9 in
Height 10 ft 0 in   Wing area 468 sq ft

*Weights:*  Tare weight 1,000 lb   All-up weight 1,680 lb

*Performance:*  Maximum speed 65 mph   Endurance $4\frac{1}{2}$ hours

The Avro 508 at the 1914 Olympia Aero Show (*J. M. Bruce/G. S. Leslie Collection*)

The Avro 510 prototype at Calshot, July 1914

# Avro 510

The Avro 510 was a large two-seat, two-bay seaplane built for the 1914 Circuit of Britain Race. A larger version of the 504 rudder proclaimed the aircraft's Avro origins but it bore no other resemblance to any previous machine built by the firm. The upper mainplane overhung the lower by more than 12 ft and the extension planes (which carried the ailerons), were braced by cables to steel-tube kingposts. Power was derived from a 150 hp Sunbeam eight cylinder watercooled engine (later named the Nubian), fitted with nose radiator and stub exhausts.

The undercarriage consisted of four steel struts connected at their lower extremities to a tubular steel rectangle, the corners of which were bolted to the attachment points of each float. These were of entirely new design with a pronounced taper aft of the single step. The tail was supported on a large wooden float with water rudder.

Built at Manchester in July 1914, the Avro 510 was despatched by rail to Calshot, starting point of the race. Following by road to supervise its erection, A. V. Roe put up for the night at Havant where the next morning he learned of England's declaration of war on Germany. The race was perforce cancelled but the Avro 510 was erected and flew well, the new float design being particularly successful. Much smoother alightings were possible than with the old flat backed pontoon-type floats.

When the trials were complete, the machine was purchased by the Admiralty and much to A. V. Roe's surprise a cheque was handed over on the spot by Capt (later Air Vice Marshal Sir Arthur) Longmore. The Admiralty also placed an order for five production Avro 510s but stipulated a taller undercarriage incorporating an extra inclined strut and using the well-tried, but entirely outmoded, flat backed floats. These were bolted direct to the struts without the complicated sub-frame of the original. To A. V. Roe's disappointment the modern floats of the prototype were also replaced.

136

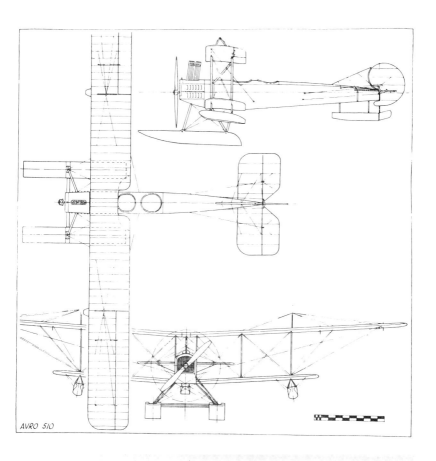

AVRO 510

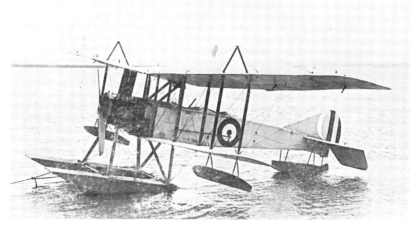

One of the five production-type Avro 510s built for the RNAS.

137

RNAS Avro 510s were fitted with a fixed fin having a curved trailing edge which fitted snugly round the leading edge of the rudder. All six were powered by the 150 hp Sunbeam and though data was published for a version with the 160 hp Gnome rotary there is no evidence that this motor was ever fitted to an Avro 510. Delivery of the production machines took place between December 1914 and April 1915 but their performance was very poor and they repeatedly failed to pass acceptance tests. Only solo flying proved possible. This resulted in all but 130 being sent to the Supermarine Works at Woolston for modification in October 1915. All the machines had been removed from the active list by March 1916.

## SPECIFICATION AND DATA

*Manufacturers:* A. V. Roe and Co Ltd, Clifton Street, Miles Platting, Manchester

*Powerplants:* One 150 hp Sunbeam Nubian

*Dimensions:* Span (upper) 63 ft 0 in (lower) 38 ft 0 in
Length 38 ft 0 in
Wing area 564 sq ft

*Weights:* Tare weight 2,080 lb    All-up weight 2,800 lb

*Performance:* Maximum speed 70 mph
Climb to 1,000 ft $4\frac{1}{2}$ minutes.    Endurance $4\frac{1}{2}$ hours

*Production:* Prototype sold to Admiralty 1914 and numbered *881*
Production machines built under contract C.P.30654/14:-

*130* delivered to RNAS Killingholme 6.12.14, to Grain 10.4.15, fitted with non-standard undercarriage and floats in mid-1915.

*131* delivered to Killingholme 5.2.15, acceptance test flights by F. P. Raynham 15.4.15, dismantled 18.10.15, to Woolston by sea 21.10.15.

*132* delivered to Killingholme 17.2.15, erected 3.15, acceptance test flights by F. P. Raynham 15.4.15, dismantled 18.10.15, to Woolston by sea 21.10.15

*133* delivered to Dundee, erected 25.3.15, preliminary trials flown 31.3.15, declared to be 'of negligible value' 3.9.15, to Woolston 26.10.15

*134* delivered to Dundee 4.4.15, acceptance test flights flown on 12.4.15, used for a few operational patrols without observer, order given to return machine to its makers 19.10.15

F. P. Raynham in the Avro 511 at Hendon on May 23, 1914. (*Flight*)

# Avro 511

Three full-sized aircraft shown on the Avro stand at the Olympia Aero Show, London, March 16–25, 1914, were a production Avro 504 seaplane, the Avro 508 pusher and the Avro 511 single-seat, single-bay biplane. This was designed specifically for fast scouting in the event of war and could be swiftly dismantled for road transport to the operational area. Heavily staggered, sparless mainplanes of cellular construction, designed and stressed by Avro's assistant designer H. E. Broadsmith, were given pronounced sweepback in an attempt to reduce the span and attain inherent stability. On this account the aircraft was promptly and unofficially dubbed 'Arrowplane' or even 'Arrowscout' by the sensational press but these names can find no place in a serious work of reference. Ailerons were fitted to all four wings and single wide-chord interplane struts were used on each side. Landing flaps were incorporated in the inboard trailing edges of the lower mainplanes and pivoted diagonally about a stout steel tube which passed through the fuselage. This device, years ahead of its time, reduced touchdown speed to 35 mph.

The Avro 511 was otherwise typically Avro with standard centre-skid undercarriage and comma-type rudder. The nose was of good streamline shape with a close fitting cowling round the 80 hp Gnome Monosoupape rotary engine. The cowling was later modified as it prevented adequate cooling. Estimated maximum speed was 95–100 mph and the machine was to have been piloted by F. P. Raynham in the Aerial Derby Race round London on May 23, 1914 (racing No.14). Storms on the eve of the race caused deterioration in the weather which led to a postponement until June 6 but Raynham managed to make one or two demonstration runs for the benefit of the few hardy spectators. When returning home on the following day he made a safe landing after the engine failed within gliding distance of

Brooklands. It had not proved as fast as had been hoped but was nevertheless entered (racing No.20) in the postponed Aerial Derby.

In preparation for this event the Avro 511 was fitted with alternative mainplanes without sweepback which Broadsmith had designed in case trouble was encountered with the swept wings. The rebuilt machine, designated Avro 514, was also equipped with a light weight, unsprung, V-type racing undercarriage without the familiar skid, but while taxying out at Brooklands to take off for Hendon on the eve of the race, an eye bolt sheared. The undercarriage collapsed, breaking the airscrew and bending the engine crankshaft as well as damaging wings and fuselage. After reconstruction at Manchester the Avro 514 was successfully flown from Southport Sands by F. P. Raynham in July 1914 but further development was ended by the outbreak of war.

## SPECIFICATION AND DATA

*Manufacturers:*  A. V. Roe and Co Ltd, Clifton Street, Miles Platting, Manchester; and Brooklands Aerodrome, Byfleet, Surrey

*Powerplant:*  One 80 hp Gnome Monosoupape

*Dimensions:*  Span 26 ft 0 in   Length 22 ft 4 in
Height 9 ft 4 in   Wing area 235 sq ft

*Weights:*  Tare weight 675 lb   All-up weight 1,165 lb

*Performance:*  Maximum speed 95–100 mph

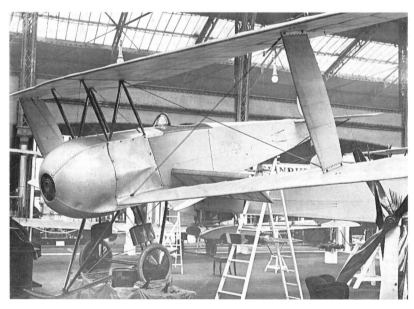

The Avro 511 at the 1914 Olympia Aero Show.

140

*8441*, second of the two RNAS Avro 519 single-seat biplanes. (*Courtesy the Royal Aeronautical Society*)

# Avro 519

Evolved from the Avro 510 seaplane and built for the Admiralty early in 1916, the Avro 519 was a single-seat biplane bomber with folding wings, a scaled-up version of the standard Avro central skid undercarriage and a large fin and rudder of the style used on the Avro 504B.

In addition to the two Avro 519s built for the RNAS a pair of two-seat Avro 519As with stout V-strut undercarriage and having no central skid were ordered for the RFC. All four machines had unique characteristics. The first Type 519, *8440*, which spent some time at Eastchurch in 1916, was fitted with side-mounted radiators. Sister machine *8441* and the first of the two 225 hp Sunbeam powered aircraft for the RFC, *1614*, were fitted with a large radiator mounted above and behind the engine. This unit not only blocked the pilot's forward view but would also have introduced high additional drag to a type known for its poor rate of climb. It is thought that it was in an attempt to correct this lack of performance that the second RFC machine, *1615*, was completed with equal-span wings approximately 43 ft in length. This machine was a Type 522, a fact confirmed by signwriting on the side of its fuselage, but despite this it was still officially referred to as a Type 519A.

This last machine, *1615*, was despatched to Hamble from Manchester on November 1, 1916, and though ready for military acceptance by December

*1614*, first of the two RFC Avro 519A two-seaters.

141

8, 1916, remained there until April 1917 when it departed along with *1614* and *8441* which were also at Hamble at that time. The fact that company reports talk of 'managing to get rid' of these three machines is a measure of their success.

Photographs taken by test pilot Capt F. T. Courtney suggest that all four machines were tested at Farnborough where they were dubbed 'The Big Avros'. *1614* was there in May 1916. Their ultimate fate is unknown.

*1615*, the Avro 522 with equal-span wings. (*J. M. Bruce/G. S. Leslie Collection*)

## SPECIFICATION AND DATA

*Manufacturers:*   A. V. Roe and Co Ltd, Park Works, Newton Heath, Manchester; and Hamble Aerodrome, near Southampton, Hants.

*Powerplants:*   One 150 hp Sunbeam Nubian
One 225 hp Sunbeam

*Dimensions:*

|  | Avro 519 | Avro 519A | Avro 522 |
|---|---|---|---|
| Span (upper) | 63 ft 0 in | 63 ft 0 in | 43 ft 0 in |
| Span (lower) | 38 ft 0 in | 38 ft 0 in | 43 ft 0 in |
| Length (150 hp Sunbeam) | 32 ft 9 in | — | — |
|  | 33 ft 3 in |  |  |
| Length (225 hp Sunbeam) | 35 ft 1¾ in | 33 ft 10 in | 33 ft 8 in |
| Height | 11 ft 8 in* | 11 ft 8 in* | — |
| Wing Area | 600 sq ft | 600 sq ft |  |

*measured to the highest point on the upper surface of the wing

*Weights:*   (Avro 519) All-up weight 3,000 lb

*Performance:*   (Avro 519) Speed 75 mph    Climb 6,000 ft in 30 mins

*Production:*   (Type 519 for RNAS) *8440* and *8441*
(Type 519A for RFC) *1614*
(Type 522 for RFC) *1615*

142

The prototype Avro 521 at Farnborough in January 1916. (*Crown Copyright Reserved.*)

# Avro 521

Designed late in 1915, the Avro 521 two-seat fighter-trainer was a hybrid embodying the features of several Avro 504 variants. In side elevation the straight top longerons proclaimed it a derivative of the 504 prototype, yet the short-span ailerons and the rudder-tail skid assembly were pure 504A, the cockpit positioning and centre-section struts were 504E, the V'-strut undercarriage was contributed by the 504G and the streamlined headrest was copied from the Avro 519. Standard Avro 504 mainplanes were shortened to a span of 30 ft, cut away at all four wing roots to improve upward and downward vision and rigged with only a single set of interplane struts on each side. The engine was a 110 hp Clerget rotary in characteristic Avro cowlings.

The initial order was for one machine, test flown at Trafford Park, Manchester, by F. P. Raynham with H. E. Broadsmith standing up in the rear cockpit and brandishing a dummy machine-gun to enable the effect of the extra drag to be assessed. Raynham found the Avro 521 longitudinally unstable and unpleasant to fly; nevertheless it was delivered to Farnborough in February 1916 and 25 production machines were ordered for the RFC.

Proposals were also made for interchangeable wings to suit different roles. Designation Avro 521A was allotted to a version with three-bay mainplanes of 42 ft span. At least one Avro 521A was built but it is thought that the Avro 521B, intended to have standard Avro 504 wings of 36 ft span, remained on the drawing board. Construction of the production batch, it is believed, was suspended due to the type's instability and that only one or two machines were completed. None was delivered to the RFC.

One Avro 521, most probably the prototype, was however at the Central Flying School, Upavon, in the summer of 1916 where it was flown amongst others by Lt H. H. Balfour (later Lord Balfour of Inchrye, PC, MC). The

143

machine was considered 'a beast to fly' and its tendency to spin off a righthand turn eventually claimed the life of Lt W. H. Stuart Garnett, a scientist pilot with the CFS Testing Flight, who spun in from 1,500 ft on September 21, 1916.

The Avro 521A had three-bay 42 ft span wings. (*RAF Museum*)

## SPECIFICATION AND DATA

*Manufacturers:*  A. V. Roe and Co Ltd, Park Works, Newton Heath, Manchester; and Hamble Aerodrome, near Southampton, Hants.

*Powerplant:*  One 110 hp Clerget

*Dimensions:*  Span 30 ft   Length 28 ft 2 in
Height 9 ft 10 in   Wing area 266 sq ft

*Weights:*  Tare weight 1,150 lb   All-up weight 1,995 lb

*Performance:*  Maximum speed 94.6 mph at sea level
Climb to 6,000 ft, 14 min
Endurance $4\frac{1}{2}$ hr

*Armament:*  One 0.303-in Lewis gun mounted on the rear cockpit

*Production:*  One prototype that for a time was painted as *1811* (believed to have been its Works Order number); and twenty-five production aircraft *7520* to *7544* to contract 87A 234, believed not all built

*Service Use:*  Evaluated at Farnborough and at CFS Upavon

The Avro 523 Pike showing the pusher airscrew installation.

# Avro 523 Pike

In 1916 A. V. Roe decided to move the Avro factory from Manchester to a waterside site convenient for the development of naval aircraft, and bought the stretch of Hampshire grassland which is now Hamble Aerodrome, together with a mile of foreshore on the adjacent Southampton Water. Manchester architect Harry Fairhurst designed the new Avro Hamble Works and a garden city of 350 houses for employees, but after the hangars and only 24 houses had been built, wartime shortage of building materials halted the scheme. Very reluctantly the company was compelled to keep its main works in Manchester and to use Hamble only for erection and as an experimental establishment.

It was to Hamble therefore that their first twin-engined machine and the first to receive a type name, the Avro 523 Pike, was sent for erection and test. Designed by Roy Chadwick to RAF Types IV, VI and VII as a long-distance photo-reconnaissance fighter or short range day or night bomber, it was powered by two opposite-handed 160 hp Sunbeam engines driving pusher airscrews. A fine example of advanced thinking, the Pike was a large three-bay biplane equipped with horizontal-tier bomb-stowage (designed personally by A. V. Roe) and carrying the pilot just ahead of the mainplanes. Gunners' cockpits fore and aft were armed with Lewis guns on rotatable ring mountings. The divided undercarriage was sprung with larger editions of the famous Avro shock absorbers, and a large comma-type rudder was hinged to a fixed fin of low aspect ratio.

Although the Pike was apparently sent to Hamble some months earlier, the aircraft was erected over a twelve-day period ending on November 11, 1916. After initial tests, new wings were called for by the Admiralty and these arrived at Hamble on January 22, 1917. Performance on a mere 320 hp was said to be very good but the Pike appeared too late. Production contracts had already been awarded to Short Bros for a standard RNAS bomber, and the RFC was interested solely in the much larger Handley Page heavy bombers then under construction.

During test flying, the Pike was sent to the RNAS experimental establishment on the Isle of Grain for demonstration before Admiralty officials but during one flight the Pike was flown with the C.G. position too far aft and

The Avro 523A with two 150 hp Green engines and tractor airscrews, at Hamble 1917, with the Pike. (*Avro*)

was so tail heavy that F. P. Raynham dared not throttle back to attempt a landing. The situation was saved through the gallantry of R. H. Dobson (later Sir Roy Dobson), who climbed out of the rear cockpit and along the top of the fuselage to transfer his weight to the bow gunner's position. The danger of stalling was averted and a successful landing made. By the end of February 1917, the Pike was ready for delivery, though it was not actually flown to Eastchurch until March 24, 1917.

A second machine, the Avro 523A, built at Manchester and initially tested at Southport, was fitted with two 150 hp Green engines like its predecessor driving pusher airscrews and cooled by nose radiators on each nacelle. Available photographs suggest it was flown both with a single fin and triple fin arrangement. The latter had two Avro 504 style comma rudders outboard which was possibly an attempt to overcome reported stability problems. On completion of four weeks of extensive test flying the machine, which was allocated the RFC serial *A316*, was despatched from Southport

The Avro 523 Pike. (*J. M. Bruce/G. S. Leslie Collection*)

to Hamble on September 11, 1916. Its exposure to the elements at Southport necessitated thorough renovation during which process it was converted to tractor configuration with revised engine mounts and rear radiators and the two outboard fins were dispensed with. It flew for the first time in this form in February 1917. Later, after the completion of official tests both machines were returned to the manufacturers to enjoy extensive experimental careers and were still in commission at Hamble in 1918. Plans to produce Avro 523B and 523C variants with higher powered Sunbeam and Rolls-Royce engines were shelved, but the Admiralty ordered an improved version which appeared in 1917 as the Avro 529.

### SPECIFICATION AND DATA

*Manufacturers:*   A. V. Roe and Co Ltd, Park Works, Newton Heath, Manchester; and Hamble Aerodrome, near Southampon, Hants.

*Powerplants:*   (Avro 523) Two 160 hp Sunbeam
(Avro 523A) Two 150 hp Green

The Avro 523A *A316* on Southport Sands in August 1916 in its original form with pusher airscrews and triple rudders. (*RAF Museum*)

147

| *Dimensions:* | Span 60 ft 0 in   Length 39 ft 1 in |
| | Height 11 ft 8 in   Wing area 815 sq ft |
| *Weights:* | (Avro 523) Tare weight 4,000 lb   All-up weight 6,064 lb |
| *Performance:* | (Avro 523) Maximum speed 97 mph |
| | Climb to 5,000 ft 9 min 30 sec |
| | Endurance 7 hours |
| *Production:* | (Avro 523) One aircraft only, Works Order number believed to be 2230. Allocated the serial *N523* after delivery to the RNAS. |
| | (Avro 523A) Two aircraft ordered to contract 87/A/329 dated April 12, 1916, and serials *A316* and *A317* allocated. It is believed that only *A316* was built and that its Works Order was 2231. |

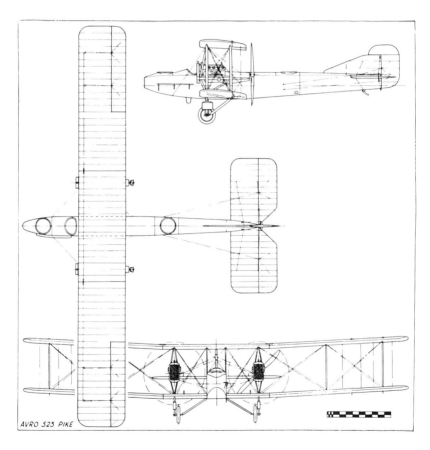

AVRO 523 PIKE

The Avro 527 with 150 hp Sunbeam engine. (*Imperial War Musuem photo Q.63792*)

# Avro 527

While the Avro 523 Pike was under construction in the Manchester Works, A. V. Roe and Co were also building a 'reconnaissance fighting biplane' for the Royal Flying Corps which had been designed in December 1915. It was essentially a modified Avro 504E fitted with a 150 hp Sunbeam engine, standard central skid and RNAS-style fin and rudder. The mainplanes were standard Avro 504K units of 36 ft span with which it was designated Avro 527, and a second version with a span of 42 ft was also considered under the designation Avro 527A. Armament consisted of a single Lewis gun mounted on a pillar in the rear cockpit.

The machine, which underwent trials at Farnborough in early 1916, was not a success, the rate of climb was poor and as on the Avro 519 the pilot's forward view was seriously obstructed this time by twin exhaust stacks in addition to the large centrally mounted radiator. There was also doubt as to the airframe's suitability for the relatively powerful 150 hp engine.

## SPECIFICATION AND DATA

*Manufacturers:*    A. V. Roe and Co Ltd, Park Works, Newton Heath, Manchester; and Hamble Aerodrome, near Southampton, Hants.

*Powerplant:*    (Avro 527 and 527A) One 150 hp Sunbeam

*Dimensions:*    (Avro 527) Span 36 ft 0 in (Avro 527A) Span 42 ft 0 in

*Production:*    (Avro 527) One aircraft only to Works Order 2100

The Avro 528 Silver King at Hamble. (*RAF Museum*)

# Avro 528 Silver King

Type number 528 was allocated to a derivative of the Avro 519 intended as a 'bomb dropper' for the Admiralty. Known as The Silver King, the machine was ordered in September 1915 with the intention of it being ready in time for Admiralty competitive trials which took place in March 1916. However not even the drawings were ready by that date and the machine was not completed until six months later.

The Avro 528 was finally despatched to Hamble from the Park Works at Manchester on September 9, 1916, but the need to correct manufacturing faults plus continual engine trouble resulted in it remaining in the workshops at Hamble until December 19, 1916.

The engine trouble persisted and the installation of a replacement engine obtained from Sunbeam failed to cure the problem. A variety of different propellers was also tried, apparently to no avail as before February 24,

The Type 528, clearly showing the large side radiators and the faired bomb racks on the lower mainplanes. (*RAF Museum*)

150

1917, the Admiralty advised the manufacturers, that they would not accept the machine 'under any circumstances'. Nevertheless they thought it suitable for experimental purposes. The Silver King was last heard of at Hamble in April 1917.

## SPECIFICATION AND DATA

*Manufacturers:*   A. V. Roe and Co Ltd, Park Works, Newton Heath, Manchester; and Hamble Aerodrome, near Southampton, Hants.

*Powerplant:*   One 250 hp Sunbeam

*Dimensions:*   Span (upper) 65 ft 0 in (lower) 55 ft 0 in
Length 33 ft 8 in
All-up weight 5,509 lb

*Production:*   One aircraft only to Works Order 2350

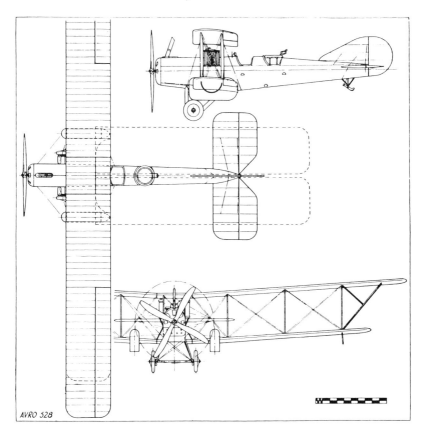

AVRO 528

3694, the sole Avro 529, at Hamble in April 1917.

# Avro 529

In 1916 the Admiralty ordered two enlarged versions of the Pike for long-range bombing duties. Unnamed and known only as the Avro 529 and 529A, they had three-bay folding wings rigged without dihedral, and although closely resembling the Pike were distinguishable from it by the rudder shape. That of the Pike was flat topped with a straight bottom edge to the balance portion, but those of the Avro 529s were curved with a semi-circular balance area.

Whereas the first aircraft was built wholly in Manchester and assembled at Hamble, the second was sent there in unfinished state to make way for increased Avro 504K production at Manchester. The Avro 529, first flown in March 1917, was powered by uncowled 190 hp Rolls-Royce Falcons mounted at mid-gap and driving opposite handed airscrews. The Avro 529A, flown at Hamble in the following October, had two 230 hp Galloway-built B.H.P. engines which were fully cowled and housed in nacelles on the lower mainplane. Radically different installations called for two distinct types of fuel systems and in the Avro 529 petrol was carried in a 140 gallon tank in the centre fuselage. On the Avro 529A each nacelle carried its own 50 gallon supply with small wind-driven pumps to raise the fuel to a 10 gallon gravity tank above the engine.

3695, the Avro 529A, identified by low set nacelles.

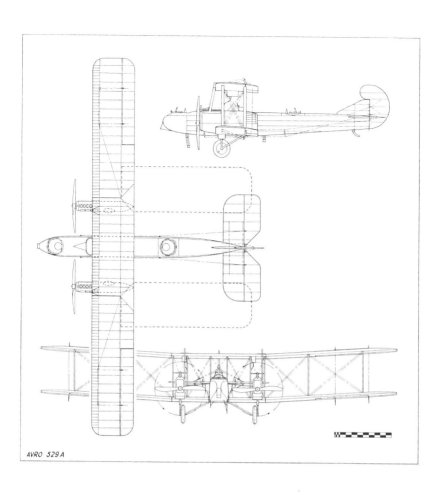

AVRO 529A

The Avro 529A *3695* at Hamble. (*Courtesy R. C. B. Ashworth*)

153

Lewis guns were mounted on Scarff rings over front and rear cockpits and the rear gunner was provided with emergency dual control. The front gunner also acted as bomb aimer and steered the pilot on to target with the aid of a Gosport speaking tube. On the 529A, which carried twenty 50 lb bombs stowed nose upwards inside the fuselage between the spars of the lower wing, he was able to use a projecting prone position in the cockpit floor.

Apart from poor elevator control (a shortcoming of both types), the performance of the Avro 529A was very good on such low power, asymmetrical flying being particularly easy. Nevertheless no production contract materialised and only the prototypes were built.

Both machines were tested at the Aeroplane Experimental Station, Martlesham Heath. The Avro 529A *3695* arrived there for its trials on October 31, 1917, but during the course of these the rudder gave way in the air on November 11, 1917, and the machine crashed. Interestingly, the same problem had occurred, without catastrophe, to the Avro 529 during initial tests in March 1917 and the rudder was strengthened as a result. This first machine was last heard of on January 19, 1918, when it was flown in comparative trials at Martlesham with the Blackburn Kangaroo prototype *B9970*, a machine which was both larger and more powerful than the Avro 529.

## SPECIFICATION AND DATA

*Manufacturers:*   A. V. Roe and Co Ltd, Park Works, Newton Heath, Manchester; and Hamble Aerodrome, near Southampton, Hants.

*Powerplants:*   (Avro 529 )   Two 190 hp Rolls-Royce Falcon
(Avro 529A)   Two 230 hp B.H.P. (Galloway-built)

*Dimensions, Weights and Performances:*

|  | Avro 529 | Avro 529A |
| --- | --- | --- |
| Span | 63 ft 0 in | 64 ft 1 in |
| Length | 39 ft 8 in | 39 ft 8 in |
| Height | 13 ft 0 in | 13 ft 0 in |
| Wing area | 922½ sq ft | 910 sq ft |
| Tare weight | 4,736 lb | 4,361 lb |
| All-up weight | 6,309 lb | 7,135 lb |
| Maximum speed | 95 mph | 116 mph |
| Climb to 5,000 ft | — | 7 min 0 sec |
| Climb to 6,500 ft | 11 min 25 sec | 9 min 50 sec |
| Ceiling | 13,500 ft | 17,500 ft |
| Endurance | 5 hours | 5 hours 15 min |

*Production:*   Prototypes only under Contract C.P.122495/16 with RFC serials *3694* (Avro 529) and *3695* (Avro 529A)

The first Type 530 in early form with small fin and rudder and large centre-section fairing. (*RAF Museum*)

# Avro 530

The Avro 530, first flown in July 1917, was a two-seat fighter which failed to secure a production contract in the face of competition from the celebrated Bristol Fighter because of non-availability of engines. The 300 hp water-cooled Hispano-Suiza was not obtainable when required and the machine flew with a 200 hp Hispano-Suiza. Even on the lower power the performance of the Avro 530 rivalled that of the Bristol and it might still have become one of the famous fighters of the First World War had not almost all 200 hp Hispano-Suiza engines been reserved for the S.E.5A.

Built at Manchester and erected and flown at Hamble, the Avro 530 was an unusually clean two-bay biplane. Its deep fuselage was of wire-braced, box-girder construction with the fabric covering stretched over formers to give a more streamlined shape. The engine mounting consisted of strutted duralumin girders. The pilot occupied the front cockpit with a single Vickers gun mounted in a large plywood fairing on top of the fuselage ahead of him. This fairing obstructed the pilot's forward view and the machine was later rebuilt with new top decking and much smaller fairing. In this form the top wing was on a level with the pilot's eyes, ensuring adequate view in all upward and forward directions while a rear gunner armed with a single Lewis gun on a Scarff mounting commanded the downward and rearward view.

The fabric-covered, wooden mainplanes were of RAF 14 section and engine cooling was by a large frontal radiator. Though the aircraft was initially flown without it, the lines of the short, blunt nose were later improved by fitting a hollow, open-fronted metal spinner. The famous Avro skid-type undercarriage gave place to a new unit comprising two narrow Vs, braced by an internal V-strut, later faired with metal sheeting to reduce drag. Landing speed was reduced by trailing-edge flaps actuated by a

The second prototype Avro 530 with 200 hp Sunbeam Arab, enlarged fin and flapless mainplanes. (*Courtesy R. C. B. Ashworth*)

handwheel in the pilot's cockpit. They were fitted to both upper and lower mainplanes between the inboard ends of the ailerons and the fuselage. Trials proved that the original small fin and rudder were inadequate and a number of different tail units were tested before the final balanced rudder arrangement was adopted.

In an attempt to solve the engine supply problem, the second prototype Avro 530 was completed with a 200 hp Sunbeam Arab engine. An unfaired, wide angle V undercarriage was fitted; there was no spinner; the tail fin was larger and more gracefully curved; and new RAF 15 section mainplanes were fitted. These were without flaps but had long-span ailerons and metal cuffs to fair the ends of the interplane struts into the wing.

In view of its deep and capacious fuselage, the Avro 530 was offered in 1920 as a high-speed touring aeroplane with comfortable tandem cockpits above a large baggage compartment. There is no evidence that this modification took place and the machine did not receive a civil registration.

The Hispano-Suiza engined Type 530 in its final form with spinner, faired undercarriage, enlarged fin and small centre-section fairing.

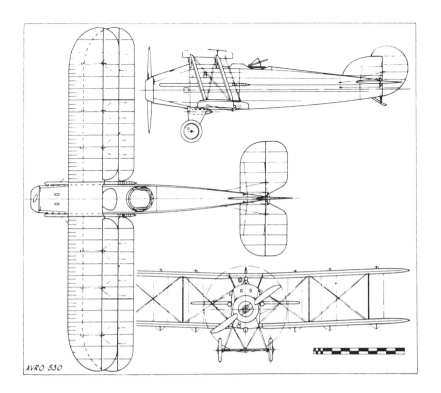

AVRO 530

## SPECIFICATION AND DATA

*Manufacturers:*  A. V. Roe and Co Ltd, Park Works, Newton Heath, Manchester; and Hamble Aerodrome, near Southampton, Hants.

*Powerplants:*  One 200 hp Hispano-Suiza (first prototype)
One 200 hp Sunbeam Arab (second prototype)

*Dimensions:*  Span 36 ft 0 in    Length 28 ft 6 in
Height 9 ft 7 in    Wing area $325\frac{1}{2}$ sq ft

*Weights:*  Tare weight 1,695 lb (1,760 lb)
All-up weight 2,680 lb (2,500 lb)

*Performance:*  Maximum speed 114 mph (118 mph)
Cruising speed 95 mph (102 mph)
Climb to 5,000 ft 6 min 30 sec (5 min 30 sec)
Ceiling 18,000 ft    Endurance 4 hours

*Production:*  Two prototypes only; Contract A.S.425/17 let on 15.5.17 and serials *B3952* and *B3953* were allocated. Two further serials, *B9431* and *B9432*, were allocated against the same contract on 26.7.17. As no identity appeared on either machine, which if any serials were actually used is not known.

*Note:* Estimated figures for proposed civil version are given in parentheses.

The Avro 531 Spider single-seat fighter. (*Avro*)

# Avro 531 Spider

First flown at Hamble in April 1918, the Spider was an unsponsored private venture single-seat fighter in which many Avro 504K components were used for speed of manufacture. To this end a shortened rear fuselage of conventional construction with spruce longerons was married to a standard Avro 504K front fuselage and the engine was a 'borrowed' 110 hp Le Rhône. There seems little doubt that the Avro company hoped that the Spider would replace the single-seat Avro 504K night fighter in the Home Defence Squadrons. To simplify rigging (a time consuming operation not acceptable to squadrons in the field) all flying and landing wires were replaced by very rigid welded steel Warren girder interplane bracing. This comprised six faired steel tubes arranged in three inverted triangles on each side, anchored to the main spars of the upper mainplane and to the front spar of the lower. Ailerons were fitted only to the upper wing, the lower being shorter and with a chord of only 2 ft 6 in.

The simple steel V-strut undercarriage was reminiscent of the second Avro 530 and the attempt made in the earlier design to improve substantially the pilot's field of vision was carried a stage further in the Spider by siting the cockpit under a circular aperture in the centre section. This was mounted close to the fuselage so that the pilot's head protruded above it. Armament consisted of a single synchronised Vickers gun on top of the fuselage and slightly to starboard of centre.

The little fighter was a delight to handle, with powerful and well harmonised controls which made it extremely manoeuvrable, and more than a match for many of its contemporaries. Performance was further enhanced by fitting a 130 hp Clerget and drawings were made for the installation of a 150 hp Bentley B.R.1 rotary or a 170 hp A.B.C. Wasp I radial. Well-known pilots were invited to fly it in off duty hours and to give their opinions, for which purpose it was at the School of Special Flying, Gosport, from April

27 to May 18, 1918, and again on July 13. In this way the Spider became such a topic of conversation that the Air Ministry could not fail to take note of it. Nevertheless it was not ordered into production because the Sopwith Snipe had already been standardised as the RAF's next single-seat fighter. The Spider was therefore used for experimental work which included benzole fuel tests at Alexandra Park in August, 1919.

A considerably modified version of the Spider was allotted type number Avro 531A. This had conventional two-bay, wire-braced mainplanes rigged with a considerable stagger and using 504K-type interplane struts. With

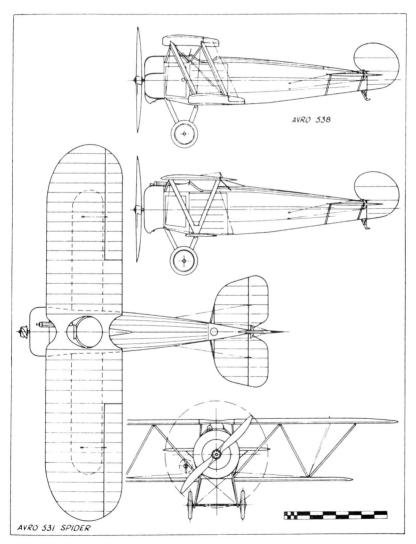

AVRO 538

AVRO 531 SPIDER

The Spider at The School of Special Flying, Gosport in 1918. (*Courtesy Bruce Robertson*)

the 130 hp Clerget rotary the Avro 531A had a performance similar to that of the Spider. While a Type 531A was reported to be under construction in early 1919, there is no means of proving that it ever existed as such and it is probable that the machine donated its fuselage, undercarriage and tail unit to the civil Avro 538, and first flew in this form.

The Avro 538 emerged from the flight shed at Alexandra Park, Manchester, in May 1919 registered *K-132*, a temporary civil marking later changed to *G-EACR*. As far as is known these letters were never carried and the machine's main adornment was the word AVRO in the usual enormous black letters. Although powered by a 150 hp Bentley B.R.1 and intended as a racer, a main spar defect limited the machine's activities to straight

The Avro 538 communications machine of the Avro Transport Company, at Birkdale Sands, Southport, 1919.

160

and level flight, and a notice to this effect was displayed in the cockpit. Bearing fleet number 7, the Avro 538 was used solely by the Avro Transport Company's chief engineer J. C. C. Taylor, who flew it around the joyriding sites in order to sign out the Avro 504Ks.

## SPECIFICATION AND DATA

*Manufacturers:*   A. V. Roe and Co Ltd, Park Works, Newton Heath, Manchester; and Hamble Aerodrome, near Southampton, Hants.

*Powerplants:*   (Avro 531 ) One 110 hp Le Rhône
                ) One 130 hp Clerget
            (Avro 531A) One 130 hp Clerget
            (Avro 538 ) One 150 hp Bentley B.R.1

*Dimensions, Weights and Performances:*

|  | Avro 531 Spider | | Avro 531A | Avro 538 |
|---|---|---|---|---|
|  | Clerget | *Bentley | Clerget | Bentley |
| Span, upper | 28 ft 6 in | 28 ft 6 in | 28 ft 0 in | 28 ft 0 in |
| Span, lower | 21 ft 6 in | 21 ft 6 in | 27 ft 0 in | 28 ft 0 in |
| Length | 20 ft 6 in | 20 ft 6 in | 20 ft 6 in | 20 ft 6 in |
| Height | 7 ft 10 in | 7 ft 10 in | 8 ft 6 in | 8 ft 6 in |
| Wing area | 189 sq ft | 189 sq ft | — | 210 sq ft |
| Tare weight | 963 lb | 1,148 lb | 960 lb | 975 lb |
| All-up weight | 1,517 lb | 1,734 lb | 1,514 lb | 1,400 lb |
| Maximum speed | 120 mph | 124 mph | 120 mph | 125 mph** |
| Climb to 3,500 ft | — | 2 min 12 sec | — | — |
| Climb to 5,000 ft | 4 min | — | 4 min | 4 min |
| Climb to 10,000 ft | — | — | — | 10 min |
| Ceiling | 19,000 ft | — | 19,000 ft | — |
| Endurance/Range | — | 2½ hours | 3 hours | 320 miles |

*Estimated figures.    **Cruising speed 108 mph

*Production:* (Avro 531) One prototype only
            (Avro 538) One aircraft only, *K-132/G-EACR*, c/n 538/1, registered to A. V. Roe and Co Ltd 25.5.19, s.o.r. 9.20

*F3492*, the Siddeley Puma engined Avro 533 Manchester Mk.II.

# Avro 533 Manchester

The Manchester of 1918, final variation on the Pike/Avro 529 theme, was a three-seat, twin-engined bomber or photographic reconnaissance fighter designed to Air Ministry requirements round two of the new 320 hp A.B.C. Dragonfly I seven-cylinder radial engines. Unlike its forebears the Manchester was constructed entirely at Hamble and its deeper, more shapely fuselage giving improved crew accommodation was but one of many refinements, others including a graceful (almost de Havilland-shaped) rudder, and ailerons balanced by means of 'park bench' auxiliary aerofoils.

Erection of the first Manchester was completed by October 1918 after which it was dismantled for covering, during which the opportunity was taken to fit two 300 hp Siddeley Puma high-compression, water-cooled engines. This was to prevent interruption of flight tests by the non-delivery of the Dragonfly engines which had run into a number of teething troubles. The Pumas arrived at Hamble in November, and thus powered, the aircraft was known as the Avro 533A Manchester Mk.II. First flights took place early in December 1918 and the Mk.II aircraft *F3492* consequently had an earlier serial than the Mk.I which followed. On December 20 *F3492* went to No.186 Development Squadron, Gosport, where it remained until at least January 9, 1919, before proceeding to Martlesham in the following March. Official trials lasted until September 1919 when *F3492* returned to Hamble to be fitted with Napier Lions, a project which did not materialise.

Delivery of the Dragonfly engines in December 1918 enabled the second airframe, *F3493*, to be completed as the Manchester Mk.I. After prolonged manufacturer's tests it was flown from Hamble to Martlesham for official trials in October 1919, the journey via Winchester, Basingstoke, London and Chelmsford occupying 90 minutes.

Apart from the engines and the revised nacelle shape of the Mk.I which decreased the effective area of the lower wing by 4 sq ft, the two marks of

Manchester differed only in their tail units. Both had balanced rudders but all tail surface areas were greater in the Mk.I which had taller vertical surfaces and an unbalanced elevator. That of the Mk.II was horn-balanced.

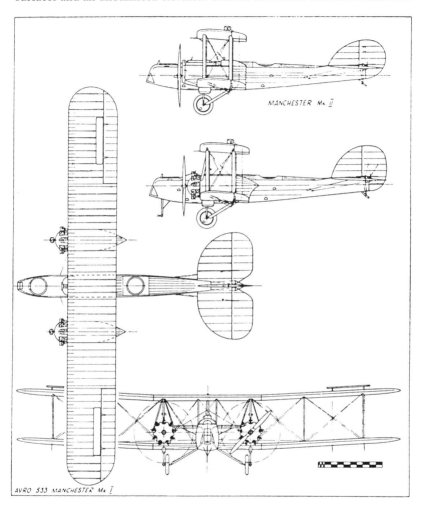

MANCHESTER Mk. II

AVRO 533 MANCHESTER Mk I

The performance of both marks was quite remarkable on comparatively low power and despite their size could be looped and spun, but the need for a bomber of this type disappeared when the war ended. A third airframe, intended as the Manchester III with two 400 hp Liberty engines, was completed but the engines were never fitted. The jigs were then dismantled and A. V. Roe's war effort was at an end.

*F3493*, the A.B.C. Dragonfly powered Avro 533 Manchester Mk.I.

## SPECIFICATION AND DATA

*Manufacturers:*  A. V. Roe and Co Ltd, Hamble Aerodrome, near South-ampton, Hants.

*Powerplants:*   (Mk.I)    Two 320 hp A.B.C. Dragonfly I
(Mk.II)   Two 300 hp Siddeley Puma high-compression
(Mk.III)  Two 400 hp Liberty 12

*Dimensions:*   Span 60 ft 0 in   Length 37 ft 0 in   Height 12 ft 6 in
Wing area (Mk.I) 813 sq ft (Mk.II) 817 sq ft

*Weights:*     (Mk.I )   Tare weight 4,887 lb   All-up weight 7,390 lb
(Mk.II)   Tare weight 4,574 lb   All-up weight 7,158 lb

*Performance:*  (Mk.I )   Maximum speed 112 mph
Climb to 10,000 ft, 14 min 20 sec
Ceiling 19,000 ft.   Endurance $5\frac{3}{4}$ hours
(Mk.II)   Maximum speed 119 mph
Climb to 10,000 ft, 16 min 30 sec
Ceiling 17,000 ft   Endurance $3\frac{3}{4}$ hours

*Production:*   *F3492* (Manchester Mk.II);
*F3493* (Manchester Mk.I);
*F3494* (Manchester Mk.III) airframe only

164

The first, short-lived, Avro 534 Baby prototype.

# Avro 534 Baby

After the Armistice A. V. Roe was impatient to return to low-powered flying and build a light aircraft of 600 lb all-up weight with an engine of 20–30 hp which could disport itself within the confines of any large field. Chief designer Roy Chadwick favoured an aeroplane with a heavier wing loading, an engine of 40–50 hp, and cross-country capability. Final design was dictated by engine availability, the only suitable one in existence being A. V. Roe's 35 hp Green which had been preserved by Mr Fred May of the Green Engine Co Ltd. It is said that this engine was fitted originally to the first Avro Type D biplane for Pixton's flight to Brighton on May 6, 1911.

The little Avro 534 was designed round this veteran powerplant and although at first named the 'Popular', soon acquired the type name Baby. The Green Engine Co completely modernised the engine and fitted aluminium pistons, new type camshaft, valve gear and oil pressure regulator. Cooling was by traditional nose radiator. The Baby was an equal-span, single bay biplane of wire-braced, fabric-covered wooden construction with ailerons on all four wings and the balance area of the famous Avro comma rudder was increased slightly to make it an accurate circle. About a dozen of these machines were built singly at Hamble and eight of them helped to lay sure foundations for the light aeroplane movement which came seven years later. Their Green engines, even lighter than the remodelled original, were specially built by Peter Brotherhood Ltd of Peterborough from a complete set of manufacturing drawings found in the Green Engine Co's archives.

The prototype Baby emerged on April 30, 1919, and it is said that its total flying life of 2 minutes ended when H. A. Hamersley spun into the Hamble foreshore from 300 ft when the ignition switches were cut inadvertently. The same pilot won the handicap section of the Aerial Derby at Hendon on June 21, 1919, at an average speed of 70·3 mph in *K-131*, usually regarded as the first Avro Baby. It certainly had the same engine but a number of minor differences identify it as actually the second machine of the type, first flown at Hamble on May 10, 1919. As if to emphasise that the Baby was no low-powered freak, Hamersley won the Victory Trophy Race at Hendon at 77 mph in July and flew nonstop from Hounslow Heath to Brussels in 2 hours 50 minutes in August, afterwards flying on to the First Air Traffic Exhibition at Amsterdam. The machine was dazzle painted and carried the words 'Avro Baby' in large white letters. The original marking *K-131* remained, but for the overseas flight the permanent registration *G-EACQ* was painted in white on the sloping decking.

On its return the elevator control system was modified so that cables previously carried within the fuselage now ran externally from double-ended cranks mounted on a cross shaft behind the pilot. The Baby then gave aerobatic displays along the South Coast to publicise the joyriding Avro 504Ks. Chadwick, who had just been taught to fly by Hamersley, frequently went cross-country in it but when flying low on January 13, 1920, an abnormal bump deposited the aircraft on the ground in the garden of the Rev Everard Verdon Roe's Hamble Vicarage. Chadwick was gravely injured and eye-witness acounts suggest that the Baby was a complete wreck and it is probable that the rebuilt aircraft incorporated only the engine and primary structure of the earlier machine. Registration *G-EACQ* was retained and many detail improvements were made. These included a raised tailplane; tapered ailerons; a slightly taller, oval shaped rudder; a new oil tank without projecting filler cap; more streamlined interplane struts and the pitot head repositioned on the top wing. H. J. 'Bert' Hinkler bought it in April 1920 and on May 31 made a sensational 650 mile nonstop flight from Croydon to Turin in 9½ hours for which he was later awarded the Britannia Trophy. He went on to Rome and flew back in easy stages, reaching Hamble on

Hinkler's famous Turin flight Baby *G-EACQ* at Hamilton, Victoria as *VH-UCQ* in 1936.

166

Avro 534A Water Baby *G-EAPS* with revised vertical tail surfaces, ready for launching at Hamble, in November 1919.

June 10. The machine was then exhibited at the Olympia Aero Show and on July 24 came second in the Aerial Derby Handicap at Hendon, piloted by the owner.

The Avro 534A Water Baby, a second machine built in October 1919, was a twin-float seaplane similar to the rebuilt prototype. It had an unbalanced rudder hinged to a large fin, and a slight reduction in lower mainplane span which imparted a slant to the interplane struts. Flown from Southampton Water, the Water Baby performed very creditably despite water soakage.

Designated Avro 534B by virtue of its plywood covered fuselage and slightly shortened bottom wing, the third Baby *G-EAUG* reverted to the perfectly circular rudder. Piloted by Hamersley it just beat Hinkler to win the 1920 Aerial Derby Handicap but was destroyed soon afterwards with serious injuries to Avro pilot D. G. Westgarth-Heslam. The control column universal joint failed during a forced landing with choked carburettor while he was en route to Martlesham to fly the Avro 547A in the Air Ministry Commercial Aeroplane Competition.

The next machine, produced in July 1920, was the Avro 543 Baby *G-EAUM* two-seater which housed pilot and passenger in an enlarged single cockpit. It was otherwise a standard Baby with the front fuselage lengthened by 2 ft 6 in and on test carried Hinkler and Chadwick to 11,000 ft. Flown by Capt T. Tulley, it averaged 73·67 mph in the 1921 Aerial Derby but was forced down at Brooklands and fared no better in the 1922 and 1923 King's Cup Races. In 1926 *'UM* went to Shoreham under the joint ownership of L. E. R. Bellairs and F. G. Miles who removed the ancient Green and attendant plumbing in favour of a 60 hp A.D.C. Cirrus I air-cooled engine, gravity fed from a large centre-section tank. A later owner R. A. Whitehead overturned it in a forced landing at Bury St Edmunds during the 1928 King's Cup Race, after which it was bought by

167

H. H. Leech for the 1929 race. He sold it to Roper Brown at Southend in 1932. A projected Cirrus I conversion of a single-seat Baby as the Avro 534G did not materialise.

All later Babies were equally remarkable. Avro 534C *G-EAXL* had the span of both wings further reduced for the Aerial Derby of July 16, 1921, but Hinkler forced landed at Sidcup, Kent. During an air test at Hamble on September 6, 1922 (eve of the first King's Cup Race), the engine cut at low altitude and Hinkler got a ducking when '*XL* fell into Southampton Water. The special Avro 534D Baby *G-EAYM* which first flew at Hamble

The two-seat Avro 543 Baby *G-EAUM* at Hamble, July 1920, in its initial form with 35 hp Green engine.

*G-EAUM* at Shoreham in 1926 with 60 hp A.D.C. Cirrus I air-cooled engine.

The clipped wing Avro 534C racer at Hamble, June 1921.

on September 14, 1921, had all-steel engine bearers, oversize radiator, extra cowling louvres, slightly taller undercarriage, and a luggage locker behind the pilot's seat. It was built to the order of Col E. Villiers, an ex-RAF pilot who flew it at Dum Dum, Calcutta, as a means of inspecting his business interests. This Baby was still flying in 1928.

Projected variants with folding wings (Avro 534E) and 100 hp Bristol Lucifer (Avro 534F) were not built, but in accordance with the Soviet practice of buying single examples of outstanding aircraft, standard Avro 534 single-seater *G-EBDA* was collected from Hamble by Russian pilot Gwaiter in May 1922. His delivery flight from London to Moscow was the first ever made between these capitals. Last of the breed to fly was the Avro 554 Antarctic Baby, a photographic survey development of the projected Le Rhône engined Avro 544 Baby two-seater. Identified by rounded wingtips it was built in 1921 for the Shackleton-Rowett South Polar Expedition. Limited shipboard stowage space called for swift dismantling and erection by gloved hands without rigging problems. Tubular steel struts therefore replaced flying wires, N-type interplane struts were used, and all bolts were extra large. An 80 hp Le Rhône rotary completely altered the shape of the nose and the tailplane was raised above the fuselage and adjustable for incidence on the ground. After trials on Southampton Water by Maj C. R. Carr, Shackleton's pilot, the Avro 554 was embarked in the *Quest* at Tower Bridge and left for the far south. Engine trouble in the *Quest* compelled Shackleton to proceed direct to Rio de Janeiro, so that he was unable to collect parts of the aircraft left at Cape Town by an earlier vessel, or to use the 554 on the expedition. The missing components were collected on the return journey and the complete aeroplane arrived back in the *Quest* on September 16, 1922.

In 1923 the Antarctic Baby was purchased by Capt R. S. Grandy on behalf of Bowring Bros Ltd of St John's and registered *G-EBFE* for test flying on wheels at Hamble. Fitted with skis, it was shipped to Newfoundland for seal spotting and occupied a platform on the stern of Bowring's sealer

169

*Neptune*. A hostile crew refused to allow it to fly but in 1924 Grandy took off from an icefloe alongside the *Eagle* and spotted a herd of 125,000 seals. The Baby was flown for three more seasons by C. S. 'Jack' Caldwell and retired in favour of an Avro Avian in 1927.

After the 1920 Aerial Derby Hinkler decided to ship the Baby *G-EACQ* to Australia and had the engine bay modified so that he could do single handed overhauls in the outback and even remove cylinders with the engine in situ. The machine was first exhibited at the Royal Sydney Easter Show and on April 11, 1921, Hinkler made the now historic 800 mile nonstop flight from Sydney to his native Bundaberg where he landed in the main street and taxied up to his garden gate. The Baby had now been registered *G-AUCQ* and during the return flight on April 27, overturned on a remote beach in tropical rain. When righted, it was towed 16 miles to Newcastle by horse team and shipped to Sydney where it was repaired and sold to H. E. Broadsmith who designed and built a set of floats to the order of a film company. Resulting from several flights from the waters of Botany Bay in 1922, he advised the company that the Baby would be unsuitable for operation in New Guinea and *'CQ* later reverted to a wheeled undercarriage with the front legs farther aft as on Villers' Avro 534D. After a period as an attraction at a Queensland garage, it passed to W. E. Hart and later to F. Fitzalan of Melbourne, to whom it was re-registered *VH-UCQ* in 1928. As late as December 1936 a flight of 200 miles from Melbourne to Hamilton, Victoria, was made by final owner J. J. Smith. Though it was withdrawn from use in 1937, J. J. Smith kept the Baby in store until he presented it to the Queensland Museum, Brisbane, where it was placed on display beside Hinkler's Avro Avian *G-EBOV* in 1972 painted as *G-EACQ*.

One Baby was used by H. G. Leigh for experiments with narrow-chord

H. J. Hinkler and H. G. Leigh at Hamble in December 1920 with the experimental 'Venetian blind' wing Baby.

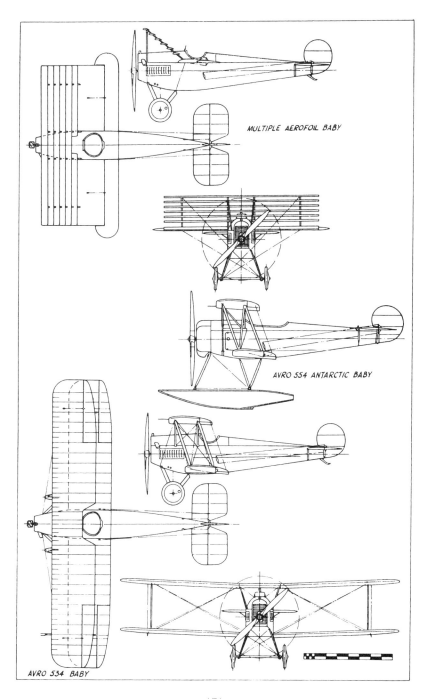

MULTIPLE AEROFOIL BABY

AVRO 554 ANTARCTIC BABY

AVRO 534 BABY

171

The tropicalised Avro 534D Baby built for India.

Maj C. R. Carr taxying the Avro 554 Antarctic Baby on Southampton Water in 1921.

multiple aerofoils at Hamble in December 1920, but a number of unused airframes remained in store until F. G. Miles bought them early in 1929. His prototype Southern Martlet *G-AAII*, first flown at Shoreham in August that year, was not (as is often supposed) a conversion of one of these. It resembled the Baby externally and used most of its metal fittings, but the timber work was completely new and the engine mounting, undercarriage and tail unit were of entirely new design.

# SPECIFICATION AND DATA

*Manufacturers:*    A. V. Roe and Co Ltd, Hamble Aerodrome, near Southampton, Hants

*Powerplants:*    (Avro 534 and 543)    One 35 hp Green
               (Avro 543)            One 60 hp A.D.C. Cirrus I
               (Avro 554)            One 80 hp Le Rhône

*Dimensions, Weights and Performance:*

|  | Avro 534 | Avro 534C | Avro 534D | Avro 543 | Avro 554 |
|---|---|---|---|---|---|
| Span (upper) | 25 ft 0 in | 20 ft 0 in | 25 ft 0 in | 25 ft 0 in | 26 ft 3 in |
| Span (lower) | 25 ft 0 in | 18 ft 0 in | 23 ft 0 in | 23 ft 0 in | 24 ft 0 in |
| Length | 17 ft 6 in | 17 ft 6 in | 17 ft 6 in | 20 ft 0 in | 22 ft 5 in |
| Height | 7 ft 6 in | 7 ft 6 in | 7 ft 6 in | 7 ft 6 in | 10 ft 3 in |
| Wing area | 180 sq ft | — | 176·5 sq ft | 176·5 sq ft | 184·5 sq ft |
| Tare weight | 625 lb* | — | 656 lb | 630 lb | 980 lb |
| All-up weight | 857 lb | — | 950 lb | 970 lb | 1,569 lb |
| Maximum speed | 78 mph | — | — | 82 mph** | 90 mph |
| Cruising speed | 70 mph | — | — | 70 mph | 70 mph |
| Initial climb | 500 ft/min | — | — | 450 ft/min | 330 ft/min |
| Range | 240 miles | — | 370 miles | 225 miles | 190 miles |

*The Leigh multiple aerofoil Baby 675 lb and 921 lb
**98 mph with A.D.C. Cirrus I engine.

*Production:*

| Constructor's No. and Registration | | Registered | Details |
|---|---|---|---|
| — | — | — | 534 Prototype; crashed at Hamble 30.4.19 |
| 534/1 | K-131 | 29.5.19 | Avro 534: later G-EACQ, first flown 16.5.19; 4.20 H. J. Hinkler; to Australia 4.21 as G-AUCQ; registered VH-UCQ 1928, struck off register (s.o.r.) 1937, exhibited in Queensland Museum, Brisbane, from 1972 |
| 534/2 | G-EAPS | 21.11.19 | Avro 534A: crashed 7.9.21 |
| 534B/1 | G-EAUG | 9.7.20 | Avro 534B: crashed at Bentley, Suffolk, while en route from Hamble to Martlesham Heath 4.8.20. wreck returned to Hamble by rail the following day. |
| 543/1 | G-EAUM | 12.7.20 | Avro 543; C of A 3.8.23, c/n amended to 5062 at engine change 1926; 11.27 L. E. R. Bellairs and F. G. Miles; 7.28 R. A. Whitehead; 9.28 H. H. Leech; 9.29 H. R. A. Edwards; 9.32 Roper Brown, Southend, sold to a Cambridge Undergraduate after C of A expiry in 1934 and flown to Cambridge on one-flight only permit; s.o.r. 12.34 |
| 534C/1 | G-EAXL | 27.6.21 | Avro 534C; crashed in Southampton Water 6.9.22 |
| 5049 | G-EAYM | 17.9.21 | Avro 534D; first flown 14.9.21, withdrawn from use at Calcutta in 1929 |
| 5062 | G-EBDA | 28.4.22 | Avro 534; sold in Russia 13.6.22 |
| 5040 | nil | — | Avro 554; built 1921; registered to the Aerial Survey Co, Newfoundland 1.2.23 as G-EBFE, to Newfoundland 1923, scrapped there 1927 |

The prototype Avro 536 *K-114/G-EACC* at Hamble in May 1919 in its original form without dorsal fin.

# Avro 536

Reference has been made in previous chapters to a unique batch of civil aircraft built in the Hamble works between April and November 1919. To satisfy the enormous demand for pleasure flights, the Avro Transport Company simply had to provide more seats and quickly. The problem was solved by giving some of these Hamble 504K variants a nine-inch increase in width to enable four passengers to sit in side by side pairs in the rear cockpit. Each occupant had his own individual windscreen, the rear windscreens being fixed to a strip of decking hinged to the starboard top longeron for ease of entry. In this form, as the Avro 536, the machine was a short-range five-seater and (as in the case of Avro 504Ls from the same production batch), extra take-off power at the higher all-up weight was given by a 150 hp Bentley B.R.1.

The Avro 536 was easily distinguishable from the 504K since the extra nine inches of width resulted in an obvious difference in the spacing of the centre section struts. Having a tricolour rudder, but no other markings apart from AVRO in large white letters, the prototype first flew at Hamble in April 1919, one of the first passengers being the Lord Chancellor who flew in it with H. A Hamersley on the 25th of that month. Seven production 536s which followed plunged immediately into the fray at southern joyriding sites: *K-104* and *K-105* at Hounslow Heath; *K-116* and *K-137* at Southsea; *K-161* at Weston-super-Mare; and *K-166* at Margate. *K-165* is believed to be that sent to the First Air Traffic Exhibition at Amsterdam. A batch of 12 was also put in hand at Manchester but only seven of these were certificated in time to earn money in 1919. Whereas the constructor's numbers of the Hamble batch were prefixed A.T.C. (Avro Transport Company), those built in Manchester were initialled B for Blackpool where three pilots carried 500 passengers in 536s on the day of their introduction.

All Avro 536s had the 504L-type fin to offset the torque of the powerful Bentley rotary except the first three production aircraft, two of which were

174

involved in serious accidents. Capt H. R. Hastings was killed when *K-105* stalled on approaching Sandhurst at the end of a charter flight from Hounslow on August 6, 1919; and Capt E. A. Sullock, on direct track from Hounslow to Southend with two passengers on September 9, suffered engine failure over Rotherhithe and put *K-104* down in Southwark Park where it broke its back. A third Avro pilot, Brig-Gen C. F. Lee CMG, who had demonstrated the 504J *C4312* at Washington in 1917, was killed when the fin-equipped *K-161* stalled when coming in to land on Weston-super-Mare sands in the same month.

Unlike other Avro 536s, the prototype boasted a large aerofoil-shaped centre-section fuel tank and after a few trial flights at Hamble, was fitted with floats and extended fin to become the sole 536 seaplane. It retained the tri-colour rudder and on July 2, 1919, began a joyriding season in the Isle of Wight as *K-114*. The pilot was Capt F. Warren Merriam who flew A. V. Roe daily to and from Hamble while he was on holiday in the island and, assisted by a 504L, completed a two months' lucrative season at Ryde, Sandown, Shanklin and Ventnor. The last two Hamble-built 536s were special aircraft; *K-139/G-EADV* was a two-seater with large fuselage fuel tank for experimental work or long-distance competition flying, and the other (23rd and last machine on the mixed production line) was converted into a cabin type known as the Avro 546 for three passengers and pilot. Main differences between this aircraft and the contemporary Avro 504M lay in the widened fuselage, open pilot's cockpit, squarish windows below the top longeron and the Bentley B.R.1 engine. Registered *G-EAOM*, the Avro 546 saw little service and only made a few flights at Hamble and West Blatchington Farm, Brighton, early in 1919–20.

When the Avro Transport Company ceased operations a few of its former pilots hired 536s and carried on in 1920 but all eventually returned to Alexandra Park for storage. Four from the tail end of the production line (*G-EAKM–'KP*), completed too late to be used commercially, were also

The prototype Avro 536 joyriding at Sandown in seaplane form in July 1919, showing its unique aerofoil-shaped centre-section tank.

*K-137/G-EADC*, a standard Avro Transport Company Avro 536 at Southsea in 1919. (*C. A. Nepean Bishop*)

The unmarked Avro 546 cabin machine, actually *G-EAOM*, at Hamble in December 1919.

stored. In 1923 F. J. V. Holmes bought '*KN* for use by Berkshire Aviation Tours Ltd and in 1925 '*KJ*, '*KM* and '*KP* were acquired by Surrey Flying Services Ltd to take over joyriding from their aged 504Ks.

Bentley rotaries were no longer in service in 1925 and the Surrey Avro 536s were fitted with Clergets. With reduced fuel loads they were very economical indeed, carrying pilot and four passengers quite satisfactorily on the company's famous 5 minute/5 shilling 'flips'. Low power also made the dorsal fin unncecessary and in 1926–27 the firm erected four additional Avro 536s *G-EBOF*, '*OY*, '*RB* and '*TF*, for which no original construction details were recorded. They were evidently the best of the airframes still

176

Surrey Flying Services' Avro 536 *G-EBOF*.

remaining in store and the unexplained constructor's number P.8 given for *G-EBOY* is believed to be a corruption of B.8, identifying it as the former *G-EAKL*. They seldom ventured far afield, although *G-EBOY* gave joy flights from the beach at Jersey in 1927 and during a barnstorming tour in 1928 '*RB* was used extensively for wing walking exhibitions.

## SPECIFICATION AND DATA

*Manufacturers:* A. V. Roe and Co Ltd, Newton Heath, Manchester; and Hamble Aerodrome, near Southampton, Hants.

*Powerplants:* (Avro 536)  One 130 hp Clerget
One 150 hp Bentley B.R.1
(Avro 546)  One 150 hp Bentley B.R.1

*Dimensions:* Span 36 ft 9 in  Length 29 ft 5 in
Height 10 ft 5 in  Wing area 335 sq ft

*Weights:* Tare weight 1,431 lb  All-up weight 2,226 lb

*Performance:* Maximum speed 90 mph  Cruising speed 70 mph
Initial climb 550 ft/min  Ceiling 12,000 ft
Range 190 miles

*Note:* The above figures apply to both Avro 536 and 546.

*Production:*
(a) **Hamble built**
*K-114/G-EACC*, c/n. A.T.C.1, C of A 3.7.19, prototype, flown as landplane 5.19 and as seaplane 7.19, s.o.r. 7.21
*K-104/G-EAAQ*, A.T.C.2, C of A 14.5.19, crashed in Southwark Park, London, 9.9.19;

*K-105/G-EAAP*, A.T.C.3, C of A 14.5.19, crashed at Sandhurst Military College 6.8.19

*K-137/G-EADC*, A.T.C.5, C of A 3.6.19, scrapped at Hamble 12.19

*K-161/G-EAGM*, A.T.C.6, C of A 12.7.19, crashed at Weston-super-Mare 1.9.19

*K-165/G-EAHA*, A.T.C.7, C of A 12.8.19, s.o.r. 9.20, believed sold in The Netherlands

*K-166/G-EAHB*, A.T.C.8, C of A 17.7.19, scrapped at Hamble 12.19

*K-116/G-EACG*, A.T.C.9, C of A 17.6.19, crashed at Manston 30.8.19

*K-139/G-EADV*, A.T.C.11, no C of A, experimental long-range two-seater registered 6.6.19, scrapped 12.19

*G-EAOM*, A.T.C.23, C of A 22.12.29, completed as Avro 546, s.o.r. 12.20

### (b) Manchester built

*K-173/G-EAID*, c/n B.1, C of A 7.8.19, stored at Alexandra Park Aerodrome, Manchester, 8.21

*K-174/G–EAIE*, B.2, C of A 7.8.19, Fleet number 19, stored at Alexandra Park 8.21

*G-EAKD*, B.3, C of A 22.8.19, stored at Alexandra Park 8.21

*K-175/G-EAIF* B.4, C of A 5.8.19, stored at Alexandra Park 8.21

*G-EAJR* B.5, C of A 20.8.19, stored at Alexandra Park 8.21

*G-EAKJ* B.6, C of A 9.9.19, based at Brighton, to Surrey Flying Services Ltd, Croydon, 4.24, s.o.r. 1.29

*G-EAKK* B.7, C of A 9.9.19, stored at Alexandra Park 8.21

*G-EAKL* B.8, C of A 19.11.19, stored at Alexandra Park 8.21, believed rebuilt as *G-EBOY* in 1926

*G-EAKM* B.9, registered 18.8.19, to Surrey Flying Services Ltd, 7.25, C of A 18.8.25, crashed at Taplow, Bucks, 4.7.28

*G-EAKN* B.10, registered 18.8.19, to F. J. V. Holmes, Monkmoor Aerodrome, Shrewsbury, 9.23, C of A 17.4.24, crashed near Brill, Bucks, 12.8.24

*G-EAKO* B.11, registered 18.8.19, stored at Alexandra Park 8.21

*G-EAKP* B.12, registered 18.8.19, to Surrey Flying Services Ltd 7.25, C of A 15.7.25, s.o.r. 1.29

### (c) Erected by Surrey Flying Services Ltd, Croydon

*G-EBOF* no c/n, C of A 26.6.26, s.o.r. 12.30

*G-EBOY* P.8, C of A 28.8.26, s.o.r. 12.30

*G-EBRB* no c/n, C of A 13.5.27, crashed at Barry, Glamorgan, 28.5.28

*G-EBTF* no c/n, C of A 1.9.27, s.o.r. 12.30

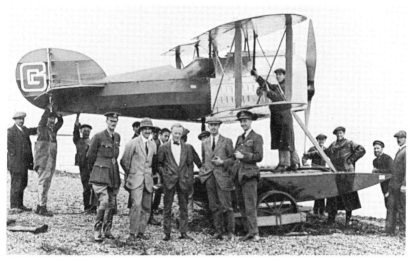

The Avro 539 racer at its first launching with the original rounded rudder.

# Avro 539

Rushed through the Hamble works in time for the 1919 Schneider Trophy Race, the Avro 539 single-seat twin-float seaplane was the smallest biplane that could be designed round the 240 hp Siddeley Puma engine. Its wooden structure was typically Avro but there was little external resemblance to any of the company's previous aeroplanes. The fuselage was a rectangular-section box-girder with deep curved fairings above and below to conform to the lines of the engine cowlings. These were a close fit with the cylinder heads projecting through them and cooling was by nose radiator.

Single-bay mainplanes with rounded tips were rigged with dihedral on the lower, shorter plane only. The tailplane was of generous area and an unbalanced rudder was hinged to a considerable dorsal fin. Four streamlined steel tubes carried two 14 ft single-step wooden floats at a track of 7 ft but there were no wingtip or tail floats. Piloted by Capt H. A. Hamersley, the Avro 539 first flew from Hamble slipway on August 29, 1919, but apart from the national *G* outlined in white on the rudder, no marks were carried despite the allocation of registration *G-EALG* eight days before. When taking off for eliminating trials at Cowes on September 3, a float was damaged by floating debris and a separate trial was arranged for September 8. This allowed time not only for repairs but for the fitment of a horn-balanced rudder, a change of fin shape and the display of full registration marks under the revised designation Avro 539A. The Schneider contest took place at Bournemouth on September 10, with the Avro 539A acting as reserve British machine to the Sopwith Schneider and the Supermarine Sea

179

Lion I. These were to compete with French and Italian entries but the race was declared void because of fog.

Deprived of an opportunity of showing its paces, the aircraft returned to Hamble where it was eventually converted into a landplane for the Aerial Derby at Hendon on July 24, 1920. A rigid V undercarriage was located well forward as on early Avro Babies, the fin area was reduced, and a small streamlined headrest fitted. Still known as the Avro 539A, *G-EALG* was flown in the race by Capt D. G. Westgarth-Heslam who forced landed drenched in fuel at Abridge, Essex.

The unlucky racer then returned to Hamble for a more extensive reconstruction to permit the installation of a 450 hp Napier Lion driving a 10 ft diameter Avro airscrew. By removing the frontal radiator it was possible to rebuild the nose with a downward slope to improve both streamlining and forward view. The three banks of cylinders projected from smoothly tapering cowlings which terminated in a conical airscrew boss, the engine being cooled by small radiator units on each side of the fuselage ahead of the cockpit. With an engine almost twice the power and weight of the original, it was necessary to shorten the nose and to strengthen the fuselage by planking it with plywood. A more robust undercarriage with rubber-in-compression shock absorbers was also necessary.

In this form the machine was re-registered *G-EAXM* under the designation Avro 539B and first flew at Hamble piloted by D. G. Westgarth-Heslam on July 13, three days before the 1921 Aerial Derby Race in which it was entered. At the end of this, its only flight, he made a perfect landing too far up the aerodrome and overshot into a railway cutting leading to the old RAF Assembly Park. The 539B was completely wrecked and the pilot was seriously injured.

Avro 539A *G-EALG* at Bournemouth on September 10, 1919, showing the horn-balanced rudder and enlarged fin. (*Flight photo 750*)

180

*G-EALG* in landplane form at Hendon on July 24, 1920, for the Aerial Derby Race. (*Flight photo 830.*)

The machine after reconstruction as the Avro 539B with Napier Lion engine, running up at Hamble on July 13, 1921.

## SPECIFICATION AND DATA

*Manufacturers:*   A. V. Roe and Co Ltd, Hamble Aerodrome, near South-ampton, Hants.

*Powerplants:*   (Avro 539)   One 240 hp Siddeley Puma
(Avro 539A)   One 240 hp Siddeley Puma
(Avro 539B)   One 450 hp Napier Lion

*Dimensions:*   Span (upper) 25 ft 6 in   (lower) 24 ft 6 in
Length (Puma) 21 ft 4 in
Height (Puma) 9 ft 9 in   (Lion) 8 ft 6 in
Wing area 195 sq ft

*Weights:*   (Avro 539) Tare weight 1,670 lb
All-up weight 2,119 lb

181

*Production:*  One aircraft only—Avro 539 *G-EALG*, c/n 539/1, first flown
29.8.19; rebuilt 1920 as Avro 539A *G-EALG*, c/n 539A/1;
rebuilt 1921 as Avro 539B *G-EAXM*, c/n 539B/1, damaged
beyond repair at Hamble 13.7.21

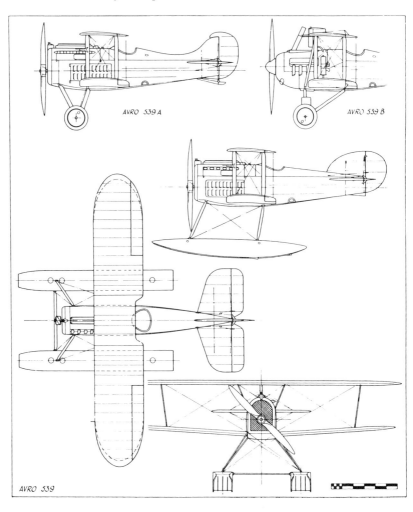

AVRO 539 A

AVRO 539 B

AVRO 539

The Beardmore-engined Avro 547 *G-EAQX*.

# Avro 547

The Avro 547 *G-EAQX* was a commercial triplane with enclosed cabin built in February 1920 and powered by a 160 hp Beardmore water-cooled engine. Engine mountings and cabin structure were of new design but almost all the remainder of the Avro 547 was built from surplus Avro 504K components. By reverting to A. V. Roe's favourite triplane formula, the span was kept to a minimum while construction was speeded and costs kept low by the ingenious use of standard 504K mainplanes, interplane struts, tail unit and undercarriage. Ailerons were fitted to all three wings, the centre pair being fitted with 'park bench' type aerodynamic balances. The tail unit employed the dorsal fin used on the Avro 504L and 536 and the undercarriage was standard apart from a longer axle and a wider rear V-strut.

The fabric-covered rear fuselage, although of generous proportions and quite unlike that of a 504K, was built in the same manner from spruce strip and used all the 504K metal fittings. Aluminium engine cowlings were used and the fuselage from nose radiator to the rear of the cabin was plywood-covered. Fuel and oil tanks were located in a special bay behind the engine and the cabin accommodated four passengers in facing pairs in adjustable, spring mounted bucket seats. With the seats removed, 113 cu ft of space was available for the carriage of light freight or mail. An entry door, complete with railway carriage-type, strap operated, opening Triplex window, was on the starboard side. Immediately behind the cabin was the pilot's open cockpit, offset to port to give adequate forward and downward view, and about two feet of the port centre wing and starboard bottom wing trailing edges were cut back to the rear spar further to improve the view with the tail down.

Capt. H. A. Hamersley flew the machine at Hamble and reported that performance and handling characteristics were much the same as those of the 504K. The airframe was already stressed for engines of higher power, so that when the rules of the Air Ministry Small Commercial Aeroplane Competition were published, it was a simple matter to build a second triplane in June 1920 and fit a 240 hp Siddeley Puma. With this engine the calculated performance made it a likely winner and the machine consequently occupied a place of honour on the Avro stand at the Olympia Aero Show in London, July 9–20, 1920. With the competition in mind, several improvements were made in the cabin, notably seven extra inches of leg room, hot and cold air control, interior lighting, upholstered bench-type seats and a trapdoor for communicating with the pilot.

Registered *G-EAUJ* under the designation Avro 547A, the machine was flown from Hamble to Martlesham by Capt H. A. Hamersley and weighed in on August 3 to compete against the Austin Kestrel, Beardmore W.B.X, Bristol Seely Puma, Sopwith Wallaby and the Westland Limousine III (eventual winner of the £7,500 prize). Hamersely was the first competitor to start the tests when he made the glide test from 500 ft next morning and covered the measured mile at 95.7 mph. Then followed reliability-with-economy, getting off and landing tests at an all-up weight of 3,683 lb, a slow run at 51.5 mph on August 12 and a measured landing run of 239 yards on the 14th. The machine failed to qualify for an award because it was not inherently stable and had failed to reach the stipulated minimum top speed of 100 mph.

In the landing trial the Avro 547A was put down rather hard and an

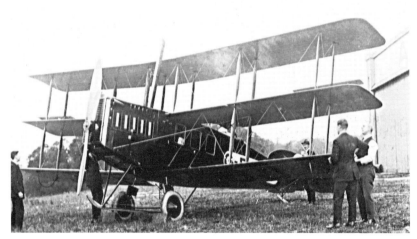

A. V. Roe and H. A. Hammersley discussing *G-EAUJ*, the Puma-engined Avro 547A.

undercarriage strut was so badly bent that a quarter of an hour later the entire undercarriage collapsed as it stood at dispersal. After repairs it was flown back to Hamble but returned to Martlesham for official trials on October 12. It was flown on this occasion by H. J. Hinkler who stopped for three days of demonstration flights at Croydon en route. The return trip on October 30 followed the same pattern, after which it was based at Hamble until dismantled sometime after its final C of A renewal in August 1921.

At the invitation of S. Instone and Co Ltd H. J. Hinkler ferried the first machine, *G-EAQX*, to Croydon on June 1, 1920, where it was flown the next day by Instone's chief pilot F. L. Barnard. He did not recommend its purchase and further demonstrations at Croydon on June 24 were equally abortive. A third 547 fuselage, built against the possible order, hung from the roof of the flight shed at Hamble until well into 1925 as mute reminder of these failures.

Nevertheless Queensland and Northern Territories Aerial Services Ltd (QANTAS) purchased *G-EAQX* in November 1920, for £2,798 for the Charleville-Katherine section of its proposed Melbourne–Darwin route, and a twice weekly service between Charleville and Cloncurry. The aircraft was crated and shipped to the Australian Aircraft and Engineering Co Ltd, the Avro agents, and on arrival was assembled at Mascot. It was first flown from there on March 2, 1921, by P. J. McGinniss (co-founder of QANTAS) but its slender main undercarriage legs gave way on landing. More than a year went by before it was repaired and fitted with stout, rubber-sprung V-strut undercarriage more suited to the unprepared landing grounds in Queensland. In this form the 547 was flown into second place in the Australian Aerial Derby at Victoria Park Racecourse, Sydney, by QANTAS manager Hudson Fysh on May 6, 1922, at an average speed of 69.5 mph. After a short period of joyriding over Sydney Harbour the machine, which was thought only safe to fly in good conditions from airfields with a perfect surface, was condemned on these and other counts, including inadequate rudder area, and the certificate of airworthiness was withdrawn. The failure of the 547 was a major setback to the fledgling QANTAS and the company resolved never to do business with A. V. Roe and Co again should no compensation be forthcoming. The fuselage was subsequently used as a hen-house in a Sydney suburb.

## SPECIFICATION AND DATA

*Manufacturers:*   A. V. Roe and Co Ltd, Newton Heath, Manchester; and Hamble Aerodrome, near Southampton, Hants.

*Powerplants:*   (Avro 547)  One 160 hp Beardmore
(Avro 547A) One 240 hp Siddeley Puma

*Dimensions:*   Span 37 ft 3 in   Length 29 ft 10 in
Height 14 ft 5 in   Wing area 498 sq ft

*Weights:*    (Avro 547)  Tare weight 2,077 lb   All-up weight 3,000 lb
             (Avro 547A) Tare weight 2,460 lb
             All-up weight 3,666 lb*

*Performance:*  (Avro 547)  Maximum speed 96 mph
                Cruising speed 83 mph
                Climb to 5,000 ft, 15 min
                Range 230 miles
              (Avro 547A) Maximum speed 95 mph
                Cruising speed 80 mph
                Climb to 10,000 ft, 19 min
                Range 280 miles

*Flown at an all-up weight of 3,683 lb at Martlesham; maximum permissible gross weight increased to 3,800 lb at C of A renewal 22.8.21

*Production:*

| Constructor's No. and Registration | C of A Issued | Details |
|---|---|---|
| 547/1    G-EAQX | nil | 2.20 A. V. Roe and Co Ltd; 11.20 Australian Aircraft and Engineering Co Ltd; to QANTAS 3.21 as *G-AUCR*; used as spares at Mascot late 1922 |
| 547A/1   G-EAUƷ | 25.8.20 | Martlesham competition 3–14.8.20; to Martlesham trials 12–30.10.20; dismantled at Hamble 1922 |
| —        — | nil | Incomplete airframe stored at Hamble until 1925 |

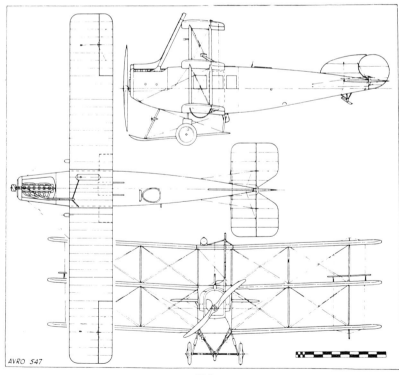

AVRO 547

The Olympia Aero Show model Avro 548 showing the wing root elevator control cranks.

# Avro 548

By 1918 successful development of the inline engine was already ending the long career of the rotary. The inline was not only less complex and more easily maintained, but less extravagant in fuel and oil. It was not therefore surprising that A. V. Roe's ingenious civil adaptations of the 504K embraced an economical engine of this type, particular as tens of surplus thousands were to be had at give-away prices.

Experiments began at Hamble in October 1919 with the Avro 545 *G-EAPR*, an experimental 504K with 90 hp Curtiss OX-5. This American eight-cylinder Vee water-cooled engine was cooled by spiral tube radiators on each side of the front cockpit in the manner of the Avro Type E prototype of an earlier era. Such an installation, with its heavy and potentially troublesome plumbing, would not have appealed to private owners and final choice fell on the air-cooled 80 hp Renault, a similar engine which drove a four bladed wooden airscrew.

Designated Avro 548, first flown at Hamble by H. A. Hamersley late in 1919, flown to Farnborough for checks on January 13, 1920, and certificated in the following March, the first Renault Avro *G-EAPQ* was a 504K with the dual control removed to carry two passengers in tandem behind the pilot. Fuel, entirely gravity fed, was carried in a large centre-section tank and a false decking covered the large rear cockpit so that each occupant had his own windscreen. This machine was the only Avro 548 to have external elevator control wires running from cranks above the lower wing root. Silver overall with polished cowlings, it graced the Avro stand at the Olympia Aero Show, London, in July 1920 without markings as the 'Avro Tourist'. The third Avro 548, *G-EALF*, was available for demonstration flights at Hendon during the Show and on July 28 F/Lt Leslie flew Prince Alfonso d'Orleans to Farnborough in it.

The trade slump killed any potential market, and a projected trainer version (Avro 553) was shelved, but the prototype was repainted in wartime drab for Capt E. D. C. Herne who used it for a photographic survey of the whole of England, the entire coastline of Belgium and France as well as all the major Belgian inland towns. When King George V visited Belfast, *'PQ* was flown 700 miles from Croydon to Belfast and back in one day, yet total repairs after 30,000 miles in 18 months amounted to only £2 for a set of control cables, and 3d for a valve spring. W. G. Pudney afterwards acquired it and ran a joyriding business at Croydon throughout 1922.

Three other Avros 548s built at Hamble were without the false decking and had a large, double rear cockpit. One was sold in Uruguay and another, *G-EAFH* (formerly *K-147*, 504K test-bed for the 170 hp A.B.C. Wasp I), spent 1921 at Swansea with the Welsh Aviation Company and won all three races at the Croydon Meeting of September 17, 1921, piloted by F. G. M. Sparks. When the firm went into liquidation, pioneer private owner Dr E. D. Whitehead Reid of Bekesbourne, Canterbury, bought it for a mere £1 10s, converted it to two-seater and flew it in and out of fields on his professional rounds until 1927. *G-EAFH* then returned to joyriding, first at Squires Gate and in 1931 at Southport sands and with the Giro Aviation Co, finally crashing there on May 31, 1935, during a low altitude aerobatic display. A. V. Roe and Co built only three other 548s, dual trainers *G-EBIT–'IV* for the North Sea Aerial and General Transport Co Reserve School at Brough in 1924.

The majority of Avro 548s were conversions made by outside firms such as the Aircraft Disposal Co which produced ten at Croydon. Only the first of these, *G-EAYD*, resembled Avro's prototype with three separate cockpits. The remainder included five for Reserve Training at Stag Lane by the de Havilland School of Flying, one of which was the former Avro Transport Company 504K *G-EAAL*. Named *Vida*, the latter eventually passed into private ownership at Stag Lane. *G-EBPJ*, privately owned in 1926 by Nigel Norman, served the Norfolk and Norwich Aero Club at Mousehold 1927–28; and *'PO* went to Newcastle Aero Club at Cramlington in the same year.

Surrey Flying Services built three; *G-EBAJ* for airborne radio telephony experiments by Marconi's Wireless Telegraph Co at Croydon and Chelmsford; *G-EBBP* for private owner Sir Derwent Hall Caine (which later in 1922 reverted to the company for instructional use); and dual trainer

The prototype Avro 548 during its 1922 Croydon joyriding season. Note the three individual cockpits.

Avro's slave aircraft *G-EAPR* in Avro 545 configuration, October 1919, with 90 hp Curtiss OX-5 engine.

*G-AABW* in 1928. The only difference between these and the genuine Avro-built 548 was the bulged under-cowling. When Marconi ceased experiments in 1926, *G-EBAJ* joined the rapidly expanding fleet of the Henderson School of Flying at Brooklands. A. B. H. Youell flew it at the next year's Bournemouth Easter Meeting, winning the Business Houses Handicap on April 16, 1927, at an average speed of 74 mph. On October 1 that year it took a prominent part in welcoming home the victorious Schneider Trophy team by flying round Croydon with suitably inscribed yellow banners attached to a crude metal framework. The Henderson School and its successor, the Brooklands School of Flying, owned nine 548s, six of which they built from spares. Although primarily intended for instructional work, the 548s always went joyriding at coast resorts such as Skegness and Canvey Island in the summer. Two, *G-EBRD* and '*SC*, shipped to South Africa for a pleasure flying season in 1927–28, took part in Cape Town's first air display on December 11, 1927.

The most important Henderson 548 was *G-EAJB*, one of Avro's original 1919 civil 504Ks which had been used at Filton for some years by the Bristol Aeroplane Co as a Lucifer engine test-bed. Standard 504K shock absorbers now replaced the special oleo units used at Bristol but '*JB* retained the 504N-type ailerons with curved trailing edge. The only other Avro 548 so fitted was Henderson's second machine *G-EBRD*, built for South Africa.

In 1925 Maj F. B. Halford of the Aircraft Disposal Co modernised the 80 hp Renault by fitting redesigned cylinder heads and valve gear which raised the power output to 120 hp. This engine, the Airdisco, was fitted into one of the company's surplus 504K airframes to create the first Avro 548A. Registered *G-EBKN*, it had greatly improved all-round performance and became the lively mount of Shoreham private owner A. G. Head. Not to be outdone in publicity by A. V. Roe and Co, donors of an Avro 504R

189

to the Lancashire Aero Club in July 1926, the Aircraft Disposal Co simultaneously presented the club with one of their 548 conversions *G-EBOK*. Soon afterwards, on October 2, T. Neville Stack flew *'OK* to victory in the Yorkshire Open Handicap Race at Sherburn, beating the Brough 548As *G-EBIT* and *'IU*. Together with *'IV*, these had been re-engined with Airdiscos but were sold to joyride concerns in 1928 along with *'OK*. *G-EBIV* went to Surrey Flying Services, Croydon, while *'IT* and *'IU* joined *'OK* at Squires Gate and there became even better known than the 504K.

The last two British 548s, *G-ABMB* and *'SV*, were built at Barton by Berkshire Aviation Tours Ltd in 1931 for the Giro Aviation Co, their sole cross-country flying being the delivery flight to Southport where they worked the beaches for several years. Both were replaced by D. H. Fox Moths in 1934–35 but remained fully rigged in the hangar at Hesketh Park until 1938.

A few Avro 548 conversions were also made overseas. The Canadian Aircraft Co Ltd of Winnipeg, importers of six 80 hp Renaults in April 1920, built three machines and retained two for charter flying. The third was converted for the McCall Hanrahan Aero Service of Calgary but crashed in less than a fortnight. In 1928 they also built the Hawk-Clark Y-Avro Mallard *G-CASY* for W. P. A. Straith, using an old 504K fuselage with a 75 hp Rolls-Royce Hawk engine and Clark Y section wings. In Australia Matthews Aviation Ltd replaced the Dyak in *G-AUBG* by an Airdisco; and *G-AUBK*, flown by E. W. Percival in the Australian Aerial Derby with an 80 hp Renault on May 6, 1922, also later received an Airdisco. The only other example, *G-AUEW*, started life as a Clerget 504K, but was modified progressively to 548 and 548A by E. W. Beckham and Courier Aircraft Ltd of Brisbane 1926–27.

The Henderson School of Flying joyriding Avro 548 *G-EBAJ* with framework for towing a 'Welcome Home' banner at Croydon when the victorious 1927 Schneider Trophy team returned from Venice. (*Flight photo 5086.*)

190

## SPECIFICATION AND DATA

*Manufacturers:*    A. V. Roe and Co Ltd, Newton Heath, Manchester, and Hamble Aerodrome, near Southampton, Hants
The Aircraft Disposal Co Ltd, Croydon Aerodrome, Surrey
Berkshire Aviation Tours Ltd, Barton Aerodrome, Manchester
The Canadian Aircraft Co Ltd, Winnipeg, Manitoba, Canada
The Henderson School of Flying Ltd, Brooklands Aerodrome, Surrey
Surrey Flying Services Ltd, Croydon Aerodrome, Surrey

*Powerplants:*    (Avro 545)   One 90 hp Curtiss OX-5
(Avro 548)   One 80 hp Renault
(Avro 548A) One 120 hp Airdisco

*Dimensions:*    Span 36 ft 0 in   Length 29 ft 5 in
Height 10 ft 5 in   Wing area 330 sq ft

*Weights and Performance:*

|  | Avro 545 | Avro 548 | Avro 548A |
|---|---|---|---|
| Tare weight | 1,241 lb | 1,338 lb | 1,460 lb |
| All-up weight | 1,829 lb | 1,943 lb | 2,150 lb |
| Maximum speed | — | 80 mph | 91 mph |
| Cruising speed | 70 mph | 65 mph | 84 mph |
| Initial climb | — | 350 ft/min | 400 ft/min |
| Ceiling | — | — | 11,200 ft |
| Range | 210 miles | 175 miles | 300 miles |

*Production:*

### (a) By A. V. Roe and Co Ltd

*G-EAPQ/H2322*, C of A 16.3.20, to W. G. Pudney 3.22, written off 19.10.22; *G-EAFH*, c/n A.T.C.14, C of A 22.6.20, to Welsh Aviation Co 5.21, Dr E. D. Whitehead Reid 3.22, to Giro Aviation Co 3.31, crashed at Southport 31.5.35; *G-EALF/J743*, C of A 8.12.20 struck off register (s.o.r.) 7.21; *G-EAVH*, c/n 548/4, C of A 15.10.20 crashed at Montevideo, Uruguay, 21.8.21; *G-EBIT–'IV\**, c/n 5100–5102, C of A 9.5.24, North Sea Aerial and General Transport Co Ltd, *'IT* and *'IU* to the Lancashire School of Aviation Ltd 2.28, *'IT* crashed at Kingstown 25.9.30, *'IU* damaged beyond repair at Rhyl 17.5.37, *'IV* to Surrey Flying Services Ltd 5.28.

*Avro 548A with 120 hp Airdisco.

### (b) By the Aircraft Disposal Co Ltd 1921–26

*G-EAAL/E4154*, *G-EBAG/H2025*, *G-EBFL/H2053*, *G-EBFM/H2070* and *G-EBHL/H2067* for the de Havilland Aircraft Co Ltd, *'AL* to T. H. Richardson as *Vida*, crashed near Stag Lane 3.6.28, *'AG* to Northern Airways Ltd 6.27, *'FL* crashed 24.7.23, *'FM* to G. L. P. Henderson 5.26 (crashed at Brooklands 20.9.28), *HL* s.o.r. after accident 6.11.25; *G-EAYD/H7428*, crashed 13.10.21; *G-EBHK/H7488* withdrawn from use 1.1.26; *G-EBKN/E449\** A. G. Head, Shoreham 2.30, parts used to rebuild Avro 504K *G-EBJE* in 1969 as *E499* for

*Avro 548A with 120 hp Airdisco

*G-EBKN*, first of the 120 hp Airdisco-engined Avro 548A machines produced by the Aircraft Disposal Company.

*G-EBRD*, an Avro 548 with tapered ailerons erected by Henderson at Brooklands for the 1927–28 South African tour.

RAF Museum; *G-EBOK*, c/n R/R3/Re/70022, Light Planes (Lancs) Ltd, to Lancashire School of Aviation Ltd 8.28 s.o.r. 1.37; *G-EBPJ/E9337* Nigel Norman, to Norfolk and Norwich Aero Club 11.27, Inland Flying Services Ltd 5.28, British Flying and Motor Services Ltd, Maylands, 10.28, crashed near Romford 31.7.28; *G-EBPO/E3387* Newcastle Aero Club, J. J. Robertson 11.27; Pleasure F/S 2.29; Cramlington Aircraft Ltd 11.29; s.o.r. 9.31

### (*c*) **By Surrey Flying Sevices Ltd 1922–29**

*G-EBAJ/E3043* first flown 17.1.22, Marconi's Wireless Telegraph Co. Ltd., to G. L. P. Henderson 7.26, crashed at Brooklands 9.4.28; *G-EBBC/H2212*, D. Hall Caine, to Surrey Flying Services Ltd. 8.22, withdrawn from use 25.11.25; *G-AABW*, c/n G516\*, Surrey Flying Services Ltd., crashed at Woolwich 19.9.29.

\*As documented.

### (*d*) **By the Henderson School of Flying Ltd 1927–29**

*G-EAJB/H2598*, ex Avro 504K, s.o.r. 1.29; *G-EBRD* scrapped in South Africa 1928; *G-EBSC* crashed in South Africa 5.28; *G-EBVE* to Brooklands School of Flying Ltd. 11.28, damaged beyond repair at Brooklands 1929; *G-EBWH* damaged beyond repair at Canvey Island, Essex 22.7.28; *G-EBWJ* to Brooklands School of Flying Ltd. 11.28; to C. B. H. Crawshaw, Hooton

5.31, sold as scrap circa 1932; *G-AADT* to Brooklands School of Flying Ltd., to E. Willox, Dyce 11.30, s.o.r. 12.31.

(*e*) **By the Berkshire Aviation Co Ltd 1931–32**
*G-ABMB/H2232*, C of A 9.7.31 and *G-ABSV*, C of A 7.4.32, for the Giro Aviation Co Ltd, scrapped at Southport circa 1940.

(*f*) **By the Canadian Aircraft Co Ltd 1920–21**
*G-CACD*, c/n 1160, C of A 5.10.20, Canadian Aircraft Co Ltd; *G-CACI/D8997*, C of A 15.6.21, ex-Avro 504K *G-CABS*; *G-CACN*, c/n 1161, C of A 27.6.21, McCall Hanrahan Aero Service, crashed at Calgary, Alberta, 6.7.21. *G-CASY*, Hawk-Clark Y-Avro Mallard, c/n 2, registered 21.5.30, s.o.r. 5.31

(*g*) **In Australia 1920–21**
*G-AUBK*, E. W. Percival 6.21, to Courier Aircraft Ltd, crashed at Ipswich, Queensland, 9.2.27; for *G-AUBG* and '*EW* see page 88.

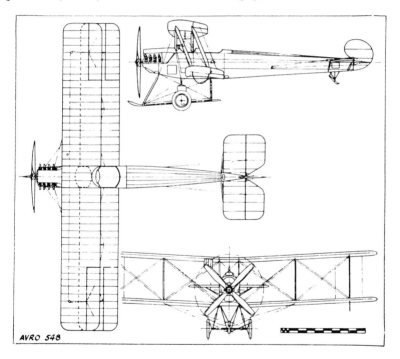

AVRO 548

193

The first prototype Avro 549 Aldershot *J6852* with dorsal fin, running up at Hamble 1922.

# Avro 549 Aldershot

The Aldershot, Avro's first entirely new postwar military aeroplane, was a long-range heavy bomber designed by Roy Chadwick and built to Air Ministry Specification 2/20 (D of R Type 4B). Powered by a single 650 hp Rolls-Royce Condor III, it was historically important as the first Avro type to have a metal fuselage, and featured a capacious plywood-covered central cabin divided into two decks. Two pilots sat side by side on the upper (with dual control) with the gunner armed with a single Scarff-mounted Lewis gun, close behind while an internal ladder gave access to the bomb aimer and radio operator in the cabin below. A 210 gallon fuel tank was located ahead of the cabin and the lower half of the nose formed a radiator compartment into which cooling air was admitted through controllable shutters.

Slightly swept, three-bay, folding wings of wooden construction were fitted with large differential ailerons aerodynamically balanced by 'park bench' aerofoils on the upper pair. A high set, variable-incidence tailplane gave the gunner a clear field of fire over and around a long dorsal fin and Avro circular rudder. The undercarriage was of the wide-track, divided type to permit the carriage of a single heavy bomb centrally under the fuselage.

Two Aldershot I prototypes, *J6852* and *J6853*, built at Hamble for competitive trials with the de Havilland Derby, were test flown by H. J. 'Bert' Hinkler early in 1922. Trials with the first prototype evidently revealed excessive rudder loads, for the dorsal fin was removed and a new rudder with enlarged balance area fitted. This was only partially effective

194

and the trouble was eventually cured by increasing the length of the fuselage by some six feet. *J6852* made its debut in lengthened form in the New Types Park at the Hendon RAF Display on June 24, 1922, and won the Handicap Race piloted by F/O C. E. Horrex. It then returned to Hamble for the installation of one of six prototype 1,000 hp Napier Cub sixteen-cylinder, water-cooled engines which the Air Ministry had ordered in 1919 at a cost of £10,000 each. This vast power unit drove a four-bladed wooden airscrew and weighed 2,450 lb so that Chadwick had not only to design new mountings and install a gas starter, but also to strengthen the aeroplane very considerably and fit a four-wheeled double undercarriage.

Amid considerable publicity and in the presence of Air Vice-Marshal Sir Geoffrey Salmond and Wing Cdr Cave Brown Cave of the Air Ministry, H. T. Vane of the Napier company and A. V. Roe himself, the machine first flew at Hamble as the Aldershot II on December 15, 1922. The great machine left the ground in three seconds and after getting the feel of the controls, Hinkler threw it about and made a downwind pass at an estimated 140 mph before coming in for an impressively slow landing. It was delivered

The first prototype Aldershot with experimental rudder and oversize horn balance. (*Courtesy C. H. Barnes*)

*J6853*, second prototype Aldershot in final form with lengthened fuselage.

Running up the 1,000 hp Napier Cub in *J6852*, modified as the Aldershot II, at Hamble in December 1922.

to the RAE, Farnborough, on January 10, 1923, and shown at the Hendon RAF Display on June 30 before despatch to Hamble on July 2 to be prepared for Sweden, where it dwarfed all other aeroplanes at the Gothenburg Aero Exhibition. After its return on October 30, the Aldershot II was displayed with a Condor-engined example at the Imperial Air Conference at Croydon on November 9–12, and spent 1923 at the RAE Engine Research Flight, where it was flown by F/Lt P. W. S. Bulman.

In 1923 fifteen Condor-powered, long-fuselage Aldershots with strengthened multi-strut undercarriage and fuel tanks under the upper wing, were ordered under the designation Aldershot III. Armament was still the single aft-firing Lewis gun but a 2,000 lb bomb load was carried internally. Specially re-formed at Andover on April 1, 1924, No.99 Squadron flew the Aldershot IIIs to Bircham Newton, Norfolk, their permanent base throughout the two short years of their career. The Aldershots' exceptional

Avro Aldershots of No.99 Squadron RAF at Bircham Newton in 1924.

196

stability made them particularly suitable for night flying and many of No.99's operations were at night. They flew past in pondrous formation at the Hendon RAF Display on June 27, 1925, but soon afterwards the Air Ministry abandoned its large single-engined bomber policy and replaced the Aldershot IIIs with twin-engined Handley Page Hyderabads.

After extended trials at Farnborough the Cub Aldershot *J6852* returned to Hamble where the standard undercarriage was replaced and the machine equipped as flying test-bed for the 850 hp Beardmore Typhoon slow revving six-cylinder, inverted inline engine. Cooled by a radiator below and behind, the Typhoon permitted a slim, streamlined nose with much improved view for the pilot. In this form the machine was known as the Avro 549C Aldershot IV and first flew at Hamble on January 10, 1927. It was demonstrated there by Hinkler on January 24 before leaving again for Farnborough. One standard Aldershot III was fitted experimentally with a set of steel wings and redesignated Avro 549M.

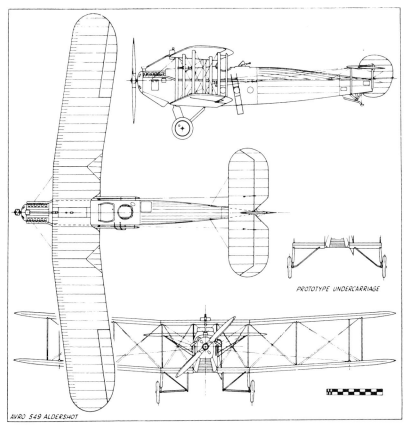

PROTOTYPE UNDERCARRIAGE

AVRO 549 ALDERSHOT

197

*J6852* in final form as the Avro 549C Aldershot IV with 850 hp Beardmore Typhoon engine.

## SPECIFICATION AND DATA

*Manufacturers:* A. V. Roe and Co Ltd, Newton Heath, Manchester; and Hamble Aerodrome, near Southampton, Hants.

*Powerplants:* (Aldershot I)   One 650 hp Rolls-Royce Condor III
(Aldershot II)  One 1,000 hp Napier Cub
(Aldershot III) One 650 hp Rolls-Royce Condor III
(Aldershot IV) One 850 hp Beardmore Typhoon I

*Dimensions:* Span 68 ft 0 in   Length 45 ft 0 in★
Height 15 ft 3 in   Wing area 1,064 sq ft

★ Prototypes originally about 39 ft.

*Weights:* (Prototypes)
Tare weight 6,027 lb   All-up weight 10,764 lb
(Aldershot III)
Tare weight 6,310 lb   All-up weight 10,950 lb

*Performance:* (Aldershot III)
Maximum speed 110 mph   Cruising speed 92 mph
Ceiling 14,500 ft            Range 625 miles

*Production:* Prototypes *J6852* and *J6853* ordered 2.12.20 to Contract 324861/20; fifteen production Aldershot IIIs *J6942–J6956* ordered 26.1.23 to Contracts 369334/22 and 375620/22

*Service use:* By No.99 Squadron, RAF, at Bircham Newton, Norfolk, 1924–26

The famous test vehicle *G-EAPR* in Avro 552A form with 180 hp Wolseley Viper engine and 504K-type undercarriage.

# Avro 552

In the course of Avro's postwar 504K modernisation programme, unused airframes *H2322* and *'23* were taken from the Manchester production line and fitted with inline engines. The first received an 80 hp Renault to become the prototype Avro 548 *G-EAPQ* and the other a 90 hp Curtiss OX-5 as the 'one-off' Avro 545 *G-EAPR*. Comparative trials led to adoption of the Renault engine for the low-powered touring variant, but the company foresaw the need for a higher powered, two-seat advanced trainer which, in seaplane form, would have a better performance than the Avro 504L.

Thousands of cheap S.E.5A power units, comprising 180 hp Wolseley Viper water-cooled engine and frontal radiator, were available from the Aircraft Disposal Co and a scheme to fit a unit of this type in the standard 504K received type number Avro 551 in October 1920. The trial installation was made in *G-EAPR* but a large aerofoil shape centre-section tank was fitted to carry additional fuel needed by the bigger engine, full dual control was provided, and tapered ailerons fitted to improve lateral control. These considerable modifications resulted in the issue of type numbers Avro 552 to the basic seaplane and 552A to the landplane version.

For the Aerial Derby at Croydon on July 16, 1921, a V-type undercarriage was fitted to *'PR* which came fifth at 102·51 mph piloted by L. R. Tait-Cox. The skid-type undercarriage was then refitted but the machine was almost immediately mounted on twin wooden floats for demonstrations at Hamble which resulted in a substantial order for Avro 552 seaplanes from the Naval Air Division of the Argentine Ministry of Marine. Assembly began at Hamble in October 1921 and after test flights from Southampton Water the machines were created for despatch to the Puerto Belgrano School at Bahia Blanca, where they were still in use in 1927.

*G-EAPR* was again modified early in 1922 as test vehicle for features then being incorporated in the company's new trainer, the Avro 504N. These (shown publicly when Hinkler flew the machine to Croydon on April

12, 1922) included twin 18 gallon fuel tanks under the top wing and the now famous N-type indestructible 6 ft track undercarriage with oil damped, rubber shock absorbers. Hinkler flew it in this form in the Croydon Races of June 3, 1922, but the early V-type undercarriage was later refitted for H. A. Hamersley's victory in the handicap section of the Aerial Derby at Hendon on August 6, 1923.

To meet a RCAF requirement for forestry patrol aircraft a contract was awarded in 1924 to Canadian Vickers Ltd for the construction of five single-seat Avro 552A landplanes followed soon after by one for nine two-seat floatplanes. The latter were developed from the temporary Avro 552B conversion of *G-EAPR* but employed floats designed by the US Naval Aircraft Factory and all fourteen aircraft were fitted with 25 gallon wing tanks to give greater range than the Avro-built machines. Their Service life was short and all had been withdrawn from use by September 1928.

Stripped of its wings, the slave aircraft *G-EAPR* was rebuilt at Hamble in 1927 as the Cierva C.8V (Avro 586) autogiro *G-EBTX*. Giratory experiments occupied 1928 and '29 but in 1930 the machine was acquired by L. G. Anderson who reconverted it at Hanworth to Avro 552A with skid undercarriage and untapered ailerons. Registered *G-ABGO* and equipped with underwing rollers, it was then used for banner towing by Inca Aviation Ltd but retained the autogiro pylon attachment points on the top longerons until its demise in 1933. Only three other 'Viper Avros' existed in England, all of which were built from spares by C. B. Field at Kingswood Knoll, Surrey, for Inca in 1932. In vivid red and yellow they were a familiar sight almost everywhere but after 1935 were operated by

L. R. Tait-Cox on the starting line of the 1921 Aerial Derby at Croydon in *G-EAPR* fitted with V-type undercarriage.

*G-EAPR* in final fixed-wing form with 504N-type undercarriage.

Root designation Avro 552 represented the original twin-float concept, in which form *G-EAPR* was flown at Hamble in 1921.

Argentine Avro 552 seaplane *E-13* at Hamble. (*J. M. Bruce/G. S. Leslie Collection*)

*G-CYGB*, the prototype Avro 552 seaplane built by Canadian Vickers, showing the U.O.1. type central wooden float designed by the Naval Aircraft Factory, Philadelphia, in 1925. (*Canadian Vickers Ltd*)

*G-EAPR* as the prototype Avro 552B with single wooden float.

Plane Advertising Ltd which kept them for a short time at Barton, Manchester.

## SPECIFICATION AND DATA

*Manufacturers:*   A. V. Roe and Co Ltd, Newton Heath, Manchester; and Hamble Aerodrome, near Southampton, Hants
Canadian Vickers Ltd, Vickers Works, Maisonneuve, Montreal, Canada
C. B. Field, Kingswood Knoll, Surrey

202

| | |
|---|---|
| *Powerplant:* | One 180 hp Wolseley Viper |
| *Dimensions:* | Span 36 ft 0 in    Length 28 ft 0 in<br>Height 10 ft 5 in    Wing area 330 sq ft |
| *Weights:* | All-up weight 2,260 lb |
| *Production:* | |

### (a) By A. V. Roe and Co Ltd

1. Prototype *G-EAPR*, ex *H2323*, C of A issued 11.7.23; converted 1927 to Cierva C.8V (Avro 586) *G-EBTX*; reconverted to Avro 552A as *G-ABGO* in 1931, C of A issued 22.4.31, owner Inca Aviation Ltd, Hanworth; crashed on take-off while banner towing, Coal Aston, Sheffield, 25.10.33.
2. At least thirteen Avro 552 seaplanes, beginning *E-1*, for Argentina 1921–22
3. At least two Avro 552 seaplanes for Bulgaria, *B-BAHA* and *B-BBAH*

### (b) By Canadian Vickers Ltd, Montreal

1. Avro 552A landplanes
   *G-CYFT*, c/n CV.10, first flown 2.12.37
   *G-CYFU* to *'FX* inclusive, c/n CV.11 to CV.14.
2. Avro 552A seaplanes
   *G-CYGB*, c/n CV.20, first flown 1.5.25
   *G-CYGC* to *'GJ* inclusive, c/n CV.21 to 28

### (c) By C. B. Field

| Constructor's No.<br>and Registration | | C of A<br>Issued | Details |
|---|---|---|---|
| nil | *G-ACAW* | 20. 6.33 | To Plane Advertising Ltd; s.o.r. 9.37 |
| 12 | *G-ACAX* | 22.12.34 | To Plane Advertising Ltd; crashed at Sandridge, Herts, 27.3.36 |
| 9 | *G-ACRP* | 3. 7.34 | To Plane Advertising Ltd; s.o.r. 3.36 |

At least two Avro 552 seaplanes were delivered to Bulgaria for use on the Black Sea coast. (*J. M. Bruce/G. S. Leslie Collection*)

203

A production Avro 555A Bison II with dorsal fin but without circular portholes forward.
(*Crown Copyright Reserved*)

# Avro 555 Bison

The Bison was an exceedingly ugly deck-landing biplane for sea reconnaissance and fleet gunnery spotting to Specification 3/21 (D of R Type 7A). Although structurally similar to other wire-braced biplanes designed by the company, its shape, purely functional and dictated by naval requirements, was little short of grotesque, largely because the pilot's cockpit was located high up in front of the top wing with the engine cowling sloping away steeply to give an unrestricted forward view when landing on an aircraft carrier. Power was provided by a 450 hp Napier Lion water-cooled engine on a special mounting which also formed a work stand when the Lion was removed from the airframe for maintenance. High-lift mainplanes were built round two spruce spars, rigged with 5 in of back stagger, and arranged to fold for stowage aboard a carrier. Interplane struts were of tubular steel streamlined with fabric over wooden formers.

The fuselage was of tubular steel construction, the central part being plywood-covered to form a cabin having large rectangular observation windows on each side. It allowed sufficient headroom for the crew to stand upright and housed all the radio and navigation equipment and even a plotting table. A rear gunner's position on a raised platform reached from the rear of the cabin was armed with a single Lewis gun on a Scarff mounting to supplement the pilot's fixed Vickers gun. Flotation bags were fitted in the rear fuselage and to provide buoyancy at the front end in the event of a forced landing at sea, fuel could be jettisoned from the 93 gallon main tank. The undercarriage was of standard Avro oil dashpot and rubber-in-compression design.

The first prototype Bison, *N153*, flown in 1921, had the upper mainplane mounted directly on top of the fuselage, three arrester wire claws (also tried on the Avro 504N *J7301*) fixed to the axle and had the tail supported by a simple rubber sprung skid. *N154*, a second prototype to Specification 33/22, shown off by Hinkler before official guests at the Cub-engined Aldershot demonstration at Hamble on December 12, 1922, had the cutaway wing roots filled in and the top mainplane raised 15 inches above the fuselage on short struts. This permitted the insertion of a sliding communication hatch in the cabin roof behind the pilot. To improve directional control and stability the rudder was enlarged and auxiliary fins were mounted under the outer ends of the tailplane. Side bracing-struts were also added to the bottom centre section, the long exhaust pipes of *N153* were abandoned and an improved metal tail skid fitted. A third prototype, *N155*, identical with *N153* but with a tail unit similar to *N154*, was shown in the New Types Park at the Hendon RAF Display on June 30, 1923. It was taken on charge at the Wireless and Photographic Flight of the RAE, Farnborough, early in 1924 but was later based at Gosport.

Twelve Bison I aircraft similar to *N153* were then built and one was shown at the Prague Exhibition of May 31–June 9, 1924. Another, *N9594*, was later converted by the Hamble works into the Avro 555B Bison I amphibian with 22 ft 4½ in mahogany boat-built central float, two small wingtip stabilising floats and retractable wheels. Performance trials on this aircraft were abandoned after preliminary handling flights at the MAEE, Felixstowe, had shown longitudinal and directional instability, unsatisfactory behaviour on the water and inadequate elevator control below 70 knots.

Main production batches to Air Ministry Specification 16/23, based on the second prototype with raised centre section, large dorsal fin replacing the small auxiliary units, and two-bladed instead of four-bladed airscrews, were designated Avro 555A Bison IA. Late production aircraft had the centre-section gap further increased but were without the undercarriage arrester claws and circular portholes forward. With these modifications the aircraft was known as the Bison II, but unlike the Bison I which had

*N153*, the first prototype Avro 555 Bison.

205

*N154*, second prototype Bison with centre-section struts and increased mainplane gap.

dihedral on both upper and lower mainplanes, the top wings of the Bison IA and II were without dihedral. First deliveries were made from Woodford to Gosport via Sealand and Farnborough (for acceptance tests) by H. J. Hinkler and A. G. B. Ellis in February 1925.

Although destined originally for deck landing, the Bison was first employed on Coastal Area reconnaissance duties, replacing Westland Walrus biplanes of No.3 Squadron, RAF, at Gosport in 1922. The type was not issued to the Fleet Air Arm until No.3 Squadron disbanded in April 1923, the first naval unit to receive the Bison II being No.423 Fleet Spotter Flight, Gosport, which later took them to the Mediterranean in HMS *Eagle*. Similar Flights, numbered 421, 421A, 421B, 447 and 448 served in the same carrier (some as target tugs), or with the Home Fleet in HMS *Furious*, and No.448 also served ashore at Hal Far, Malta. All were superseded by Fairey IIIFs in 1929.

The Avro 555B Bison I amphibian. (*Crown Copyright Reserved*)

Before final retirement the early Bison I *N9592* was transferred from Gosport to Farnborough where it served with the Engine Research Flight for a year on engine and radiator tests.

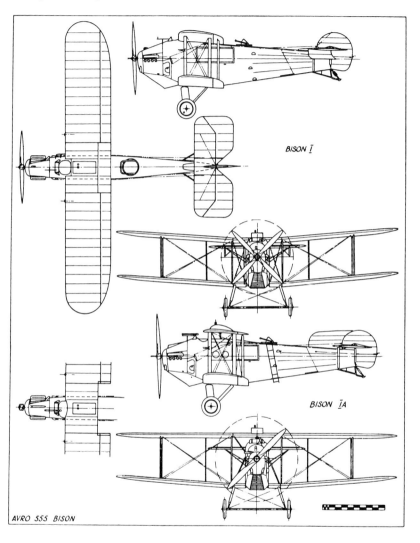

BISON I

BISON IA

AVRO 555 BISON

207

# SPECIFICATION AND DATA

*Manufacturers:*   A. V. Roe and Co Ltd, Newton Heath, Manchester; and Hamble Aerodrome, near Southampton, Hants

*Powerplant:*   One 480 hp Napier Lion II

*Dimensions, Weights and Performances:*

|  | Avro 555 Bison I | Avro 555A Bison II | Avro 555B amphibian** |
|---|---|---|---|
| Span | 46 ft 0 in | 46 ft 0 in | 45 ft 10 in |
| Length | 36 ft 0 in | 36 ft 0 in | 37 ft 4½ in |
| Height | 13 ft 6 in* | 14 ft 2 in | 14 ft 10½ in |
| Wing area | 620 sq ft* | 630 sq ft | 620 sq ft |
| Mainplane gap | 6 ft 9 in* | 8 ft 3 in | 6 ft 9 in |
| Tare weight | 4,160 lb | 4,116 lb | 4,972 lb |
| All-up weight | 5,800 lb | 6,132 lb | 6,244 lb |
| Maximum speed | 110 mph | 108 mph | — |
| Cruising speed | 90 mph | 90 mph | — |
| Initial climb | 600 ft/min | 450 ft/min | — |
| Ceiling | 14,000 ft | 12,000 ft | — |
| Range | 340 miles | 360 miles | — |

*Bison IA 13 ft 10 in, 630 sq ft and 8 ft 0 in respectively.
**Felixstowe Report F/11 dated 20.8.25.

*Production:*

**Prototypes:** *N153, N154* (dismantled at Hamble 4.28), *N155*

**Avro 555 Bison I.** Twelve aircraft built at Manchester to Air Ministry order 1922: *N9591–N9602.* (*N9592* to the Engine Research Flight, RAE, 28.2.24; *N9594* rebuilt as the Avro 555B Bison I amphibian; others rebuilt as Bison IA.)

**Avro 555A Bison II.** Forty-one aircraft built at Manchester in four batches: *N9836–N9853* (18 aircraft) ordered July 1924. Delivery flights Sealand–Farnborough: *N9836* on 20.4.25, *N9838* (Hinkler) 28.2.25, *N9839* (Ellis) 28.2.25, *N9840* (Ellis) 5.3.25.
*N9966–N9977*   (12 aircraft) December 1924.
*S1109–S1114*   (6 aircraft) November 1926.
*S1163–S1167*   (5 aircraft) February 1927.

*Service Use:* (*a*) RAF 1922–23: No.3 Squadron, Gosport. (*b*) Fleet Air Arm 1923–29: Fleet Spotter Flights Nos.421, 421A, 447 with HMS *Furious*, Home Fleet; Nos.421B, 423, 448 with HMS *Eagle*, Mediterranean Fleet.

The first prototype Avro 557 Ava *N171* (rounded wingtips) flying past at the Hendon RAF Display on July 2, 1927. (*P. T. Capon*)

# Avro 557 Ava

First conceived in November 1921 as the Avro 556 torpedo bomber to Specification 16/22 (D of R Type 9), the Avro 557 Ava was a large, three-bay biplane designed by Roy Chadwick and intended originally for very-long-range coastal defence work or night bombing. The bombing role was eventually shelved and the first Ava prototype, *N171*, was completed purely for coastal work. Gun positions were built into the nose and the rear fuselage aft of the wings, the space under the tail was covered by a third gunner in a retractable 'dustbin', and the machine could carry 2,000 lb of bombs internally or a single 21-in Whitehead torpedo between the twin under-carriage units.

Powered by two uncowled 650 hp Rolls-Royce Condor III water-cooled engines gravity fed from fuel tanks immediately above them, the Ava was of wooden construction with folding wings and dual control for two pilots side by side in an open cockpit. The rudders were possibly the largest of the famous Avro comma type ever built and formed part of an enormous biplane tail. The Ava was initially flown with triple rudders but the central one was soon removed and the twin rudder arrangement became standard.

Although built at Hamble in 1924 the machine did not appear in public until numbered 14 in the New Types Park at the Hendon RAF Display on July 3, 1926. A second Ava prototype, *N172*, shown at the Hendon Display on July 2, 1927, was largely similar to the first, but was of metal construction throughout and identified by square-cut instead of rounded wingtips.

The adoption of the 18-inch British Admiralty Mk.VIII as the standard

209

The second Ava, *N172*, with torpedo in position showing the square cut wingtips. (*P. T. Capon*)

naval torpedo made the size of the aircraft unnecessary and there was no production.

It is a point of interest that another set of drawings, still in existence and also numbered Avro 557, depict a single-seat monoplane. This project, dated January 5, 1923, or nearly nine months before the Ava, envisaged an Avro 552 fuselage (complete with Wolseley Viper engine), mounted on an Avro 504N undercarriage and attached to a parasol wing wire-braced to a central kingpost. Although the scheme was dropped and the type number reallotted, performance calculations gave an estimated tare weight of 1,600 lb, all-up weight 2,450 lb, maximum speed 110 mph, initial climb 1,000 ft/min and ceiling 20,000 ft.

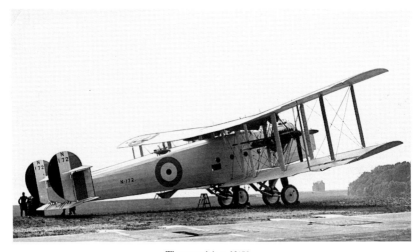

The second Ava, *N172*.

210

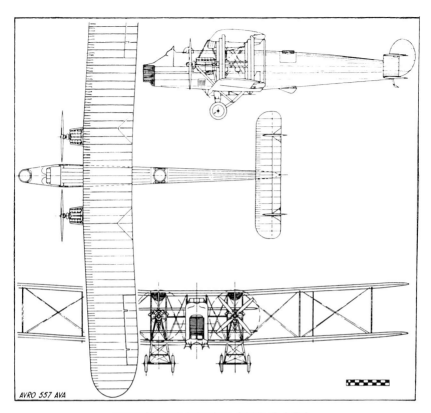

AVRO 557 AVA

## SPECIFICATION AND DATA

*Manufacturers:* A. V. Roe and Co Ltd, Newton Heath, Manchester; and Hamble Aerodrome, near Southampton, Hants

*Powerplants:* (Avro 556 project) One 1,000 hp Napier Cub
(Ava) Two 650 hp Rolls-Royce Condor III

*Dimensions:* (Avro 556 project) Span 95 ft 0 in    Length 58 ft 3 in
(Ava *N171*) Span 96 ft 10 in    Length 61 ft 9 in
Height 19 ft $7\frac{3}{4}$ in
Wing area 2,163 sq ft
(Ava *N172*) Span 95 ft 4 in

*Weights:* (Ava *N171*) Tare weight 12,760 lb★    All-up weight
19,920 lb
(Ava *N172*) Tare weight 13,304 lb    All-up weight
20,465 lb

★13,020 lb at Martlesham trials.

*Production:* Two prototypes only, *N171* and *N172*, of wood and metal construction respectively. *N172* was completed and weighed at Hamble on 21.4.27 and first flown next day.

211

The Avro 558 ultra-light biplane No.5 with B and H Vee twin-engine at Lympne, October 1923, (*Flight*)

# Avro 558

The unnamed Avro 558 was a small biplane, two examples of which were built at Hamble for the *Daily Mail* performance trials for light single-seaters held at Lympne October 8–13, 1923. Chief designer Roy Chadwick chose the biplane configuration on account of its small overall dimensions, low structural weight, narrow chord mainplanes and small c.p. travel. A. V. Roe thought otherwise and designed a clean cantilever monoplane under designation Avro 560.

The Avro 558s had heavily staggered, RAF 15 section, high aspect ratio mainplanes braced by circular-section wire. They were supported on solid spruce I-type interplane and centre-section struts of streamline section into the slotted ends of which were riveted V-shaped duralumin plates bolted to fittings on the spars. The pilot sat on the floor of a conventional wire-braced, fabric-covered wooden fuselage with his head projecting through a hole in the hinged plywood decking. To keep down head resistance still further the undercarriage, comprising two 22 in diameter bicycle wheels mounted on a steel-tube axle sprung by rubber cord, was located inside the fuselage with only the lower half of the wheels protruding. Their track was so narrow and the bottom wing so near the ground that strong wingtip skids were needed.

Entered by A. V. Roe and Co and flown by H. J. Hinkler, the first (unregistered) Avro 558 No.5, was powered by a B and H direct-drive, twin-cylinder, air-cooled Vee-type motorcycle engine. The second *G-EBHW* No.11, built for G. S. Bush and H. A. Hamersley (who flew the machine), was also equipped with a motorcycle engine, a 500 cc twin-cylinder, horizontally-opposed Douglas, complete with external flywheel and driving the airscrew through a $2\frac{1}{2}$:1 chain reduction gear. This was by far the better performer of the two and on the opening day of the trials Hamersley completed four laps of the $12\frac{1}{2}$ mile Lympne circuit and reached a height of 6,750 ft. He then exploited its high flying potential and although he failed to beat the A.N.E.C. I in this respect, 13,850 ft reached on October 13 was no mean achievement in turbulent conditions. For this he received the Duke of Sutherland's £100 prize.

A temperamental engine prevented Hinkler from making any laps of the circuit in No.5 and when Lt Barrett flew it on October 13, he was forced to land by the high winds and the machine was damaged. After the competition No.5 was taken back to Hamble where the nose of the fuselage was modified to take a 698 cc Blackburne Tomtit engine. The close proximity of the lower wing to the ground undoubtedly made landing difficult in long grass

The second Avro 558, *G-EBHW*, with 500 cc Douglas flat-twin engine.

The second Avro 558, No.11/*G-EBHW*, at Hendon on October 27, 1923, with raised undercarriage and wingtip skids. (*H. H. Grant*)

213

No.5, the first Avro 558, in modified form with 698 cc Blackburne Tomtit engine and V-type undercarriage.
(*Avro*)

or on rough surfaces and both machines were modified accordingly. No.5 was fitted with a light-weight strutted undercarriage with aircraft wheels, while No.11 was raised on its existing bicycle wheels by means of two wide vertical struts, probably those removed from the Avro 560 monoplane. It was raced in this form at the Royal Aero Club Light Plane Demonstration at Hendon on October 27, 1923, by H. A. Hamersley, who flew a low and stylish race in high wind and came third.

H. J. Hinkler in the cockpit of No.5 at Lympne.

214

# SPECIFICATION AND DATA

*Manufacturers:*    A. V. Roe and Co Ltd, Newton Heath, Manchester; and Hamble Aerodrome, near Southampton, Hants

*Powerplants:*    One B and H
One 500 cc Douglas
One 698 cc Blackburne Tomtit

*Dimensions:*    Span 30 ft 0 in    Length 19 ft 6 in
Wing area 166 sq ft

*Weights:*    Tare weight 294 lb    All-up weight 480 lb

*Production:*    Two aircraft only, 1923 Lympne trials No.5; and No.11, c/n 5089, registered to G. E. Bush and H. A. Hamersley 19.9.23 as *G-EBHW*, a registration which eventually lapsed

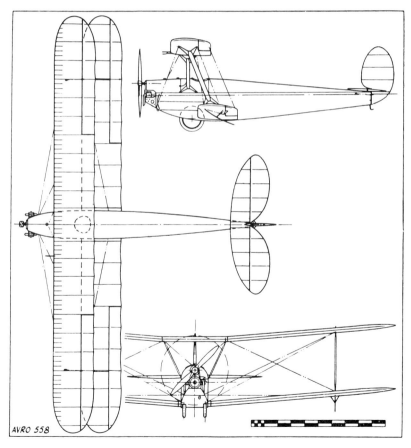

AVRO 558

215

The Avro 560 ultra-light monoplane with upright Tomtit engine as flown at Lympne, October 1923.
*(Courtesy the Royal Aeronautical Society)*

# Avro 560

In addition to the Avro 558 biplanes, the Hamble works also produced an ultra-light, high aspect ratio cantilever monoplane which was flown in the 1923 Lympne trials by H. J. Hinkler. Known as the Avro 560 and said to have been designed personally by A. V. Roe, it received competition No.6 and distinguished itself during the meeting by completing 80 laps of the $12\frac{1}{2}$ mile circuit (1,000 miles) without a forced landing. Its fuel consumption worked out at 63.3 mpg and at one stage of the trials the machine completed 10 laps (125 miles) nonstop. A second ultra-light monoplane, the Avro 559, was not completed.

The fuselage of the Avro 560 was of typical Avro fabric-covered, wooden construction with a tapered, biconvex section, cantilever mainplane bolted directly to the top longerons with the pilot's cockpit between the spars. A 698 cc Blackburne Tomtit upright Vee twin air-cooled engine was bolted to a duralumin plate on the front end of the fuselage and the undercarriage, unlike those of the biplanes, consisted of two short struts projecting below the fuselage and carrying two light wooden wheels on a rubber sprung steel axle. The tailplane was a cantilever unit built in two halves which bolted together through the fuselage as on the 558 and the altimeter was inside the wing root so that there were no pipelines to disconnect when the wing was removed.

Provision was made for the substitution of an alternative mainplane of reduced span to give higher speeds for competition purposes when required. Unfortunately the Lympne officials ruled that with the short-span wing it would rank as a different aeroplane. They would not therefore allow the change because the machine had not been separately entered in that condition.

Hinkler flew the Avro 560 again, this time fitted with the reduced span mainplane, at the RAeC Light Plane Demonstration at Hendon on October 27, 1923, but was forced down with engine trouble. Wear on the inlet valve stems had been a continuous problem with this engine, and when the aircraft was taken on Air Ministry experimental charge as *J7322* for assessment at Martlesham against the Parnall Pixie II and the D.H.53

216

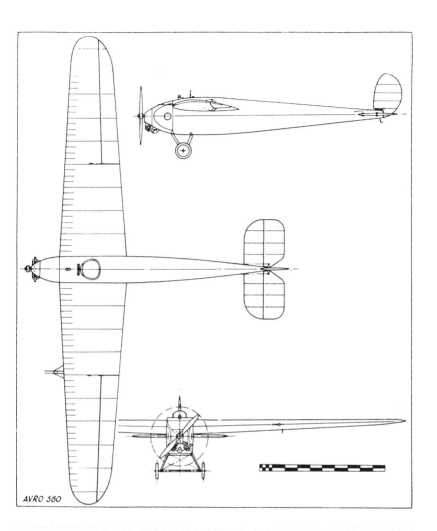

The Avro 560 at Martlesham in 1924 with V-type undercarriage, inverted Tomtit engine and serial *J7322*.

H. J. Hinkler with the Avro 560 at Lympne. (*British Aerospace*)

Humming Bird in 1924, one of the new Blackburne Tomtit inverted engines was fitted. It was also given an orthodox strutted undercarriage with aircraft wheels of the type fitted to Avro 558 No.5, and the rear circular portholes filled in. At a time of stringent economy the RAF needed a cheaply run aircraft of this kind for practice flying and communication but choice fell on the D.H.53 and no further Avro 560 monoplanes were built.

## SPECIFICATION AND DATA

*Manufacturers:*  A. V. Roe and Co Ltd, Newton Heath, Manchester; and Hamble Aerodrome, near Southampton, Hants

*Powerplants:*  One 698 cc Blackburne Tomtit upright engine
One 698 cc Blackburne Tomtit inverted engine

*Dimensions:*  Span 36 ft 0 in   Length 21 ft 0 in
Wing area 138 sq ft

*Weights:*  Tare weight 285 lb   All-up weight 471 lb

*Production:*  One aircraft only, 1923 Lympne trials No.6, remodelled in 1924 and transferred to the RAF as *J7322* under Contract 487256/24

218

The first Avro 561 Andover, *J7261*, taxying out at the Hendon RAF Display on June 28, 1924.

# Avro 561 Andover

Built to RAF order to replace D.H.10s on the Cairo–Baghdad desert air route, the Andover could be equipped alternatively as passenger transport or ambulance. It used the same folding mainplanes, undercarriage and tail unit as the Avro 549 Aldershot but the fuselage was entirely new. This was built in three sections and comprised a steel-tube cantilever engine mounting and shutter-equipped radiator compartment, an oval-section wooden monocoque cabin amidships and a fabric-covered tubular-steel after-section to fair it neatly into the tail.

The cabin portion, 22 ft long, 4 ft 9 in wide and with 6 ft headroom, accommodated up to 12 passengers in wicker chairs (six each side of a central gangway) or six stretcher cases, and was built up from large oval rings and stringers covered inside and out with plywood. The air space between provided insulation against temperature variations and noise. Large openable windows ran the length of each side and entry was via a rectangular trapdoor in the starboard side.

The pilot sat in an open cockpit just below the leading edge of the centre section with the navigator alongside and at a slightly lower level with direct access to the cabin through a door in its forward bulkhead. Fuel was carried in two large aerofoil section slipper-type gravity tanks on top of the wing, while long multiple RAE perforated exhaust pipes acted as silencers.

When the desert air route was transferred to Imperial Airways, the order was cut back and only three Andovers were built initially, the first of which, *J7261*, was shown in the New Types Park and flown past at the Hendon RAF Display on June 28, 1924. All three then went into service at RAF Halton. Early in 1925 a fourth machine, the purely civil Avro 563 12-passenger version (also named Andover) was built to Air Ministry order. It was the first Avro machine to be built specially for airline service on main routes and was largely similar to the military transport with six single seats down each side of a central gangway, but with lavatory and luggage accommodation in the rear. The Avro 563 was registered *G-EBKW* and after airworthiness test flights at Hamble and Gosport in March 1925, was loaned to Imperial Airways at Croydon for cross-Channel proving flights during the summer of that year.

## SPECIFICATION AND DATA

*Manufacturers:*   A. V. Roe and Co Ltd, Newton Heath, Manchester; and Hamble Aerodrome, near Southampton, Hants

*Powerplants:*   (Avro 561) One 650 hp Rolls-Royce Condor III
(Avro 563) One 650 hp Rolls-Royce Condor III

*Dimensions:*   (Avro 561) Span 68 ft 0 in    Span (folded) 27 ft 6 in
Length 51 ft 3 in   Height 15 ft 3 in
Wing area 1,062 sq ft
(Avro 563) Span 68 ft 0 in    Span (folded) 27 ft 6 in
Length 51 ft 7 in   Height 16 ft $1\frac{1}{2}$ in
Wing area 1,064 sq ft

*Weights:*   (Avro 561) Tare weight 6,980 lb★   All-up weight 11,500 lb★
(Avro 563) Tare weight 6,800 lb    All-up weight 10,685 lb
★6,987 lb and 11,793 lb at Martlesham trials.

*Performances:*   (Avro 561) Maximum speed 110 mph   Ceiling 13,500 ft
Range 460 miles
(Avro 563) Maximum speed 110 mph   Cruising speed 90 mph
Initial climb 400 ft/min   Ceiling 10,000 ft

*Production:*   (*a*) For the RAF—three aircraft only *J7261* to *J7263* to Contract 458918/23.
(*b*) Civil—one aircraft only, *G-EBKW* c/n 5097, registered to the Air Council 27.2.25, C of A issued 21.4.25, loaned to Imperial Airways 1925, handed over to the RAF 1.27 as *J7264*

The Avro 563 Andover civil transport (*P. T. Capon*)

The Avro 563 Andover *G-EBKW* after transfer to the RAF as *J5264*. (*Courtesy Philip Jarrett*)

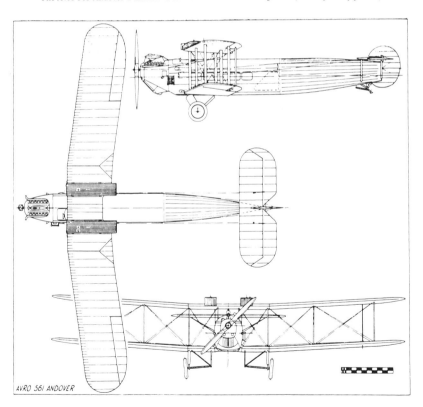

AVRO 561 ANDOVER

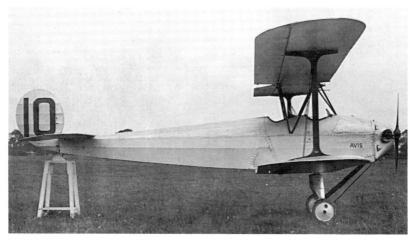

The Avro 562 Avis in early form with 32 hp geared Bristol Cherub II driving a wooden airscrew.

# Avro 562 Avis

The Avis, Avro entry for the Air Ministry's Two Seat Light Aeroplane Trials held at Lympne September 29–October 4, 1924, was a small equal-span, single-bay biplane slightly reminiscent of the Avro 514 of 1914 with circular rudder and single I-type interplane struts. The fuselage was the usual wire-braced, fabric-covered Warren girder with plywood top decking, and the wings were designed to fold to comply with the rules of the competition. A pair of steel V-shaped jury struts were provided to support the inner ends when folded. Ailerons ran the full length of all four wings, the upper pair being linked to the lower by rods at the inner end so that all four could be depressed to act as flaps on final approach by means of an ingenious worm drive mechanism. A long-travel oleo undercarriage with front radius rods completed a very business-like little aeroplane.

Although first flown at Hamble with a 35 hp Blackburne Thrush direct-drive, three-cylinder radial, an alternative mounting was built to enable a 32 hp Bristol Cherub II geared horizontally-opposed engine to be substituted when required. Remembering the previous year's disappointment when competition regulations prevented the Avro 560 monoplane from flying at Lympne with the short-span mainplane, the Avis biplane was entered as two separate aeroplanes, No.10 with the Cherub and No.11 with Thrush. In the event this precaution was unnecessary as the Thrush was not used.

When the machine was delivered at Lympne by road on September 28, the Cherub had not yet been installed but this work was completed during the next two days. Unfortunately snags were encountered and the engine appeared to give only half power. After several attempts during the afternoon of September 30, Hinkler managed to get the Avis airborne, but not daring

222

to venture round the course, was eliminated from the competitions. Nevertheless, overnight the Cherub was converted to direct-drive and performance was such that on October 1 Hinkler gave flights to Director of Civil Aviation Sir Sefton Brancker and Air Vice-Marshal Sir Geoffrey Salmond. Next day Avro enterprise was at last rewarded when, in a field of 13 aircraft, Hinkler won the Grosvenor Challenge Trophy and £100 by flying the Avis eight times round the $12\frac{1}{2}$ mile course at an average speed of 65·87 mph.

With his wife as passenger, Hinkler then flew the Avis triumphantly back to Hamble with a night stop at Croydon on October 6 and a fuelling stop at Farnborough next day.

The Avis in 1925 with direct-drive Cherub and duralumin airscrew.

The Avis at the 1926 Lympne Trials with 1,500 cc Blackburne Thrush three-cylinder radial.

223

The Avis was at Martlesham for trials in March and April 1925, appearing again in public at the Lympne Meeting on August 1, 1925, still with direct-drive Cherub, which this time drove a duralumin airscrew specially made for it by Avro. Hinkler, very familiar with the $12\frac{1}{2}$ mile circuit, came third in the International Light Aeroplane Holiday Handicap at 64·8 mph and fifth in the Grosvenor Challenge Trophy Race at 65·32 mph. At this stage the Avis cowlings differed from those of the previous year because the cylinder heads of the direct-drive Cherub were lower in relation to the thrust line of the airscrew than those of the geared engine. It also bore civil registration *G-EBKP* allocated to it in December 1924.

As 'second string' to Avro's new Avian prototype for the Two Seat Light Aeroplane Trials at Lympne, September 12–17, 1926, the Avis reverted to a Thrush engine, this time the new and slightly heavier 1,500 cc (38 hp) model. Painted yellow and flown by Wing Cdr W. Sholto Douglas (later Lord Douglas of Kirtleside), the machine averaged 51·25 mph to Shoreham and back on the first day but was eliminated when the undercarriage was damaged in a forced landing on the second.

In the following year Avros refitted the direct-drive Cherub I and disposed of the Avis to private owner E. L. O. Baddeley who kept it only a few months before advertising it for sale for £250. The price dropped to £100 in the following August and the machine was eventually acquired by T. S. Baldwin, garage proprietor of Totnes, Devon, who finally scrapped it at the end of 1931.

The Avis at the 1926 Lympne meeting.

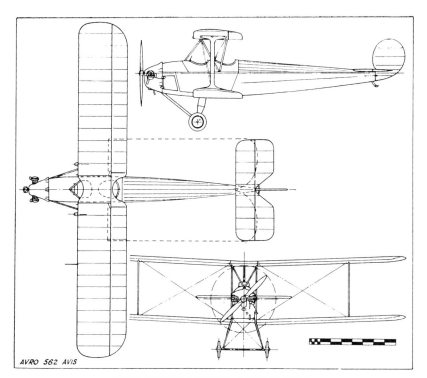

AVRO 562 AVIS

## SPECIFICATION AND DATA

*Manufacturers:*  A. V. Roe and Co Ltd, Newton Heath, Manchester; and Hamble Aerodrome, near Southampton, Hants

*Powerplants:*  One 1,096 cc (35 hp) Blackburne Thrush
One 1,500 cc (38 hp) Blackburne Thrush
One 1,096 cc (32·6 hp) Bristol Cherub I direct-drive
One 1,096 cc (32·6 hp) Bristol Cherub II geared

*Dimensions:*  Span 30 ft 1 in    Span (folded) 9 ft 0 in
Length 24 ft 0 in  Height 9 ft 0 in
Wing area 246 sq ft

*Weights:*  (1,096 cc Thrush)
             Tare weight 590 lb  All-up weight 995 lb
(1,500 cc Thrush)
             Tare weight 606 lb  All-up weight 1,050 lb
(Cherub I)  Tare weight 565 lb  All-up weight 943 lb
(Cherub II) Tare weight 575 lb  All-up weight 960 lb

*Performance:*  Maximum speed 75 mph

*Production:*  One aircraft only, *G-EBKP* c/n 5105, registered to A. V. Roe and Co Ltd 19.12.24; C of A issued 1.2.26; sold 10.27 to E. L. O. Baddeley; to T. S. Baldwin, Baldwin's Garage, Totnes, Devon 10.28; scrapped 12.31

225

The Avenger in its first, Avro 566, form.

# Avro 566 Avenger

The Avenger was a private venture single-seat fighter designed by Roy Chadwick and first flown at Hamble by H. J. Hinkler on June 26, 1926. It was a single-bay biplane powered by a 525 hp direct-drive Napier Lion VIII turning a two-bladed wooden airscrew, and cooled by Lamblin radiators built into the underside of the upper mainplane. The mainplanes were built up from two spruce spars with plywood ribs, fabric-covered, rigged with N-type interplane struts and fitted with ailerons on the top wing only.

One of the cleanest biplanes built up to that time, the Avenger was unique in its day by virtue of its oval-section semi-monocoque fuselage of elm frames and spruce longitudinals, double planked with mahogany, fabric-covered and varnished. Tailplane and fin were cantilever units bolted to stub spars built integral with the fuselage. The pilot's seat was beneath a cut-out in the trailing edge of the centre section and the undercarriage was of normal cross-axle type with oleo and rubber-in-compression front legs and rubber sprung tail skid. Fuel from a 56 gallon fuselage tank was fed to the engine via a small gravity tank in the centre section.

In company with the Gloster Gorcock and Hawker Hornbill fighter prototypes, the Avenger disported in civil markings *G-EBND* at the Hendon RAF Display on July 3, 1926. None of the three was adopted for the Royal Air Force and in the following year '*ND* was entered for the King's Cup Race by Sir Kenneth Crossley, chairman of Crossley Motors Ltd which had a considerable financial interest in A. V. Roe and Co. When the impossibly high handicap speed of 244 mph was announced, Crossley's pilot F/Lt S. L. G. 'Poppy' Pope reluctantly scratched the Avenger from the race.

The original design aimed at wide overseas appeal by providing for wings with differing characteristics to suit a number of diverse roles. Advantage was taken of this feature in May 1928 when the Avenger returned to Hamble to be fitted with smaller, equal-span mainplanes, and streamlined, I-type interplane struts for racing purposes. To improve the rate of roll when cornering, ailerons were fitted to all four wings, the main undercarriage legs were raked slightly forward and a new 553 hp Napier Lion IX engine driving an Avro metal airscrew was installed under improved cowlings.

In this form, as the Avro 567 Avenger II, it was aerobatted by F/Lt F. L. Luxmoore DFC at the Hampshire Air Pageant, Hamble, on May 27–28 and Blackpool Meeting at Squires Gate on July 6, 1928. Next day Schneider Trophy pilot F/Lt S. N. Webster averaged 180·25 mph in the Open Handicap Race and came second to an Avro Avian, his speed on the straight being such that A. V. Roe entered the machine for the King's Cup Race at Hendon on July 20, 1928. Flown by F/O J. 'Mutt' Summers, it won £100 for fastest time in the race and touched down at Brooklands next day in

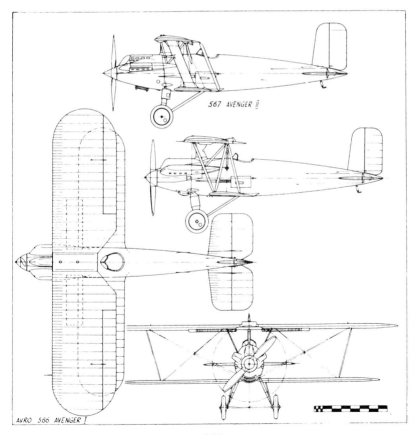

13th place, having averaged 149 mph over the 1,096 miles to Renfrew and back.

Proposals were also made in 1927 to fit the Avenger with wings of RAF 30 section as the Avro 569; with a 570 hp geared Napier Lion XI as the Avro 583; and to incorporate other extensive modifications under type number Avro 602, but all these schemes came to nought. Still in Avro 567 configuration the Avenger left for Bucharest on September 6, 1928, in company with the Vickers Vivid *G-EBPY* for demonstration before the Rumanian authorities. No orders were received and the Avenger returned to Hamble, where it remained until Air Service Training took over in May 1931 and dismantled it for use as an instructional airframe.

The modified Avro 567 Avenger II taking off from Hendon in the King's Cup Race on July 20, 1928.
(*The Aeroplane*)

## SPECIFICATION AND DATA

*Manufacturers:*  A. V. Roe and Co Ltd, Newton Heath, Manchester; and Hamble Aerodrome, near Southampton, Hants.

*Powerplants:*  (Avro 566) One 525 hp Napier Lion VIII
(Avro 567) One 553 hp Napier Lion IX

*Dimensions:*  (Avro 566) Span (upper) 32 ft 0 in (lower) 28 ft 0 in
Length 25 ft 6 in  Height 10 ft 3 in
(Avro 567) Span 28 ft 0 in  Length 25 ft 6 in
Height 9 ft 9 in  Wing area 244 sq ft

*Weights:*  (Avro 566) Tare weight 2,368 lb  All-up weight 3,220 lb
(Avro 567) All-up weight 3,414 lb

*Performances:*  (Avro 566) Maximum speed 180 mph
Cruising speed 130 mph
Initial climb 2,100 ft/min  Ceiling 22,000 ft

*Production:*  One aircraft only, Avro 566 *G-EBND* c/n 5109, C of A issued 11.7.26, to Martlesham 10.26, converted to Avro 567 in 1928, to instructional airframe 1931

228

The Avro 571 Buffalo I *G-EBNW*, showing the rounded wingtips and ailerons on the lower mainplane only.

# Avro 571 Buffalo

This was a two-seat, private venture deck landing, torpedo carrying and bombing landplane to Specification 21/23, powered by a 450 hp Napier Lion VA and first flown at Hamble in 1926. Intended as a Blackburn Dart replacement, the Buffalo was a single-bay folding biplane which used much of the wing structure of the Bison II. Wing spars were of spruce, with spruce and duralumin ribs, tubular steel drag struts and steel tie-rod internal bracing. Ailerons were fitted to the lower mainplane only and the tailplane was adjustable for incidence. The fin and rudder were those of the Bison II and the wide-track divided undercarriage was sprung by long-travel oleo and rubber-in-compression shock absorbers.

The fuselage, of entirely new design, was of tubular steel construction with duralumin decking and fabric sides, in which the pilot sat high up under a cut-out in the centre section with an excellent forward view for landing on an aircraft carrier. The second crew member sat behind, with access to both the radio cabin and a prone bombing (or camera) position in the bottom of the fuselage. Armament consisted of one Vickers gun on the side of the fuselage firing through the airscrew, and twin Lewis guns on a Scarff mounting on the rear cockpit. Flotation bags were located in the rear fuselage and a dump valve was fitted to the 160 gallon main fuel tank so that it could provide extra buoyancy in case of a forced alighting at sea.

229

Early in the Buffalo's career, the Bison fin and rudder were replaced by a large rectangular unit. Following competitive trials at Martlesham with the Blackburn Ripon and Handley Page H.P.31 Harrow built to the same specification, from which the Ripon emerged triumphant, the Buffalo was flown back to Hamble in 1927 to be fitted with an entirely new set of mainplanes. Designed to improve performance and handling qualities, the new wings were entirely of metal, more rectangular, and fitted with four Frise ailerons and controllable Handley Page slots. Thus equipped and re-engined with a 530 hp Napier Lion XIA, it was known as the Avro 572 Buffalo II.

*G-EBNW* rebuilt as the Avro 572 Buffalo II with rectangular wings and four Frise-type ailerons.

The Buffalo II as a seaplane in military marks, Hamble 1928. (*P. T. Capon*)

230

In July 1928 the Buffalo II was acquired by the Air Ministry and converted at Hamble into a seaplane with single-step, V-bottomed duralumin floats and flown to Felixstowe. A purely bomber version in landplane form, considered under type number Avro 597, was not proceeded with.

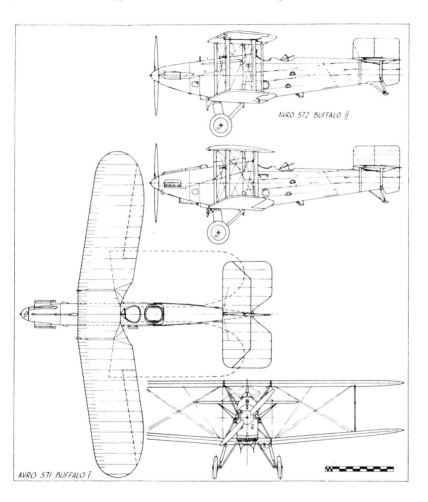

AVRO 572 BUFFALO II

AVRO 571 BUFFALO I

## SPECIFICATION AND DATA

*Manufacturers:*  A. V. Roe and Co Ltd, Newton Heath, Manchester; and Hamble Aerodrome, near Southampton, Hants.

*Powerplants:*  (Avro 571 Buffalo I)  One 450 hp Napier Lion VA
(Avro 572 Buffalo II) One 530 hp Napier Lion XIA

231

The Buffalo I with torpedo in position beneath the fuselage.

*Dimensions:*   (Avro 571) Span 46 ft 0 in   Length 36 ft 6 in
                                    Height 13 ft 9 in
             (Avro 572) Span 46 ft 0 in
             Length 37 ft 3 in, (seaplane) 38 ft 6 in
             Height 14 ft 0 in, (seaplane) 14 ft 2 in
             Wing Area 684 sq ft

*\*Weights:*   (landplane) Tare weight 4,233 lb   All-up weight 7,430 lb
             (seaplane)   Tare weight 4,684 lb   All-up weight 7,871 lb

*\*Performance:*   (landplane)
             Maximum speed 135 mph   Cruising speed 105 mph
             Initial climb 770 ft/min   Ceiling 13,700 ft
             Range 650 miles
             (seaplane)
             Maximum speed 130 mph   Cruising speed 100 mph
             Initial climb 640 ft/min   Ceiling 11,000 ft
             Range 400 miles

                                   \*Avro 572 Buffalo II

*Production:*   One aircraft only, Avro 571 Buffalo I *G-EBNW*, c/n
             R3/BTC/30021, rebuilt as Avro 572 Buffalo II in 1927,
             converted to seaplane at Hamble and transferred to the
             MAEE, Felixstowe, in 1928 as *N239*

F. T. Courtney flying the Avro 574 (Cierva C.6C) 504K derivative at Hamble in June 1926.

# Avro 574, 586 and 587
# (Cierva C.6C, C.8V, and C.6D/C.8R)

Don Juan de la Cierva, Spanish inventor of the world's first practical rotating wing, slow landing, non-stalling aircraft, started experimenting at Madrid in 1920 with a converted 1911 Deperdussin monoplane. He called this the Cierva C.1, but it would not fly. Problems of control arising from unbalanced lift also led to the failure of his C.2 (Hanriot fuselage) and C.3, but in 1922–23 he enjoyed limited success with C.4 and C.5. The Spanish Government became interested and advanced money which enabled Cierva to build his C.6A single-seat research machine. This was basically an Avro 504K (110 hp Le Rhône) with a wider-than-standard undercarriage, without mainplanes and fitted instead with a four-bladed articulated rotor (Göttingen 429 section) mounted on a pylon of steel tubes. The rotor was not engine driven but was kept in motion purely by the forward speed of the machine, a characteristic which led Cierva to invent the name 'Autogiro'. Directional control was by a normal 504K rudder but the elevator was horn balanced and the ailerons, mounted on outriggers, were standard Bristol Fighter units. For later trials an early pre-production 504N oleo undercarriage was obtained from Avros.

Construction took place at the Military Aircraft Works, Madrid, and the C.6A was first flown at Cuatro Vientos by Lt A. Gomez Spencer of the Spanish Flying Corps in May 1924. Experiments continued until December 9 when Capt J. Loriga reached an altitude of 650 ft in the course of a test flight, made an almost vertical descent and landing, and remained in perfect control at a forward speed of only 15 mph. The top speed was estimated at a useful 68 mph and on December 12 Loriga made the now historic first Autogiro cross-country flight of $7\frac{1}{2}$ miles from Cuatro Vientos to Getafe, scene of Cierva's earlier tests with the C.1. An almost exactly similar 504K derivative, the Cierva C.6B (110 hp Le Rhône) was flown at Cuatro Vientos by Loriga in 1925.

At the invitation of H. E. Wimperis, Director of Scientific Research at the Air Ministry, Cierva took the C.6A to England where Capt F. T. Courtney convincingly demonstrated it to a distinguished Farnborough gathering on October 15, 1925. As on all early Autogiros, the length of take-off run was considerably reduced by spinning the rotor with ropes. Extensive tests at the RAE by Sqn Ldr R. A. de Haga Haig AFC and exhibition flights by Courtney before French officials at Villacoublay, near Paris (January–February 1926), led the British Air Ministry to order two similar machines from A. V. Roe and Co to Contract 680624/26.

Built at Hamble under designations Cierva C.6C (Avro 574) and C.6D (Avro 587), they were similar to the C.6A and B with ailerons on outriggers, but had 130 hp Clerget engines instead of Le Rhônes. The C.6C, first flown at Hamble by Courtney on June 19, 1926, in RAF markings without serial number, flew as *J8068* before King George V at the Hendon RAF Display with the same pilot on July 3. Stub-wings (with ailerons) were later added in an attempt to relieve the rotors of part of the load in forward flight but although successful flights were made at Worthy Down on January 1, 1927, fatigue at the blade roots, caused by rigidity of the blades in the plane of rotation, resulted in the loss of a blade in flight at Hamble six days later. The machine crashed from 120 ft but Courtney was only slightly hurt and the rudder survived to be fitted eventually to a later type, the C.8L Mk.I.

Historically important as the first two-seat Autogiro, the Avro 587 (or Cierva C.6D), was first flown with a four-bladed rotor but without marks by F. T. Courtney at Hamble on July 29, 1926. Next day Cierva became

The Avro 587 (Cierva C.6D) with four-bladed rotor, Hamble 1927. (*Courtesy the Royal Aeronautical Society*)

The Avro 587 (after conversion to become the Cierva C.8R) flying over the Avro 586 (Cierva C.8V) at Hamble in 1927. (*Topical Press*)

the first passenger to fly in a rotating wing aircraft and on September 5 the noted German pilot Ernst Udet flew it at Tempelhof, Berlin, whither it had been taken by surface transport. On its return it was remodelled as the Cierva C.8R with tapered paddle-shaped rotor blades of increased chord and incorporating drag hinges to decrease the risk of fatigue failure at the roots. Stub-wings were also fitted. Work was completed on October 15 and H. J. 'Bert' Hinkler flew it early in 1927 with an experimental large area three-bladed rotor and in September that year with an exploratory two-bladed unit which set up excessive vibration and was hastily removed.

In 1926 the Autogiro research programme had also been joined by the two-seat Avro 552A slave aircraft *G-EAPR* (180 hp Wolseley Viper) stripped of wings and equipped with a similar rotor and control system to the C.8R. Tested initially by Hinkler this machine was designated C.8V (Avro 586). Main differences from the C.8R were the dorsal fin, a C.G. adjustment which permitted it to be flown solo from the front seat, and eventually a rotor with reduced blade chord which much improved the performance. Later it was equipped with a primitive tricycle undercarriage and in January 1927 with a four-wheeled chassis. The original two-wheeled undercarriage was replaced in August 1927 and in the following month the machine was allotted registration *G-EBTX* as a civil aircraft. Hinkler flew it to Croydon and back for demonstrations on October 20, 1927, but in 1930 it was reconstructed at Hanworth as an Avro 552A once more, a unique event described in the appropriate chapter.

# SPECIFICATION AND DATA

*Manufacturers:*  A. V. Roe and Co Ltd, Newton Heath, Manchester; and Hamble Aerodrome, near Southampton, Hants.
Spanish Military Aircraft Works, Getafe Aerodrome, Madrid

*Powerplants:*  (C.6A and C.6B)     One 110 hp Le Rhône
(C.6C, C.6D and C.8R) One 130 hp Clerget
(C.8V)                One 180 hp Wolseley Viper

*Dimensions, Weights and Performances:*

|  | Avro 574 (C.6C) | Avro 587 (C.6D) | Avro 587 (C.8R) | Avro 586 (C.8V) |
|---|---|---|---|---|
| Rotor diameter | 36 ft 0 in | 36 ft 0 in | 39 ft 8 in | 39 ft 8 in |
| Length | 34 ft 4¼ in | — | — | — |
| Tare weight | 1,490 lb | 1,915 lb | 1,637 lb* | 2,005 lb** |
| All-up weight | — | — | 2,212 lb | 2,768 lb |
| Initial climb | — | — | — | 270 ft/min |
| Rotor speed | 140 rpm | — | — | — |

*1,676 lb with large area three-bladed rotor 10.6.27.
**1,994 lb with four-wheeled undercarriage 15.1.27.

*Production:*

| Constructor's No. and Markings | Type | Details |
|---|---|---|

## (a) By the Spanish Military Aircraft Works

| nil | C.6A | First flown at Cuatro Vientos 7.23, to England 1925 |
|---|---|---|
| nil | C.6B | First flown at Cuatro Vientos 1925 |

## (b) By A. V. Roe and Co Ltd

| nil  *J8068* | C.6C | First flown 19.6.26, crashed at Hamble 7.2.27 |
|---|---|---|
| 5114  nil | C.6D | First flown 29.7.26, rebuilt 1927 as the C.8R |
| 5114  *G-EBTW* | C.8R | Registered 9.9.27, scrapped 1929 |
| 5113  *G-EBTX* | C.8V | Formerly Avro 552A *G-EAPR*, registered 9.9.27, reconverted to Avro 552A in 1930 as *G-ABGO* |

The Avro 586 (Cierva C.8V) with experimental four-wheeled undercarriage, January 1927. (*Courtesy the Royal Aeronautical Society*)

The Avro 575 (Cierva C.8L Mk.I) *J8930* with rudder from the earlier Avro 574 (Cierva C.6C). (*P. T. Capon*)

# Avro 575, 611 and 617 (Cierva C.8L)

Experimental Autogiro flying already described was the beginning of a long association between the Cierva Autogiro Co Ltd (formed on March 24, 1926) and A. V. Roe and Co Ltd who built the machines at Hamble. Promising results with the C.6s and C.8s (vide Avro 574 etc), led to Air Ministry Contract 698109/26 for a further prototype based on the Lynx-engined Avro 504N. This was fitted with a rotor having four paddle-type, fabric-covered, blades of 3 ft mean chord, built from tubular steel spars with spruce ribs, and running on four ball races. Fuel, carried under the top wing of the 504N, was perforce transferred to a 24 gallon fuselage tank with gravity feed. On this and three subsequent machines of the type, rotor spinning before take-off was either by a rope wound round the hub, or by fast taxying.

Known as the Avro 575 (Cierva C.8L Mk.I), the new machine comprised a 504N-type fuselage with standard tail unit and engine installation but the elevator was horn balanced and a pylon comprising four steel tubes was mounted over the front cockpit. The undercarriage was the usual unbreakable N-type, widened and equipped with long-travel, oleo and rubber-in-compression shock legs attached to the top instead of the bottom longerons. Lateral control was by ailerons hinged to a tubular steel boom.

First flown at Hamble by H. J. Hinkler in 1927, it bore RAF roundels and serial *J8930*, but has spread confusion among historians ever since because it used the rudder of the crashed Avro 574/Cierva C.6C from which the number *J8068* had not been obliterated. Cierva, who had just qualified as a pilot with the Hampshire Aeroplane Club at Hamble on Avro Avians, converted to rotary-wing machines under the tutelage of Hinkler.

237

Thenceforward he took an ever increasing part in autogiro development flying so that on September 30, 1927, it was the designer himself who delivered the Cierva C.8L Mk.I from Hamble to Farnborough, making the first cross-country flight by a rotary-winged aircraft in the UK in the process. Flight tests commenced at Farnborough with a C.8V-type rotor having blades of only 1 ft 9 in mean chord. This proved unsuccessful and *J8930* flew again with the original rotor on January 11, 1928. It remained at Farnborough until April 1930 and was written off at Andover about two months later.

A civil equivalent, the C.8L Mk.II (Avro 611) *G-EBYY*, was built in 1928 to the order of Air Commodore J. G. Weir, chairman of the Cierva Company, without whose financial backing most of the development work would have been impossible. The civil machine was similar to the first but part of the flying load was taken by a short-span, thick-section, fixed-wing carrying the ailerons. The wide-track undercarriage used the same long-travel shock absorbers but was attached to the front spar of the auxiliary wing and each half of the axle was hinged to a 504K-type skid. Rotor bracing differed in detail from that of the Mk.I and the engine, this time a Lynx IV, was more closely cowled. Dual control, tail trim and rotor lateral control gears were also fitted.

The civil Avro 611 (Cierva C.8L Mk.II).

The C.8L Mk.II was flown for the first time by Hinkler at Hamble early in May 1928 but Cierva damaged it at the Hamble Air Pageant on the 28th of that month. With the original unbalanced rudder and dorsal fin removed in favour of a standard comma-type balanced rudder, it faced the starter in the King's Cup Race at Hendon on July 20, flown by the newly appointed Cierva test pilot A. H. Rawson who was forced to retire from the race after landing at Caldecote, near Nuneaton, through fuel shortage. On August 7 Rawson began a 3,000 mile tour of the principal British civil and Service aerodromes and visited the grounds of the owner's estate at Dalrymple, near Turnhouse.

The Italian Government's Avro 617 (Cierva C.8L Mk.III) at Hamble before delivery.

Then on September 18 *G-EBYY* became the first rotating wing aircraft to cross the Channel when Cierva, with the editor of the French aviation journal *L'Aéronautique* as passenger, flew the machine from Croydon to Le Bourget. After demonstrations Cierva picked up Rawson and left for Berlin via Brussels on October 3. Rawson returned with another passenger via Amsterdam on October 13 and brought the total mileage for the tour to 1,450. Although it retained British markings, *G-EBYY* returned no more to its native land and is believed to have spent some time with Weymann-Lepère who later built the more advanced C.18 Autogiro. The C.8L Mk.II has remained ever since in the Musée de l'Air, Paris, except for a brief period on exhibition at the Brussels Aero Show in 1950.

Harold Pitcairn's Cierva C.8L Mk.IV *NC418*.

Publicity deriving from these exploits resulted in two overseas orders, the first being the Lynx IV powered C.8L Mk.III (Avro 617) built for the Italian Government and test flown by A. H. Rawson in September 1928. The Mk.IV (or C.8W), a single machine built for the USA and flown at Hamble in November 1928, was fitted with a 225 hp Wright Whirlwind J-5 for aircraft manufacturer Harold F. Pitcairn who had visited Hamble earlier in 1928, bought the American rights, and established the Pitcairn-Cierva Autogiro Co Inc at Bryn Athyn, Pennsylvania. The C.8L Mk.IV was shipped to the USA in December 1928, made the first Autogiro flight in the USA when Pitcairn demonstrated it at Pitcairn Field, Willow Grove, Pennsylvania, in January 1929, and the first cross-country flight in the USA from Pitcairn Field to Langley Field, Virginia, in the following May. At the end of its active life in 1931 the C.8L Mk.IV was presented to the Smithsonian Institution, Washington, where it was still in storage in 1990.

## SPECIFICATION AND DATA

*Manufacturers:*    A. V. Roe and Co Ltd, Newton Heath, Manchester; and Hamble Aerodrome, near Southampton, Hants.

*Rotor design:*    The Cierva Autogiro Co Ltd, Bush House, Aldwych, London W.C.2

*Powerplants:*    (C.8L Mk.I)    One 180 hp Armstrong Siddeley Lynx
(C.8L Mks.II and III)
                        One 180 hp Armstrong Siddeley Lynx IV
(C.8L Mk.IV)    One 225 hp Wright Whirlwind J-5

*Dimensions:*    (All marks) Rotor diameter 39 ft 8 in
                    Length 36 ft 0 in   Height 14 ft 9 in

*Weights:*    (C.8L Mk.I) All up weight 3,535 lb
            (C.8L Mk.II) Tare weight 1,650 lb   All-up weight 2,470 lb

*Performance:*    (C.8L Mk.I)
                Maximum speed 68 mph   Initial climb 110 ft/min
            (C.8L Mk.II)
                Maximum speed 100 mph   Cruising speed 85 mph
                Initial climb 500 ft/min   Range 255 miles
            (C.8L Mk.III)
                Maximum speed 106 mph   Initial climb 750 ft/min

*Production:*    One aircraft of each mark.

C.8L Mk.I    *J8930*, first flown July 1927, to the RAE 30.9.27, written off at Andover about 6.30

C.8L Mk.II    *G-EBYY*, first flown 5.28, registered 21.6.28 to J. G. Weir, no c/n or C of A, sold in France 4.30, preserved at the Musée de l'Air, Paris

C.8L Mk.III    For the Italian Government, first flown 9.28

C.8L, Mk.IV    First flown 11.28, sold in the USA to H. Pitcairn, as *NC418*, preserved in the Smithsonian Institution, Washington, from 1931

Avro 581 Avian prototype with 70 hp Armstrong Siddeley Genet built for the 1926 Two Seat Light Aeroplane Trials.

# Avro 581 Avian Prototype

In January 1926 the Air Ministry placed a further Autogiro contract with Avro, this time for two machines of new design, not derived from the 504K. The smaller of the two, designated Avro 576, had a slim plywood covered, square-section, fuselage without top decking in the rear but of orthodox proportions forward to accommodate a single pilot. A 70 hp Armstrong Siddeley Genet radial engine was faired into the flat-sided fuselage by large external bulges, that on the port side housing the oil tank. A wide-track, N-type oleo undercarriage gave exceptional stability on the ground, and control was by ailerons on braced outriggers in conjunction with normal rudder and elevators. There was no fin and the oval-shaped rudder, similar to that fitted to the Avro 558, was a more refined version of the famous comma type. The pylon consisted of three steel tubes mounted about the cockpit and supporting a 30 ft diameter rotor having four untapered blades coupled to a fixed head by drag hinges.

Numbered *J8931* and known as the C.9 in the Cierva series, the Avro 576 was first flown by Hinkler at Hamble in September 1927. Half-length untapered blades were tried at Farnborough in September 1928.

A second fuselage, identical at the forward end, but with two seats and a curved rear decking, was completed at Hamble as an orthodox biplane for the *Daily Mail* two-seat light aeroplane trials held at Lympne September 10–18, 1926. With an eye on the club and private owner market then being opened up, designer Roy Chadwick retained the 70 hp Genet because it was the most powerful unit available within the maximum engine weight allowance of 170 lb. Known as the Avro 581 Avian and registered *G-EBOV*, the machine was chiefly remarkable for a very low structural weight which gave a tare weight to all-up weight ratio of less than 0·5. For competition purposes the Avian had a generous wing area of 294 sq ft, and the whole single-bay wing structure was of the simplest possible concept and used thick-section mainplanes with square cut tips. The centre section was mounted on four tall wooden struts which gave an exaggerated mainplane gap of 5 ft 3 in. Ailerons were fitted only to the lower plane and fuel was carried in the front fuselage to leave the upper mainplane unencumbered. For ease of housing and to comply with competition rules, the wings folded about the rear spar to reduce the overall width to 9 ft 6¼ in. Folding was by quick release bolts in the front root end fittings but temporary jury struts were necessary to support the front corners of the wing cellule. The undercarriage was of new design with the front legs sprung by rubber blocks in streamlined fairings. Large diameter wheels with narrow tread high-pressure tyres were fitted to a steel cross-axle, while for ease of handling during the folding and 'housing' tests, a small detachable roller was clamped to the tail skid.

The Avian was a most promising entry in which H. J. Hinkler flew 1,074 miles in three days and despite a leaking fuel tank, gained second place in three of the six tests. He averaged 68·75 mph for the 312 mile, three-lap cross-country to Shoreham on September 12; 69·75 mph for three laps of the 366 mile Hastings–Eastbourne circuit on September 13; and 78·63 mph over the 396 mile six-lap course via Dover, Manston, North Foreland and Reculver on September 14. Unfortunately the machine was eliminated when the duralumin drive of the single magneto sheared and Hinkler forced

The Avro 576 (Cierva C.9) Autogiro *J8931* at Hamble, September 1927. (*Courtesy the Royal Aeronautical Society*)

242

H. J. Hinkler flying the prototype Avian in Avro 581A form with A.D.C. Cirrus II engine. (*Flight*)

landed at Iford Hill, near Lewes. As partial compensation Hinkler won the Society of Motor Manufacturers and Traders Race and £200 on September 18 by averaging 90 mph over six laps of the Lympne course.

A proposal to remove the biplane wing structure and enter the Avian for the Grosvenor Trophy Race that afternoon as a strut-braced, low-wing monoplane under the designation Avro 588, did not materialise. Nor did a further suggestion to equip it with floats as the Avro 589. In actual fact the machine returned to Hamble where the span was reduced from 32 to 28 ft and the nose was slightly lengthened to take an 85 hp A.D.C. Cirrus II inline engine, gravity fed from a large centre-section tank, to support which additional sloping struts were fitted. To compensate for the extra side area forward it was necessary to fit a triangular fin and enlarged unbalanced rudder. In this form the Avian was redesignated Avro 581A and sold to Hinkler who flew it at the Bournemouth Easter Meeting, April 15–18, 1927, winning the 'Kill Joy Stakes' at 89 mph, the Hotels Handicap at 90 mph and the Holiday Handicap at 93 mph. Limited production initially envisaged under the type number Avro 581B, then began at Hamble in a sufficiently modified form to warrant an entirely new designation. These machines are therefore dealt with in their own chapter under designation Avro 594 Avian I.

In the following July the Avian prototype *G-EBOV* was fitted with a wide-track, divided undercarriage of Hinkler's own invention which moved back as the wings were folded, imparting the twofold advantage of keeping the wheels under the C.G. so that the tail was easier to lift with the wings folded, and of lowering the engine to make it more accessible for maintenance. Later a long-range tank was fitted in the front cockpit and Hinkler left Croydon at 5.27 a.m. on August 27, 1927, to fly 1,200 miles to Riga in Latvia in $10\frac{3}{4}$ hours, the longest nonstop flight by a light aeroplane up to that time. After an inspection by the Latvian Air Force which ultimately led to an order for Avian trainers, and the completion of business for Wm. Beardmore Ltd, Hinkler flew back to Hamble in easy stages.

*G-EBOV* at Croydon in February 1928 with the special wings from the Avro 594C altitude machine, and wide-track undercarriage in readiness for Hinkler's Australia flight.

This flight provided fuel consumption figures which convinced Hinkler that '*OV* was capable of taking him home to Australia. A more rugged, non-folding divided undercarriage, the RAF 28 section Avro 594C wings

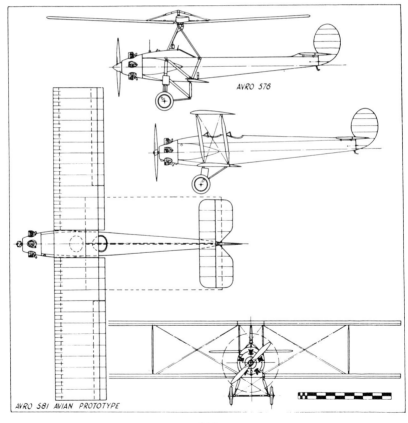

244

from the altitude record machine (see page 250) and Fairey metal airscrew were then fitted and the type number amended to Avro 581E. Hinkler took off from Croydon at 6.48 a.m. on February 7, 1928, and arrived at Darwin 15½ days later, having covered 11,005 miles in a flying time of 128 hours with night stops at Rome, Malta, Tobruk, Ramleh, Basra, Jask, Karachi, Cawnpore, Calcutta, Rangoon, Victoria Point, Singapore, Bandoeng and Bima. He undertook a further 200 hours of touring in Australia with his wife as passenger, reached Sydney on March 10 and arrived home at Bundaberg in April. They left almost immediately to make the long flight across the Bass Strait and met W. N. Lancaster and his Avian III *Red Rose* (see page 251) at Launceston on May 7. For these outstanding achievements Hinkler was awarded the Britannia Trophy for a second time and was made an Hon RAAF Squadron Leader.

The famous Avian prototype was not registered in Australia and although still in good condition after more than 35,000 miles flying, was placed in Brisbane Museum still in its British marks *G-EBOV* to remain a permanent monument to its immortal owner and to Chadwick's design genius.

## SPECIFICATION AND DATA

*Manufacturers:*   A. V. Roe and Co Ltd, Newton Heath, Manchester; and Hamble Aerodrome, near Southampton, Hants.

*Powerplants:*   (Avro 576)   One 70 hp Armstrong Siddeley Genet
(Avro 581)   One 70 hp Armstrong Siddeley Genet
(Avro 581A and E) One 85 hp A.D.C. Cirrus II

*Dimensions, Weights and Performances:*

|  | Avro 576 | Avro 581 | Avro 581A | Avro 581E |
|---|---|---|---|---|
| Span | 30 ft 0 in* | 32 ft 0 in | 28 ft 0 in | 28 ft 0 in |
| Length | 24 ft 6 in | 24 ft 3 in | 24 ft 3 in | 24 ft 3 in |
| Height | — | 8 ft 3 in | 8 ft 6 in | 8 ft 6 in |
| Wing area | — | 294 sq ft | 245 sq ft | 245 sq ft |
| Tare weight | 816 lb | 750 lb | — | — |
| All-up weight | 1,073 lb | 1,580 lb | — | — |
| Maximum speed | — | 70 mph | — | — |

*Rotor diameter.

*Production:*

Avro 576   One aircraft only, *J8931*, to Contract 698108/26, first flown at Hamble 1927, to the Science Museum 1.30

Avro 581   One aircraft only, *G-EBOV*, c/n 5116, registered to A. V. Roe and Co Ltd 7.7.26, C of A issued 8.9.26, converted to Avro 581A and sold to Hinkler 7.4.27, converted to Avro 581E and flown to Australia 2.28, s.o.r. 1.30, preserved in Brisbane Museum

The first Avro 584 Avocet, *N209*, with triangular fin and unbalanced rudder.

# Avro 584 Avocet

Designed to Air Ministry Specification 17/25 issued in June 1926, the Avocet was a single-seat fleet fighter of all metal, stressed skin construction powered by a 180 hp Armtrong Siddeley Lynx IV supercharged engine driving a metal airscrew. The fuselage was a constant diameter light alloy tube of riveted duralumin sheets, tapering only at the tail, and positioned at mid-gap by a number of steel struts. It was a single-bay sesquiplane with N-type interplane struts and full-span Frise-type ailerons on the upper mainplane only.

The wing structure did not fold but was designed for quick dismantling and stowage aboard ship. Erection was simply a matter of bolting the halves of the upper wing together and attaching the lower wing panels to the bottom centre section. There were no rigging problems, wing bracing being of the Warren truss type without wires.

Interchangeable wheel and float undercarriages made the Avocet equally suitable for operation from the deck of an aircraft carrier or for catapulting from a cruiser. Catapult points were built into the fuselage, a special headrest added, and a pick-up ring fitted ahead of the cockpit for use when the crane retrieved it from the water. Armament consisted of two Vickers guns, one on each side of the fuselage in a special trough and firing forward through the airscrew.

The Avocet was not ordered into production as on such low power its performance was unimpressive and only two prototypes, *N209* and *N210*, were built. They were identical except for the vertical tail surfaces, *N209* having a large triangular fin and unbalanced rudder while *N210* had a truncated fin and large horn-balanced rudder. For manufacturer's trials they were completed initially as landplane and seaplane respectively, *N209* flying at Hamble on wheels in December 1927 and *N210* on floats in the

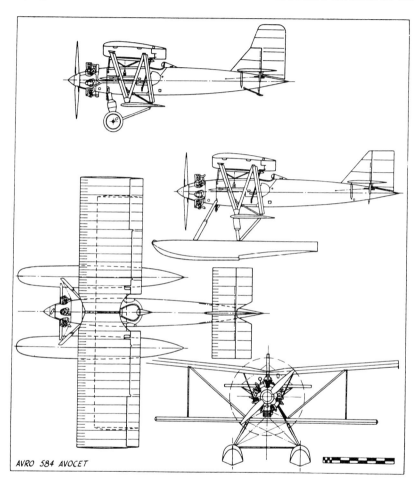

AVRO 584 AVOCET

following April. Wheels were fitted to *N210* in June 1928 and both Avocets went to Martlesham to be evaluated for the Fleet Air Arm in February 1929. In September of that year *N210*, with floats refitted, was placed on the strength of the High Speed Flight and went to Calshot as a practice machine for Schneider Trophy pilots.

## SPECIFICATION AND DATA

*Manufacturers:* A. V. Roe and Co Ltd, Newton Heath, Manchester; and Hamble Aerodrome, near Southampton, Hants

*Powerplant:* One 180 hp Armstrong Siddeley Lynx IV

*Dimensions:*

|  |  |  |
|---|---|---|
|  | Span 29 ft 0 in | Wing area 308 sq ft |
| (*N209* floats) | Length 27 ft 6 in | Height 11 ft 10 in |
| (*N210* wheels) | Length 24 ft 6 in | Height 11 ft $8\frac{3}{8}$ in |

*Weights:* (*N209* landplane) Tare weight 1,621 lb
(*N210* landplane) Tare weight 1,669 lb★
All-up weight 2,495 lb

★1,678 lb at Martlesham trials.

The second Avocet, *N210*, with small fin and large balanced rudder.

248

The RAE Aero Club's Avro 594 Avian I.

# Avro 594 Avian

A production version of the Avian prototype (Cirrus II), laid down as the Avro 581B, eventually appeared in April 1927 as the Avro 594. Only two were built, *G-EBQN* for the Royal Aircraft Establishment Aero Club, Farnborough, and a demonstrator '*QL*, flown in the 1927 King's Cup Race and at the Zürich International Meeting by Dudley Watt. Later it was presented to the Lancashire Aero Club to replace Avro Gosport *G-EBNF*. Aimed at the private owner and flying club market, they were considerably strengthened versions of the original and were later known as Avian Is. They resembled the prototype in Avro 581A form with folding wings and narrow-track, cross-axle undercarriage, but had slightly rounded wingtips and at last forsook the Avro circular rudder.

Both '*QN* and '*QL* were certificated in time to compete at the Bournemouth Easter Meeting, April 15–18, 1927, piloted by Wing Cdr W. Sholto Douglas and F/Lt J. A. Gray respectively, the latter coming second to Hinkler's prototype in the Holiday Handicap Race at 89·5 mph. They raced several times that year but by May 1927 were already outmoded by *G-EBRC*, first of nine Avro 594 Avian IIs which featured Hinkler's patent folding, wide track, divided undercarriage mounted on small triangular stub-wings. The thrust line of the Cirrus II engine was lowered still further to decrease drag and improve forward view. As before, the fuselage was a flat-sided plywood box needing none of the periodic trueing up of the wire-braced girder type.

Piloted by Dudley Watt *G-EBRC* won the altitude race at the Copenhagen Flying Meeting, Kastrup, on September 4, 1927, by reaching 12,750 ft in 90 minutes, but on the return flight to Hamble compass trouble put him south of track so that '*RC* ran out of fuel and met a watery end off Woody Point, Ventnor, Isle of Wight. The third Avian II, '*RS*, was built for Mrs S. C. Elliott-Lynn whose efforts to publicise the type amounted almost to a crusade. Leaving the Avro aerodrome at Woodford at 03.20 hrs on July 19, 1927, she covered 1,300 miles round England with 79 landings (many of them touch-and-go, often in fields) via Sealand, Bournemouth, Lympne, Norwich, Nottingham and Leeds, finally landing at Cramlington, Newcastle, at 21.27 hrs. In the next few weeks she completed a 3,000 mile European tour to Poland and back which ended with a flight from Breslau to Bromley, Kent, where the fuel ran out. Despite these exertions Mrs Elliott-Lynn and 'RS were at the Zürich International Meeting August 12–21 and on a tour of Scotland for the Air League in September.

Next off the production line was G-EBSD, powered by the second of the hand-made 100 hp Avro Alpha radial engines as a 'dark horse' for the Hinkler to fly in the King's Cup Race at Hucknall on July 30, 1927. With this engine it was designated Avro 594A Avian II but a cracked carburettor casing eliminated it from the race. In furtherance of the Avian proving and publicity programme, RAF 28 section wings with rounded tips were fitted and in this form, as the Avro 594C, it was flown to a lightplane record height with passenger of 19,200 ft by Mrs Elliott-Lynn on October 8. The Alpha engine ran successfully at full throttle for two hours during the climb but fog formed over Woodford and the flight terminated in a field at Frodsham, Cheshire. In the summer of 1928 'SD was used for joyriding in Somerset by Taxiplanes Ltd before a short period in private ownership.

Decorated in red and gold, one of the Cirrus engined Avian IIs was presented to the Aero Club of South Africa by the Shell Company and made many notable flights with the Cape Town Flying Club, first as G-UAAC and later as ZS-AAC. Three with 75 hp Armstrong Siddeley Genet II radials were supplied to Australian order, G-AUGA for E. W. Percival and G-AUFY and 'FZ for Wings Ltd who ran a flying school at Broken Hill, NSW. G-AUFY was later fitted with a 105 hp Genet Major I from the crashed Avro 619 Five VH-UNK (see page 279).

The Lancashire Aero Club's Avian II fitted with Hinkler's patent folding undercarriage.

*G-EBSD* in single-seat form as the Avro 594C with Avro Alpha engine and altitude record mainplane.

*J9182*, c/n 125, the RAF's sole Avro 594B Avian III (80 hp Armstrong Siddeley Genet II).

Avian development moved swiftly to the Mk.III, the first being *G-EBTU*, taken from the Avian II production line in September 1927 to be modified and fitted with overload fuel tanks for Capt W. N. Lancaster's flight to Australia. Apart from slim tubular steel interplane and centre-section struts the Avian III airframe was identical to that of its predecessor. A scheme to fit RAF 15 section wings under the designation Avro 600 was discarded and the chief difference between the two marks lay in the engine installation, the Cirrus II now being set still lower to bring the cylinder heads into line with the fuselage decking to permit the use of improved cowlings merging cleanly into a conical spinner. Named *Red Rose*, county symbol of Lancashire, the Avian III 'prototype' had a considerable career.

251

Accompanied by Mrs Keith Miller, Capt Lancaster left Croydon on October 14, 1927, and made good time until forced down at Ur of the Chaldees with a sheared magneto drive. Persistent magneto trouble, serious damage when a blocked fuel line caused engine cut on take-off at Muntok in the Dutch East Indies on January 10, 1928 (followed by shipment back to Singapore for repairs), delayed their arrival at Darwin until March 19. They were passed by Hinkler in the record breaking Avian prototype '*OV* at Singapore but met him again when both Avians were at Launceston, Tasmania, on May 7, '*TU* having crossed the Bass Strait from Melbourne in 6½ hours on April 29. *Red Rose* remained in Australia as *VH-UTU* under several ownerships until burned out on the ground at Singleton, NSW, in 1936.

One more pre-production and 31 production Avian IIIs were built, including *G-EBUG* which Lady Heath (the former Mrs Elliott-Lynn) shipped to South Africa in December 1927 for a leisurely solo flight from the Cape to Croydon, March–May, 1928. She later sold it in the USA to Miss Amelia Earhart, probably as *NC7083*. A notable flight in the opposite direction began on July 29, 1928, when Lt P. Murdoch left Croydon to deliver Avian III *G-EBVU* to the *Cape Argus*. Such was the Avian's sturdiness and reliability that he completed the flight without incident on August 12 and straightaway flew the machine back as far as Bulawayo. Final Avian IIIs were *J9182* tested at Martlesham March–May 1929 and later attached to No. 32 Squadron, Kenley: six seaplanes for Western Canadian Airways Ltd, Winnipeg; and *G-EBXJ* for H. J. V. Ashworth, Tollerton.

In preparation for the King's Cup Race at Brooklands on July 20–21, 1928, E. W. Percival's *G-EBYR* and two works Avians '*YO* and *YP* were fitted with the A.D.C. Company's newest engine, the 90 hp Cirrus III, under the designation Avian IIIA. They had little success but Percival and

G. H. Storck's Avro 605 Avian IIIA seaplane *NX6663*, c/n 169, *Seattle Spirit* at Hamble in September 1928.

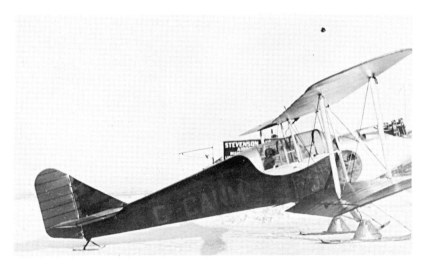

Originally supplied to Western Canada Airways on floats in 1928, *G-CANM*, c/n 128, was later flown on skis with cabin top and built-up rear fuselage.

Lady Heath were 2nd and 4th respectively in *'YR* and *'ZM* at the French Light Aeroplane Trials at Orly, September 10–21, 1928. Some 58 Avian IIIAs were built, including 16 for the American Avian distributors, Air Associates Inc of New York. One of these, licence number *392*, owned by well-known aircraft designer M. A. Northrop, was flown by film star Lya de Putti, while *7900*, owned by N. C. Durrant, was flown at Detroit, Michigan, by Ford Motor Company pilots. Considerable sales were also effected in the Commonwealth and one machine evaluated by the South African Air Force at Roberts Heights was responsible for a substantial order for a later mark. *VR-TAG*, acquired by the Director of Surveys, Tanganyika, was the first of a small fleet of miscellaneous Avro aeroplanes which completed the aerial mapping of that territory 1928–31. One Avian IIIA, intended as *G-AAAP*, was fitted with metal floats and sold to American owner G. H. Storck as *NX6663 Seattle Spirit* for an ambitious 27,000 mile world flight via India, the Far East and the Aleutians. He left Southampton Water on September 15, 1928, but overturned on take-off from Bastia, Corsica, on September 22. The machine was afterwards shipped to the USA and later flew as *NC6663*.

To cover seaplane versions the Avian designation system was extended to include type number 605, the pure Avro 605 representing the float-equipped Cirrus-engined Avian III or IIIA. Type numbers 605A and 605B were reserved for Alpha and Genet engined machines but were never used. Avian IIIA landplane *G-EBZD*, kept at Croydon initially by Airways Publications Ltd, was unique in having an 80 hp Genet II, and in common with all Genet Avians, whatever the mark, was designated Avro 594B.

Later in 1928 the undercarriage radius rods were repositioned forward of the main legs and attached to a common anchorage under the mid-point of the engine bulkhead. This produced a very robust structure, much superior to the old, which became standard and was also fitted to a number of Avian IIs and IIIs when they came up for overhaul and modernisation. With this undercarriage, and horn-balanced ailerons (and at a later date with wide-chord strut fairings and low-pressure Goodyear Airwheels), the wooden Avian became the Mk.IV and reached the limit of its development.

Avian IV production was initiated by three machines, G-AAAT with Cirrus III for A.D.C. Aircraft Ltd; G-AADL with 80 hp Genet II for J. D. Siddeley whose companies held a controlling interest in A. V. Roe and Co Ltd; and G-AABX *Comète* with Cirrus III for Lancashire cricketer P. T. Eckersley. Almost all other Avian IVs, amounting to some 90 aircraft, were fitted initially with the Cirrus III although several acquired 105 hp Cirrus Hermes Is or 115 hp Hermes IIs at a later date and in one instance

Avian IV G-AADL, c/n 182, in early form with 80 hp Armstrong Siddeley Genet II.

The Cirrus Engine Company's Avian IV G-AAAT, c/n 172, with prototype 105 hp Cirrus Hermes I.

254

The Alpha Club's rebuilt Avro 594A Avian II *G-ADEO* flying near Hamble in 1935.

(*G-AAHK*, flown by J. C. Cantrill for Pinchin, Johnson and Co Ltd), a 100 hp de Havilland Gipsy I. Handley Page slots were an optional extra.

Flying *G-AAAT*, T. Neville Stack got both the Avian IV and his company's 105 hp Hermes I engine off to a good start by covering the 620 miles between Croydon and the Berlin Aero Show in the record nonstop time of 4 hr 52 min on October 19, 1928. Only a handful of these machines were absorbed by the British market and the majority went overseas, notably to Air Associates Inc for erection in New York, and to the Whittlesey Manufacturing Co of Bridgeport, Connecticut. Many imported Avians, subject of Group 2 Approval ATC 2–39 dated October 11, 1929, survived until at least 1941, often with locally contrived engine installations, as for example *NC6882* (100 hp Wright Gipsy) and *NX603E* (95 hp Menasco B-4). Two Avro 594B Avian IVs *CF-CAQ* and *'AR* with Genet II engines were used by the Ottawa Flying Club, the first being presented by Avro director J. D. Siddeley (later Lord Kenilworth), owner of the similar machine *G-AADL*.

Avian IV sales embraced Argentina, Australia, Brazil, Mexico, Norway, South Africa and Spain. *X-CRIA Amoy*, one of 14 imported into China by the S.K. Engineering Company to form initial training equipment of the Chinese Naval Air Service at Amoy, Fukien Province, was flown from Croydon to Shanghai by Messrs Johannsen and Wen Lin Chen. It arrived at Shanghai on May 28, 1929, the only trouble experienced being a forced landing at Swingate Downs, Dover, soon after the start on March 2. Another was flown to Norway by Alf Gunnestad in June 1929 as *N-38* and later operated as *LN-ABF* with the 1933–34 Norwegian Antarctic Expedition. One survey flight discovered and named Princess Astrid Land. Twenty

255

years later in 1949 *SE-ADT* (formerly H. B. Chantrey's Heston-based *G-AAHD*) and *SE-AEM* (ex *G-EBXJ*) were still flying in Sweden.

In 1929 an Avian IV fuselage was used at Hamble in the construction of the Cierva C.17 Autogiro (Avro 612). It was not successful but work continued with the Avro 612 Hydrogiro and the Cierva C.17 Mk.II, both with Avian fuselages and Avro Alpha engines. It is not certain if the latter was completed and flown, most of its life being spent as one of Air Service Training Ltd's instructional airframes at Hamble. A team of AST engineers rebuilt it in 1935 as the Alpha-engined Avian *G-ADEO*. Apart from narrow-chord struts and the Mk.IV undercarriage it was equivalent to the original Avro 594A Avian II but its owners (the 25 strong Alpha Club) called it the Alpha 25 with constructor's number A.25/1.

At the outbreak of the Second World War, ten wooden Avians were impressed by the RAF for instructional use at Schools of Technical Training, and one Gipsy II Avian IV *VH-UKD* was similarly used by the RAAF. The only British survivors were two which escaped war service, Cirrus Avian IIIA *G-EBZM* and Genet II Avian IIIA *G-ACGT*. Both were still preserved in 1990, the latter being that sold originally in Ireland as *EI-AAB*. It returned to Gatwick in May 1933, thus following a sister machine *EI-AAA/G-ABPU* which was repatriated in 1931 and flown in the 1932 King's Cup Race by J. F. Legard.


## SPECIFICATION AND DATA

*Manufacturers:*  A. V. Roe and Co Ltd, Newton Heath, Manchester; and Hamble Aerodrome, near Southampton, Hants.
The Whittlesey Manufacturing Co, Bridgeport, Connecticut, USA

*Powerplants:*  One 85 hp A.D.C. Cirrus II
One 80 hp Armstrong Siddeley Genet II
One 90 hp A.D.C. Cirrus III
One 95 hp Menasco B-4
One 100 hp Avro Alpha
One 100 hp de Havilland Gipsy I
One 100 hp Wright Gipsy
One 105 hp A.D.C. Cirrus Hermes I
One 105 hp Armstrong Siddeley Genet Major
One 115 hp A.D.C. Cirrus Hermes II

*Dimensions:*  Span 28 ft 0 in
Length 24 ft 3 in   (seaplanes) 25 ft 0 in
Height 8 ft 6 in   (seaplanes) 9 ft 6 in
Wing area 245 sq ft

*Weights and Performances:*

| | Avian II | Avian III | Avian IIIA and IV | Avian IIIA seaplane |
|---|---|---|---|---|
| Tare weight | 907 lb | 875 lb* | 935 lb | 1,053 lb |
| All-up weight | 1,467 lb | 1,600 lb* | 1,435 lb | 1,600 lb |
| Maximum speed | 98 mph | 97 mph | 102 mph | 97 mph |
| Cruising speed | 82 mph | 80 mph | 87 mph | 82 mph |
| Initial climb | — | 650 ft/min** | 750 ft/min | 480 ft/min |
| Ceiling | 15,000 ft | 15,000 ft** | 18,000 ft | 13,000 ft |
| Range | 325 miles | 400 miles | 400 miles | 400 miles |

*Red Rose 930 lb and 1,726 lb respectively; standard seaplane 1,015 lb and 1,600 lb
**J9182 (Genet II) 330 ft/min and 6,500 ft; standard seaplane (Cirrus III) 400 ft/min and 11,000 ft maximum speed 91 mph

*Production:*
### (a) Avro 594 Avian I (Cirrus II)

| Constructor's No. and Registration | | C of A Issued | Details |
|---|---|---|---|
| R3/AV/100 | G-EBQN | 12.4.27 | RAE Aero Club, Farnborough, impressed 1.40 as 2081M |
| R3/AV/117 | G-EBQL | 12.4.27 | To Light Planes (Lancs.) Ltd* 11.27 to replace Avro Gosport, G-EBNF, rebuilt as Avian IV, crashed at Barton 18.11.33 |

### (b) Avro 594 Avian II (Cirrus II)

| R3/AV/118 | G-EBRC | 13.5.27 | Demonstrator, ditched off Ventnor, Isle of Wight 6.9.27 |
|---|---|---|---|
| R3/AV/119 | G-EBRR | 14.7.27 | Light Planes (Lancs.) Ltd*, crashed 1.29 |
| R3/AV/120 | G-EBRS | 18.7.27 | Mrs S. C. Elliott-Lynn, to Basle Air Transport 8.27, believed as CH-202 |
| R3/AV/122 | G-UAAC | 25.8.27 | Aero Club of South Africa, later ZS-AAC |
| R3/AV/124 | G-EBTP | 1.9.27 | H. Hollingdrake, Woodford, to South Africa 2.29, as ZS-AAN |

### (c) Avro 594A Avian II (Alpha)

| R3/AV/121 | G-EBSD | 28.7.27 | Temporarily Avro 594C 10.27, Taxiplanes Ltd 6.28, F. S. Lee 1.29, L. M. J. Balfour 1.30, crashed 1932, broken up at Hanworth 3.33 |
|---|---|---|---|

### (d) Avro 594B Avian II (Genet II)

| R3/AV/123 | G-AUGA | 22.9.27 | Initially to E. W. Percival, later VH-UGA, burned out at Essendon, Victoria 28.2.39 |
|---|---|---|---|
| R3/AV/126 | G-AUFY | 1.12.27 | Initially to Wings Ltd, Broken Hill, NSW, fitted with Genet Major 1931, s.o.r. 8.41 |
| R3/AV/127 | G-AUFZ | 1.12.27 | As 'FY above, converted to Avian IV (Cirrus III), s.o.r. 12.47 |

### (e) Pre-production Avro 594 Avian III (Cirrus II)

| R3/AV/125 | G-EBTU | 23.9.27 | Red Rose, sold in Australia 5.28 as VH-UTU, burned on ground at Singleton, NSW, 6.6.36 |
|---|---|---|---|
| R3/AV/128 | G-EBTY | 23.9.27 | J. P. Drew; to Scottish Flying Club 10.28; D. K. Fairweather 1.29 (all Renfrew); R. E. Horrox, Nether Thorpe 10.34; rebuilt as Avian IV (Hermes II); Light Planes (Lancs.) Ltd* 12.38; H. V. Armstrong, Woodford 8.39; impressed 12.39 as 2077M |

*Trading as the Lancashire Aero Club.

*G-AUGA*, one of three Genet II powered Avro 594B Avian IIs built for Australia.

## (f) Production Avro 594 Avian III (Cirrus II)

| Constructor's Numbers commencing R3/CN/101 | Aircraft markings |
|---|---|
| 101–125 | *G-EBUG, G-AUHC,* Señor Juan Acuna, *G-EBVA★, G-CAWI,* Argentina, *G-EBVI, M-CCAC, G-UAAS, G-IAAX, G-EBVU, 'VZ, 'WP, 'WK, G-CAUH, G-EBWR, 'WU, 'WW,* J. F. Costa, *G-AUHK, G-EBXD, M-CDAA, G-EBXE, 'XO, J9182★★* |
| 127–133 | *G-CANL-'NQ, G-EBXJ* |

★Temporarily Avro 605 Avian seaplane.
★★To Contract 787176/27 with Armstrong Siddeley Genet II serial number A.S.48.

## (g) Production Avro 594 Avian IIIA (Cirrus III)

| Constructor's Numbers | Aircraft markings |
|---|---|
| 134–150 | *G-EBYA,* Air Associates *NC6881, '82★, 7012, '13, 7154, '55, 7289, '90, 7625, G-AUHZ, 'IK, 'IL,* Air Associates *NC7869* and *392, G-CAQA, CF-AFQ* |
| 151–171 | *G-EBYM/M-CAAE, G-EBYN/M-CDDD, G-EBYO-'YR, M-CDAD,* Air Associates *NC7626,* Argentina, *G-UAAZ, G-EBZM, 'ZD★★, G-NZEE, G-CAVB, G-AUHY,* South African Air Force, Air Associates *NC7900, G-UAAT, 'AU, G-AAAP/NX6663, EI-AAA★★, 'AB★★* |
| 173–177 | *G-AABZ/VR-TAG, G-NZAV, G-UABB, ZS-ADM, G-AAAU* |
| 181 | *G-AABU* |
| 184–189 | *G-AUJF, 'JG,* Air Associates *NC10075, '76, NC367, '362* |
| 192–193 | *G-AUIU, 'IV* |
| 198–200 | *M-CPAA, ZK-AAN, G-UAAK* |
| 233–235 | *G-EBXX-'XZ* |

★Air Associates Avian Special with 100 hp Wright Gipsy to ATC2-207 dated 1.5.30, all-up weight 1,450 lb
★★Armstrong Siddeley Genet II.

## (h) Production Avro 594 Avian IV

| Constructor's Numbers | Aircraft markings |
|---|---|
| 172, 182, 183 | *G-AAAT, 'DL\*, 'BX* |
| 190–191 | Air Associates *NC540E, PP-TCB* |
| 194–197 | Air Associates *NC502E, '03E, NC541E, '49E* |
| 201–227 | *G-AUKD, 'JZ,* Argentina, *G-AADF, G-AUKR,* Argentina, China (13), *X-CRIA, CF-CAQ\*\*, 'AR\*\*, G-AAEC,* Argentina, *G-UAAV, M-WIII,* Aero Club of Yucatan (Mexico) |
| 232, 236, 237 | *G-AAGR, 'CE, 'CF* |
| 242–247 | Air Associates *NC550E, NC600E–'03E†, NC648E* |
| 248–281 | Whittlesey Body Co. *NC649E, '71E–'73E, NC11048, NC674E–76E, NC818E– '21E, NC833E–'35E, NC221H, NC836E, NC222H–'24H, NC321H, NC632E, NC524K, '25K, NC710K, '11K, NC550K–'53K, NC712K, '13K, NC577K, NC737K* |
| 303–304 | *ZS-AAG, G-AAGP* |
| 317–320 | *G-AAHK\*\*\*, 'HD, 'HE, 'HN* |
| 323 | *N-38/LN-ABF* |
| 325–328 | *G-AAIJ/M-CIAA,'IK/M-CAIA, VH-UMW, 'RM* |
| 330 | *G-AAIX* |
| R3/AV/423 | *G-ACBV* |

*Genet II, later Cirrus III.   **Genet II.   ***Later Gipsy I.
†Avian Special with 95 hp Menasco B-4 to ATC2-307 dated 29.11.30, all-up weight 1,525 lb

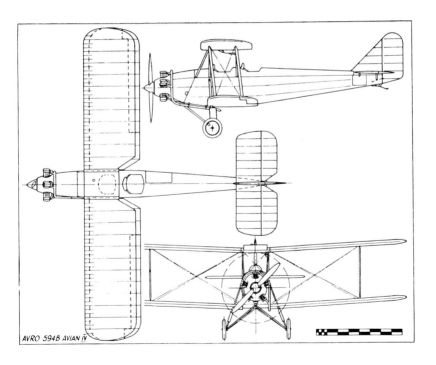

AVRO 594B AVIAN IV

The Avro 604 Antelope.

# Avro 604 Antelope

Construction of the Antelope two-seat, high-performance day bomber was preceded by an elaborate wood and canvas mock-up erected at Hamble early in 1928 which rivalled even Broadsmith's Avro 590 mock-up for realism. The Antelope itself, flown at Hamble in November that year, was built to Air Ministry Specification 12/26 and fitted with a 480 hp Rolls-Royce F.XIB eight-cylinder, water-cooled V-type engine for selective competition with the Hawker Hart and Fairey Fox II. Issued in May 1926 the Specification called for a seemingly impossible top speed (for those days) of 160 mph.

Intensive evaluation began at Martlesham on September 13, 1928, but though the Antelope and Fox II were among the most advanced two-seat military biplanes of their day, only the Hart was ordered into production.

The Antelope was a single-bay biplane with Frise-type ailerons on the upper wing only, and short-span, narrow-chord lower mainplane. The staggered, fabric-covered metal wings were slightly swept back and the centre section struts formed an inverted V. The wing roots of the upper wing tapered to a very thin section at the point of attachment to ensure maximum forward view for the pilot, and aft of his seat was the gunner's cockpit with a single Lewis gun on a patent wind-balanced, small diameter Avro gun ring. Additional armament consisted of a fixed, forward-firing Vickers gun and bombs on racks under the lower wing aimed by the gunner from a prone position in the fuselage bottom. The fuselage itself was a rigid structure built of duralumin sheeting riveted to a framework of L-section dural strip, but strut and root end fittings were of stainless steel while the engine mounting and variable incidence tailplane were of welded steel tubing.

260

The Antelope at Hamble before the fitting of undercarriage fairings. (*P. T. Capon*)

The engine drove a two-bladed Fairey F.R.608 fixed-pitch metal airscrew and was cooled by a chin-type radiator with controllable shutters. Sixty-five gallon main and 25 gallon gravity fuel tanks were housed in the fuselage behind the engine bulkhead, and the low-drag undercarriage was of the long-travel, oleo and rubber-in-compression type.

The Antelope was exhibited at the Olympia Aero Show, London, July 16–27, 1929, and despite its failure to secure a production contract, went to No.100 Squadron, Bicester, for Service trials. It returned to Hamble in July 1930 for dual control to be fitted, afterwards ending its days at the

The Antelope with Rolls-Royce Kestrel engines, Gloster-Hele-Shaw-Beacham variable-pitch airscrew and repositioned radiator.

RAE, Farnborough, as test-bed for the early Gloster-Hele-Shaw-Beacham variable-pitch airscrews. For this purpose it was twice re-engined, first with a 525 hp Rolls-Royce Kestrel IB and later with a 477 hp supercharged Kestrel IIS, but for greater airscrew efficiency the radiator was repositioned under the rear of the engine bay. Initial test flying at the RAE was undertaken on September 29, 1930, by H. H. Leech and Maurice McCudden and the machine remained in service at Farnborough until September 1933.

## SPECIFICATION AND DATA

*Manufacturers:*    A. V. Roe and Co Ltd, Newton Heath, Manchester; and Hamble Aerodrome, near Southampton, Hants

*Powerplants:*    One 480 hp Rolls-Royce F.XIB
One 525 hp Rolls-Royce Kestrel IB
One 477 hp Rolls-Royce Kestrel IIS

*Dimensions:*    Span (upper) 36 ft 0 in, (lower) 32 ft 0 in
Length 31 ft 2 in   Height 10 ft 9 in
Wing area 377 sq ft

*Weights:*    (Bomber, weighed 21.7.28)
Tare weight 2,859 lb   All-up weight 4,538 lb
(Trainer, weighed 19.7.30)
Tare weight 2,898 lb   All-up weight 4,550 lb

*Performance with Rolls-Royce F.XIB* (throttle-gated to 3,000 ft):
Maximum speed 173 mph   Cruising speed 145 mph
Initial climb 1,470 ft/min   Ceiling 22,000 ft
Range 580 miles

*Production:*    One prototype only, *J9183*, to Contract 762628/27

The Avro 612 (Cierva C.17) built from Avian IIIA components with 90 hp A.D.C. Cirrus III.

# Avro 612 and 620 (Cierva C.17)

Encouraging results with the Cierva C.8L Mk.II prompted the construction at Hamble of a smaller version for private owners or flying clubs. Based on the Avro Avian IIIA with 90 hp A.D.C. Cirrus III engine and known as the Cierva C.17, the new Autogiro used a similar rotor system to its predecessor, the wire-braced paddle blades with flapping and drag hinges having proved the most satisfactory arrangement up to that time. The rotor was mounted on a tripod of faired steel tubes and was started in the usual way either by rope spinning or fast taxying. A fixed monoplane wing carrying full-span unbalanced ailerons was braced to the top longeron by V-struts and formed an anchorage for a wide-track undercarriage comprising two Avian IIIA half units. A standard Avian tailplane was used but the fin and rudder were severely truncated to give adequate rotor clearance.

Internally the machine resembled any other Avian IIIA with the addition of a Vickers hand pump for transferring fuel from the main to gravity tank, and a rotor revolution counter.

The Avro 612/Cierva C.17 was first flown by Juan de la Cierva on October 23, 1928, but proved to be underpowered and was subsequently dismantled at Hamble where the major components were still in evidence in 1934. A second example, the Avro 620 Cierva C.17 Mk.II, with the slightly more powerful 100 hp Avro Alpha radial engine, was constructed early in 1929 but proved no more successful than the first. A further example then appeared as test vehicle for Cierva's C.12 rotor system, similar to the C.17 Mk.II but with blades of parallel chord. The pylon was initially a forward leaning wide-chord strut, which later gave way to a pyramid of narrow steel tubes. An unbalanced rudder was used without fin and the tips of the fixed wing were turned up at a considerable dihedral angle. This feature in conjunction with the parallel-chord blades establish the C.12 as the link between the C.17 and later designs, despite the apparent inversion of numerical sequence.

Cierva first flew the C.12 at Hamble during 1929 and from Southampton Water on April 25, 1930, after it had been converted to single-seater and mounted on Avian metal floats. In this form as the Hydrogiro, it was the first rotary-winged seaplane. As detailed in another chapter, an Alpha-engined Autogiro was reconstructed at Hamble in 1935 as the Avro 594 Avian II *G-ADEO*. This was clearly the former C.17 Mk.II *G-AAGJ* but no records survive to identify the C.12 as an intermediate modification of this machine, although this was almost certainly the case.

The Avian-derived Alpha-engined C.12 Hydrogiro ready for flight at Hamble on April 25, 1930.

## SPECIFICATION AND DATA

| | |
|---|---|
| *Manufacturers:* | A. V. Roe and Co Ltd, Newton Heath, Manchester; and Hamble Aerodrome, near Southampton, Hants |
| *Rotor design:* | The Cierva Autogiro Co Ltd, Bush House, Aldwych, London W.C.2 |
| *Powerplants:* | (C.17 Mk. I)  One 90 hp A.D.C. Cirrus III |
| | (C.17 Mk. II) One 100 hp Avro Alpha |
| | (C.12)      One 100 hp Avro Alpha |
| *★Dimensions:* | Rotor diameter 33 ft 3¼ in   Length 28 ft 9 in |
| | Height 11 ft 1 in |
| *★Weights:* | Tare weight 1,010 lb     All-up weight 1,445 lb |
| *★Performance:* | Maximum speed 90 mph   Cruising speed 70 mph |
| | Initial climb 500 ft/min   Range 210 miles |
| | Rotor speed 130 rpm |

★C.17 Mk.I.

| | |
|---|---|
| *Production:* | One aircraft only of each type |
| C.17 Mk.I | *G-AABP*, no c/n recorded, first flown 23.10.28, dismantled at Hamble 12.31 |
| C.17 Mk.II | *G-AAGJ*, c/n 5129, registered 19.4.29, converted to Avian II *G-ADEO* in 1935 |
| C.12 | Possibly a modification of the C.17 Mk.II, unregistered, first flown 1929, first flown as Hydrogiro 25.4.30 |

Avro 616 Avian IVM *VR-HAA*, c/n 361, at Hong Kong in 1930. The metal fuselage can be recognised by the prominent stringers.

# Avro 616 Avian IVM

A strengthened Avian IV with welded steel-tube fuselage, produced in 1929 to meet overseas requirements, was designated Avro 616 Avian IVM. The redesign used the same type of fuselage construction as the Avro Tens and Fives at that time going through the Manchester works. This consisted of welded circular-section longerons and struts, with diagonal strut bracing in the side panels and wire bracing top and bottom. The sides were then rounded out with fabric over wooden stringers and the top with a curved plywood decking. For a weight penalty of some 114 lb an extremely robust structure was obtained, more easily inspected internally or repaired than the wooden version, and far more suitable for operation in remote areas.

Martlesham trials of the first Avian IVM *G-AACV* (90 hp A.D.C. Cirrus III), begun on March 23, 1929, showed it to be light on the controls, easy to fly and to have good aerobatic qualities. The Cirrus was not quite powerful enough and early production Avian IVMs had either the 105 hp A.D.C. Cirrus Hermes I or an Armstrong Siddeley Genet Major five-cylinder radial of 100 hp. They also had variable-incidence tailplanes.

One Avian IVM *J9783* was supplied to the Air Ministry under Contract 924141/29 for comparative trials with the Hawker Tomtit.

Large batches of Genet Major Avians IVMs were despatched to Canada in 1929–30 for erection by the Ottawa Car Manufacturing Co Ltd which later obtained Canadian manufacturing rights and built about 18 with 135 hp seven-cylinder Genet Major Is and Goodyear Airwheels. Most of the imported Avian IVMs were used by flying clubs, private owners and one-man 'outback' transport concerns, often on skis or floats but ten were used for RCAF initial training at Camp Borden. The Whittlesey Manufacturing Co, importers of Avian IIIs into the USA, reached agreement with A. V.

Manchester-built Avian IVM seaplane *CF-AHV*, c/n 299, with 100 hp Armstrong Siddeley Genet Major five-cylinder radial on the Ottawa River 1931.

Roe and Co on December 24, 1928, for the manufacture of the Avian IVM (Cirrus III) under licence and tooled up for the production of 2,000 machines a year. Their name was changed to the Whittlesey Body Co on April 18, 1929, and A.T.C. Memo 2–176 (equivalent to a Special Category C of A) was issued to the Whittlesey Avian IVM on January 31, 1930, but only about ten were built before receivers were appointed in the following December.

Other exports were handled by Mina SA in Mexico; Malayan Motors Ltd, Singapore; Ferrand and Rayson in Buenos Aires; and the Holmes Motor Co Ltd in Cape Town. A batch of six Genet Major Avian IVMs were based at Tallinn by the Estonian Air Force in 1929, the year in which the South African Air Force placed a contract for 20 similar machines for basic training. Ten of these were eventually disposed of to clubs and private owners as *ZS-AGK* to *'GP* and *'GR* to *'GU*, five of which (*'GK* to *'GN* and *'GS*) were impressed with new serials *2029–2033* during the Second World War.

Henlys (1928) Ltd of Heston handled Avian IVM sales in the United Kingdom (demonstrator *G-AATL* Hermes I), and soon popularised them among private owners and sold several to the Liverpool, Lancashire and other major flying clubs. Air Service Training Ltd used *G-ABKA*, *'KB*, *'SC* and *'UN* for instructional purposes at Hamble but *'KA* was destroyed when its wingtip flares set fire to long grass during a night landing on June 11, 1932. The second machine *'KB* acquired floats each summer for seaplane training on Southampton Water. These machines were the first of a small number fitted with the 135 hp seven-cylinder Genet Major I, which included A. J. A. Wallace Barr's *G-ABME*, which, in the hands of F/Lt E. A. Healy, averaged 122·5 mph in the 1931 King's Cup Race and 130·75 mph in the 1932 event. It was fitted later with a close-fitting long-chord NACA cowling.

Despite these activities, the Avian IVM's chief role lay overseas, as in Australia (where *VH-UOE* was acquired by Charles Ulm), in New Zealand, Kenya, and in Egypt where the Shell Company kept Genet Major engined

266

*G-AATV*. This was the first of four metal Avians used by petrol companies for sales promotion, the others being the British Petroleum Co's *G-ABIB Peri* flown by J. C. C. Taylor and the Anglo American Oil Co's *G-ABDN* and *'IE*. In common with many late production Avians, they were powered by 115 hp Cirrus Hermes IIs and boasted Handley Page slots. *G-ABIE High Test* also had an extra 110 gallon fuselage tank for Tommy Rose's attempt on the England–Cape record which started at Lympne at dawn on February 11, 1931. He was eventually forced to land 30 miles south of Luxor with sand in the engine during the return journey in the following May.

*G-ABIC/VR-TAD Tanganyika*, fitted with tropical filters and Vickers-Potts oil cooler, joined its wooden brethren on the vast job of mapping the

Canadian-built Genet Major Avian IVM *CF-CFB*, c/n 65258, on skis. (*B. van Sickle*)

Avian IVM 133 built in Canada by the Ottawa Car Manufacturing Co for the RCAF with seven-cylinder 135 hp Genet Major I and Goodyear Airwheels.

267

H. F. 'Jim' Broadbent flying the record breaking Sports Avian *VH-UQE Dabs* near Melbourne in 1931.

territory, and *SE-ACP* (Hermes II) was flown out to Gothenburg Aero Club by famous Swedish pilot Gosta Andree, in June 1931, but China was the largest single customer for the Hermes model. Large numbers were shipped via the Far East Aviation Co in 1930–33, including one land machine and one seaplane for the Hong Kong Flying Club while others bore Hong Kong registrations for training Defence Force pilots at Kai Tak or onward ferrying to the Kwangtung Government flying school at Canton, or the Kwangsi Air Force at Luichow. A small number were single-seaters with a compartment for 43 lb of mail in place of the front cockpit. Their fuel capacity was raised to 35 gallons and the 'prototype', *VR-HAC* (Hermes I), completed Martlesham trials in August 1930.

To cater for sporting owners wanting 'better than standard' performance, a Hermes I version known as the Sports Avian appeared in 1930 with straight axle undercarriage, cut-away top decking and racing windscreens. It also had the top centre section gap filled by a flap, hinged to give easy access to the rear cockpit. Flown by F/Lt J. Oliver and J. C. Cantrill, the first two Sports Avians *G-AAWI* and '*YU* took part in the King's Cup Race at Hanworth on July 5, 1930, but both forced landed in Gloucestershire due to bad weather.

Sports Avian *VH-UQE Dabs* (Gipsy II), despatched to Australian National Airways in June 1931, was the machine in which H. F. 'Jim' Broadbent made a record one-day solo flight round four States on August 12, 1931, and completed a record 7,600 mile round-Australia flight of 7 days 8 hours 15 minutes on September 6. It was still flying in Australia 30 years later. *G-AAXH*, another of the type, was test flown by R. L. Palmer at Hanworth in 1936 with an experimental reversed tricycle undercarriage designed by British Landing Gears Ltd and built by the Rollason Aircraft

268

Co. This device allowed the Avian to be flown on to the ground with no 'hold off' at speeds considerably in excess of the stall.

R. H. Dobson's 1930 King's Cup entry, *G-AABS*, was a standard Genet Major Avian IVM fitted with a Sports Avian undercarriage in which D. S. Green averaged 106·4 mph round Britain and came fifth. This machine was one of three trial installation IVMs *G-AABR*, *'BS* and *'BT*, the first of which was used in 1930 for experiments with a closely-cowled Genet Major. After the 1930 King's Cup Race, *'BS* was flown with Class B marking *K-2* to test special 30 ft span wings without centre section gap destined for the long-range, single-seat Avian IVA *Southern Cross Junior G-ABCF* which Sir Charles Kingsford Smith had ordered for his attempt to lower Hinkler's England–Australia record. With the 120 hp de Havilland Gipsy II the Avian IVA had a still air range of 1,860 miles at 92 mph cruising speed, achieved by supplementing the 24 gallon centre-section tank with a welded aluminium tank holding 91 gallons in a specially strengthened fuselage. With such a machine the attempt could hardly fail, and 'Smithy' left Heston at dawn on October 9, 1930. He reached Darwin in triumph 9 days 21 hours later but soon disposed of the machine to Guy Menzies who used it for the first solo eastbound crossing of the Tasman Sea to New Zealand. He landed upside down in a swamp at Hari Hari near Hokitika at the completion of a 10 hour 15 minute, 1,235 mile flight on January 7, 1931. After repair at Wigram, *'CF* was shipped back to Sydney where L. Palmer and A. James were killed when it crashed on April 12, without the allotted Australian marks *VH-UPT* being taken up.

A second long-range single seater, *VH-UQG Southern Cross Minor*, built for Kingsford Smith later in 1931, was known as the Avian V. It differed considerably from the first because the fuselage was that of a standard, instead of a Sports model, Avian IVM and the wings were of standard 28 ft span, but the engine was again a Gipsy II. He left Melbourne on

Avian IVM *G-AAXH*, c/n 456, at Hanworth in 1936 with B.L.G. reversed tricycle undercarriage.
(*E. J. Riding*)

*G-AAYV*, the first Avro 625 Avian Monoplane, with Genet Major I radial.

*G-AAYW*, the second Avian Monoplane, with Cirrus Hermes I. (*Flight photo 8865*)

Kingsford Smith's famous long-range Avian IVA *Southern Cross Junior G-ABCF*.

September 21, 1931, to attempt a record trip to England but was compelled to give up in Turkey through illness. W. N. Lancaster, former pilot of the Avian III *Red Rose*, then acquired *Southern Cross Minor*, re-registered as *G-ABLK*, for an attempt on the England–Cape Town record. He left Lympne at dawn on April 11, 1933, and landed at In Salah on the trans-Saharan motor track next day, after which he disappeared and it was not until 29 years later, in March 1962, that a French desert patrol found his mummified body and the wreck of the Avian V some 170 miles south of Reggane.

Competing against the Sports Avian in the 1930 King's Cup Race were two special Avro 625 wire-braced, single-seat, low-wing racing monoplanes using Sports Avian fuselages equipped with wide-track N-type under-carriages, later faired to resemble the trousered type. The first Avian Monoplane *G-AAYV*, flown by F. Tomkins, was powered by a Genet Major and the other, '*YW*, by a Cirrus Hermes I. Handicapped out of the race, Tomkins retired but T. Neville Stack came 48th in '*YW* at an average speed of 119·7 mph. The Genet Major model was then reconstructed as a standard biplane but '*YW* was acquired by F/Lt R. L. R. Atcherley who fitted a 115 hp Hermes II and kept it at RAF Market Drayton until ATA Captain W. L. Handley bought it in June 1940 and flew it to Elmdon.

The last three Avians were produced in the summer of 1933 for the Merseyside Aero and Sports Co, operators of the Liverpool Aero Club, Speke. Fitted with de Havilland engines for uniformity with the rest of the club fleet, they were a Sports Avian *G-ACGV* with Avian IVM under-carriage (120 hp Gipsy III) and two standard Avian IVMs *G-ACIF* (100 hp Gipsy I) and *G-ACKE* (120 hp Gipsy II). The last had been built for Australian National Airways in February 1930 as *VH-UOB* but was re-

The Liverpool Aero Club's unique D. H. Gipsy III powered Sports Avian *G-ACGV*, c/n 649. (*E. J. Riding*)

271

engined and registered in the United Kingdom for the first time in September 1933.

Only four metal Avians were impressed by the RAF in 1940. All became instructional airframes and included the ex-Liverpool *G-ACGV*, presented to the RAF by owner Dr J. W. A. Hunter, and *G-ACNK* (Genet Major) which originated in South Africa and spent the major portion of its British registered life with RAF officers serving in the Near East.

Several machines survived the war, including Sports Avians *VH-UQE* and *ZK-ACM* (still flying in Australia and New Zealand respectively in 1963), and the Gipsy II Avian IVM *G-ACKE* which Mr Percy Blamire had carefully preserved at Queens Road Garage, Coventry. Overhauled at Walsall in 1948, it passed eventually to H. M. Woodhams at Baginton where it was seriously damaged when struck by a Tiger Moth on July 26, 1950. The late H. R. A. Edwards' Sports Avian *G-ABEE* also flew at Bassingbourn in 1948 but was in poor condition and eventually donated its fuselage to *'KE*.

### SPECIFICATION AND DATA

*Manufacturers:* A. V. Roe and Co Ltd, Newton Heath, Manchester
The Ottawa Car Manufacturing Co Ltd, Canada
The Whittlesey Body Co Inc, Bridgeport, Connecticut, USA

*Powerplants:* One 90 hp A.D.C. Cirrus III
One 100 hp de Havilland Gipsy I
One 100 hp Armstrong Siddeley Genet Major (five-cylinder)
One 105 hp A.D.C. Cirrus Hermes I
One 115 hp A.D.C. Cirrus Hermes II
One 120 hp de Havilland Gipsy II
One 120 hp de Havilland Gipsy III
One 135 hp Armstrong Siddeley Genet Major I (seven-cylinder)

*Dimensions:* Span (Avian IVA) 28 ft 0 in (Avro 625) 30 ft 0 in
Length 24 ft 3 in (seaplane) 25 ft 0 in
Height 8 ft 6 in (seaplane) 9 ft 6 in
Wing area 245 sq ft (Avian IVA) 262 sq ft

*Weights and Performances:*

|  | Avian IVM | Avian IVA | Sports Avian | Avro 625 |
|---|---|---|---|---|
| Tare weight | 1,000 lb* | 1,100 lb | 1,005 lb | 942 lb†† |
| All-up weight | 1,600 lb** | 2,225 lb | 1,600 lb | 1,351 lb†† |
| Maximum speed | 100 mph† | 115 mph | 120 mph | — |
| Cruising speed | 90 mph | 92 mph | 105 mph | — |
| Initial climb | 600 ft/min | 485 ft/min | — | 1,000 ft/min |
| Ceiling | 12,500 ft | 12,500 ft | — | — |
| Range | 360 miles | 1,860 miles | 420 miles | — |

*Prototype (Cirrus III) 1,049 lb; Gipsy I 988 lb; single-seat mailplane 1,100 lb; seaplane (Genet Major I) 1,353 lb
**Mailplane 1,610 lb; Whittlesey Avian IVM (Cirrus III) 1,579 lb; seaplane (Genet Major I) 1,850 lb
†Hermes II and Genet Major I 115 mph; seaplanes with these engines 109 mph
††With Genet Major.

*Production:*

## (a) **Avian IVMs by A. V. Roe and Co Ltd**

| Constructor's Numbers | Aircraft markings |
|---|---|
| 178–180 | *G-AABR, 'BS, 'BT* |
| 239–240 | *G-AACV*, Mexico |
| 282–302 | RCAF *92, 93, 94/CF-CAZ, 95/CF-CAY, 96, 97, 98/CF-AEZ, 99/CF-CAJ, 100, 101*, Canada, *CF-CBA*, Canada (2), *132, 125, CF-CBD, CF-AHV, CF-CBC, CF-CBJ* |
| 305–316 | Mexico, Canada, *126/CF-CDG, 127/CF-CDU, 128/CF-CDH, 129/CF-CDE*, Canada, *CF-CDL, 'DJ, 'DQ, 'DR, G-AAHJ* |
| 324, 329, 332 | *G-AAKA*, Mexico, *VT-ABD* |
| 334–354 | South African Air Force *504–523, G-AAWF* |
| 361–368 | *VR-HAA, 'AB*, Estonian Air Force *116–121* |
| 369, 385, 386 | *VH-UMX, ZS-ABQ, ZK-ABJ* |
| 372, 387 | *VH-UOE*, airframe to Hamble |
| 414–417 | *VH-UOB/G-ACKE, G-AATL, 'VM, 'VP* |
| 418, 420, 422 | *G-AAWH, G-ABCD, 'CO* |
| 425–434 | *RCAF 92–101* |
| 435, 438 | *G-AATV, G-AAUN/VR-TAA* |
| 443–452 | Canada (10) |
| 453 | Airframe to Brooklands |
| 465–466 | *M-CEAA, VR-HAC* |
| 469–472 | China (3), *G-ABDP* |
| 475, 479, 486 | *VR-HAD, G-ACNK, G-ABIC* |
| 489, 491, 494 | *G-ABHL, 'IE, VR-HAG* |
| 495, 500, 503 | *VR-HAH, G-ABIW, 'KA* |
| 504, 522, 529 | *G ABKB, 'LF, 'ME* |
| 530, 532 | *SE-ACP, G-ABMO* |
| 533 | Airframe to Avro, Hamble |
| 534–535 | China (2) |
| 554–557 | *VR-HAI, 'AJ, 'AL, 'AK* |
| 559–560 | *VR-HAM, 'AN* |
| 562–568 | *G-ABSC*, China (6) |
| 577–579 | *VR-HAO, 'AP, 'AS* |
| 580, 587, 588 | *VR-HAT, G-ABUN, 'VL* |
| 590–591 | *VR-HBB, 'BC* |
| 598–605 | *VR-HBJ, 'BI, 'BO, 'BL, 'BS, 'BT, 'BM, 'BP* |
| 608–619 | *VR-HBV, 'BW, 'BY, 'BU, 'BR*, China, *VR-HCG, 'CF, 'CB, 'CC*, China (2) |
| 656 | *G-ACIF* |

## (b) **By the Ottawa Car Manufacturing Co Ltd**
At least the following constructed using fuselages manufactured by A. V. Roe and Co Ltd

| Constructor's Numbers | Aircraft markings |
|---|---|
| 316–321 | *CF-CDV, 'DT*, RCAF *141/CF-CDW, 142, 143/CF-CDX, 144/CF-CDL* |
| 65249–65259 | *CF-CFC, 'FH, 'FI, 'EW*, untraced, *CF-CEX-'FB, 'EV* |

## (c) **By the Whittlesey Body Co Inc**

| Constructor's Numbers | Aircraft markings |
|---|---|
| At least 100–106 | *NC530M, NC199N, NC804N-NC806N, NC47V, NC48V* |

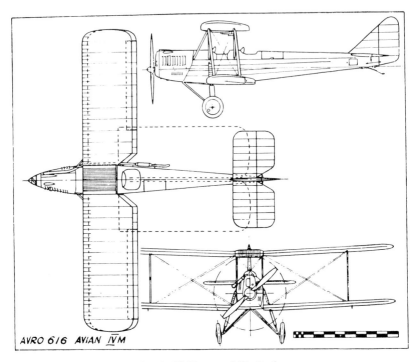

AVRO 616 AVIAN IVM

## (d) Sports Avians by A. V. Roe and Co Ltd

| Constructor's Numbers | Aircraft markings |
|---|---|
| 419, 421, 423 | *G-AAYU*, *G-ABCE*, '*DN* |
| 424 | *G-ABEA* |
| 454–456 | *G-AAWI*, Mexico, *G-AAXH* |
| 473–474 | *G-ABEE*, '*ED* |
| 490 | *G-ABIB* |
| 499, 501, 505 | *ZK-ACM*, *G-ABIM*, '*KI* |
| 531, 576, 649 | *VH-UQE*, *G-ABSS*, *G-ACGV* |

## (e) Avro 625 Avian Monoplanes

| Constructor's No. and Registration | C of A Issued | Details |
|---|---|---|
| 459 *G-AAYV* | 27. 6.30 | Genet Major I; converted to biplane 1931, to J. R. Ford, Broxbourne 5.38, scrapped 1939 |
| 460 *G-AAYW* | 27. 6.30 | Hermes I: to F/Lt R. L. R. Atcherley 9.30, fitted Hermes II, W. L. Handley 6.40, scrapped during the war |

## (f) Long range aircraft for Sir Charles Kingsford Smith

| Constructor's No. and Registration | C of A Issued | Details |
|---|---|---|
| 467 *G-ABCF* | 26. 9.30 | Avian IVA; Australian Flight 10.30, Tasman Flight 1.31, allotted *VH-UPT*, crashed at Mascot 12.4.31 |
| 523 *G-ABLK* | 21. 7.31 | Avian V *Southern Cross Minor*; abortive Australia–UK Flight 9.31 as *VH-UQG*, to W. N. Lancaster 4.33 restored as *G-ABLK*, lost in the Sahara 13.4.33, wreck discovered 3.62 |

274

Avro 618 Ten *VH-UNA Southern Sun* leaving Sydney for Croydon with the Christmas mail on November 16, 1931.

# Avro 618 Ten and Variants

In 1928 R. H. Dobson, H. E. Broadsmith and other Avro key personnel spent some time in the works of N. V. Nederlandsche Vliegtuigenfabrik (Fokker), Amsterdam, examining drawings, design data and production processes and their favourable report led to the acquisition of a licence to build the Fokker F.VIIb/3m for sale throughout the British Empire (excluding Canada). Worldwide success of this rugged, three-engined, high-wing transport resulted from combining a one-piece, thick-section, ply-covered cantilever wing with a welded steel-tube, fabric-covered fuselage. Paradoxically these were the very features distrusted by the British authorities. Fortunately the British Air Ministry was already in possession of a Netherlands-built F.VIIa/3m, *J7986*, delivered in May 1926 by Fokker's chief test pilot Grasé, who had astonished spectators by looping it on arrival over Martlesham. A series of tests during which it defeated all attempts to break it eventually cleared the way for the certification of the Avro-built version. Although generally similar to the Dutch original, it differed slightly in detail to meet British airworthiness requirements, notably in the downward tilt to the thrust line of the nose engine. Powered by three 240 hp Armstrong Siddeley Lynx IVB radials, it was known as the Avro 618 Ten, so called because it carried eight passengers and two crew.

Total production amounted to 14 aircraft, including five for Australian National Airways Ltd founded in 1929 by Sir Charles Kingsford Smith and Charles Ulm. The first of these was exhibited at the Olympia Aero Show, London, in July 1929 and later received British marks *G-AADM* for test flying at Woodford. By way of compliment to 'Smithy's veteran Fokker flagship *Southern Cross*, the new machines were named *Southern Sky, Star, Moon, Cloud* and *Sun* respectively for use on the daily, six hour, 500 mile Brisbane–Sydney service opened on January 1, 1930, and the daily 480 mile Sydney–Melbourne route inaugurated on June 1.

On April 29, 1931, *Southern Sun* (Capt P. Lynch Blosse) and *Southern Star* (Capt J. A. Mollison) helped distribute the first experimental England–Australia air mail by collecting the bags from Kingsford Smith and the *Southern Cross* at Brisbane and flying them to Sydney and Melbourne respectively. The same Avro Tens returned to Brisbane with the first northbound mail on April 23–24 and two others performed a similar function for the second service when *Southern Moon* (Capt P. G. Taylor) left Darwin on May 14 for Sydney where *Southern Sky* (Capt E. Chaseling) picked up the mail for Melbourne.

The cost of the search for *Southern Cloud* (Capt W. T. Shortridge), which disappeared over the Strathbozie Mountains between Sydney and Melbourne on March 21, 1931, and a falling-off in traffic, forced ANA to close down, the last major operation being the special 1931 Christmas mail flight which carried 52,780 packets weighing 1,340 lb to England. *Southern Sun* (Capt G. U. Allan) left Hobart, Tasmania, on November 15, picked up the Australian mail and left Darwin northbound on the 23rd, but the machine was severely damaged in a take-off accident at Alor Star on the 26th. By flying long forced stages in *Southern Star*, Kingsford Smith saved the situation and landed the mail at Croydon on December 16. After an extremely rapid top overhaul by Avros at Hamble, the Avro Ten left again on January 1, 1932, and arrived at Darwin on the 19th.

On its return from Croydon *Southern Star* was sold to the Hart Aircraft Co Ltd which opened a twice weekly Melbourne–Flinders Island–Launceston service with it on April 4, 1933. But the mystery of the disappearance of *Southern Cloud* remained unsolved. It was not until 27 years later on October 26, 1958, that the wreck was located near the top of a 5,000 ft mountain in the Toolong Range. A maker's plate inscribed 'Avro 10 No. 1' (confirming it as *VH-UMF* ex *G-AADM*) was still readable.

Avro Tens *VH-UNJ* and *'PI*, built for the Queensland Air Navigation Co Ltd of Brisbane, inaugurated a thrice weekly Townsville service on April 1, 1930, and the Lismore and Grafton routes on August 12. When the company closed down in January 1931, these and the former ANA *Southern Sky* were taken over by New England Airways Ltd, the firm responsible for the Brisbane–Narromine sector of the first regular England–Australia air mail service, flown by *City of Grafton*, formerly *Southern Sky* (Capt K. Virtue) on December 21, 1934.

The slump which closed ANA also brought the Hart Tasmania service to an end in February 1934, its single Avro Ten *VH-UMG* being transferred to Australian Transcontinental Airways Ltd for a new Adelaide–Darwin service opened by Capt J. Chapman on August 19, 1935. This venture was equally short-lived and ceased on October 11 the same year. When New England Airways also closed down, its small fleet of Tens was acquired by Airlines of Australia Ltd, Sydney.

A change of name also occurred when Charles Ulm bought the old *Southern Moon* from the liquidators of ANA in 1932 and called in Wing Cdr L. J. (later Sir Laurence) Wackett who rebuilt it at Cockatoo Island

Dockyard as a long-range machine similar to *Southern Cross*. The mainplane was lengthened and the airframe strengthened to take a series of 260 gallon fuel tanks, and the Lynx engines gave way to three 330 hp Wright Whirlwind J6-7 radials. Restyled *VH-UXX Faith in Australia*, the machine was wheeled out on June 1, 1933, first flown on June 14 and left Sydney for a projected world flight on June 24 with Ulm, P. G. Taylor and G. U. Allan as crew. Engine trouble prevented them reaching England in record time and *'XX* did not land at Heston until 17 days later on July 10. Further bad luck at Portmarnock Strand, Dublin, where the undercarriage collapsed under the weight of fuel and the tide engulfed the machine on the eve of take-off for the Atlantic crossing, necessitated reconstruction by Avros at Woodford using an entirely new fuselage having standard passenger windows. *Faith in Australia* was then flown to Brooklands where Ulm decided to abandon the world flight. Instead he left the Fairey aerodrome at Heathrow on October 12 and successfully reduced the England–Australia record time to 6 days 17 hr 45 min by arriving at Derby, WA, at midnight on the 19th.

During the night of December 3–4 *VH-UXX* made her first passage of the Tasman Sea in the course of which two lady passengers were carried to New Plymouth. After a barnstorming tour of New Zealand, Ulm made the returning crossing with mail on February 2, 1934, after which the aircraft made two more special return mail crossings (April 11/14, May 11/July 12) and later flew the first experimental air mail to New Guinea. After the loss of Ulm in the Pacific in an Airspeed Envoy in November 1934, *'XX* languished in its old hangar at Mascot until equipped with neon signs in 1935 for night advertising over Sydney. In 1941 Stephens Aviation Ltd took it to Wau for goldfields work and in the early days of the Japanese

Charles Ulm, P. G. Taylor and crew at Woodford in October 1933 with the rebuilt Avro Ten *Faith in Australia* (three 330 hp Wright Whirlwinds).

277

invasion it made many evacuation flights between New Guinea and Australia. Although it escaped the Japanese this historic aeroplane was left to rot away behind a hangar at Townsville, Queensland.

In April 1931 the sixth Avro Ten, *G-AASP*, was delivered to Imperial Airways Ltd, named *Achilles* and despatched to Cairo on long-term charter to the Iraq Petroleum Transport Co Ltd for the desert pipeline patrol. A second machine, *G-ABLU*, delivered in June 1931 and named *Apollo*, also went to Iraq. Both Avro Tens returned to European charter work in June 1933, but were based occasionally at Le Bourget to operate the Zürich service. *Apollo* was burned out after striking a radio mast between Ghent and Bruges while flying the Brussels–Croydon service on December 30, 1938, but *Achilles* survived until the early part of the Second World War.

In an attempt to establish air routes in India, four Avro Tens were built in 1931 for Indian State Airways, but financial stringency led to the abandonment of the scheme and the order was cut back to a single aircraft, *VT-ACT*, for the use of the Viceroy. Two of the frustrated machines were sold immediately to the Egyptian Army Air Force and left Heston in British marks at dawn on January 11, 1932, piloted by Messrs Clarkson and Cameron, but in September 1934 one at last found its way to the Karachi–Lahore service of Indian National Airways Ltd. The Viceregal Ten was used in 1937 to fly British Air Ministry officials over the Southern Shan States to survey a proposed air route to China. The fourth machine of the original Indian order remained in the Avro works until completed as *G-ACGF* in April 1933 to the order of John Sword to supplement Airspeed Ferries on the Renfrew–Belfast and Renfrew–Speke scheduled services of Midland and Scottish Air Ferries Ltd.

Last of all the Avro Tens was *K2682*, delivered to the Wireless and Equipment Flight at the RAE, Farnborough, on July 27, 1936.

Exhibited alongside the Avro Ten at Olympia in 1929 was a scaled-down version designed entirely by Roy Chadwick and his team. Powered by three Armstrong Siddeley Genet Majors, it would maintain 5,500 ft on two engines and because it accommodated pilot and four passengers, was known

*K2682*, the sole RAF Avro 618 Ten.

278

Wilson Airways' Avro 619 Five *VP-KAE* with the original cockpit canopy.

as the Avro 619 Five. After the show it was slightly modified for Wilson Airways Ltd, Nairobi, Kenya, as *VP-KAE Knight of the Grail* for use on local services. The long ferry flight from Heston was made in October 1929 by T. Campbell Black, and a second machine *VP-KAD Knight Errant* followed in February 1930.

Avro 624 Six prototype *G-AAYR* with flat windscreen and high mounted nacelles. (*Flight photo 8874*)

A third Avro Five *VH-UNK* was shipped to Brisbane to join the Avro Tens of the Queensland Air Navigation Co Ltd and the fourth and final machine was the British demonstrator *G-AASO*. This was flown in the King's Cup Race of July 5, 1930, by F/Lt S. L. G. Pope but was not really suitable for racing and retired at its home base, Woodford. Two months later *'SO* also flew to Kenya to replace the first Wilson machine and continued on the African services in British marks until it was damaged beyond repair in a forced landing 12 miles from Broken Hill while en route from Salisbury on January 18, 1932.

A projected single-engined Avro Five (Armstrong Siddeley Panther), the Avro 628 mailplane was not proceeded with.

A slightly larger version with widened cockpit for two pilots side-by-side with dual controls, increased cabin headroom, lavatory at the rear, and engine nacelles fitted directly to the underside of the mainplane, appeared

279

The third Avro Six, *G-ABBY*, remodelled for Air Service Training Ltd, in 1931 with underslung nacelles and angled windscreen. (*The Aeroplane*)

in May 1930 as the Avro 624 Six. Registered *G-AAYR*, the Avro Six was subjected to exhaustive test flying at Woodford and Heston, as a result of which the outboard engines were refitted in underslung nacelles in the manner of the Avro Five. The flat cockpit windscreen was also replaced by a metal framed structure with angled panels to deflect the rain. Test flying in this condition took place at Woodford with Class B marking *K-5* superimposed on the registration, and as a result of demonstrations at Heston later in 1931, the machine was sold with one other to the Far East Aviation Co Ltd for delivery to China. A third Avro Six, *G-ABBY*, remodelled in 1933 as a hybrid Five/Six with underslung nacelles and angled windscreen as a navigators' flying classroom for Air Service Training Ltd, remained in service at Hamble until taken over by No.11 Air Observers' Navigation School in the early days of the Second World War.

A further high-wing development, not readily recognisable as a Fokker derivative, was the twin-engined Avro 642/2m, known initially as the Avro Eighteen. This machine used the Avro Ten mainplane lowered to the shoulder position with two 460 hp Armstrong Siddeley Jaguar VID radial engines mounted on the leading edge. Aerodynamically it was a much cleaner design than the Ten, and when first built had a glazed semi-circular nose to the pilot's compartment but this was damaged in a gale and replaced by a conventional stepped windscreen. As indicated by the original designation, accommodation was for two crew and 16 passengers. The prototype, *G-ACFV*, delivered to Midland and Scottish Air Ferries Ltd at Renfrew in April 1934, was followed by the only other machine of the type. This was *VT-AFM*, the Avro 642/4m variant powered by four Armstrong Siddeley Lynx IVC engines. Named *Star of India* and built to the order of the Indian Government to Air Ministry Specification C.11/30 as replacement for the Avro Ten *VT-ACT*, it was flown out by Nevill Vintcent to whom it was handed over at Croydon on December 9, 1934. The Avro 642/4m was a seven-seater used as personal aircraft of the Viceroy, Lord Willingdon, and differed from *G-ACFV* in having a pilot's door on the port side of the front fuselage and full-length clear view windows in place of portholes. It remained in service at Delhi for several years but was withdrawn after a vehicle damaged a wingtip in 1940 and revealed white ant activity inside the wing.

When Midland and Scottish Air Ferries Ltd ceased operations, *G-ACFV* was sold to Commercial Air Hire Ltd of Croydon and formed the mainstay of the early morning Continental newspaper delivery flights during 1935–36. Later in 1936 W. R. Carpenter and Co Ltd bought it for mail services in New Guinea, where it continued in service with Mandated Airlines Ltd until the Japanese destroyed it in 1942.

The military potential of the Avro 642 was not overlooked and type number Avro 655 was allotted to a projected bomber (two Jaguar VIA)

The Avro 642/2m *G-ACFV* with original semicircular nose.

The Avro 642/2m *G-ACFV/VH-UXD* at Brisbane during its delivery flight to New Guinea in 1936.

The Viceroy's Avro 642/4m *VT-AFM Star of India* at Croydon, December 1934. (*Flight photo*)

281

with front and rear gunners. Preliminary layouts were made in November 1933 but the machine was not built.

## SPECIFICATION AND DATA

*Manufacturers:*   A. V. Roe and Co Ltd, Newton Heath, Manchester; and Hamble Aerodrome, near Southampton, Hants

*Powerplants:*   (Avro 618)   Three 240 hp Armstrong Siddeley Lynx IVB or IVC
Three 330 hp Wright Whirlwind J6-7

(Avro 619)   Three 105 hp Armstrong Siddeley Genet Major

(Avro 624)   Three 105 hp Armstrong Siddeley Genet Major

(Avro 642/2m)   Two 450 hp Armstrong Siddeley Jaguar VID

(Avro 642/4m)   Four 215 hp Armstrong Siddeley Lynx IVC

*Dimensions, Weights and Performances:*

|  | Avro 618 | Avro 619 | Avro 624 | Avro 642/2m | Avro 642/4m |
|---|---|---|---|---|---|
| Span | 71 ft 3 in* | 47 ft 0 in | 51 ft 0 in | 71 ft 3 in | 71 ft 3 in |
| Length | 47 ft 6 in | 35 ft 9 in | 36 ft 0 in | 54 ft 6 in** | 54 ft 6 in |
| Height | 12 ft 9 in | 9 ft 6 in | 9 ft 6 in | 11 ft 6 in | 11 ft 6 in |
| Wing area | 772 sq ft* | 333 sq ft | 360 sq ft | 728 sq ft | 728 sq ft |
| Tare weight | 6,020 lb*** | 3,062 lb | 3,058 lb | 7,360 lb | 8,731 lb |
| All-up weight | 10,600 lb*** | 4,620 lb | 5,000 lb | 11,800 lb | 12,250 lb |
| Maximum speed | 115 mph | 118 mph | 113 mph | 156 mph | 150 mph |
| Cruising speed | 100 mph | 98 mph | 95 mph | 125 mph | 130 mph |
| Initial climb | 675 ft/min | 650 ft/min | 500 ft/min | 970 ft/min | 750 ft/min |
| Ceiling | 16,000 ft | 15,000 ft | 14,000 ft | 17,500 ft | 15,000 ft |
| Range | 400 miles | 400 miles | 400 miles | 600 miles | 560 miles |

*Faith in Australia* approximately 75 ft
**Original curved nose 53 ft 0 in
***K2682 5,743 lb and 10,225 lb respectively; *Faith in Australia* 16,000 lb

*Production:*

### (a) Avro 618 Ten
Fourteen aircraft as follows: c/n 229 *VH-UMH*, C of A 5.9.29, ANA *Southern Sky*, to New England Airways 8.33 as *City of Grafton*, s.o.r. 1.36; 230 *VH-UMG*, 3.9.29, ANA *Southern Star*, to Hart 3.33, to ATA 9.35, beyond repair Mascot 21.11.36; 231 *VH-UMI*, 10.10.29, ANA *Southern Moon*, rebuilt 2.33 as *VH-UXX Faith in Australia* c/n IA, to Eastern Air Transport Ltd 8.35, Kingsford Smith Air Service Ltd 6.38, Stephens Aviation Ltd, in New Guinea 5.41, derelict at Townsville Q. 1942; 241 *G-AADM*, 26.8.29, to ANA as *VH-UMF Southern Cloud*, lost in the Strathbozie Mts 21.3.31; 371 *VH-UNJ*, 27.11.29, Queensland Air Navigation Co Ltd, to New England Airways 1.32 as *City of Brisbane*, to Airlines of Australia Ltd, s.o.r. 6.40; 384 *G-AASP*, 23.4.31, Imperial Airways Ltd *Achilles*, destroyed 3.4.40; 388 *VH-UNA*, 5.3.30, ANA *Southern Sun*, crashed at Alor Star in Malaya 26.11.31; 468 *VH-UPI*, completed

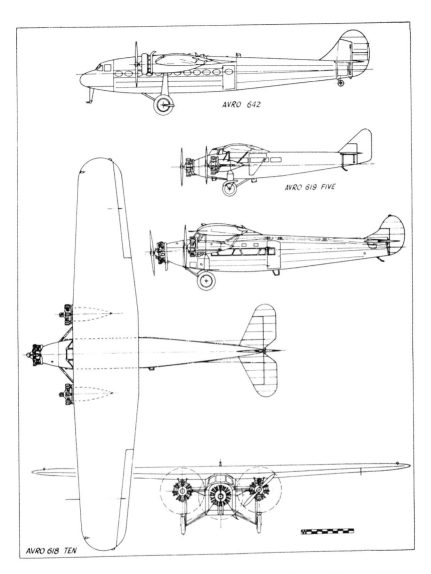

AVRO 642

AVRO 619 FIVE

AVRO 618 TEN

24.6.30, Queensland Air Navigation Co Ltd, to New England Airways 12.31 as *City of Sydney*, to Airlines of Australia Ltd, s.o.r. 9.38; 524 *VT-ACT*, C of A 6.11.31, Indian State Airways; 525 *G-ABSP*, 22.12.31, to Egyptian Army Air Force 1.32 as *F200*, crashed at Assuit in Egypt 10.12.33; 526 *G-ABSR*, 29.12.31, to Egyptian Army Air Force 1.32 as *F201*, to Indian National Airways 9.34 as *VT-AFX*; 527 *G-ACGF*, 3.5.33, Midland and Scottish Air Ferries Ltd, s.o.r. 12.46; 528 *G-ABLU*, 18.6.31, Imperial Airways Ltd *Apollo*, crashed at Ruysselede in Belgium 30.12.33; *K2682* completed 3.7.36 to Works Order 3302 and delivered to the RAF 24.7.36 under Contract 164779/32, used by the

Wireless and Equipment Flight at the RAE, Farnborough 27.7.36–28.10.36.

*Note:* Australian National Airways machines had Lynx IVB, and construction sequence was by C of A date with c/n 241 first.

(b) **Avro 619 Five**

Four aircraft as follows: c/n 228 *VP-KAE*, C of A 3.10.29, Wilson Airways Ltd *Knight of the Grail*, withdrawn from use 10.35; 370 *VH-UNK*, 16.12.29, Queensland Air Navigation Co Ltd, crashed at Maryborough, Q, 31.12.30; 383 *G-AASO*, 10.3.30, damaged beyond repair at Broken Hill, Kenya, 18.1.32; 436 *VP-KAD*, 22.1.30, Wilson Airways Ltd *Knight Errant*, broken up at Nairobi 10.32.

(c) **Avro 624 Six**

Three aircraft as follows: c/n 457 *G-AAYR*, 25.6.30, converted to six-seat Avro Five, to China via Hong Kong 12.31 as *VR-HAQ*; 458 *G-ABBY*, 8.4.31, converted to six-seat Avro Five for AST Ltd 5.33, scrapped at Hamble 3.41; 575 *VR-HBF*, 14.1.32, Far East Aviation Co Ltd, sold in China.

(d) **Avro 642/2m**

One aircraft as follows: c/n 642 *G-ACFV*, C of A 29.1.34, Midland and Scottish Air Ferries Ltd *Marchioness of Londonderry*; wrecked at Cerrig-y-Druidion, Merioneth, Wales, 4.6.34; rebuilt for Commercial Air Hire Ltd 5.35; to W. R. Carpenter Ltd, Wau, NG 9.36 as *VH-UXD*; to Mandated Airlines Ltd 3.37; destroyed by enemy action 11.3.42.

(e) **Avro 642/4m**

One aircraft as follows: c/n 773 *VT-AFM*, 8.12.34, Indian Government *Star of India*; to the RAF 1939 as *L9166*; dismantled at Delhi 1940.

Registration VP-KAH was reserved for the Avro Five G-AASO by Wilson Airways but never used. (*Avro*)

*K1230*, first Avro 621 Trainer delivered to the Air Ministry, flying over Gosport in 1933. (*Flight photo 12311*)

# Avro 621 Tutor

Tests made at Newton Heath with Fokker-type welded steel structures had shown that they were far stronger than the wooden equivalent and that the tubes did not corrode internally as had been feared. In extremes of temperature overseas, the advantages of a rugged, non-warping structure of this kind were obvious and numerous metal Avians were already behaving very satisfactorily in Canada, Australia, Africa and elsewhere. This form of construction was selected therefore for the Avro 621 two-seat basic trainer, designed in 1929 by Roy Chadwick to replace the grand old 504N in RAF service. The new aircraft was a heavily staggered, equal-span biplane of strictly conventional appearance, with enlarged Avian-type horn-balanced rudder. It was powered by an uncowled 155 hp Armstrong Siddeley Mongoose IIIA five-cylinder radial behind which the rectangular section of the basic fuselage structure was brought up to streamlined form by large fabric-covered removable inspection panels. Mainplanes, also fabric-covered, were of all steel construction, wire-braced and supported on narrow-chord N-type interplane struts. Handley Page slots were standard and Frise-type ailerons were fitted to the lower mainplane only. Twin oil damped rubber-in-compression undercarriage shock absorbers were housed in wide streamlined fairings.

Designated Avro 621 Trainer and allotted civil markings *G-AAKT*, the prototype was submitted to Martlesham in December 1929 and first shown in the New Types Park at the Hendon RAF Display on June 28, 1930, and then entered in the King's Cup Race of July 5 by the designer. Flown by J. L. N. Bennett Baggs, it averaged 108·3 mph from Hanworth to Woodford where it retired, but although no racer its handling qualities were superb, rivalling even those of the 504N. Two batches of Trainers *K1230–K1240*

285

and *K1787–K1796* were then ordered by the Air Ministry to Specification 3/30 for Service trials at Gosport; No.3 FTS, Grantham; and elsewhere during 1930. In March of that year three others were supplied to the Irish Army Air Corps, which bestowed its own name Triton, for instructional purposes at Baldonnel. One other was supplied in civil marks as *VH-UOL* to Australian National Airways Ltd.

The original design provided for the alternative installation of a 215 hp Armstrong Siddeley Lynx IVC and this engine was fitted to the majority of production aircraft. Two further prototypes *G-AARZ* and *'TU* were built with this engine and given enlarged and rounded rudders. Flown initially as *G-AARZ* but later as *K-4*, the first of these was otherwise similar to the first machine *'KT* and forerunner of special camera-equipped specimens *G-ABAP, 'AR* and *'HA* which the Director of Surveys, Tanganyika, added to his Avian fleet. Standard Avro 621s were supplied to the Ottawa Car Co Ltd and the Far East Aviation Co Ltd which needed them urgently for demonstration to the expanding Royal Canadian and Kwangsi Air Forces respectively.

Prototype trials, and the testing to destruction of works aircraft, *G-ABFL*, led to the adoption of the Avro 621 in June 1932 as the standard RAF trainer under the Service name of Avro Tutor. Contracts were initially to Specification 18/31, but as a result of Martlesham trials with *K1797* and the remaining prototype *G-AARZ*, later batches were to Specification 25/32 with the undercarriage moved forward $4\frac{3}{4}$ in, Dunlop intermediate pressure wheels, brakes, Frise ailerons on all four wings, and duplicated bracing wires. By 1934 developed Tutors were in production to Specification 24/34 with low-drag undercarriages, Goodyear Airwheels, Townend rings, and eventually (after tests with *K3189* in November 1933) a tie-rod between the ailerons as well as the original balance cable. Performance tests with

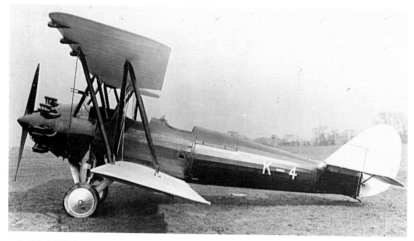

*K-4/G-AARZ*, first prototype Avro 621 Tutor, with rounded rudder and ailerons on the lower mainplane only.

*K2893*, the Avro 646 Sea Tutor trials aircraft. (*Crown Copyright Reserved*)

A production Avro 621 Tutor with four Frise ailerons, long-travel undercarriage and Dunlop wheels. (*Flight photo 12934*)

the Townend ring were made with *K1797*, but beginning with *K3219* all had this refinement. Brakes and a tail wheel were adopted for the final RAF batches after trials with *K3248* but the Avro 621 Mk.II, *K3308*, fitted with two-bay wings and tested at Martlesham in 1936, was the only one of its type.

At least two of the original RAF Mongoose Trainers were sold to civil operators in 1934 and several others became instructional airframes. Survivors were posted to the Air Navigation School at Andover in 1935 but were struck off charge and broken up in 1937. Main Tutor production to meet RAF and overseas orders progressed very rapidly by means of newly devised mass production methods using jig-built components to ensure complete interchangeability. It ceased in May 1936 with the completion of the 795th aircraft. All construction work took place in the Newton Heath works, but as soon as engine, centre section and undercarriage had been fitted, the Tutors were towed 15 miles behind a lorry to Woodford Aerodrome for rigging and flying. They were issued to the Central Flying School; the Flying Training Schools; the RAF College, Cranwell; the University and Auxiliary Squadrons; and in later years to the Elementary and Reserve Training Schools. They took over the formation, aerobatic and inverted flying turn at the Hendon RAF Display, beginning with a CFS team flying *K3237–K3242* at the display of June 26, 1933.

Two early model Tutors, *113* and *114*, ordered by the Danish Navy, arrived at Copenhagen in crates on January 4, 1932. Locally designated L.B. IV, they were later brought up to late production standard and supplemented by *115* equipped with long-chord cowlings and revised aileron circuit without the connecting strut or cable. Tutor *115* was delivered without covering as a pattern for licence production by Orlogsvaerftet (Danish Naval Shipyard) but only three were built in Denmark. Skis from a Hawker Danecock were fitted to one of them in 1938.

As a result of trials in Greece with civil demonstrator *G-ADMG*, a large batch was sold to the Greek Air Force; two were also acquired by the Polish Ministry of Communications, Warsaw, in May 1935; and two others, *701* and *702*, were evaluated at Roberts Heights by the South African Air Force,

A Greek Air Force Tutor showing the aileron link strut fitted to late production aircraft.

The experimental two-bay Avro 621 Tutor Mk.II *K3308*.

Danish Navy Tutor *115* with long-chord cowling.

which then acquired a licence to build 57 machines at the Aircraft and Artillery Depot, Pretoria. Improved versions similar to the Egyptian and Brazilian Avro 626s (see page 296), considered in March 1935 as the Avro 662 with Lynx and as the Avro 669 with Cheetah IX, remained only projects.

Early production Tutors *G-ABIR* and '*IS* were used for advanced flying instruction at Hamble by Air Service Training from 1931 until the outbreak of war. As at CFS, they were used to teach blind flying techniques first developed on the old hooded 504Ns, and during 1934 were brought up to the full modification standard of later RAF batches. Trials at Hamble and the MAEE, Felixstowe, with the civil seaplane prototype *G-ABGH* (Lynx IVC) led to the temporary use of '*IR* for seaplane instruction in the summer of 1932 and to the placing of an Air Ministry order for one trials aircraft and 14 production Avro 646 Sea Tutors to Specification 26/34. Equipped with floats built to Specification 17/33, they were delivered during 1934–36 and used for waterborne trials at Felixstowe and by the Seaplane Training School, Calshot, until withdrawn in April 1938.

In the winter of 1932–33, civil Tutors *G-ABZP* and '*ZR*, supplied to Sir Alan Cobham's Circus for aerobatic joyrides, joined the prototype machine *G-AARZ* on a South African tour piloted by C. W. Bebb, Martin Hearn and others. After the loss of '*ZR* in a fatal crash, the other two were shipped back to the UK in readiness for the 1934 season during which '*RZ* was damaged beyond repair. In the same year *G-ACOV* (formerly *K1791*, one of the original RAF Mongoose Trainers ) was overhauled for similar use by Air Pageants Ltd and in 1936 an even earlier specimen, *K1231*, was converted at Eastleigh for private owner T. C. S. Westbrook and registered *G-ADYW*. This was later used by Grimsby Aviation Ltd by whom it was scrapped in 1940. Air Service Training machines '*IR* and '*IS* served with No.3 EFTS, Hamble, until impressed at the end of 1941 and eventually handed over to the Air Training Corps as instructional airframes. In April 1940 this fate befell *G-AFZW* (formerly *K3237*, starboard outer machine of the 1933 RAF Display aerobatic flight) belonging to Portsmouth, Southsea and Isle of Wight Aviation Ltd.

Among redundant Service stocks after the war were a number of Tutors, of which three were disposed of to civilians. The first, *G-AHSA* ex *K3215*, was converted at Weston-super-Mare for the Darlington and District Aero Club in February 1947; *K6105* was rebuilt as *G-AKFJ* by W. Sturrock, Avro manager at Bracebridge Heath, near Lincoln, in 1948; but *K3363*, the actual machine used in the comic event at the 1935 RAF Display, languished untouched at Croydon for some years without becoming *G-AIYM*. Sole surviving Tutor in the UK in 1990 was *G-AHSA*, preserved in flying condition with original serial *K3215* by the Shuttleworth Trust.

## SPECIFICATION AND DATA

*Manufacturers:* A. V. Roe and Co Ltd, Newton Heath, Manchester; and Hamble Aerodrome, near Southampton, Hants

Orlogsvaerftet (Danish Naval Shipyard), Copenhagen, Denmark

South African Air Force, Aircraft and Artillery Depot, Pretoria

*Powerplants:* One 155 hp Armstrong Siddeley Mongoose IIIC (designated Mongoose IIIA in civil machines)
One 215 hp Armstrong Siddeley Lynx IV
One 215 hp Armstrong Siddeley Lynx IVC

*Dimensions, Weights and Performance:*

|  | Avro 621 | | Avro 646 Sea Tutor |
|---|---|---|---|
|  | Mongoose IIIC | Lynx IVC |  |
| Span | 34 ft 0 in | 34 ft 0 in | 34 ft 0 in |
| Length | 26 ft 7¾ in | 26 ft 4½ in | 29 ft 3 in |
| Height | 9 ft 7 in | 9 ft 7 in | 11 ft 6 in |
| Wing area | 302 sq ft | 301 sq ft | 300 sq ft |
| Tare weight | 1,535 lb | 1,844 lb | 2,218 lb |
| All-up weight | 2,182 lb* | 2,493 lb* | 2,894 lb |
| Maximum speed | 104 mph | 120 mph* | 92 mph |
| Cruising speed | 95 mph | 97 mph | 95 mph |
| Initial climb | 725 ft/min* | 910 ft/min | 430 ft/min |
| Ceiling | 12,400 ft | 16,000 ft | 12,000 ft |
| Range | 380 miles | 250 miles | 240 miles |

*G-AAKT 1,571 lb, 2,230 lb, and 650 ft/min respectively
**Avro 621 Mk.II *K3308* all-up weight 2,687 lb

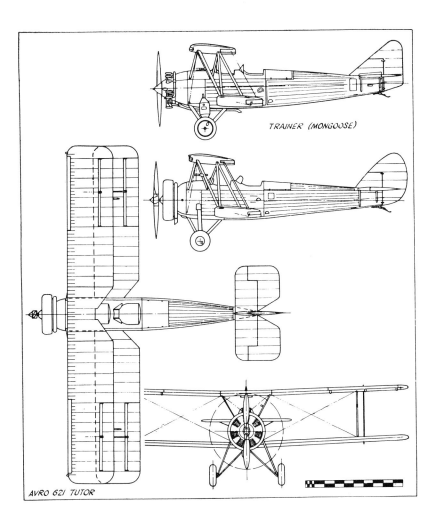

TRAINER (MONGOOSE)

AVRO 621 TUTOR

*Production:*
## (*a*) Avro 621 prototypes, civil and export orders

| Constructor's Numbers | Aircraft markings |
|---|---|
| 321, 332, 410–413 | *G-AAKT, G-AARZ/K-4,* Irish *A.7-A.9, VH-UOL* |
| 437, 463, 464, 477 | *G-AATU, CF-ANQ*/RCAF *224, VR-HAF, G-ABFL* |
| 485, 497, 498 | *G-ABGH, G-ABIR*/HM504, *G-ABIS*/HM505 |
| 506–516 | RCAF *184, 189, 186, 187, 185, 188,* Kwangsi Air Force (5) |
| 550, 551, 774 | Danish Navy *113-115* |
| 624, 625, 638, 641 | *G-ABZP, 'ZR,* S.A.A.F. *701, 702* |
| 795, 826, 827 | *G-ADMG*/Greek Air Force E-69, Poland (2) |
| 891–919 | Greek Air Force *E-50* to *E-68* and *E-70* to *E-79* |

291

(b) **Avro 621 survey version**

Three aircraft for the Director of Surveys, Tanganyika: c/n 461, 462, 487; *G-ABAP*, *'AR* and *'HA*; Cs of A issued 18.7.30, 30.9.30 and 4.3.31; to Tanganyika 2.32 as *VR-TAB*, *'AC* and *'AE*; impressed locally 1940.

(c) **Avro 621 Trainers** (Mongoose IIIC)

Eleven aircraft *K1230–K1240* requisitioned 3.30; a further ten *K1787–K1796* requisitioned 10.30. (Civil conversions: *K1231* for T.C.S. Westbrook as *G-ADYW*, C of A issued 23.6.36, to Grimsby Aviation Ltd, scrapped at Waltham 1940; *K1791* for Air Pageants Ltd, as *G-ACOV*, C of A issued 29.5.34, crashed 12.34).

(d) **Avro 621 Tutors** (Lynx IVC)

| Contract | Quantity | Serials | Contract | Quantity | Serials |
|---|---|---|---|---|---|
| — | 1 | *K1797★* | 195190/32 | 94 | *K3381–K3474* |
| 113780/31 | 18 | *K2496–K2513* | 350988/34 | 40 | *K4798–K4837* |
| 195190/32 | 30 | *K3189–K3218* | 411542/35 | 40 | *K6087–K6126★★* |
| 195190/32 | 153 | *K3219–K3371* | 411542/35 | 5 | *K8168–K8172* |

★Wrecked in landing collision 24.4.35.     ★★All delivered to No.2 ASU

(Civil conversions: *K3215* to Darlington and District Aero Club Ltd, as *G-AHSA*, C of A issued 20.7.47, preserved by the Shuttleworth Trust; *K3237* to Portsmouth, Southsea and Isle of Wight Aviation Ltd as *G-AFZW*, C of A issued 3.4.40, to No.15 MU, Wroughton, 29.4.40 as *AV980*, instructional airframe 1.41 as *2427M*; *K3363* by road to Burton-on-Trent 1950 before conversion to *G-AIYM*; *K6105* to W. Sturrock, Bracebridge Heath, as *G-AKFJ*, C of A issued 17.12.47, to Doncaster Ultra Light Group 1948, crashed at Doncaster 30.7.49.)

(e) **Avro 646 Sea Tutors**

| Contract | Quantity | Serials | Contract | Quantity | Serials |
|---|---|---|---|---|---|
| 174901/32 | 1 | *K2893★* | 335645/34 | 2 | *K3475–K3476* |
| 261030/33 | 9 | *K3372–K3380* | 419033/35 | 3 | *K6923–K6925* |

Also four engineless airframes in 1934 and three in 1936.
★Trials aircraft initially with Short metal floats, later with Avro-built floats.

(f) **Total production by A. V. Roe and Co Ltd**

Complete aircraft 1930–36: 436 military, 49 civil. Engineless airframes 1932–36: 303 military. Civil airframes: six in 1931 and one in 1938. Total production 795 aircraft.

(g) **Avro 621s built under licence**

*South Africa:* Fifty-seven aircraft, serials believed *703–759*.
*Denmark:* Three aircraft, *116–118*, Orlogsvaerftet c/n 86–89, on Danish Navy charge 24.6.35, 6.4.37 and 13.4.37 respectively. These and the Avro-built

South African built Tutor SAAF *740*.

*114* and *115* were stored during the German occupation and believed destroyed when saboteurs blew up their hangar 22.11.43.

*Service Use:* (with specimen serials)
   (Tutors) Central Flying School, Upavon, *K3203*, '*05*, '*37–'42*, '*48*, '*61–*
'*65*, *K3362–'65*, '*69*; School of Air Pilotage, Andover, *K1233*, '*34*, *K1787–*
'*96*; No.2 FTS, Digby, *K4809*; No.3 FTS, Grantham, *K1230*, '*33*, '*39*,
*K2496–K2513*, *K2353*, *K4816*; No.5 FTS, Sealand, *K3233*, '*43–'47*, '*49–*
'*52*, '*63*, '*65*, '*66*, '*68*, '*70–'72*, *K3449*; No.11 FTS Wittering, *K3403*, '*73*;
RAF College, Cranwell, *K3198*, *K3205*, *K3461*; No.23 ERFTS, Rochester,
*K3244*, '*64*, *K3331*, '*67*, *K3419*; Oxford University Air Squadron, *K3271*,
'*95*, *K3442–'44*, '*50*, *K4620*, *K4798*, '*99*, *K4820*, '*23*; Cambridge UAS,
Duxford, *K3225*, '*26*, '*60*, '*74*, '*78–'83*, *K3341*, *K3430*, '*31*, '*36*, '*70*, *K4798*,
*K4830*, '*32*; London UAS, *K3215*, '*48*, '*71*, *K3302*, '*07*, '*91*, *K3406*, '*53*,
'*73*, '*74*, *K4828*, '*29*, *K6123*, '*24*; No.600 Sqn AAF, Hendon, *K3266*,
*K3326*, '*84*, *K3471*; No.601 Sqn AAF, Hendon, *K3360*, *K3442*; No.605
Sqn AAF, Castle Bromwich, *K3309*, *K3458*; No.609 Sqn AAF, *K3433*;
No.610 Sqn AAF, *K3307*, '*11*; No.614 Sqn AAF, *K6104*; No.24 (Communications) Sqn, Hendon, *K6090*; Hong Kong Volunteer Air Force, Kai
Tak, *K3309*, *K3439–'41*; RCAF School of Army Co-operation, Camp
Borden.
   (Sea Tutors) Seaplane Training Sqn, Calshot, *K2893*, *K3373–'77*; DTD
trials *K3372*; stored *K3378–'80*.

A Cheetah V powered Avro 626 of the Brazilian Air Force. (*Flight photo 13892*)

# Avro 626 and Variants

To satisfy the needs of foreign air forces having only limited financial resources, the Tutor was redesigned in 1930 and offered as the unnamed Avro 626, with conversion kits to make it suitable for initial flying training, or bombing, photographic, gunnery, wireless, night flying, navigation, blind flying and seaplane instruction. Although the machine remained a two-seater, a third cockpit or gunner's position was provided aft of, and in communication with, the rear cockpit.

An early demonstrator, *G-ABFM*, was taken in crates by cargo steamer to the British Empire Trade Exhibition in Buenos Aires in January 1931, where it was flown by Capt Norman Macmillan as a landplane at the Argentine Air Force base; and on both wheels and floats at the naval base at Bahia Blanca. The same pilot then made the first all-British crossing of the Andes during a round trip from Buenos Aires to Bahia Blanca, Neuquen (North Patagonia), Chillan, Santiago and Mendoza. On its return *G-ABFM* was commandeered on the spot by the Argentine military authorities to help quell a provincial uprising, and performed so well that 14 additional Avro 626s were purchased a few months later.

Resulting from the Avro company's brilliant appraisal of overseas requirements and the untiring efforts of their globetrotting demonstrators *G-ABGG, 'JG, 'RK* and *G-ACFW*, the 626 went into large-scale production. *G-ACFZ*, a seaplane with Short all-metal floats and flown initially from Hamble slipway, was demonstrated and sold in Brazil in 1933; *G-ADKZ* and *'UJ* in Czechoslovakia and Austria respectively in 1935; and six others were ferried to Austria in British marks 1936–37. Considerable foreign contracts resulted and when production ceased in 1939, Avro 626s were in service with the air forces of Argentina, Austria, Belgium, Brazil, Canada, Chile, Czechoslovakia, Egypt, Greece, the Irish Free State, Kwangsi

Provincial Government (South China) and Lithuania. Four for Estonia were supplied with interchangable float undercarriages after waterborne trials at Hamble with *142*. The first for Chile was flown over the Andes in December 1934 by Avro chief test pilot H. A. Brown in mid-winter at an all-up weight of 3,250 lb.

After the delivery of 26 aircraft, the Portuguese Government aircraft factory OGMA acquired a licence to build Avro 626s locally for the Navy and 5a Arma. In 1935 the Ringhoffa-Tatra concern in Czechoslovakia also acquired a licence to build the Avro 626. These aircraft were to be designated Tatra T-126 and appear in two versions: Czechoslovak aircraft with 355 hp Avia Rk. 17 engines and aircraft for export to Turkey and the Balkans with standard British-made 260 hp Cheetah Vs. However problems with the Avia powerplant resulted in construction of the almost complete prototype being abandoned along with the whole production programme. In Canada some RCAF machines e.g. *225*, were equipped with twin metal skis, cabin tops and Arctic cowlings with controllable shutters.

The Avro 626 was not a civil type and the demonstrators bore civilian marks purely for test or to facilitate their passage abroad. The exceptions were *G-ABRK*, flown by the Earl of Amherst at Heston, and *G-ABYM*, the Air Service Training radio trainer. Apart from a trip to Cairo in December 1933 for the Circuit of the Oases Rally piloted by W. D. Campbell (who handed over to F/Lt R. P. Pope on arrival) it was in constant use at Hamble until scrapped in 1939. Rally competitors were shepherded across the desert by four Egyptian Army Air Force Avro 626s, ten of which had been delivered a month previously for survey work and anti-hashish patrols over the Sinai Desert. Egyptian pilots were given a familiarisation course at Lympne before a formation delivery flight begun on November 18, but two crashed and burned in fog in France and replacements were built later.

*G-ABGG*, one of the early-type Avro 626s used by A. V. Roe and Co as a demonstrator.

Egyptian Army Air Force Avro 626s (with aileron link struts) ready for delivery at Lympne, November 1933. (*Flight photo 10809S*)

The Avro 626 civil floatplane demonstrator *G-ACFZ* at Hamble before despatch to Brazil.

All the Egyptian Avro 626s, including ten delivered in 1937 to form No.1 (General Purpose) Squadron, were of an improved type with 260 hp Armstrong Siddeley Cheetah V. Seventeen with this engine and inscribed 'Exercito' later joined demonstrator *G-ACFZ* in Brazil.

The only versions significantly different from standard were the Avro Prefect and the Avro 637. The first was a specialised navigation trainer developed for the RAF via a conversion of the Tutor *K3221* illustrated on page 287. Seven built to Specification 32/34 replaced the old Mongoose Trainers at the School of Air Navigation, Andover, in 1935. They were merely two-seat Tutors brought up to full Avro 626 condition (but without the third cockpit), and equipped with tail wheels and modified aileron circuits. During their Service life these machines were known simply as

Avro Prefects without type number, to distinguish them from the Avro 626. The only other Prefects were four supplied to the RNZAF in 1935, but these were variants having the third cockpit and were referred to as Avro 626s. After the Second World War, two Prefects *K5069* and *K5066* were overhauled by Southern Aircraft (Gatwick) Ltd and flown a little in 1946 as civil machines. In New Zealand, *NZ203* was converted for private owner J. Frogley at Havelock North in 1947 as *ZK-APC* and remained airworthy until 1958. After more than twenty years in storage it was rebuilt to flying condition as *NZ203* at RNZAF Ohakea.

The Avro 637 was a lightly armed frontier patrol aircraft with rounded wingtips giving slightly increased span. Only eight were built, all supplied to the Kwangsi Air Force at Luichow, South China, by the Far East Aviation Co, Hong Kong, following demonstrations at Yunnanfu by Capt G. S. Jones-Evans DFC in 1934. The development vehicle for the Avro 637 was *G-ABJG*, which in B conditions as K-10, was modified repeatedly during 1932–33 until the desired configuration was arrived at, and then submitted for Air Ministry trials at Andover in 1934. The pilot, who occupied the front seat and was protected by a tunnel-like windscreen, was armed with one Vickers gun on top of the fuselage. His observer in the rear was provided with one Lewis gun on an Avro low-drag mounting. A large additional fuel tank was installed in the front fuselage and the engine was a Cheetah V driving a metal airscrew. As well as 400 rounds of ammunition the machine would carry six 20 lb bombs and vertical camera, or four bombs and radio equipment. If required, the rear decking could be hinged to take a stretcher case behind the pilot.

*225*, an RCAF Avro 626 with skis, enclosed heated cockpits, and Arctic engine cowling.

# SPECIFICATION AND DATA

*Manufacturers:*    A. V. Roe and Co Ltd, Newton Heath, Manchester
Oficinas Gerais de Material Aeronautico, Alverca do Ribatejo, Portugal

*Powerplants:*    (Avro 626) One 215 hp Armstrong Siddeley Lynx IVC
One 260 hp Armstrong Siddeley Cheetah V
(Avro 637) One 260 hp Armstrong Siddeley Cheetah V

*Dimensions, Weights and Performances:*

|  | Avro 626 (Lynx IVC) | | Avro 626 (Cheetah V) | | Avro 637 |
|---|---|---|---|---|---|
|  | landplane | seaplane | landplane | seaplane |  |
| Span | 34 ft 0 in | 34 ft 0 in | 34 ft 0 in | 34 ft 0 in | 36 ft 0 in |
| Length | 26 ft 6 in | 29 ft 4 in | 26 ft 6 in | 29 ft 4 in | 27 ft 3 in |
| Height | 9 ft 7 in | 11 ft 6 in | 9 ft 7 in | 11 ft 6 in | 9 ft 9 in |
| Wing area | 300 sq ft | 300 sq ft | 300 sq ft | 300 sq ft | 314 sq ft |
| Tare weight | 1,765 lb | 2,026 lb | 2,010 lb | 2,305 lb | 1,987 lb |
| All-up weight | 2.750 lb | 2,735 lb | 2,667 lb | 2,963 lb | 3,127 lb |
| Maximum speed | 112 mph | 108 mph | 130 mph | 120 mph | 135 mph |
| Cruising speed | 95 mph | 90 mph | 108 mph | 100 mph | 115 mph |
| Initial climb | 880 ft/min | 675 ft/min | 1,000 ft/min | 850 ft/min | 990 ft/min |
| Ceiling | 14,800 ft | 14,000 ft | 16,800 ft | 13,700 ft | 16,000 ft |
| Range | 240 miles | 240 miles | 210 miles | 200 miles | 540 miles |

*Note:* Figures quoted for the Avro 626 are for aircraft equipped for initial flying instruction. Those for the Avro 637 are for an unarmed aircraft, performance figures for the two main roles being given below.

|  | Maximum speed | Cruise | Climb | Ceiling | Range |
|---|---|---|---|---|---|
| With bombs | 130 mph | 110 mph | 900 ft/min | 14,000 ft | 300 miles |
| Fighter | 137 mph | 116 mph | 1,160 ft/min | 17,500 ft | 450 miles |

*Production:*

## (a) Avro 626 prototypes, civil and export orders

| Constructor's Numbers | Aircraft markings |
|---|---|
| 476, 478, 496, 553 | *G-ABGG/K-7,'FM,'JG/K-10,'RK* |
| 569, 570, 620, 634 | *VR-HAU,'AW,'BZ,'CA* |
| 622, 643, 648, 862 | *G-ABYM, G-ACFZ,'FW, G-ADKZ* |
| 868 | *G-ADUJ* |
| 923–925, 982–984 | *G-AEGA–'GC, G-AVEI–'VK* |

Demonstration aircraft: *G-ABRK* Persia; *G-ACFW* Belgium; *G-ACFZ* Finland and Brazil.

## (*b*) **Avro 626 military production**

| Constructor's Numbers | For | Serials | Constructor's Numbers | For | Serials |
|---|---|---|---|---|---|
| 517–521 | China | | 828–847 | Chile | *1 to 20* |
| 536–549 | Argentina | | 869, 890 | Portugal | |
| 571–574 | China | | 927–929 | RCAF | *225 to 227* |
| 593–596 | Estonia | *141, 143, 144, 142* | 930–938 | Greece | *TT1 to TT9* |
| 668–677 | Egypt | *J300 to J309* | 952–966 | Brazil | *1 to 15* |
| 680 | Egypt | *J310* | 996–1007 | Portugal | |
| 687–690 | Ireland | *A.10 to A.13* | 1070–1078 | RCAF | *266 to 274* |
| 695, 793 | Egypt | *J311, J312* | 1089–1090 | Lithuania | |
| 703, 797 | Lithuania | | 1091–1098 | Portugal | |
| 761–770 | Egypt | *J320 to J329* | 1099–1110 | Greece | *TT10 to TT21* |
| 783–790 | Belgium | *A-1 to A-8* | 1123–1126 | Portugal | |
| 799, 942, 950 | Egypt | *J330, J331, J328\** | 1152 | Egypt | *J332\*\** |
| 822–825 | Belgium | *A-9 to A-12* | | | |

\*Replacement aircraft with duplicated serial.
\*\*Delivered 4.40 to Works Order 21050 with Avro 652 Mk.II *SU-AAO*.

## (*c*) **Avro Prefect**

*K5063–K5069* to Air Ministry Specification 32/34 under Contract No. 368655/34, delivered to the RAF January–July 1935; *NZ201–NZ204*, c/n 809–812, under Contract No.36122/34 for the Royal New Zealand Air Force July 1935. (Civil conversions: *K5069* to *G-AHRZ*, C of A issued 27.7.46, broken up at Gatwick 1948; *K5066* to *G-AHVO*, C of A issued 9.7.46, broken up at Hastings 1950; *NZ203* to *ZK-APC* for J. Frogley 1947, airworthy until 1958, presented to the RNZAF Museum 1980, rebuilt to flying condition at Ohakea as *NZ203*, first flight 8.7.85

Avro Prefect *K5066* which in later years flew in civil guise as *G-AHVO*. (*Flight photo 11629S*)

### (d) Avro 637

Eight aircraft, c/n 635–637, *VR-HCH*, *'CL* and *'CE*, Cs of A issued 24.5.33; c/n 662–664 unregistered, c/n 665 *VR-HCP*, c/n 681 unregistered, Cs of A issued 2.11.33, 6.11.33, 6.11.33, 15.1.34 and 15.12.33, supplied to the Kwangsi Air Force, Luichow, South China, by the Far East Aviation Co Ltd, Hong Kong; Chinese serials around and about *112*.

*G-ABJG/K-10* the Avro 637 development vehicle.

A standard Avro 637 with 'tunnel-type' windscreen for the Kwangsi Air Force, South China.

The Avro 627 Mailplane in standard form, 1931.

# Avro 627 Mailplane

The Avro 604 Antelope was followed through the Newton Heath works by a second airframe, c/n 5125, intended as a private venture two-seat fighter variant designated Avro 608 Hawk and powered by a Bristol Jupiter radial engine. Antelope mainplanes, interplane and centre-section struts, tail unit and undercarriage were retained, but instead of being metal clad, the welded steel tube basic fuselage structure was rounded out with removable fabric-covered panels to conform to the shape of the engine as on the Tutor series.

Armanent, largely similar to that of the Antelope, consisted of two synchronized forward-firing Vickers guns and a single Lewis on an Avro low-drag, rotatable mounting. To permit the gunner to stand over his weapon without undue drag penalty, the rear cockpit was set deep in the curved rear decking.

In accordance with normal practice for private venture military proto-types, application was made for civil registration and the marking *G-EBWM* was allotted on February 29, 1928. This lettering was never used because the Hawk remained incomplete until redesigned to take the 540 hp Armstrong Siddeley Panther II radial under designation Avro 622 in April 1930.

Following a visit by an Avro representative to Canadian Airways, who had started their Prairie Air Mail service between Winnipeg, Calgary and Edmonton in 1930, a possible requirement for a mail plane was foreseen. Designs were consequently amended still further and the Avro 622 was completed as the Avro 627 Mailplane. Roy Chadwick equipped the Mailplane for ski or float operation, installed night flying equipment, inertia starting and a large 40 cu ft fire-and-waterproof mail compartment in the front fuselage. Powered by a 525 hp Armstrong Siddeley Panther IIA in a

301

double Townend ring, the machine was capable of long stages up to 560 miles. Pilot comfort in extremely low temperatures was therefore of considerable importance and with this in mind the cockpit was positioned well aft, to give an exceptional view in all directions. It was also provided with exhaust heating, adjustable seat and rudder bar, as well as such emergency and navigation equipment as existed at that time.

The Avro 627 was painted yellow overall, certificated on August 2, 1931, and demonstrated at Heston on August 10 for the benefit of the Air Minister, Col Shelmerdine. It was then shipped to Canada for operational trials, during which the fitting of a Pratt & Whitney Hornet in place of the Panther was recommended, but unfortunately its arrival coincided with a Canadian Government decision to reduce drastically the annual allotment to civil aviation. Canadian Airways was thus unable to afford new equipment and the Avro 627 returned to England in time for exhibition and demonstration at the Hendon SBAC Show on June 27, 1932. Entered by Sir John Siddeley and flown by Avro chief test pilot H. A. Brown, the machine came 29th in the King's Cup Race at Brooklands on July 8–9, 1932, but set up the fastest speeds ever recorded in the race up to that time, averaging 175·5 mph to Woodford and back on the first day and 176·0 mph round shorter circuits on the second.

The machine's military potential was still evident but a further scheme for a Panther engined Avro 630 day bomber based on the Mailplane was eventually shelved, and the Mailplane itself returned to Woodford to re-emerge in June 1933 as the Avro 654 high-performance single-seat test-bed for the 700 hp Armstrong Siddeley Tiger IV engine. The rear centre-section struts were faired in and the undercarriage modified and equipped with long-travel oleo legs. A skid replaced the tail wheel. On 30 per cent more power, performance was spectacular and in November 1933 a flight observer's cockpit was fitted in place of the mail compartment, but the aeroplane's operational life was short and dismantling followed in 1934.

The Mailplane in November 1933 as the two-seat Avro 654 Armstrong Siddeley Tiger test-bed.

## SPECIFICATION AND DATA

*Manufacturers:*     A. V. Roe and Co Ltd, Newton Heath, Manchester

*Powerplants:*     (Avro 608)    One 425 hp Bristol Jupiter
                     (Avro 622)    One 540 hp Armstrong Siddeley Panther II
                     (Avro 627)    One 525 hp Armstrong Siddeley Panther IIA
                     (Avro 654)    One 700 hp Armstrong Siddeley Tiger IV

*Dimensions:*     Span (upper) 36 ft 0 in, (lower) 32 ft 0 in
                     Length 30 ft 10 in    Height 10 ft 10 in
                     Wing area 381 sq ft

*Weights:*     Tare weight 3,077 lb    All-up weight 5,150 lb

*Performance:*     Maximum speed 170 mph    Cruising speed 147 mph
                     Initial climb 1,200 ft/min    Ceiling 19,000 ft
                     Range 560 miles

*Note:* The above weight and performance figures refer to the standard Avro 627

*Production:*     One aircraft only, conversion of unfinished Avro 608 Hawk *G-EBWM*, c/n 5125. Completed as Avro 627 Mailplane *G-ABJM*, c/n 502, C of A issued 2.8.31, converted 11.33 to Avro 654, dismantled 5.34

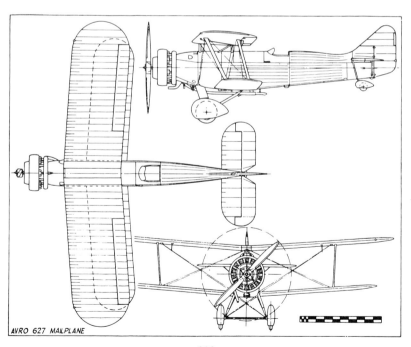

AVRO 627 MAILPLANE

The prototype Avro 631 Cadet showing the short nose. (*The Aeroplane*)

# Avro 631 and 643 Cadet

Produced in 1931 as a smaller version of the Tutor for club or private use, the Avro 631 Cadet bore a remarkable resemblance to the earlier machine, but differed slightly because wing and control surface structures were of wood. Registered *G-ABRS* in October 1931, the prototype made its first public appearance when Avro chief test pilot H. A. Brown gave an aerobatic display at the opening of Skegness Aerodrome on May 14, 1932, and Roy Dobson flew it into fourth place in a local race at 114 mph. The Irish Army Air Corps, first foreign purchaser of the Avro 621, ordered six Cadets straight from the drawing board and these had already been delivered when the prototype made its debut.

Modifications considered in March 1932 for an Avro 633 Cadet Fighter, suitable for air forces of the smaller nations, were never made, and the type remained only a project. The standard Cadet was also offered as a seaplane but none, in fact, became marine aircraft.

Although retaining the roomy cockpits and thoroughbred handling qualities of a generation of Avro trainers, the Cadet was fitted with the 135 hp Armstrong Siddeley Genet Major I seven-cylinder radial and was consequently more expensive to run than contemporary two-seat light aeroplanes. Also the staggered wings did not fold and the type found little favour as a private aircraft, the sole examples being the smart blue *G-ABVV* in which Maj J. E. D. Shaw commuted between Kirbymoorside and Heston; *'YC* kept initially at Hamsey Green aerodrome, Surrey, by Gardners, the prewar air racing family; and *'ZF* flown by F. G Miles at Woodley.

By far the largest user was Air Service Training, Hamble, which quickly found it the almost perfect small aeroplane for ab initio flying instruction, aerobatics or blind flying, and in the years 1932–34 the number of black and silver Cadets at Hamble reached a total of 17. All but six were still active at the outbreak of war in 1939 and remained on the strength of No.3 ERFTS, Hamble, in camouflage with civil markings until moved to Watchfield in 1940 and eventual impressment as ATC instructional airframes in 1941–42. AST's associate, the Far East Aviation Co, acquired the prototype Cadet *G-ABRS* in October 1934 for service with the Avian IVMs of the Far East Aviation School at Hong Kong. Later three others joined it and a fourth was demonstrated in China. The Irish Army Air Corps acquired a seventh, serial *C.7*, with inverted fuel system which survived until 1950 when it was sold to a private owner and registered *EI-AFO*. The Portuguese Government acquired one Cadet for evaluation in 1934 leaving as the only other purchaser the Lancashire Aero Club, whose second Cadet *G-ACMG*, lost in a crash, was replaced by *G-ABYC* bought from Gardner.

The Avro 643 Cadet, introduced early 1934, was an improved model with slightly more rotund fuselage and raised rear seat. Only eight were built including *G-ACZA* demonstrated far and wide by Henlys' test pilot A. ('G.B.') Golding-Barrett; one ferried to the Spanish concern Constructiones Aeronauticas SA as *EC-W26*; *G-ADEG* and *'FD* for flying clubs at York and Bristol; *G-ADEX* for the Hon R. F. Watson and *'IE* for Sir William Firth. The Avro 643 was merely the forerunner of the final and most widely used variant, the Avro 643 Mk.II Cadet\* with the more powerful 150 hp Genet Major IA. To accept this engine the front fuselage was lengthened by six inches and at the same time wing spars were

*This designation has been misquoted frequently as Avro 643 Cadet Mk.II.

The Hon R. H. Casey DSO, MC, flying an Avro 643 Mk.II Cadet of the RAAF in 1938.

Avro 643 Mk.II Cadet *VH-BJB*, formerly *A6-34* of the RAAF, with Wackett Trainer canopy. (*N. Wiltshire*)

strengthened; bracing wires were taken to the front wing root fitting for ease of parachute escape from the front cockpit; and full blind flying equipment was fitted as standard.

*G-ADJT*, the prototype Avro 643 Mk.II, was demonstrated at Croydon in September 1935 before sale in France. It was followed by *PP-TAF* for a Brazilian private owner and two for the Perak Flying Club. Major production, however, was for Air Service Training and the Royal Australian Air Force. Those of the former served at No.3 ERFTS, Hamble, and No.9 ERFTS, Ansty, near Coventry, but in the early days of the war were moved to Watchfield and impressed, meeting the same fate as their sister machines, the Avro 631s. Proposals for an even later variant, the Genet Major engined Avro 663 Cadet Trainer, were dropped in the face of changing requirements arising from the Expansion Scheme.

In the British Isles two Avro 643s *G-ACIH* and *G-ADIE* alone flew again after the war. Both were resident at Weston Aerodrome, Leixlip, Eire, from which the latter made a 200 mile trip to Waterford and back after restoration by Mr M. Marron to attend the Tara Air Rally of June 4–5, 1960. They later became *EI-ALU* and *'LP* respectively and though no longer airworthy remained extant in 1990.

Thirty-four Avro 643 Mk.II Cadets, built at Manchester for the Australian Air Board, were delivered in three batches in November 1935, December 1937 and February 1939. Unlike the AST machines they were equipped with tail wheels and inverted fuel systems for use by the RAAF at No.1 FTS, Point Cook, and by No.21 (City of Melbourne) and No.22 (City of Sydney) Citizen Air Force Squadrons. Survivors were sold in 1946 when 16 flew in civil marks, seven initially with the Newcastle Aero Club, NSW. Four were still extant in 1963, *VH-BJB* with the sliding hood from a Wackett Trainer, *VH-AFX* and *'FY* which were re-engined in that year with 220 hp Jacobs R-755 radials for crop spraying operations in Queensland and another crop-sprayer *VH-PRT*. The last and *VH-AFX* were still airworthy in 1986.

*Manufacturers:*    A. V. Roe and Co Ltd, Newton Heath, Manchester

*Powerplants:*      (Avro 631)    One 135 hp Armstrong Siddeley Genet Major I
                    (Avro 643)    One 135 hp Armstrong Siddeley Genet Major I
                    (Avro 643 Mk.II)
                                  One 150 hp Armstrong Siddeley Genet
                                  Major IA
                                  One 220 hp Jacobs R-755

*Dimensions, Weights and Performances:*

|  | Avro 631 | Avro 643 | Avro 643 Mk. II |
|---|---|---|---|
| Span | 30 ft 0 in | 30 ft 2 in | 30 ft 2 in |
| Length | 24 ft 9 in | 24 ft 9 in | 24 ft 9 in |
| Height | 8 ft 9 in | 8 ft 9 in | 8 ft 10 in |
| Wing area | 261¼ sq ft | 262 sq ft | 262 sq ft |
| Tare weight | 1,180 lb | — | 1,286 lb |
| All-up weight | 1,900 lb | 2,000 lb | 2,000 lb |
| Maximum speed | 118 mph | — | 116 mph |
| Cruising speed | 100 mph | — | 100 mph |
| Initial climb | 600 ft/min | — | 700 ft/min |
| Ceiling | 13,000 ft | — | 12,000 ft |
| Range | 350 miles | — | 325 miles |

*Production:*
### (a) **Avro 631 Cadet**

| Constructor's No. and Registration | | C of A Issued | Details |
|---|---|---|---|
| 558 | *G-ABRS* | 15. 3.32 | Sold to Far East Aviation School 10.34 as *VR-HCS* |
| 581–86 | *C.1-C.6* | nil | Irish Air Corps |
| 589 | *G-ABVV* | 28. 5.32 | Fatal crash at Welburn, Yorks, 30.5.39 |
| 592 | *G-ABVU* | 8. 6.32 | Lancashire Aero Club, scrapped at Barton 5.51 |
| 597 | *G-ABWJ* | 18. 6.32 | Demonstrator, sold in Brazil 1.37 as *PP-TJC* |
| 621 | *G-ABYC* | 27. 7.32 | Yardley and Co Ltd; to Lancashire Aero Club 1935; scrapped Barton 5.51 |
| 623 | *G-ABZF* | 4.10.32 | Merseyside Aero and Sports Ltd, Hooton: to F. G. Miles, Woodley, crashed at Liverpool 10.6.36 |
| 678 | — | 27.12.33 | For China via Far East Aviation Co Ltd |
| 682 | *G-ACMG* | 3. 1.34 | Lancashire Aero Club; damaged beyond repair at Adlington, Cheshire 2.12.34 |
| 683 | *VR-HCL* | 6. 1.34 | ⎫ To Far East Aviation Co Ltd for operation by Far East Flying |
| 684 | *VR-HCM* | 8. 1.34 | ⎬ School, Hong Kong |
| 685 | *VR-HCN* | 8. 1.34 | ⎭ |
| 727 | — | nil | To the Portuguese Government 6.34 |
| 730 | *C.7* | nil | Irish Air Corps; to R. A. Clark 8.50 as *EI-AFO* |

Air Service Training fleet: c/n 606–607, *G-ABWS, 'XU*; 628–633 *G-ACCH–'CN*; 692–693, *G-ACNE–'NF*; 701–702, *G-ACRY, 'RZ*; 724, 806, 805, 813, *G-ACUH, G-ADAU, 'AV, 'CX*.

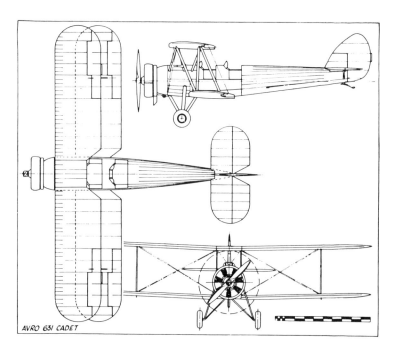

AVRO 631 CADET

## (b) Avro 643 Cadet

| Constructor's No. and Registration | | C of A Issued | Details |
|---|---|---|---|
| 657 | G-ACIH | 9. 3.34 | To Iona National Airways 4.61 as EI-ALU |
| 758 | G-ACXJ | 12. 9.34 | Demonstrator, scrapped during war |
| 778 | EC-W26 | 29.11.34 | Constructiones Aeronauticas SA Spain |
| 794 | G-ACZA | 23. 1.35 | To the Perak Flying Club 1.38 |
| 817 | G-ADEG | 8. 4.35 | York Aviation and Country Club; scrapped at Tollerton 1950 |
| 819 | G-ADFD | 24. 5.35 | Bristol Aeroplane Club; to Ferndown School ATC, Wimborne, Dorset, 1951; scrapped 1961 |
| 820 | G-ADEX | 29. 5.35 | Hon R. F. Watson; to L. C. Lewis 1.37; sold abroad 9.37 |
| 848 | G-ADIE | 5. 6.35 | Sir W. Firth; North of Ireland Aero Club 9.38; re-registered 9.60 as EI-ALP |

## (c) Avro 643 Mk. II Cadet

| Constructor's No. and Registration | | C of A Issued | Details |
|---|---|---|---|
| 849 | G-ADJT | 14. 9.35 | Sold in France 3.38 as F-AQMX |
| 867 | PP-TAF* | nil | To José Daniel de Camargo, Brazil 11.35 |
| 920 | VR-RAK | 16. 3.36 | Perak Flying Club Ltd |
| 921 | VR-RAL | 11. 3.36 | Perak Flying Club Ltd |

*Duplicating registration of Avro 671 Cierva C.30A c/n 738.

Air Service Training fleet: c/n 870–889, G-ADTF–'TZ; 922, 926, 949, G-AEAR, 'IR, 'NL.

Avro 643 Mk.II Cadet *VH-AFY* at Archerfield, Brisbane, in January 1964, equipped for crop spraying as a single-seater with trailing-edge nozzles and 220 hp Jacobs R-755 engine. (*J. Hopton*)

## (*d*) **Avro 643 Mk. II Cadet (RAAF)**

| Constructor's Number | Aircraft markings |
|---|---|
| 850–861 | *A6-1* to *A6-12* (Cs of A issued 29.10.35 to 2.1.36) Civil conversions; 851 *VH-APV*; 854 *VH-AEG*; 857 *VH-AEJ*; 859–861 *VH-AMM*, *'FW*, *'FX* |
| 986–995 | *A6-13* to *A6-22* (Cs of A issued 15.12.37 to 3.2.38) Civil conversions: 990 *VH-AGH*; 991 *VH-AEH/VH-PRV*; 994 *VH-AFZ* |
| 1058–1069 | *A6-23* to *A6-34* (Cs of A issued 18.11.38 to 28.2.39) Civil conversions: 1058 *VH-AHH*; 1060 *VH-AEI/VH-PRU*; 1062 *VH-AHW*; 1063 *VH-APW*; 1066–1069 *VH-AFY*, *'GC/VH-PRT*, *'EL*, *VH-BJB**|

*Fitted with Wackett Trainer sliding canopy.

Avro 643 Cadet *EI-ALP*, last flown in June 1977, was undergoing restoration in 1990.

*A.14*, first Avro 636 for the Irish Army Air Corps.

# Avro 636

The unnamed Avro 636 two-seat fighter trainer, designed by Roy Chadwick in November 1934 and built in 1935, was not only the ultimate development of the Avro 621 theme, but also the only Avro aeroplane to show visible evidence of the firm's absorption into the Hawker Siddeley Group. Its fuselage structure was of welded steel-tube and all fuel and oil lines, control rods and cables, were accessible by removing curved, fabric-covered outer panels in true Tutor tradition. The fabric-covered metal mainplanes and tailplane, however, were constructed by the Armstrong Whitworth riveted system, and the aircraft was almost identical in size, weight and external appearance to the Armstrong Whitworth A.W. 35 Scimitar single-seat fighter.

The Avro 636 was a heavily staggered, single-bay biplane with wings and tail unit built up from spars and ribs of high tensile steel strip and equipped with Frise-type ailerons on top and bottom wings. Powered by a 420 hp Armstrong Siddeley Jaguar IV, the machine was designed to reproduce the flying characteristics of contemporary single-seat fighters and thus be suitable for fighter pilot tactical training, or for dual or solo advanced aerobatics. With the rear seat faired over, it could be used purely as a fighter, for which purpose it was equipped with two forward-firing Vickers guns projecting from the hump which raised the cockpits above the level of the engine cowling. In this role it was, like the Scimitar, powered by an Armstrong Siddeley Panther radial in an Armstrong Whitworth two-piece, long-chord cowling and designated Avro 636A.

It was one of the cleanest biplanes ever built. Fuel was carried on the front fuselage to leave the upper wing free of all projections, while the undercarriage—revolutionary for those days—was equipped with low-pressure airwheels (with neatly faired Dunlop brake drums), mounted on cantilever oleo legs attached to the bottom longeron and taken upwards inside the fuselage to meet at the mid point of a cross-strut between the top longerons. This also formed an anchorage for the engine mounting.

Construction of the first Avro 636, laid down as a civil demonstrator and registered *G-ADHP* in May 1935, was abandoned, but as in the case of the Avro 631 Cadet, the first (and in this instance, the only) customer was the Irish Army Air Corps, purchaser of four machines in December 1934. These were powered by four old 460 hp Armstrong Siddeley Jaguar VIC unsupercharged engines originally procured in 1930 for installation in four Vickers Vespa IV Army Co-operation biplanes supplied to the Free State in March of that year. Despite the reservation of type number Avro 667 for the Jaguar VIC machine, it was always referred to as the Avro 636 but performance was rather less dramatic than it would have been with the Panther's extra 180 hp. Nevertheless it was a remarkable aeroplane, having a top speed of 175 mph and controls which were light, positive and well harmonised throughout a wide speed range. The four Irish machines were delivered to Baldonnel in August 1935 and remained in service there for several years, at least two (including *15*) taking part in air firing exercises at Gormanston, Co. Meath in 1938.

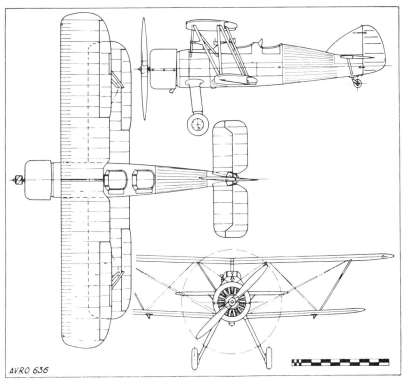

AVRO 636

## SPECIFICATION AND DATA

*Manufacturers:*   A. V. Roe and Co Ltd, Newton Heath, Manchester

*Powerplants:*   (Avro 636)   One 420 hp Armstrong Siddeley Jaguar IV
                 (Avro 636A) One 680 hp Armstrong Siddeley Panther XI
                 (Avro 667)   One 460 hp Armstrong Siddeley Jaguar VIC

*Dimensions:*   Span (upper) 33 ft 0 in  (lower) 27 ft 3 in
               Length 27 ft 6 in  Height 11 ft 7 in
               Wing area 261 sq ft

*Weights:*   (Avro 636A)   Tare weight 2,970 lb   All-up weight
                                             3,924 lb
               (Avro 667)    Tare weight 2,766 lb   All-up weight
                                           3,721 lb

*Performance:*   (Avro 636A)   Maximum speed 230 mph
                                 Cruising speed 195 mph
                                 Initial climb 2,000 ft/min
                                 Ceiling 32,000 ft   Range 290 miles
               (Avro 667)    Maximum speed 175 mph
                                 Initial climb 1,200 ft/min
                                 Ceiling 18,000 ft

*Production:*   (*a*) Avro 636—one civil demonstrator *G-ADHP*, c/n 821,
                 registered to A. V. Roe and Co Ltd 27.5.35, construction
                 abandoned, s.o.r. 12.36
             (*b*) Avro 667—four fighter trainers for the Irish Army Air
                 Corps July 1935, *A.14* to *A.17*, c/n 863–866 (prefix *A*
                 dropped by 1938)

Formation of the Irish Army Air Corps Avro 636s.

312

Avro 638 Club Cadet *G-ACHO* of the Airwork School of Flying, over Heston in 1933.
(*The Aeroplane*)

# Avro 638 Club Cadet and Variants

A version of the Cadet for clubs and private owners, introduced in 1933, was known as the Avro 638 Club Cadet. Its structure was identical with that of the Avro 631 but the stagger was greatly reduced so that the wings could fold for economy in hangar space. The prototype, *G-ACAY*, first flew at Woodford in May 1933 but only 15 others were built, all for the home market, and the first production machine *G-ACGY* went to the Lancashire Aero Club which was already operating two Avro 631s. Three others, *G-ACHN–'HP*, delivered from Woodford to Airwork Ltd at Heston in formation on June 21, 1933, were joined a month later by *G-ACTX* and '*TZ*. The five white and green Club Cadets served the Airwork School and its successor, the Airwork Flying Club Ltd, for many years during which they were fitted with 130 hp de Havilland Gipsy Major inline engines. Being of smaller frontal area than the seven-cylinder Armstrong Siddeley Genet Major Is fitted originally, the Gipsy reduced fuel consumption.

A few Club Cadets were used privately, notably *G-ACHW* by S. P. Tyzack; '*NY* by Lord Londonderry; and *G-ADBC* at Manorbier by the Earl of Essex. The majority of these soon gravitated to the clubs, however, the largest fleet being that of the Southend Flying Club which, at the outbreak of war in 1939, owned *G-ACAY*, '*HW*, '*JZ*, '*TB* and '*TX*. Together with some private aircraft they were removed in 1940 to the local Middleton Garage where tail units and other projecting parts taking too much space were simply sawn off. In 1935 the Southend club also acquired the Club Cadet Special *G-ACIL*, built originally to the order of prominent Renfrew pilots, Douglas and the Hon Mrs Margaret Fairweather, whose names later became legendary in Air Transport Auxiliary. *G-ACIL*, fitted with a 140 hp Cirrus Hermes IVA and most powerful Club Cadet, first

313

Airwork's Club Cadet *G-ACHN* after conversion to D.H. Gipsy Major engine, 1936.
(*The Aeroplane*)

*G-ACGA*, the only Avro 639 Cabin Cadet completed. (*Flight photo 10218S*)

flew at Woodford with Class B marking *K-11*. It was destroyed in a serious accident soon after it went to Southend.

An enclosed version designated Avro 639 Cabin Cadet was built on the same lines as the open model but the fuselage filled the whole mainplane gap and the 28 gallon fuel tank, normally carried in the centre section, was repositioned under the floor. It was flown at Woodford and Hamble under B conditions as *K-14* and later as *G-ACGA* during 1933–34 but did not go into production.

A final variant, the Avro 640 Cadet three-seater, was also fitted with folding wings, but whereas the Avro 639 seated three with pilot in front, the 640 had the front fuselage widened to seat two passengers side-by-side in an open cockpit in front of the pilot for joyriding work. The first four Avro 640s were powered by 140 hp Cirrus Hermes IVs and slightly

314

antedated the Club Cadet. They were delivered to the Scottish Motor Traction Co Ltd at Renfrew in April–May 1933 for pleasure flying in the Highlands and Islands.

Only nine Avro 640s were constructed and the remaining five, powered by 135 hp seven-cylinder Genet Major Is, were not easily distinguishable from Club Cadets. *G-ACFX*, first with Genet Major I, was delivered to Midland and Scottish Air Ferries Ltd in June 1933 but was later sold abroad. The remaining four comprised *G-ACJX*, Heston-based demonstrator of Cadet distributors Henlys (1928) Ltd; and *G-ACLU*, *'PB* and *'OZ* for Sir Alan Cobham's National Aviation Day Displays. One red, one white and one blue, they were used for formation passenger flights and for dropping parachutists. When the Scottish Motor Traction Co Ltd ceased flying operations in 1935, *G-ACFU* was sold to Tom Campbell Black and went on tour with C. W. A. Scott's Flying Display, while the other three joined the ex-Cobham *'PB* with Utility Airways Ltd. They gave seasonal pleasure flights in the Liverpool, Manchester, Southport and Blackpool area until 1939, when they were stored with several other machines under the grandstand at Hooton Park Racecourse, and were lost when it was destroyed by fire on July 8, 1940.

No Avro 640s survived the war and the only Club Cadet to do so in airworthy condition was the former Airwork *G-ACHP*. Its four stablemates *'HO*, *'NY*, *'TZ* and *'ZS* were shipped abroad in 1941 and remain untraced, but *'HP* was used by Saunders-Roe Ltd throughout the war for

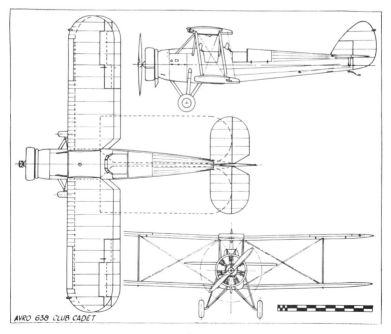

AVRO 638 CLUB CADET

*G-ACFH*, the first Avro 640 Cadet three-seater, flying in Scottish Motor Traction Co colours. (*Flight*)

communicating between their Cowes and Eastleigh factories. For this purpose it was impressed by the RAF and camouflaged as *HM570*. After overhaul by Saunders-Roe in June 1946 it flew for ten more years, mainly as mount of the Vintage Aeroplane Club, until wrecked at Denham on January 1, 1956.

## SPECIFICATION AND DATA

*Manufacturers:*    A. V. Roe and Co Ltd, Middleton, Manchester

*Powerplants:*    (Avro 638)  One 130 hp de Havilland Gipsy Major I
                                      One 135 hp Armstrong Siddeley Genet Major I
                                      One 140 hp Cirrus Hermes IVA
                  (Avro 639)  One 135 hp Armstrong Siddeley Genet Major I
                  (Avro 640)  One 135 hp Armstrong Siddeley Genet Major I
                                      One 140 hp Cirrus Hermes IV

*Dimensions, Weights and Performances:*

|  | Avro 638 | Avro 639 | Avro 640 |
|---|---|---|---|
| Span | 30 ft 2 in | 30 ft 2 in | 30 ft 0 in |
| Length | 24 ft 9 in | 24 ft 9 in | 24 ft 9 in |
| Height | 8 ft 9 in | 8 ft 9 in | 8 ft 9 in |
| Wing area | 262 sq ft | 262 sq ft | 261¼ sq ft |
| Tare weight | 1,244 lb | — | 1,140 lb |
| All-up weight | 2,000 lb | — | 1,855 lb |
| Maximum speed | 115 mph | — | 110 mph |
| Cruising speed | 100 mph | — | 95mph |
| Initial climb | — | — | 700 ft/min |
| Ceiling | — | — | 13,500 ft |
| Range | 325 miles | — | 325 miles |

*Production:*
## (a) **Avro 638 Club Cadet**

| Constructor's No. and Registration | | C of A Issued | Details |
|---|---|---|---|
| 626 | G-ACAY | 2. 6.33 | Southend Flying Club, broken up 1940 |
| 650 | G-ACGY | 6. 6.33 | Lancashire Aero Club, sold abroad 2.39 |
| 651 | G-ACHN★ | 22. 6.33 | Airwork Ltd, crashed during the war |
| 652 | G-ACHO★ | 26. 6.33 | Airwork Ltd, shipped abroad 6.41 |
| 653 | G-ACHP★ | 26. 6.33 | Airwork Ltd, impressed 7.42 as *HM570* for Saro; to Vintage Aeroplane Club 1952; crashed at Denham 1.1.56 |
| 654 | G-ACHW | 3. 8.33 | Southend Flying Club, broken up 1940 |
| 655 | G-ACHY | nil | Construction abandoned |
| 661 | G-ACIL★★ | 18. 7.33 | Initially *K-11*; Southend Flying Club, crashed at Thundersley, Essex, 22.12.35 |
| 667 | G-ACJZ | 16. 9.33 | Southend Flying Club, broken up 1940 |
| 686 | G-ACNY | 24. 3.34 | Airwork Ltd, shipped abroad 6.41 |
| 704 | G-ACTB | 1. 6.34 | Southend Flying Club, broken up 1940 |
| 718 | G-ACTX | 27. 6.34 | |
| 719 | G-ACTY | nil | Construction abandoned |
| 720 | G-ACTZ★ | 14. 7.34 | Airwork Ltd, shipped abroad 2.41 |
| 797 | G-ACZS | 8. 2.35 | Airwork Ltd, shipped abroad 6.41 |
| 807 | G-ADBC | 7. 2.35 | Sold in France 4.37 as *F-AQCJ* |
| 816 | G-ADEH | 10. 4.35 | York Aviation and Country Club Ltd, scrapped at Tollerton 1950 |

★Re-engined with Gipsy Major I circa 12.36.       ★★Cirrus Hermes IVA.

## (b) **Avro 639 Cabin Cadet**

| 639 | G-ACGA | nil | Also flown as *K-14*, scrapped 1936 |
|---|---|---|---|

## (c) **Avro 640 Cadet three-seater**

| 640 | G-ACFH★ | 28. 4.33 | Scottish Motor Traction Co Ltd; to Utility Airways Ltd 7.35, burned at Hooton 8.7.40 |
|---|---|---|---|
| 644 | G-ACFS★ | 18. 5.33 | |
| 645 | GACFT★ | 18. 5.33 | |
| 646 | G-ACFU★ | 18. 5.33 | Initially SMT Co Ltd; to T. Campbell Black 7.35, crashed at Leigh, Lancs, 2.8.37 |
| 647 | G-ACFX | 23. 6.33 | Midland and Scottish Air Ferries Ltd; to the Perak Flying Club 11.36 as *VR-RAJ* |
| 666 | G-ACJX | 14.10.33 | Henlys' demonstrator, dismantled 11.34 |
| 679 | G-ACLU | 11. 4.34 | National Aviation Day; sold abroad 4.39 |
| 696 | G-ACPB | 11. 4.34 | National Aviation Day; to Utility Airways Ltd 7.35, burned at Hooton 8.7.40 |
| 697 | G-ACOZ | 11. 4.34 | National Aviation Day; scrapped 1941 |

★140 hp Cirrus Hermes IV.

The Maharajah of Vizianagram's Avro 641 Commodore *VT-AFN*.

# Avro 641 Commodore

Experience gained in building and flying the little three-seat Avro 639 Cabin Cadet led in 1934 to the construction of a larger version accommodating up to five people. Two pilots sat in front with a central control column having swing-over spectacle-type aileron control so that the machine could be flown from either seat, and two passengers (or three with less luggage) sat in the rear. Known as the Avro 641 Commodore, it was a direct descendant of the well-tried Tutor and was of the same form of metal construction. The usual system of heavily staggered mainplanes was employed together with rigid N-type interplane struts, but Frise-type ailerons were used, and then only on the lower wing.

Powered by an electrically started 215 hp Armstrong Siddeley Lynx IVC driving a Fairey Reed metal airscrew, the Commodore was equally suitable for taxi work or as a luxury class private aeroplane. Fuel for a useful range of 500 miles was carried in two 25 gallon tanks in the upper wing roots so that smoking could be permitted in the cabin. America had already established a lead with this class of tourer and a number of US cabin types had already been seen in the UK, notably *G-ACGJ*, Lady Hay Drummond Hay's Waco UIC which arrived in June 1933. Due to its Tutorial origins the Commodore bore a striking, but entirely coincidental, resemblance to the Waco although the American machine probably inspired the Avro's newer features—the stout tubular metal strut in place of landing wires; faired, spatted undercarriage; and long-chord engine cowling.

Businesslike in appearance and with a robust performance, the Commodore was years before its time and so far ahead of the demand that only six were sold. These were built in the Avro works at Failsworth, Manchester, and the silver prototype, *G-ACNT*, was delivered to private owner

318

W. Westhead at Woodford on May 24, 1934. Later in the day he flew it south to Heston, social focus of private flying in those days, and destined to be the home base of all five British-registered Commodores. Capt the Earl of Amherst's red and grey *'RX*, which joined the prototype a few weeks later, was used later for taxi work by the British Air Navigation Co Ltd (BANCO). Then followed the white and green *G-ACUA* for Airwork Ltd, blue and silver *'UG* for Maj J. E. Durrant Shaw; and finally *'ZB* for Henlys (1928) Ltd who were to handle Commodore sales.

Only one more Commodore was, in fact, completed; this was *VT-AFN* sold in India to the Maharajah of Vizianagram in October 1934. The remaining half-finished airframes were broken up in the works, a fate which also overtook *'FN* which had proved unsuitable for operation in India and returned to England in 1935. After a year in private hands the prototype was repurchased by the manufacturers and redoped in red and grey for use as a 'hack'. It was dismantled at Woodford in October 1939 and there seems little doubt that, after storage during the Second World War, it was broken up along with the company's Avro 626 *G-ACFW* in 1950.

In June 1934 a scheme was considered under type number Avro 665 whereby a Commodore fuselage with Lynx IVC engine was to be equipped

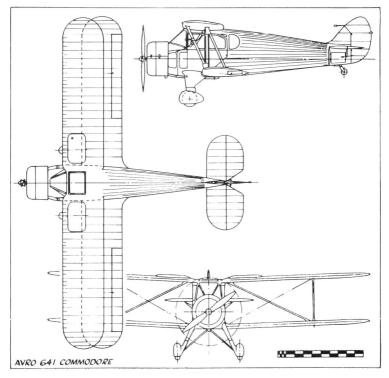

AVRO 641 COMMODORE

with a three-bladed rotor and flown as the four-seat Cierva C.33 Autogiro, but the aircraft was not completed.

In 1935 Airwork sold its Commodore *G-ACUA* to an Egyptian private owner at Almaza, Cairo, where it was joined a few months later by BANCO's *'RX*, which had been sold to V. H. Tait, an RAF officer serving in Egypt. This, too, passed into Egyptian hands in 1936 but soon afterwards both Commodores were taken over by the Egyptian Army Air Force which had ample stocks of interchangeable Avro 626 spares and was well able to maintain them for communications work.

In England, Maj Shaw's private *'UG* was based at Kirbymoorside, Yorks, in connection with his interest in Slingsby Sailplanes Ltd, which from March 1936 *'ZB* operated from Whitley Aerodrome, Coventry, as a liaison 'hack' between the Armstrong Whitworth factory and RAF squadrons working up on the new A. W. Whitley bombers. At the outbreak of war both Commodores were impressed and camouflaged, *'ZB* being posted for service with No.51 OTU, Cranfield, until struck off charge in 1942. *G-ACUG* on the other hand was issued to Air Transport Auxiliary for training duties at White Waltham where it stalled in a crosswind on the approach with fatal results for the pilot in the summer of 1941.

## SPECIFICATION AND DATA

*Manufacturers:*    A. V. Roe and Co Ltd, Failsworth, Manchester; and Woodford Aerodrome, Cheshire

*Powerplants:*    One 215 hp Armstrong Siddeley Lynx IVC

*Dimensions:*    Span 37 ft 4 in    Length 27 ft 3 in
Height 10 ft 0 in    Wing area 307 sq ft

*Weights:*    Tare weight 2,237 lb    All-up weight 3,500 lb

*Performance:*    Maximum speed 130 mph    Cruising speed 110 mph
Initial climb 700 ft/min    Ceiling 11,500 ft
Range 500 miles

*Production:*

| Constructor's No. and Registration | | C of A Issued | Details |
|---|---|---|---|
| 691 | G-ACNT | 18. 5.34 | Prototype, dismantled at Woodford 13.10.39, believed broken up at Woodford 1950 |
| 700 | G-ACRX | 3. 7.34 | To Egypt 1936 as SU-AAS, later to the Egyptian Army Air Force |
| 721 | G-ACUA | 11. 8.34 | To Egypt 1936 as SU-AAU, later to the Egyptian Army Air Force |
| 722 | G-ACUG | 28. 9.34 | Impressed 15.2.41 as DJ710; to HQ Training Ferry Pilots' Pool, crashed at White Waltham 10.8.41 |
| 729 | G-ACZB | 24. 4.35 | Impressed 27.8.41 as HH979; initially to RAF, Cranfield; 3.42 to No.6 MU Brize Norton; 6.42 to No.51 OTU, Cranfield; s.o.c. 17.8.42 |
| 759 | VT-AFN | 16.10.34 | Maharajah of Vizianagram, broken up at Woodford 1935 |

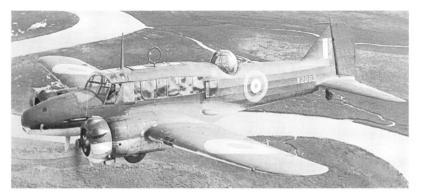

Avro 652A Anson I *W2083* flying in wartime colours in Australia. (*Department of Air*)

# Avro 652A Anson Mks. I–X

In the early thirties American high-performance aeroplanes set a fashion which quickly spread to Europe, where the new twin-engined, low-wing formula with retractable undercarriage was rapidly adopted by several manufacturers. The significance of these developments was not lost on G. E. Woods Humphery, managing director of Imperial Airways, and on May 18, 1933, he submitted a specification to Sir John Siddeley of the Avro company for a small, but fast, long-range charter aircraft of this type. Enthusiasm at Manchester was such that by August 1933 a design study had been prepared and approved for a four-passenger aircraft powered by two Armstrong Siddeley Cheetah radials, cruising at 150 mph over a still air range of 600 miles.

So was born the Avro 652, Roy Chadwick's brilliant adaptation of the Avro-Fokker airframe in which the well tried, one-piece wooden mainplane was merely moved from the high to the low wing position. Its welded steel-tube fuselage was rounded out by fabric over wooden formers, and the undercarriage (retracted by 140 turns of a chain driven, low-pitch screw gear) moved forwards and upwards into streamlined engine nacelles. The 270 hp Cheetah V engines were housed in smooth, long-chord cowlings and drove Fairey Reed metal airscrews. Each of the four passengers had an individual circular window and two crew sat side by side with dual control behind a gently sloping, five-panel windscreen.

While the Avro 652 was in the design stage, the Air Ministry invited the Avro company to tender for a twin-engined coastal patrol landplane for the large expansion programme made necessary by events in Europe. Their specification resembled that of the Imperial Airways machine so closely that it was a comparatively simple matter to prepare designs for an Avro 652A military version. These were submitted to the Air Ministry on May 19, 1934.

321

Ava, second of Imperial Airways' Avro 652 charter aircraft in original form with horn balanced rudder.
(*The Aeroplane*)

Imperial Airways' Avro 652, *Avalon* with mass-balanced rudder fitted. (*BOAC*)

Powered by 295 hp Cheetah VIs in helmeted cowlings, the Avro 652A had an estimated cruising range of 600 miles at 160 mph and was offered with a gunner's position (with single Lewis) in the roof above the main spar; or a hand-operated turret (of the type used on the A. W. Whitley) aft of the wings. A bomb load of 360 lb could be carried in the centre section and the pilot had a single Vickers gun on the port side, but the Avro 652A was otherwise similar to the civil version except that the windows were now square and the entry door was in the starboard side. Competition within the aircraft industry was fierce, but prototype orders were placed only with A. V. Roe and Co and the de Havilland Aircraft Co for one Avro 652A (with turret) and one D.H.89M to be delivered in March 1935.

When the first Avro 652 for Imperial Airways was flown for the first time at Woodford on January 7, 1935, by F. B. Tomkins, few adjustments were found necessary and its handling qualities were in the true Avro tradition, surpassing even those of the firm's classic biplanes. Both Avro 652s, *G-ACRM Avalon* and *'RN Avatar* (almost immediately changed to *Ava*) were delivered at Croydon on March 11, 1935, and the military Avro 652A prototype *K4771* first flew on March 24 piloted by S. A. 'Bill' Thorn. Service trials conducted by the Coast Defence Development Unit at Gosport in competition with the D.H.89M *K4772* between May 11 and 17 favoured the Avro 652A, and earned it a place in the New Types Park at the Hendon RAF Display on June 29, 1935. Further Martlesham trials, however, showed that a 25 per cent increase in tailplane span and a reduction in elevator area was desirable.

An alternative design—the Avro 664—was then dropped, and following a decision made on May 25 to adopt the Avro 652A as standard equipment, Air Ministry Specification 18/35 was written round it and a contract placed for 174 aircraft. The production prototype *K6152*, first flown at Woodford by Geoffrey Tyson on December 31, 1935, was thereupon given the Service name Anson Mk.I. Typical of the thousands of Ansons which were to fly millions of miles during the Second World War, *K6152* had a higher continuous line of cabin windows giving uninterrupted all-round view, a further increase in tailplane span and 350 hp Cheetah IX engines in seven-lobed NACA cowlings. Armament remained the same as on *K4771*. The rudder, horn-balanced on *K4771* and the two civil machines, was now mass-balanced and this modification was incorporated in all three earlier machines in September 1935. After the first few aircraft, wing trailing-edges were made detachable at the rear spar to simplify transportation.

In Imperial Airways service the Avro 652 cruised at the unprecedented speed of 165 mph and flew the long Croydon-Brindisi route with monotonous regularity for several years until sold to Air Service Training as navigation trainers. Their work continued at Hamble with No.11 Air Observer's Navigation School until impressed in February 1941 for RAF service with No.1 School of Photography, Farnborough. Five months later they were handed over to the Royal Navy and ended their days with No.811 Squadron, Lee-on-Solent.

To fulfill an RAAF order for twelve Ansons, *K6212–K6223* were deleted from the RAF contract, reserialled *A4-1* to *A4-12* and delivered in Melbourne by ss *Orani* on November 19, 1936. The first was test flown by Wing Cdr A. W. Murphy at Laverton on December 2 as a prelude to their issue to Nos.2, 3 and 5 (General Reconnaissance) Squadrons at Laverton, Victoria and Richmond, NSW. The Australian order was later increased to 48, the last ten of which were the first Ansons fitted with Sperry blind flying panels. In Britain the first Ansons (*K6153–K6162*) were delivered to No.48 Squadron, Manston, in February 1936 and commissioned on March 6, a date historically important as that on which the RAF puts its first monoplane and first retractable undercarriage into squadron service.

*K4771*, the Avro 652A prototype. (*Crown Copyright Reserved*)

The Avro 652 Mk. II *SU-AAO* built for the Egyptian Government.

Armament included two 100 lb and four 20 lb bombs, or flares and smoke floats.

Later in 1936 two further contracts were placed for a total of 135 aircraft during the construction of which metal-framed ailerons and steeper windscreens with opening direct-vision panels were introduced and (beginning with *K8720*) hydraulically-operated Schrenk flaps were fitted to steepen the glide. Diversions from this batch were three to the Finnish Air Force and one to the Estonian Air Force. In October 1936 a special Anson, *SU-AAO*, was cleared for a take-off weight of 8,000 lb and flown to Egypt in civil marks so that the Egyptian Army Air Force might test its suitability for a proposed Bomber Transport Squadron. The entry door was certainly on the port side but its official designation Avro 652 Mk.II was scarcely justifiable in view of its almost complete external similarity to an Anson I. Also additional to RAF production were two more Anson Is (serials *21* and *22*) for the Irish Army Air Corps in May 1938. War cut short an order for 25 placed by the Turkish Government and only six were delivered, but 12 were flown out to the Greek Air Force in British civil marks in June 1939. Many of these were captured by the Germans when the British withdrew from Greece on April 4, 1941, but a few managed to escape to Egypt to form the nucleus of a Light Bomber Squadron. A number of RAF Anson Is transferred to the Royal Iraqi Air Force in 1938–39 remained in service until destroyed in the Rashid Ali uprising of May 2, 1941.

Anson I deliveries to the RAF proceeded rapidly and five complete squadrons (Nos.206, 220, 224, 233 and 269) flew past in mass formation at the Hendon RAF Display of June 26, 1937. For $3\frac{1}{2}$ years they formed the backbone of Coastal Command and although already obsolescent when war was declared, adopted an unexpectedly warlike attitude, first evinced by an Anson I of No.500 Sqn, Detling, which bombed a German U-boat on September 5, 1939. Ansons of this squadron carried two additional machine-guns firing through the side windows and the CO's machine had a 20 mm anti-submarine cannon in the bottom of the fuselage. In September one of No.269 Squadron's Ansons shot down a Dornier Do 18 flying-boat and in June 1940 three Ansons on patrol over the English Channel not only survived an attack by three Messerschmitt Bf 109s but by surreptitiously throttling back, succeeded in destroying two and damaging the third as they overshot. In July 1940 a Bf 110 fighter, an He 115 seaplane and an He 111 bomber were also shot down by Ansons.

When the Lockheed Hudsons arrived Ansons were withdrawn from front-line service although a number were fitted with early ASV radar and remained with Air Sea Rescue Squadrons until 1942. The majority were relegated to instructional duties which they performed with distinction at Flying Training, Navigation and Air Gunnery Schools until the end of the war. Those fitted with dual control for pilots' twin conversions generally had the A.W. hand-operated turret removed, but it was retained as an astrodrome on flying classroom Ansons used by W/T operators and navigators until the aircraft next came up for major overhaul. The balance of the 2,476 Ansons Is built under six Air Ministry contracts placed in 1937–40 were completed as turretless trainers. Later when the Blackburn Bothas and other types used by the Air Gunnery Schools were no longer considered satisfactory, they were replaced by 313 Anson Is specially built with Bristol B.1 Mk.VI turrets, hydraulically-operated by electric motors under the floor. Training Ansons had twin landing lights in the leading edge of the mainplane in place of the single unit in the nose and a number were loaned to the USAAF in England for communications duties, e.g. *AX623* at Steeple Morden.

Supplementary orders were placed in 1939 for 1,500 more Anson Is (later increased by a further 800), 40 of which were loaned to Australia for use by Nos.2, 4 and 6 (Bomber) Squadrons RAAF, while others were supplied to the SAAF under Specification 33/35. In 1940 they replaced Junkers Ju 86s on shipping patrol work off East Africa with No.60 Sqn. and on anti-submarine work off the Cape with Nos. 31, 32 and 33 Flights, SAAF. One, serial *3158*, was fitted with floats as a non-flying seamanship trainer for Sunderland squadrons using Congella flying-boat base, Durban. Dutch air crews who fled to the UK in 1940 were also given Ansons with which to form No.320 Sqn, Coastal Command, and after the war were presented

The South African Air Force Anson I seamanship trainer *3158* at Congella, Durban, circa 1942.

325

The Anson IV prototype *R9816* with Wright Whirlwind engines and variable-pitch airscrews, February 1942. (*Crown Copyright Reserved.*)

with surplus machines to take home for the newly unified Royal Netherlands Air Force.

Ansons were delivered in numbers to schools of the Commonwealth Air Training Plan in Canada, Australia and elsewhere, and by January 20, 1945, shipments to Australia had reached a figure variously given as 1,028 and 1,034 Ansons (including the original 48). About 450 were in long-term storage in 1948, and *W2599* was still preserved in full training yellow by Marshall Airways Ltd at Bankstown, Sydney, as late as 1963. Many were lost at sea, as for example *R9712*, *AW620* and *AX302* sunk during shipment to Canada, Australia and South Africa respectively. Large numbers of elderly squadron Ansons, as well as new aircraft in the *N*, *R* and *W* series were sent to Canada but U-boat activity and the shortage of Cheetah IX motors led to the construction of complete Ansons in that Dominion. They were fitted with 330 hp Jacobs L6MB engines under designation Anson Mk.II, but as an interim measure some British-built aircraft were Jacobs-powered to become Anson Mk.IIIs, and 223 airframes were built specially for shipment to Canada to be fitted with 300 hp Wright Whirlwind R-760-E1 radials. These were known as Anson Mk.IVs, the trial installation for which was made in England in *R9816*.

The all-Canadian Anson Mk.II had revised windows and a Vidal plastic-bonded nose, while both the Anson Mks.II and III had parallel undercarriage radius rods in place of the old single fork type, as well as Dowty hydraulic retraction and flap systems. The prototype Anson II, *7069*, adapted from an Anson I by Federal Aircraft Ltd and first flown on August 21, 1941, was the first of 1,832 built by six sub-contractors. Fifty were supplied to the USAAF in 1943 for advanced crew training as the Model AT-20 with 330 hp Jacobs R-915-7 engines.

To husband stocks of steel it was decided to abandon Avro-Fokker tradition and build an all-wood version with the fuselage entirely of Vidal moulded plywood. Trainees were increased to five and 'greenhouse' windows replaced by three circular portholes. A prototype fuselage made by Vidal at Bristol, Mass, and equipped with major components from Anson Mk.I RCAF *6013* (ex-RAF *N9943*) flew in 1942 as the first Anson Mk.V, *8649X*.

326

The fifty USAAF Anson IIs were known as Federal AT-20s.

Production of 1,050 turretless navigation trainers began immediately at three aircraft plants, and a single Anson Mk.VI gunnery trainer, *13881* with Bristol B.1 Mk.VI turret was also built. Both marks were powered by the 450 hp Pratt & Whitney Wasp Junior R985-AN12B or AN14B radials driving Hamilton or Hoover constant-speed airscrews. Marks-VII, VIII and IX were reserved for later Canadian variants which did not materialise. The Anson Mk.Vs remained in RCAF and Royal Canadian Navy service until the late '50s when the last four flew from Uplands to Trenton, three for civilian disposal and *12518* for preservation by the RCAF.

Production of 7,195 Anson Mk.Is ordered from A. V. Roe and Co. was speeded by the establishment of a shadow factory at Yeadon, Yorks, where the output reached 130 aircraft a month in 1943–44. They included a batch of 20 urgently needed by the RAF in Egypt in 1943, which were temporarily disguised as civil machines *G-AGGJ* to *'HD* and given BOAC markings for an audacious delivery flight in camouflage from Croydon to Lisbon and thence to Aboukir via Takoradi and the trans-African route.

The all-up weight of the Anson was steadily increased from 7,342 lb for the prototype in 1935, to 8,000 lb in September 1938 when the crew was increased from three to four, and to 9,300 lb in 1941 (by which time the bomb load had been increased to two 250 lb bombs), finally to 9,850 lb in

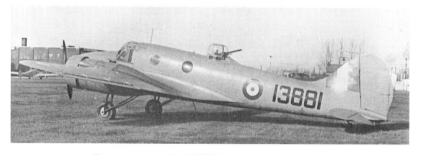

The unique Anson Mk.VI RCAF *13881* at Cartierville, Quebec.

*11561*, an Anson II of the SBA Training Flight No.33 SFTS, Carberry, Manitoba, Canada. (*Courtesy J. M. Bruce.*)

Royal Canadian Navy Anson V *12435*.

1943 for a number equipped with Bristol B.1 Mk.VI turrets as combined navigation and armament trainers. Engine-overheating then led to the fitting of smooth 'Oxford' type cowlings.

The Anson Mk.X (prototype *NK753*), introduced in 1943, was virtually a Mk.I with cabin floor strengthened to support heavy freight. Some early production aircraft had full military equipment and the Bristol Turret but the majority were without such adornment for Nos.4 and 5 AODU and Air Transport Auxiliary post D-Day freight runs to the Continent. Many Mk.Xs. had transparent nose caps and smooth engine cowlings, modifica-

Anson I *G-AGGY*, one of twenty temporarily demilitarized and ferried to Egypt by BOAC in 1943.

tions retrospectively incorporated in a large number of Anson Mk.Is, a considerable fleet of which flew nearly ten million miles with the ATA Air Movements Flight, distributing and collecting ferry pilots. Capt Douglas Fairweather, founder of the Flight and former owner of Avro Cadet Special *G-ACIL*, was a middle-aged Anson devotee who chain-smoked his way through any weather to get his exhausted and sleeping loads back to base, often with Service hitch hikers 'strap hanging' in the gangway. He and a

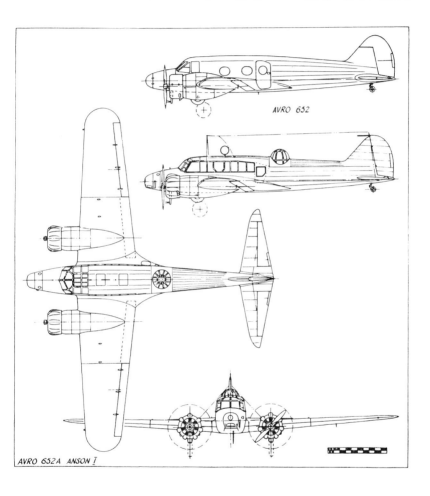

AVRO 652

AVRO 652A ANSON I

nursing sister lost their lives somewhere in the Irish Sea in Anson I *N4875* on April 4, 1944, while trying to reach Prestwick in appalling weather to pick up a serious hospital case.

After the war surplus Anson Mk.Is were sold in small numbers to the air forces of Belgium (e.g. *NA3* ex *EG208*), Egypt (e.g. *NK581*), Iran, Israel,

Norway, The Netherlands (*D-1* to *D-9*), Portugal and Saudi Arabia. The largest number, 223, was sold to France to equip the Air Navigation and Bombing School at Cazoux, patrol squadrons in Syria and Equatorial Africa, the advanced Flying School at Cognac, and the Aéronavale. While no Ansons were supplied direct to the British Royal Navy, a number were transferred from the RAF postwar for Air Observer training.

With its quite remarkable reputation as a reliable and easily maintained work horse, the war surplus Anson Mk.I was the natural choice of countless small charter firms which sprang up in the years immediately following the war. This resulted in the civil registration of 98 in the UK and 140 in Australia alone. Similarly Anson Mk.Vs served Spartan Air Services Ltd, Ottawa, and other Canadian concerns for more than two decades and one, *OY-DZI*, was used as an ambulance in Denmark by Zone Redningskorpset. Others were ferried to Central and South America for civil use.

Civil conversion was simply a matter of installing six or eight seats and reducing the enormous glazing to three or four square or circular windows on each side, although Air Service Training's *G-AHNS* and *'NT* remained in standard form for twin conversion and navigation training. Other long-term Anson users were the Fairey and Hunting survey organisations; the College of Aeronautics, which used three at Cranfield as flying laboratories

Anson I *214*, ex RAF aircraft *NK437*, reconditioned at Woodford for the Portuguese Government in 1947.

and equipped *G-AIPC* for flight testing aerofoil sections above the cabin roof; the Cambridge University Aeronautical Laboratory, which used *MG467* for boundary layer suction experiments in 1950; and the Straight Corporation, which used 10 for school work and scheduled services. The tourist trade kept the Anson-equipped mushroom concerns in business for a year or two but lasting success came principally to Blue Line Airways Ltd, Tollerton, with five; British Air Transport, Redhill, with six; and Transair, Croydon, which at one time or another owned eleven, mainly windowless freighters for the early morning Continental mail and newspaper run prior to 1953.

Overseas the Anson gave sterling service with C.L. Air Surveys in Kenya; Gulf Aviation, Bahrain; Nanyang Airways, Singapore; Trans Arabian Airways, Amman; and Airwork, Nairobi. Many were fitted with underwing spray bars or hoppers for agricultural work and pest control in North and Central Africa. Others were used for communications by oil companies in the French Sahara and flew in the markings of many South American, Asian and European countries.

Regrettably glued joints do not last indefinitely and the Anson's wooden mainplane inevitably deteriorated with age. Thus in 1960 when the ARB decided to grant no more Cs of A to Anson Mks.I and X for passenger work, the old war horse rapidly disappeared from British skies, the last being *G-ALXC* and *G-AMBE* which landed their final loads of vegetables at Speke for the Federated Fruit Co in April 1961; and Derby Aviation's *G-AMDA* which made a geophysical survey of Southern England with a towed magnetometer in 1954–5 and ended its flying career in 1962 with the London School of Flying at Elstree before going to a museum at Staverton in 1963.

In Australia, where short-lived enterprises had given the Anson an even more complex commercial history than in the UK, the final ban came at midnight on June 30, 1962. The major Anson users, Flinders Island Airways Ltd and Brain and Brown Ltd of Moorabbin, Melbourne, had provided essential ferry services to Tasmania and the Bass Strait islands for many years with *VH-BSF*, *'FIA* and *'IC*; while in Western Australia, Woods Airways Ltd had run the Perth-Rottnest Island link with *VH-WAB* and *'AC*. These and *VH-AGA*, *'BEL* and *'MMH* belonging to other taxi concerns were relegated to inland work when over-water passenger flights were banned on January 1, 1962. On the final day six months later, *VH-BSF*, *FIA* and *'IC* made a farewell formation flight over Melbourne while *VH-BEL* and *'MMH* circled Perth together for the last time.

## SPECIFICATION AND DATA

*Manufacturers:*  A. V. Roe and Co Ltd, Newton Heath and Chadderton, Manchester; Woodford Aerodrome, Cheshire; and Yeadon Aerodrome, Yorks
Federal Aircraft Ltd, Montreal, Canada
Canadian Car and Foundry Co Ltd, Amherst, Nova Scotia, and Cartierville, Montreal
de Havilland Aircraft of Canada Ltd, Downsview Airport, Toronto, Canada
National Steel Car Corporation, Malton, Ontario, Canada (later renamed Victory Aircraft Ltd)
Ottawa Car and Aircraft Co Ltd, Ottawa, Canada
MacDonald Bros, Stevenson Field, Winnipeg, Canada

| | | | |
|---|---|---|---|
| *Powerplants:* | (Avro 652) | Two 270 hp Armstrong Siddeley Cheetah V | |
| | (Avro 652 Mk.II) | Two 310 hp Armstrong Siddeley Cheetah IX | |
| | (Avro 652A prototype) | Two 290 hp Armstrong Siddeley Cheetah VI | |
| | (Anson Mks.I and X) | Two 335 hp Armstrong Siddeley Cheetah IX | |

*Powerplants:*    (Avro 652)    Two 270 hp Armstrong Siddeley Cheetah V

(Avro 652 Mk.II)    Two 310 hp Armstrong Siddeley Cheetah IX

(Avro 652A prototype)    Two 290 hp Armstrong Siddeley Cheetah VI

(Anson Mks.I and X)    Two 335 hp Armstrong Siddeley Cheetah IX

(Anson Mk.II) Two 330 hp Jacobs L6MB

(AT-20)    Two 330 hp Jacobs R-915-7

(Anson Mk.III) Two 330 hp Jacobs L6MB

(Anson Mk.IV) Two 300 hp Wright Whirlwind R-760-E1

(Anson Mks.V and VI)    Two 450 hp Pratt & Whitney Wasp Junior R985-AN12B (automatic mixture control) or AN14B (manual control)

*Dimensions:*    Span 56 ft 6 in    Length 42 ft 3 in
Height 13 ft 1 in    Wing area 463 sq ft

*Weights and Performances:*

| | Avro 652 | Anson I | Anson V and VI | Anson X |
|---|---|---|---|---|
| Tare weight | 5,100 lb | 5,375 lb | 6,693 lb | — |
| All-up weight | 7,400 lb | 7,665 lb* | 9,460 lb | 9,450 lb |
| Maximum speed | 195 mph | 188 mph | 190 mph | 175 mph |
| Cruising speed | 165 mph | 158 mph | 145 mph | 140 mph |
| Initial climb | 770 ft/min | 960 ft/min | 1,500 ft/min | — |
| Ceiling | 21,500 ft | 19,000 ft | 21,450 ft | — |
| Range | 790 miles | 660 miles | 580 miles | — |

*Avro 652 Mk.II, Anson G.R. Mk.I, Anson Mk.II and Mk.III 8,000 lb

*Production:*

### (a) By A. V. Roe and Co Ltd

**Avro 652**: Two aircraft for Imperial Airways Ltd
   *G-ACRM Avalon*, c/n 698, C of A issued 1.3.35; to Air Service Training Ltd 7.38; impressed 2.41 as *DG655*; to No. 811 Sqn 7.41
   *G-ACRN Avatar* (changed to *Ava*), c.n 699, C of A issued 8.3.35; to Air Service Training Ltd 7.38; impressed 2.41 as *DG656*, damaged in ground collision with Chesapeake, Lee-on-Solent, 1.10.41
**Avro 652 Mk.II**: One aircraft for the Egyptian Army Air Force.
   *SU-AAO*, c/n 891 (duplicating c/n of Greek Avro 621 serial *E-50*), C of A issued 4.11.36; to Egyptian Army Air Force as *W204*
**Avro 652A Prototype**: One aircraft to Air Ministry Specification G.18/35
   *K4771*, first flown at Woodford 24.3.35; to Martlesham 13.4.35; Service

trials, Gosport, 11-17.5.35; Hendon RAF Display 29.6.35; at Martlesham till 1937; at RAE, Farnborough 8.39

**First RAF production batch** of 174 aircraft to amended Specification 18/35 under Contract No. 421119/35: *K6152–K6325* (*K6212–K6223* to the RAAF as *A4-1* to *A4-12*, c/n 967–978).

**Second RAF production batch** of 106 aircraft ordered 1936 under Contract No. 497338/36: *K8742–K8847* (*K8792–K8812* to the RAAF as *A4-13* to *A4-33*, c/n 1008–1028; *K8840–K8844* as *A4-34* to *A4-38*, c/n 1053–1057)

**Third RAF production batch** of 39 aircraft delivered 28.7.37–25.10.37 under contract No. 497339/36: *K8703–K8741* (*K8738–K8740* to Finland as *AN101–AN103*, c.n 939–941; *K8741* to Estonia as *158*, c/n 951)

**Irish Army Air Corps** batch of four aircraft ordered 1937: *A.19* and *A.20*, c/n 980–981, delivered ex Woodford 20.3.37; *A.21* and *A.22*, c/n 1033–1034, delivered ex Woodford 19.1.38

**Fourth RAF production batch** of 28 aircraft ordered 1937 under Contract No.633200/37: *L7046–L7073*

**Fifth RAF production batch** of 98 aircraft ordered 1937 under Contract No. 690658/37, the first in which the serial 'black out' technique was used: *L7903–L7932*, *L7945–L7977*, *L7991–L7994*, *L9145–L9165*, *N1330–N1339* (*L7913–L7922* to the RAAF as *A4-39* to *A4-48*, c/n 1079–1088)

**Royal Hellenic Air Force** batch of 12 aircraft ordered 1938: *TT51–TT62*, flown out as *G-AFTU* to *G-AFTW*, *G-AFUH* to *G-AFUJ*, *G-AFUM* to *G-AFUO*, and *G-AFUR* to *G-AFUT*, c/n 1111–1122, Cs of A issued between 12.5.39 and 15.6.39

**Sixth RAF production batch** of 850 aircraft ordered 1938 under Contract No.766119/38: *N4856–N4899*, *N4901–N4948*, *N4953–N4989*, *N4995–N5044*, *N5047–N5094*, *N5096–N5125*, *N5130–N5178*, *N5182–N5220*, *N5225–N5274*, *N5279–N5318*, *N5320–N5359*, *N5361–N5385*, *N9526–N9575*, *N9587–N9621*, *N9640–N9689*, *N9713–N9752*, *N9765–N9790*, *N9815–N9858*, *N9870–N9919*, *N9930–N9956*, *N9972–N9999* (*N9947–N9952*, c/n 1127–1132, to Turkey 5.40)

**Seventh RAF production batch** of 200 aircraft ordered 1939 under Contract No.B12565/39: *R3303–R3351*, *R3368–R3413*, *R3429–R3476*, *R3512–R3561*, *R3581–R3587*

**Eighth RAF production batch** of 300 aircraft ordered 1939 under Contract No.B32842/39: *R9567–R9611*, *R9627–R9670*, *R9685–R9725*, *R9739–R9781*, *R9798–R9846*, *R9864–R9899*, *R9928–R9969*

**Ninth RAF production batch** of 1,000 aircraft ordered 1939 under Contract No.61695/39: *W1505–W1524*, *W1529–W1540*, *W1544–W1570*, *W1576–W1618*, *W1627–W1676*, *W1690–W1736*, *W1751–W1800*, *W1814–W1863*, *W1875–W1924*, *W1932–W1971*, *W1986–W2025*, *W2031–W2072*, *W2078–W2099*, *W2109–W2158*, *W2163–W2212*, *W2216–W2245*, *W2252–W2291*, *W2298–W2347*, *W2355–W2398*, *W2403–W2452*, *W2457–W2592*, *W2598–W2646*, *W2651–W2665*

**Tenth RAF production batch** of 1,770 complete Anson Mk.Is, 57 Mk.I airframes and 223 Mk.IV airframes ordered 1940 under Contract No. B137211/40: *AW443–AW492*, *AW506–AW540*, *AW586–AW635*, *AW653–AW697*, *AW739–AW758*, *AW778–AW812*, *AW833–AW882*, *AW897–AW941*, *AW963–AW982*, *AX100–AX149*, *AX163–AX187*, *AX218–AX267*, *AX280–AX324*, *AX343–AX372*, *AX396–AX445*, *AX466–AX515*, *AX535–AX584*, *AX607–AX656*, *DG689–DG737*,

*DG750–DG787, DG799–DG844, DG857–DG880, DG893–DG942, DG956–DF987, DJ103–DJ149, DJ162–DJ190, DJ205–DJ248, DJ263–DJ298, DJ314–DJ361, DJ375–DJ417, DJ430–DJ478, DJ492–DJ529, DJ545–DJ589, DJ603–DJ639, DJ656–DJ700, EF805–DF839, EF858–EF890, EF903–EF941, EF952–EF993, EG104–EG148, EG165–EG195, EG208–EG246, EG251–EG280, EG293–EF335, EG350–EF396, EG412–EG447, EG460–EG507, EG524–EG561, EG583–EG616, EG629–EG655, EG672–EG704*

**Eleventh RAF production batch** increasing Contract No.B137211/40 by 1,550 Anson Mk.I aircraft: *LS978–LS999, LT112–LT160, LT175–LT210, LT231–LT258, LT271–LT307, LT334–LT378, LT410–LT459, LT472–LT503, LT521–LT549, LT575–LT610, LT641–LT682, LT701–LT745, LT764–LT797, LT823–LT849, LT872–LT899, LT921–LT961, LT978–LT999, LV122–LV167, LV199–LV230, LV252–LV300, LV313–LV332, MG102–MG147, MG159–MG199, MG214–MG256, MG270–MG314, MG327–MG368, MG381–MG423, MG436–MG478, MG490–MG536, MG549–MG596, MG613–MG656, MG669–MG701, MG714–MG757, MG770–MG813, MG826–MG874, MG888–MG928, MG962–MG999, MH103–MH135, MH149–MH196, MH210–MH237* (23 diverted to the RNZAF as *NZ401–NZ423* included *LT349/NZ410*, later civil as *ZK-BCL*)

**Twelfth RAF production batch** increasing Contract No.B137211/40 by a further 800 Anson Mk.I aircraft: *NK139–NK187, NK199–NK244, NK260–NK303, NK315–NK356, NK368–NK406, NK419–NK462, NK475–NK516, NK528–NK568, NK581–NK623, NK636–NK679, NK692–NK738, NK750–NK793, NK806–NK848, NK861–NK906, NK919–NK958, NK970–NK999, NL112–NL155, NL169–NL208, NL220–NL251*

**Avro 652 Anson Mk.I** aircraft ferried to Egypt in BOAC markings 1943: *G-AGGJ* to *G-AGGP* and *G-AGGR* to *G-AGHD*, temporarily demilitarised with c/n 1152–1171, Cs of A issued 3.6.43 to British Overseas Airways Corporation. The aircraft reverted to military serials *LT191, 192, 203, 204, 236, 255, 256, 257, 307, 340, EG677, LS985, LT279, 115, 176, 234, 276, 281, EG651* and *LS989* respectively on arrival at Aboukir. (Note: c/n of *G-AGGJ* duplicates that of the final Egyptian Avro 626)

**Avro 652A Anson Mk.X**

(i) 103 aircraft laid down as Anson Mk.Is but completed as Ansons Mk.Xs: *NK352–NK354, NK356, NK368–NK369, NK426–NK428, NK431–NK433, NK438–NK439, NK443, NK446–NK449, NK487–NK493, NK528–NK534, NK657–NK661, NK664–NK668, NK695, 696, 699, 700, 703, 705, 706, 722, 725, 728, 731, 734, 737, 751, NK766–NK772, NK775, 778, 781, 784, 786, 787, 789, 791, 793, 819, 820, 823, 824, 827, 828, 831, 832, 835, 838, 841, 844, 847, 862, 865, 920, 921, 924, 925, NK930–NK935, NL112–NL116*

(ii) 17 Anson Mk.Is converted to Anson Mk.Xs after delivery: *AW871, MG471, MH192, MH231, NK178, 183, 234, 262, 500, 567, 702, 707, 710, 712, 716, 727* and *814*

*Note:* All British-built Ansons were constructed at Newton Heath with the exception of *W2612–W2646, W2651–W2665, DG689–DG727*, and all *EF, EG, LS, LT, LV, MG, MH, NK* and *NL* batches which were built at Yeadon.

## (b) Anson Mk.II aircraft for the Royal Canadian Air Force

| Serial range | Manufacturer | Serial range | Manufacturer |
|---|---|---|---|
| 7069 | Federal | 8404–8463 | Ottawa Car |
| 7070–7173 | Canadian Car | 8464–8648 | McDonald Bros |
| 7174–7498 | de Havilland | 11181–11281 | Canadian Car |
| 7499–7622 | National Steel | 11282–11380 | McDonald Bros |
| 8203–8353 | National Steel | 11381–11580 | Victory Aircraft |
| 8354–8403 | Canadian Car | | |

*Note:* Fifty aircraft were procured by United States Army Air Force in the fiscal year 1943 and given the designation Federal AT-20. Serials *43–8181* to *43–8230*. Thirty-nine of these are known to have been ex RCAF *7114–7, 7119–23, 7126, 7128–30, 7170, 7172, 7248, 7381–2, 7461–3, 7569, 7585, 7590, 8204, 8245, 8333, 8340–1, 8343, 8348, 8350–1, 8354, 8357, 8378, 8387,* and *8394*

## (c) Anson Mk.II aircraft for the RAF in Canada

| Serial range | Manufacturer |
|---|---|
| *FP687–FP947* | National Steel/Victory Aircraft |
| *FP948–FP997* | de Havilland |
| *FP998–FP999* | MacDonald Bros |
| *JS100–JS132* | MacDonald Bros |
| *JS133–JS218* | Canadian Car |

## (d) Anson Mk.V aircraft for the Royal Canadian Air Force

| Serial range | Manufacturer | Serial range | Manufacturer |
|---|---|---|---|
| 8649 | Federal | 11681–11930 | Canadian Car |
| 11581 | Canadian Car★ | 11931–12628 | McDonald Bros |
| 11582–11630 | Canadian Car | 13231–13250 | Canadian Car |
| 11631–11680 | McDonald Bros | | |

*Note:* All Canadian Car and Foundry production at Amherst, Nova Scotia, except ★ at Cartierville.

### (e) The Anson Mk.VI
One aircraft only, RCAF serial *13881*, built by Federal Aircraft Ltd

### (f) Reconditioned aircraft
Ten ex-RAF Anson Mk.Is reconditioned by A. V. Roe and Co Ltd 5.47 for the Portuguese Government as *213* to *222*, c/n 1334–1339 (ex *NK182, 437, 444, 476, 483* and *484*); and c/n 1370–1373 (ex *MG690, 692, 696* and *221*) to Works Orders 35970 and 36651

*Service Use:* (Units which used the Anson in numbers, with codes in parentheses)
   *Coastal Command:* Nos.42 (AW), 48 (XZ), 86 (BX), 206 (WD,VX), 217 (YQ, MW), 220 (Hu), 221, 224 (PW), 233 (EY), 269 (WP, UA), 320 (TD), 321, 500, (SQ, MK), 502 (KQ, YG), 608 (PG, OY) and 612 (DJ) Squadrons; Nos.1, 3, 6 and 8 OTUs; No. 3 School of General Reconnaissance; No.1693

Flight. *Bomber Command:* Nos.7 (MG), 51, 58, 61, 109 (ZP, HS), 144 (PL) and 148 (BS) Squadrons; Nos.1 to 6 Bomber Group Pools; Nos.10 (UY), 11 (TX), 12, 13 (SL), 14, 15, 16 (GA), 17 (WJ) and 19 (XF) OTUs. *Fighter Command:* No.62 OTU *Air Sea Rescue;* Nos.275, 276 (AQ), 278 (MY), 280 (MF, YF), 281 (FA), 282 and 293 Squadrons. *Special Duties:* Nos.138 and 161 Squadrons (agent recovery), No.1473 Flight (radio counter-measures), Nos.516 and 544 Squadrons (Combined Operations). *Training Units:* Nos.6, 7, 11, 12, 15, 16, 18, 28, 29, 33, 37 and 39 E and RFTS; AST, Hamble; CFS and Air Navigation school (prewar); Nos.6, 9, 10 and 11 Flying Training schools; Nos.2, 3, 4, 7, 8, 10, 12 and 13 Air Gunners Schools; Nos.2, 3, 4, 5, 7 and 12 Air Observers Schools; Nos.3, 5, 6, 7, 11, 14, 15, 17, 18 and 20 (Pilot) Advanced Flying Units; Nos.1, 7 and 10 (Observers) Advanced Flying Units; Nos.10 and 11 Radio Schools; No.1 Staff Pilots Training Unit; Nos.2 (FFM), 3 (Z), 5 (FFI), 7 (FFN) and 10 (FFT) Air Navigation Schools; No.19 Flying Training School (FAG) (postwar); School of Air Traffic Control (FDY); Central Navigation School. *Air Transport Auxiliary:* Nos.1 to 16 Ferry Pools and the Air Movements Flight. *Commonwealth Air Training Plan:* Flying Schools in Canada, Australia, South Africa, Southern Rhodesia and New Zealand. *RAAF Coastal Patrol:* Nos.1, 2, 6, 12, 13, 14, 21, 22, 23, 25, 33, 34, 35, 66, 67, 71, 73 and 92 Squadrons. *SAAF:* Nos.31, 32 and 33 Flights, Nos.35 and 60 Squadrons. *Miscellaneous Units:* Nos.510 (later the Metropolitan Communications Sqn) and 575 Squadrons; Middle East Communications Squadron; Free French Group Artois (West Africa). *Royal Navy:* No.758 Squadron; Air Observers School.

Ansons were also used singly or in small numbers by numerous Station Flights and other units, and in the early postwar years the Anson Mk.I was used by the RAF College, Cranwell and many of the re-formed Reserve Flying Schools.

LT112, a late production Anson 1 with Bristol Turret. (*Avro*)

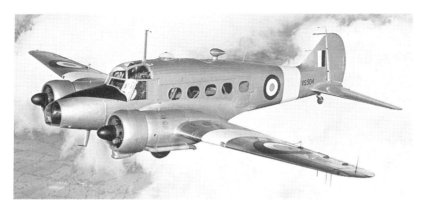

Avro 652A Anson T. Mk.20 navigation trainer *VS504*. (*Avro*)

# Avro 652A Anson Mks.11 to 22

In 1944 the roof of the Anson cabin was raised to increase internal headroom, the 'greenhouse' glazing was replaced by three square windows on each side and flaps and undercarriage were hydraulically operated as on the Canadian Mk.II. The modernised Anson was built in two versions— Mk.11 with two 395 hp Armstrong Siddeley Cheetah 19s driving fixed-pitch Fairey-Reed metal airscrews, and Mk.12 with two 420 hp Cheetah 15s turning Rotol constant-speed airscrews. The two marks were only distinguishable externally because spinners were fitted to the variable-pitch airscrews of the Mk.12.

Anson 11 production, beginning with *NK790* in May 1944, reached a total of 90 and continued parallel with the completion of 16 Anson Mk.1s as Anson Mk.12s and the construction of a further 264 Anson Mk.12s beginning with *PH528*. Several were completed as ambulances with hinged wing root fillets on the port side to allow stretchers to be pushed into the cabin. *NK870*, the first Anson Mk.11 ambulance, flew on July 30, 1944, and the first Anson Mk.12 ambulance, *NL153*, on October 27 of that year. The prototype Anson Mk.12 *NL152* (first flown at Woodford on September 5, 1944) and *NL246*, the last production Anson Mk.11, became civil in the autumn of 1944 as *G-AGLB* and *'LM* for temporary use by Air Attachés in Madrid and London respectively. *NL152* later reverted to the RAF for communication duties until scrapped at Aldergrove in 1963, the only survivors of either mark then being Anson Mk.11s *G-ALIH* equipped with large nose scanner for radar development work by E. K. Cole Ltd, Southend; and *G-ALXH* used for aerial mapping by BKS Air Survey Ltd.

In 1945 A. V. Roe and Co fitted Anson Mk.12 *MG159* with nine seats and five oval windows to satisfy the Brabazon XIX feeder-liner specification of 1943. It thus became known as the Avro 652A Nineteen and was handed over to the Associated Airways Joint Committee as *G-AGNI* for evaluation on internal air routes. Anson Mk.12 *G-AGLB* was then recalled from Madrid for similar conversion, but retained its square windows. A VIP general transport version of this variant, ordered by the RAF as the Avro C. Mk.19 and built at Yeadon, appeared in two versions, Series 1 with wooden wings, and Series 2 with metal tailplane and tapering, fabric-covered, metal mainplane of one foot greater span. The first 25, originally laid down as Anson Mk.12s, were followed by a contract for a further 160, of which 67 (commencing *TX223*) were Series 2. Orders were placed later for 124 Series 2 aircraft but not all were delivered, 23 Series Is being diverted to civil orders, one Series 2 to the Afghan Government and nine others to the RAF as Anson T. Mk.20 trainers. A few Series 2 machines, e.g. *VP514*, were equipped with vertical cameras for P.R. work, while others, e.g. *VL353*, had the perspex nose of the T. Mk.20. Mark numbers 13 and 14 were reserved for turreted gunnery trainers and 15 and 16 for navigation and bombing training versions, but none of these was built. Designation Anson Mk.18 was given to a batch of 12 general purpose aircraft equipped for police duties, liaison, transport and survey work by the Royal Afghan Air Force 1948–56. A second batch of 12, with opaque nose caps and DF loops repositioned farther aft, were delivered to the Indian Government as civil aircrew trainers under designation Anson

Anson Mk.11 *NK870* with Armstrong Siddeley Cheetah 19s and fixed-pitch airscrews.

Anson Mk.12 *NL175* with Cheetah 15s and variable-pitch airscrews.

Royal Afghan Air Force metal-winged Anson Mk.18 *YA-B.252.*

Mk.18C. Despite their earlier mark numbers, both these types were derived from the Mk.19, the prototype Mk.18 being a conversion of *VP511*, a production Anson C.Mk.19 Series 2.

The largest fleet of civil Avro 19 Series 1 aircraft was that of Railway Air Services Ltd which operated 14 on routes from Croydon to the North, Dublin, the Isle of Man and Belfast until 1947. The Ministry of Civil Aviation also maintained six at Gatwick for airport radio calibration and for instrument rating tests. Five were supplied to Egypt, one for Royal use and the others for airline service with Misrair; two to the Emperor of Ethiopia (*G-AGUH* and *'UI*); and others were sold to Hunting Air Travel Ltd, Sivewright Airways Ltd and Westminster Airways Ltd. *G-AIKM*, originally the Rochester-based charter machine of Short Bros and Harland Ltd, later became *Star Visitant*, crew trainer of British South American Airways. Eventually these proud fleets dispersed to the four winds and by 1959 all the survivors had been absorbed by the aircraft industry as 'hacks',

Indian Government Anson Mk.18C civil aircrew trainer *VT-CXZ. (Avro)*

339

*G-AGUH* by Armstrong Siddeley Motors Ltd, *'WE* by the Decca Navigator Co Ltd, *G-AHIC* by the College of Aeronautics, Cranfield, as an aerodynamic test vehicle (with experimental aerofoil sections flown vertically on the roof), *'XK* by Hawker Aircraft Ltd, and *'YN* by Armstrong Whitworth Aircraft Ltd.

The first production civil Avro 19 Series 1, *G-AGPG*, built at Yeadon in June 1946, remained in the service of A. V. Roe and Co for 16 years. They converted it to Series 2 in 1952 and sold it to Skyways Ltd, Lympne, ten years later. Production of the Avro 19 Series 2 for civil purposes was limited to 14 aircraft as shown in the data section.

Many civil and Service Anson C. Mk.12 and 19 machines were eventually modernised to Series 2 and fitted with the metal wing, as were several civil Mk.11s. This was also common to the last three Anson variants, the T. Mk.20, 21 and 22. Built to Air Ministry Specification T.24/46 as a general purpose trainer for Southern Rhodesia, the Anson T. Mk.20 (prototype *VM305* possessed several distinguishing features. For navigation training an astrodome was fitted on top of the fuselage, a moulded perspex nose was fitted for practice bomb-aiming, and bombs were carried in racks under the wings. The DF loop, situated just behind the pilot's cabin on the Avro 19, was moved back level with the fourth window. A small number of reserve Anson T. Mk.20s which remained in the UK were flown without bomb racks.

The Anson T. Mk.21 to Air Ministry Specification T.25/46 (prototype *VS562*, first flown in May 1948), produced as a navigation trainer accommodating a crew of six for use in the British Isles by Flying Training Command, was identical externally to the T. Mk.20 but had an opaque metal nose cap. Last came the T. Mk.22, a radio trainer to Specification T.26/46 for the instruction of air signallers (prototype *VM306* flown in June 1948). It resembled the T.Mk.21 but was without astrodome and could be identified further by the positioning of the DF loop above the second cabin window. In 1955 the prototype was used for airborne radar experiments with a bulbous nose of the type fitted to Ekco's *G-ALIH*. Anson T. Mks.20, 21

*G-AGUI*, an Avro 19 Series 1 aircraft supplied to the Ethiopian Government in 1945. (*Avro*)

340

*VM306* after modification to become the prototype Anson T. Mk.22.

and 22 differed from the Avro 19 and all earlier British marks because the engine nacelles carried no external oil coolers and had the exhaust pipes on the outboard instead of inboard sides. There were also fewer metal frames supporting the glazing of the pilots' cabin.

Seventeen years after going into production, the 11,020th and last Anson—the T. Mk.21 *WJ561*—was test flown by Avro chief test pilot J. H. Orrell on May 15, 1952, and handed over to the RAF by Sir Roy Dobson on the 27th. The career of an aircraft which had already eclipsed that of the immortal 504K was by no means over, however, and in 1954 the Fairey Aviation Co operated T. Mk.20 *VS512* on survey work in Central Africa as *VP-YOF*. After 1958 it was used for the same purpose in the UK as *G-ANWW* at a time when obsolete RAF Anson C. Mk.19s were also being released for commercial use. Six flown to North Africa in 1958–59 were used on local services in Algeria, while others equipped overseas air forces, e.g. three to the Southern Rhodesian Air Force, but by December 1962 only about 100 remained in military service. A mere handful were left in civil employ, notably Avro 19 Series 2 *VH-RCC*, formerly *G-AHXK*, flown from Gatwick to Australia October 1–27, 1962, by Richard Cavill of

Avro 19 Series 2 (tapered wing) *G-AKDU* at Heany, Southern Rhodesia, in 1947 with pest control spray gear under the fuselage.

341

Nicholas Air Charter Ltd, and wooden Anson I *VH-BAF* of Brain and Brown Airservices Pty, Moorabin, Victoria, rebuilt with tapered metal wing from *VH-BIX/VM375*. *VH-BAF* survived to become the last airworthy Anson in Australia, appearing at airshows such as that at Ballarat, Victoria, on February 22, 1987.

A further ten former RAF Ansons were allocated civil registrations in 1967 but none was used commercially. The following year, after a record breaking 32 years the type was finally withdrawn from RAF service, an occasion marked by a flypast of six Ansons of the Southern Communications Squadron at Bovingdon on June 29. 1968 also saw a further six Ansons

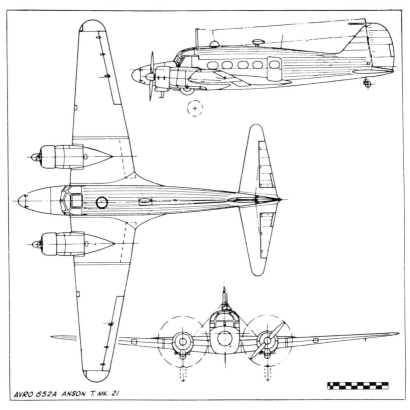

AVRO 652A ANSON T. MK. 21

civilianised, two of these, *G-AWMG* and *'MH*, were used for relief flights between the island of Fernando Po and Biafra, where *'MG* crashed on September 6, 1968, and another, *G-AWRS*, saw service with Kemps Aerials Surveys. The last Anson to be civilianised, T.Mk.21 *G-BFIR*, formerly *WD413/7881M*, was flown to East Midlands on January 21, 1978, after spending twelve years as an instructional airframe at 23 MU Aldergrove. Following an accident later the same year it was rebuilt using parts from Avro 19 Series 2 *G-AHIC* and was still airworthy in the late eighties.

## SPECIFICATION AND DATA

*Manufacturers:*   A. V. Roe and Co Ltd, Newton Heath and Chadderton, Manchester; and Yeadon Aerodrome, Yorks

*Powerplants:*   (Anson Mk.11) Two 395 hp Armstrong Siddeley
                       Cheetah 19
            (Anson Mk.12) Two 420 hp Armstrong Siddeley
                       Cheetah 15
            (Anson Mk.18) Two 420 hp Armstrong Siddeley
                       Cheetah 17
            (Anson Mks.18C, 19, 20, 21 and 22)
                       Two 420 hp Armstrong Siddeley
                       Cheetah 15

*Dimensions:*   (Anson Mks.11, 12 and 19 Series 1)
                       Span 56 ft 6 in   Length 42 ft 3 in
                       Height 13 ft 10 in   Wing area 463 sq ft
            (Anson Mks.18, 18C, 19 Series 2, 20, 21 and 22)
                       Span 57 ft 6 in   Length 42 ft 3 in
                       Height 13 ft 10 in   Wing area 440 sq ft

*Weights and Performances:*

|  | Mks.11, 12, 19 Series 1 | Mks.18, 18C, 19 Series 2, 20, 21, 22 |
|---|---|---|
| Tare weight | 7,419 lb | 6,576 lb |
| All-up weight | 10,500 lb* | 10,400 lb** |
| Maximum speed | 190 mph | 171 mph |
| Cruising speed | 167 mph | 149 mph |
| Initial climb | 730 ft/min | 700 ft/min |
| Ceiling | 15,000 ft | 16,000 ft |
| Range | 610 miles | 660 miles |

        *Anson Mk.11 9,700 lb    **Anson T. Mk.22 10,306 lb

*Production:*

**Anson Mk.11:** Ninety aircraft laid down as Anson Mk.I but completed at Yeadon as Ansons Mk.11s. *NK790, NK870–NK875, NK940, NK986–NK999, NL125, NL128, NL129, NL132, NL133, NL136, NL137, NL140,*

RAF Avro C.19 Series 2 *VM306* with experimental radar scanner in the nose. (*Courtesy Air Pictorial*)

343

*NL141, NL144, NL145, NL148, NL149, NL181–NL208, NL220–NL246.*
Civil conversions: *NL132/G-ALIF; NL182/G-ALIG; NL186/G-ALIE; NL229/G-ALIH; NL231/G-AMBC; NL246/G-AGLM*

**Anson Mk.12:** Sixteen aircraft laid down as Anson Mk.I but completed at Yeadon as Anson Mk.12s. *MG159, NK150, NK151, NL152, NL153, NL171, NL172, NL175, NL176, NL179, NL180, NL247–NL251.* Civil conversions: *MG159/G-AGNI*, c/n 1214; *NL152/G-AGLB*, c.n 1205

Major production comprised 255 aircraft built at Yeadon under Contract No.3077. *PH528–PH569, PH582–PH626, PH638–PH679, PH691–PH735, PH747–PH789, PH803–PH840.* Civil conversions: *PH599/ZK-AXY; PH806/SU-ADJ*, c/n 1272

**Anson C. Mk.19 Series 1:** Seven aircraft converted at Yeadon from Anson Mk.12s before delivery. *PH814–PH816, PH827, PH829, PH830, PH839.* Civil conversion: *PH830/G-AIRV*

Thirteen aircraft laid down at Yeadon as Anson Mk.12 but completed as C. Mk.19s. *PH841–PH845, PH858–PH865.* Civil conversions: *PH845/G-AVTA, PH858/G-AIIA; PH860/G-AGWD,* c/n 1285 to Egyptian *VN889.SU-ADN Tanta*

Main production comprised 85 aircraft built at Yeadon under Contract No.5037. *TX154–TX197, TX201–TX222, TX224–TX235, TX237–TX252, TX255.* Diverted to civil production before delivery: *TX201* and *TX202,* c/n 1286 and '87, to the Ministry of Civil Aviation as *G-AGWE* and *'WF; TX240–TX245; TX246/G-AHKC/SU-ADQ* c/n 1327, Misrair *Mona; TX247; TX248* and *TX249/G-AHKD* and *'KE,* c/n 1328–29, Misrair *SU-ADP Radwa* and *'DO Arafat; TX250–TX252, TX255*

Civil conversions: *TX157/G-AVCK; TX166/G-AWML; TX176/ G-AVGR;TX182/G-AVIJ;TX211/G-AVHU;TX213/G-AWRS;TX227/ G-AWMH*

**Anson C. Mk.19 Series 2:** Production at Yeadon totalled 158 aircraft comprising 34 originally laid down as Series 1s—*TX223, TX253, TX254, TX256, TX257, VL285–VL313, VL333–VL363;* 95 aircraft to Contract No.5680—*VM305–VM342, VM351–VM394, VM406–VM418;* 30 aircraft to Contract No.6103—*VP509–VP538;* a further 100 aircraft to Contract No.1396—*VV740–VV789* and *VV805–VV854* were cancelled. Diversions from Contract: *VL356, VM335* and *'37* to SRAF as *SR29–SR31; VL358–VL363, VM305, VM410–VM418* to Anson T. Mk.20; *VP511* to prototype Anson Mk.18 for the Afghan Government. Civil conversions: *VL298/G-AMNA; VL336/G-AJDH; VL348/G-AVVO; VL349/G-AWSA; VM330/G-AVPP; VM336/G-AFLN,* c/n 1508; *VM351/G-AWSB; VM360/G-APHV; VM373/G-AKUD,* c/n 1449; *VP509/G-AVVP; VP512/G-AKFE; VP519/G-AVVR*

**Anson Mk.18:** Prototype *VP511* and thirteen aircraft built at Yeadon for the Afghan Government comprising 12 production aircraft *YA-A.251* to *YA-L.262,* c/n 1465–1476 and one other, *YA-A.251,* c/n 1509, supplied later to replace c/n 1465

**Anson Mk.18C.** Twelve aircraft built at Yeadon for the Director General of Civil Aviation, India. *VT-CXT* to *VT-CYE,* c/n 1477–1488, British Cs of A issued 8, 18, 21, 29 and 31.3.49; 5 and 13.4.49; 3.5.49; 2, 5 and 10.8.49; 13.7.49 and 10.8.49 respectively.

**Avro 19 Series 1 civil and overseas production:** c/n 1212, *G-AGPG*, C of A issued 6.8.45, Avro communications; 1214, *G-AGNI*, 23.1.45, Associated Airways Joint Committee; 1241, *G-AGPU*, 15.10.45, Air Attaché in Lisbon
c/n 1271, *G-AGPB*, C of A issued 3.1.46, Ministry of Civil Aviation, 1272, *SU-ADJ*, 26.9.45, see page 344, 1273–74, *G-AGUH* and *'UI*, 2.1.46, Imperial Ethiopian Air Force *IEAF.120–121*; 1275–78, *G-AGUD*, *'UE*, *'UX*, *'VA*, 23.11.45, Railway Air Services Ltd; 1285, *G-AGWD*, not taken up, see page 344; 1286–87, *G-AGWE* and *'WF*, 12.6.46, Ministry of Civil Aviation
c/n 1312, *OO-ANT*, C of A issued 3.5.46, John Mahieu Aviation, Brussels; 1317–25, *G-AHIB-'IJ*, 14.5.46–11.7.46, Railway Air Services Ltd; 1327–29, *G-AHKC-'KE,* see page 344; 1330–31, *G-AGZS* and *'ZT*, 1.10.46 and 1332, *G-AGWA*, 24.6.46, Ministry of Civil Aviation
c/n 1351–53, *G-AHXK-'XM*, Hunting Air Travel Ltd *Eland, Oryx* and unnamed; 1357–58, *OO-APN* and *'PX*, 10.9.46, John Mahieu Aviation; 1359, *G-AHYN*, 13.8.46, Sivewright Airways Ltd *Salfordia*; 1360, *G-AHYO*, 16.8.46, Westminster Airways Ltd; 1363, *OO-APG*, 26.6.47, John Mahieu Aviation

**Avro 19 Series 2 civil and overseas production:** c/n 1313–1315 Irish Air Corps *141–143*; c/n 1333, *G-AHKX*, C of A issued 17.12.46, Smiths Aircraft Instruments Ltd; 1361–62, *OO-CFA* and *'FB*, 13.12.46. Cie Chemins de Fer du Congo Supérieur, *'FA* later *OO-DFA* and *OO-VIT*, to UK as *G-AYWA* 14.4.71; 1364, *G-AIKM*, 31.10.46, Short Bros and Harland Ltd; 1369, *CF-FEQ*, 7.1.47, A. V. Roe Canada Ltd: 1375, *G-AIYK*, 24.1.47, Hunting Air Travel Ltd; 1376, *G-AIXE*, 17.3.47, Sivewright Airways Ltd; 1377, *VT-CLI*, 22.5.47, Indian Air Survey and Transport Ltd: 1383, *VT-CKA*, Bharat Airways, not taken up; 1384, *VT-CJZ*, 18.4.47, Bharat Airways Ltd; 1423–24, *G-AKDU* and *'DV*, 25.9.47, Sec of State for the Colonies, Southern Rhodesia, 1507, *LV-FBR*, test flown as *G-11-50*, for Argentina

**Anson T. Mk.20:** Sixty aircraft built at Yeadon and comprising prototype *VM305* and nine other aircraft *VM410–VM418* diverted from C. Mk.19 Series 2 production; 48 aircraft to Contract No. 811—*VS491–VS534, VS558–VS561*; and two aircraft to Contract No.1396—*VV866, VV867*. Civil conversions: *VM305/G-APTL; VS512/G-ANWW; VS514/ G-APCF; VS519/G-APCG; VS558/G-APCH; VS559/G-APCI; VS561/ G-APCJ;VV866/G-APCK*

**Anson T. Mk.21:** 252 aircraft built at Yeadon and comprising 30 to Contract No.1396—*VS562–VS591;* and 222 aircraft to Contract Nos.1019, 2473, 3634 and 5343—*VV239–VV264, VV293–VV333, VV880–VV919, VV950–VV999, WB446–WB465, WD402–WD418, WD437–WD458★, WJ509–WJ519, WJ545–WJ561*. Civil conversions: *VV297/G-AVEV; VV958/G-AWMG; WD413/G-BFIR*

*★Contract for 22 aircraft cancelled 13.7.50.

Production Anson T. Mk.21 *VV313*. (*Avro*)

**Anson T. Mk.22:** Fifty-four aircraft built at Yeadon comprising prototype *VM306* and 53 under Contract Nos.1019 and 3634—*VS592–VS603, VV358–VV370, VV371–VV381\*, VW100–VW114\*, WD419–WD422, WD433–WD436*

\*Contract for 26 aircraft cancelled.

*Service Use:* (unit codes used up to 1950 in parentheses)

Anson C. Mk.11, 12, 19 and later 21, with a small number of C. Mk.20 and 22, were used widely for communications and almost every RAF Station Flight had at least one. The more important users were No.31 Squadron (CB) (later the Metropolitan Communications Squadron); No.58 (OT); No.81 (photographic reconnaissance); and Nos.173 and 527 Squadrons

Communications Flights: Bomber Command (4Z), Coastal Command, Fighter Command, Flying Training Command (FKN), Reserve Training Command (RCA), Technical Training Command (TWY), Central Flying School (FDI), Central Bomber Establishment (XE), Empire Flying School (FCV), Empire Air Armament School (FGC), Central Fighter Establishment, Transport Command, Maintenance Command, Northern Ireland (QU), Fighter Weapons School, RAF Technical College, School of Land/Air Warfare, Radio Warfare Establishment (V7), No.1689 Flight (9X), Middle East Communications Squadron, Aden Communications Flight, Far East Communication Squadron, Air Electronic School and the following Group Communications Flights—Nos.1 (3V), 3 (3S), 11, 12 (WQ), 13, 18 (2V), 19 (G2), 21 (FKO), 22, 23 (FKP), 24, 27 (TSO), 38, 43 (1B), 61 (RCE), 62 (RCF), 63 (RCG), 64 (RCH), 66 (RCI), 84 (EP)

Anson T. Mk.20: Used mainly by No.3 Air Navigation School, Thornhill, Southern Rhodesia, (coded Z) but a few remained in the UK.

Anson T. Mk.21: Nos.1 (RCM), 3 (RCK), 5 (RCY), 7 (RCP), 8 (RCQ), 9 (RCZ), 10 (RSB), 11 (RCR). 12 (RCB), 14 (RCL), 15 (RCD), 16 (RCS), 17 (RCJ), 18 (RCT), 22 (RCU), 23 (RSA), 24 (RCV), 25 (RCW) and 48 Reserve Flying Schools; Nos.1 (FFI, FFJ) and 2 (FFP) Air Navigation Schools; Nos.1 and 2 (N) Basic Air Navigation Schools; No.19 FTS (FAG) (later the RAF College); School of Flying Control (FDY)

Anson T. Mk.22: Nos.1 (TCR) and 4 (TMA, TSM) Radio Schools; No.1 Air Signallers School; the Air Electronic School

346

The Parnall Parasol *K1229* with the Avro 661 wing. (*Crown Copyright Reserved*)

# Avro 661

Two Parasol monoplanes *K1228* and *K1229* (one 200 hp Armstrong Siddeley Lynx IV), were designed and built by George Parnall and Co at Yate, Glos, and delivered to Farnborough on August 20 and October 15, 1930, respectively for full-scale tests on wing sections by the Aerodynamics Dept of the RAE. Parnalls also supplied a series of 42 ft span wings, all of rectangular planform and aspect ratio 6, but of varying section, which could be mounted on a 'floating' rig of steel struts to enable lift and drag to be measured with a dynamometer.

In 1934 it was decided to test the new Zap split flaps, the hinges of which moved along rails as the flap was lowered. A wing of RAF 28 section equipped with this flap system and ordered from A. V. Roe and Co to Air Ministry Specification 15/34 under type number Avro 661, was built to designs supplied by the Zap Development Corporation, and *K1229* was sent to Woodford for it to be fitted. Apart from a gap in the centre, the flap extended over the whole span, and 'park bench' ailerons were mounted above it.

*K1229* was weighed at Woodford on completion on December 1, 1934, and returned to Farnborough on January 28, 1935, in company with Cierva C.30A (Avro 671) *K4775*. Tests ran from February 22 to August 14 when the Avro wing was replaced by the standard Göttingen 387 test wing. The aircraft did not fly again after F/O A. E. Clouston forced landed at Sutton Green on March 31, 1936.

Span 32 ft 0 in Length 28 ft 0 in Wing area 294 sq ft All-up weight (Avro 661 wing) 3,070 lb

# Avro 671 (Cierva C.30A)

Early in 1934 A. V. Roe and Co acquired a licence to build the Cierva C.30A two-seat Autogiro (140 hp Armstrong Siddeley Genet Major IA), including the whole rotor system, at Manchester. Developed from the C.19 Mk.V via the C.30 *G-ACFI* (erected at Hanworth by National Flying Services from a C.19 fuselage), the C.30P prototype *G-ACKA* (built entirely by Airwork, Heston) and three pre-production C.30Ps *G-ACIM-'IO* (built by Avro at Manchester), the C.30A featured a wide-track knuckled undercarriage, folding rotor blades and reverse aerofoil section on the port tailplane to counteract rotor torque.

One of the first orders for the type, placed by the Air Ministry on February 14, 1934, was for ten (later twelve) for investigation into its Army Co-operation potential. Airframe and engine Service names were Rota I and Civet I respectively. Deliveries took place between August 24, 1934, and May 23, 1935—production being to Specification 16/35, written around the aircraft in 1935 at the time that it was belatedly given the type number Avro 671.

Production of the C.30A also went ahead in France where 25 were built by Loiré et Olivier as the LeO C.301 with 175 hp Salmson 9NE; and in Germany where Focke-Wulf built 40 with Siemens engines.

*K4230*, the first Rota, was issued to the Directorate of Technical Development in 1934. It went to Martlesham for trials on February 5, 1935, and subsequently had external flotation bags for deck landing trials on HMS *Furious* on September 9, and later still on *Courageous*. *K4296*, first of the two additional Rota Is, was fitted with Short metal floats and flew for the first time from the Medway at Rochester piloted by A. H. Marsh on April 15, 1935. Unlike any other of the type, *K4296* was equipped with a rudder to assist the tilting rotor head during turns with heavy float undercarriage. It was ferried to the Marine Aircraft Experimental Establishment, Felixstowe, by the same pilot in the following month.

Civil and export production of the Avro-built C.30A amounted to 66 aircraft, distribution being via the Cierva base at Hanworth. The first, *G-ACUI*, delivered to Hanworth in July 1934 was sold to the Marquis of Dufferin and Ava at Heston in 1935 and a total of 37 were of British registry. Others were sold to the Hon Mrs Victor Bruce, Hanworth (*'VX*); Austin Dobson MP, Woodford (*'WN*); and The Earl of Essex (*'YE*). Instructional machines included *G-ACUT* of Airwork which performed with C. W. A. Scott's Flying Display in 1936 and the antics of another *'YH* were a popular feature of National Aviation Day Displays in 1935–36. In 1938 the latter was used for banner towing by Aerial Sites Ltd. In the course of time the type fell from favour with private owners and at least 16 British registered examples were sold in Australia, France, Germany, Italy, the Netherlands, Poland and Switzerland, so that by 1939 the Autogiro Flying Club, Hanworth, alone remained a major operator with a fleet consisting of *G-ACUI*, *'WM*, *'WO*, *'WP*, *'WR* and *'WS*.

Among the export orders were two sold in China through the Far East Aviation Co, Hong Kong; three for India comprising *VT-AFF* for Prince Ghanshyam Singh Ji and two for Tata Air Lines; *LY-LAS* for the Lietuvos Aero Klubos, Lithuania; one for Glavinprom, Moscow; and *VH-USR* for A. T. Modingly in Australia.

An important line of research into direct take-off, without forward run, begun at Hanworth in 1933, culminated in the perfection of Cierva's Autodynamic rotor head which allowed the rotor to speed up beyond take-off revolutions with the blades at zero incidence. By suddenly applying positive pitch, sufficient excess lift was created for the machine to leap some 20 ft into the air. This device, together with long-travel undercarriage and rudder, was fitted to Avro built C.30A *G-ACWF*, demonstrated on Hounslow Heath by A. H. Marsh on July 23, 1936.

The Avro-built Cierva C.30P *G-ACIN* showing the pre-production undercarriage design.

The float-equipped Avro 671 Rota I *K4296*.

Most C.30As surviving in the United Kingdom in 1939 were stored at Hanworth and Hamble until impressed in small batches for radar calibration duties. This involved orbiting a marker in a pre-arranged position at sea at minimum speed and was a risky commitment necessitating fighter escort,. While stationed at Duxford with the autogiro section of No.74 (Signals) wing under Sq Ldr R.A.C. Brie, they calibrated every coastal radar station from Orkney to the Isle of Wight. Early in 1941 the unit rebuilt six C.30As (*DR622–DR624* and *HM580–HM581*) from dismantled airframes, bringing the total of C.30As on war service to 17, including four of the original Rotas, *K4232*, *'33*, *'35* and *'39*. In February 1942 they reformed as No.1448 Flight, Halton, under Sq Ldr A. D. Marsh, were renamed No.529 Squadron in June 1943, and moved to Henley-on-Thames in August 1944.

During 1945 the twelve survivors, which included three old Rota Is, were sold for civil use by No.5 MU, Kemble, and the majority were later overhauled at Eastleigh by the Cierva Autogiro Co Ltd. Two went to Southern Aircraft (Gatwick) Ltd who then built one serviceable machine for AB Helikopterflyg, Stockholm, and three (*G-ACXW*, *G-AHMI* and *'MJ*) were commissioned by the Fairey Aviation Co in 1946 as a means of pilots gaining rotary wing experience during the development of their Gyrodyne helicopter.

The last serviceable examples were *G-AHTZ* of Rota Towels Ltd and G. S. Baker's *G-ACUU*, both of Elmdon, Birmingham. The former civilianised at Gravesend by Essex Aero Ltd in 1946, was burned out on March 4, 1958, but *'UU*, withdrawn from use in April 1960, was still extant at Duxford in 1990. Others similarly preserved include Rota Is *K4232* at the RAF Museum, Hendon, and *K4234/G-AHMJ* by the Shuttleworth Trust, Old Warden; *AP507* (the one-time *G-ACWP*) at the Science

Museum, London; *G-ACXA* originally sold in Italy in August 1935, subsequently used by the Regia Aeronautica as *MM30030* during the war, and now exhibited at the National Museum of Science and Technology, Milan, as *I-CIER*; *SE-AEA* exported to Sweden in September 1934 and originally equipped with skis is suspended from the roof of the Technical Museum, Stockholm; *SE-AFI* is displayed at Schiphol Airport, Amsterdam, *LV-FBL* in Buenos Aires and *VH-USR* at Bankstown, NSW.

## SPECIFICATION AND DATA

*Manufacturers:*   A. V. Roe and Co Ltd, Newton Heath, Manchester
Loiré et Olivier in France
Focke-Wulf in Germany

*Designer:*   The Cierva Autogiro Co Ltd, Bush House, Aldwych, London
WC2

*Powerplant:*   One 140 hp Armstrong Siddeley Genet Major IA

*Dimensions:*   Rotor diameter 37 ft 0 in    Length 19 ft 8½ in
Height 11 ft 1 in

*Weights:*   Tare weight 1,220 lb    All-up weight 1,900 lb

*Performance:*   Maximum speed 110 mph    Cruising speed 95 mph
Rotor speed 200–240 rpm    Take-off run 12 yd
Initial climb 700 ft/min    Range 285 miles
Service ceiling 6,600 ft

*Production:*
(a) **Avro 671 Rota I**
Ten (later 12), ordered by the Air Ministry 14.2.34, delivered between 24.8.34 and 23.5.35 to Specification 16/35: *K4230–K4239* and *K4296* (delivered Rochester–Felixstowe on floats 15.4.35) and *K4775*.

(b) **Civil and export C.30As**

| Constructor's Numbers | Aircraft markings |
|---|---|
| 705–717 | *G-ACUI,'VC,'VX*/*PH-ASA*,*G-ACWF,'WG*/*F-AOHY*,*G-ACWH,'WI*/*F-AOIO*, *G-ACWJ*/*PH-HHH*, *G-ACWK*/*D-EKOM*, *G-ACWL*/*D-EKOP*, *G-ACWM–'WO* |
| 725, 726, 728 | *G-ACUT,'UU,'WP* |
| 731–745 | *G-ACWR,'WS*/*G-AHUC*/*SE-AZA,'WT*/*F-AOLK*, China (1), *LN-BAD*/*SE-AFI*, *G-ACWU*/*HB-MAB*, *G-ACXW*, *PP-TAF*, *OK-ATS*, *SE-AEA. VT-AFF*, *'FS,G-ACXG*/*PH-ARA,G-ACXV,'YP*/*SP-ANN* |
| 748–750 | *VT-AFQ, G-ADKY*, Danish Army *M.1*/*SE-AKW* |
| 752–757 | *G-ACWZ,'XA*/*I-CIER*/*MM.30030*,*G-ACXB*,'*XC,EA-SCA,'CB* |
| 760, 771, 772 | *G-ACXR,'YH,'XP*/*VH-USQ* |
| 775–777 | *G-ACYE, YC*/*F-AOHZ,LY-LAS* |
| 779–782 | Russia (1), *G-ADCK*/*VH-UUQ*, Spanish *41–2, 41–3* |
| 791, 792, 798 | *G-ACZV, VH-USR, G-ADBJ* |
| 800–804 | French Air Ministry (5) |
| 808, 815 | China (1), *OE-TAX* |
| 818, 985 | Belgian Air Force (1), Danish Army *M.2* |
| 1029–1032 | Yugoslav Air Force Nos.*1* and 2, Argentina (2) |

351

Egyptian Army Air Force Avro 674 *K509*. (*Courtesy J. A. Bagley*)

# Avro 674

To assist in the RAF Expansion Programme 1935–37, A. V. Roe and Co built 287 Hawker Audax army co-operation biplanes (Rolls-Royce Kestrel engines) to Air Ministry Specification 34/34. These were standard aircraft and did not receive an Avro type number. Later, as the result of an Anglo-Egyptian Treaty signed in 1936 which gave the Egyptian Army Air Force and the RAF joint responsibility for the air defence of Egypt, the Sudan and the Canal Zone, the Egyptian Government ordered six modernised Audaxes powered by 750 hp Armstrong Siddeley Panther VIA radials. Construction of these special aircraft was also entrusted to A. V. Roe and Co which, in view of the amount of redesign, allotted its own type number Avro 674. Delivery in March 1937 was followed by a second contract for 18 (Panther X), completed between February and May 1938.

## SPECIFICATION AND DATA

*Manufacturers:*    A. V. Roe and Co Ltd, Newton Heath, Manchester

*Designers:*    Hawker Aircraft Ltd., Canbury Park Road, Kingston-on-Thames, Surrey

*Powerplant:*    One 750 hp Armstrong Siddeley Panther VIA or X

*Dimensions:*    Span 37 ft 3 in    Height 10 ft 5 in
Wing area 348 sq ft

*Production:*    *K400–K405*, c/n 943–948, delivered 3.37 to Avro Works Order 17523; *K501–K518*, c/n 1035–1052, delivered 2.38–5.38 to Avro Works Order 19177

Avro 679 Manchester IA *L7515* of No.207 Squadron.

# Avro 679 Manchester

Second Avro type to bear the name Manchester, the Avro 679 was designed in 1937 to Specification P.13/36, in which the Air Ministry outlined its requirements for a new generation of twin-engined medium bombers. Of the several tenders received, only the Avro 679 and Handley Page H.P.56 were selected for construction and contracts were placed for two prototypes of each. Powerplants in each case were the new and untried Rolls-Royce Vulture 24-cylinder, X-type water-cooled engines. Nominally of 1,760 hp, but developing 1,845 hp in low supercharger gear at 5,000 ft, these were the largest engines produced by Rolls-Royce and consisted of two Peregrine engines (ultimate development of the famous Kestrel), mounted on a common crankcase and developing almost double the power of the Merlin. As sufficient Vulture engines were not ready in time, the H.P.56 was abandoned in 1937 in favour of a four Merlin version later built in quantity as the H.P.57 Halifax. This left the Manchester as the successful tender to the Specification and in 1938 a large production programme was initiated at Manchester.

Manned by a crew of seven, the Manchester was an advanced aeroplane weighing more than 20 tons and capable of carrying heavy bomb loads at high speed. It was a mid-wing, all-metal, cantilever monoplane with two-spar, flush riveted wing and semi-monocoque fuselage of flattened circular section. The flight crew was grouped in a forward cabin under a transparent canopy fitted with bullet-proof glass panels, warmed by air ducted from a small coolant radiator in the wing. The captain and fire controller sat on the port side, the navigator farther aft at a chart table to starboard, and the radio operator in the rear near the astrodome. Armament on production aircraft consisted of eight ·303 Browning guns in Nash and Thompson hydraulically-driven nose, tail and dorsal turrets, while the bottom of the centre fuselage was one vast bomb bay closed by hydraulically-operated doors. The powerful hydraulic system (an entirely novel feature in those days) also retracted the large Dowty undercarriage and operated split trailing-edge flaps, radiator and air intake shutters. Bomb loads varied inversely with the range, the maximum for each being five tons (11,200 lb) and 2,000 miles respectively.

Avro chief test pilot H. A. Brown captained the unarmed prototype *L7246* on its maiden flight at Ringway on July 25, 1939, but after tests at Boscombe Down a shark-style central fin was fitted to the twin ruddered tail. Much of the prototype's life was spent at the RAE, Farnborough, in perfecting a catapult launching and arrested landing technique which was specially designed for the Manchester but, in the end, never used.

A second prototype, *L7247*, flown at Ringway on May 26, 1940, was armed with six ·303 guns in Fraser Nash nose, tail and ventral turrets. The last was quickly replaced by an F.N.7 Botha-type dorsal turret, cut down in height to reduce drag, and the crude central fin was soon replaced by a more rounded wide-chord unit. At the same time, metal-covered ailerons and elevators were replaced on both prototypes by fabric-covered components, *L7247* also having experimental servo elevator balance tabs and new wingtips which increased the span by 9 ft 11 in to 90 ft 1 in.

Production of the Manchester I to Specification 19/37 began in July 1939 with a contract for 200, deliveries commencing with *L7276* on August 5, 1940. Construction also began at the new Metropolitan-Vickers works at Trafford Park, Manchester, but on December 23, 1940, the first Metro-Vick machine, together with twelve others on the production line and valuable tool and jigs, were destroyed by German bombing.

*L7246*, first prototype Manchester with original twin ruddered tail unit. (*Crown Copyright Reserved*)

*L7247*, second prototype Manchester with early form of central fin. (*Crown Copyright Reserved*)

The Service career of the Manchester began in November 1940 with No.207 Squadron, Waddington, Lincs, where the station CO, the late Air Marshal Sir John Boothman, quickly discovered that rotation of the dorsal turret in flight disturbed the airflow and set up destructive vibration in the central fin. Nevertheless the Manchester was a fine aircraft with handling qualities which drew unstinted praise from pilots. Its first operational flight to Brest on the night of February 24–25, 1941, was followed by participation in the 1,000 bomber raid on Cologne and regular operations over Germany which culminated in the award of a Victoria Cross to F/Lt L. T. Manser, captain of *L7301* of No.50 Squadron, for his part in a raid on May 30, 1942.

Similar in layout to the Vulture, the 2,100 hp Napier Sabre was suggested as an alternative powerplant for a projected Manchester II but although one airframe was delivered to D. Napier and Son Ltd at Luton, the scheme was dropped before the engines were installed. With wings removed the aircraft then became a Sabre engine test stand. Another version of the Manchester II with two 2,520 hp Bristol Centaurus radials actually had the engines installed, but was not flown due to preoccupation with the more attractive Manchester III. This was a standard Manchester fitted by agreement with the Air Ministry with a redesigned centre section carrying two 1,145 hp Rolls-Royce Merlins Xs, and new outer wing sections mounting two further Merlins. Serialled *BT308*, this aeroplane became the first prototype Avro 683 Lancaster, but during trials at Boscombe Down and in the light of operational experience by No.207 Squadron, was fitted with a 33 ft span tailplane with enlarged twin fins. The new tail proved superior to the old triple fin arrangement and was fitted retrospectively to all Manchester Is which then became Manchester IAs, cleared for take-off at an increased weight of 56,000 lb and armed with two nose, two dorsal and four tail guns. Integral fuel tanks, unsatisfactory in combat, were also replaced by the self-sealing variety.

Recurrent failure of the insufficiently developed Vulture engine unfortunately brought the career of this promising aeroplane to a premature end. Absolute priority given to Merlin production made it impossible for the manufacturers to divert any of their resources to eliminating Vulture teething troubles (such as the fatigue failure of connecting-rod bolts) and production was discontinued. Manchester deliveries therefore ceased when

355

Avro had built 156 and Metropolitan-Vickers 44, their last Bomber Command operation being a raid on Bremen during the night of June 25–26, 1942.

## SPECIFICATION AND DATA

*Manufacturers:*  A. V. Roe and Co Ltd, Newton Heath, Manchester; and Woodford Aerodrome, Cheshire
Metropolitan-Vickers Ltd, Trafford Park, Manchester

*Powerplants:*  (Manchester I and IA) Two 1,760 hp Rolls-Royce Vulture I
(Manchester II)  Two 2,100 hp Napier Sabre I
Two 2,520 hp Bristol Centaurus
(Manchester III)  Four 1,145 hp Rolls-Royce Merlin X

*Dimensions, Weights and Performances:*

|  | Prototypes | Manchester I | Manchester IA |
|---|---|---|---|
| Span | 80 ft 2 in | 90 ft 1 in | 90 ft 1 in |
| Length | 68 ft 4 in | 68 ft 10 in | 68 ft 10 in |
| Height | 19 ft 6 in | 19 ft 6 in | 19 ft 6 in |
| Wing area | 1,057½ sq ft | 1,131 sq ft | 1,131 sq ft |
| Tare weight | 25,959 lb | — | — |
| All-up weight | 45,000 lb | 50,000 lb | 56,000 lb |
| Cruising speed | 294 mph | — | — |
| Ceiling | — | 19,200 ft | — |
| Range | — | 1,630 miles* | — |

*Maximum range, bomb load 8,100 lb   With maximum load of 10,350 lb, range 1,200 miles.

*Production:*

**Prototypes:** Two aircraft ordered 8.9.36 to Air Ministry Specification P.13/36 under Contract No.624973/37 and built to Works Order 5667: *L7246*, first flown at Ringway 25.7.39; *L7247*, first flown at Ringway 26.5.40.
**Built by A. V. Roe and Co Ltd to Works Order No. 5723:** Order placed 12.37 to Air Ministry Specification 19/37 under Contract No. B648770/37. Delivered from 31.7.40 as Manchester I and from *L7420* as IA, production terminated at 156 aircraft. *L7276–L7325, L7373–L7402, L7415–L7434, L7453–L7497, L7515–L7526.* (*L7517* damaged by fire 19.11.41 and deleted from Contract) *L7285, L7289, L7293* and *L7297*, diverted to Contract No.B10962/39 for armament development, were returned to the original Contract and completed and delivered as standard Manchester Is.
**Built by Metropolitan-Vickers Ltd to Works Order No.8060:** Order placed 1939 to Air Ministry Specification 19/37 for 100 Manchester Is under Contract No.B108750/40. Delivered to A. V. Roe and Co Ltd for assembly and test from 10.3.41, but production terminated at 44 aircraft. *R5768–R5797, R5829–R5841.* (*R5768–R5780* were destroyed on the production line by enemy bombing 23.12.40, and new machines were given the same serials at the end of the Contract, *R5768–R5776* assembled at Woodford and the remainder at Ringway.)

**Cancelled Orders:** (Fairey Aviation) *R4525–R4554, R4572–R4611, R4630–R4649, R4670–R4694, R4710–R4744*; (Armstrong-Whitworth) *R5273–R5320, R5339–R5380, R5397–R5426, R5448–R5477*

**Conversions to Manchester Mk.IA by A. V. Roe and Co Ltd:** *L7276, '77, '79–'94, '96–'99, L7301, '05, '08, L7385, '86, '89–'91, '94–'98, L7417, '18*

**By Rollaston Aviation Ltd and Tollertons Ltd:** *L7399–L7402, '15, '16*

**Trials aircraft:** A. V. Roe and Co Ltd *L7280* (F. N. Turret), *L7281* (trial modifications), *'87, L7305, '20, '97*; A and AEE, Boscombe Down *L7276, '77. '81. L7320, R5830; AFDU*, Wittering *L7303*; AFEE *L7392*; RAE, Farnborough *L7279, '85, L7400*; Rolls-Royce Ltd, Hucknall *L7293, '95* for flame damper tests (burned out 26.5.41), *'97*; TDU, Gosport *L7276, '92, R5773, '74*

*Service Use*: (with squadron codes in parentheses and giving representative serial numbers).

Bomber Command Squadrons. No.9: *L7386, L7425, R5784, R5838*. No.44: *L7382, L7430, R5790*. No.49 (EA): *L7281, L7387, L7420, L7524, R5771, R5836*. No.50 (VN): *L7289, L7301, L7415, L7516, R5778, R5833*. No.57: *L7460, R5796*. No.61 (QR): *L7276, L7307, L7426, L7518, R5787, R5832*. No.83 (OL): *L7285, L7385, L7418, L7522, R5768, R5830*. No.97 (OF): *L7282, L7306, L7421, R5783*. No.106 (ZN): *L7390, L7417, L7515, R5770, R5839*. No.207 (EM): *L7278, L7300, L7419, L7523, R5782*. No.408: *L7401, R5835*. No.420: *L7402, R5769*. Training Units: No.25 OTU; Nos.1654, 1656, 1660, and 1661 HCU; No.1485B and GS.

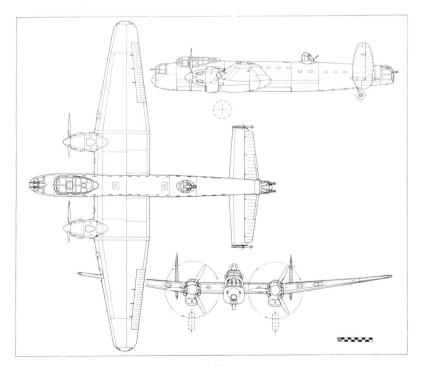

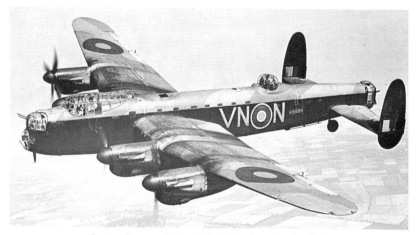

Avro 683 Lancaster I *R5689* of No.50 Squadron. (*The Aeroplane*)

# Avro 683 Lancaster

In a letter to A. V. Roe and Co in December 1945 Air Chief Marshal Sir Arthur Harris, chief of Bomber Command, declared that the Lancaster was the greatest single factor in winning the Second World War. This undoubted truth, based on the fact that the Lancaster delivered 608,612 tons (or two thirds of the total bomb load dropped after the beginning of 1942), was the more remarkable when it is remembered that the aircraft came into existence almost fortuitously as a direct result of the failure of the twin-engined Manchester. Arising from the urgent need to replace the Vulture engines, one standard Manchester airframe, complete with central fin and 22 ft span tailplane (but without dorsal turret), was fitted with four underslung, 1,145 hp Rolls-Royce Merlin X engines. First referred to as the Manchester III, and finally as the Lancaster prototype, it was serialled *BT308*, first flown at Woodford on January 9, 1941, and delivered to the A and AEE, Boscombe Down, for acceptance tests on January 27. Before its major trials, however, the central fin was removed and the aircraft fitted experimentally with large twin oval fins at the ends of a 33 ft span tailplane. A second, or 'productionised' prototype, *DG585*, was flown on May 13, 1941, and thereafter all airframes laid down as Manchesters were completed as Lancasters.

Powered by four 1,280 hp Merlin XXs, the first production Lancaster I, *L7527*, flew for the first time at Woodford on October 31, 1941. It was equipped with de Havilland three-bladed, constant speed, fully-feathering airscrews; internal wing tanks of 2,154 gallons total capacity; nose, tail, dorsal and ventral turrets; and self-inflating dinghy. Entry was via a ladder to a door in the starboard side of the rear fuselage. With 7,000 lb of bombs in its capacious vitals and operating at a maximum loaded weight of 65,000 lb, the Lancaster I had a maximum range of 2,530 miles and a performance so outstanding that production far in excess of the original Manchester contracts was straightaway initiated. Construction on such a scale was made possible by the formation of the Lancaster Group of shadow factories tooled up by Sir W. G. Armstrong Whitworth Aircraft Ltd, Austin Motors Ltd, Metropolitan-Vickers Ltd and Vickers-Armstrong Ltd. To supplement output at Woodford, the parent company opened a second factory at Yeadon, Yorks, where Their Majesties King George VI and Queen Elizabeth named Lancaster Is *R5489* and *R5548 George* and *Elizabeth* respectively on March 26, 1942. By the end of the war the full total of completed Lancasters reached the impressive figure of 7,374 and peak monthly production reached in August 1944 was 293 exclusive of spares.

No.44 (Rhodesia) Squadron, Waddington, which received the Lancaster prototype *BT308* for crew training in September 1941, later became the first Lancaster squadron, the first operational sortie being to lay mines in Heligoland Bight on March 3, 1942. The prototype was then transferred to the RAE, Farnborough, for ballistics experiments and in 1943 was used by the National Gas Turbine Establishment to air test a Metro-Vick F2/1 turbojet mounted in the tail. The second Lancaster squadron, No.97 based at Woodhall Spa, joined with No.44 on April 17, 1942, in sending 12 machines on the first of the Lancaster's innumerable spectacular raids, a low-level daylight attack on the M.A.N. diesel factory at Augsburg in which seven Lancasters were shot down and Sq Ldr J. D. Nettleton was awarded the Victoria Cross. The great daylight raid on the Le Creusot arms factories on October 17, 1942, by Nos. 49 and 57 Squadrons, was also the work of Lancaster Is. They also inaugurated the first of several new and revolutionary bombing techniques when No.83 Squadron and the Pathfinder Force raided Flensburg on the night of August 18–19, 1942.

To ensure continuous Lancaster production in the event of an interruption in Merlin supplies, provision was made for the alternative installation of 1,650 hp Bristol Hercules VI radial engines. *DT810*, the first with Hercules, Avro-built and designated Lancaster II, had a top speed of 270 mph and a large contract was therefore placed with Armstrong Whitworth who delivered the first production Lancaster II, *DS601*, at Sywell in October 1942. It transpired that Merlins remained in plentiful supply and as the Hercules was needed urgently elsewhere, the Lancaster II contract was repeatedly

Lancaster prototype *BT308* with the original Manchester-type tail assembly. (*Crown Copyright Reserved*)

Lancaster II, four Bristol Hercules VI, *DS604* of No.61 Squadron.

cut back until the total built was but 300. They remained in service over Europe with Nos.61, 115, 408, 426, 432 and 514 Squadrons until the autumn of 1944 and also with Nos.1668 and 1678 Heavy Conversion Units.

Apart from minor changes such as the gradual filling in of the 13 small slit windows on each side and the fitting of bulged bomb doors, the Lancaster airframe remained virtually unchanged throughout its life. Thus the Lancaster III with American-built Packard Merlin 28 engines was outwardly identical to the Mk.I and the first Lancaster III, *W4114*, was forerunner of 2,990 examples built to supplement Lancaster I production. They were, in turn, augmented by 430 Lancaster Xs, a version of the Packard Merlin Lancaster III built by Victory Aircraft Ltd at Malton, Canada, and ferried across the Atlantic to be fitted with turrets and issued to the RAF or British-based RCAF units. The first, flown on August 6, 1943 (16 months after the receipt of drawings), made a 9 hr 30 min Atlantic crossing to the UK on September 17.

Without doubt the war's finest Lancaster epics were the breaching of the Möhne and Eder dams on the night of May 16–17, 1943, by 17 Lancaster IIIs of No.617 Squadron, Scampton, led by Wing Cdr Guy Gibson (who won the VC); and the sinking of the German battleship *Tirpitz* in a Norwegian fjord on November 12, 1944, by a combined force of 31 Lancasters of Nos.9 and 617 Squadrons under Wing Cdr J. B. Tait. The celebrated 'Dam Busters' used special low-flying techniques (developed by *ED817* with cutaway belly) and a type of revolving cylindrical skip bomb invented by Dr Barnes N. Wallis, but the *Tirpitz* was sunk by a single 12,000 lb 'Tallboy' bomb which the Lancaster alone could carry. Beginning with the 8,000 lb bombs dropped on Essen on the night of April 10–11, 1942, the vast bomb bay of the Lancaster was progressively adapted to carry bombs of ever increasing size, culminating in the fearsome 22,000 lb 'Grand Slam' used by Sq Ldr C. C. Calder to wreck the Bielefeld Viaduct from a No.617 Squadron Lancaster on March 14, 1945. Aircraft modified to carry a single 8,000 lb, 12,000 lb or 22,000 lb bomb carried no H2S radar and were powered by Merlin 22s or 24s under the designation Lancaster

B. Mk.I (Special).

Development beyond the major Lancaster I/III/X sequence was directed towards increasing the range for operation in the Far East against Japan. Mock-ups of 1,200 gallon saddle tanks, fitted on top of the centre fuselage, were test flown on Lancaster Is *HK541* and *SW244*, but the scheme was dropped in favour of a plan to refuel en route from tanker aircraft equipped with apparatus manufactured by Flight Refuelling Ltd. Designs were also put in hand for extensively redesigned long-range versions with Merlin 68s and 85s to be known as the Lancaster IV and V. These were to be fitted with a Bristol B.17 turret mounting two 20 mm cannon, the trial installation for which was made in Lancaster III *JB456* in May 1944. Orders for 250 aircraft were placed with Vickers-Armstrongs Ltd but all were cancelled at the end of 1944 as by that time the designs had been finalised as the Lincoln I and II. A similar fate befell the Avro 684 and 686 high-altitude Lancaster replacement projects with four Rolls-Royce Merlin engines.

There were various attempts at improving the Lancaster's already impressive fire power, including trials with Mk.I *LL780* and Mk.III *RF268* with 20 mm cannon in dorsal and ventral barbettes remotely controlled from a rear aiming position. Revised armament was not introduced, however, until the Lancaster VII which had two ·50 calibre guns in a Glenn Martin dorsal turret situated farther forward than the Nash and Thompson of the Lancaster III.

Among the Lancaster's last offensive actions in Europe was the tactical bombing of enemy troops in support of the Normandy landings in June 1944, final operational sorties on April 25, 1945, being a daylight attack on Hitler's mountain retreat at Berchtesgaden and a night raid on oil installations at Vallo, Norway. Total wartime sorties amounted to 156,000 at a very low rate of loss. On March 21, 1945, Bomber Command had 56 squadrons of Lancasters, totalling 745 aircraft in front-line service, and when hostilities ended many of these and the 296 machines at OCUs were put to the task of repatriating 75,000 prisoners of war.

Designations Lancaster VIII and IX were never used but a considerable number of aircraft in the *SW* and *TW* series were specially equipped by

Lancaster I *HK541* with 1,200 gallon saddle tank mock-up for the Far East war. (*Avro*)

361

Lancaster VI was the designation applied to a small number of Lancaster Is powered by four Rolls-Royce Merlin 85 or 102 engines in annular cowlings. *DV170* is illustrated. (*Rolls-Royce*)

Armstrong Whitworth as the Lancaster B. Mk.I (F.E.) and repainted with white upper surfaces for service with 'Tiger Force' in Burma. Made redundant by the end of the war in the Far East, many served with the peacetime RAF. Those of No.35 Squadron, Graveley, made a goodwill tour of the USA July 9–August 29, 1946, and a number of others were modified for photographic-reconnaissance under the designation P.R. Mk.I. With turrets removed these formed the equipment of No.82 Squadron which completed the aerial survey of East, Central and West Africa in 1946–52.

A number of Lancasters IIIs were sent to Eastleigh, Southampton, in July 1946 to be modified for air-sea rescue duties as A.S.R. Mk.3s equipped with airborne lifeboats. Some were further modified at a later date for maritime reconnaissance as G.R. Mk.3s (later M.R. Mk.3), initially with Packard Merlin 28 and 38, but when these became obsolete, with Packard Merlin 224. They served with Coastal Command and RCAF Squadrons, including Nos.37 and 38 in Malta whose last M.R. Mk.3, *RF273*, was flown back to England in February 1954. Another of this mark, *RF325*, withdrawn from use at the School of Maritime Reconnaissance, St Mawgan, on October 15, 1956, was the RAF's last Lancaster. In order that this famous type should not be forgotten, Lancaster I *R5868*, veteran of 137 wartime sorties with Nos.83 and 467 Squadrons, was then selected for preservation and mounted at the main gate of RAF Scampton, its former base.

Lancaster Xs which had been flown back from Europe by No.6 Group in June 1944 saw considerable postwar service in Canada with the RCAF in six special variants—the Lancaster 10-B bomber; 10-PR photographic-reconnaissance (ten conversions for No.408 Squadron, Rockliffe, two of which had radio altimeters for a 911,000 square mile survey of Northern Canada); 10-ASR air-sea rescue (twelve conversions 1949); 10-BR bomber reconnaissance (winterised conversions of the last four 10-ASRs plus *FM221* as prototype of the main batch converted in 1949); 10-MR maritime reconnaissance to succeed 10-BR (prototype *KB919* first flown December 29, 1950); 10-N navigation trainer (three converted); and 10-O Avro Orenda engine test-bed (*FM209*). The last three RCAF Lancasters were withdrawn from service on April 1, 1964—23 years after the prototype's first flight.

The three Lancaster 10-Ns, *FM206 Northern Cross*, *FM208 Polaris* and *KB826 Orion* of the RCAF Central Navigation School, made a number of training flights to the UK between March 1954 and June 1957, and in September 1962 the 10-ASR *FM104* again crossed the Atlantic to participate in the Battle of Britain Display at Cottesmore. A number of Lancaster Xs have been preserved in Canada including *KB944* in the Canadian National Aeronautical Collection, Ottawa, and *FM213*, rebuilt to flying condition by the Canadian Warplane Heritage at Hamilton, Ontario, where it made its first post-restoration flight on September 11, 1988. *W4783 George*, veteran of 90 operations over Germany, and flown to Australia in 1944, was later allotted RAAF serial *A66-2* and is preserved in the Australian War Museum at Canberra. *A66-1*, only other Lancaster with RAAF marks, and formerly *ED930 Queenie VI*, was flown out by the same route in the previous year by F/Lt P. S. Isaacson and an Australian crew. It arrived at Sydney on June 4, 1943, and flew nonstop from Melbourne to Ohakea, New Zealand, in 7 hr 39 min on June 11.

Lancaster III *JB456* with two 20 mm Hispano guns in a Bristol B.17 dorsal turret.

Lancaster A.S.R. Mk.III *RF310* with airborne lifeboat, December 1945. (*Crown Copyright Reserved.*)

Lancaster I *A66-1*, one of only two Lancasters to carry RAAF marks.

Lancaster X *KB944* is preserved at Ottawa in near wartime condition. (*K. M. Molson*)

RCAF Lancaster 10-ASR *FM104* on its visit to the United Kingdom in 1962. (*B. N. Stainer*)

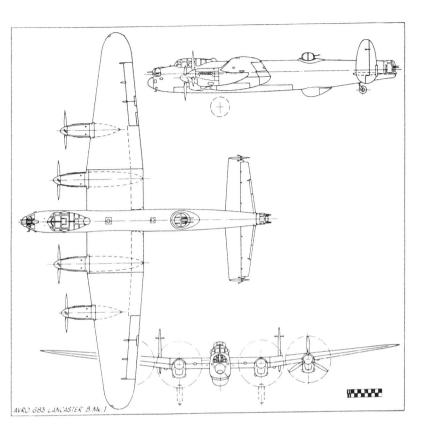

AVRO 683 LANCASTER B.Mk.1

War surplus Lancasters found a ready market among foreign powers and A. V. Roe and Co overhauled fifteen Metro-Vick machines which were flown to Buenos Aires to equip Air Regiment No.1 (Bomber), Argentine Air Force. In March 1952 fifty-four Mks.1 and 7 were also reconditioned at Woodford and Langar, Notts, for the French Aéronavale. Dorsal turrets were removed, ventral ASV radar installed; and long-range tanks, extra rear windows and lifeboat pick-up points were fitted. With Western Union serials commencing *WU01*, they went into French overseas service with Nos.24F (Laun-Bihoue) and 25F Squadrons for maritime reconnaissance from bases in North Africa to assist RAF Coastal Command in protecting Atlantic shipping. Others served with Nos.9S and 10S Squadrons of the 95th Flotille, Tontouta, New Caledonia. Five additional Austin-built Lancaster VIIs supplied in December 1953 for special duties were serialled *FCL.01* to '05.

# SPECIFICATION AND DATA

*Manufacturers:*    A. V. Roe and Co Ltd, Newton Heath, Manchester; and Woodford Aerodrome, Cheshire; and Yeadon Aerodrome, Yorks

Sir W. G. Armstrong Whitworth Aircraft Ltd, Baginton Aerodrome, Coventry and (from 1945) Bitteswell Aerodrome, Warwicks

Austin Motors Ltd, Longbridge Works, Birmingham

Metropolitan-Vickers Ltd, Mosley Road Works, Manchester

Vickers-Armstrong Ltd, Castle Bromwich Aerodrome, Birmingham; and Hawarden Aerodrome, Chester

Victory Aircraft Ltd, Malton, Ontario, Canada

*Powerplants:*    (Prototypes)    Four 1,145 hp Rolls-Royce Merlin X

(Lancaster I)    Four 1,280 hp Rolls-Royce Merlin XX, 22 or 24

(Lancaster B. Mk. I Special)

       Four 1,280 hp Rolls-Royce Merlin 22 or 24

(Lancaster II)    Four 1,650 hp Bristol Hercules VI or XVI

(Lancaster III)    Four 1,300 hp Packard Merlin 28; 1,480 hp Merlin 38; or 1,640 hp Merlin 224

(Lancaster VI)    Four 1,750 hp Rolls-Royce Merlin 85 or 102

(Lancaster VII) Four 1,620 hp Rolls-Royce Merlin 24

(Lancaster X)    Four 1,300 hp Packard Merlin 28; 1,480 hp Merlin 38; or 1,640 hp Merlin 224

*Dimensions:*    Span 102 ft 0 in    Length 69 ft 4 in

Height 20 ft 6 in    Wing area 1,297 sq ft

*Weights:*    (Lancaster I, III and X) Tare weight 36,457 lb

                               All-up weight 50,000 lb★

(Lancaster VII)           All-up weight 68,000 lb

★Range 1,550 miles with 22,000 lb (10 ton) bomb at a take-off weight of 72,000 lb

*Performances:*    (Lancaster I, III and X)

           Maximum speed 287 mph

           Cruising speed 200 mph

           Initial climb 250 ft/min    Ceiling 19,000 ft

           Maximum range 2,530 miles

(Lancaster II)    Maximum speed 270 mph

(Lancaster VII) Maximum speed 275 mph

           Maximum range (for Aéronavale long-range conversions) 3,800 miles

*Production:*

Three Avro-built prototypes *BT308*, *DG585* and *DT810* ordered to Contract No.B135521/40, followed by 7,374 production aircraft as follows: A. V. Roe and Co Ltd 3,670; Sir W. G. Armstrong Whitworth Aircraft Ltd 1,329; Austin Motors Ltd 330; Metropolitan-Vickers Ltd 1,080; Vickers-Armstrong Ltd 535; Victory Aircraft Ltd 430

*(a)* **By A. V. Roe and Co Ltd**

(i) 1,070 aircraft ordered 1940 to Air Ministry Specification under Contract No.B69274/40, and bulit at Manchester to Works Order No.7671: (Lancaster B. Mk.I) *L7527–L7549, L7565–L7584, R5482–R5517, R5537–R5576, R5603–R5640, R5658–R5703, R5724–R5763, W4102–W4140, W4154–W4201, W4230–W4279, W4301–W4340, W4355–W4384, ED303–ED334.* (Lancaster B. Mk.I and III) *ED347–ED396, ED408–ED453, ED467–ED504, ED520–ED569, ED583–ED631, ED645–ED668, ED688–ED737, ED749–ED786.* (Lancaster B. Mk.III) *ED799–ED842, ED856—ED888, ED904–ED953, ED967–ED999, EE105–EE150, EE166–EE202*

(ii) 2,050 Lancaster B. Mks.I and III ordered 1941 to Air Ministry Specification under Contract No1807 and built at Manchester and Yeadon to Works Order No.8545: *JA672–JA718, JA843–JA876, JA892–JA941, JA957–JA981, JB113–JB155, JB174–JB191, JB216–JB243, JB275–JB320, JB344–JB376, JB398–JB424, JB453–JB488, JB526–JB567, JB592–JB614, JB637–JB684, JB699–JB748, ND324–ND368, ND380–ND425, ND438–ND479, ND492–ND538, ND551–ND597, ND613–ND658, ND671–ND715, ND727–ND768, ND781–ND826, ND839–ND882, ND895–ND936, ND948–ND996, NE112–NE151, NE163–NE181, PA964–PA999, PB112–PB158, PB171–PB213, PB226–PB267, PB280–PB308, PB341–PB385, PB397–PB438, PB450–PB490, PB504–PB542, PB554–PB596, PB609–PB653, PB666–PB708, PB721–PB768, PB780–PB823, PB836–PB881, PB893–PB936, PB949–PB998, PD112–PD139, RE115–RE140, RE153–RE188, RE200–RE222, RE225–RE226, SW319–SW345, SW358–SW377, TX263–TX273 (RE115–TX273* built at Yeadon; *PB780–PB936* all B. Mk.I; *PD112–PD139* delivered as B. Mk.I (Special); *PB579* crashed on test flight 11.9.44 and erased from Contract, Avro test pilot S. H. Gleave killed)

(iii) 550 Lancaster B. Mks.I and III ordered 1942 to Air Ministry Specification under Contract No.2010 and built at Yeadon to Works Order No.8589: *LM301–LM346, LM359–LM395, LM417–LM448, LM450–LM493, LM508–LM552, LM569–LM599, LM615–LM658, LM671–LM697, LM713–LM756, ME295–ME337, ME350–ME395, ME417–ME458, ME470–ME503, ME517–ME551*

*(b)* **By Sir W. G. Armstrong Whitworth Aircraft Ltd**

(i) 910 Lancaster B. Mk.I aircraft ordered 1941 to Air Ministry Specification under Contract No.239/SAS/C4(C) and built at Whitley, Coventry 1943; *LL740–LL758, LL771–LL813, LL826–LL867, LL880–LL923, LL935–LL977, LM100–LM142, LM156–LM192, LM205–LM243, LM257–LM296, NF906–NF939, NF952–NF999, NG113–NG149, NG162–NG206, NG218–NG259, NG263–NG308, NG321–NG367, NG379–NG421, NG434–NG469, NG482–NG503, RF120–RF161, RF175–RF197, SW297–SW316, TW647–TW671, TW858–TW873, TW878–TW911*

(ii) 300 Lancaster B. Mk.II aircraft ordered 1941 to Air Ministry Specification under Contract No.239/SAS/C4(C) and built at Whitley, Coventry 1942–43: *DS601–DS635, DS647–DS692, DS704–DS741, DS757–DS797, DS813–DS852, LL617–LL653, LL666–LL704, LL716–LL739*

(iii) 119 Lancaster B. Mk.I and III aircraft ordered 1941 to Air Ministry Specification under Contract No.239/SAS/C4(C) and built at Whitley Coventry 1945: *RF198–RF216, RF229–RF273, RF286–RF326, SW283–SW296*

*(c)* **By Austin Motors Ltd**
(i)   150 Lancaster B. Mk.I aircraft ordered 1942 to Air Ministry Specification under Contract No.2827 and built at Longbridge Works, Birmingham: *NN694–NN726, NN739–NN786, NN798–NN816, NX548–NX589, NX603–NX610*
(ii)  180 Lancaster B. Mk.VII aircraft ordered 1942 to Air Ministry Specification under Contract No.2827 and built at the Longbridge Works, Birmingham: *NX611–NX648, NX661–NX703, NX715–NX758, NX770–NX794, RT670–RT699*

*(d)* **By Metropolitan-Vickers Ltd**
(i)   57 Lancaster B. Mk.I aircraft originally ordered as Manchesters under Contract No.B982866/40, built at the Mosley Road Works, Manchester: *R5842–R5868, R5888–R5917*
(ii)  400 Lancaster B. Mk.I and III aircraft ordered 1940 to Air Ministry Specification under Contract No.B69275/40 and built at the Mosley Road Works: *W4761–W4800, W4815–W4864, W4879–W4905, W4918–W4967, W4980–W5012, DV155–DV202, DV217–DV247, DV263–DV312, DV324–DV345, DV359–DV407*
(iii) 487 Lancaster B. Mk.I aircraft ordered 1941 to Air Ministry Specification under Contract No.2221 and built at the Mosley Road Works: *ME554–ME596, ME613–ME650, ME663–ME704, ME717–ME759, ME773–ME814, ME827–ME868, PD198–PD239, PD252–PD296, PD309–PD349, PD361–PD404, PD417–PD444, SW243–SW279*
(iv)  136 Lancaster B. Mk.I aircraft ordered 1941 to Air Ministry Specification under Contract No.2221 and built at the Mosley Road Works: *RA500–RA547, RA560–RA607, RA623–RA627, RA787–RA806, TW915–TW929*

*(e)* **By Vickers-Armstrong Ltd**
(i)   200 Lancaster B. Mk.I aircraft originally ordered 30.9.41 as B.Mk.IIs, built at Castle Bromwich 1943–44 under Contract No.1336: *HK535–HK579, HK593–HK628, HK644–HK664, HK679–HK710, HK728–HK773, HK787–HK806*
(ii)  200 Lancaster B. Mk.I aircraft ordered 17.7.43 and built at Castle Bromwich under Contract No.1336: (100 built) *PP663–PP695, PP713–PP758, PP772–PP792.* (100 cancelled) *PP793–PP806, PP820–PP866, PP880–PP918*
(iii) 235 Lancaster B. Mk.I aircraft ordered 1943 under Contract No.2791 and built at Chester: *PA158–PA198, PA214–PA239, PA252–PA288, PA303–PA351, PA365–PA396, PA410–PA452, PA473–PA478* and *PA509*
(iv)  100 Lancaster B. Mks.IV and V ordered 17.12.43 and a further 150 ordered 6.44: *SR707–SR749, SR766–SR790, SR814–SR851, SR864–SR907* (Contract cancelled 12.44 and aircraft not built)

*(f)* **By Victory Aircraft Ltd**
430 Lancaster B. Mk.X aircraft ordered 1942 and built at Malton, Ontario, Canada: *KB700–KB999, FM100–FM229*

*(g)* **Reconditioned by A. V. Roe and Co Ltd**
Fifteen Metro-Vick aircraft for the Argentine to Works Order SALES 106: *B–031* to *B–045*, c/n 1450–1464, test flown as *G-11-14* to *G-11-28*, ex *PA375, 376, 377, 350, 348, 349, 344, 369, 346, 365, RA625, 798, 788, 789* and *PA378.* Nine Lancaster B. Mk. III for Egypt 1950 converted at Bracebridge Heath to

Works Order 1054: *1801–1809*, c/n 1510–1518, test flown as *G-11-60* to *G-11-68*, ex *PA476, 441, SW308, TW893, PA435, 391, TW890, SW313* and *TW656*. Five Lancaster B. Mk.VII for France 12.53 to Works Order 1670: *FCL.01* to *FCL.05*, c/n 1521–1525, ex *RT693, NX738, RT689, 673, 679* and *693*, believed test flown as *G-11-69* to *G-11-73*.

*Service Use:*

Lancaster B. Mk.I: Nos.7, 9, 12, 15, 35, 44, 49, 50, 57, 61, 70, 75, 82, 83, 90, 97, 100, 101, 103, 104, 106, 115, 138, 148, 149, 150, 153, 156, 166, 167, (VL), 170, 178, 186, 189, 195, 207, 210, 218, 227, 262, 300, 405, 407, 408, 419, 424, 427, 429, 433, 434, 460, 463, 466, 467, 514, 550, 576, 582, 617, 622, 625, 626, 627, 630, 635 and 683 Squadrons: No.1677 Flight (HM); Bomb Ballistics Unit (OR); Radio Warfare Establishment (V7). Lancaster B.Mk.I (F.E.): Nos.7, 9, 35, 49, 90, 115, 138, 148 (AU), 149, 207, 214 (QN) and 425 Squadrons; No.230 OCU (A3); Central Bombing Establishment (DF); Central Gunnery School (FJS) Empire Air Navigation School (FGE); Empire Flying School (FCX); Radio Warfare Establishment (4S). Lancaster B. Mk.I (Special): Nos.15 and 617 Squadrons, Lancaster B. Mk.II: Nos. 61, 115, 408, 432, 514 and 627 Squadrons: Nos.1651, 1653–1656, 1659–1662, 1665–1668 HCU. Lancaster B. Mk.III: Nos.7, 9, 12, 15, 21, 35, 44, 49, 50, 57, 61, 75, 83, 90, 97, 100, 101, 103, 106, 115, 138, 148, 149, 150, 153, 156, 166, 170, 189, 195, 203, 207, 218, 227, 231, 262, 300, 405, 419, 420, 424, 426, 427, 429, 431, 432, 433, 460, 462, 466, 467, 514, 550, 576, 582, 617, 619, 621 and 622 Squadrons; Bomber Command Instructors' School (WB); Empire Air Armament School (FGA); Empire Flying School (FCX); Nos.1, 3, 5 and 6 LFS Lancaster B. Mk.III (Special): No.405 Squadron. Lancaster ASR Mk. III: Nos.37, 179 (OZ) and 203 Squadrons. Lancaster GR Mk.III: Nos.18, 120 (BS), 170 (TC), 203 (CJ) and 621 Squadrons. Lancaster MR Mk.III: Nos. 37, 38 (RL), 210 (OZ), 224 (XB), 404, 405 and 408 Squadrons; Air-Sea Warfare Development Unit (P9); No.1 School of Maritime Reconnaissance; Nos.6, 111 and 132 OTU (K7); No.236 OCU (K7). Lancaster B. Mk.VI: No.635 Squadron. Lancaster B. Mk.VII: Nos.9, 35, 40, 57, 104 (EP), 214 (QN), 427, 460 and 617 Squadrons. Lancaster B. Mk.VII (F.E.): Central Flying School (FDI); Empire Air Armament School (FGC); Empire Air Navigation School (FGG); Empire Flying School (FCX); Station Flight, Scampton (YF); No.20 MU (QX). Lancaster MR Mk.X: Nos.61, 101, 115, 404, 405, 407, 420, 424, 425, 428, 431 and 434 Squadrons; No.2 MOTU Lancaster PR Mk.X: Nos.408, 413 and 419 Squadrons.

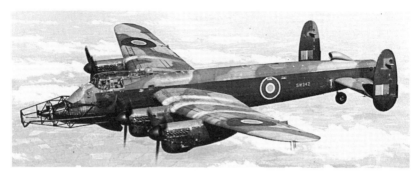

Lancaster III *SW342* with Armstrong Siddeley Mamba propeller-turbine in a nose-mounted icing rig, and Adder turbojet in the tail. (*Armstrong Siddeley*)

# Avro 683 Lancaster (civil and experimental)

With armament removed, the war surplus Lancaster made an ideal test vehicle and was used in some numbers by aircraft and engine manufacturers bent on perfecting new equipment and new engines for postwar civil and military use. The first, *G-AGJI*, was delivered to the BOAC Development Flight at Hurn on January 20, 1944, and with neat fairings replacing front and rear turrets (but initially retaining wartime camouflage), was first used for developing equipment for new postwar transport aircraft. Later the Merlin 22s gave place to Merlin 102s with annular radiators for test under operating conditions before their installation in the new Avro 688 Tudor Is. In this form *G-AGJI* was equivalent to one version of the Lancaster VI.

Four of the six Lancaster Is acquired by the British South American Airways Corporation from the Ministry of Supply in 1946 were converted into freighters by A. V. Roe and Co at Bracebridge Heath, Lincoln, and fitted with elongated noses of the type employed on the Avro 691 Lancastrian, but the tail turrets were merely silvered over. They proved uneconomic in operation and were pensioned off after only a year, their main task having been the transport of perishable goods and South American cotton samples. Airtech Ltd of Thame acquired one of them (*G-AGUM*) for the trial installation of an outsize ventral pannier intended for carrying vehicles or other awkward loads on the Berlin Air Lift. One of BSAA's two unconverted Lancasters went to the BOAC Development Flight in September 1946 as *G-AHVN* to continue the test programmes initiated by *G-AGJI*.

Four Lancaster IIIs released to Flight Refuelling Ltd in August 1946 were converted at Staverton into two pairs of tanker and receiver aircraft with bulk storage tanks and power-driven hose reels. Registered *G-AHJT* to '*JW*', they went to Ford (and later Tarrant Rushton) to assist in perfecting the company's airborne refuelling techniques, earlier developed with Lancaster IIIs *NE147, ND648* and *PP992*. The last two of these were flown

370

after the war under B conditions as *G-33-1* and *2* respectively. The commercial application of this system was demonstrated in co-operation with BSAA on 22 trans-Atlantic flights during the period May–August 1947. Flown by Air Vice-Marshal D. C. T. Bennett, the first service left London on May 28, 1947, refuelling in mid-Atlantic from an Azores-based Lancaster tanker, and completed the 3,355 mile flight to Bermuda nonstop. In 1948 the two tanker aircraft *G-AHJU* and *'JW*, plus *'VN* acquired from BOAC, were flown to Germany for a year's service on the Berlin Air Lift during which they completed 757 sorties.

Seven other Lancasters were allotted British civil marks immediately postwar but with two exceptions were broken up for spares. The first, a camouflaged B. Mk.I (Special), arrived at White Waltham in July 1947 and a month later was flown to Italy as *G-AJWM* under British European Airways ownership as a trainer for Alitalia Lancastrian crews. The other aircraft, Lancaster I *G-AKAB Sky Trainer*, was used for the same purpose by Skyways Ltd at Dunsfold. Much later New Caledonia based French Navy Lancaster VII *WU-15* was acquired by two private individuals in 1964, registered *G-ASXX*, and ferried from Sydney to Biggin Hill April 25–May 13, 1965. Surplus RCAF Lancaster Xs were also used for survey work in Canada by Spartan Air Services of Ottawa as *CF-IMF* and *'MG*,

Lancaster I test bed *G-AGJI* in its original form with Merlin 22 engines.

Lancaster Freighter *G-AGUL Star Watch* of British South American Airways Corporation being loaded at London Airport in 1946. (*The Aeroplane*)

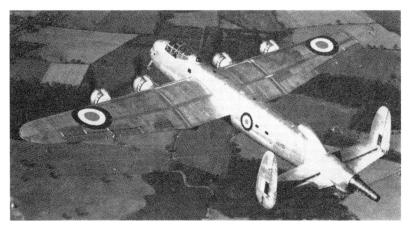

Lancaster II *LL735* flying with Metro-Vick Beryl gas-turbine engine mounted in the tail.
(*Charles E. Brown*)

and the famous *Polaris FM208* was acquired by World Wide Airways Inc of Dorval as *CF-KHH*. Another *CF-TQC*, partially converted to a water bomber after retirement from RCAF service in 1964, and flown occasionally until 1972, was ferried to Scotland to join the Strathallan Collection as *G-BCOH* in May 1975.

In normal civil use the Lancaster was powered by four 1,640 hp Rolls-Royce Merlin T.24 engines as used in the Avro 685 York.

In addition to important contributions to the reshaping of air transport in the years immediately after the Second World War, the Lancaster also served as flying test-bed for final marks of the historic Merlin engine; for the new generation of gas-turbine engines; and for aerodynamic research. Three aircraft employed at Filton for flight testing control systems for the eight-engined Bristol Type 167 Brabazon 1 in 1945–46 were Lancaster I *PP745* (power operated elevators); Lancaster II *DS708* (servo controls); and Lancaster III *RE131* (scaled-down version of the entire Brabazon control system). Lancaster I *PA474*, transferred to the College of Aeronautics, Cranfield, on its retirement from No.82 Squadron in 1954, and used initially as a flying laboratory with aerofoil sections mounted vertically on top of the fuselage, flew at Cranfield on October 2, 1962, with a section of laminar flow wing for the Handley Page H.P. 117 in the test rig. Lancaster III *ME540* was fitted by Boulton Paul Ltd with a gust alleviation device in the nose in 1951–52.

Three other Lancasters played a key role in postwar navigation, signals and armament development. Most famous of these was Lancaster I *PD328* (named *Aries*), delivered to the Empire Air Navigation School, Shawbury, in 1944 for long-range navigation liaison flights. In nine 24 hour working days, Avro's aircraft repair depot at Waddington, Lincs, stripped and polished it, fitted Lancastrian nose and tail sections, a Lincoln undercarriage, and extra fuel tanks in nose and bomb bay. powered by four 1,280 hp Rolls-

Royce Merlin 24s, captained by Wing Cdr D. C. McKinley DFC, and carrying over a ton of the newest navigational aids, it had the distinction of being the first British service aeroplane to circumnavigate the earth when it flew to Auckland, New Zealand, via Montreal and San Francisco and back via Australia, Ceylon, Aden, Cairo and Malta. This 41,454 mile flight was completed on December 14, 1944.

After special Arctic modifications it was flown to Iceland on May 16, 1945, to make a series of research flights over the North Geographic and Magnetic Poles to confirm true positions calculated by the Astronomer Royal, and to help in the development of the Greenwich Grid system of polar navigation. The homeward trip was made by Wing Cdr McKinley nonstop from Whitehorse, Yukon, to Shawbury over the Magnetic Pole on May 25–26.

Piloted by Sq Ldr A. A. Imrie, *Aries* flew 4,076 miles nonstop from Prestwick to Rivers, Manitoba, on June 7 on a liaison visit to the Canadian Central Navigation School; flew to the Mediterranean in September; and in January 1946 Wing Cdr C. M. Dunnicliffe DSO, DFC used it for the first Cairo–Cape Town nonstop flight and reduced the England–Cape record to 32 hr 21 min. A second tour to the Pacific which began at Blackbushe on August 22 that year with Sq Ldr J. E. Aldridge as captain, lasted six weeks and covered much the same route as in 1944. Three FAI point-to-point records were established:

| | | |
|---|---|---|
| London–Karachi | 3,945 miles in 19 hr 14 min |
| London–Darwin | 8,639 miles in 45 hr 35 min |
| London–Wellington | 11,647 miles in 59 hr 50 min |

Her final mission, begun on October 24, 1946, was a three-week, 12,000 mile tour through Canada and the USA, and in February 1947 *Aries* was withdrawn from use after covering 200,000 miles on major flights alone.

*Iris* was a Lancaster I (F.E.) equipped at the Central Signals Establishment, Watton, with the fullest possible range of radio and radar aids (including Rebecca, Babs, Loran, Gee, radio altimeter and compass, SBA, etc) for the calibration and regular checking of radio and radar services in Home and Overseas Commands. In this connection the aircraft made an

Lancaster III *NG465* with Rolls-Royce Dart propeller-turbine engine in nose icing rig. (*Rolls-Royce*)

373

extensive tour of Africa and the Near East in August 1948. *PB875 Thor* fulfilled a similar function at the Empire Air Armament School, Manby, where it was fitted with the newest blind bombing and gunnery devices. Captained by Wing Cdr M. H. de L. Everest, it left on an armament demonstration mission to Australia and New Zealand on March 25, 1946.

Noteworthy on account of Lincoln-type rudders and the absence of ventral radar blister, dorsal and tail turrets, the former No.617 Sqn Lancaster B. Mk.VII *NX739* was maintained by Eagle Aviation at Blackbushe for several years on behalf of the Ministry of Supply as a photographic aircraft for 'shooting' fast new types being test flown at Farnborough. It was dismantled in 1957.

*Civil conversions:*
### (a) In the United Kingdom

*DV379/G-AGJI*, C of A 12.1.44, BOAC Development Flight, broken up at No.39 MU, Colerne 12.47; *PP689/G-AGUJ*, 12.3.46, BSAAC *Star Pilot*, dismantled at Langley 1949; *PP688/G-AGUK*, 30.1.46, BSAAC *Star Gold*, reduced to spares at Langley 1947; *PP690/G-AGUL*, 1.4.46, BSAAC *Star Watch*, crashed at London Airport 23.10.47; *PP751/G-AGUM*, 6.5.46, BSAAC *Star Ward*, to BOAC 9.49, dismantled at Dunsfold 12.49; *PP744/G-AGUN*, civilianised 7.46 as *G-AHVN* for the BOAC Development Flight, to Flight Refuelling Ltd 3.49, scrapped at Tarrant Rushton 1.50; *PP746/G-AGUO*, returned to the RAF before conversion; *LL809/G-AHJT*, 13.5.46, Flight Refuelling Ltd tanker aircraft, scrapped at Tarrant Rushton 1.50 with receiver *LM681/G-AHJU* and receiver *LM639/G-AHJV*; *ED866/G-AHJW*, 13.5.46, Flight Refuelling Ltd tanker, crashed near Andover 22.11.48; *PP741/G-AJWM*, 19.7.48, sold to Alitalia by BEA 30.11.48; *PP739/G-AKAB*, 10.10.47, Skyways Ltd *Sky Trainer*, scrapped at Dunsfold 11.48; *NX611/WU-15/G-ASXX*, registered 10.64 to M. D. N. Fisher and W. R. Snadden, delivered to Biggin Hill 13.5.65, later became the gate guardian at RAF Scampton. On display at the Lincolnshire Aviation Heritage Centre, East Kirkby, in 1990; *KB889/*

374

*G-LANC*, Mk.X, unairworthy, registered 31.1.85 to aircraft collector Douglas Arnold, to the Imperial War Museum, Duxford, for static exhibition 14.5.86

*Note:* *HK557*, *PP743*, *PP742* and *PP734* were obtained by Flight Refuelling Ltd 6.47 and flown to Tarrant Rushton as *G-AKAJ–'AM* to be used as spares. *NX726*, a Lancaster VII which had been allotted marking *G-ALVC*, was reduced to spares for the Yorks of Eagle Aviation Ltd at Luton 1.50

(*b*) **In Canada**

*FM222/CF-IMF*, Mk.10ASR ex No.103 RU, Greenwood, NS, disposed of to Spartan Air Services Ltd 16.3.56, permit for ferrying Camp Borden–Ottawa 19.3.56, restricted C of A 7.6.56, s.o.r. 29.12.59; *KB907/CF-IMG* and *KB909/CF-IMH*, Mk.10ASR ex-Eastern Air Command, to Spartan 16.3.56, ferrying permits Camp Borden–Ottawa 19.3.56 and 26.3.56 respectively, conversion not proceeded with; *FM208/CF-KHH*, Mk.10N ex-Maritime Air Command, Summerside, PEI, to Ajax Aircraft Ltd, Toronto, 28.5.57, to World Wide Airways Inc and equipped for bulk transport of diesel fuel, last reported Dorval 7.60; *KB976/CF-TQC*, Mk.10, retired from RCAF service 1964, to Strathallan Aircraft Collection as *G-BCOH* 1975, sold to Charles Church 1.87, in storage at RAE Thurleigh in 1990.

*Engine test-beds:*

*R5849*  Lancaster I  To Rolls-Royce Ltd, Hucknall; flown with four 1,770 hp Merlin 600 engines in annular cowlings

*BT308*  Prototype  To Rolls-Royce Ltd, Hucknall 28.2.42; flown with Metropolitan-Vickers F.2 axial-flow gas-turbine in the rear fuselage with large air intake above it; s.o.c. at RAE Farnborough 30.5.44

*JB675*  Lancaster III  To Rolls-Royce Ltd, Hucknall; flown with two 1,770 hp Merlin 621 for the Avro Tudor I inboard, and two 1,760 hp Merlin 620 for the Canadair C-4 outboard

*LL735*  Lancaster II  To Metropolitan-Vickers Ltd to replace *BT308*; first flown with F.2/1 gas-turbine in the tail 29.6.43. Flew with 3,500 lb st F.2/4 Beryl in the tail 1945

*ND784*  Lancaster VI  To Power Jets Ltd; equipped for mounting a variety of test engines in the bomb bay and known as the 'Lancaster Universal Test Bed'. Flown at the RAE 4.43 with four Merlin XXs and one 2,600 lb st Armstrong Siddeley ASX in the bomb bay; later with four 1,750 hp Merlin 85s in annular cowlings and one Armstrong Siddeley Mamba in the nose

The Lancaster X Avro Orenda test bed *FM209*.

NG465    Lancaster III    To Rolls-Royce Ltd, Hucknall 8.46; first flown by R. T. Shepherd 10.10.47 with 1,000 hp + 325 lb st Dart test engine No.5 in the nose; two 100 gallon water tanks later installed in the rear fuselage for water droplet artificial icing flight programme; flown 3.49 with Dart No.15; 2.51 with Dart No.3; and 1.53 with Dart No.30; destroyed in forced landing at Holinwell Golf Course, Mansfield 22.1.54

PP791    Lancaster III    To Rolls-Royce Ltd, Hucknall; flown with four 1,770 hp Merlin 600

RE137    Lancaster III    To Armstrong Siddeley Motors Ltd, Baginton, 1947; flown with two 3,670 hp Python propeller-turbines driving eight-bladed contra-rotating airscrews outboard

SW342    Lancaster III    Modified by Air Service Training Ltd, Hamble, 1.49 to take a nose-mounted Armstrong Siddeley Mamba propeller-turbine; delivered to Bitteswell for icing tests. Flown 5.52 with four 1,640 hp Merlin 24s, Mamba driving a cropped airscrew inside the icing rig, and Adder turbojet in the tail for scale after-burning tests, dismantled 8.56

TW911    Lancaster III    To Armstrong Siddeley Motors Ltd; first flown at Bitteswell 3.1.49 with two 1,610 hp Merlin 24s inboard and two 3,670 hp Python I propeller-turbines outboard. A 400 gallon extra fuel tank was fitted in the bomb bay and the wing trailing-edge was extended rearwards as far as the outer nacelles

80001    Lancaster    Equipped as a test-bed for the Royal Swedish Air Force by Air Service Training Ltd, Hamble to Avro Works Order 1080, c/n 1520, and first flown 24.4.51. Fitted in Sweden with one 7,360 lb st Stal Dovern turbojet in a ventral pod; later air tested reheat Ghost for Saab J 29; crashed 8.5.56

FM205    Lancaster X    Converted by A. V. Roe (Canada) Ltd as test-bed for two 3,000 lb st Avro Chinook T.R.4 Mk.II axial-flow engines in the outer nacelles but this engine never flew

FM209    Lancaster X    Converted as above for air testing Avro Orenda axial-flow engines in the outer nacelles

KB848    Lancaster X    RCAF trials with Ryan Firebee missiles mounted under wingtips

Avro 685 York C.1 *G-AGNP Manchester* in its original BOAC blue, gold and polished metal livery. (*BOAC*)

# Avro 685 York

To exploit more fully the Lancaster's long-distance load carrying capability while retaining its fine handling qualities, designer Roy Chadwick conceived the idea of a pure transport version which used the same mainplane, power units, undercarriage and tail assembly. He therefore designed an all-metal, square section fuselage having twice the cubic capacity of the original, and because the project was a private venture, had the prototype (named York) in the air for the first time at Ringway on July 5, 1942—just five months after the drawings were issued to Avro's experimental department.

The agreement between Britain and the USA by which the latter should produce all wartime transport aircraft made it impossible to sanction materials or labour for the York. Nevertheless the successful result of trials with the camouflaged prototype *LV626* at Boscombe Down in August 1942 led to a contract for three further prototypes and a limited number of production York C. Mk.1s to Air Ministry Specification 1/42. Whereas the first prototype, *LV626*, was an unfurnished freighter, the second, *LV629*, completed with full complement of passenger seats, was based at Woodford until broken up there in 1948. The third prototype, *LV633 Ascalon* which had square instead of round windows, was delivered to No.24 Squadron, Northolt, as a flying conference room for Mr (later Sir) Winston Churchill but a reservation for civil registration *G-AGFT*, believed for this aircraft, was not taken up. The fourth York, *LV639*, fitted with dropping doors in the floor and evaluated by the AFEE, Ringway, as a paratroop transport, was found unsuitable due to slipstream wash along the fuselage. *Ascalon*, posted to the Far East Communication Flight at Changi, Singapore, in 1946, was later replaced by *MW295 Ascalon II* which paid an official visit to New Zealand in February 1957.

First and second prototypes had twin fins and rudders as on the Lancaster but subsequent prototypes and all production aircraft (known in the RAF as the York C. Mk.1) had a third central fin to compensate for increased fuselage side area forward of the C.G. A third fin was fitted later to the first prototype *LV626* when it flew as the first—and only—York C. Mk.2 with four 1,650 hp Bristol Hercules VI radials.

Absolute priority given to Lancaster production resulted in the construction of only three Yorks in 1943. This increased to three per month in 1944 but its designer did not live to see it in large-scale production in 1945–48. Most early examples were VIP transports, the first two, *MW100* and *MW101* (also with No.24 Squadron), alone covered more than half a million miles carrying Cabinet Ministers and high ranking officers to wartime conferences at Cairo, Teheran, Yalta and Moscow, as well as on other official business. The Prime Ministerial *Ascalon* carried Churchill and numerous Allied commanders Northolt–Gibraltar–Algiers on May 25, 1943, and was used soon afterwards by King George VI on his tour of Service units in North Africa and the Mediterranean area. On posting, its duties were taken over by *MW100* which, together with *MW104*, was eventually disposed of as spares in 1953. They were then given civil marks *G-ANAA* and *'AB* and flown (*'AA* without the central fin) to Stansted to be broken up as spares. *MW107*, personal transport of Field-Marshal Smuts, transferred to the South African Air Force in 1945 as *4999 Oubaas*, was frequently at Northolt. *MW140 Endeavour* performed a similar function for HRH the Duke of Gloucester 1945–46 during his period of office as Governor-General of Australia. The RAAF serial group *A74*, reserved for Yorks, was never used and *Endeavour* retained its RAF numbering.

Five other early Yorks were combination passenger/freighters 'borrowed' from RAF production and allotted to BOAC as *G-AGJA–'JE*. They seated 12 passengers in the rear of the cabin (with the freight forward) and inaugurated the first UK–Cairo route via Morocco on April 22, 1944.

Production continued at Ringway until October 1945 when the jigs were transferred to the Yeadon factory. Here the last 77 examples were built, *PE108* the final York being completed in April 1948. Production for the RAF (including the five for BOAC) amounted to 208 Yorks comprising five passenger transports, 114 pure freighters and 64 passenger/freighters. The first RAF squadron wholly equipped with Yorks was No.551 at Lyneham in 1945 but by 1948 this and No.24 had been joined by seven others wholly or partially York equipped for service on the world-wide trunk routes of

The first prototype Avro 685 York, *LV626*, as first flown with twin rudders.

*LV626* after the addition of the central fixed fin and conversion to York C. Mk.2 with four Bristol Hercules VI radials. (*Bristol*)

RAF Transport Command. During the Berlin Air Lift these squadrons carried 230,000 tons of supplies in 29,000 sorties.

Included in a batch of 45 Yorks built after the war were a further 25 (*TS789–TS813*) for RAF/BOAC joint services; 12 for British South American Airways (*G-AHEW–'FH*); five 24-passenger machines for Flota Aerea Mercante Argentina (FAMA) for operation between Buenos Aires and London in competition with BSAA; and three 30-passenger machines for Skyways Ltd; bringing total York production to 256. One additional York, *FM400*, built by Victory Aircraft Ltd at Malton, Canada, for the RAF in 1945, differed from British-built Yorks because the cabin floor did not slope when the aircraft was airborne in the cruise and as a result the cabin windows were all the same level.

In 1946 the joint services were handed over to BOAC and after overhaul at Croydon and Hamble, the Yorks were painted in BOAC livery as *G-AGNL–'OF* and *'SL–'SP*, with the M Class names given in the data section. Thirteen were fitted as 12-berth sleepers for the UK–Johannesburg 'Springbok' service, five being loaned to South African Airways 1946–47. Seven were also transferred temporarily to BSAA in 1948. Nine of the original BSAA Yorks were taken over when that company was absorbed by BOAC in 1949 but the entire fleet was withdrawn from passenger carrying on October 7, 1950. A few maintained the London–Singapore freight run in modern decor and flew replacement engines to stranded BOAC aircraft. Thirteen years' continuous service during which the York fleet flew 44 million miles and carried 90,000 passengers, ended on November 22, 1957, when the last two BOAC Yorks *G-AGJC Malmesbury* and *'SO Marston* were flown to Stansted for delivery to Skyways.

They joined a considerable number of secondhand and RAF surplus Yorks including the Canadian-built *FM400* (acquired by Skyways in June 1948 as *G-ALBX Sky Dominion*) on long-distance War Office trooping contracts under the ownership of the Lancashire Aircraft Corporation Ltd, Eagle Aviation Ltd, Skyways Ltd, Surrey Flying Services Ltd, Air Charter Ltd, and Scottish Airlines (Prestwick) Ltd. As the Anglo-Egyptian Treaty of 1936 allowed only military aircraft to land in the Canal Zone, the Yorks were given temporary RAF serials in the *WW-XJ* range. The longest trooping run was the regular London-Fiji service flown fortnightly by Air Charter Ltd whose Yorks covered 24 million passenger-miles on this contract in 12 months.

At the time of the Berlin Air Lift, most surviving civil Yorks were owned by Skyways Ltd, whose original machine *G-AHFI Skyway* completed 147 sorties before crashing at Gatow; *'LV Sky Courier* no fewer than 467 sorties and *G-ALBX* a like number. Many RAF Yorks exceeded these figures and when replaced in 1948 were ferried to Silloth, Aldergrove or Kirkbride for reduction to produce, but three were retained by the Transport Command Development Unit, Benson, until 1956 and about 30 others were disposed of to civil operators. Hunting-Clan Air Transport Ltd and Dan-Air Services Ltd became York operators for the first time, the former opening a UK-Africa York freight service on July 23, 1955. The noise level in the York left much to be desired and by 1963 only three certificated examples remained in the UK and all were retired by October 1964.

The RAF's last operational York, *MW295 Ascalon II*, flew home from the Far East in March 1957 but was sold almost immediately to Trans-Mediterranean Airways as *OD-ACQ* and ferried to Beirut as *G-APCA*. It was one of many which worked out their useful lives on the pilgrim traffic

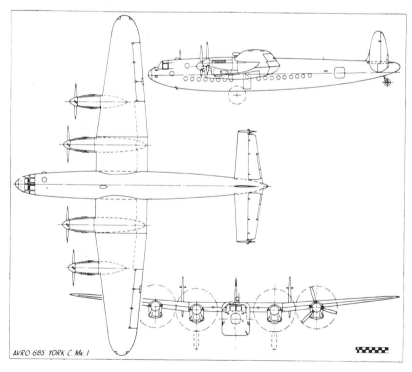

AVRO 685 YORK C. Mk. I

to Mecca or on local airline services in Jordan, Saudi Arabia or Iran. Skyways disposed of three Yorks to Persian Air Services in 1955 for freighting between Beirut and Teheran and the oil centres of Abadan and Kuwait, as well as to Basle, Switzerland, via Brindisi. Others were used by Air Liban and Middle East Airlines, including *OD-ACN*, formerly General Smuts' *Oubaas* which MEA obtained from Tropic Airways Ltd, who had flown it as a 54-seater on the Johannesburg–Amsterdam services as *ZS-DGN* since 1952.

Twelve Yorks completely overhauled by A. V. Roe and Co in 1955 were flown to Canada via Prestwick to airlift men and materials to the DEW Line sites along the Arctic Circle. During the operation they were flown by bush operators but on its completion were sold for airline work with Maritime Central Airways, Arctic Wings Ltd, Trans-Air Ltd, Associated Airways Ltd, and Pacific Western Airlines Ltd. Almost the last Yorks to leave RAF service, *MW137* and *234*, were acquired by the French Aéronavale and based at Le Bourget for general transport duties 1954–55.

## SPECIFICATION AND DATA

*Manufacturers:*   A. V. Roe and Co Ltd, Newton Heath, Manchester; Ringway Aerodrome, Manchester; Woodford Aerodrome, Cheshire; and Yeadon Aerodrome, Yorks
Victory Aircraft Ltd., Malton, Ontario, Canada

*Powerplants:*   (York C. Mk.1) Four 1,620 hp Rolls-Royce Merlin T.24
Four 1,620 hp Rolls-Royce Merlin 502
(York C. Mk.2) Four 1,650 hp Bristol Hercules VI

*Dimensions:*   Span 102 ft 0 in   Length 78 ft 6 in
Height 16 ft 6 in   Wing area 1,205 sq ft

*Weights:*   Tare weight 42,040 lb   All-up weight 68,000 lb

*Performance:*   (York C. Mk.1) Maximum speed 298 mph
Cruising speed 233 mph
Initial climb 1,500 ft/min
Ceiling 26,000 ft   Range 2,700 miles

*Production:*

**Four prototypes built at Manchester under Contract No.2087/C4A**: *LV626*, first flown at Ringway 5.7.42, converted to sole York C. Mk.2, to No.1 ATS 1945 as *5554M*; *LV629* with passenger furnishings to No.4 S. of TT 1948 as *6554M*; *LV633* Churchill's *Ascalon*, Far East Communication Flight 1946, broken up at North Coates Fittes 1954; *LV639* paratroop version, to No.11 S of TT, Hereford, 1947 as *6466M*

**York C. Mk.1 (passenger version)** built at Manchester 1944 to Specification C.1/42 under Contract No.2429/C4A: *MW100–102, 104, 106, 107, 109–112, 114–120, 122–128, 140*. Individual aircraft: *MW112* Rolls Royce Ltd, Hucknall, engine silencing tests; *MW140* Governor-General, Australia,

Civil conversions (1953–57): *MW100/G-ANAA*, *MW104/G-ANAB*, *MW107* (SAAF *4999 Oubaas*)/*ZS-DGN/OD-ACN*; *MW110/G-AMUS* Air Charter *New Britain*, *t/s *XF919*

*Trooping serial.

**Civil Yorks for BOAC**: *MW103, 108, 113, 121, 129* diverted 1944 as *G-AGJA–'JE*, c/n 1207–1211. *G-AGJA Mildenhall*, later BSAA *Star Fortune* and BOAC *Kingston*, t/s *WW541* and *WW508*; *'JB Marathon*, t/s *WW503*; *'JC Malmesbury*, t/s *WW504*; *'JD Mansfield*; *'JE Middlesex*, later BSAA *Star Way* and BOAC *Panama*, t/s *WW580*

**York C. Mk.1 (freight version)** built at Manchester 1944–45 to Specification C.1/42 under Contract No.2429/C4A; *MW105, 130–139, 141–149, 161–168, 170–172, 174–177, 179–185, 187–189, 191, 192, 194, 195, 200, 202, 203, 205, 207, 210, 223, 225, 228, 231, 232, 234, 235, 237–271, 284–290, 293, 294, 297, 299, 302, 305–309*. Civil conversions (1952–56): *MW135/CF-HMV*; *MW136/CF-HMW*; *MW138/G-AMRI* Surrey F/S *New Enterprise/OD-ACD*; *MW139/G-ANAW*; *MW141/G-ANXJ*; *MW143/G-ANTI*; *MW147/CF-HMZ*; *MW149/G-ANTJ*; *MW167/CF-HMX*; *MW177/G-ANTH*; *MW183/G-AMUU* Air Charter *Nouvelle Calédonie*, t/s *XD668*; *MW185/G-AMUT/CF-HTM*; *MW203/CF-HMU*; *MW210/G-ANYA*; *MW231/G-ANGL/EP-ADA*; *MW232/G-ANTK*; *MW237/CF-HMY*; *MW253/G-ANVO*, t/s *XJ264*; *MW254/G-ANGF/OD-ADL*; *MW258/G-ANXN* Aviation Traders *New Charter*; *MW287/CF-HIP*; *MW290/CF-HAS*; *MW294/CF-HIQ*; *MW302/G-AMVZ*; *MW308/G-AMUL*, t/s *XF284*

**York C. Mk.1 (passenger/freighter version)** built at Manchester and Yeadon 1945–48 to Specification C.1/42: *MW169, 173, 178, 186, 190, 193, 196–199, 201, 204, 206, 208, 209, 222, 226, 227, 229, 230, 233, 236, 272, 291, 292, 295, 296, 298, 300, 301, 303, 304, 310–333, PE101–PE108*. Civil conversions (1952–57): *MW178/G-ANXK*; *MW193/G-ANSY*, t/s *XG929*; *MW196/G-ANXL*; *MW199/G-AOAN*; *MW226/G-AMUV* Air Charter *New Venture II*, t/s *XD669*; *MW227/G-ANXM*; *MW233/CF-HFP*; *MW236/G-ANAC*; *MW291/CF-HFQ*; *MW292/G-AMVY*; *MW295/G-APCA/OD-ACQ/EP-ADE*; *MW302/G-AMVZ*; *MW318/G-ANXO*; *MW321/G-AMUN*, t/s *XD667*; *MW323/G-AMXM/OD-ADM*; *MW326/G-AMRJ* Surrey F/S *New Era II*, t/s *XG897/OD-ACE*; *MW327/G-ANRC*, t/s *XG898*, *MW322/G-AMUN*, t/s *XF285*

**York C. Mk.1 for joint RAF Transport Command/BOAC use** built at Yeadon 1945–46: *TS789–TS802/G-AGNL–'NZ*, c/n 1213–1227; *G-AGNL Mersey*, t/s *WW581*; *'NM Murchison*, t/s *WW511/XA192*; *'NN Madras*, later South African Airways *ZS-BGU*, BSAA *Star Crest*, BOAC *Atlantic Trader*, t/s *WW465*; *'NO Manton*, t/s *WW577* and *WW576*; *'NP Manchester*, temporarily *ZS-BRA*, t/s *WW509*, later *OD-ABT/OD-ACZ*; *'NR* temporarily *ZS-ATP Springbok*, later BOAC *Moira*; *'NS Melville*, temporarily *ZS-BTT*, later BSAA *Star Glory* and BOAC *Pacific Trader* t/s *WW466*; *'NT Mandalay*, temporarily *ZS-ATU*, t/s *WW514*; *'NU Montgomery*, temporarily *ZS-ATR Impala*, later BSAA *Nassau*, BOAC

*Nassau*, Air Charter *New Endeavour*, t/s *XD670*, *OD-ACO*; *'NV Morville* (later *Middlesex*); *'NW Morecambe*, temporarily *ZS-ATS Sable*, later BOAC *Caribbean Trader*, t/s *WW581*, later *EP-ADB*; *'NX Moray*, later BSAA and BOAC *Lima*, t/s *WW582*; *'NY Melrose*, t/s *WW510*; *'NZ Monmouth*, temporarily *ZS-BRB*

*TS803–TS808/G-AGOA–'OF*, c/n 1228–1233: *G-AGOA Montrose*, t/s *WW542*; *'OB Milford*, t/s *WW501*; *'OC Malta*, later BSAA *Star Path*; *'OD Midlothian*, t/s *WW576* and *WW577*, later *EP-ADC/OD-ACP*; *'OE Medway*; *'OF Macduff*, temporarily *ZS-ATT*, t/s *WW579*

*TS809–TS813/G-AGSL–'SP*, c/n 1236–1240: *G-AGSL Morley*, t.s *WW579*; *'SM Malvern*, t/s *WW540*; *'SN Marlow*, t/s *WW578*; *'SO Marston*, t/s *WW467*; *'SP Marlborough*, later *Santiago*

**York C. Mk.1 for British South American Airways Corporation** built at Yeadon 1946. *G-AHEW–'FH*, c/n 1300–1311: *G-AHEW Star Leader*; *'EX Star Venture*; *'EY Star Quest*, t/s *WW506* later *JY-ABZ*; *'EZ Star Speed*; *'FA Star Dale* t/s *WW504*; *'FB Star Stream*, t/s *WW499* and *WW586*, temporarily *JY-AAC* in 1957; *'FC Star Dew*, t/s *WW507*, later *OD-ACJ/HZ-CAA/EP-ADD*; *'FD Star Mist*, t/s *WW500*, later *OD-ADB*; *'FE Star Vista*, t/s *WW468* and *WW578*; *'FF Star Gleam*, t/s *WW503*; *'FG Star Haze*, t/s *WW468*; *'FH Star Glitter*, t/s *WW502*, later *OD-ADA*

**York C. Mk.1 for Skyways Ltd** built at Yeadon 1946. *G-AHFI Skyway*, c/n 1316; *G-AHLV Sky Courier*, c/n 1340; *G-AIUP Sky Consul*, c/n 1374

**York C. Mk.1 for Flota Aerea Mercante Argentina (FAMA)** built at Yeadon 1946. *LV-XGN*, c/n 1354, re-registered *LV-AFV* after delivery, to Surrey F/S 1951 as *G-AMGL New Era*, t/s *XA192*; *LV-XGO*, c/n 1355, operated as *LV-AFY*, to Surrey F/S 1952 as *G-AMGM New Venture*; *LV-XGP*, c/n 1356, operated as *LV-AFZ*, to Eagle Aviation Ltd 1951 as *G-AMGK*, t/s *XA191* and *WW512*, temporarily *OD-ABV* in 1954; *LV-XIG*, c/n 1365 crashed 23.12.46; *LV-XIH*, c/n 1366, crashed 25.7.47

**York C. Mk.1 Special** built for RAF Transport Command by Victory Aircraft Ltd, Toronto, Canada 1945. *FM400*, c/n PC4494, to Skyways Ltd 1948 as *G-ALBX Sky Dominion*, crashed at Wunsdorf, Germany, 19.6.49

*Service Use:* (With Unit codes in parentheses)
RAF Transport Command: Nos.24, 40 (LE), 51 (TB), 59 (BY), 99, 206, 232, 242 (KY), 246 (VU), and 511 Squadrons. Training Units: No.241 OCU (YY), 1332 (T) CU, 1384 (T) CU India H.Q. Communications Flight.

The first production Avro 688 Tudor 1, *G-AGRC*, with the early type of tail unit. (*BOAC*)

# Avro 688 Tudor I

In the autumn of 1943 it was clear that an interim type would be needed for the North Atlantic route until the big Brabazon Type I (Bristol 167), Type 3 (Avro 690 and 692—also referred to as the Avro XXII and XXIII), Type 3A (Avro 693) and Type 4 (D.H. 106) transports were ready. To meet this requirement A. V. Roe and Co conceived the idea of the Avro 687 (or Avro XX) with a circular-section pressurised cabin but otherwise based on the Lancaster IV (or Lincoln) with four-Merlin layout but using a single fin in place of the twin unit. To cover this suggestion the Air Ministry issued Specification 29/43 to the company in March 1944, calling for a 72,000 lb transport to carry a 3,760 lb payload for 4,000 miles, cruising at 235 mph at 25,000 ft.

Heavy military commitments delayed detail design until the following June, but as work proceeded Lancaster conversion was abandoned and an entirely new 12-passenger type, the Avro 688 Tudor 1, emerged. Two prototypes were ordered in September 1944 and the first, *TT176/G-AGPF* powered by four 1,750 hp Rolls-Royce Merlin 102 engines, made its first flight at Woodford piloted by S. A. Thorn and J. H. Orrell on June 14, 1945. It was the first British pressurised transport but initial tests were made without pressurisation and with the tail wheel fixed. Trials continued at Woodford until April 1946 while work proceeded apace on 14 production aircraft (increased to 20 in April 1945) ordered for BOAC by the Ministry of Supply in November 1944. Flights trials with the prototype and the first and second production aircraft, *G-AGRC* and *'RD*, revealed directional and longitudinal instability (resulting in the fitment of larger fins, rudders and tailplanes), and pre-stall wing buffeting (cured by extending the wing root fillets and inner engine nacelles, and by sealing the wing leading-

384

edge/fuselage junction). Airfield limitations at Woodford restricted proto-type trials with 'PF to an all-up weight of 65,000 lb, but when flown at Boscombe Down at the maximum take-off weight of 80,000 lb, a considerable landing bounce was apparent, corrected by fitting a shortened undercarriage. Boscombe Down also estimated the still air range at 3,600 instead of the expected 4,000 miles and attempts were made to improve matters by cleaning up the airframe and replacing the Merlin 600s (civil equivalent of the original Merlin 102s) by the more efficient Merlin 621s with reversible-pitch capability.

The unhappy Tudor 1 was not only the subject of protracted modifications but also victim of extremely high ideals set by BOAC for its first postwar airliner. At the final design conference on March 12–13, 1946, the Corpor-ation called for no fewer than 343 changes in layout and decor, even though the whole production programme was already in serious disorder after two years of ever-changing decisions. Modifications recommended after unsatisfactory consumption tests and tropical trials at Nairobi in December 1946 with the second production Tudor 1 *G-AGRD* were incorporated in the seventh aircraft, '*RI*, tested at Boscombe Down in February 1947. These included sealed engine cowlings, smooth de-icer pipes and increased engine compression ratio, while to improve airflow over the wing still further, the inner nacelles were extended beyond the trailing edge.

Despite the fact that a ceremony had taken place at London Airport on January 21, 1947, when the fourth production aircraft *G-AGRF* (Capt S. W. A. Scott) was chosen as flagship of the future Tudor fleet and named *Elizabeth of England* by HRH Princess Elizabeth, the Tudor was judged incapable of operating over the Atlantic and was finally rejected by the Corporation on April 11, 1947. At the same time the Australian Government abandoned its intention of building twelve Tudors in Australia to equip a transport squadron, even though a wooden mock-up had been constructed and serial group *A76* had been allotted.

A considerable number of production Tudors which had taken shape at Woodford included *G-AIYA* and *G-AJKC* which were despatched to Sir W. G. Armstrong Whitworth Aircraft Ltd at Baginton, Coventry, to be fitted with luxury day and night accommodation for nine passengers as

Tudor 1 *G-AGRE*, later the ill-fated Tudor 4 *Star Ariel*, showing the revised tail unit.

British South American Airways' Tudor 4 *G-AHNN Star Leopard.*

Tudor 3 transports for the personal use of Cabinet Ministers. They returned to Woodford with RAF markings *VP301* and *VP312* respectively.

Four airframes were completed as Tudor 4s to the requirements of British South American Airways Corporation for whom the front fuselage was lengthened by 6 ft, the flight engineer's position removed and the seat pitch decreased to enable 32 passengers, mail and freight to be carried. Conversions of early Tudor 1s *G-AGRD* and *'RE* which retained the flight engineer and carried 28 passengers were designated Tudor 4B. The 4s and 4Bs were supplied to BSAA to Specification 28/46B and the first example *G-AHNJ Star Panther*, was flown for the first time at Woodford by S. A. Thorn on April 9, 1947. The second aircraft *G-AHNK Star Lion*, flown at Woodford on September 29 by J. H. Orrell, was immediately delivered to London by the same pilot so that its inaugural 16,500 mile demonstration and route proving flight to South America and back might begin next day. Piloted by Air Vice-Marshal D. C. T. Bennett via Lisbon, Dakar, Natal, Rio de Janeiro, Buenos Aires and Santiago, *Star Lion* returned on schedule and without incident on October 9. The fleet then settled down on the BSAA London–Bermuda route, but after the unexplained loss of *G-AJNP Star Tiger* northeast of Bermuda on the night of January 29–30, 1948, and of *G-AGRE Star Ariel* between Bermuda and Jamaica on January 17, 1949, the remainder were stripped of furnishings and pressurisation and relegated to freight duties under designations Tudor Freighter 4 or 4B.

During the Berlin Air Lift the Corporation completed 261 sorties with *G-AGRG, 'RH* and *'RJ* stripped as Tudor Freighter 1s, but when the operation ended in August 1949 the entire fleet was withdrawn from service and stored at Woodford. Later the aircraft were moved to Tarrant Rushton and Ringway but a number of new Tudors still in the Avro works were sold as scrap and broken up in R. J. Coley's yard at Dukinfield, Cheshire.

The second prototype *TT181/G-AGST* took part in the original modification programme and was subsequently rebuilt as a Tudor 4. Later still it was fitted with four 5,000 lb st Rolls-Royce Nene 4 turbojets in paired nacelles under the designation Tudor 8 and transferred to military marks

The second prototype Tudor 1 in its final form as the Tudor 8 *VX195* with four Rolls-Royce Nene 5 turbojets.

as *VX195*, flying for the first time on September 6, 1948, and demonstrated at the Farnborough SBAC Show by J. H. Orrell a few days later. It was then handed over to Boscombe Down for test and eventually relegated to the 'outback' at Farnborough where it was broken up in 1951 and the fuselage donated to Teddington Controls Ltd as a static test rig.

Prolonged negotiations by Aviation Traders Ltd resulted in the purchase of all the surviving Tudors, comprising four Freighter 1s *G-AGRG–'RJ*; four Freighter 4Bs *G-AHNI, 'NL, 'NM* and *'NO*; and the two Freighter 3s *G-AIYA* and *G-AJKC*, as well as 88 new Merlin engines, on September 2, 1953. They were intended to replace Air Charter's long-range Yorks, and *G-AGRI* and *'RG* were rushed into service and by the following month *'RI* had already made a number of overseas flights from Northolt with temporary RAF serial *XF739*. Between December 1953 and January 1954 all the other Tudors were flown to Southend for overhaul, followed a month later by the component parts of *G-AGRF, G-AHNK* and *'NN* by road from Hurn. Drastic modifications of *'RI* by upgrading the engines to Merlin 623, re-routing hydraulic and pneumatic lines, fitting Shackleton-type wheels and providing 42 rearward-facing seats, resulted in the issue of an unrestricted passenger carrying C of A in February 1954. Eventually all except *G-AGRJ* and *G-AJKC* were reconverted for passenger carrying but the War Office would not permit trooping by converted aircraft. In the following year therefore *'RG El Alamein* and *G-AIYA* were lengthened into Tudor 4s by Aviation Traders Ltd at Stansted and modified to the same standard as *'RI*, which they joined on the Colonial coach service from Stansted to Idris (Tripoli) and Lagos.

The utility of *G-AGRH Zephyr, G-AHNI, 'NM* and *'NO* was further improved by large 6 ft 10 in by 5 ft 5 in rectangular freight doors designed, constructed and tried out on the fuselage of *G-AHNK* by Aviation Traders

387

at Southend. With these doors in the port side and a permitted increase in all-up weight to 83,600 lb the aircraft were renamed Avro Super Trader (or 4B) and granted a full C of A in March 1955. The prototype installation was made in 'NI in April 1954 and later two of the improved Merlin 723 engines were tried experimentally in 'RH.

The resuscitated Super Traders made many outstanding long-distance charter flights, notably to Christmas Island in the Pacific, and fully justified their owners' faith in the soundness of the basic design. In August 1958 G-AHNM *Cirrus* flew as far as Christchurch, New Zealand, to collect Bristol Freighter spares. They remained in service until 1959 when 'RG was burned out after swinging on take-off at Brindisi and 'RH struck the 14,547 ft summit of Mt Suphan Dag in east Turkey while en route to Woomera, Australia.

## SPECIFICATION AND DATA

*Manufacturers:*  A. V. Roe and Co Ltd, Greengate, Middleton, Manchester; and Woodford Aerodrome, Cheshire

*Powerplants:*  (Tudor 1, first prototype)
                                                 Four 1,750 hp Rolls-Royce Merlin 102
           (Tudor 1)              Four 1,750 hp Rolls-Royce Merlin 102A
                                                   Four 1,740 hp Rolls-Royce Merlin 600
  (Tudor 1, 3, 4, 4B) Four 1,770 hp Rolls-Royce Merlin 621
                                                   Four 1,760 hp Rolls-Royce Merlin 623
           (Tudor 8)              Four 5,000 lb st Rolls-Royce Nene 5

*Dimensions, Weights and Performances:*

|  | Tudor 1 | Tudor 3 | Tudor 4 | Tudor 4B | Tudor 8 |
|---|---|---|---|---|---|
| Span | 120 ft 0 in | 120 ft 0 in | 120 ft 0 in | 120 ft 0 in | 120 ft 0 in |
| Length | 79 ft 6 in | 79 ft 3 in | 85 ft 3 in | 85 ft 3 in | 79 ft 3 in |
| Height | 20 ft 11 in* | 20 ft 11 in | 20 ft 11 in | 20 ft 11 in | 20 ft 11 in |
| Wing area | 1,421 sq ft | 1,421 sq ft | 1,421 sq ft | 1,421 sq ft | 1,421 sq ft |
| Tare weight | 47,960 lb | 38,923 lb | 49,441 lb | 50,322 lb** | 34,724 lb |
| All-up weight | 71,000 lb | 78,761 lb | 80,000 lb | 82,000 lb** | 80,000 lb |
| Maximum speed | 260 mph | 282 mph | 282 mph | 282 mph | 385 mph |
| Cruising speed | 210 mph | 210 mph | 210 mph | 210 mph | 350 mph |
| Initial climb | 700 ft/min | 800 ft/min | 800 ft/min | 635 ft/min | 2,930 ft/min |
| Ceiling | 26,000 ft | 27,400 ft | 27,400 ft | 23,500 ft | 44,000 ft |
| Range | 3,630 miles | 4,000 miles | 4,000 miles | 3,500 miles** | 1,720 miles |

*Height 24 ft 0 in with original undercarriage.
**Super Trader 4 and 4B 45,375 lb, 83,600 lb and 1,300 miles respectively.

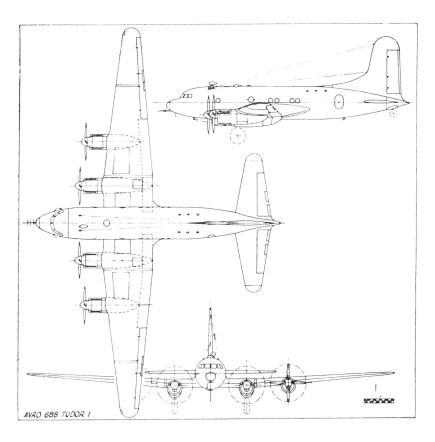

AVRO 688 TUDOR I

*Production:*
  (*a*) **Tudor 1**

| Constructor's No. and Registration | | Details |
|---|---|---|
| 1234 | G-AGPF | Initially *TT176*, C of A 18.11.47, to MoS 1949 as *VX192*, scrapped at Woodford 12.50 |
| 1249 | G-AGST | Initially *TT181*, rebuilt as Tudor 4 and later as Tudor 8 *VX195*, broken up at Farnborough 1951 |
| 1251 | G-AGRC | First flown 12.1.46, scrapped at Woodford 12.48 |
| 1252 | G-AGRD | Development aircraft, C of A 22.11.46, scrapped at Woodford 3.49 |
| 1253 | G-AGRE | To Boscombe Down 8.46, C of A 25.9.46, to Woodford 11.46 for prototype Tudor 4B conversion |
| 1254 | G-AGRF | C of A 6.12.46, BOAC *Elizabeth of England*, converted to Tudor 4B in 1948 |
| 1255 | G-AGRG★ | C of A 10.1.47, BSAA Tudor Freighter 1 *Star Cressida*, converted to Super Trader 4 in 1956 |
| 1256 | G-AGRH★ | C of A 10.12.46, BSAA Tudor Freighter 1, converted to Super Trader 4B in 1956 |
| 1257 | G-AGRI★ | C of A 3.2.48, Air Charter Ltd trooping 10.53 as *XF739*, dismantled at Southend 10.54 |
| 1258 | G-AGRJ★ | C of A 24.2.47, dismantled at Stansted 8.56 |
| 1259 | G-AGRK | Transferred to the MoS as TS874 and TS875 respectively and eventually scrapped at Woodford |
| 1260 | G-AGRL | |

Super Trader 4B *Trade Wind G-AHNI* of Air Charter Ltd. The hinges of the freight door are visible forward of the ladder.

## (b) Tudor 3

| Constructor's No. and Registration | | Details |
|---|---|---|
| 1367 | G-AIYA★ | Temporarily *VP301* in 1948, C of A 14.2.50, converted 5.54 to Tudor 1 |
| 1368 | G-AJKC★ | Temporarily *VP312* in 1948, C of A 14.2.50, scrapped at Southend 8.56 |

## (c) Tudor 4 and 4B

| Constructor's No. and Registration | | Details |
|---|---|---|
| 1253 | G-AGRE | BSAA *Star Ariel*, C. of A 12.11.48, lost in the Western Atlantic 17.1.49 |
| 1254 | G-AGRF★ | C of A 8.12.48, dismantled at Hurn 1953, components by road to Southend |
| 1255 | G-AGRG★ | C of A 31.1.54, converted to Super Trader 4 *El Alamein* for Air Charter Ltd 7.56, burned out at Brindisi 27.1.59 |
| 1256 | G-AGRH★ | C of A 25.10.55, converted 7.56 to Super Trader 4B *Zephyr*, crashed on Mt Suphan Dag, Turkey 23.4.59 |
| 1341 | G-AHNH | Construction abandoned |
| 1342 | G-AHNI★ | BSAA *Star Olivia*, C of A 24.2.50, converted to Super Trader 4B *Trade Wind* for Air Charter Ltd in 1956, scrapped at Stansted 6.59 |
| 1343 | G-AHNJ | BSAA *Star Panther*, C of A 18.7.47, reduced to spares at Ringway 1953 |
| 1344 | G-AHNK★ | BSAA *Star Lion*, C. of A 30.9.47, reduced to spares at Ringway 1953 |
| 1345 | G-AHNL★ | C of A 14.2.50, converted to Super Trader 4B in 1956, scrapped at Southend 2.60 |
| 1346 | G-AHNM★ | C of A 6.3.50, converted to Super Trader 4B *Cirrus* for Air Charter Ltd in 1956, scrapped at Stansted 6.59 |
| 1347 | G-AHNN★ | BSAA *Star Leopard*, C of A 23.3.48, to spares at Ringway 1953 |
| 1348 | G-AHNO | C of A 24.2.50, converted to Super Trader 4B *Conqueror* for Air Charter Ltd 1956, scrapped at Stansted 8.59 |
| 1349 | G-AHNP | BSAA *Star Tiger*, C of A 5.11.47, lost in the Western Atlantic 30.1.48 |
| 1350 | G-AHNR | Construction abandoned |

★Acquired by Aviation Traders Ltd 2.9.53.

*Note:* All Tudor 1 and 4 aircraft were allotted BSAA Star class names but only those actually used are recorded above. Cs of A were not issued to *G-AGST,* '*RC,* '*RK,* '*RL, G-AHNH* and '*NR*

Avro 689 Tudor 2 prototype *G-AGSU* with original tail unit, taking off from Woodford for an early test flight on April 3, 1946. (*BOAC*)

# Avro 689 Tudor 2

The Tudor 2 (or Avro XXI) was designed originally as a stretched version of the Tudor 1 to carry 60 passengers for BOAC as the Avro 689 and for BEA as the Avro 699. To this end the fuselage diameter was to be increased by 1 ft and the length by 25 ft, with the flying surfaces, powerplants and undercarriage remaining unchanged. In November 1944, while the aircraft was still in the design stage, BOAC, QANTAS and South African Airways decided to standardise it on all the Commonwealth routes and the original BOAC order for 30 was increased to 79. By May 1945, however, aerodynamic considerations and the operators' changing requirements had increased the length to no less than 105 ft 7 in, making the Tudor 2 the largest aircraft produced in Britain up to that time.

Four months of flight testing followed the maiden flight of the Tudor 2 prototype *G-AGSU* at Woodford by S. A. Thorn and J. H. Orrell on March 10, 1946. It then went to Boscombe Down for certification trials and the original Rolls-Royce Merlin 102s were changed for the civil equivalent designated Merlin 600 Special. Teething troubles similar to those of the Tudor 1 were soon encountered and '*SU* returned to Woodford in September 1946 for rearward extension of the inner nacelles and the fitting of the enlarged type of fin and rudder. Increases in structural weight resulting from the stretching processes and subsequent modifications had by this time reduced performance to the point where the Tudor 2 could no longer operate from aerodromes east of Calcutta or south of Nairobi. QANTAS and South African Airways were thus compelled to re-equip with American types and the Tudor 2 order was reduced to 50, at which stage tragedy overtook the prototype which crashed on take off from Woodford on August 23, 1947, due to incorrect assembly of the aileron circuit, an accident which cost the lives of Avro's famous chief designer Roy Chadwick and test pilot S. A. 'Bill' Thorn.

In an attempt to recover some of the lost performance, the first production Tudor 2 *G-AGRX* was completed with four 1,750 hp Bristol Hercules 120 radial engines, redesignated Tudor 7 and first flown on April 17, 1946, in time for that year's Radlett SBAC Show. When the shortened undercarriage

Tudor 2 *G-AGRY* flew initially in military markings as *VX202*.

was fitted in June 1948 the engine nacelles were tilted to give greater airscrew clearance and the aircraft used for cabin heating tests before delivery to the Ministry of Supply in March 1949 as *VX199* for use at the Telecommunications Research Establishment, Defford.

Merlin-powered Tudor 2 development continued with the second production aircraft *G-AGRY* which the MoS sent to Nairobi for tropical trials as *VX202*. These proved unsatisfactory and orders were cut back drastically to 18, made up of two Tudors 2s for experimental work, ten earmarked for completion with tricycle undercarriages as Avro 711A Traders to Specification 23/48, and six to BSAA requirements as Tudor 5s to Specification 39/46. The experimental machines *G-AGRZ* and '*SA* were loaned to the RAE, Farnborough, and Rolls-Royce Ltd, Hucknall, respectively and used military marks for pressurisation, airscrew and engine development but the Trader programme was shelved.

Powered by four 1,770 hp Rolls-Royce Merlin 621s, the Tudor 5s were identified by circular instead of square windows and were equipped to carry 44 passengers by day or 36 by night (28 seated, 8 sleeping). Painted in full BSAA livery, they were delivered to the company's engineering base at Langley but did not go into scheduled service. Instead, they were stripped of furnishings and used as tankers on the Berlin Air Lift, the first, *G-*

British South American Airways Tudor 5 *G-AKCB Star Kestrel*. (*E. J. Riding*)

*AKBY*, being sold to Airflight Ltd of Blackbushe, which had already acquired Tudor 2 *G-AGRY*. After 85 trips from Wunsdorf to Gatow, each time carrying 9¾ tons of mixed freight, the latter also became a tanker and in just over a year the immense total of 3,167 tanker sorties was flown by the seven 'large' Tudors, *G-AKBY* being landed on one occasion successfully by Air Vice-Marshal Bennett on the trimmers alone after taking off with the elevator locked.

On their return to England the aircraft were refurnished for passenger work but *'BY* crashed with a loss of 80 lives due to incorrect loading on March 12, 1950, when approaching to land at Llandow at the end of a charter flight from Dublin. *G-AKCA* flew to Montreal in 1952 and appeared for a short time in the colours of Lome Airways as *CF-FCY* before returning to Stansted; while *'CC* and *'CD* were disposed of to William Dempster Ltd and converted to 52-seat layout for London–Johannesburg tourist flights. After *'CC* was damaged beyond repair when landing at Bovingdon from Castel Benito on October 26, 1951, its sister machine went

The Tudor 7 *G-AGRX* with revised tail unit.

to Stansted, where it was gradually broken up with other Tudor 5s to provide spares for Air Charter's Super Traders and for Tudor 2 *G-AGRY* which made 13 trooping flights to the Suez Canal Zone for this company as *XF537* in September 1953.

Designation Tudor 6 was reserved for six aircraft ordered by the Argentine airline FAMA for operation over the South Atlantic with 32–38 day or 22 night passengers. Although airframe numbers were allotted and application made for Cs of A they were not completed. Also derived from the Tudor 2 were six aircraft powered by four Rolls-Royce Nene turbojets and equipped with tricycle undercarriages. First referred to as the Avro 689 Tudor 9, this variant was eventually built as the Avro 706 Ashton high-altitude research type described later in this book.

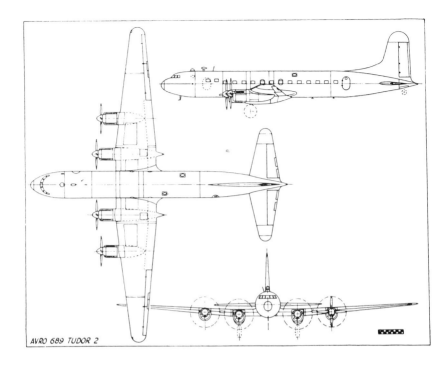

AVRO 689 TUDOR 2

## SPECIFICATION AND DATA

*Manufacturers:* A. V. Roe and Co Ltd, Greengate, Middleton, Manchester; Ringway Aerodrome, Manchester; and Woodford Aerodrome, Cheshire

*Powerplants:* (Tudor 2) Four 1,750 hp Rolls-Royce Merlin 102
Four 1,740 hp Rolls-Royce Merlin 600A
Four 1,770 hp Rolls-Royce Merlin 621
(Tudor 5) Four 1,770 hp Rolls-Royce Merlin 621
(Tudor 7) Four 1,750 hp Bristol Hercules 120

*Dimensions:* Span 120 ft 0 in   Length 105 ft 7 in
Height 24 ft 3 in   Wing area 1,421 sq ft

*Weights:* (Tudor 2 and 5)
Tare weight 46,300 lb   All-up weight 80,000 lb
(Tudor 7) Tare weight 51,625 lb   All-up weight 80,000 lb

*Performance:* (Tudor 2 and 5)
Maximum speed 295 mph
Cruising speed 235 mph
Initial climb 740 ft/min   Ceiling 25,550 ft
Range 2,330 miles

394

(Tudor 7) Maximum speed 270 mph
Cruising speed 200 mph
Initial climb 750 ft/min    Ceiling 25,100 ft
Range 2,800 miles

*Production:*

### (a) **Tudor 2**

| Constructor's No. and Registration | | Details |
|---|---|---|
| 1235 | G-AGSU | Prototype, destroyed at Woodford 23.8.47 |
| 1250 | G-AGSV | Intended as prototype Avro 711A Trader, construction abandoned |
| 1262 | G-AGRY | Initially *VX202*, C of A 1.9.48, to Airflight Ltd 9.48, to Fairflight Ltd 4.50, to Air Charter Ltd 1953, temporarily *XF537*, scrapped at Stansted 7.59 |
| 1263 | G-AGRZ | To MoS 1.51 as *VZ366*, to Flight Refuelling Ltd 11.53 as *G-AGRZ*, to Aviation Traders Ltd for spares 3.54, scrapped 7.59 |
| 1264 | G-AGSA | To MoS 1.49 as *VZ720* on loan to Rolls-Royce Ltd, Hucknall, scrapped at Farnborough 10.53 |

*Note:* The following reservations for Tudor 2s were not taken up: *G-AJJV* to *'KB*, c/n 1395–1401; *G-AKTH* to *'TT*, c/n 1425–1436; *G-AKUE–'UP*, c/n 1437–1448

### (a) **Tudor 5**

| Constructor's No. and Registration | | Details |
|---|---|---|
| 1417 | G-AKBY | Airflight Ltd, C of A 24.9.48, crashed at Llandow 12.3.50 |
| 1418 | G-AKBZ | BSAA *Star Falcon*, C of A 3.11.48, scrapped at Stansted 7.59 |
| 1419 | G-AKCA | BSAA *Star Hawk*, C of A 7.12.48, temporarily to Lome Airways as *CF-FCY* in 1952, scrapped at Stansted |
| 1420 | G-AKCB | BSAA *Star Kestrel*, C of A 31.12.48, scrapped at Stansted 7.59 |
| 1421 | G-AKCC | BSAA *Star Swift*, C of A 26.1.49, William Dempster Ltd *President Kruger*, damaged at Bovingdon 26.10.51 |
| 1422 | G-AKCD | BSAA *Star Eagle*, C of A 11.2.49, scrapped at Stansted 1956 |

### (c) **Tudor 6**

Six aircraft, c/n 1386–1391, ordered by Flota Aerea Mercante Argentina (FAMA), were not built

### (d) **Tudor 7**

| Constructor's No. and Registration | | Details |
|---|---|---|
| 1261 | G-AGRX | First flown 17.4.46, to MoS 3.49 as *VX199*, to Flight Refuelling Ltd 11.53 as *G-AGRX*, Aviation Traders Ltd as spares 3.54, scrapped at Stansted 9.59 |

### (e) **Avro 711A Trader**

Prototype *G-AGSV*, c/n 1250, and nine production aircraft comprising *G-AGSB* to *'SG*, c/n 1265–1270 (registered 9.45 to the Ministry of Supply and Aircraft Production) and *G-AJJS* to *'JU*, c/n 1392–1394 (registered to the Ministry of Supply 3.47). None of these was completed

# Avro 691 Lancastrian

To prepare for a Canadian transatlantic service, M. B. Barclay and G. B. Lothian, senior Trans-Canada Air Lines captains, were seconded to the RAF/BOAC North Atlantic ferry in 1941 but it was not until two years later that such a service was established. Initial equipment was the British built Lancaster III *R5727* which had been flown to Canada in August 1942 to assist in the tooling for local production. Following a tour of bases in the United States to show off this then new British bomber it returned to Malton in March 1943, where Victory Aircraft faired over the nose and tail turrets and removed the mid-upper. Stripped of camouflage and provided with three extra windows at the rear, it was handed over to TCA for evaluation and given Fleet No.100. Known affectionately as 'Old TCA 100', it made experimental freight runs from Moncton to Goose Bay piloted by Capt Barclay and quickly proved its ability to carry loads of up to 14,000 lb over great distances at reasonable speed.

It was then flown back to England where A. V. Roe and Co completed its demilitarisation and replaced the turrets by streamlined wooden fairings designed and supplied by Victory Aircraft. Unlike the nose cones of later conversions, that of TCA 100 was quite short and housed the navigator under a glazed roof. Extra fuel tanks increased the still-air range to 4,000 miles and seats for ten passengers were installed. Re-camouflaged, registered *CF-CMS* and piloted by Capt R. F. George, it inaugurated the TCA-operated Canadian Government Trans Atlantic Air Service on July 22, 1943, by flying 4 tons of Forces' mail nonstop Dorval-Prestwick in the record time of 12 hrs 26 min. The machine was then cleared for passenger carrying, was granted a British C of A on September 1, 1943, and on March 3, 1944, set up a westbound record to Montreal of 12 hr 59 min carrying 3,611 lb of mail, 435 lb of freight and four passengers.

These successes prompted the acquisition of additional aircraft and two Canadian-built Lancaster Xs were allocated for civil conversion by TCA and delivered stripped of military equipment and with turret openings faired over. TCA then installed dual controls, airline standard instrument

'Old TCA 100' *CF-CMS*, the original demilitarised Lancaster from which the full Lancastrian modification was developed.

panels and radio equipment, bomb-bay fuel tanks and fairings, and the astrodromes were moved forward. Known as Lancaster X Transports, they were joined in 1944 by five more Lancaster Xs converted by Victory Aircraft at Malton, which produced a more elegant version, the Lancaster XPP, with longer, all-metal, semi-monocoque nose which increased the mail capacity to $3\frac{1}{2}$ tons. One TCA conversion, *CF-CMU*, was lost over the Atlantic with British Admiralty officials in December 1944, and *CF-CMS* was burned out in a take-off accident at Dorval in June 1945 during trials with four Merlin 85 engines in Lincoln-type annular cowlings. The remaining six plied twice weekly between Dorval and Prestwick until September 16, 1946, when the route was extended to London and became a public scheduled service, but the aircraft were quite uneconomic in civil use and were replaced in 1947, having completed 1,900 ocean crossings.

An outstanding long-distance flight was made by *CF-CMW* (Capt G. B. Lothian) which left Prestwick on July 9, 1946, with a crew of four and ten passengers and flew to Vancouver in an elapsed time of 28 hrs 23 min with a single refuelling stop at Dorval.

The first BOAC Lancastrian 1, *G-AGLF*.

A more sophisticated conversion with 500 gallon fuel tanks in the bomb bay but outwardly similar to the Victory machine, was put into production by A. V. Roe and Co. in 1944 under the designation Avro 691 Lancastrian 1. It was intended as an interim type for BOAC's Australian route until the Tudors were ready, and the first aircraft, *VB873/G-AGLF*, was handed over to the Corporation's Development Flight at Hurn early in 1945. Two months later Capt R. G Buck's record breaking 3½ day flight to New Zealand in this machine heralded a new era of fast Commonwealth schedules. Although 32 aircraft from the tail end of Lancaster production were reserved for BOAC, only 20 were completed, the last delivery being in October 1945. Registered *G-AGLS* to 'MM (less 'MI), they operated jointly with QANTAS on the Kangaroo service in RAF Transport Command coding, Australian crews taking over at Karachi. The inaugural eastbound service was flown by *G-AGLV/OKZV* (Capt E. Palmer) ex-Hurn on May 31, 1945, while the westbound machine *G-AGLS/OKZS* left Sydney on June 2. After the loss at sea north of the Cocos Islands on March 24, 1946, of *G-AGLZ* (Capt Thomas) in which Jack Dobson, son of A. V. Roe's managing director, was flying to Australia to organize Lincoln production, the Lancastrians settled down to a career of high utilisation. With accommodation for only nine passengers and carrying a limited quantity of mail, the type was anything but economic in operation, nevertheless an estimated annual loss of £1.4m on the Kangaroo route was accepted as the price of maintaining a fast British prestige service to Sydney.

The Lancastrian was also the first British commercial aeroplane with South Atlantic capability, and on October 5, 1945, Capt O. P. Jones left Hurn in *G-AGMG* to survey the route which had long been a British ambition. The ease with which the Lancastrian crossed the ocean to Buenos Aires, and continued over the Andes to Santiago and Lima, resulted in the delivery of six Lancastrian 3s *G-AGWG* to 'WL for the establishment of a regular BSAA service in the following year. The Mk.3 had additional windows and seats for 13 passengers.

RAF commitments to India, the Far East and Australia were met by equipping Transport Command with nine-seat Lancastrian C. Mk.2s to Specification C.16/44. They were similar to the civil Lancastrian 1 but the total RAF order (deliveries began on October 16, 1945) included twenty 10–13 seat Lancastrian C. Mk.4s, equivalent to the civil Lancastrian 3. Production ceased at the 82nd aircraft at the end of 1946 and the last to leave Woodford were 12 civil examples of which five, collected by BEA and flown to White Waltham for ferrying to Alitalia, were named after Mediterranean winds, for a weekly Rome–Montevideo South Atlantic service which began on June 2, 1948. The remaining seven, comprising three which formed the initial equipment of Silver City Airways Ltd, and four sold to Skyways Ltd, were used for long-distance charters to South Africa, Australia and the Far East. Skyways also commissioned eight ex-RAF Lancastrian C. Mk.2s and 4s in 1947–48, of which five were sold to BSAA and BOAC to alleviate fleet shortages caused by the failure of the

Argentine Air Force Lancastrian 4 *T-102* at Ezeiza Airport, Buenos Aires, on May 24, 1960. (*Marcelo W. Miranda*)

Tudor. Three additional Lancastrian C. Mk.4s were overhauled by A. V. Roe and Co for Flota Aerea Mercante Argentina (FAMA) but in 1949 these were taken over by the Argentine Air Force and served as VIP transports with the V Brigada Aeria at Villa Mercedes.

Four of BOAC's early Lancastrian 1s, sold to QANTAS in November 1947, continued on the Kangaroo service in Australian marks and from December 16 between Sydney and Japan on a weekly flight for the RAAF. One was fitted with a ventral pannier for carrying spare engines and the service was extended to Tokyo on October 15, 1948. A few weeks later a machine captained by L. R. Ambrose made the first direct flight across the Indian Ocean from Perth to Johannesburg, reached on November 20 via the Cocos Islands and Mauritius. Mauritius was also a scheduled stop on the shuttle service operated by Skyways in 1949 between Nairobi and Reunion with ex-British Lancastrian 1s *VP-KFD* and *'GT*.

Skyways Lancastrian 2 *G-AKFH* was registered to the company's East African subsidiary as *VP-KFD* from March 1948 until April 1949.

During the milk shortage of 1947 four Skyways Lancastrians were used for carrying milk in churns from Belfast/Nutts Corner to Liverpool/Speke and later, on the Berlin Air Lift, Flight Refuelling Ltd was called in to specialise in the bulk delivery of petrol and diesel oil. Five former BOAC/BSAA machines and four TCA aircraft specially ferried from Montreal, were equipped at Ford, Sussex, with 2,500 gallon fuselage tanks, and the combined fleet made a total of 3,600 sorties, while five Skyways tankers made an additional 2,000. Their useful lives ended with the airlift and the veterans were flown back to Hurn, Dunsfold and Tarrant Rushton

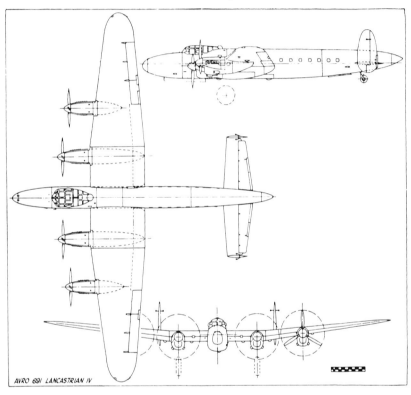

AVRO 691 LANCASTRIAN IV

and broken up in 1951. An attempt to establish a charter company (Onzeair Ltd) in Pakistan using two TCA Lancastrians, *CF-CMW* and '*MX*, and two Skyways aircraft, *G-AJPP* and *G-AKJO*, ended with the loss of '*MW* on August 1, 1948, near the end of its Montreal–London–Karachi delivery flight.

Although primarily a transport type the Lancastrian C. Mk.2 had a notable career as a long-range navigation trainer with the Empire Air Navigation School, Shawbury. Typical of this work were the 36 day, 34,000 mile round the world flight made by *VM701* (Air Vice-Marshal Fiddament) ex Blackbushe on November 12, 1945; and 12,500 mile Northolt–Wellington

*VH742* flying on the power of two Rolls-Royce Nene 1 turbojets, 1946. (*Flight photo 20644S*)

flight by *VM726* (Sq Ldr J. Adams) March 6–8, 1946. The latter returned to Northolt 6 days 13 hrs 15 min later and was the first aircraft to circumnavigate the globe in less than a week.

The development of larger gas-turbines called for test vehicles able to lift large quantities of fuel, and two surplus Lancastrian 1s from the civil production line were modified at Hucknall by Rolls-Royce Ltd to take two 5,000 lb st Nene 1 turbojets in the outer nacelles. *VH742*, first flown at Hucknall by Sq Ldr R. T. Shepherd on August 8, 1946, was the first commercial type in the world to fly solely on jet power. After exhibition at the Radlett SBAC Show in September 1946 it made a record flight from London to Le Bourget on the Nenes alone in 50 mins at 263 mph on November 18 piloted by Shepherd and carrying Roy Chadwick as passenger. The return flight from Villacoublay on November 22 occupied only 49 min.

Similar conversions of two Lancastrian C. Mk.2s to take two 5,000 lb st D.H. Ghost engines were made at Hatfield by the de Havilland Engine Co from drawings supplied by Rolls-Royce, but to accommodate the large Ghost nacelles, the ailerons and flaps were considerably shortened. *VM703*, first flown by John Cunningham and C. D. Beaumont on July 24, 1947,

RAF Lancastrian C. Mk.2 *VM704* equipped as test-bed for Tudor powerplants outboard and Shackleton inboard. (*Rolls-Royce*)

401

appeared at that year's Radlett SBAC Show and later completed rocket assisted take-off trials at Hatfield with two Walter 109-500 'cold' peroxide units under the fuselage. The second Ghost test bed, *VM729*, was used for reheat research and together the two aircraft flew 425 hours, giving valuable jet experience in readiness for the Ghost Vampire and Comet.

Two other Lancastrian C. Mk.2s were flown with Rolls-Royce Griffon piston engines inboard driving six-bladed, contra-rotating airscrews on test for the Shackleton, while *VM704* later flew with Tudor-type Merlin 600 power-plants in the outer nacelles. Two others flew with Rolls-Royce Avon turbojets and the last, *VM733*, modified by Air Service Training, had two Armstrong Siddeley Sapphires outboard and first flew on January 18, 1950, during delivery from Hamble to Boscombe Down by F/Lt P. Fowler.

## SPECIFICATION AND DATA

*Manufacturers:*  A. V. Roe and Co Ltd, Greengate, Middleton, Manchester; and Woodford Aerodrome, Cheshire
Victory Aircraft Ltd., Malton, Toronto, Canada

*Powerplants:*  Four 1,635 hp Rolls-Royce Merlin T.24/2 (later up-rated to T.24/4)
Four 1,750 hp Rolls-Royce Merlin 85
Four 1,635 hp Rolls-Royce Merlin 500

*Dimensions:*  Span 102 ft 0 in   Length 76 ft 10 in
Height 19 ft 6 in   Wing area 1,297 sq ft

*Weights and Performances:*

|  | Mks.1 and 2 | Mks. 3 and 4 | Nene test-bed |
|---|---|---|---|
| Tare weight | 30,426 lb | 30,220 lb | — |
| All-up weight | 65,000 lb | 65,000 lb | 62,570 lb |
| Maximum speed | 310 mph | 315 mph | — |
| Cruising speed | 230 mph | 245 mph | 265 mph★ |
| Initial climb | 750 ft/min | 950 ft/min | — |
| Ceiling | 30,000 ft | 25,500 ft | 25,000 ft |
| Range | 4,150 miles | 2,820 miles | 800 miles★ |

★On two Nene engines only.

*Production:*

### (*a*) Exploratory conversions 1943–44
CF-CMS   TCA 100, ex *R5727*, C of A 1.9.43, burned out at Dorval 6.45
CF-CMT   TCA 101, ex *KB701* ⎫ Conversions by TCA at Montreal, '*MU*
CF-CMU   TCA 102, ex *KB702* ⎭ lost eastbound over the Atlantic 30.12.44

### (*b*) By Victory Aircraft Ltd, Toronto 1944
CF-CMV   TCA 103, ex *KB729*, to Flight Refuelling Ltd 9.47 as *G-AKDO*
CF-CMW   TCA 104, ex *KB730*, to Onzeair Ltd, Karachi, as *AP-ACM*, crashed at Manipur, Pakistan, 1.8.48
CF-CMX   TCA 105, ex *FM184*, to Onzeair Ltd, Karachi

*CF-CMY*    TCA 106, ex *FM185*, to Flight Refuelling Ltd 1.48 as *G-AKDP*, crashed en route Berlin–Hamburg 10.5.49

*CF-CMZ*    TCA 107, ex *FM186*, to Flight Refuelling Ltd 3.48 as *G-AKDR*

*CF-CNA*    TCA 108, ex *FM187*, to Flight Refuelling Ltd 12.47 as *G-AKDS*

### (c) Lancastrian C. Mk.1s by A. V. Roe and Co Ltd

Twenty-three aircraft for the RAF under Contract No.4780 to Works Order 9126: *VB873* prototype, *VD238*, *VD241*, *VD253*, *VF145–VF148*, *VF152–VF156*, *VF160–VF167*, *VH737* and *VH742*

Twenty-one transferred to BOAC 1945 as follows: c/n 1172 *G-AGLF*, ex *VB873*, C of A 7.2.45, unnamed, Skyways *Sky Diplomat* 5.46, beyond repair in Iraq 11.5.47; 1173 *G-AGLS*, ex *VD238* ex *PD141*, 9.3.45, *Nelson*, scrapped at Hurn 1.51; 1174 *G-AGLT*, ex *VD241* ex *PD142*, 20.3.45, *Newcastle*, scrapped at Hurn 1.50; 1175 *G-AGLU*, ex *VD253* ex *PD143*, 29.3.45,unnamed, beyond repair at Hurn 15.8.46; 1176 *G-AGLV*, ex *VF163*, 13.4.45, unnamed, Skyways *Sky Lane* 5.46, temporarily *VP-KGT* in 1949, scrapped 3.52; 1177 *G-AGLW*, ex *VF164*, 26.4.45, *Northampton*, scrapped at Hurn 1.51; 1178 *G-AGLX*, ex *VF165*, 14.5.45, unnamed lost in the Indian Ocean 23.3.46; 1179 *G-AGLY*, ex *VF166*, 29.5.45, *Norfolk*, scrapped at Hurn 1.51; 1180 *G-AGLZ*, ex *VF167*, 2.6.45, *Nottingham*, to QANTAS 11.47 as *VH-EAU*; 1181 *G-AGMA*, ex *VF152*, 11.6.45, *Newport*, scrapped at Hurn 2.51; 1182 *G-AGMB*, ex *VF153*, 15.6.45, *Norwich*, crashed at Singapore 27.8.48; 1183 *G-AGMC*, ex *VF154*, 21.6.45, unnamed crashed at Sydney 2.5.46; 1184 *G-AGMD*, ex *VF155*, 29.6.45, *Nairn*, to QANTAS 7.47 as *VH-EAS*; 1185 *G-AGME*, ex *VF156*, 3.7.45, *Newhaven*, scrapped at Hurn 1.50; 1186 *G-AGMF*, ex *VF160*, 25.7.45, unnamed, crashed at Broglie, France, 20.8.46; 1187 *G-AGMG*, ex *VF161*, 21.8.45, *Nicosia*, scrapped at Hurn 1.51; 1188 *G-AGMH*, ex *VF162*, 28.8.45, unnamed, crashed Karachi 17.5.46; 1189 *G-AGMJ*, ex *VF145*, 11.9.45, *Naseby*, scrapped at Hurn 1.51; 1190 *G-AGMK*, ex *VF146*, 20.9.45, *Newbury*, scrapped at Hurn 1.51; 1191 *G-AGML*, ex *VF147*, 26.9.45, *Nicobar*, to QANTAS 9.47 as *VH-EAT*; 1192 *G-AGMM*, ex *VF148*, 3.10.45, *Nepal*, wrecked at Castel Benito 7.11.49

*Note:* G-AGMN to ’MY, c/n 1193–1204, ex *VF149–VF151* and *VF137–VF144*, were intended for BOAC but not completed.

*VH737* and *VH742*, ex *PD193* and *PD194*, were loaned to Rolls-Royce Ltd, Hucknall, in 1946 as flying test-beds for the Nene 1 turbojet

### (d) Lancastrian C. Mk.2s for the RAF

Thirty-three aircraft to Specification C.16/44 under Contract No. 5328 to Works Order 9199; *VL967–VL981*, *VM701–VM704*, *VM725–VM738*. Used by No. 24 Squadron and the Empire Air Navigation School

Civil conversions: *VL971/G-AKPY*, C of A 16.3.48, BOAC *Natal*; *VL972/ G-AKPZ*, 9.3.48, BOAC *Nile*; *VL973/G-AKSN*, 9.5.49, Skyways *Sky Consort*; *VL974/G-AKSO*, 6.4.49, Skyways *Sky Kingdom*; *VL977/G-AKMW*, 23.12.47, BSAA *Star Bright*, Skyways *Sky Empire* 1949; *VL978/G-AKTC*, BSAA spares; *VL979/G-AKFI/G-AJPP*, 1.12.47, Skyways *Sky Consort*; *VM737/G-AKRB*, 1.3.48, BOAC *Nyanza*; *VM738/G-AKTB*, 28.4.48, BSAA *Star Glory*, to Flight Refuelling 1949; *G-AKFH*, 23.10.47, Skyways *Sky Scout*, temporarily *VP-KFD* 3.48–4.49, burned out at Gatow, Berlin, 26.6.49; *G-AKTG*, BSAA, spares

(e) **Lancastrian 3s**

Eighteen aircraft, initially to BSAA order, under Contract No. 5820 to Works Order 9265: c/n 1279 *G-AGWG*, C of A 5.12.45, *Star Light*, crashed in Bermuda 13.11.47; 1280 *G-AGWH*, 9.1.46, *Star Dust*, lost in the Andes 2.8.47; 1281 *G-AGWI*, 24.1.46; *Star Land*, to Flight Refuelling 1.49; 1282 *G-AGWJ*, 28.1.46, *Star Glow*, crashed at Bathurst, Gambia, 30.8.46; 1283 *G-AGWK*, 15.2.46, *Star Trail*, crashed in Bermuda 5.9.47; 1284 *G-AGWL*, 13.2.46, *Star Guide*, to Flight Refuelling 1.49

With the absorption of BSAA by BOAC the remaining 12 were delivered as follows: c/n 1288 *G-AHBT*, C of A 23.8.46, Silver City Airways *City of New York*, Skyways *Sky Ranger* 7.47; 1289 *G-AHBU*, 16.9.46, Skyways *Sky Path*, crashed at Nutts Corner 3.10.47; 1290 *G-AHBV*, 18.9.46, Silver City *City of Canberra*, to Skyways 3.49; 1291 *G-AHBW*, Silver City *City of London*, to QANTAS 1.48 as *VH-EAV*; 1292 *G-AHBX*, 2.4.47, to Alitalia 2.48 as *I-AHBX Maestrale*; 1293 *G-AHBY*, 2.4.47, to Alitalia 11.47 as *I-AHBY Libeccio*; 1294 *G-AHBZ*; 6.11.46, Skyways *Sky Ambassador*, to Onzeair Ltd 3.49 as *AP-ACQ*; 1295 *G-AHCA*, 6.11.46, Skyways, burned at Dunsfold 8.12.46; 1296 *G-AHCB*, 8.1.47, to Alitalia 7.47 as *I-AHCB Grocale*; 1297 *G-AHCC*, 12.12.46, Skyways *Sky Chieftain*; 1298 *G-AHCD*, 10.1.47, BSAA *Star Valley*, to Alitalia 12.47 as *I-AHCD Sirocco*; 1299 *G-AHCE*, 2.4.47, to Alitalia 8.47 as *I-DALR Borea*

(f) **Lancastrian C. Mk.4s for the RAF**

Eight aircraft under Contract No.5666 to WO 9243: *TX283–TX290*
Civil conversions by Skyways: *TX284/G-AKFF*, C of A 10.9.47, *Sky Ruler*, BSAA *Star Flight* 1948, to Flight Refuelling 1949; *TX285/G-AKLE* used for spares; *TX286/G-AKFG*, 29.9.47, *Sky Minister*, BSAA *Star Traveller* 1948, to Flight Refuelling 1949; *G-AKJO*, 25.10.47, *Sky Envoy*, to Onzeair Ltd 7.48
Civil conversions by A. V. Roe and Co for FAMA, Argentina: *TX288/ LV-ACS*, c/n 1382, C of A 17.1.47; *TX287/LV-ACU*, 1402, 6.4.47; *TX289/ LV-ACV*, 1403, 19.5.49. Transferred to V Brigada Aeria, one serialled *T-102*

(g) **Lancastrian engine test-beds**

*VH742*   Converted at Hucknall, first flown 14.8.46 with two 5,000 lb st Rolls-Royce Nene 1 outboard
*VH737*   Second Nene conversion similar to above
*VM703*   Converted at Hatfield, first flown 24.7.47 with two 5,000 lb st de Havilland Ghosts outboard
*VM729*   Second Ghost conversion similar to above
*VM704*   Flown with two 2,450 hp Rolls-Royce Griffon 57 inboard and two Merlin T.24/4 outboard. Later with two 1,770 hp Merlin 600s
*VM728*   Second Griffon conversion similar to above
*VM732*   Originally for Rolls-Royce Merlin exhaust tests, converted at Hucknall to take two Rolls-Royce Avons outboard and shown at Farnborough 7.9.48
*VL970*   Second Avon conversion similar to above
*VM733*   Converted by Air Service Training to take two Armstrong Siddeley Sapphires outboard, first flown Hamble-Boscombe Down 18.1.50, still flying at Bitteswell 6.54

Lincoln B. Mk.2 *RF385* of No.57 Squadron.

# Avro 694 Lincoln

In 1943 an improved Lancaster was designed for the Pacific War with better performance, heavier armament and very long range. Overall dimensions were increased, more powerful engines installed and the whole design so extensively modified that it emerged as a new type. The intention to call it the Lancaster IV when fitted with four 1,750 hp Rolls-Royce Merlin 85s, and Lancaster V with the Packard Merlin 68A equivalents, was dropped therefore in favour of new designations Avro 694 Lincoln 1 and 2 respectively.

The Lincoln anticipated Air Ministry Specification B.14/43 to which it was built and the unarmed prototype *PW925* first flew at Ringway, piloted by Capt H. A. Brown, on June 9, 1944. Similar in structure to its predecessor, it used a standard Lancaster tail unit (with enlarged rudders) to speed production, but flush riveting gave place to the mushroom type and a sturdier Dowty undercarriage carried the extra weight. Merlin 85 engines drove Rotol three-bladed airscrews and were arranged as detachable power units in low-drag, armour plated cowlings with annular radiators of the type airtested in Lancaster VI *ND784/G* and TCA's civil conversion *CF-CMS*.

*PW925* was fitted later with a Glenn Martin mid-upper turret, but subsequent prototypes *PW929* and *PW932* and all production Lincolns had the Bristol Type 17 Mk.II, with Boulton Paul F and D type in nose and tail, all mounting (in the Lincoln B. Mk.1) twin 0·50 in machine-guns. Two 0·50 in guns in the nose turret of the Lincoln B. Mk.2 were remotely controlled by the bomb aimer, two others were in the tail and one in a ventral position. The mid-upper mounted two 20 mm British Hispano cannon. Twelve Lincoln B. Mk.1s were converted to Mk.2 by Short Bros and Harland Ltd in 1947. The alternative fitment of H2S Mk.IIIG or IVA radar bomb sights gave rise to two sub-variants, the Lincoln B. Mk.2 (IIIG) and B. Mk.2 (IVA).

Range varied from 1,470 miles with 14,000 lb bomb load to 4,450 miles with 3,000 lb. Flown by a crew of seven, it had the magnificent handling qualities of the Lancaster but came too late for service against the Japanese. Contracts awarded to the Lancaster Group for 800 Lincolns were consequently cut back to a small number for use as standard heavy bombers in the postwar RAF. Production initiated by A. V. Roe and Co at Manchester and Yeadon was completed by Armstrong Whitworth.

Lincolns were first issued to No.57 Squadron, East Kirkby, Lincs, and No.44 Squadron, Mildenhall, for Service trials in September 1945 and the type made its first public appearance when B. Mk.2 *RE325* was demonstrated at a Farnborough 'At Home' on October 29 that year. Three Lincolns which flew 20,000 miles from Scampton to Santiago, Chile, and back in October 1946 were the first of many globetrotters. Sixteen Lincolns of No.617 Squadron flew nonstop Binbrook–Gander on July 23, 1947, flew over New York in formation, and visited Los Angeles and Canada before returning on September 9. No.44 Squadron flew to Southern Rhodesia in June 1948; No.97 to Singapore in the same year; and six from No.9 Squadron took part in Exercise 'Sunrise' in the Canal Zone before paying a goodwill visit to Pakistan in October 1949.

All 20 Lincoln squadrons (of which 15 flew in mass formation at the Farnborough RAF Display in July 1950), were normally UK-based but in March 1950 No.97 Squadron, Waddington, was the first of several detached to Tengah, Singapore, for bombing operations against terrorists in Negri Sembilan. They performed a similar service in Kenya against the Mau Mau in 1954. Historically important as the RAF's last piston-engined bomber, the Lincoln was completely replaced in front-line service by 1955. The last in RAF use were *RA685*, *RF398*, *RF461*, *RF505* and *RF570* which formed a Flight of No.151 Squadron, Signals Command, Watton. They made a farewell flight over East Anglia on March 12, 1963, after which two went to Hullavington for preservation and the others to No.23 MU, Aldergrove, where the majority of their predecessors had been broken up.

The first prototype Lincoln *PW925*. (*Avro*)

The unique Canadian-built Lincoln *FM300* at Malton in October 1945. (*Courtesy K. M. Molson*)

The Lincoln 3 was an Air-Sea Rescue project which appeared eventually in a much modified form as the Avro 696 Shackleton. The B. Mk.4 announced in April 1947 was merely a B. Mk.2 with Merlin 85s, the next designation being Lincoln B. Mk.15, a Canadian version of the B. Mk.1 laid down by Victory Aircraft Ltd in 1946 after RCAF tests at Edmonton with *RE258* and *SX924*. All were scrapped in the factory, by then taken over by A. V. Roe and Co, except the first, *FM300*, which, fitted with Rolls-Royce Merlin 68 engines, flew for the first time on October 25, 1945. Fifty-four examples of the Lincoln Mk.30(B) were constructed at Melbourne by the Australian Government Aircraft Factory, five from British parts (the first flown on March 17, 1946), and the remainder entirely built in Australia. Twenty-four of the latter had Merlin 102s and 30 had Australian-built Merlin 85s under the designation Lincoln Mk.30A(B). The 18 Lincolns of No.10 Squadron, Garbutt, were returned to the factory in 1952 to be fitted

Royal Australian Air Force Lincoln Mk.31(MR) *A73-55* with nose extension. (*RAAF*)

407

with a 6 ft fuselage extension housing additional radar gear for anti-submarine work as Lincolns Mk.31(MR). In 1961 all RAAF Lincolns were grounded and the majority flown to Archerfield, Brisbane, to be melted down. The last to fly was *A73-61*.

In March 1947 an RAAF Lincoln penetrated farther south than any previous Australian aeroplane to photograph a proposed explorers' base at Macquaue Island, Antarctica. Another named *Nyhuan* (*Pathfinder*) surveyed the site of the world famous Woomera missile range. The Australian Lincoln's main offensive opportunity was against Malayan terrorists and for this purpose No.1 Squadron RAAF was based alongside the RAF at Singapore. Several, including *A73-66*, were fitted with four rocket projectiles under each wingtip for strafing jungle hideouts. In a peaceful role, *A73-39* was used for rain making experiments in 1958.

The career of the British Lincoln paralleled that of the Lancaster and a number were operated by the Central Bomber Establishment, Marham, and the Empire Air Armament, Navigation and Radio Schools at Manby, Shawbury and Debden. Their names *Excalibur, Crusader, Thor II, Aries II* and *Mercury II* perpetuated those of their illustrious forebears. During 1946–49 they made long-distance liaison flights to the Commonwealth and

*Aries III RE367* of the Empire Air Navigation School, Shawbury, with Lancastrian nose and tail. (*Flight photo 25077S*)

USA to demonstrate the latest bombing tactics, defensive armament and navigation aids. *Aries II*, with Lancastrian-type nose and tail, made a round trip to Australia during October–December 1947 to make researches into the earth's magnetic field but in 1948 was destroyed by fire and replaced by *Aries III*.

The Lincoln's performance at altitude and its ample accommodation for test equipment made it an ideal vehicle for flight-testing the new generation of British propeller-turbines. Other experimental Lincolns included *RF533* fitted in 1954 with a stepped canopy for observing rain erosion of a Javelin radome in the nose; *RA657* used to perfect Flight Refuelling's probe and drogue apparatus; *RE284* flown with a scale Brabazon undercarriage and *RF322* maintained by Eagle Aviation Services Ltd, Blackbushe, as a camera ship in succession to Lancaster *NX739*. *RE366* and *RF395* were converted into U. Mk.5 target drones, and two (one in civil marks) were converted for

408

Napier Icing Research Lincoln *RF342/G-APRJ* with aerofoil test section in position on the fuselage.
(*Flight photo 39293S*)

de-icing research in 1956 by the Napier Flight Development Establishment, Luton, and flown with 6 ft specimen wing sections mounted vertically on top of the fuselage and wetted by a 36 nozzle spray mat fed from water tanks in the bomb bay.

The Argentine Air Force acquired 30 (12 ex-RAF Lincoln B. Mk.2s and 18 new aircraft) to supplement Lancasters of Air Regiment No.1 and the first (serial *B-001*) was exhibited in Buenos Aires in October 1947. *B-003*, rebuilt at Langar, Notts, in 1948 with Lancastrian extremities and named *Cruz del Sud* for South Polar research flights with temporary civil marks *LV-ZEI*, was the first true Avro 695 Lincolnian. Paraguay also commissioned Field Aircraft Services Ltd to convert Lincoln 2s *RF417, RE376*

*ZP-CBR-97*, second of the abortive Paraguayan Lincolnian freighters.

and *RF458* to the same standard and to fit ventral freight holds. With civil marks *ZP-CBP-96* to *'BS-98* they were intended for carrying meat, but were scrapped when the scheme fell through. *G-ALPF*, sole British aircraft of this kind, was converted by Airflight Ltd at Langley (C of A June 22,

409

Lincoln B. Mk.4 *SX971* with ventral mounted Rolls-Royce Derwent and retractable tail wheels. (*Air Service Training*)

1949) from Lincoln 2 *RE290* and fitted with ventral pannier for use by Surrey Flying Services on the Berlin Air Lift. After one freight sortie it was converted for the bulk uplift of fuel oil and made 45 tanker sorties before returning to Southend to be scrapped in 1952.

## SPECIFICATION AND DATA

*Manufacturers:*    A. V. Roe and Co Ltd, Greengate, Middleton, Manchester; and Woodford Aerodrome, Cheshire; and Yeadon Aerodrome, Yorks

Metropolitan-Vickers Ltd, Mosley Road Works, Manchester

Sir W. G. Armstrong Whitworth Aircraft Co Ltd, Whitley, Coventry

Victory Aircraft Ltd, Malton, Ontario, Canada

The Australian Government Aircraft Factory, Fishermens Bend, Melbourne

Lincoln B. Mk.2 *RF403* with Armstrong Siddeley Python propeller-turbines in the outer nacelles. (*Hawker Siddeley*)

410

Lincoln B. Mk.2 *RF402* equipped for Napier Naiad propeller-turbine icing trials, 1948. (*Napier*)

*Powerplants:*   (B. Mk.1)   Four 1,750 hp Rolls-Royce Merlin 85
                        Two 1,750 hp Rolls-Royce Merlin 85B and two
                         1,750 hp Rolls-Royce Merlin 66
           (B. Mk.2)   Four 1,750 hp Packard Merlin 68, 68A or 300
           (B. Mk.4)   Four 1,750 hp Rolls-Royce Merlin 85
           (B. Mk.15) Four 1,750 hp Packard Merlin 68A
           (Mk.30(B)) Four 1,750 hp Rolls-Royce Merlin 85
                         Four 1,750 hp Rolls-Royce Merlin 102

*Dimensions:*   Span 120 ft 0 in   Height 17 ft $3\frac{1}{2}$ in
              Length 78 ft $3\frac{1}{2}$ in; with Lancastrian nose and tail 85 ft 0 in;
                Mk.31(MR) 84 ft $3\frac{1}{2}$ in
              Wing area 1,421 sq ft

*Weights:*   (B. Mk.1) Tare weight 43,778 lb   All-up weight 82,000 lb
          (B. Mk.2) Tare weight 44,148 lb   All-up weight 82,000 lb

*Performance:*   Maximum speed 295 mph at 15,000 ft
              Cruising speed 238 mph at 15,000 ft
              Initial climb 820 ft/min   Ceiling 22,000 ft
              Maximum range 3,750 miles
              Range 2,640 miles (with 14,000 lb of bombs at 215 mph at
                20,000 ft)

The Tyne test-bed Lincoln *G-37-1*. (*Rolls-Royce*)

*Production:*

### (a) By A. V. Roe and Co Ltd at Manchester

Three prototypes to Air Ministry Specification B.14/43: *PW925, PW929* and *PW932*, also 162 aircraft under Contract No.1807: *RE227–RE268, RE281–RE288* (B. Mk.1); *RE289–RE325, RE338–RE380, RE393–RE424* (B. Mk.2). (*PW932* scrapped at Cranfield 1961)

### (b) By A. V. Roe and Co Ltd at Yeadon

Six aircraft for the RAF under Contract No.3858: *SS713–SS714* (B.Mk.1); *SS715–SS718* (B. Mk.2)

### (c) By Metropolitan-Vickers Ltd

Seventy-nine aircraft under Contract No.2221: *RA628–RA655* (B. Mk.1); *RA656–RA658, RA661–RA693, RA709–RA724* (B. Mk.2)

### (d) By Sir W. G. Armstrong Whitworth Aircraft Ltd

Two hundred aircraft under Contract No.239: *RF329–RF370, RF383–RF427, RF440–RF485, RF498–RF539, RF553–RF577* (B. Mk.2)

Sixty aircraft under Contract No.4069: *SX923–SX958, SX970–SX993* (B. Mk.2 modified to Mk.4 after delivery)

Twenty-one aircraft under Contract No.3388: *WD122–WD133, WD141–WD149* (B. Mk.2).

Eighteen diverted to A. V. Roe for the Argentine under Works Order SALES 104 as *B-013* to *B-030*, c/n 1489–1506

### (e) By Victory Aircraft Ltd at Malton, Ontario

Five aircraft *FM300–FM304* laid down but only *FM300* completed. First flown 25.10.45. (possibly its only flight) On charge at No.1 Equipment Depot, Weston, Ontario, 17.8.46 but remained stored in the Avro Canada works at Malton until at least 4.3.47

### (f) By the Australian Government Aircraft Factory

Twenty-four Mk.30(B): *A73-1* to *A73-24*. Thirty Mk.30A(B): *A73-25* to *A73-54*. Eighteen conversions to Mk.31(MR) reserialled *A73-55* to *A73-73*

### (g) Reconditioned by Short Bros and Harland Ltd at Belfast

Twelve Lincoln B. Mk.2 for the Argentine under Works Order SALES 104/17: *B-001* to *B-012*, Avro c/n *1405–1416*, ex *RE343, RE349–RE356, RE408–RE410*

*Service Use* (Squadron codes in parentheses):

Bomber Command: Nos.7(MG), 9, 12(PH), 15(LS), 35(TL), 44(KM), 49(EA), 50(VN), 57(DX), 61(QR), 83(OL), 90(WP), 97(OF), 100(HW), 101(SR), 115(KO), 116, 138(NF), 148(AU), 149(OJ), 192, 199, 207(EM), 214(QN), 245, 527, 617(KC). Other Units: No.230 OCU, Air Sea Warfare Development Unit, Bomber Command Instructors' School, Central Bomber Establishment, Radio Warfare Establishment, Empire Air Armament School, Empire Test Pilots' School, Central Gunnery School, Radar Reconnaissance Flight, Radar Bombing School, No.1426 Flight, Aden, No.90 Group. To Australia for special trials: *RA638, 640, 644, 648, RE258, 259, 339, 418, RF403, 423*

*Named Lincolns:*

*Aries II*     *RE 364*, Empire Air Navigation School, Shawbury; Lancastrian nose and tail; named 3.47 by Lady Coningham; to Singapore 7.3.47, nonstop Habbaniyah, Iraq, Shawbury 30.3.47, to South Africa 30.4.47, to Montreal 11.8.47, to New Zealand 20.10.47, to the Far East 27.1.48; destroyed by fire 1948

| *Aries III* | *RE367*, replaced *Aries II* 12.48 |
| *Crusader* | *RF498*, Central Bomber Establishment, Marham; to South Africa 26.10.46, to the Far East and Australasia 26.10.47, to South Africa 16.2.48, to Canada and USA 1.4.49, to *7021M* |
| *Excalibur* | *RF844*, Central Bomber Establishment, Marham; to the Far East, Australia and New Zealand 9.9.46 |
| *Mercury II* | *RE414*, Empire Radio School, Debden, replacing Halifax VI *Mercury*; to Canada and USA 27.5.47, to the Far East and Australasia 22.1.48, to South Africa 19.9.48, to Canada 18.1.49 |
| *Thor II* | *RF523*, Empire Air Armament School, Manby, replacing Lancaster *Thor I*; to Canada and USA 2.11.46, to the Far East 18.4.47, to Canada and USA 26.9.47, to South Africa 22.1.48, to New Zealand 10.5.48, to the Far East 18.1.49 |

*Lincoln test beds:*

| *RA643* | Equipped as test-bed for Bristol Phoebus turbojet 1947 by D. Napier and Son Ltd, Luton. Test engine mounted in bomb bay, extensive flying at Filton |

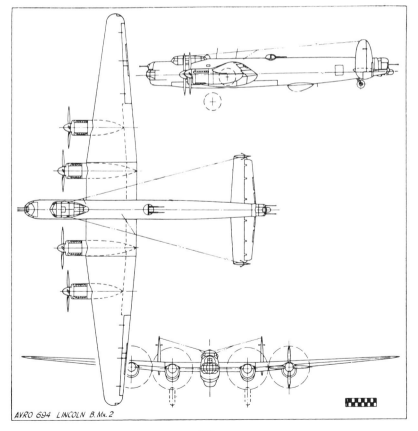

AVRO 694 LINCOLN B.Mk.2

| RA716 | Fitted by the Engine Division of the Bristol Aeroplane Co Ltd with two 2,400 hp Bristol Theseus 11s in outer nacelles, first flown at Filton by A. J. Pegg 17.2.47; at Martlesham 3.55 with Rolls-Royce Avons outboard, to No.23 MU, Aldergrove 4.57 |
|---|---|
| RE339 | Similar conversion with two 2,180 hp Bristol Theseus 21s (with heat exchangers) in outer nacelles |
| RE418 | Second Theseus 21 conversion, loaned to RAF Transport Command for scheduled services from Lyneham to the Middle East beginning 21.5.48 |
| RF342 | Fitted with Lancaster nose to continue Napier icing research begun by *RF402* (below), but equipped with four 200 gallon fuselage water tanks. Tested Beverley, Caravelle, Britannia and Comet wingtips. Civil as *G-APRJ* for flight to France 1.59; to Class B 1960 as *G-29-1* with Buccaneer tail test section; flown to College of Aeronautics, Cranfield, 11.62 as *G-36-3*; last flight Cranfield to Southend as *G-APRJ* 9.5.67, displayed at the British Historic Aircraft Museum painted as *G-29-1*. By road to Blackbushe to join Doug Arnold's Warbirds of the Great Britain Collection 11.11.83, later moved to Bitteswell; sold to Aces High Ltd, North Weald, and restored to register as *G-APRJ* 19.8.86 but remained dismantled. In storage at RAE Thurleigh in 1990. |
| RF368 | Fitted with two Bristol Proteus in the outer nacelles |
| RF402 | Converted by D. Napier and Son Ltd, Luton, 1948 for icing trials with dummy Napier Naiad in the nose. Reverted to standard 9.56 for use by the Napier Icing Research Unit and flown with vertically mounted Beverley wingtip on top of fuselage, and 36-nozzle spray mat supplied from two 60 gallon water tanks. Allotted registration *G-APRP* 1.59, to spares for *RF342* in 1960 |
| RF403 | Fitted with two Armstrong Siddeley Pythons in outer nacelles by Air Service Training Ltd, Hamble |
| RF530 | Flown at Luton 1946 with one 1,500 ehp Napier Naiad propeller-turbine in the nose |
| RF533 | Flying laboratory at RAE for development of radar and fire control systems |
| SX971 | One Rolls-Royce Derwent fitted under the bomb bay by Air Service Training Ltd, Hamble, first flown 10.50 by F/Lt P. R. Fowler. To counteract afterburner heat the under fuselage was sheathed with stainless steel and twin retractable tail wheels fitted. Flown Farnborough-Hullavington for scrapping 4.12.56 |
| SX972 | Converted 6.49 as *RA716* (above) with two 3,200 hp Bristol Proteus in outer nacelles |
| SX973 | Flown with one Napier Nomad 1 in the nose, trials completed 1954. A scheme to equip a further Lincoln test-bed with two Nomads was allotted type number Avro 717 |
| G-37-1 | Converted ex *RF533* (above) and strengthened at Hucknall and flown with prototype 4,500 hp Rolls-Royce Tyne in the nose 1956 in connection with the Vickers Vanguard development programme. Flown at the Farnborough SBAC Show 9.9.56 on the Tyne alone, with all four Merlins shut down and propellers feathered |

414

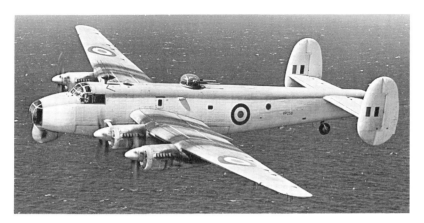

Avro 696 Shackleton M.R.1. *VP256* of RAF Coastal Command. (*Avro*)

# Avro 696 Shackleton

Planned originally as the anti-submarine Lincoln 3, the Shackleton was developed to meet a 1946 Coastal Command requirement for a long-range maritime reconnaissance aircraft to replace lend-lease Fortress and Liberator machines handed back to the USA. It used many Tudor assemblies and was fitted with the Lincoln mainplane and undercarriage, but the tailplane was moved from low- to mid-wing position and the vertical surfaces enlarged. The new stressed skin fuselage was shorter, wider and deeper than the Lincoln's and power was supplied by two 2,450 hp Rolls-Royce Griffon 57As inboard and two 57s outboard, all driving D.H. Hydromatic six-bladed contra-rotating airscrews.

Conforming to Air Ministry Specification R.5/46 and known as the Shackleton G.R.1 (later M.R.1), the prototype *VW126* was first flown at Woodford by Avro chief test pilot J. H. Orrell on March 9, 1949. It was armed with a 20 mm Hispano cannon on each side of the nose, two more in a Bristol B.17 mid-upper turret, and two 0·50 in machine-guns in the tail. Depth charges and/or bombs were housed in the bomb bay and the normal crew was ten. A large chin-type radome housed the ASV scanner and *VW126* also had a flight-refuelling intake under the tail. Two further prototypes, *VW131* and *VW135*, followed, and the first production aircraft, *VP254*, to Specification 42/46 flew on October 24, 1950. After entering service via No.120 Squadron and No.236 OCU, Kinloss, in February 1951 the Shackleton M.R.1 gradually replaced the Lancaster M.R.3 and formed the equipment of several new Coastal Command squadrons.

The second production batch, delivered in 1952, was fitted with Griffon 57A engines throughout, resulting in a widening of the outer nacelles and change in designation to M.R.1A. Total M.R.1 and M.R.1A production was 77 aircraft. Operational experience showed the need for improved radar

*VW131*, the second prototype Shackleton, with its bomb doors open. (*Avro*)

and the ineffectiveness of the nose and tail armament. This was consequently removed from existing Shackletons, to supersede which the aerodynamically cleaner M.R.2 was produced with a 10 ft streamlined nose housing twin 20 mm cannons above a bomb aimer's position equipped with optically flat panels. A new radome with 360 degree scan was sited in a semi-retractable 'dustbin' aft of the bomb doors, a transparent tail cone was fitted, and twin retractable tail wheels replaced the single fixed unit. These improvements were first flown on the prototype *VW126* which served as the M.R.2 aerodynamic test vehicle. The next aircraft, *WB833*, a modified M.R.1A, first flew as an M.R.2 on June 17, 1952, and an early example *WL796*, complete with Saro Mk.3 lifeboat, was flown at the 1953 Farnborough SBAC Show with three engines feathered.

The first of 69 Shackleton M.R.2s entered Coastal Command service in the UK and Malta later in 1952 after which long-distance flights were made by No.42 Squadron to South Africa and the Far East in April 1953; No.206 Squadron made a 40,000 mile goodwill tour to Fiji in 1954; and four M.R.1As of No.228 Squadron visited Brazil, Venezuela and Colombia in 1955. Those of No.240 Squadron swept the Pacific during the atomic tests at Christmas Island and Malta-based Shackletons were used as troop transports during the intervention in Egypt in November 1956. A projected

Shackleton M.R.1A *WB833* after modification to M.R.2 standard.

416

meteorological version of the Shackleton M.R.2 was allocated the type number Avro 713.

The withdrawal of the last Sunderland flying-boats created a need for a modernised Shackleton and work began on the M.R.3 version in 1954. Similar in appearance to the M.R.2, it was equipped with a tricycle undercarriage and duplicated landing wheels; a modified mainplane with revised planform; improved ailerons; wingtip auxiliary tanks; and clear vision flight deck canopy. Twin nose-mounted 20 mm cannon were reintroduced but the mid-upper turret was omitted in favour of eight rocket projectiles or sonobuoys under the wings.

The M.R.3 could remain airborne for 18 hours, or in special circumstances 24 hours, so that it was necessary to carry a duplicated crew and provide a

South African Air Force Shackleton M.R.3 *1720*, c/n 1520.

soundproofed ward room for off duty periods. The link with naval tradition was strengthened by painting all Shackletons in battleship grey. *WR970*, the first M.R.3, flew on September 2, 1955, and appeared at that year's SBAC Show but contracts were cut back in 1956 and the first machines did not reach the squadrons until 1957. From bases in Northern Ireland, Southwest England, Gibraltar and Malta the M.R.3s settled down to unpublicised, unspectacular but incessant patrolling of the sea lanes and in February 1959 an aircraft of No.206 Squadron (F.Lt D. R. Foster) remained airborne for the record time of 24 hr 21 min during a patrol to the Canaries. In November 1962 three M.R.3s of No.120 Squadron took part in Exercise Main Run III and made a goodwill tour of the Caribbean.

A visit to Durban by four Shackleton M.R.2s of No.204 Squadron in June 1955 for a South African air-sea exercise resulted in eight M.R.3s from the initial production batch being supplied to the SAAF, with serials *1716* to *1723*, in the face of strong American competition. The first two were handed over at Woodford on May 16, 1957, and after crew training at St Mawgan and a joint tactical exercise over the North Sea with Coastal Command, were flown to D.F. Malan Airport, near Cape Town, to equip No.35 Squadron. One, *1718*, was lost in a crash in the Steyskloof Mountains of Cape Province on August 8, 1963, but the remaining seven aircraft

417

continued their ocean patrols until, beginning with *1723* in 1977, they were progressively grounded as their 4,400 hour spar lives were reached. By the end of 1983 only three were airworthy and the type was officially withdrawn from service on November 23, 1984, an occasion marked by the survivors *1716*, *1721* and *1722* making a flypast at D.F. Malan, their base for 27 years.

Although largely superseded by the M.R.3 with its improved submarine plotting equipment, the earlier marks continued in service and a number of elderly Shackleton M.R.1 and 1As were modified internally to reproduce the radio and navigation layout of the M.R.3 under the designation T.Mk.4 for use by the Maritime Operational Training Unit, Kinloss. Modifications to the engines, electronic equipment and accommodation of the M.R.2s produced the M.R.2 Phases 1, 2 and 3. The latter had M.R.3 navigation and offensive equipment together with a Mk.3 exhaust system to eliminate soot traces on the wings and were known unofficially as the Shackleton M.R.2C. This mark equipped No.205 Squadron FEAF, at Singapore in 1962.

Phase modifications were also applied to the M.R.3. with Phase 2 involving provision of new electronics and diesel exhaust detection equipment to aid submarine detection. The fitting of Viper 203 turbojets in the rear of the outboard nacelles to boost available power for take-off and provision of improved navigational equipment produced the Phase 3 machine. All M.R.3s were brought up to this standard with the exception of the single machine operated by the RAE.

Following the examples of previous Avro 'heavies', the Shackleton was also used experimentally. *WL789* was flown at St Mawgan in 1954 with a MAD (Magnetic Anomaly Detection) 'stinger' tail; and the same year one

M.R.1 was equipped, but did not fly with two 3,135 hp Napier Nomad 2 engines in the outer nacelles. A production version, the Avro 719 Shackleton Mk.4 with four Napier Nomad E.145 engines, was not built. One other aircraft used for research until its retirement in 1973 was the RAE's M.R.3 *WR972*. Employed mainly on parachute development work for which an observer was provided with a modified tail position, its tasks during the 1960s included testing escape parachutes for Concorde flight-test crews and ground towing the supersonic airliner's drag parachute.

Deficiences in the RAF's ability to detect low flying aircraft led to the development of the final version of the Shackleton, the A.E.W.2. Conceived in 1967, the first of twelve M.R.2s to be converted to this standard, *WL745*, flew for the first time in its new guise on September 30, 1971. The main radar came from redundant Fairey Gannet A.E.W.3s and was housed in a large and distinctive ventral radome. All the aircraft went to No.8 Squadron which was reformed at Kinloss in January 1972 but moved to Lossiemouth in August the following year.

The majority of the M.R.1 and 1As were flown to No.23 MU at Aldergrove and scrapped in the early 1960s but the later marks of Maritime Reconnaissance Shackleton remained in service until progressively replaced by the Hawker Siddeley Nimrod beginning in 1969. The last UK-based M.R.3, *XF703* of No.42 Squadron, was withdrawn from service in September 1971 and those based in Malta with No.203 Squadron followed soon afterwards. A number of M.R.2s, however remained in service at Honington with No.204 Squadron until it was disbanded on April 28, 1972.

Once the venerable RAE Shackleton T.4 *VP293 Zebedee* was withdrawn from service and flown to Strathallan for preservation in December 1975, only the No.8 Squadron Early Warning aircraft remained operational. On

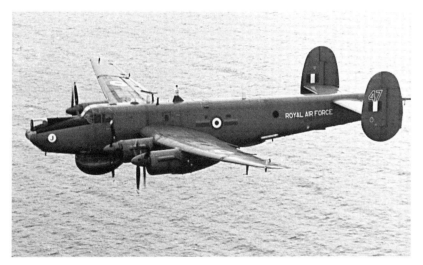

Shackleton A.E.W.2 *WL747* of No.8 Squadron, RAF Lossiemouth. (*Crown Copyright reserved*)

419

March 9, 1989, the six remaining A.E.W.2s took part in the flypast at Woodford to mark the 40th Anniversary of the Shackleton's first flight. Final withdrawal of the type from RAF service was scheduled for June 30, 1991, the day that No.8 Squadron would re-equip with Boeing Sentry A.E.W.1s.

## SPECIFICATION AND DATA

*Manufacturers:*  A. V. Roe and Co Ltd, Greengate, Middleton, Manchester; and Woodford Aerodrome, Cheshire

*Powerplants:*  (M.R.1)  Two 2,450 hp Rolls-Royce Griffon 57 and two Griffon 57A
(Other marks) Four 2,450 hp Rolls-Royce Griffon 57A

*Dimensions, Weights and Performances:*

|  | Shackleton M.R.1 | Shackleton M.R.2 | Shackleton M.R.3 |
|---|---|---|---|
| Span | 120 ft 0 in | 120 ft 0 in | 119 ft 10 in |
| Length | 77 ft 6 in | 87 ft 3 in | 92 ft 6 in |
| Height | 17 ft 6 in | 16 ft 9 in | 23 ft 4 in |
| Wing area | 1,421 sq ft | 1,421 sq ft | 1,421 sq ft |
| Tare weight | — | — | 57,800 lb |
| All-up weight | — | 86,000 lb | 100,000 lb |
| Maximum speed | — | — | 302 mph |
| Cruising speed | — | — | 260 mph |
| Initial climb | — | — | 850 ft/min |
| Ceiling | — | — | 19,200 ft |
| Range | — | — | 4,215 miles |

*At 200 mph at 1,500 ft

*Production:*

**Prototypes**: *VW126, VW131* and *VW135* to Air Ministry Specification 5/46 (*VW126* later aerodynamic test vehicle for Shackleton M.R.2, scrapped at No.23 MU, Aldergrove 1957)

**Shackleton M.R.1**: Twenty-nine aircraft to Specification 42/46, *VP254–VP268, VP281–VP294*

**Shackleton M.R.1A**: Forty-eight aircraft built at Chadderton, *WB818–WB837, WB844–WB861, WG507–WG511, WG525–WG529*

**Shackleton M.R.2**: Sixty-nine aircraft built at Chadderton, *WG530–WG533, WG553–WG558, WL737–WL759, WL785–WL801, WR951–WR969*

**Shackleton M.R.3**: Thirty-four aircraft built at Chadderton, *WR970–WR990, XF700–XF711, XF730.* (*WR970*, first flown 2.9.55, crashed at Foolow, Derbyshire, 7.12.56, Avro test pilot J. B. Wales and crew killed)

**Shackleton M.R.3**: Eight aircraft for the South African Air Force, serials *1716–1723,* c/n 1526–1533

*Conversions*

**Shackleton T.4** (from M.R.1A): *VP258, VP259, VP292, WB819, WB820, WB822, WB826, WB831, WB832, WB837, WB844, WB847, WB849, WB858, WG511* and *WG527*

**Shackleton A.E.W.2** (from M.R.2): *WL741, WL745, WL747, WL754,*

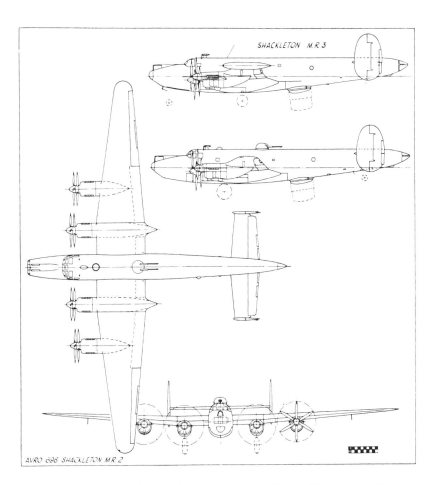

SHACKLETON M.R.3

AVRO 696 SHACKLETON M.R.2

*WL756, WL757, WL790, WL793, WL795, WR960, WR963* and *WR965*
*Service Use:* (Individual aircraft often served with so many different squadrons
that it is only possible to quote representative serial numbers)

Home-based Squadrons. No.8: A.E.W.2s listed above. No.42: *WG510,
WL737, WR952.* No.120: *VP259, WB828, WG511, WL745, WR987,
XF703.* No.201: *WR975, XF707.* No.203: *WV860, WG507, WR973,
XF704.* No.204: *VP284, WB850, WL751, WR951.* No.206: *WB826,
WG508, WR982, XF702,.* No.210: *WG555, WL797, WR971, XF700.*
No.220: *VP257, WB821, WL737, WR969.* No.224: *VP256, WB852,
WG532, WL741.* No.228: *WG557, WR959.* No.240: *VP287, WB835,
WG529, WL738.* No.269: *VP255, WB818, WG509, WL746.* Overseas
Squadrons. No.37: *WG556, WL744.* No.38: *WL740, WR954.* No.205:
*VP291, WB825, WG525, WL750.* No.35 Squadron S.A.A.F.: *1716–1723.*
Training. No.236 O.C.U. (later M.O.T.U.): *VP262, WB830.* Air Sea
Warfare Development Unit: *VP288, WB856, WG553, WL789.* Aeroplane
and Armament Experimental Establishment: *VP258, WB858.* Royal Air-
craft Establishment: *VP293, WG557, WR972*

# Avro 698 Vulcan

Developed to a 1947 Air Staff requirement (specification B.35/46) calling for a high-altitude bomber to carry a nuclear warload at speeds approaching Mach 1, the Vulcan was the world's first large delta-wing aircraft. Radical departure from convention enabled Roy Chadwick to design an aircraft which met an exacting specification yet at the same time was comparatively small and landed relatively slowly. Regrettably he did not live to see the tender accepted on November 27, 1947, or the completion of the design in the following September.

Of all-metal, stressed skin construction, the wing was some 7 ft thick at the root end enabling drag to be kept to a minimum by enclosing engines, undercarriage, fuel and bomb load entirely within it. Trailing-edge flaps were unnecessary as landings were made at high angles of attack and defensive armament was neither needed nor fitted. Although unusual in appearance the Vulcan was structurally orthodox with two-spar mainplane, backward retracting nose wheels, forward retracting eight-wheel bogie main units, and turbojets grouped close to the centre line. A conventional rudder was hinged to a swept fin but the other controls consisted of two pairs of ailerons and elevators on the trailing edge of the wing, with gate-type air-brakes extending above and below. A braking parachute was fitted as standard.

Due to the unavailability of the Bristol Olympus turbojets for which it had been designed, Vulcan prototype *VX770* was completed with four 6,500 lb st Rolls-Royce Avon R.A.3s and the first flown in August 30, 1952, by Avro chief test pilot Wing Cdr R. Falk, who startled the aviation world by rolling it at the Farnborough SBAC Show a few days later. Such success derived from Avro's far sighted test programme with five small Avro 707 delta-wing research aircraft which were, in effect, third-scale models. They gave valuable data on the Vulcan's probable flight characteristics, and two of them—the all-red Avro 707A *WD280* and all-blue Avro 707B *VX790*—emphasised the docility of deltas by flying a patriotic formation with the all-white Vulcan prototype during its SBAC debut. *VX770* reappeared at the 1954 Show with 8,000 lb st Armstrong Siddeley Sapphires and in 1957–58 with 15,000 lb st Rolls-Royce Conway R.Co.7s.

The second prototype *VX777*, fitted with 9,750 lb st Bristol Olympus 100s, flew for the first time on September 3, 1953. The Vulcan 'V Bomber' had been ordered into quantity production for the RAF before the prototype had flown and though the first production aircraft *XA889* (first flown on February 4, 1955) was initially powered by Olympus 100s it was later re-engined with the 11,000 lb st Olympus 101s that were fitted to subsequent machines. Production models were also made slightly longer in the nose to avoid the need for shortening the nose leg before retraction. Boscombe Down trials showed that application of *g* at altitude could initiate buffeting which could lead to fatigue failure of the outer wings. In October 1955 therefore *VX777* was flown with leading edge sweepback reduced from 52 to 42 degrees at half-span but increased further outboard. The few existing Vulcans were immediately modified in this way and beginning with *XA890*, had extended engine nacelles.

Designated Vulcan B. Mk.1 the new deltas entered service with No.230 OCU in May 1956 and No.83 Squadron in July 1957. Planned re-equipment was completed in 1960 when Nos.101 and 617 also received the Vulcan B. Mk.1.

During the first overseas Vulcan flight, *XA897* flew from Boscombe Down to Melbourne via Aden and Singapore on September 9, 1956, in 23 hrs 9 min, but its tragic crash on final approach to London Airport, at the end of the flight on October 1, marred an impressive performance. In March 1958 *XA908* toured the Central African Federation.

The advent of powerful 16,000 lb st Olympus 200 (flown in Vulcan B. Mk.1 *XA891* at the 1958 Farnborough SBAC Show) made possible the much more advanced Vulcan B. Mk.2 with increased span and intended as a launching platform for the Avro Blue Steel 'stand-off' bomb or the Douglas Skybolt missile. Best use of the increased power was made by reducing the thickness/chord ratio of the wing extremities and further increasing the compound taper of the leading edge. Buffeting limitations were removed by fitting elevons in place of conventional ailerons and elevators. A Rover auxiliary power plant made the Mk.2 independent of outside services and the effective range was extended by providing for air refuelling from Vickers Valiant tankers. The second prototype *VX777*, became the B. Mk.2 aerodynamic test vehicle and first flew with the new wing and toed-out jet-pipes for the later Olympus engines on August 31, 1957.

The first production Vulcan B. Mk.2 *XH533* flew in August 1958 and deliveries began in 1960 to Nos.27, 83 and 617 Squadrons and B. Mk.1 aircraft from the last two were then taken over by Nos.44 and 50.

The power of the B. Mk.2 was gradually increased until the 20,000 lb st

423

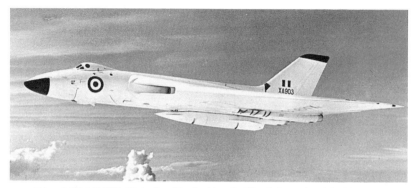

Vulcan B.Mk.1 *XA903* with the Avro Blue Steel 'stand-off' bomb that equipped the B.Mk.2.

Olympus 301 raised the top speed and operating altitude to the aerodynamic limits of the airframe. Designation B.Mk.2A was applied to the late production aircraft having this engine. One aircraft went to Edwards Air Force Base in the USA in July 1961 to check the compatibility of the Vulcan and Skybolt electrical systems, but after that missile was abandoned in 1963, Blue Steel became the standard war load. It was first fitted to the 15th production Mk.1 aircraft, *XA903*, and shown publicly at the 1962 SBAC Show on *XL361*. The Service development trials were conducted by No.617 Squadron, Scampton, which fired the first training rounds at Woomera late in 1963. With its fighter-like manoeuvrability and ability to release Blue Steel one hundred miles from the target, the Vulcan B.Mk.2 was at the time one of the finest medium bombers in service anywhere and a formidable deterrent.

After the B.Mk.2s had entered service the remaining B.Mk.1s were modified to B.Mk.1A standard. This involved the fitting of an extended tail

Vulcan B.Mk.1 *XA889* with modified leading edge planform. (*Avro*)

424

cone, upgraded electronics and a flat Electronic Counter Measures aerial plate between the two starboard jet-pipes.

Many spectacular long-distance flights with air refuelling emphasised the Vulcan's incredible ability to reach remote places of the earth in less than a day, as for example the 8,500 mile nonstop, $17\frac{1}{2}$ hour UK–Karachi and return flight by a No.617 Squadron aircraft in April 1961: UK–Gan nonstop a month later; Scampton–Sydney nonstop in 20 hr 3 min in June 1961; the 3,674 miles London–Aden point-to-point record by a Vulcan of No.101 Squadron in 6 hrs 14 min on March 30, 1962; and Waddington–Perth nonstop by three aircraft of No.101 Squadron in July 1963. Others took part in Operation Skyshield II in October 1961 and Western Ranger flights to the USA. One each from Nos.27, 83 and 617 Squadrons, Scampton, flew to the Antipodes in November 1962 to fly past at the Commonwealth Games and to participate in the RNZAF 25th Anniversary celebrations. On the return trip No.617 Squadron's machine established a Goose Bay–Scampton record of 3 hr 46 min at an average speed of 656 mph.

After the destruction of the Conway R.Co.7 test-bed *VX770* during a high-speed run at the Battle of Britain Display at Syerston in September 1958, a 1,000 hr endurance programme with the R.Co.11 was carried through at Hucknall in *XA902*. This aircraft was used later for Rolls-Royce Spey development and flew from Hucknall on October 12, 1961, piloted by Rolls-Royce chief test pilot J. Heyworth, with Conways fitted outboard and the Rolls-Royce Spey by-pass engines (for the D.H.121 Trident, B.A.C. One-Eleven and Buccaneer S.2) inboard.

Specially instrumented, *XA894* was equipped as test-bed for the Olympus 22R powerplant of the supersonic T.S.R.2., the additional engine being

The Vulcan FTB *XA903* with an Olympus 593 in a Concorde engine pod underneath the fuselage.
(*Rolls-Royce*)

*XA894* with supersonic Bristol Olympus test engine in ventral pod with bifurcated air intake.
(*S. P. Peltz*)

The Rolls-Royce/Turbo-Union RB.199 engine of the Panavia Tornado beneath Vulcan FTB *XA903*.
(*Rolls-Royce*)

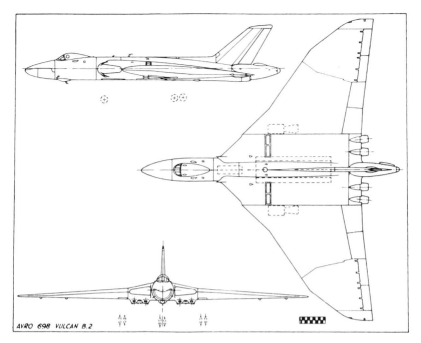

AVRO 698 VULCAN B.2

carried in an underslung pod with bifurcated air intake. After almost eighty hours of test flying the aircraft was burned out on the ground at Filton on December 3, 1962. It was not until January 1964 that a replacement engine test bed, *XA903*, was delivered to Bristol Patchway. Employed on Concorde development work, *XA903* logged over 400 hours of test flying with an Olympus 593, in a Concorde engine pod beneath the fuselage, before the supersonic airliner flew. The same aircraft was modified in 1973 to carry a Rolls-Royce/Turbo-Union RB.199 mounted in an exact replica of the starboard half of a Tornado. Some 285 hours of test flying was completed in this, its final form, before the aircraft was retired in March 1979. One Vulcan B.Mk.2, *XH557*, was used by Bristol Siddeley for routine engine development flying in the early 1960s.

Together with the Victor, the Blue Steel equipped Vulcans B.Mk.2s provided the United Kingdom's Nuclear Deterrent until the role was taken over by Royal Navy submarines equipped with Polaris missiles in 1967. Subsequently the Blue Steels were withdrawn and the Vulcans switched to a conventional bombing role. The Vulcan B.Mk.1As were all withdrawn from service by 1968 and the three Squadrons (Nos.44, 50 and 101) re-equipped with B.Mk.2s.

The Vulcan took on a new role when No.27 Squadron, reformed at Scampton on November 1, 1973, was equipped with B.Mk.2s modified for the long distance strategic reconnaissance role previously undertaken by the Handley Page Victors of No.543 Squadron. These aircraft were designated Vulcan B.Mk.2MRR and remained in service for ten years.

Throughout the 1970s detachments of Vulcans from Nos.9 and 35 Squadrons were based with the Near East Air Force at Akrotiri, Cyprus, as part of Britain's contribution to CENTO. Aircraft from other squadrons ventured abroad to make a major impression at a number of military exercises. Four machines (one each from No.230 OCU and Nos.44, 101 and 617 Squadrons) participated in the USAF strategic bombing and navigation competition 'Giant Voice' held at Barksdale AFB, Louisiana, in November 1974. Competing against Boeing B52s and General Dynamics FB-111s, the Vulcans won two out of a possible three trophies, the best result the RAF had achieved since the normally annual event began in 1951. Vulcans were again in the USA in November and December 1978 taking part in only the second ever night 'Red Flag' air warfare exercise held at Nellis AFB, Nevada. Here good use was made of the aircraft's Terrain Following Radar and Electronic Counter Measures equipment to penetrate the sophisticated ground and fighter defences surrounding target areas in the 10 million acre range.

Delivery of *XH554* to the RAF Regiment's Fire Training School at Catterick on June 9, 1981, marked the start of the Vulcan retirement programme but it was in the twilight of its career during the Falklands War that the Vulcan was to fulfil its design role and be used for live bombing of an enemy target.

On May 1, 1982, *XM607*, operating from Wideawake Airfield on Ascension Island flew no less than 3,400 miles, aided by air-to-air refuelling from Handley Page Victor K.2 tankers to successfully drop a full load of twenty-one 1,000 lb bombs on the runway at Port Stanley airfield in the Falklands. Operation 'Black Buck 1', as it was known, was followed by further equally remarkable long-range missions against the Argentinian Forces occupying the islands. A second attack on Port Stanley airfield 'Black Buck 2' was flown by *XM607* on May 3/4, 1982, and caused considerable damage to airfield installations and parked aircraft as did 'Black Buck 7' flown on June 12. Another Vulcan, *XM597*, equipped with two anti-radiation Shrike missiles mounted on under-wing pylons, knocked out the main Argentinian radar on the islands on May 30 in operation 'Black Buck 5'. The same aircraft, on this occasion, carrying four Shrikes flew another mission ('Black Buck 6') against enemy radar installations on the island on June 2/3 but on its return journey the refuelling probe broke. Short of fuel,

Vulcan K.2 *XH560* refuelling a Panavia Tornado

a diplomatically embarrassing diversion to Rio de Janeiro was executed and a week passed before the Vulcan was released.

The 'Black Buck' missions stretched the RAF's flight refuelling capabilities to their limit resulting in a decision being made to augment the fleet with Vulcan tankers. Designated Vulcan K.2s, six aircraft were converted in 1982 and operated by No.50 Squadron until the unit, the last to operate the Vulcan, was disbanded in early 1984. The last B.Mk.2 squadron, No.44, had been disbanded on December 31, 1982.

Despite its withdrawal from active service the formation of the Vulcan Display Flight, equipped with *XH558* and based at Waddington, enabled the majestic delta to continue thrilling crowds at summer airshows throughout the eighties and into the nineties.

## SPECIFICATION AND DATA

*Manufacturers:*  A. V. Roe and Co Ltd, Greengate, Middleton, Manchester; and Woodford Aerodrome, Cheshire; restyled the Avro-Whitworth Division of Hawker Siddeley Aviation wef July 8, 1963

*Powerplants:*  (First prototype)
Four 6,500 lb st Rolls-Royce Avon R.A.3
Four 8,000 lb st Armstrong Siddeley Sapphire
Four 15,000 lb st Rolls-Royce Conway R.Co.7
(Second prototype)
Four 9,750 lb st Bristol Olympus 100
(Vulcan B.Mk.1)
Four 11,000 lb st Bristol Olympus 101
Four 12,000 lb st Bristol Olympus 102
Four 13,500 lb st Bristol Olympus 104
Four 17,250 lb st Rolls-Royce Conway R.Co.11 (*XA902* only)
Four 16,000 lb st Bristol Olympus 200 (*XA891* only)
(Vulcan B.Mk.2)
Four 16,000 lb st Bristol Olympus 200 (*XH533* only)
Four 17,000 lb st Bristol Olympus 201
Four 20,000 lb st Bristol Olympus 301

*Dimensions, Weights and Performances:*

|  | Vulcan B.Mk.1 | Vulcan B.Mk.2 |
| --- | --- | --- |
| Span | 99 ft 0 in | 111 ft 0 in |
| Length | 97 ft 1 in | 99 ft 11 in |
| Height | 26 ft 6 in | 27 ft 2 in |
| Wing area | 3,554 sq ft | 3,964 sq ft |
| All-up weight | 170,000 lb | 200,000 lb |
| Maximum speed | 625 mph | 645 mph |
| Cruising speed | 607 mph | 620 mph |
| Service ceiling | 55,000 ft | 60,000 ft |
| Range | 3,000 miles | 4,600 miles |

*Production:*

### (a) **Prototypes**

*VX770*, first flown with Avons 30.8.52, later with Sapphires and Conways; crashed at Syerston, Notts, 14.9.58. *VX777* first flown 3.9.53, later became aerodynamic test vehicle for the Vulcan B.2, first flown as such 31.8.57.

### (b) **Vulcan B.Mk.1**

Forty-five aircraft built at Woodford, *XA889–XA913*, *XH475–XH483*, *XH497–XH506* and *XH532*

### (c) **Vulcan B.Mk.2**

Eighty-nine aircraft built at Woodford, *XH533–XH539*, *XH554–XH563*, *XJ780–XJ784*, *XJ823–XJ825*, *XL317–XL321*, *XL359–XL361*, *XL384–XL392*, *XL425–XL427*, *XL443–XL446*, *XM569–XM576*, *XM594–XM612*, *XM645–XM657*

*Conversions*

Vulcan B.Mk.1A: *XA895*, *XA900*, *XA901*, *XA904*, *XA906*, *XA907*, *XA909–XA913*, *XH475–XH483*, *XH497–XH506* and *XH532*

Vulcan B.Mk.2MRR: Nine aircraft including *XH534*, *XH537*, *XH558*, *XH560*, *XH563* and *XM570*

Vulcan K.2: *XH558*, *XH560*, *XH561*, *XJ825*, *XL445* and *XM571*

*Service Use:* (with representative serial numbers).

Vulcan B.Mk.1 and 1A Squadrons: No.44 (Scampton) *XA896*, *XH501*. No.50 (Waddington) *XA909*, *XH483*. No.83 (Scampton) *XA901*. No.101 (Waddington) *XA913*, *XH532* and No.617 (Scampton) *XH483*, *XH497*. Also No.230 OCU (Finningley) *XA896*, *XA900*, *XH504* and RAE (Farnborough) *XA892*

Vulcan B.Mk.2 Squadrons: No.9 (Coningsby) *XH557*, *XJ780*, *XL389*, *XM646*. No.12 (Coningsby) *XM597*, *XM602*. No.27 (Scampton) *XM595*, *XJ824*, *XL444*. No.35 (Coningsby) *XH561*, *XJ783*, *XL445*, *XM572*. No.83 (Scampton) *XJ782*, *XL443* and No.617 (Scampton) *XH554*, *XL361*, *XM595*. Also No.230 OCU (Finningley) *XH559*, *XL319*, *XL359*

*Civil registered Vulcans:* (None flew after initial delivery in military marks): *XM575*, arrived East Midlands 21.8.83, registration *G-BLMC* reserved mid-1984 by Loughborough and Leicestershire Aircraft Museum for proposed ferry flight to Bruntingthorpe. Remained at East Midlands and preserved in the Aeropark. *XL426* arrived Southend 19.12.86, registered to R. E. Jacobsen (t/a The Vulcan Memorial Flight) as *G-VJET* 7.7.87. *XM655* arrived Wellesbourne Mountford 11.2.84, registered to R. E. Jacobsen as *G-VULC* 27.2.84, re-registered in USA as *N655AV* 3.9.85, restored as *G-VULC* 25.9.87

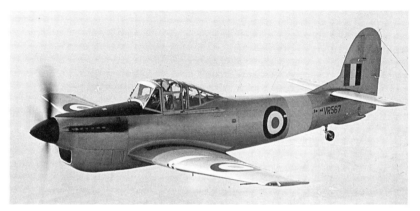

Avro 701 Athena T. Mk.2 *VR567. (Avro)*

# Avro 701 Athena

Designed by S. D. Davies, the Athena T. Mk.1 was a three-seat advanced trainer with propeller-turbine built to Air Ministry Specification T.7/45, as was the Boulton Paul Balliol, its main competitor. Intended to replace the Percival Prentice as the standard RAF basic trainer, it was an all-metal, low-wing monoplane which used the same aerofoil section as the Hawker Tempest in order to reproduce fighter-style handling qualities. Work began in March 1947 but after the first fuselage and wing structure had gone to Farnborough for strength tests, changing requirements of RAF Training Command and non-availability of turbine engines led to the replacement of the original Specification by T.14/47 stipulating a change of power plant to the 1,280 hp Rolls-Royce Merlin 35, large stocks of which were held in store. Considerable redesign resulted in the Athena T. Mk.2 on which the mainplane had been moved forward 27 inches to compensate for the greater weight of the piston engine.

Nevertheless work continued at Manchester on the installation of Armstrong Siddeley Mamba and Rolls-Royce Dart gas turbines in three Mk.1 airframes. These small-diameter engines gave a much improved view over the nose but required a large-diameter jet-pipe ejecting through the fuselage side aft of the starboard wing root on the Mamba powered *VM125* and *VM132*, and under the fuselage on the Dart engined *VM129*. *VM125* was first flown at Woodford on June 12, 1948, by J. H. Orrell.

The centre section of the T. Mk.2 housed an inward retracting Lockheed undercarriage, main fuel tanks, ·303 in Browning gun, 300 rounds of ammunition and a G.45B camera gun. It was also made immensely strong to minimise damage in the event of a wheels-up landing and was equipped with attachment points for bomb racks or 45 gallon drop tanks as well as access doors to the internal engineering. Although provision was made for folding wings they were not built as the naval requirement was withdrawn

431

before the first Athena flew. Engine cooling was by beard-type Morris radiator, and a target-towing point was situated under the tail.

Delivery of two Merlin powered Athena T. Mk.2 prototypes *VW890* (first flown on August 1, 1948) and *VW892* to Boscombe Down for performance tests, and tropical trials at Khartoum with *VW890*, was followed by evaluation of two production aircraft, *VR566* and *VR567*, at the Central Flying Establishment in October 1949. Whereas the first and third prototype T. Mk.2s and all the turbine-powered machines had triangular fins and small unbalanced rudders, the second T. Mk.2 *VW891*, was fitted with a balanced rudder of greater area hinged to a larger fin. This rudder was a feature of all production aircraft but with fin cut back giving the tail unit a tall angular appearance. The canopy was also shortened by moving the radio forward and eliminating the third seat.

The Athena T. Mk.2 replaced the Harvard for armament training at the RAF Flying College, Manby, for which purpose provision was made for two 60 lb rocket projectiles under each wing. Production was abandoned after the construction of 15 aircraft, but one machine was given temporary civil status as *G-ALWA* in February 1950 for a demonstration tour of India. It returned to Croydon on May 13, reverted to the Ministry of Supply as *VR569* and was demonstrated at the Farnborough SBAC Show in the following September by Avro test pilot J. Nelson.

Athena T. Mk.2 first prototype *VW890* with the original canopy and tail unit. (*Crown Copyright Reserved.*)

Second prototype, *VW891*, with increased fin and rudder area. (*Crown Copyright Reserved.*)

432

The Mamba-powered Athena T. Mk.1 *VM125*. (*Avro*)

The Athena T. Mk.2 civil demonstrator for *G-ALWA/VR569*, c/n 1519. (*Avro*)

## SPECIFICATION AND DATA

*Manufacturers:*  A. V. Roe and Co Ltd, Greengate, Middleton, Manchester; and Woodford Aerodrome, Cheshire

*Powerplants:*  (T. Mk.1)  One 1,010 hp Armstrong Siddeley Mamba 1
(T. Mk.1A)  One 1,400 hp Rolls-Royce Dart 1
(T. Mk.2)  One 1,280 hp Rolls-Royce Merlin 35

*Dimensions:*  (T. Mk.1)  Span 40 ft 0 in   Length 36 ft 6 in
Height 11 ft 11 in   Wing area 270 sq ft
(T. Mk.2)  Span 40 ft 0 in   Length 37 ft 3½ in
Height 12 ft 11 in   Wing area 270 sq ft

*Weights:*  (T. Mk.1 Mamba) Tare weight 5,067 lb
All-up weight 7,191 lb
(T. Mk.2)  Tare weight 6,540 lb  All up weight (dual) 9,043 lb, (gunnery) 9,101 lb, (navigation) 9,189 lb (bombing) 9,383 lb
(*G-ALWA*)  Tare weight 5,884 lb
All-up weight 8,210 lb

433

*Performances:*    (T. Mk.1 Mamba)
                   Maximum speed 291 mph at 20,000 ft
                   Cruising speed 256 mph    Initial climb 2,640 ft/min
                   Ceiling 34,800 ft    Range 620 miles
                   (T. Mk.2)
                   Maximum speed 293 mph at 20,000 ft
                   Cruising speed 223 mph    Initial climb 2,050 ft/min
                   Ceiling 29,000 ft    Range 550 miles

*Production:*
   (*a*) **Athena T. Mk.1**
Three aircraft to Specification T.7/45: *VM125* (Mamba) first flown at
Woodford 12.6.48, shown at 1948 SBAC Show; *VM129* (Dart) first flown
17.9.49, shown at 1949 SBAC Show; *VM132* (Mamba) first flown 12.12.49
   (*b*) **Athena T. Mk.2 prototypes**
Four aircraft to Specification T.14/47: *VW890* first flown 1.8.48, to Boscombe
Down; *VW891* tail modifications and tropical trials; *VW892* shown at 1949
SBAC Show thence to Boscombe Down; *VW893* to Empire Test Pilots' School,
Farnborough
   (*c*) **Athena T. Mk.2 production**
Fifteen aircraft: *VR566–VR580*. (*VR569* temporarily civil as *G-ALWA*, c/n
1519, C of A issued 2.2.50, reverted to *VR569* for SBAC Show 9.50 after
Indian sales tour.) Two further aircraft, *VR581* and *VR582*, were not built

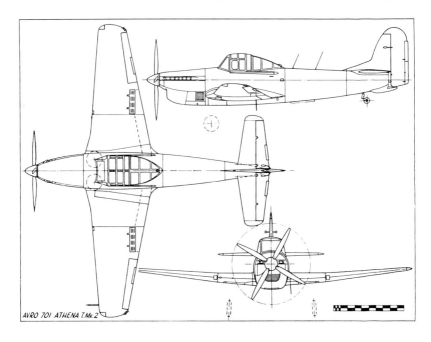

AVRO 701 ATHENA T.Mk.2

The Avro 706 Ashton Mk.1 *WB490*. (*Avro*)

# Avro 706 Ashton

Flight trials of the Tudor 8 with paired Rolls-Royce Nenes in single nacelles showed the need for a tricycle undercarriage to keep the jets clear of the ground when taxying. Designs were therefore put in hand for a Tudor 9 transport, based on the Tudor 2, but equipped with four turbojets and nose wheel undercarriage. This type did not see the light of day, but the Ministry of Supply placed an order for six somewhat similar research aircraft with tall, angular fins and rudders and powered by four 5,000 lb st Nene 5s and 6s. Known as Avro 706 Ashtons, they utilised Tudor 2 airframes but were given thicker skins and were shortened to Tudor 1 length due to the amount of knowledge accumulated with the Tudor 8 in this configuration. They differed from each other in detail, being intended for a wide variety of experimental flying and comprised one Ashton 1 *WB490*, first flown in September 1950; one Ashton 2 *WB491*; three Ashton 3s *WB492*, *WB493* and *WE670*; and one Ashton 4 *WB494*. The first two had the Tudor 2 pressure cabin with rear pressure bulkhead aft of the entrance door but on the remainder this was moved forward of the door to shorten the pressurised section.

The six Ashton aircraft and their contributions to the advancement of aeronautical knowledge are listed below.

*WB490*  Ashton Mk.1, first flown 1.9.50; demonstrated at the 1950 Farnbor-ough SBAC Show by J. H. Orrell; to the A and AEE, Boscombe Down, 1954, for high-altitude turbojet research; long-range tanks fitted under the outer wings and special autopilot installed; still flying 12.56, dismantled at Woodford and the fuselage used for internal pressure tests.

435

*WB491*  Ashton Mk.2 first flown 2.8.51, flown at the 1951 Farnborough SBAC Show by J. H. Orrell and J. Nelson; to the RAE, Farnborough, for pressurisation, refrigeration, humidification and temperature control investigation. Converted at Luton by D. Napier and Son in 1954 as a universal engine test-bed for the National Gas Turbine Establishment; flown with a Rolls-Royce Avon in a ventral pod. In 1955 the pod was replaced by the 17,500 lb st Rolls-Royce Conway R.Co.12 Mk.508 nacelle (with icing rig) for the Boeing 707–420, first flown at Luton by a Napier pilot and also at that year's SBAC Show; flown 1956 with Armstrong Siddeley Sapphire nacelle with icing rig.

*WB492*  Ashton Mk.3, first flown 6.7.51, to the Radar Research Establishment, Defford, for radar bombing research with large under-wing bomb containers and advanced radar bomb sight in a ventral radome.

Ashton Mk.3 *WB492* of the Radar Research Establishment, Defford, with wing-mounted bomb containers and ventral radar bomb sight. (*Avro*)

The Olympus Ashton Mk.3 *WB493* landing at Filton, 1955. (*Bristol*)

436

Ashton Mk.3 *WE670* equipped for icing tests with podded Rolls-Royce Avon. (*Rolls-Royce*)

*WB493* Ashton Mk.3, first flown 18.12.51. to the RAE, Farnborough, for high-altitude brush wear investigations and instrument development. To the Bristol Engine Division, Filton, in 1955 as test-bed for advanced marks of reheat Bristol Olympus turbojets. An Olympus was mounted outboard of each nacelle and in 1957–58 the aircraft flew with the port Olympus replaced by the Bristol Orpheus.

*WB494* Ashton Mk.4, first flown 18.11.52, fitted with pressurised ventral bomb-aimer's pannier and under-wing bomb containers at the RAE Farnborough 1954–55 for visual bombing research; Sapphire de-icing trials 4.58–2.59.

*WE670* Ashton Mk.3, first flown 9.4.52, used by the Orfordness branch of the RAE for bomb ballistics research; modified by Napier at Luton 1955 and flown at Wymeswold and Hucknall with one Rolls-Royce Avon R.A.14 under the fuselage with water spray gear for intake icing trials.

The Ashton Mk.4 *WB494* equipped with under-wing bomb containers.

437

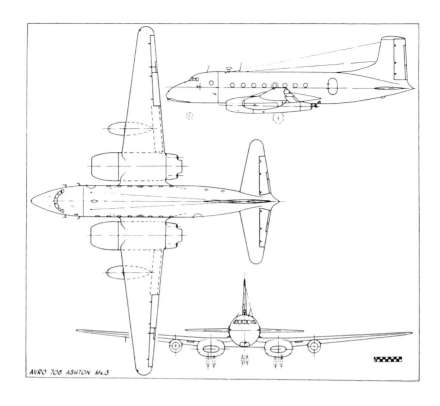

AVRO 706 ASHTON Mk.3

## SPECIFICATION AND DATA

*Manufacturers:*   A. V. Roe and Co Ltd, Greengate, Middleton, Manchester; and Woodford Aerodrome, Cheshire

*Powerplants:*   Four 5,000 lb st Rolls-Royce Nene 5 and 6

*Dimensions:*   Span 120 ft 0 in    Length 89 ft $6\frac{1}{2}$ in
Height 31 ft 3 in    Wing area 1,421 sq ft

*Weights:*   (Mk.1)   All-up weight 72,000 lb

*Performance:*   (Mk.1)   Maximum speed 439 mph
Cruising speed 406 mph

The low-speed model Avro 707B *VX790* which retained the dorsal air intake. (*Hawker Siddeley*)

# Avro 707

The Avro 707 was a small delta-wing research monoplane powered by a single Rolls-Royce Derwent turbojet, built in 1949 to Specification E.15/48 to provide data for the Avro 698 Vulcan. It was a single-seater of all-metal, stressed skin construction with sharply tapering mainplane and a dorsal engine air intake faired into a swept fin. Control was by normal rudder combined with four control surfaces hinged to the trailing edge of the wing, the inboard pair acting as elevators and the outers as ailerons. Retractable air-brakes were provided above and below the wing, and the cockpit canopy was from a Gloster Meteor.

In RAF marks *VX784*, the Avro 707 was first flown at Boscombe Down on September 4, 1949, by Avro test pilot S. E. 'Red' Esler who spent the next day putting in sufficient flying for the 707 to qualify for inclusion in that year's SBAC Show. He flew it to Farnborough for static exhibition on September 6 but during a test flight on September 30, crashed near Blackbushe and was killed.

A second aircraft, Avro 707B *VX790*, intended for research into the low-speed stability characteristics of delta wings, was first flown on September 6, 1950, by Avro chief test pilot R. J. Falk, who then flew it at the SBAC Show. Basically similar to the ill-fated Avro 707, the 707B was also Derwent powered but incorporated a wing having 51 degrees of leading-edge sweep-back. To speed construction it used an Avro Athena main undercarriage and a Hawker P.1052 nose wheel leg lengthened by 9 in to give sufficient take-off incidence. It proved an outstandingly docile aeroplane which completed 100 hours of research flying at Dunsfold before going in September 1951 to Boscombe Down where it was flown by Air Marshal J. N. Boothman and subsequently cleared for flying by selected civilian and Service pilots. J. H. Orrell demonstrated the 707B at the 1952 SBAC Show and a year later it formed an exhibit at the Hatfield RAeS Garden Party.

High-speed data were obtained with a third delta aircraft, *WD280*, designated Avro 707A and first flown at Boscombe Down by R. J. Falk on June 14, 1951. It was designed for operation at the highest possible subsonic speed because speeds greater than that of sound required excessive engine power as well as power operated controls.

Although nominally a 'low speed' aircraft, the Avro 707B had been flown fast enough for the canopy to set up turbulence around the dorsal air intake and to cause partial starvation of the engine. The 707A was consequently built with wing-root intakes, making it virtually a one-third scale model of the Vulcan, with which it flew in formation at the 1952 SBAC Show.

In late 1951 a second Avro 707A, *WZ736*, (maiden flight February 20, 1953) was ordered for general research by the RAE together with four side-by-side two-seaters, designated Avro 707C, for RAF delta training. In the event only one Avro 707C, *WZ744*, was completed, like *WZ736*, at the Avro repair organisation's premises at Bracebridge Heath, Lincolnshire. The aircraft first flew at nearby Waddington on July 1, 1953, and two months later made its public debut at the 1953 SBAC Show flying in formation with its three single-seat brethren.

Avro 707A *WD280* flew at the 1953 Paris Aero Show and was later used as test vehicle for the compound sweepback modification subsequently built into the leading edge on all Vulcans. It was afterwards shipped to Australia for investigations into airflow over delta wings at low speed by the Aeronautical Research Laboratories of the Department of Supply and flown from a base at Avalon, Victoria. With serial number repositioned on the nose, it was suspended from the laboratory roof for public exhibition at Avalon in February 1961 and gave a spirited flying display at the Laverton RAAF base on September 16, 1962.

The second Avro 707A, *WZ736*, was employed by the RAE on automatic throttle development while the two-seat Avro 707C was transferred to RAE Bedford, for supersonic tests in 1958 and flew with a fly-by-wire electric servo system duplicating the normal control circuits.

Veteran of fourteen years of experimentation, this machine was retired in 1967, the same year as *WZ736* and *WD280*. All three have been preserved.

Avro 707 prototype *VX784* at Farnborough, September 1949, showing the Gloster Meteor cockpit (*Courtesy the Royal Aeronautical Society*)

The high-speed model Avro 707A *WD280*, first of the delta experimentals to feature wing root air intakes.
(*Avro*)

## SPECIFICATION AND DATA

*Manufacturers:* A. V. Roe and Co Ltd, Greengate, Middleton, Manchester; and Woodford Aerodrome, Cheshire

*Powerplants:* (Avro 707 and 707B) One 3,500 lb st Rolls-Royce Derwent 5
(Avro 707A and 707C) One 3,600 lb st Rolls-Royce Derwent 8

*Dimensions, Weights and Performances:*

|  | Avro 707 | Avro 707A | Avro 707B | Avro 707C |
|---|---|---|---|---|
| Span | 33 ft 0 in | 34 ft 2 in | 33 ft 0 in | 34 ft 2 in |
| Length | 30 ft 6 in | 42 ft 4 in | 42 ft 4 in | 42 ft 4 in |
| Height | — | 11 ft 7 in | 11 ft 9 in | 11 ft 7 in |
| All-up weight | 8,600 lb | 9,500 lb | 9,500 lb | 10,000 lb |

The two seat Avro 707C *WZ744*. (*Avro*)

441

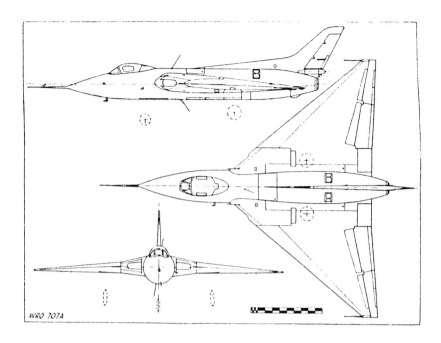

AVRO 707A

*Production:*

Avro 707, *VX784*, first flown at Boscombe Down 4.9.49, crashed near Blackbushe 30.9.49

Avro 707B, *VX790*, low-speed model, first flown at Boscombe Down, 6.9.50, withdrawn from use (wfu) 1960 and scrapped at Bedford

Avro 707A, *WD280*, first high-speed model, first flown 14.7.51; to the Australian Department of Supply for boundary layer tests 1958, wfu 1967, preserved in a suburban back garden at Williamstown, Victoria

Avro 707A, *WZ736*, second high-speed model, first flown 20.2.53, wfu 1967, preserved in the Manchester Museum of Science and Industry

Avro 707C, *WZ744*, two-seat familiarisation aircraft, first flown 1.7.53, wfu 1967, preserved in the Cosford Aerospace Museum

442

*C-91.2500*, first of six Avro 748 Series 2 transports built for the Brazilian Air Force. (*Avro*)

# Avro 748

Following a company decision to re-enter the civil market after many years of military production, an Avro project design team under J. R. Ewans explored a number of layouts for a short/medium-range feederliner. In 1958 the first project to bear type number Avro 748 appeared as a twin 1,000 hp propeller-turbine 20-seater with a span of 75 ft and operating at a maximum gross weight of 18,000 lb. Low- and high-wing versions were considered but market research revealed insufficient interest in an aircraft of this size and the project was scaled up into the Dakota replacement class. This also permitted the use of Rolls-Royce Dart engines of proven reliability.

In January 1959 the Hawker Siddeley group decided to build the Avro 748 in this form as a private venture and a month later the Chadderton Works began construction of four prototypes, two for static tests and two for flight trials. Work proceeded rapidly and the first flying prototype, *G-APZV*, was flown at Woodford for the first time by chief test pilot J. G. Harrison only 18 months later on June 24, 1960.

An all-metal, low-wing, pressurised monoplane of orthodox appearance and Avro fail-safe construction with circular-section fuselage, it accommodated up to 44 passengers in four-abreast seating with central gangway. The outer panels of the two-spar mainplane were attached to a centre section built integral with the fuselage, and to give adequate ground clearance to large diameter airscrews and avoid cut-outs in the spars, the Dart engines were mounted high up in closefitting cowlings with the jet-pipes passing over the wing. The forward retracting, twin-wheel undercarriage was housed in a bulbous compartment ahead of the leading edge, creating the now familiar Avro 748 cranked engine nacelle.

443

To support its claim to be a Dakota replacement, the Avro 748 was designed for a balanced field length of 3,400 ft, obtained by the use of large-diameter airscrews, powerful brakes, electrically-operated Fowler flaps of special design, and large fin and rudder. Reliability resulted from the use of the 1,740 hp Dart 514 powerplant and Rotol gearbox of the Vickers Viscount 800, the A. W. Argosy's 12 ft four-bladed airscrews, and Vickers Vanguard pressurisation equipment.

Carrying full instrumentation and water tanks which enabled the C.G. to be changed from the aft to forward limit in three minutes, the first prototype completed 60 hr flying by its 20th flight. Five weeks on the ground for modification and maintenance were followed by an appearance at the Farnborough SBAC Show on September 5, 1960, and the issue of a C of A next day. The completion of the third airframe as the second flying prototype *G-ARAY*, flown at Woodford by J. G. Harrison on April 10, 1961, considerably speeded the test programme. This partly furnished aircraft had the forward freight door on the port instead of starboard side. Performance trials with this aircraft at Nicosia and Madrid in July 1961 were followed by the installation of the more powerful Dart R.Da.7 engines to permit operation from aerodromes of up to 8,500 ft elevation. Thus powered it became the prototype Avro 748 Series 2 and first flew on November 6, 1961. It was named *Pride of Perth* on March 7, 1962, and next day left for tropical trials at Nairobi in Kenya and Kano in Nigeria.

Before the first aircraft had been completed, Skyways Coach-Air Ltd and BKS Air Transport Ltd ordered three and two Avro 748s respectively. The Indian Government also signed a manufacturing agreement whereby Hindustan Aeronautics Ltd assembled Avro 748s for use by the Indian Air Force and the Indian Airlines Corporation from British-built components at Kanpur. The first HAL 748 was flown on November 1, 1961, and named *Subroto* after a former Indian Chief of Staff. Three further Series 1s were erected before production switched to the Series 2, the first, *BH1048*, making its maiden flight on January 28, 1964. Production terminated with the eighty-fifth Series 2 machine early in 1984.

Destined for Skyways Coach-Air Ltd, *G-ARMV*, the first production Avro 748 Series 1, made its initial flight at Woodford on August 31, 1961, and appeared at the Farnborough SBAC Show a few days later. A demonstration tour to Jordan and Syria preceded the handing over to Skyways for 160 hours of route proving between Lympne, Beauvais, Lyon and Montpellier. Satisfactory static tests with the second and fourth airframes then led to the issue of a full British C of A on December 7, 1961, and to the clearance of the Series 1 at an increased all-up weight of 36,800 lb and the series 2 (with structural strengthening) at 42,000 lb, permitting them to operate as 48 and 52-seaters respectively. The maximum take-off weight of the Series 2 was further increased to 43,500 lb in September 1963 and to 44,495 lb in October 1965 enabling *G-ATEH, 'EI, 'EJ* and *'EK* to be supplied to Channel Airways as 62-seaters.

Fatigue tests having shown the wing to be slightly over-strength, pro-

*G-ARRW*, the first of two Avro 748 Series 1s delivered to BKS Air Transport in 1963–64.

duction aircraft were built with a 3 ft 6 in increase in span. *LV-PIZ*, second production aircraft and first of nine ordered by Aerolineas Argentinas in March 1960, first flew on December 10, 1961, and was delivered to the Argentine by Avro test pilot Colin Allen. The 11,300 mile flight via Stornoway and the North Atlantic route was completed in 8 days and *LV-PIZ* arrived at Ezeiza Airport, Buenos Aires, on Janaury 26, 1962. The co-pilot was Capt Arturo Micelli who ferried all subsequent Argentine 748s. At a ceremony in the following month the Bishop of Lomas named the first machine *Ciudad de Bahia Blanca*, the rest of the fleet also receiving names of the cities they would serve. All were given permanent registrations on arrival and three additional Avro 748s were ordered in 1963.

In an effort to exploit what was a most promising design, layouts were produced for a number of specialized variants, the chief of which were:

Avro 748E A stretched Series 2 with 6 ft fuselage extension to operate at an all-up weight of 43,000 lb and carry up to 60 passengers.

Avro 748 Super E High-performance variant of the above powered by two 2,400 hp Rolls-Royce Dart R.Da.10s

HAL 748 Series 2, *VT-DXJ Rameshwaram* of Indian Airlines.

445

The prototype Hawker Siddeley 748MF *G-ARRV* flying with the rear doors and ramp open as the aircraft appears in the supply dropping role. (*Hawker Siddeley*)

Avro 748F   A civil freight version of the Series 1 with freight door and strengthened floor

Avro 757    A military freight version of the Series 1 to Indian Air Force requirements. Also known as the Avro 748M

Avro 758    Layout made for the Indian Air Force for a high-wing assault version of the Avro 757 with a 2 ft increase in fuselage diameter, swing-tail rear loading, underslung nacelles, and undercarriage retracting into the fuselage. Span 97 ft 4 in, All-up weight 43,600 lb. Cruise 230 knots at 20,000 ft.

Avro 778    A version with two aft-mounted 7,000 lb st Bristol BS.75 turbofan engines using the Avro 748E structure but with reduced span for high speed. All-up weight 50,000 lb.

While all of these variants remained only projects, a heavier and more powerful version of the 748 with upswept tail and rear loading door, announced as the Avro 748MF (Military Freighter), but known internally as the Avro 780, was built for the RAF. The excellent performance of the Series 2 prototype *G-ARAY* during tests from unprepared surfaces, including deeply rutted mud, at Martlesham in February 1962 secured the order for the 748MF in the face of competition from the Handley Page Dart Herald. Six Avro 748 Series 2 were also ordered for RAF Transport Command, two to be operated by the Queen's Flight. The type name Andover, first used by the Avro 561 in 1924, was allotted to RAF Avro 748s, the 748MF being the Andover C.Mk.1 and the 748 Series 2 the C.C.Mk.2.

Powered by two Rolls-Royce Dart R.Da.12s driving 14 ft 6 in Dowty-Rotol airscrews, the 748MF was equipped with a widened centre section, larger wheels, and a reinforced floor for carrying wheeled vehicles. So that

446

the rear ramp could be brought on a level with the tail boards of freight lorries or loading ramps for access to ground level, undercarriage height could be varied hydraulically. Alternative internal layouts in the STOL support role were for 40 paratroopers, 48 fully-equipped troops, or casualty evacuation for 15 sitting and 18 stretcher cases. To speed completion of the first Avro 748MF, the first prototype Series 1 *G-APZV* returned to the Engineering Development Department at Chadderton for conversion on August 2, 1962. Piloted by J. G. Harrison, it was airborne from Woodford for 2 hr 5 min on December 21, 1963, in the course of its maiden flight as the re-titled Hawker Siddeley 748MF prototype, *G-ARRV*. The first of thirty-one production Andover C.Mk.1s for the RAF, *XS594*, flew on July 9, 1965.

Three squadrons were equipped with Andover C.1s, No.46 at Abingdon, No.52 at Seletar and No.84 at Sharjah, with training being undertaken by the Andover Conversion Unit at Abingdon. Defence cuts in 1975 resulted in the end of the type's role as a tactical transport with the RAF, but six aircraft were converted for use in the electronic calibration role with No.115 Squadron at Brize Norton and were redesignated Andover E.3s. Others were used by the RAE and the ETPS and for communications and medical evacuation duties by No.32 Squadron. In 1976 ten stored machines were sold to the Royal New Zealand Air Force, four going to No.1 Squadron, Whenuapai, and six to No.42 Squadron at Ohakea where they replaced Bristol Freighters and Douglas Dakotas. At least two, *NZ7622* and *NZ7628*, were used as VIP transports.

An order for three Avro 748 Series 2s (intended as *VR-AAU–'AW*) placed by the Aden Airways Ltd in April 1960 was cancelled in May 1962 and the machines absorbed into an order for six for the Brazilian Air Force Special Transport Group. These were all ferried by the North Atlantic route for use mainly on a shuttle service between Brasilia and Rio de Janeiro.

Skyways Coach-Air introduced its first Series 1 *G-ARMV* into service on the Lympne-Beauvais ferry on April 1, 1962, but leased its second machine *G-ARMW* (delivered the following month) to BKS Air Transport, pending delivery of its own Avro 748s. *G-ARMW* inaugurated the BKS Yeadon-London service on October 1, 1962, cut flying time by one third and produced a 49 per cent increase in traffic. This machine served Belfast from March 6, 1963, and joined the first BKS-owned aircraft *G-ARRW* on April 27. On October 28, 1963, Avro 748 Series 1 *G-ASJT* was delivered to Smith's Aviation Division, Staverton, for autopilot development and in 1970 was transferred to the RAE Farnborough as *XW750*.

An unobstructed cabin with 6 ft $3\frac{1}{2}$ in headroom permitted several luxurious interior layouts, one of which was built into *G-ARAY* early in 1963. It then left on a 40,000-mile world tour as a result of which one was supplied to the King of Thailand and three commercial models to Thai Airways. VIP versions of the Hawker Siddeley 748, as the aircraft was designated after July 1, 1963, were also supplied to the Presidents of

The freight door equipped H.S.748 Series 2A *FAE 738* of the Ecuadorian Air Force.

Argentina, Brazil, Ecuador, Venezuela and Zambia, the Sultan of Brunei and to No.34 Squadron RAAF Fairburn for Government use. Eight navigation trainers were also supplied to the RAAF as flying classrooms, the first *A10-601*, flown on February 21, 1968, being registered briefly as *G-AVZD* for certification trials of the Dart R.Da.8.

Two special aircraft, *G-AVXI* and '*XJ*, were used by the Civil Aviation Flying Unit, Stansted, for radio calibration work and seven aircraft, *D-AFSD* to *D-AFSJ*, were supplied to the Bundesanstalt für Flugsicherung for the same purpose in West Germany.

A new version, the H.S.748 Series 2A with 2,290 eshp Dart R.Da.7s, was announced in June 1967, the prototype *G-AVRR* making its maiden flight on September 5, 1967. Like *G-ARAY* before it this aircraft spent much of its early life on lease to potential customers. *G-AZJH*, a convertible passenger/freight version with a large rear cargo door giving entry width of 8 ft 9 in first flew at Woodford on December 31, 1971. Later in 1972 it was camouflaged for demonstration to the Royal Malaysian Air Force and also to the Belgian Air Force who later ordered three similar aircraft. Other freight door equipped aircraft were supplied to a number of operators including Bahamsair and the Air Forces of Brazil and Ecuador.

One H.S.748, *G-BCDZ*, first flown at Chester on February 18, 1977, was equipped as a maritime patrol aircraft with radar (housed below the front fuselage), bubble observation windows on each side and increased fuel capacity to give an 11 hour patrol endurance. Named Coastguarder, it carried a crew of five, two pilots, one tactical navigator and two observers.

However no orders for the variant were received and the prototype reverted to airline configuration.

Nationalisation resulted in Hawker Siddeley Aviation becoming part of British Aerospace in April 1977 and the 748 changed its name for the second time, becoming the BAe 748. Under the new banner development of the highly successful airliner continued and in June 1979 the final production version, the Series 2B, was flown for the first time. Improvements included extended drag reducing wingtips giving an overall span of 102 ft 5 in, updated flightdeck instrumentation, new 'wide-body' interior, engine hush-kits and a 2,000 lb increase in payload.

In the mid-eighties, with forest fires becoming an increasing problem in

G-BNJK, the unique Macavia 748 Turbine Tanker water bomber, dropping half its 2,000 US gallons load of water. (*Courtesy Photographic Section, Cranfield Institute of Technology*)

many parts of the world, the US firm of Macair International Ltd conceived the idea of converting secondhand 748s into water bombers. With assistance from the Cranfield Institute of Technology a prototype conversion took place. Capable of carrying 2,000 US gallons of water, the Macavia 748 Turbine Tanker *G-BNJK* (c/n 1594) made its public debut at Cranfield on November 12, 1987. Though a technical success no orders were received despite a sales tour to France, Australia and the USA.

After more than three hundred and seventy 748 series aircraft had been built, production ceased in 1988 and the last aircraft was delivered in February 1989. However a development of the aircraft, the Pratt & Whitney PW100 powered BAe ATP, remains in production at Woodford. A quarter of the parts of this new machine are common with the 748, the last aircraft to carry the Avro designation.

449

# SPECIFICATION AND DATA

*Manufacturers:* A. V. Roe and Co Ltd, Greengate, Middleton, Manchester; and Woodford Aerodrome, Cheshire; restyled the Avro-Whitworth Division of Hawker Siddeley Aviation wef July 1, 1963, and British Aerospace (Commercial Aircraft) Ltd wef April 29, 1977
Hindustan Aeronautics Ltd, Kanpur, India

*Powerplants:* (Avro 748 Series 1)
Two 1,740 eshp Rolls-Royce R.Da.6 Dart 514
(Avro 748 Series 2)
Two 2,105 eshp Rolls-Royce R.Da.7 Dart 531
(Avro 748MF) Two 2,970 eshp Rolls-Royce R.Da.12 Dart Mk.201C

*Dimensions, Weights and Performances:*

|  | Prototypes | Series 1 | Series 2 | Avro 748MF |
|---|---|---|---|---|
| Span | 95 ft 0 in | 98 ft 6 in | 98 ft 6 in | 98 ft 3 in |
| Length | 67 ft 0 in | 67 ft 0 in | 67 ft 0 in | 78 ft 0 in |
| Height | 24 ft 10 in | 24 ft 10 in | 24 ft 10 in | 30 ft 1 in |
| Wing area | 795 sq ft | 811 sq ft | 811 sq ft | 831 sq ft |
| Tare weight | 19,444 lb | 22,614 lb | 25,600 lb | 27,914 lb |
| All-up weight | 33,000 lb | 38,000 lb | 44,495 lb | 50,000 lb |
| Maximum cruise | 230 knots | 255 knots | 284 knots | 224 knots |
| Maximum range | 1,630 nm | 1,565 nm | 1,695 nm | 1,150 nm |

*Production:*

(*a*) **Prototypes**

1. *G-APZV*, c/n 1534, first flown 24.6.60, Special Category C of A 6.9.60, to Chadderton works 2.8.62 for prototype Avro 748MF conversion. Re-registered *G-ARRV* with new c/n 1548, wfu 3.69
2. Unregistered, static test airframe, pressurisation tests in A.W. rig 12.59; full pressure tests in water tank, Woodford 2.60; later tested to destruction
3. *G-ARAY*, c/n 1535, Chadderton–Woodford for assembly 5.3.61, first flown 10.4.61, Special Category C of A 29.5.61, first flown as Series 2 prototype 6.11.61, Hawker Siddeley executive aircraft 1963, leased to prospective customers 2.65 to 6.67. Sold for airline use 7.67, wfu 10.89, scrapped 5.90
4. Unregistered, static test airframe, fatigue test at Chadderton 7.61 when 48,000 cycles (equivalent to 72,000 hrs flying) were completed before failure

(*b*) **Avro 748 Series 1**

(c/n 1536–1538) Skyways Coach-Air, *G-ARMV* to *G-ARMX*, first flown 31.8.61, 8.5.62 and 19.10.62, Cs of A issued 30.3.62, 28.5.62 and 9.4.63 respectively; (1539–1547) Aerolineas Argentinas, *LV-PIZ*/*LV-HGW Ciudad de Bahia Blanca*, first flown 10.12.61/C of A issued 9.1.62,, *LV-PJA*/*LV-HHB Corrientes* 20.2.62/6.3.62, *LV-PRJ*/*LV-HHC Concordia* 2.4.62/13.4.62, *LV-PUC*/*LV-HHD Salta* 21.4.62/31.4.62, *LV-PUF*/*LV-HHE San Juan* 9.6.62/20.6.62, *LV-PUP*/*LV-HHG Mar del Plata* 29.6.62/6.7.62, *LV-PVH*/*LV-HHH Neuquen* 14.7.62/27.7.62, damaged in forced landing 4.9.62 when the cabin door struck the rudder during investigations into accidental door-opening in flight, and *LV-PVI/LV-HHI Rio Gallegos* 20.7.62/30.7.62; (1549) BKS Air Transport, *G-ARRW* 10.12.61/18.4.63; (1556–1558) Aerolineas Argentinas, *LV-PXD/LV-IDV Ciudad de Montevideo* 19.7.63/13.8.63, *LV-PXH/LV-IEE* 6.9.63/30.9.63 *Ciudad de Sante Fe*, and *LV-PXP/LV-IEV Ciudad de Gualequay Chu* 24.10.63/15.11.63; (1559) S. Smith and Sons (England) Ltd, *G-ASJT* 11.10.63/20.10.63; (1560) BKS Air Transport, *G-ASPL* 31.3.64/14.4.64

(c) **Avro/Hawker Siddeley 748 Series 2**

(c/n 1550–1555) Brazilian AF, *C-91.2500*, first flown 27.8.62/delivered 17.11.62; *C-91.2501* 16.1.63/26.2.63, *C-91.2502* 22.2.63/20.3.63, *C-91.2503* 19.3.63/19.4.63, *C-91.2504* 10.6.63/4.7.63, *C-91.2505* 30.8.63/28.9.63, (1561–1562) Queen's Flight, Andover CC.Mk.2, *XS789* and *XS790*; (1563–1566) RAF Transport Command, Andover CC.Mk.2, *XS791–XS794*; (1567–1569)

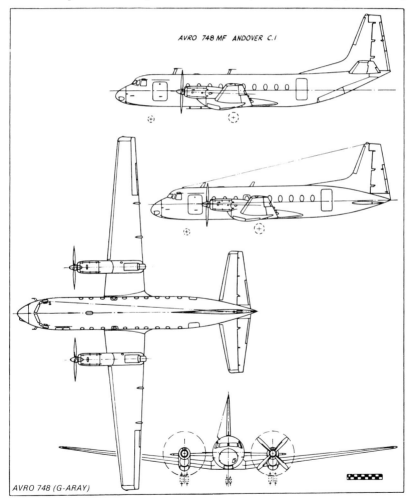

AVRO 748 MF ANDOVER C.I

AVRO 748 (G-ARAY)

451

Thai Airways, *HS-THA* to *HS-THC*; (1570) Thai Royal Flight, *HS-TAF*; (1571) Air Ceylon, *4R-ACJ*; (1576) BKS Air Transport, *G-ATAM*; (1577–1582) LAV, *YV-C-AME*, *'MI*, *'MO*, *'MY*, *'MF* and *'MC*; (1583–1584) LIAT, *VP-LIK* and *VP-LIP*; (1585–1588) Channel Airways, *G-ATEH* to *G-ATEK*; (1589–1590) Austrian Airlines, *OE-LHS* and *OE-LHT*; (1591) Venezuelan Ministry of Defence, *0111*; (1592–1593), Autair International Airways, *G-ATMI* and *G-ATMJ*; (1594) COPA, *HP-432*; (1595–1596) RAAF, *A10-595* and *A10-596*; (1597) Argentine AF, *T-01*; (1598–1599) Aeromaya, *XA-SEV* and *XA-SEY*; (1600) Zambian AF, *AF-601*; (1601–1608) RAAF, *A10-601* to *A10-608*; (1609–1612) Bahamas Airways, *VP-BCJ* to *VP-BCM*; (1613) Fiji Airways, *VQ-FAL*; (1614–1622) LAN-Chile, *CC-CEC* to *CC-CEK*; (1625–1632) Varig, *PP-VDN* to *PP-VDU*; (1636–1643) Philippine Airlines, *PI-C1014* to *PI-C1019* and *PI-C1021* to *PI-C1022*; (1644) Thai Airways, *HS-THD* to *HS-THF*; (1656) BFS, *D-ASFD*; (1659–1660) Philippine Airlines, *PI-C1023* and *PI-C1024*; (1661) Fiji Airways, *VQ-FBH*; (1662) COPA, *HP-484*; (1663–1664) Philippine Airlines, *PI-C1025* and *PI-C1026*; (1670) LIAT, *VP-LAA*; (1693) Thai Airways, *HS-THG*; (1707–1708) Thai Airways, *HS-THH* and *HS-THI*; (1709–1710) Royal Australian Navy *N15-709* and *N15-710*; (1711) BFS, *D-AFSE*; (1715) Thai Royal Flight, *HS-TAF*; (1723–1727) BFS, *D-AFSF* to *D-AFSJ*

(*d*) **Hawker Siddeley/British Aerospace 748 Series 2A**

(1633–1634) Varig, *PP-VDV* and *PP-VDX*; (1635) Hawker Siddeley, *G-AVRR*; (1647) Mount Cook Airlines, *ZK-CWJ*; (1657–1658) Avianca, *HK-1408* and *HK-1409*; (1661 and 1665) Fiji Airways, *VQ-FBH* and *VQ-FBK*; (1666–1667) Air Malawi, *7Q-YKA* and *7Q-YKB*; (1668) Transair, *CF-MAK*; (1669) AMOCO, *CF-AMO*; (1671–1672) Royal Nepal Airlines, *G-AXVZ/9N-AAU* and *9N-AAV*; (1673–1675) SAESA, *XA-SAB*, *'AC* and *'AF*; (1676–1677) Zambia Airways, *9J-ABJ* and *9J-ABK*; (1678) Rousseau Aviation, *G-AYDH/F-BSRA*; (1679) Chevron Oil, *G-AYFL/CF-CSE*; (1680) Zambia Airways, *9J-ABW*; (1681) Hawker Siddeley, *G-AYIR*; (1682–1684) Ecuadorian AF *FAE 682*, *FAE 684* and *FAE 001*; (1685–1686) Ghana Airways, *9G-ABX* and *9G-ABY*; (1687) SATA, *G-AYIM/CS-TAG*; (1688) Zambian AF *AF-602*; (1689) Mount Cook Airlines, *ZK-DES*; (1690–1692) South African Airways, *ZS-SBU*, *'BW* and *'BV*; (1694) Brunei Government, *AMDB-110*; (1695–1696) Merpati Nusantara *G-AZAE/PK-MHM* and *PK-MHR*; (1697) Hawker Siddeley, *G-AYYG*; (1698) Hawker Siddeley, *G-AZJH*; (1699) Air Gaspe, *CF-AGI*; (1700–1701) Hawker Siddeley, *G-AYVR* and *G-AYYH*; (1702–1705) SATENA, *FAC1101* to *FAC1104*; (1706) Air Botswana, *A2-ZGF*; (1712) Mount Cook Airlines, *ZK-MCA*; (1713) Hawker Siddeley, *G-BBGY*; (1714) Polynesian Airlines, *5W-FAO*; (1716) Air Illinois, *G-BAFY/N748LL*; (1717–1720) Hawker Siddeley, *G-BASZ*, *G-BABJ*, *G-BBLN* and *G-BBPT*; (1721) SATA, *CS-TAH*; (1722) Bouraq, *G-BBTA/PK-IHR*; (1728) Tanzanian Government, *5H-STZ*; (1729–1734) Brazilian AF, *C91-2506* to *C91-2511*; (1735) Bouraq, *G-BCDM/PK-KHL*; (1736–1737) British Airways, *G-BCOE* and *G-BCOF*; (1738–1739) Ecuadorian AF, *FAE 738* and *FAE 739*; (1740) Williamson Diamonds, *5H-WDL*; (1741–1743) Belgian AF, *CS-01* to *CS-03*; (1744–1745) LAV, *YV-45C* and *YV-46C*; (1746) Hawker Siddeley, *G-BDVH*; (1747–1748) Guyana Airways, *8R-GEU* and *8R-GEV*; (1749–1750) Cameroon AF, *TJ-XAF* and *TJ-XAH*; (1751–1753) Tanzanian AF, *G-BETZ/JW9008*, *G-BETY/JW9009* and *G-BETX/JW9010*; (1754) Upper Volta Government, *XT-MAL*; (1755) Air Liberia, *EL-AIH*; (1756–

1759) TTAS, *9Y-TFS*, *'FT*, *'FX* and *'GD*; (1760) Linhas Aereas de Guine-Bissau, *J5-GAT*; (1761) Bahamasair, *C6-BEB*; (1762) LIAT, *VP-LAZ*; (1763–1765) Bahamasair, *C6-BED* to *C6-BEF*; (1766–1767) TTAS, *G-BGMN/9Y-TGH* and *G-BGMO/9Y-TGI*; (1769) Air Senegal, *6V-AEO*; (1770) Transkei Airways, *G-BGPR/ZS-XGE*; (1771) Royal Nepal Airlines, *9N-ABR*; (1775) Upper Volta AF, *XT-MAN*; (1777) SATA, *CS-TAO*

   *(e)* **British Aerospace 748 Series 2B**
   (1768) British Aerospace, *G-BGJV*, prototype, first flown 22.6.79; (1772–1773) Air Madagascar, *5R-MJA* and *5R-MJB*; (1774) Bouraq, *G-BKLD/PK-IHO*; (1776) SATENA, *FAC-1108*; (1778–1779) Air Niger, *5U-BAR* and *5U-BAS*; (1780) Air Madagascar, *5R-MTI*; (1781) Cascade Airways, *N117CA*: (1782) Air Virginia, *G-BICK/N748AV*; (1783) Air Illinois, *N749LL*; (1784–1786) DLT, *D-AHSA* to *D-AHSC*; (1787–1788) Bouraq, *G-BKLE/PK-IHP* and *G-BKLF/PK-IHW*; (1789) Cascade Airways, *G-BJGI/N118CA*; (1790) Air Illinois, *G-BJTL/N749AV*; (1791) DLT, *G-BKAL/D-AHSD*; (1792) Air Virginia, *G-BJTM/N750AV*; (1793–1795) Bouraq, *G-BKLG/PK-IHT*, *G-BKLH/PK-IHM* and *G-BKLI/PK-IHN*; (1796) Airline of the Marshall Islands, *G-BKIG/MI-8203*; (1797) DLT, *D-AHSF*; (1798–1799) British Airways, *G-HDBA* and *'BB*; (1800–1803) LIAT *G-BLGJ/V2-LCQ*, *V2-LCR*, *G-BLYL/V2-LCS* and *V2-LCT*; (1804–1805) Cameroon Airlines, *TJ-CCF* and *TJ-CCG*; (1806–1807) Makung Airlines, *G-BPEP/B-1771*, and *G-BPIW/B-1773*

   *(f)* **748s built in India by Hindustan Aeronautics Ltd**
   Four Series 1 and eighty-five Series 2 aircraft erected from Manchester-built components: Series 1: (c/n 500) *BH572*, *Subrato* first flown 1.11.61 as *VT-DRF*; (501) *BH573*, *Jumbo*; (502) *BH574*; (503) *BH1047*; Series 2: (504) *BH1048*, first flown 28.1.64; (505) *BH1010*; (506) *VT-DUO*; (507–509) *BH-1011* to *BH-1013*; (510) *H-913*; (511–515) *VT-DXF* to *VT-DXJ*; (516–517) *H-914* to *H-915*; (518–525) *VT-DXK* to *VT-DXR*; (526–530) *H-1030* to *H-1034*; (531–538) *H-1175* to *H1182*; (539) *H-1386*; (540–549) *VT-EAT* to *VT-EBC*; (550–568) *H-1512* to *H1530*; (569–578) *H-2175* to *H-2184*; (579–588) *H2372–H2381*

   *(g)* **Avro/Hawker Siddeley 748MF Andover (Avro Type 780)**
   One prototype *G-ARRV* (c/n 1548) first flown 21.12.63, C of A issued 4.9.64; followed by 31 production aircraft for the RAF *XS594* to *XS597* (1572–1575), *XS598* to *XS613* and *XS637* to *XS647*
*Notes:* (i) *XS599*, *XS600*, *XS602*, *XS604*, *XS608*, *XS611*, *XS612*, *XS613*, *XS638*, *XS645* to the RNZAF as *NZ7620* to *NZ7629* in 1976; (ii) *XS603*, *XS605*, *XS610*, *XS639*, *XS640* and *XS641* converted to Andover E.3; (iii) *XS607* registered to Hawker Siddeley as *G-BEBY* 7.76 to 9.76 for sales tour of India 8.76

*Service Use:* (individual aircraft often served with a variety of squadrons, hence only representative serial numbers are given)
   No.32 Squadron, *XS597*, *XS639*; No.46 Squadron, *XS596*, *XS599*, *XS600*; No.52 Squadron, *XS606*, *XS607*, *XS608*; No.84 Squadron, *XS595*, *XS642*, *XS645*; No.115 Squadron, Andover E.3 conversions listed above; Andover Conversion Unit, Abingdon, *XS601*, *XS602*, *XS603*; No.241 OCU *XS599*, *XS638*, *XS640*; No.242 OCU, *XS610*, *XS645*; RAE Farnborough, *XS646*; A&AEE, Boscombe Down, *XS594*, *XS601*; Empire Test Pilots School, *XS606*; Also No.1 Squadron RNZAF Whenuapai, and No.42 Squadron RNZAF, Ohakea

# Construction for Other Manufacturers

Success came to the Autogiro, largely as a result of several years of joint experiment at Hamble by A. V. Roe and Co and the Cierva Autogiro Co, in the course of which standard Avro biplanes of various types were shorn of mainplanes and equipped with rotors. These machines, along with the Cierva C.30A constructed under licence at Manchester as the Avro 671, are described in the main body of the book by virtue of their having Avro type numbers as well as the Cierva designations. In addition one other Cierva Autogiro, the C.19, designed and built at Hamble beginning in 1929, was associated with A. V. Roe and Co. Following the transfer of the Avro design office to Manchester at the end of 1928, some of the staff remained at Hamble working under contract to the Cierva company. This resulted in Avro constructor's numbers being allocated to the C.19s but because the machines were wholly designed and built by the Cierva Autogiro Co no Avro type number was allocated. For completeness the production details for the C.19 are listed below:

## (a) Cierva C.19 Mk.I

| Avro Constructor's No. and Registration | | C of A Issued | Details |
|---|---|---|---|
| 5130 | G-AAGK | 2.8.29 | Sold abroad 1.30 |
| 5131 | G-AAGL | 30.8.29 | Crashed at Haldon, Teignmouth, 21.9.29 |
| 5132 | G-AAHM | 22.3.32 | Converted to C.19 Mk.IV, crashed at White City Stadium, London, 29.9.32 |

## (b) Cierva C.19 Mk.II

| | | | |
|---|---|---|---|
| 5133 | G-AAKY | nil | Sold in the USA to H. Pitcairn 12.29, believed as NC311V |
| 5134 | G-AAKZ | 26. 9.29 | Crashed at Sherburn-in-Elmet. 31.5.31 |
| 5135 | G-AALA | 24.12.29 | Converted to C.19 Mk.III, crashed 5.32 |
| 5136 | G-AAUA | 1. 8.30 | C.19 Mk.IIA, sold abroad 3.31 |

## (c) Cierva C.19 Mk.III

| | | | |
|---|---|---|---|
| 5137 | G-AAYN | nil | Sold abroad 10.30 |
| 5138 | G-AAYO | 10. 9.30 | On RAF charge 6.11.30 as K1696, soc 21.2.31 |
| 5139 | G-AAYP | 10. 9.30 | To C.19 Mk.IV, scrapped 1932 |
| 5140 | G-ABCK | 14.10.30 | To New Zealand 12.30 as ZK-ACL, crashed Oamaru 5.31, wreck shipped to the UK. |
| 5141 | G-ABCL | 20.10.30 | Crashed at Hounslow Heath 29.11.30 |
| 5142 | G-ABCM | 13.12.30 | Delivered Hamble-Farnborough 5.1.31, on RAF charge 16.1.31 as K1948, soc 14.3.34 |

## (d) Cierva C.19 Mk.IV

| Avro Constructor's Numbers | Aircraft markings |
|---|---|
| 5143–5145 | G-ABFZ, 'GB, 'GA |
| 5148–5153 | G-ABUC/VR-SAR, 'UD, 'UE, 'UF, 'UG/SE-ADU, 'UH/VH-USO |
| 5154–5159 | G-ABXD, 'XE. 'XF/J-BAYA, 'XG, 'XH/EC-W13/EC-ATT, 'XI/Spanish Air Force 49–1 |

*Note:* The single Cierva C.19 Mk.V *G-ABXP* had neither constructor's number nor C of A and was scrapped in 1935

Apart from Cierva Autogiros, the only non-Avro aircraft to be honoured with type numbers were the Parnall Monoplane for which the Company built the Avro 661 experimental mainplane in 1934; and the Egyptian Army Air Force Hawker Audax aircraft which went through the works in 1937–38 as Avro 674s. Chapters on these aircraft can also be found in the main section of the book.

In addition A. V. Roe and Co built the following aircraft wholly designed by other manufacturers:

(i) 287 Hawker Audax biplanes: *K5120–K5176, K5561–K5585, K5586–K5603, K7307–K7486* and *K8311–K8335*

(ii) 1,005 Bristol Blenheims IVs: *L6594–L6843, N3522–N3545, N3551–N3575, N3578–N3604, N3608–N3631, R2770–R2799, Z5721–Z5770, Z5794–Z5818, Z5860–Z5909, Z5947–Z5991, Z6021–Z6050, Z6070–Z6104, Z6144–Z6193, Z6239–Z6283, Z6333–Z6382, Z6416–Z6455, Z9533–Z9552, Z9572–Z9621, Z9647–Z9681, Z9706–Z9755, Z9792–Z9836,* and *AE449–AE453*

(iii) The single production Hawker Tornado *R7936* (first flown August 29, 1941); and

(iv) 75 English Electric Canberras: *WJ971–WJ995, WK102–WK146,* and *WK161–WK165*

# Aircraft Designed by A. V. Roe Canada Ltd

Formed late in 1945 when A. V. Roe and Co acquired Victory Aircraft Ltd of Malton, Ontario, which had already built 1,168 Avro aircraft comprising 736 Ansons, 430 Lancasters, one York and one Lincoln.

The new firm's first aircraft, the Avro Canada C-100 Canuck, was the first jet fighter designed in Canada and was designated CF-100 in the Royal Canadian Air Force CF- series. The C-105 Arrow also received an RCAF designation, the CF-105.

## Avro Canada C-100 Canuck

*(Canadian National Defence)*

Normally known by its RCAF designation, CF-100, the C-100 was an all-metal two-seat twin-engined, long-range all-weather fighter designed for Arctic defence 1947–48. *18101*, first of two Rolls-Royce Avon powered CF-100 Mk.1 prototypes, first flown at Malton by W. A. Waterton January 19, 1950. *18103*, the first of five pre-production Mk.2 (Avro Orenda Mk.1 turbojets) flew June 20, 1951. Two of these were equipped as Mk.2T dual trainers.

First RCAF production batch of 76 Mk.3s (Mk.3 and 3B Orenda 8s and Mk.3A Orenda 2s) equipped with tip tanks and armed with eight 0.5-in. guns in a ventral tray, included a number of Mk.3T trainers. Main production began with Mk.4A (Orenda 9s) with longer nose housing the Hughes APG-40 fire control system. Armed solely with 2.75-in Mighty

Mouse rockets, 48 in a ventral pack and 58 in wingtip pods, Prototype, *18112*, flown by Jan Zurakowski October 11, 1952, and first production machine flew on October 24, 1953. Final examples were Mk.4B (Orenda 11) three of which, *18320–22*, arrived at CFE, West Raynham, Norfolk, for evaluation March 27, 1955. *18321–22* were shown at the 1955 Farnborough SBAC Show.

Production of the Mk.5, a lightened and more powerful PRU fighter version with increased span for improved high altitude performance, included 53 for the Belgian Air Force (deliveries began in December 1957). The prototype Mk.5, *18323*, originally known as the Mk.4C, flew in September 1954 and construction ceased in December 1958 with the 692nd aircraft, but a considerable number of Mk.4Bs were converted to Mk.5s, and seven were modified to carry Sparrow missiles under the designation Mk.5M.

## SPECIFICATION AND DATA

*Powerplants:*    (Mk.1)   Two 5,700 lb st Rolls-Royce Avon RA.2
               (Mk.2)   Two 6,000 lb st Avro Canada Orenda 1
               (Mk.3 and 3B) Two 6,000 lb st Avro Canada Orenda 8
               (Mk.3A) Two 6,000 lb st Avro Canada Orenda 2
               (Mk.4A) Two 6,300 lb st Avro Canada Orenda 9
               (Mk.4B and Mk.5) Two 7,300 lb st Avro Canada Orenda 11

*Dimensions, Weights and Performances:*

Mk.1   Span 52 ft 0 in, length 52 ft 6 in, height 14 ft 6 in, wing area 540 sq ft, tare weight 19,185 lb, all-up weight 31,877 lb, maximum speed 550 mph at 40,000 ft, initial climb 9,800 ft/min.

Mk.2   Span 52 ft 0 in, length 52 ft 3 in, height 14 ft 6 in, wing area 540 sq ft, all-up weight 33,100 lb.

Mk.3   Span 52 ft 0 in (57 ft 6 in with tip tanks), length 52 ft 3 in, height 14 ft 6 in, wing area 540 sq ft, all-up weight 34,000 lb.

Mk.4   Span 49 ft 11 in (53 ft 7 in with rocket pods), length 54 ft 2 in, wing area 540 sq ft, tare weight 24,408 lb, all-up weight 35,500 lb, (Mk.4B) maximum speed 600 mph at 10,000 ft and initial climb 8,000 ft/min.

Mk.5   Span 57 ft 3 in (60 ft 10 in with rocket pods), length 54 ft 2 in, wing area 591 sq ft, tare weight 23,100 lb, all-up weight 33,528 lb, maximum speed 560 mph at 30,000 ft, initial climb 8,750 ft/min, combat ceiling 45,000 ft, range 2,000 miles

*Production:*

(CF-100 Mk.1) RCAF *18101–18102*; (Mk.2) *18103*, *18104* and *18106*; (Mk.2T) *18105* and *18107*; (Mk.3) *18139*, *18148–18149*; (Mk.3A) *18113*, *18115–18134*; (Mk.3B) *18135–18138*, *18140–18147* and *18150–18182*; (Mk.3D) *18114*; (Mk.3T) *18108–18111*; (Mk.4) *18112*; (Mk.4A) *18183–18319*, (Mk.4B) *18320–18474*, *18477–18479* and *18481–18513*; (Mk.5) *18475–18476*, *18480*, *18514–18684*, Belgian Air Force *AX-1* to *AX-53* and RCAF *18739–19792*

*Service Use:* By nine RCAF home defence squadrons including Nos.419, 423, 425, 428 and 445, and by four squadrons of No.1 Air Division in Europe; also by the 1st All-Weather Interceptor Wing, Belgian Air Force, Beauvechain

*British civil aircraft:* One aircraft only, CF-100 Mk.4B RCAF *18393*, registered to O.A. Haydon-Baillie 18.3.75 as *G-BCYK*. Delivered to Duxford 29.3.75 and grounded. Now preserved in RCAF marks by the Imperial War Museum at Duxford.

## Avro Canada C-101

A projected twin-engined navigation trainer for the Royal Canadian Air Force.

## Avro Canada C-102 Jetliner

*(Avro Canada)*

A 50-passenger medium-range transport similar to the Avro Tudor 8. Designs begun in 1946 envisaged the use of two Rolls-Royce Avon turbojets the non-availability of which led, in the autumn of 1947, to the fitting of four 3,600 lb st Rolls-Royce Derwent 5s.

Prototype *CF-EJD-X* first flown at Malton by Avro chief test pilot J. H. Orrell on August 10, 1949, belly landing at Malton due to undercarriage failure on August 16, 1949, repaired and completed 10 hrs flying before public demonstration on October 5, 1949. Re-engined with Derwent 8s (starboard outer, port inner) and Derwent 9s for Toronto–Ottawa flight on April 11, 1950 in 36 min at 418 mph; and New York mail flight on April 19, 1950. Flew 150 hours by December 1950, reached 39,800 ft and exceeded 500 mph in level flight.

No orders were received and construction of the partially built second prototype was abandoned. The prototype, however, was used for observing C-100 tests and remained operational until November 1956.

### SPECIFICATION AND DATA

Span 98 ft. 1 in., length 82 ft. 5 in., wing area 1,097 sq. ft., tare weight 27,427 lb., all-up weight 55,000 lb., maximum speed at 30,000 ft. 417 m.p.h., cruising speed at 30,000 ft. 376 m.p.h., initial climb 2,220 ft./min/., ceiling 40,300 ft., maximum range 1,680 miles.

## Avro Canada C-103

A projected afterburner-equipped twin-engined, swept-wing version of the C-100 Canuck for the RCAF. No prototype or production contracts were placed and the C-103 was not built.

## Avro Canada C-104

Initial design studies were for an all-weather interceptor fighter to replace the CF-100 Canuck. The wings were heavily swept-back, there was a conventional swept all-moving tail and the twin engines were to be stacked one above the other in the same style as on the English Electric Lightning. This configuration was however abandoned in favour of the delta layout that eventually evolved into the Avro Canada C-105 Arrow.

## Avro Canada C-105 Arrow

*(Avro Canada)*

This was an all-metal, twin-turbojet all-weather fighter which originated from a 1952 RCAF requirement to which Avro Canada submitted alternative C-104 Mk.1 single-engined and C-104 Mk.2 twin-engined delta wing designs. Designated CF-105 by the RCAF, the C-105 Arrow was a development of the C-104 Mk.2, with two 23,000 lb st Pratt & Whitney J75s specified for the two prototypes, and two 28,000 lb st Orenda Iroquois for production machines.

First prototype, *25201*, first flown at Malton on March 25, 1958, by Jan Zurakowski, exceeded 1,000 mph on the level during its seventh flight. Pre-production batch of 37 ordered in June 1958. Second prototype, *25202*, completed in September 1958 was followed by *25203–25205*.

In February 1959, after some £108 million has been spent on the development of the Arrow airframe and Iroquois engine, the whole programme was dropped in favour of Bomarc surface to air missiles. One Mk.2 aircraft, *25206*, with 26,000 lb st Avro Orenda Iroquois 2s was completed but not flown.

## SPECIFICATION AND DATA

(Mk.1) Span 50 ft 0 in, length 77 ft 9½ in, height 21 ft 3 in, wing area 1,225 sq ft, tare weight 48,923 lb, all-up weight 68,600 lb, maximum speed with reheat at 40,000 ft 1200 mph, initial rate of climb with reheat 39,000 ft/min, combat ceiling 50,000 ft.

### Avro Model 1 Avrocar

(*US Air Force photo*)

Nicknamed 'The Saucer', the Avrocar was an 18 ft diameter disc-shaped, two-seat, Coanda effect VTOL research vehicle powered by three Continental J69 turbojets. These drove a 5 ft diameter central fan designed to create a peripheral air cushion for a vertical take-off and aft deflected thrust was expected to allow transition to forward flight during which normal aerodynamic lift would occur. Design expectations were for a range of 1,000 miles and a maximum speed of 300 mph.

The programme was initially funded by A. V. Roe Canada and the Canadian Government but in 1955 the project was taken over by the US Department of Defense as the Weapon Systems 606A (WS606A) and the machine allotted the US Army designation VZ-9V.

After seven years of development one of the two prototypes was tested at Malton on December 12, 1959, by Waldeck Potocki. It however only rose a few feet on an air cushion and failed to achieve sufficient velocity to sustain itself in true flight. In 1960, the second machine was sent to the NASA Ames Research Center in California for wind-tunnel tests before performing no better than its twin during free tests on May 17, 1961. Though the failure was put down to insufficient power it was concluded that even if re-engined the Avrocar would have suffered serious stability problems in forward flight at high speeds and the project was terminated. The two aircraft, both of which carry the serial *58-7055*, now reside in museums, one in the US Army Transportation Museum at Fort Eustis, Virginia, and the other in the National Air and Space Museum, Washington, DC.

## SPECIFICATION AND DATA

Three 1,000 lb st Continental J69 (licence-built Turboméca Marboré) turbojets, diameter 18 ft, central fan diameter 5ft, height 5 ft 1 in, tare weight 3,600 lb, all-up weight 5,650 lbs.

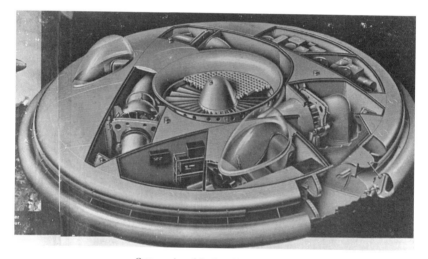

Cutaway view of the Avro Model 1 Avrocar.

462

# Avro Projects

Although the designation system introduced by A. V. Roe with the type number Avro 500 in 1912 had reached the Avro 784 by the time that it was replaced by the Hawker Siddeley designation system in 1963, only about 30 per cent of the possible designs were actually built. The remaining designations mainly represent unbuilt projects, but it must be remembered that in several instances they were passed over and not used at all, in others they were applied to sub-assemblies built for other aircraft constructors, and in a number of cases (where an earlier design study was abandoned), were used twice. This Appendix lists all projects including those where construction of a prototype was abandoned before completion.

Avro Mono-Plane
> Advertised along with the Bi-Plane below in the Avro catalogue 'The Aviator's Storehouse' of 1910. Length 27 ft, Span 36 ft, Height 7 ft 6 in, weight (without engine) 200 lb, wing area 220 sq ft. The following engines were offered as options: 20 hp Avro, 20 hp JAP, 35 hp JAP, 35 hp Green or 40 hp Avro

Avro Bi-Plane
> Length 21 ft, Span 29 ft, Height 7 ft 6 in, weight (without engine) 250 lb, wing area 350 sq ft. Engines options as for the Mono-Plane above.

Avro 505  Type number not used.

Avro 506  Also known as Type J. Layout made in 1913 for a two-seat, twin-float seaplane similar to the Avro 508 and powered by a 160 hp or 200 hp Gnome pusher. A machine-gun was mounted in the nose. Span 70 ft 0 in, Length 44 ft 0 in, Height 15 ft 5 in, Wing area 980 sq ft. All-up weight 3,800 lb. Endurance 4 hr

Avro 507  Designation allocated to a set of mainplanes built for a Mr Leigh in July 1913. He is believed to have been the purchaser of an experimental Avro 534 Baby in 1920

Avro 509  Type number first used for a set of tanks and strut sockets supplied to the Walsh brothers for the first Walsh flying boat, built at Orakei, Auckland, in August 1913. Evidently these components were later considered unworthy of a special type number as the designaton Avro 509 was reissued in November 1913 to a projected radio equipped twin-float seaplane. This was a three-seater, three-bay biplane with two 120 hp Austro-Daimler engines outboard and a heavy calibre gun in the nose. A contract, to the value of £3,384, for one prototype was awarded by the Admiralty in January 1914 and serial 94 was allocated. However the machine was not built, possibly because

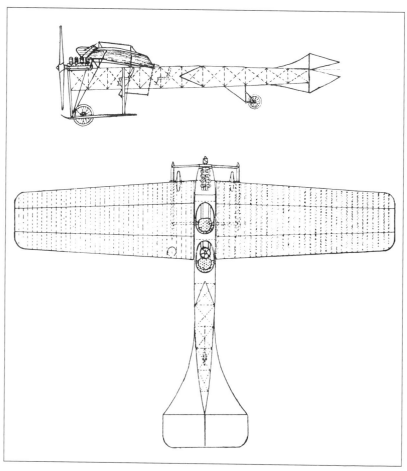

The Avro Mono-Plane project of 1910.

of there being insufficient capital available to finance its construction. Span (upper) 80 ft 0 in, (lower) 56 ft 0 in. Length 44 ft 3 in. Wing area 931 sq ft. Tare weight 2,800 lb. All-up weight 4,510 lb. Maximum speed 70 mph.

Avro 512    A projected landplane with one 65 hp Austro-Daimler engine. Span 26 ft 0 in.

Avro 513    A design study made in March 1914 for a two seat, twin-float bomber seaplane powered by two 80 hp Gnome engines. Wings were designed to fold, and floats and flying surfaces were interchangeable with those of the Avro 510. Span (upper) 72 ft 0 in, (lower) 47 ft 0 in. Length 36 ft 6 in.

Avro 515    Layout for a biplane with one 150 hp Sunbeam engine, September 1914.

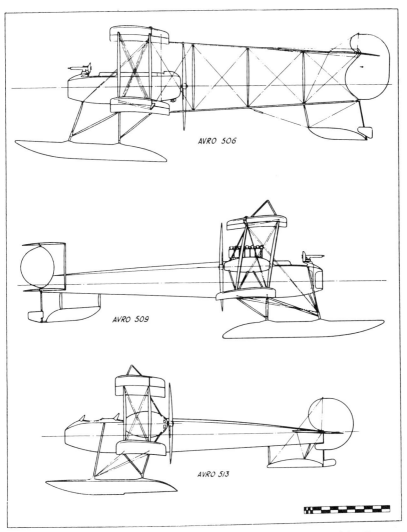

AVRO 506

AVRO 509

AVRO 513

Avro 516   A monoplane with one 80 hp Gnome considered in January 1915.

Avro 517   Layout for a biplane version of the Avro 516, February 1915

Avro 518   A projected single-seater with one 150 hp Sunbeam engine, May 1915

Avro 520   Designs for a single-seat landplane with one 150 hp Sunbeam engine for the Royal Navy, May 1915.

Avro 524   A projected scout with one 80 hp engine.

Avro 525   Layout for a single-seat ground attack fighter to RAF Type II; November 1915.

| Avro 526 | Similar to the Avro 525 but with monoplane tail unit. |
|---|---|
| Avro 532 | This has been widely quoted as a postwar single-seat racer, a mistaken belief based on the false assumption that the sporting version of the Avro 531A had been allotted the next Avro type number. This was not so, the civil machine inquestion being the Avro 538. Drawings dated April 14, 1918, show the true Avro 532 as a projected two-seater (one 350 hp A.B.C. Dragonfly radial) to RAF Types IIIA, IIIB and IVB, adaptable as short-range reconnaissance fighter, artillery spotter or long-distance photographic aircraft. Span 40 ft 0 in. Length 27 ft 10 in. |
| Avro 535 | Design study made in April 1919 for an Avro contender for the *Daily Mail* £10,000 prize for the first transatlantic flight. It would have been an unstaggered biplane with one 275 hp Rolls-Royce Falcon III and an enclosed cabin for the crew. Forestalled by Alcock and Brown's crossing in a Vickers Vimy, the Avro 535 was not built. Span 45ft 0 in. Length 36 ft 3 in. |
| Avro 537 | Designs made in March 1919 for a transport biplane for pilot and ten passengers, powered by two 300 hp high-compression Siddeley Puma engines in outboard nacelles. Span 70 ft 0 in. Length 46 ft 0 in. |
| Avro 541 | A projected twin-float fleet reconnaissance seaplane to RAF Type XXI, September 1919. It was envisaged as a folding wing sesquiplane powered by one 450 hp Napier Lion. Span 40 ft 0 in. Length 30 ft 0 in. Height 12 ft 10 in. |
| Avro 542 | Layout made in October 1919 for a passenger transport with one 450 hp Napier Lion engine. |
| Avro 550 | Reserved either for a projected three-seat reconnaissance triplane to Specification 37/22; or a 15-passenger European civil transport with three Rolls-Royce Condors to Specification 40/22. |
| Avro 553 | A training version of the Avro 548 (80 hp Renault) |
| Avro 556 | Coastal defence torpedo bomber to Specification 16/22 (D of R Type 9) powered by one 1,000 hp Napier Cub. Development abandoned in favour of the Avro 557 Ava |
| Avro 559 | Light monoplane for the 1923 Lympne trials |
| Avro 564 | Preliminary designs for a two-seat fighter monoplane with thick section elliptical wing, powered by one 650 hp Rolls-Royce Condor III, July 1924. |
| Avro 565 | A version of the Avro 564 powered by one 450 hp Napier Lion, July 1924. |
| Avro 568 | Projected all-metal single-seat fighter, November 1925. |
| Avro 569 | Avro 566/567 Avenger with RAF 30 section wing. |
| Avro 570 | Layout for a single-seat seaplane, November 1925. Span 32 ft 0 in. Length 29 ft 3 in. |
| Avro 573 | Design study for a large commercial biplane with folding wings and three Bristol Jupiter engines to joint Imperial Airways and Air Ministry Specification 26/24. Intended for the Cairo- |

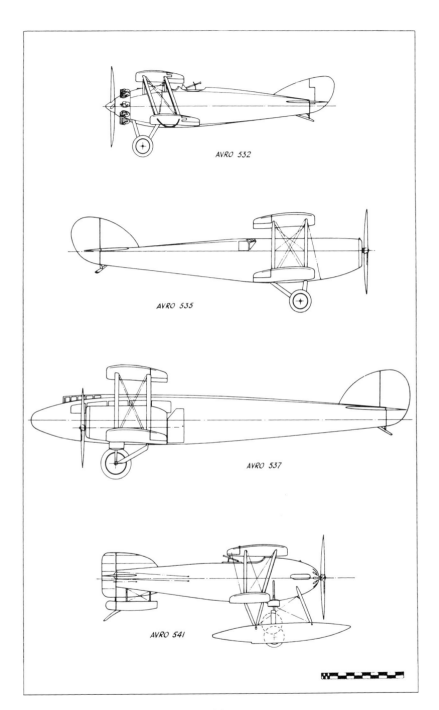

AVRO 532

AVRO 535

AVRO 537

AVRO 541

467

Baghdad desert air mail route, the aircraft resembled an enlarged three-engined Andover with double freight doors on the port side. Choice fell on the de Havilland D.H.66 Hercules and the Avro 573 was not built. Span 100 ft 0 in. Length 60 ft 6 in. Height 18 ft 8 in.

Avro 577   A projected general purpose landplane, January 1926.

Avro 578   Seaplane version of the Avro 577. Span 48 ft 0 in. Length 37 ft 9 in.

Avro 579   Projected Avro 562 Avis with RAF 15 wing section.

Avro 580   Layout for a heavy bomber powered by four Bristol Jupiter radial engines, February 1926.

Avro 583   Avro 566/567 Avenger with 570 hp geared Napier Lion XI

Avro 588   70 hp Armstrong Siddeley Genet powered monoplane version of the Avro 581 Avian Prototype

Avro 589   Avro 588 seaplane.

Avro 590, 591 and 592   Variations on a single basic layout for high-performance Army Co-operation two-seat, two-bay biplanes (one 450 hp Bristol Jupiter VI) to Australian Government Specifications A.C.35, 36 and 37, October 1927. H. E. Broadsmith took the Avro 590, 591 and 592 drawings to Australia and campaigned vigorously to get them adopted for local manufacture, even to the extent of building a full-size, wood and canvas mock-up at Melbourne. No orders rewarded this enterprise because a British military commission at that time in Australia insisted that in time of war all Australia's needs could be supplied by Britain.

The full-scale mock-up of the projected Avro 590 Army Co-operation biplane built at Melbourne by H. E. Broadsmith in 1927.

Avro 593   A two-seat seaplane version of the Avro 590–592 series, powered by one Armstrong Siddeley Jaguar radial, October 1927.

Avro 595   A projected two-seat land or seaplane reconnaissance fighter to Specification O.22/26, February 1927.

Avro 596   The three-seat bomber version of the Avro 595.

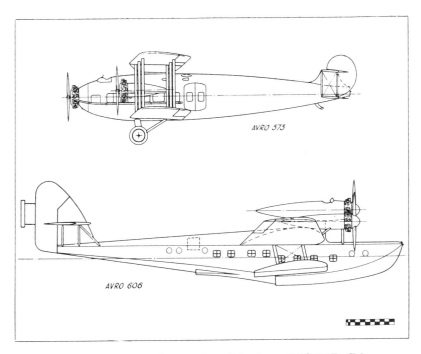

Avro 597   Landplane bomber version of the Avro 571/572 Buffalo

Avro 598 and 599   Type numbers allocated to designs for a two-seat trainer to Australian Government Specification. Although not built, they were given the names Warregull Mk.I and Mk.II respectively.

Avro 600   Avro 594 Avian with RAF15 section wings.

Avro 601   Projected two-seat reconnaissance landplane powered by one 450 hp Napier Lion, April 1927.

Avro 602   Extensively modified version of the Avro 566/567 Avenger.

Avro 603   Designs for three-engined, eight-passenger monoplane for West Australian Airways. H. E. Broadsmith conducted negotiations in Australia in May 1927 but the design was eventually turned down in favour of Vickers Viastra IIs delivered in 1931.

Avro 606 and 607   Schemes drawn up in October 1927 to Air Ministry Specification 4/27 for Imperial Airways flying-boats for the Mediterranean section of the new India air route. Large three-engined monoplanes were envisaged, the Avro 606 with square-section and the Avro 607 with circular-section hull. The production contract was awarded to the Short Calcutta and neither of the Avro designs was built. (Avro 606) Three 505 hp Bristol Jupiter VIII. Span 110 ft 0 in. Length 80 ft 0 in. All-up weight 21,050 lb. Maximum speed 120 mph (Avro 607) Span 96 ft 4 in.

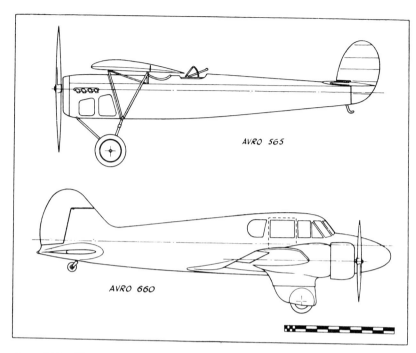

AVRO 565

AVRO 660

Avro 608    Two-seat biplane fighter known as the Hawk. Powered by one
            425 hp Bristol Jupiter engine. Construction of prototype
            *G-EBWM* abandoned. Airframe used in development of Avro
            622 and subsequently the Avro 627 Mailplane.

The Avro 608 Hawk.

Avro 609    Preliminary designs for a three-seat, general purpose military
            seaplane based on the Avro 608 Hawk and powered by one

Bristol Jupiter radial, December 1927.

Avro 610  A projected high-wing cabin monoplane, similar to the de Havilland D.H.75 Hawk Moth, to be powered by any engine of 200 hp, e.g. the Armstrong Siddeley Lynx, Wright Whirlwind or Bristol Titan. Pilot and four passengers sat in a glazed cabin beneath a one-piece mainplane mounted directly on top of a welded steel-tube fuselage. An alternative shoulder-mounted scheme with glazed cabin roof was also considered. The fin and rudder were typically Avro Avian. Span 43 ft 6 in. Length 27 ft 6 in. Height 8 ft 6 in. Wing area 266 sq ft. Tare weight 1,800 lb. All-up weight 3,140 lb. Maximum speed 123 mph. Cruising speed 110 mph. Initial climb 700 ft/min. Ceiling 15,500 ft.

The projected Avro 610 five-seat monoplane.

Avro 613  Layout made to Air Ministry Specification B.19/27 in May 1928 for a night bomber powered by two Armstrong Siddeley Jaguar IV radial engines. Contract 841675/28 awarded for prototype and serial *J9249* allotted but there were no detailed designs and the machine was not built. Of note is that Specification B.19/27 also applied to the Handley Page Heyford and Fairey Hendon prototype and these machines were built.

Avro 614 and 615  Type numbers allotted in June 1928 to preliminary designs for a high-wing commercial monoplane powered by three 180 hp Armstrong Siddeley Lynx IV radials. A sole pilot occupied an open cockpit ahead of a one-piece, thick-section, strut-braced mainplane and the outboard engine nacelles were above each wheel. Avro 615 was the proposed twin-float version, but when the Fokker licence was acquired, both projects were shelved in favour of the Avro 619 Five.

Avro 622  540 hp Armstrong Siddeley Panther II powered fighter-bomber version of the Avro 608 Hawk, April 1930. Converted into the Avro 627 Mailplane *G-ABJM* before completion.

Avro 623  Layout for a survey or general purpose single- or two-seat, high-wing monoplane with one Armstrong Siddeley Lynx or Cheetah radial.

Avro 628    Mailplane version of the Avro Five powered by a single Armstrong Siddeley Panther, August 1930

Avro 629    Single-engined mailplane

Avro 630    Armstrong Siddeley Panther engined day bomber developed from the Avro 627 Mailplane, September 1931.

Avro 632    A project considered in September 1932 for a Fleet torpedo bomber/reconnaissance aircraft with one Armstrong Siddeley Tiger radial to Air Ministry Specification S.9/30. Choice fell on the Hawker Osprey and the Avro 632 was not built. Span 46 ft 0 in.

Avro 633    Single-seat fighter version of Avro Cadet.

Avro 634    A projected two-seat low-wing monoplane, May 1932. Span 30 ft 0 in. Length 24 ft 9 in.

Avro 635    Layout for a low-wing cabin monoplane with one Armstrong Siddeley Lynx IVC, July 1932. Span 39 ft 0 in. Length 28 ft 4 in.

Avro 644    A projected two-seat reconnaissance bomber with one Armstrong Siddeley Jaguar radial, 1933. Span 36 ft 0 in. Length 26 ft 6 in.

Avro 645    A projected six-seater powered by two 340 hp Armstrong Siddeley Double Mongoose (Serval) radials.

Avro 647 and 648    These were low-wing projects with six seats and two 140 hp Armstrong Siddeley Genet Major IA radials, June 1933. Span 50 ft 0 in and 46 ft 0 in respectively.

Avro 649    Layout for a 17-seat seaplane with four 240 hp Armstrong Siddeley Lynx radials

Avro 650    A projected eight-seat monoplane with four 140 hp Armstrong Siddeley Genet Major radials, July 1933.

Avro 651    A project considered in August 1933 for a monoplane with one Armstrong Siddeley Jaguar VI radial in the nose and two 240 hp Armstrong Siddeley Lynx IVC outboard.

Avro 653    A projected long-range seaplane with four Armstrong Siddeley Cheetah IIA radials, October 1933.

Avro 655 and 656    These were projects for low-wing bombers powered by two Armstrong Siddeley Jaguar VIA radials.

Avro 657    Layout for a high-performance military aircraft, December 1933.

Avro 658    Layout for a three-seat, low-wing monoplane with one 140 hp Armstrong Siddeley Genet Major IA radial.

Avro 659 and 660    Scaled-down versions of the Avro 652 transport powered by two 140 hp Armstrong Siddeley Genet Major IA radials, and fitted with fixed trousered undercarriages. The Avro 659 was not proceeded with but a mock-up of the Avro 660 was built in January 1934 and construction of a prototype reached the stage where c/n 723 and registration *G-ACUN* were allotted. Maximum speed 165 mph, cruise 140 mph, range 420 miles.

Avro 662   Special Armstrong Siddeley Lynx powered Avro Tutor

Avro 663   Avro Cadet Trainer

Avro 664   Twin-engined monoplane. Development abandoned in favour of the Anson

Avro 665   Cierva C.33 Autogiro employing Avro 641 Commodore fuselage, June 1934

Avro 666   A layout made in October 1934 for a Fleet Air Arm fighter/dive-bomber to Specification O.27/34 and powered by one Armstrong Siddeley Tiger radial. Span 39 ft 0 in. Length 32 ft 10½ in.

Avro 668   Following the abandonment of the Avro 665 Commodore-type Cierva C.33 Autogiro, designs went ahead in February 1935 for the Avro 668 twin-engined, rotary-wing cabin aircraft having an entirely new fuselage of Avro design. Equipped with three-bladed rotor, it would have been the C.37 in the Cierva series but was not built.

Avro 669   Special Armstrong Siddeley Cheetah powered Avro Tutor, March 1935

Avro 670   Preliminary designs drawn up in October 1935 for an Army Co-operation aircraft to Air Ministry Specification A.39/34.

Avro 672   A projected twin-engined reconnaissance aircraft to Air Ministry Specification G.24/35 and M.15/35. Span 56 ft 3 in.

Avro 673   Layout for a twin-engined advanced gunnery trainer with 200 hp de Havilland Gipsy Six, October 1935.

Avro 675   A projected twin-engined reconnaissance aircraft to Air Ministry Specifications G.24/35 and M.15/35, May 1936, powered by Armstrong Siddeley Terrier engines.

Avro 676 and 677   Layouts for low-wing advanced trainers with Rolls-Royce Kestrel engines, made to Air Ministry Specification T.6/36 in May and June 1936 respectively. Construction did not take place due to the adoption of the Miles Master I.

Avro 678   A scheme for a twin-airscrew fighter, powered by a single Rolls-Royce Merlin engine, August 1936.

Avro 680   Layout prepared in April 1939 for a four-engined heavy bomber to Air Ministry Specification B.1/39. There were no detail drawings and the type was not built.

Avro 681 and 682   Type numbers allotted to heavy bomber projects.

Avro 684   'Stratosphere bomber' with four Rolls-Royce Merlin engines

Avro 686   High-altitude bomber. Lancaster replacement, October 1944

Avro 690   Avro XXII, Transport with six Rolls-Royce Merlin 100s. August 1944.

Avro 696   Avro XXIII, Transport with six Rolls-Royce Merlin 100s. September 1944.

Avro 693   Projected medium/long-range propeller-turbine transport for the Commonwealth routes. The design emerged finally as a large turbojet aircraft with four Rolls-Royce Avons and having a wing area of 2,700 sq ft but was cancelled in 1947.

Avro 697     Projected medium-range Empire transport, June 1947.
Avro 700     Layout made in January 1945 for a 12-seat low-wing transport with two 475 hp Armstrong Siddeley Cheetah 26.
Avro 702     Preliminary designs made in January 1945 for a Canadian aircrew trainer to RCAF Specification 4/10.
Avro 703     Projected 36-seat turbojet powered transport for Trans-Canada Air Lines, September 1947
Avro 704     Designs for a two-seat trainer powered by two Rolls-Royce Derwent turbojets, November 1947.
Avro 705     Projected transport with tricycle undercarriage and four Rolls-Royce Nene turbojets.
Avro 708     Long-range Empire transport
Avro 709     Long-range Empire transport. A version of the Tudor 2.
Avro 710     Half-scale Delta
Avro 711     Trader. Tricycle undercarriage development of Tudor 4.
Avro 712     Lincoln meteorological aircraft.
Avro 714     Designs for a basic trainer powered by a single turbojet.
Avro 715     A projected 8–10 seat four-engined passenger transport.
Avro 716     Avro Shackleton Mk.3 Development of M.R.3 with four 2,500 hp Rolls-Royce Griffon Mk.57a.
Avro 717     Lincoln test-bed with two Napier Nomad engines.
Avro 718     A military transport powered by four Bristol Olympus 3s. June 1951.
Avro 719     Shackleton Mk.4 with four Napier Nomads, November 1951.
Avro 720     Designs for a mixed powerplant delta fighter commenced in 1954 to Ministry of Supply Specification 137. Interception with D.H. Firestreak missiles was to be made on the power of one Armstrong Siddeley Screamer rocket, the aircraft then returned to base on an Armstrong Siddeley Viper unit. Prototype *XD696*, nearly complete, scrapped in the 1956 economy drive. Span 27 ft $3\frac{1}{2}$ in. Length 48 ft 6 in.

The incomplete Avro 720 rocket interceptor prototype *XD696*, in the Avro works 1956. (*Avro*)

Avro 721   Preliminary designs for a low-level bomber, October 1952.

Avro 722   The Avro Atlantic long-range, four-turbojet, delta transport considered in December 1952. Based on the Vulcan it was to carry up to 113 tourist class passengers from London to New York in under 7 hours. Span 121 ft 0 in. Length 145 ft 0 in. All-up weight 200,000 lb. Cruise 600 mph.

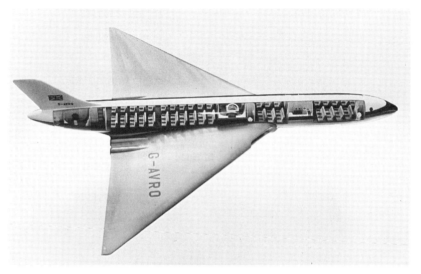

The projected Avro 722 Atlantic long-range transport. (*Avro*)

Avro 723   A projected 'DC-3 replacement' powered by four Alvis Leonides radials, May 1953.

Avro 724   Designs for a VTOL aircraft as alternative to the Avro Canada Avrocar, June 1953.

Avro 725   Projected advanced trainer based on the Avro 720 and powered by a single de Havilland P.S.35 or Bristol BE.26 engine, October 1953.

Avro 726   A light delta-wing fighter powered by a single de Havilland P.S.35 or Armstrong Siddeley P1.51 turbojet, November 1953.

Avro 727   Ground attack fighter to NATO Specification, February 1954, Avro 720 delta-wing and new fuselage housing one Bristol Orpheus turbojet and two 20 mm cannon. Abandoned when contract was awarded to the Fiat G.91. Span 27 ft 3½ in. Length 35 ft 9½ in.

Avro 728   De Havilland Gyron Junior powered naval interceptor development of the Avro 720, March 1955.

Avro 729   All-weather fighter powered by one de Havilland Gyron Junior, January 1955.

Avro 730    Preliminary designs in 1955 for a supersonic bomber of stainless steel sandwich construction to Specification R.B.156D powered by eight Armstrong Siddeley P.176 engines. One configuration had length 159 ft, height to top of tail 30·22 ft, wing area 2,100 sq ft., aspect ratio 2.05, maximum fuselage diameter 9.35 ft, undercarriage track 41.063 ft. Gyron Junior flying-scale models were envisaged.

Avro 731    Three-eighths scale experimental and development aircraft for the Avro 730, with two D.H. Gyron Juniors, October 1955.

Avro 732    Supersonic bomber with four turbojets, July 1956.

Avro 733    Type number of Avro-designed Shackleton-type mainplane for the A.W.650 Argosy transport (four Rolls-Royce Darts). Span 115 ft 0 in.

Avro 734    Decoy counter-measures aircraft powered by one Armstrong Siddeley P.176, November 1956.

Avro 735    Design study for a supersonic passenger aircraft developed from the Vulcan. Powered by eight turbojets, November 1956.

Avro 736    A propeller-turbine transport aircraft powered by four Napier E.223 or Armstrong Siddeley P1.82 engines, January 1957.

The wind-tunnel model of the Avro 739 low-level strike aircraft. (*British Aerospace*)

Avro 737    A four-engined STOL aircraft powered by Napier E.223 or Armstrong Siddeley P1.82 engines, January 1957.

Avro 738    Designs for a weapons system, 1957.

Avro 739    Low level supersonic aircraft, 1957.

Avro 740    Design study for a short-haul, swept-wing, 70-passenger transport to a British European Airways specification issued in 1956, with three turbojets (either the 13,500 lb st Bristol Olympus 551 or Rolls-Royce RB.141) grouped round a butterfly tail.

Aircraft to have been built jointly with Bristols as the Bristol 200 but was abandoned when BEA ordered the D.H.121 Trident. Length 109.6 ft, height 28.2 ft, span 109.6 ft.

Avro 741  Twin Bristol Orpheus powered executive jet or feeder aircraft, July 1957.

Avro 742  A jet-flap transport powered by three Bristol BE.53s, July 1957.

Avro 743  A long-range military freighter powered by four Bristol Orion propeller-turbines, July 1957.

Avro 744  Nuclear powered aircraft studies 1957.

Avro 745  NATO maritime patrol or reconnaissance aircraft with four Rolls-Royce Dart propeller-turbines, August 1957.

Avro 746  Propeller-turbine jet-flap research aircraft powered by a single Bristol BE.53, August 1957.

Avro 747  Passenger or freight transport with two Rolls-Royce Dart propeller-turbines, October 1957.

Avro 749  VTOL transport for British European Airways, February 1958.

Avro 750  Jet airliner with either two or four engines, February 1958.

Avro 751  Three-engined jet airliner, March 1958.

Avro 752  VTOL assault aircraft, March 1958.

Avro 753  Freighter with wing of Avro 745, May 1958.

Avro 754  Civil transport with Avro 745 wing, May 1958.

Avro 755  Deflected-slipstream STOL aircraft, June 1958.

Avro 756  Long-range military transport powered by four Rolls-Royce Tynes, July 1958.

Avro 758  Layout made for the Indian Air Force for a high-wing assault version of the Avro 748 with 2 ft increase in fuselage diameter, swing-tail rear loading, underslung nacelles, and undercarriage retracting into the fuselage. Span 97 ft 4 in. All-up weight 43,600 lb, Cruise 230 knots at 20,000 ft. February 1959.

Avro 759  Narrow Delta wing research glider, October 1958.

Avro 760  Supersonic civil airliner, November 1958.

Avro 761  1958 design study for turbofan Viscount replacement with a high tail and 35 deg of sweepback with Rolls-Royce R.B.163 rear-mounted engines. 65 passengers, AUW 70,000 lb, cruise 480 knots over 500 mile stage lengths.

Avro 762  Advanced Weapons System, November 1958.

Avro 763  VTOL Jeep, December 1958.

Avro 764  VTOL military transport version of the A.W.650 Argosy, February 1959.

Avro 765  VTOL lift fan fighter.

Avro 766  Long-range military transport with four turbojets.

Avro 767  Joint project with Bristol Aircraft for a four-jet airliner.

Avro 768  Early Warning Aircraft.

Avro 769  VTOL Weapons system version of the Avro Vulcan.

Avro 770  STOL assault transport.

The Avro 771 twin turbo-fan transport. (*British Aerospace*)

Avro 771   Similar design to Avro 761, powered by two 7,350 lb st Bristol
           Siddeley BS.75 turbojets. 60 economy class seats. Span 77 ft 5
           in, length 80 ft 4 in, height 24 ft 3 in, wing area 800 sq ft, cruise
           495 knots, all-up weight 47,000 lb, range with maximum payload
           (12,000 lb) 500 nm.
Avro 772   Car ferry transport.
Avro 773   STOL military freighter.
Avro 774   Long-endurance weapons system.
Avro 775   Maritime reconnaissance aircraft to replace Shackleton. Powered
           by two Rolls-Royce Tyne propeller-turbine and one rear-
           mounted Rolls-Royce RB.168 turbofan.
Avro 776   Version of the Avro 775 having three rear-mounted RB.178
           turbofans. Span 135.716 ft, length 129.25 ft, height 36.5 ft.
Avro 777   Designation not used.
Avro 778   Development of the Avro 748 with two rear-mounted RB.178
           turbofans.
Avro 779   High-wing STOL freighter development of the Avro 748.
Avro 781   Shortened twin-turbofan development of the Avro 748.
Avro 782   Equivalent Avro 781 development of the Avro 748MF.
Avro 783   STOL version of the Avro 748MF to NATO requirements.
Avro 784   Maritime reconnaissance aircraft with four propeller-turbines.

The Avro 784 was the last type number issued under the Avro name.
Subsequent projects from the same design office were allocated Hawker
Siddeley (H.S.) designations and are outside the scope of this book.

# Avro Blue Steel

Developed by the Weapons Research Division of A. V. Roe and Co to meet Air Staff Operational Requirement OR1132, the Blue Steel stand-off bomb was designed to deliver a nuclear warhead in the megaton range and be carried beneath either an Avro Vulcan B.Mk.2 or Handley Page Victor B.Mk.2. After launch at 40,000 ft one hundred miles from its target, and thus well outside the range of local defences, the stainless-steel missile was designed to dive to 32,000 ft before its single Bristol Siddeley Stentor rocket engine (burning hydrogen-peroxide and kerosene) would fire and carry it up to 70,500 ft from where it would dive to its target, guided throughout by its Elliot inertial navigation system. Modifications to allow low level launches were applied in December 1962 following the cancellation of the US ALBM (air launched ballistic missile) Skybolt.

First ordered in March 1956, the stand-off bomb, which later became known as Blue Steel, was undergoing trials by 1959, with test firings taking place at both RAE Aberporth and the Woomera range in South Australia. No.18 Joint Services Trial Unit at Scampton and No.4 JSTU at Edinburgh Field, Australia, were given the responsibility of bringing the weapon up to operational status. The first Squadron to receive Blue Steel was No.617 flying Vulcan B.Mk.2s from Scampton in 1962 followed in 1963 by Nos.27 and 83, also flying Vulcan B.Mk.2s from the same base and Nos.100 and 139 flying Victor B.Mk.2s from Wittering. The Blue Steel equipped V-

Blue Steel with a Vulcan in the background. (*S. P. Peltz*)

Bomber force provided Britain's nuclear deterrent until 1967 when the role was taken over by the Royal Navy's Polaris submarines. The weapon, however, remained in RAF service for a further three years, the last Blue Steel sortie being flown by No.617 Squadron on December 21, 1970.

## SPECIFICATION AND DATA

*Manufacturers:* The Weapons Research Division of A. V. Roe and Co Ltd

*Powerplant:* One Bristol Siddeley Stentor Rocket engine

*Dimensions:* Wing span 13 ft, foreplane span 6 ft 6 in, length 35 ft, maximum body diameter 4 ft 2 in

*Weight:* 16,500–17,000 lb

*Range:* 100 miles    Maximum speed: Mach 1.6 (estimated)

*Number ordered:* 57

Blue Steel missiles awaiting deployment in the MSSB (Missile Servicing and Storage Building) at RAF Scampton in 1963 (*S. P. Peltz*)

# Avro Motor Vehicles

## The Avro Car

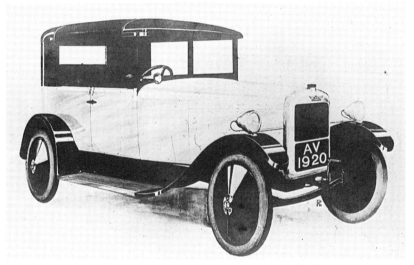

*(The National Motor Museum)*

Following the large-scale cutback in aircraft orders at the end of the First World War, A. V. Roe and Company sought to diversify their business into motor-car production.

The three-seat Avro Car, was announced in November 1919, by which time a number of prototypes had been built and production tooling was under way. Materials originally purchased for the construction of Avro 504Ks were to be used and the cars produced at the Newton Heath Works which had been extended before the armistice to facilitate construction of 500 aircraft a month.

The Avro Car had an enclosed body built on a pressed steel chassis, though at least one prototype convertible model was built. The four-cylinder water-cooled engine, rated at 10 hp, had a Zenith carburettor with petrol fed by gravity from a tank located under the dashboard. Of note was the Avro designed gearbox which was of the double differential type with three epicyclic gears, two forward and reverse, which were always in mesh. Top gear was direct.

A small number of Avro cars were completed before production was halted as a result of Crossley Motors taking a financial interest in the Avro Company.

*Body*: three-seater, with detachable sprung seats mounted in an enclosed shell which had a light ash frame and aluminium panelling. *Windows and Doors*: two doors with four windows, all on hinged guides. The four-part windscreen also opened as did the rear window. *Engine*: 1,330 cc, 10 hp four-cylinder with a large bonnet giving easy access. *Gear Box*: Avro patent differential type providing three forward speeds plus reverse. *Suspension*: Quarter elliptic springs at the front with cantilever springs at the rear. *Wheelbase*: 8 ft 6 in. *Track*: 4 ft. *Tyres* 760 × 90 mm. *Weight*: 14 cwt *Price*: £425 with self starter, £395 without.

## The Avro Monocar (1923)

Designed by A. V. Roe in 1923, the single-seat Avro Monocar was intended to be a substitute for the motorcycle and being priced at a modest £75 the hope was that it would provide a means of transport for the masses. It had two wheels, with outriders which provided support when the machine was at rest. Motive power was provided by a 2.75 hp Barr and Stroud engine, with kick start, a three-speed gearbox and chain drive. Its cruising speed was 25 mph and fuel consumption was 100 mpg. The driver sat in a well-padded adjustable seat, with space behind for luggage, and protection from the elements was afforded by the enclosed body and collapsible hood. To demonstrate that the driver was exposed to neither engine nor road dirt, A. V. Roe made a point of wearing a light grey suit during tests. In the

event only the prototype Monocar, *HO9530*, was built and the vehicle never entered production. It was later fitted with a modified body with streamlined sloping front and open back.

## The Avro Monocar (1926)

In 1926 A. V. Roe designed a further monocar, but like its predecessor only the prototype was built. This model, which had registration number *OT3664*, was however used extensively by its designer for commuting between Manchester and Hamble, clocking up some 30,000 miles in the process. In 1953 it was donated to the Science Museum and was housed at the Museum's Wroughton out-station in 1990.

Powered by a 350 cc Villiers two-stroke engine with three-speed gearbox, the machine has a pressed-steel frame with a light alloy body and windscreen to give protection from the weather. A low bucket seat was provided for the rider who controlled the machine by a handle-bar. A third, and once again different, monocar was subsequently built by A. V. Roe in the workshops at his home and used constantly until shortly before his death.

### SPECIFICATION AND DATA

*Length*: 7 ft 6 in. *Wheels* 19 × 3.5. *Engine*: 350 cc two stroke; drip lubrication; magneto ignition, kick start. *Gearbox*: Sturmey-Archer three-speed with gated quadrant control. *Final Drive*: shaft drive through two fabric disc couplings. *Suspension*: coil springs front and rear. *Steering*: rod levers from steering column. *Controls*: foot brake (rear); hand brake (front); gear change; lubrication rate; throttle; mixture; clutch. *Brakes*: expanding shoe front and rear. *Chassis*: two welded steel box sections longtitudinally, with bolted transverse struts, the right hand section being extended into a curved cantilever to the front wheel. Rear wheel suspension on aluminium alloy casting pivoted to the main chassis which also acted as the main drive shaft housing. *Luggage*: rear compartment with hinged lid provided both interior and external storage.

# Individual Histories of British Civil Avro 504Ks

This section is arranged to show former RAF serial and/or constructor's number, registration, date of issue of Certificate of Airworthiness, all owners, and disposal. Unless subsequently changed the home base is given only when an operator is first mentioned.

Abbreviations: AC—Aircraft Co Ltd; A.S.—Aircraft Services Ltd; AT & T—Aircraft Transport and Travel Ltd; Av Co—Aviation Co Ltd; Avro— A. V. Roe and Co Ltd; BAT—Berkshire Aviation Tours Ltd; dbr—damaged beyond repair; EW—Engineering Works Ltd; FS—Flying Services Ltd; G.W.—Grahame-White Aviation Co Ltd; L & P—London and Provincial Aviation Co Ltd; NAL—Northern Air Lines; NAT—Northern Air Transport Ltd; NS—North Sea Aerial Navigation Co (later Aerial and General Transport Co Ltd); RAeS—Royal Aeronautical Society; s.o.r.—struck off register; S of F—School of Flying Ltd; W.B.—William Beardmore and Co Ltd; wfu—withdrawn from use.

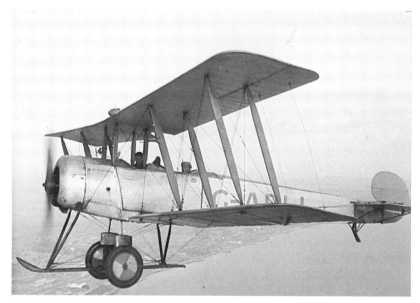

Avro 504K *G-ABLL* was built in 1926 as *J8333*.

*E4222/G-EAAK*, 9.5.19, Avro, Hounslow, wfu 5.20; *E4154/AL*, 29.5.19, Avro, Southsea, 2.23 Vickers Ltd, Brooklands, 1925 to Avro 548; *E3289/AM*, 9.5.19, Avro, Hounslow, wfu 5.20; *E4225/AN*, 5.5.19, Avro, Weston-Super-Mare, wfu 5.20; *D6205/AX*, 12.5.19, G.W., Hendon, wfu 5.21; *C724/AY*, 7.5.19, G.W., 9.24 Lady Ulica Beecham, Hendon, 5.25 Liverpool Av Co, 4.26 Southern Counties Av Co "Jake", Brooklands; 10.26 F.G. Miles Shoreham: 4.27 L.J. Skytrips Ltd., 7.30 L.R.G. Errington, Bekesbourne, crashed 1931

*E3480/G-EABA*, 27.5.19, G.W., wfu 5.21; *E4137/BE*, 18.5.19, G.W., 9.23, E.F. Edwards, Whitley Bay, crashed near Cambridge 12.5.24; *C748/BF*, 11.7.19, G.W., wfu 7.21; *C749/BG*, 30.5.19, G.W., wfu 5.21; *B8758/BH*, 7.8.19, G.W., wfu 8.21; *E4359/BJ*, 19.5.19, Avro No.3★, Blackpool, sor 5.20; *D8287/BK*, Avro, Southport, sor 5.20; *E4324/BL*, 19.5.19, Avro, Alexandra Park, sor, 5.20; *E4360/BM*, 19.5.19, Avro No.2, Southport and Isle of Man, sor 5.20; *C723/BN*, 9.5.19, G.W., wfu 5.21; *D6202/BO*, 27.5.19, G.W., to Canada 5.20 as *G-CAAE*; *F9802/BP*, 18.5.19, G.W., to Belgium 7.21; *D6201/BT*, nil, L & P, Stag Lane, sor 8.19; *D6229/BV*, 18.5.19, Avro, crashed 12.19; *C747/BW*, 25.5.19, G.W., wfu 7.22; *E4230/BX*, 20.5.19, G.W., 8.22 Manchester Av Co, Alexandra Park, sor 8.23

*E6765/G-EACA*, 18.6.19, G.J. Lusted, Shoreham, 2.21 H. Sykes, Kingsbury, crashed near Stag Lane 1.10.21; *E1671/CB*, nil, Avro, sor 9.20; *E4224/CD*, 16.5.19, Avro, crashed 12.19; *D9298/CL*, 10.6.19, J.D.V. Holmes, East Hanney, crashed near Northampton 21.7.19; *D9341/CS*, 20.5.19, Avro, sor 5.20; *E4233/CV*, 24.6.19, Vickers Ltd, Joyce Green, crashed 4.20; *E1663/CW*, 2.6.19, Avro, Southsea, ditched in the sea 11.19

*E4221/G-EADA*, 19.5.19, Avro, 1923 to Avro 504N; *E1665/DD*, 25.5.19, Avro, sor 5.20; *E3502/DH*, 31.5.22, West of Scotland Av Co, 5.22 Kingwill and Jones Flying Co, wfu 6.26; *E3292/DI*, 25.5.19, Avro No.6, Morecambe, sor 5.20; *E4336/DM*, 10.6.19, Avro, Southsea, to Belgium 8.21; *E3293/DN*, 5.6.19, Avro, to Belgium 7.21; *F8706/DO*, 16.6.19, Central AC, Northolt, crashed 12.19; *E3481/DP*, 11.8.19, Central AC "White Wings", 10.21 Midland Av Co, 3.23 Manchester Av Co, 3.24 Northern Av Co, Alexandra Park, crashed at Morecambe 27.7.26; *D7588/DQ*, 6.6.19, Central AC, Irish Air Corps 6.22; *D6245/DR*, 10.7.19, Bournemouth Av Co, crashed at Werrington, Northants. 24.6.20; *H2507/DS*, 24.6.19, Vickers Ltd, crashed 4.20; *D9329/DU*, 1.7.19, Central AC, 9.20 J.M. Drysdale, Caversham, 8.23 D.M. Matthews 9.23 J.E.A. Binnie, Renfrew, 7.24 N.S. McConnell, Renfrew, wfu 10.24; *E4343/DW*, 24.6.19, Avro, wrecked by gale at Rhyl 8.19; *E3408/DY*, 7.8.19, Navarro Av Co, 5.20 Astra EW, Hendon, sold in South Africa 1.21

*D9304/G-EAEA*, 3.7.19, Navarro Av Co, 5.20 Astra EW, sold in South Africa 1.21; *B8774/EB* 3.7.19, Navarro Av Co, 7.20 S. Summerfield,

★Avro Transport Company fleet numbers are given where known.

crashed at Norwich 25.9.21; *E3501/EC*, 1.9.19, Cambridge S. of F., Hardwicke, to Australia 8.19, became *G-AUDQ* in 1921; *D9018/EN*, 13.6.19, Avro No.11, Southport, crashed 1.20; *E4362/EO*, 13.6.19, Avro No.10, Morecambe, sor 6.20; *H2586/EV*, 24.6.19, Avro, wfu 6.20; *H2560/EY*, 1.7.19, Vickers Ltd, crashed 4.20; *H2561/EZ*, 30.6.19, Vickers Ltd, crashed 4.20

*E1660/G-EAFC*, 10.7.19, Avro No.16, wrecked by gale at Rhyl 8.19; *E4329/FD*, 25.6.19, Avro No.12, Southport (flew as *D4329*), 3.20 J. Blake and Co, Liverpool, wfu 6.20; *D7648/FE*, 10.7.19, Avro, crashed 8.9.21; *E3363/FP*, 1.7.19, Central AC, to Australia 12.21 as *G-AUFP*; *E4180/FQ*, 7.8.19, T.J. Rogers, 9.21 Stallard Airways, Herne Bay, crashed at Penshurst, Kent, 26.11.21; *D9340/FS*, 10.7.19, Avro No.15, Southport, sor 7.20; *H2583/FU*, 10.7.19, South African Aerial Transport Co, sold in South Africa 7.19; *H2584/FV*, as for 'FU; *H2591/FW*, as for 'FU; *H6543/FX*, nil, Golden Eagle Av Co, Squires Gate, wrecked by gale 8.19, rebuilt as *G-EASG*

*H5173/G-EAGB*, 15.12.19, Aerial Photos Ltd, Edinburgh, 8.22 Midland Av Co, crashed at Evesham 10.9.23; *H5172/GC*, 12.8.19, L & P, 12.19 Aerial Photos, 3.23 Manchester Av Co, sor 3.24; *D5499/GD*, nil L & P, damaged and reconstructed as *G-EALE*; *E4234/GI*, 14.8.19, Central AC, crashed at Twickenham 19.3.20; *C746/GJ*, 2.8.19, Central AC, crashed at Twickenham 12.19; *D9343/GO*, 2.8.19, Avro, crashed at Southport 20.8.19; *D6217/GT*, 2.8.19, Kingsbury Av Co, 5.20 Astra EW, 8.20 Oxfordshire Av Co, crashed 3.21; *H6598/GV*, 2.8.19, N.S., Leeds, crashed at Olivers Mount, Yorks, 3.8.20; *H6599/GW*, 2.8.19, N.S., Leeds crashed

Avro Transport Company joyriding 504Ks in 1919.

486

at Scarborough 7.20; *D8984/GZ*, 7.8.19, C.A. Crichton, Sunderland, sor 7.20

*E4340/G-EAHK*, 12.8.19, Bournemouth Av Co, 2.20 J.W. Gibson, 2.21 J. Barnes wfu 8.21; *E4118/HL*, 12.8.19, Cambridge S. of F., 10.20 Leatherhead Av Co, Croydon, 3.23 Manchester Av Co, crashed at Dunham Massey 30.6.23; *E1707/HM*, 2.8.19, T.D. Lewis, crashed 12.19; *H1959/HO*, 7.8.19, H.V. David; crashed at Aberystwyth 28.8.19; *E1611/HU*, 7.8.19, Aerial Photos, Edinburgh, 5.22 W.L. Woodward, Castle Bromwich, crashed at Turnhouse 28.4.22; *H2297/HV*, 7.8.19, Aerial Photos, Edinburgh, wfu 8.21; *E3364/HW*, 6.9.19, Handley Page Ltd, Cricklewood, crashed in Southwark Park, London, 31.3.20; *E3366/HX*, 6.9.19, Handley Page Ltd, sor 8.21; *H7513/HY*, 26.8.19, West of Scotland Av Co, 9.23 W.B., Renfrew, wfu 8.28; *H2411/HZ*, 26.8.19, West of Scotland Av Co, 8.21 F.J.V. Holmes, crashed 1.3.23

*F8717/G-EAIA*, 26.8.19, West of Scotland Av Co, 8.20 Border Av Co, 3.23 R. Atkinson, sor 3.24; *D9303/IB*, 12.8.19, J.D.V. Holmes, 6.20 Anderson and Pool Av Co, Ipswich, wfu 8.20; *E1675/IG*, nil, Aerial Photos, Edinburgh, sor 10.19; *H2595/IH*, 8.8.19, Avro, Amsterdam, to Belgium 7.21, *H2596/II*, 7.8.19, Avro, crashed at Yarmouth 1.8.20; *H2597/IJ*, 7.8.19, Avro, Amsterdam, wfu 7.20; *E3359/IO*, 22.9.19, AT & T, Hendon, sor 8.20; *E4143/IP*, nil, AT & T, sor 8.20; *E4144/IQ*, 28.8.19, AT & T, scrapped 11.20; *E4164/IR*, 28.11.19, AT & T, 9.21 Surrey FS, Croydon, crashed at Hayling Island 11.8.23; *E4170/IS*, nil, AT & T, sold abroad 4.20; A.A.E.C.1 to 4/*IV* to *IY*, nil, Australian Aircraft and Engineering Co. Ltd, Sydney, *IV* to *G-AUCB* and *IY* to *G-AUBE* 6.21

*H2549/G-EAJE*, 1.8.19, J.D. Atkinson, to DDL, Copenhagen, 1921 as *T-DOLM*; *H2556/JF*, 1.8.19, J.D. Atkinson, to Danish Army 11.21 as '*Avro 1*'; *H1956/JG*, 14.7.19, Eastbourne Av Co, 3.22 T. Baden Powell, crashed at Penshurst, Kent, 20.8.22; *D7619/JK*, 29.8.19, Central AC, 5.21 Vulcan Av Co, crashed 8.21; *E1728/JP*, 14.8.19. Navarro-Wellesley Av Co, 5.20 Astra EW, sold abroad 1.21; *H2587/JQ*, 20.8.19, Avro, Amsterdam, 8.20 H. W. B. Hansford, Lyme Regis, crashed at Honiton, Devon, 28.9.20; *H2592/JU*, 20.8.19, Avro Amsterdam, 5.22 Gnat Aero Co, Shoreham, 8.28 J.C. Don, Shoreham, dbr Brighton, 21.7.29; *H2594/JZ*, 27.8.19, Avro, Brighton, 11.22 W.G. Pudney, Canvey, Essex, 7.23 D. M. Matthew, crashed 11.8.23

*H2588/G-EAKB*, 26.8.19, Avro, sor 8.20; *E4246/KR*, 19.9.19, Avro, crashed in France 20.9.19; *J803/KV*, 17.9.19, Avro to Switzerland 9.19 as *CH-10*; *H2593/KW*, 26.8.19, Avro, Hamble, wfu 8.20; *H2600/KX*, 18.9.19, Avro, Brighton, 12.20 B.A.T., East Hanney, 6.29 NAL, Barton, 8.33 L.J. Rimmer, dismantled at Hooton 9.34; *H2599/KY*, 9.9.19, Avro, wfu 8.20; *E3297/KZ*, 9.9.19, Avro, Brighton, sor 9.20

*E1640/G-EALA*, 7.10.19, Avro, 7.22 R. Taylor, crashed 21.8.22; *H1925/LD*, 10.6.19, Eastbourne Av Co, 5.22 R.H. Leavey (Provincial FS), crashed at Kennington 27.8.22; *D5499/LE*, 26.8.19, Aerial Photos, 8.22 Midland Av Co, crashed at Burton, Cheshire 30.3.23

*E3399/G-EAMI*, 19.9.19, W.G. Pudney, crashed at Banbury 16.4.21; *J747/MN*, 26.9.19, Avro, sor 9.20; *J746/MO*, 26.9.19, Avro, Brighton, to Chile 9.21; *J745/MP*, 11.10.19, Avro, sor 10.20; *J748/MQ*, 7.10.19, Avro, crashed at Rhyl 14.10.20; *E3724/MZ*, 26.9.19, Avro, 5.23 F.P. Raynham, 7.24 M.W. Piercy, 6.25 Earl of Kinnoull, crashed at Le Bourget 9.6.25

*H2318/G-EANC*, nil, Avro, sor 10.20; *J749/ND*, 26.9.19, Avro, sold in Belgium 6.21; *J751/NE*, 25.10.19, Avro, sold in Chile 9.21; *J752/NF*, 3.10.19, Avro, sor 10.20; *J753/NG*, 7.10.19, Avro, sold in Belgium 6.21; *H2514/NN*, 13.4.20, Sir P. Sassoon, Lympne, 3.20 H. Sykes, 9.20 Adastral Air Lines, crashed in France; *J756/NO*, 11.10.19, Avro, sor 10.20; *J754/NP*, nil, Avro, to the Japanese Navy 9.21; *J755/NQ*, 11.10.19, Avro 4.20 Border Av Co, crashed on the shores of the Solway Firth 1.12.21; *E3358/NT*, 4.10.19, GN Ltd, Brooklands, sor 10.20; *J757/NX*, 25.10.19, Avro, to the Japanese Navy 9.21; *J758/NY*, 7.11.19, as for 'NX; *J759/NZ*, 3.10.19, as for 'NX

*J760/G-EAOA*, *J761/OB*, *J762/OC* and *J763/OD*, nil, Avro, to the Japanese Navy 9.21; *E3505/G-EAOE*, nil, Lt-Col R. B. Bourdillon, Farnborough 1920, 5.22 B. Martin, Cleethorpes, crashed at Cleethorpes 12.6.22; *E3021/G-EAQU*, 18.2.20, A.A. Mitchell, Edinburgh, sor 2.21; *E9443/QV*, 18.2.20, A.A. Mitchell, crashed at Kelso, Roxburgh, 25.5.20

*G-EARP*, 6.4.20, Pudney-Brettel-Owen Co, wfu 3.21; *H6551/RZ*, 12.4.20, Bournemouth Av Co, crashed at Bournemouth 7.8.20

*F9809/G-EASA*, 12.4.20, Bournemouth Av Co, 11.21 S. Summerfield, crashed at Doncaster 28.4.22; *F9810/SB*, 12.4.20, Bournemouth Av Co, 5.25 C.P.B. Ogilvie, Hendon, crashed near Ripley, Yorks, 12.26; *D5858/SF*, 9.4.20, Cobham and Holmes Av Co, 7.20 O.P.Jones, 3.22 F.J.V. Holmes, 6.29 NAL, Barton, 8.33 L.J. Rimmer, dismantled at Hooton 1937; *H6543/SG*, 22.4.22, Golden Eagle Av Co, 7.21 J. S. Boumphrey, 7.22 Liverpool Av Co, crashed at Great Bookham, Surrey, 2.9.26

*F9802/G-EATB*, 22.6.20, A.R. Van den Bergh, written off 26.8.21; *E3045/TU*, 28.2.21, C. L. Pashley, Shoreham, 9.27 Gnat Aero Co, crashed at Shoreham 5.9.27; *D6387/TV*, 26.6.20, International Av Co, crashed 11.20; *E3022/TZ*, nil, J.M. Drysdale, re-registered *G-EAVC*

*E3022/G-EAVC*, nil, W.R. Bailey, scrapped 1.21; *E6757/VD*, nil, Handley Page Ltd, to Brussels 16.8.20; *E1644/VI*, 25.7.21, W.A. Hadden, wfu 8.24; *E3672/G-EAWI*, 1.4.21, Surrey FS, crashed near Croydon 9.21; *D2035/WJ*, 22.3.21, Surrey FS, wfu 2.22; *E3671/WK*, 22.6.21, Welsh Av Co, Swansea, 4.22 Evan Williams, crashed in Swansea Bay 3.10.22; *E9341/WL* and *E9245/WM*, 20.4.21 and 29.3.21, Welsh Av Co, 4.22 Evan Williams, sor 4.23; *D9058/G-EAXY*, 9.7.21, Royal Aero Club, Croydon, wfu 7.23; *H6608/G-EAYB*, 22.7.21, Royal Aero Club, Croydon, crashed at Croydon 14.6.23; *H6609/YC*, 22.7.21, Royal Aero Club, Hendon, crashed at Croydon 16.5.22; *H7426/G-EAZF*, *H6605/ZG*, *H6611/ZK* and *H6601/ZL*, nil, Aircraft Disposal Co Ltd, sold in Belgium 11.21 (*ZF* and *ZL* crashed on test at Croydon and were replaced); *H2516/ZQ*, *H2553/ZR*, *H2558/ZS*, *H2509/ZU* and *H2565/ZV*, nil, Aircraft Disposal Co Ltd, sold in Belgium 1.22; *H2295/G-EAZW*, 22.8.22, Manchester Av Co, 3.24 Northern Av Co, crashed at Cleckheaton, Yorks, 3.5.24; *E1860/ZX*, 24.7.22, Manchester Av Co, 3.24 Northern Av Co, crashed at Manchester 2.8.24

*H7467/G-EBAF*, nil, Aircraft Disposal Co Ltd, Croydon, sold in Belgium 1.22; *F9783/AV*, 20.4.22, Leatherhead Av Co, crashed at Slough 20.8.22; *AY*, nil, H. Sykes, 7.22 A. Fraser, Kingsbury, sor 7.23; *E1843/G-EBBF*, 16.7.23, H. Sykes, 7.22 A. Fraser, wfu 7.24; *H6653/BP*, nil, Aircraft Disposal Co Ltd, sold in Belgium 4.22; *H221/G-EBCB*, 2.5.22, Kingwill and Jones Flying Co, written off 2.29; *H6656/CC*, *H7487/CD* and *H2065/CF*, nil, Aircraft Disposal Co Ltd, sold in Belgium 5.22; *E3379/CK*, 29.4.22, F.J.V. Holmes, 1.23 F. Neale, Epping, 2.25 B. Roberts, 5.26 H. Sykes, sor 1.28; *E9227/CL*, 20.4.22, W.R. Bailey, Newport, crashed at Rogerstone, Monmouth, 6.5.22; *H7482/CO*, nil, Aircraft Disposal Co Ltd, sold in Belgium 5.22; *H6547/CQ*, 22.5.22, Leatherhead Av Co, 12.22 Manchester Av Co, crashed at Barrow-in-Furness 24.8.23; *H7474/CR*, *H2062/CS* and *H2071/CT*, nil, Aircraft Disposal Co Ltd, sold in Belgium 7.22; *H2060/G-EBDC* and *H2052/DJ*, nil, Aircraft Disposal Co Ltd, sold in Belgium 5.22; *F2284/G-EBDP*, 22.6.22, Surrey FS, wfu 7.25; *E3291/ G-EBEL*, 15.8.22, London Av Co Ltd, sold abroad 1.23; *C691/EO*, nil, A.S.J. Chapman, written off 8.24

*G-EBFV*, 14.5.23, F.J.V. Holmes, 10.23, W.B., crashed 6.10.24; *E1850/FW*, 28.5.23, Surrey FS, crashed at Bunford, Yeovil, 17.9.26; *H6602/G-EBGH*, nil, Manchester Av Co, crashed at Broughton Grange 5.6.23; *H2416/GI*, 12.6.23, Manchester Airways, sor 6.24; *E9358/G*, 26.6.24, Aircraft Disposal Co Ltd, sold abroad 6.24; *R/LE/10390/G-EBGY*, 25.7.23, W.B., crashed 12.6.24; *R/LE/10407/GZ*, 25.7.23, 10.29, L.J. Rimmer, dismantled at Hooton 1934; *G-EBHB*, nil, Manchester Airways, sor 8.24; *R3/CL/10365/G-EBHE*, 11.4.23, L.J. Rimmer, crashed 1.37; *E3794/HM*, 21.8.23, Surrey FS, crashed at Port Talbot 31.6.27

*E1826/G-EBII*, 12.11.23, Surrey FS, sor 11.24; *G-EBIN*, 4.1.24, F.J.V. Holmes, crashed at Plymouth 25.7.24; *R/LE/12663/G-EBIS*, 9.2.24, W.B., 2.29 North British Av Co, Hooton, crashed at Rainhill 22.4.35; *IZ*, 19.5.24, Cornwall Av Co, St. Austell, wfu 3.33; *G-EBJE*, 21.1.26, Southern Counties Av Co, 1.26 J.R. Cobb, Brooklands, 8.26 F.G. Miles, 7.28 Southern Aircraft Ltd, Shoreham, sor 12.34, rebuilt 1963 for the RAF Museum as *E449*; *E2969/G-EBKB*, 13.9.24; F.J.V. Holmes, 4.29, NAL, 8.33 L.J. Rimmer, ditched off Scarborough 3.9.31; *E3382/KR*, 24.3.25, F.J.V. Holmes, 8.27 C.L. Kent, 5.30 Wolverhampton AC, crashed at Church Lawton, Cheshire, 22.7.32; *KS*, 1.6.25, Southern Counties Av Co, sor 2.28; *E3386/KX*, 9.5.25, F.J.V. Holmes, 7.29 NAL, 8.33 L.J. Rimmer, crashed at Great Crosby,

Lancs. 21.7.34; *R/LE/18615/G-EBLA*, 1.7.25, N.S., Brough, 4.28 A.G. Cooper, crashed into sea at Weymouth 29.5.28

*G-EBNH*, 6.4.26, T.J. Carslake, Hooton, 5.27 South Wales Airways, crashed at Bridgend, Glam, 7.5.28; *F8864/NR*, 16.3.26, Cornwall Av Co, wfu 2.30; *E448/NU*, 23.4.26, Aircraft Disposal Co Ltd, to the Finnish AF 9.26 as *AV-57*; *F8865/G-EBOB*, 2.6.26, F.J.V. Holmes, wfu 3.29; *G-EBQR*, 14.4.27, Western Aviation Ltd, Cheltenham, 4.33 Aviation Tours Ltd, sor 4.37; *H2234/G-EBSE*; 29.7.27, Cornwall Av Co, crashed at Margate 27.7.29; *H257/SG*, 29.7.27, South Wales Airways, 5.28 Western Av Ltd, sor 11.34; *H2365/SJ*, 16.4.28, A.H. Matthews, Maylands, 7.34 North British Av Co, sor 5.35; *D6330/SL*, 27.8.27, F.J.V. Holmes, 5.30 NAT, Barton, crashed 9.5.32; *H9859/SM*, 10.8.27, F.J.V. Holmes, 5.28 J. Bunning Ltd, Pontypool, wfu 5.29; *G-EBVL*, 9.1.28 L.E.R. Bellairs, Shoreham, 7.28 Southern Aircraft Ltd, 8.31 F.C. Fisher, Christchurch, scrapped 1939; *G-EBVW*, 18.5.28, F.J.V. Holmes, Shrewsbury, 7.29, NAL, dismantled at Hooton 12.31; *G-EBWF*, 21.3.28, L.J. Skytrips Ltd, 5.29 Alliston Av Co, scrapped at Hornchurch, Essex, 12.32; *WO*, 26.7.28, Dr M.C. Wall, Woodley, 11.28 Phillips and Powis Ltd, Woodley, crashed at Reading 1.4.29

*G-EBXA*, 4.4.28, W.B., 7.29 North British Av Co; wfu 12.33; *XV*, 26.5.28, Western Av Ltd, 4.33 Aviation Tours Ltd, wfu 4.37; *G-EBYB*, 26.5.28, Gnat Aero Co, 3.30 Southern Aero Club, Shoreham, dismantled 2.33; *G-EBYE*, 30.6.28, Henderson S. of F., Brooklands, 8.28 Midland Aero Flights Ltd., 11.28 R.H. Jackson, 1.30 Brooklands S of F, crashed at Brixton, London, 2.2.31; *G-EBYW*, 3.9.28, Surrey FS, 5.30 Aviation Tours Ltd, 5.34 Kinmel Bay FS, Rhyl, sor 3.38; *G-EBZA*, 13.7.28, L.J. Skytrips Ltd, 8.30 L.R.G. Errington, sor 12.31; *H2262/ZB*, 2.10.26, Surrey FS, 11.32 M.W. Allenby, Wilmington, sor 11.33

*G-AAAF*, 7.9.28, Cornwall Av Co 8.33 Surrey FS, 6.35 H.V.K. Atkinson, Witney, 8.35 Flying Hire Ltd, Chilworth, burned at Gatwick 1939,

Cheltenham-based Western Aviation's Avro 504K *G-EBQR*.

490

*G-AACA*, 3.11.28, L.J. May, 2.29 Brooklands S of F, 6.32 F.J.V. Holmes, sor 12.33; *F8811/CG*, 12.11.28, L.J. Anderson, sor 1.32; *G-AACW*, 27.7.29, Southern Aircraft Ltd, 11.30 Home Counties AS, Shoreham, crashed at Horley, Surrey, 25.1.31; *G-AACX*, 20.11.28, Dominion Aircraft Ltd, Gatwick, crashed 4.29; *J8373/G-AADY*, 23.2.29, Henderson S of F, 10.29 W. Cornell, 11.30 D.A.N. Watt, Ford, wfu 12.31; *G-AAES*, 29.3.29, T.J. Carslake, burned at Hooton 1935; *G-AAEZ*, 27.3.29, Aeroplane Services Ltd, Castle Bromwich, 5.30 H.C. Howard, 8.31 NAL, 8.33 W. Mackay, sor 12.34

*G-AAFE*, 31.5.29, Inland FS, Maylands, wfu 12.30; *J8375/FJ*, 3.4.29, Henderson S of F, 5.30 H.C. Howard, 11.30 Mrs E. M. Watt, Ford, wfu 12.31; *J8379/FT*, 26.3.29, A.B. Forsyth, 5.29 Inland FS, sor 3.31; *G-AAGB*, 17.4.29, Surrey FS, crashed at Telscombe 12.7.34; *G-AAGG*, 6.5.29; Phillips and Powis Ltd, 3.31 Rollason Av Co, Croydon, wfu 12.35; SP/1312(sic)/*G-AARV*, 7.11.30, S. Payne Jnr., crashed at Bekesbourne 2.1.31; *F2540/G-AASS*, 16.5.30, L.G. Anderson, Hanworth, 11.30 South Wales Airways, crashed at Swansea and submerged by tide 1.8.31; *F9819/ST*, 11.1.30, E. Brown, sor 12.32; *G-AASX*, 7.5.30, Alliston Av Ltd, 7.30 R.M. Stobie, Brough, sor 12.32; *G-AATY*, 17.3.30, Wolverhampton AC, scrapped at Driffield 1937.

K.A.S.1/*G-AAUJ*, 28.3.30, Kent AS, Kingsdown, crashed at Harrogate 5.10.32; K.A.S.2/*G-AAUK*, 28.3.30, Kent AS, crashed at Epsom Downs 3.6.31; K.A.S.3/*G-AAUL*, 21.5.30, Kent AS, crashed at Dovercourt, Essex, 2.8.31; *F9720/G-AAVW*, 18.9.30, L.G. Anderson, 1.31 L.D. Trappitt, sor 12.35; *G-AAWB*, nil, Kent AS, not converted; K.A.S.5/*G-AAWC*, 21.5.30, Kent AS, 9.30 P.H. Meadway, sor 12.32; K.A.S.4/*G-AAWD*, 16.6.30, Kent AS, dismantled 10.36; *H9833/G-AAYH*, 6.6.30, NAT, to Eire 3.32 as *EI-AAM*; *H9861/YI*, 29.5.30, Cornwall Av Co, sor 12.31; *G-AAYM*, 9.6.30, Surrey FS 4.33 Aviation Tours Ltd, 8.33 L.J. Rimmer, sor 12.34

*G-ABAA*, 11.9.30, G & H Aviations Ltd, Stag Lane, 3.33 Luff's Aviation Tours Ltd, 5.36 Williams and Co, Squires Gate, dismantled at Brooklands 1939, rebuilt 1950 and flown as '*H2311*', subsequently stored, to the Manchester Museum of Science and Industry in 1989; *G-ABAB*, 4.7.30, G & H Av Ltd, 6.32 R.O. Roch, last flight 16.10.32; *J8353/AU*, 19.6.30, H. Sinclair, Chelmsford, burned in hangar fire at Broomfield, Chelmsford, 18.9.32; *J8348/AV*, 9.7.30, NAT, crashed at Holyhead, 9.30; *J8347/AW*, 21.6.30, NAT, sor 12.33; *G-ABAY*, 7.8.30, Surrey FS, wrecked at Croydon 13.1.35; *H202/G-ABBF*, 2.7.31, Rollason Av Co, 11.30 Mrs E.M. Watt, Ford, 7.31 R.E. Pancoast-Bliss, Croydon, 10.31 Southend Flying Club, dismantled at Bekesbourne 7.32

*G-ABGI* 12.6.31, Mrs V. Brailey, 8.33 L.J. Rimmer, sor 1.36; *G-ABGJ*, nil, Mrs V. Brailey, sor 12.34; *J8342/G-ABHI*, 7.3.31, NAT, 4.32 Cornwall Av Co, sor 1.34; *J8343/HJ*, 7.3.31 and *J8351/HK*, 24.3.31, NAT, 8.33 L.J. Rimmer, crashed at Hooton 1933; *J8371/HP*, 14.3.31, NAT to Eire 3.32 as

*EI-AAN*; K.A.S.6/*G-ABJF*, 30.3.31, P. Turner, 3.32 Thanet Av Ltd, sor 5.34

*J8333*/*G-ABLL*, 3.6.31, NAT, 8.33 L.J. Rimmer, crashed at Lowton Moor, Lancs., 30.8.34; *H3086*/*LV*, 16.5.31, R.H. Thomas, Wenvoe, S. Wales, scrapped 1936; *H3087*/*LW*, 16.5.31, R.H. Thomas, 8.33 South Wales Airways, sor 1.34; *E348*/*G-ABML*, nil, Calder Valley Aero Club, Burnley, not converted; K.A.S.7/*G-ABOL*, nil, Kent AS, crashed 12.32; *G-ABSL*, 5.5.32, C.B. Field, Kingswood Knoll, Surrey, 8.32 Modern Airways Ltd, 4.33 L.J. Rimmer, sor 8.36; *H1986*/*SM*, 15.6.32, C.B. Field, 10.32 E.L. Gandar Dower, Shoreham, sor 12.37; *H2965*/*SN*, 7.7.32, C.B. Field, 7.32 L & P, Herne Bay, 8.33 L.J. Rimmer, 12.34 P/O F.B. Chapman, Gosport, sor 4.38

*G-ABTX*, nil, J. McKay, not converted; *J8365*/*G-ABUK*, 7.4.32, NAT, crashed at Hedon, Hull, 3.9.32; *E9353*/*G-ABWK*, 27.6.32, Essex Flying Club, Abridge, 8.33 Kinmel Bay AS, sold abroad 12.35; *G-ABYB*, 7.9.32 Essex AC, Orsett, 10.32 H.M. Talbot-Lehmann, Chelmsford, sor 6.33; *G-ABZC*, 5.4.33, Devonshire Aviation Tours Ltd, crashed at Chard, Somerset, 30.4.33; *G-ACAU*, 26.4.33, C.B. Field, sor 3.37

*G-ACNB*, nil, The Shuttleworth Trust, Old Warden, registered 29.10.81 but flown as *E3404* from 1955 after rebuild and conversion from Avro 504N by Avro Apprentices. Re-registered 18.4.84 as *G-ADEV* (believed to be its true identity) and subsequently flown as *H5199*, the original military serial of '*EV*; H.A.C.1/*G-ATXL* (replica), registered 19.7.66 to V.H. Bellamy, Kings Sombourne, Hants, to Cole Palen Collection, Old Rheinbeck, NY, as *N2939* 12.70

A wing walker on the Cornwall Aviation Company's Avro 504K *G-AAAF* at Shoreham in 1932. (*D.L. Brown*)

# GENERAL INDEX

Listing civil and military operators, agents, sub-contractors, countries, principal cities, aerodromes and events, together with certain VIPs and those individuals closely linked with A. V. Roe, the Avro company or the development of aviation. (The abbreviation AF used throughout indicates Air Force).

Armstrong Whitworth, 55, 115, 123, 310, 320, 325, 340, 359, 362, 366, 367, 385, 406, 410, 412
Arrow Aviation Co, 97
Associated Airways, 381
Atcherley, F/Lt R.L.R., 271, 274
Auckland, 96, 109, 110, 373, 463
Austin Motors Ltd, 359, 365, 366, 368
Australia, 66, 193, 244, 251, 252, 257, 258, 266, 268, 269, 272, 274, 277, 278, 285, 321, 325, 326, 330, 331, 336, 341, 342, 349, 363, 373, 374, 378, 381, 385, 388, 398, 407, 408, 412, 449, 468, 469, 486
Australian Aerial Derby Race, 86, 87, 185
Australian Government Aircraft Factory, 407, 410, 412
Australian Aircraft and Engineering Co, 70, 85, 86, 87, 109, 185, 186, 487
Australian Flying Corps, 85
Australian National Airways, 268, 271, 275, 276, 282, 284, 286
Australian Transcontinental Airways, 276
Autogiro Flying Club, 349
Auto Aero Services Ltd, 86
Aviation Commerce Ltd, 105, 106
Aviation Traders Ltd, 387, 390, 395
Avro Schools Ltd, xvii
Avro School (Brighton) Ltd, 24
Avro Strainer, xviii
Avro Transport Co, xix, xxi, 75–78, 88, 89, 95, 101, 107, 108, 111, 114, 160, 161, 174–176, 188, 485, 486
Ayr, 62, 63, 78

Baden-Powell, B.F.S, xiv
Baghdad, 219, 466–467
Bahamasair, 448, 452, 453
Bahrain, 331
Baldonnel, 93, 286, 311
Balfour, Lt H.H. (Lord Balfour), 143
Barnwell, Sqn Ldr F.S., 86
Barnwell, R.H., 43
Barrow-in-Furness, 19, 20, 48, 489
Barton, 202, 257, 307, 487, 488, 490
Beardmore, Wm., & Co, 80, 243, 489
Bedford, (RAE) 414, 440
Bekesbourne, 188, 485, 491
Belgium, 88, 119, 188, 284, 298, 485, 487–489

Belgian Air Force, 88, 123, 294, 299, 329, 351, 448, 452, 458, 459
Bennett, AVM D.C.T., 371, 386, 393
Berkshire Aviation Co, 81, 83, 176, 191, 193
Berlin, 235, 239, 255, 403
Berlin Air Lift, 370, 371, 379, 380, 386, 392, 400, 410
Bermuda, 109, 371, 386, 404
Bermuda and West Atlantic Aviation Co, 109
BFS, 448, 452
Bicester, 261
Biggin Hill, 371, 374
Binbrook, 406
Bitteswell, 331, 414
BKS Air Survey Ltd, 337
BKS Air Transport, 444, 445, 447, 451, 452
Black, Tom Campbell, 279, 315, 317
Blackburn Aeroplane and Motor Co., 53
Blackbushe, 373, 374, 393, 400, 408, 414, 439
Blackpool, xix, 6, 11, 13, 14, 75, 76, 125, 174, 227, 485
Bleriot & Spad Aircraft Works, 60, 61
Blue Line Airways, 330
Border Aviation Co, 79, 487, 488
Borwick and Sons, 26
Boscombe Down, 354, 355, 357, 358, 377, 385, 387, 389, 391, 402, 404, 423, 432, 434, 435, 439, 440, 453
Boston, Mass., 14, 15
Botha, Gen T.E., 100
Boulton & Paul, 67, 372
Bourget, Le, 80, 112, 239, 278, 381, 401, 488
Bournemouth Aviation Co, 77, 487, 488
Bournemouth Flying School, 121
Bovingdon, 342, 393, 395
Bowring Bros Ltd, 169
Bracebridge Heath, 290, 292, 368, 370, 440
Brain & Brown Ltd, 331, 342
Brancker, Sir Sefton, 130, 223
Brazil, 119, 306–308, 416
Brazilian Naval Air Service, 101, 123
Brazilian AF, 294, 443, 447, 448, 451
Brearley, Norman, 85
Brighton, 49, 54, 76, 112, 165, 175, 178, 487, 488

Clifton Street, xviii, 35, 52
Coal Aston, 203
Cobb, John, 80, 489
Cobham, Sir Alan, 78, 83, 84, 119, 289, 315
Cole, E.K., Ltd, 337, 340
Colerne, 374
Commercial Air Hire Ltd, 281
Commonwealth Air Training Plan, 326, 336
Constructiones Aeronauticas SA, 305, 308
Copenhagen, 91, 119, 123, 249, 288, 487
Cornwall Aviation Co, 82–84, 121, 489–492
Cosmos Engineering Co, 113, 115
*Courageous*, HMS, 348
Courier Aircraft Ltd, 190, 193
Cottesmore, 363
Courtney, F.T., 89, 142, 233, 234
Cranfield, 320, 330, 340, 372, 414, 449
Cranwell, 59, 62, 72, 125, 288, 293, 336
Crossley Motors, xvii, xix, 130, 226, 481
Croydon, 74, 77, 79, 83, 85, 88, 89, 92, 105, 106, 114, 116, 118, 129, 166, 178, 185, 188–190, 196, 199, 200, 220, 223, 235, 239, 243, 244, 252, 253, 255, 276, 278, 280, 281, 290, 306, 323, 327, 330, 339, 379, 432, 488, 489, 491, 492
Curragh, 62, 63
Curtiss of Marblehead, 15
Czech AF, 294

Dan-Air Services, 380
DDL, 91, 92, 487
Denmark, 91, 92, 119, 123, 288, 330, 351
Danish Army, 92, 351, 487
Danish Naval Shipyard, 119, 122, 288, 290
Danish Navy, 91, 92, 113, 119, 123, 288, 289, 291, 292
Darlington & District Aero Club, 290, 292
Darwin, 373
Davidson, G.L.O., xiv
Davies, S.D., 431
Davis, Capt Duncan, 63, 76
Dayton-Wright Airplane Co, 103

Debden, 408, 413
Decca Navigator Co, 340
de Havilland Aircraft Co, 322
de Havilland Aircraft of Canada, 331, 334
de Havilland Engine Co, 401
de Havilland School of Flying, 188
Denham, 316, 317
Dempster, William, Ltd, 393
Derby Aviation, 331
Detling, 324
Digby, 117, 124, 293
Diggers Co-op Aviation Co, 85
Dobson, R.H. (Sir Roy), xix (P), xxi, 145, 269
Douglas, Wing Cdr W. Sholto (Lord Douglas), 224, 249
Dover, 62, 108, 242, 255
Dublin, 83, 277, 339, 393
Dundee, 138
Dunsfold, 371, 374, 400
Duxford, 125, 293, 350, 375
Dyce, 192

Eagle Aviation, 374, 375, 379, 383, 408
*Eagle*, H.M.S., 206, 208
Eastbourne Aviation Co, 60, 61, 70, 71, 77, 108–110, 487
Eastchurch, 3, 35, 39, 49–51, 56, 141
Eastern Aircraft Factory, 65
Eastleigh, 350, 362
Earhart, Amelia, 252
East Hanney, 83, 489, 487
East Kirkby, 406
East Retford, 72
Ecuadorian AF, 448, 452
Edwards, M.F., 26
Egypt, 65, 66, 266, 283, 320, 327, 328, 334, 339, 344, 352, 416
Egyptian Army AF, 278, 283, 294, 295, 296, 299, 320, 324, 329, 332, 352, 368, 456
Elizabeth, H.R.H. Princess, 385
Elliott-Lynn, Mrs S.C. (Lady Heath), 249, 250, 252, 253, 257
Ellis, A.G.B., 127, 128, 206
Elmdon, 271, 350
Esler, S.E., 439
Essex Aero Ltd, 350
Essex Aviation Co, 80
Essex Flying Club, 81, 492
Estonian AF, 93, 132, 266, 273, 298, 324, 333

# INDEX OF AIRCRAFT AND MISSILES

# INDEX OF AERO ENGINES